FirstPerson

FirstPerson

New Media as
Story, Performance, and Game

Edited by Noah Wardrip-Fruin and Pat Harrigan

Designed by Michael Crumpton

The MIT Press

Cambridge, Massachusetts

London, England

This book was set in Adobe Chapparal and ITC Officina by Michael Crumpton and was printed and bound in the United States of America.

Library of Congress Cataloging-in-Publication Data

First person : new media as story, performance, and game / edited by Noah Wardrip-Fruin and Pat Harrigan.

p. cm.

Includes bibliographical references and index.

ISBN 0-262-23232-4 (hard : alk. paper)

I. Wardrip-Fruin, Noah. II. Harrigan, Pat.

GV1469.17.S63F57 2003

794.8—dc21

2003048784

10 9 8 7 6 5 4 3 2

Contents

Contents

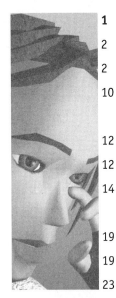

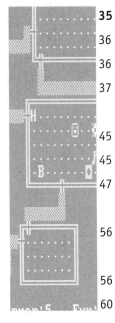

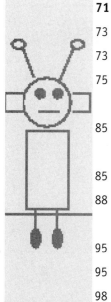

Contents

Dedication

Noah and Pat dedicate their work to their siblings,
Nathan, Katie, Becky, and Sam.

Michael dedicates his work to his father,
Charles.

Acknowledgments

We would like to thank everyone who helped make this book possible — but that list is far too long, so we'll content ourselves with the following:

Doug Sery, Katherine Innis, Deborah Cantor-Adams, Valerie Geary, and everyone else at MIT Press; Joseph Tabbi, Ewan Branda, Anne Burdick, Matthew Thornton, and others at *electronic book review;* those who supported this work, directly or indirectly, at Brown University, New York University, University of Baltimore, Royal Melbourne Institute of Technology, and the Johnston Center for Integrative Studies at the University of Redlands; Carrie Rainey, Marjetta Geerling, Jane McGonigal, Elan Lee and others who made non-institutional contributions of time and support; our essayists and respondents; our families and friends.

Thank you all,
Noah, Pat, and Michael

Introduction
Noah Wardrip-Fruin and Pat Harrigan

In addition to their long nonwired histories, game equipment and literature now exist as forms of computer-based experience. We might say they exist both as "new media" and perhaps "physically" or in "real life." Game equipment and literature are not the only concerns of *First Person*, but they are central — let's start with them.

It is now the case that the market for computer games (handheld games, arcade games, games for PCs and consoles) dwarfs that of their physical counterparts (card and board games, sports equipment, tabletop role-playing games). Meanwhile, the market for computer literature seems nonexistent. But is it really? Many of the most popular computer games, those that have pushed the industry's growth (until its revenue is not just larger than that for non-computer games, but rivals the feature film industry's box office revenue) clearly have some form of story as a major component. The first big game hit of the 2000s wasn't a descendent of the abstract *Tetris;* it was *The Sims*™ — a system for generating stories about suburban life. Similarly, in the 1990s, the first massively popular CD-ROM was *Myst* — in which players uncovered the story of an intricate and beautiful world.

But maybe these are overly facile categorizations. Couldn't it be argued that *The Sims* is a resource-management experience, and that *Myst* is an exploration and puzzle-solving experience — that the gameplay is the central experience, and that generated or embedded stories are at best "themes" (which could be switched out for others), or even distractions? Isn't it the case that *Counter-Strike* — which speeds up the essential multiplayer interaction and removes the replayability-limiting story — is a better game than *Half-Life*, on which it is based? *Counter-Strike*, after all, was created by players, who might be better guides to what makes a good gaming experience than the creators of narrative games (who may be in the unfortunate throes of what Eric Zimmerman calls "cinema envy"). Yet it was players who, in the first year of this new century, kept sending games with strong story components — *The Sims*, the book-derived *Harry Potter*, the mythic, multi-act *Black and White* — to the tops of the charts.

This line of questioning, about the relationship between stories and games, is one of the major themes of *First Person*, and is addressed by theorists and practitioners from a wide variety of backgrounds.

Yet we began by talking about *literature*. Surely "story" is not all there is to literature in new media; if we are talking of literature, where is text — where are the words? The Sim characters for which the game is named don't utter sentences that tell a story — much less language that edifies or entertains — but rather communicate through icons and gibberish to indicate what is on their simple minds. And this seems appropriate for the roles these proto-characters play. But this begs the question: what about the times when some more complex linguistic form is called for? Settembrini, in Mann's *The Magic Mountain*, may insist that form is

The new media field includes those who learned the term "first person" as the name for a grammatical tense and literary point of view; those who use it to describe the well-known cinematic POV; those who associate it with the movement of a virtual "camera" through a computer graphic scene; those who mainly utter it as the first two words in the computer game genre of the "first person shooter"; and even those for whom it evokes images of invention and discovery, as in "arguably, the first person to make it work." As creative exploration continues, and the new media field evolves, our meanings for "first person" will no doubt continue to evolve — but there seems little chance it will leave our vocabulary.

Tabletop games pose their own game/story questions. Roleplaying games such as *Dungeons and Dragons* or *Unknown Armies* can be viewed as specialized machines for generating stories; but there is a wide spectrum of gaming complexity available even here, from simple percentile-based rules (*Call of Cthulhu/Delta Green*) to the infinitely expandable *GURPS* line of gaming supplements. We might say that "rules-heavy" systems incline toward the game, and "rules-light" systems toward story.

folderol, but the editors of this volume respectfully disagree. Text in new media — fiction, poetry, performance — must have some utility other than in the form of the cut-scene, although to find it we may have to look outside the mainstream. If *The Sims* and *Black and White* are the surprisingly good summer blockbusters (or the better bestsellers), we still may still wish to locate the art films (or the small presses).

This is another major concern of this project: the exploration of new textual experiences — and other new literary/linguistic experiences — created by artists, poets, programmers, and fiction writers. Our concerns are broader than those found in 1990s surveys of "hypertext,"[1] yet are more focused than a rundown of abstruse textual possibilities. In *First Person* we provide examples of textual/literary practices (including hypertexts) that in their internal procedures or audience interaction can be thought of as performance or gameplay, or that provoke us to reconsider these terms. Although far from exhaustive, this survey counterpoints the "story-game" discussion, and opens up for examination some of the most noteworthy intersections of new media and literary practice.

First Person is organized as a series of imagined panel presentations,[2] which are extraordinary in two respects. First, they gather a selection of field leaders and rising stars from a wider range of backgrounds (theoretical, technical, and artistic) than are commonly found together at any conference. Second, these panels incorporate exceptional audience members who — virtual microphones in hand — respond to each contributor, encouraging them to review fundamental aspects of their argument, reevaluate claims, or expand on statements too-lightly delivered. Each author then offers a final statement to her or his respondents.

From these presentations and their follow-up discussions we have created the *First Person* book and web site, constructed as an experiment in publication. The web site — created in collaboration with *electronic book review* — will build over time, while the book will be released, unsurprisingly, all at once. All the panel presentations will appear both online and in print; the first set of audience responses will appear only in print, and the next set of responses and the authors' final statements will appear only online. From there the online discussion will continue to grow — with expanding "first person" commentary from another level of thoughtful readership: including, perhaps, you.

1. A term now generally used more narrowly than intended by its creator, Ted Nelson. See the section "Hypertexts and Interactives" in this volume.

2. Not surprising, considering that many of these essays began life as presentations at conferences such as ACM SIGGRAPH, Digital Arts and Culture, and ACM Hypertext.

References

Call of Cthulhu. Sandy Peterson; Chaosium. 1981.

Delta Green. Dennis Detwiller, Adam Scott Glancy and John Tynes; Pagan Publishing. 1997.

Dungeons and Dragons. Gary Gygax and Dave Arneson; Tactical Studies Rules (TSR). 1974.

GURPS. Steve Jackson et al.; Steve Jackson Games. 1986.

Unknown Armies. Greg Stolze and John Tynes; Atlas Games. 1999.

Contributors

Noah Wardrip-Fruin, editor
Pat Harrigan, editor

Espen Aarseth
Mark Bernstein
Mark Bernstein and Diane Greco
John Cayley
Chris Crawford
J. Yellowlees Douglas
J. Yellowlees Douglas and Andrew Hargadon
Johanna Drucker
Markku Eskelinen
Mary Flanagan
Gonzalo Frasca
Matt Gorbet
Diane Gromala
N. Katherine Hayles
Mizuko Ito
Henry Jenkins
Natalie Jeremijenko
Jesper Juul
Brenda Laurel
Bryan Loyall
Michael Mateas
Jon McKenzie
Nick Montfort
Stuart Moulthrop
Janet Murray
Celia Pearce
Simon Penny
Ken Perlin
Rita Raley
Rebecca Ross
Warren Sack
Richard Schechner
Bill Seaman
Phoebe Sengers
Andrew Stern
Stephanie Strickland
Lucy Suchman
Eugene Thacker
Camille Utterback
Victoria Vesna
Jill Walker
Adrianne Wortzel
Will Wright
Eric Zimmerman

Cyberdrama

Janet Murray, who coined the term *cyberdrama,* uses it to discuss a new type of storytelling —
and a new type of story — that she sees emerging as the computer becomes an expressive
medium. Cyberdrama appears to tell the story of our lives now, much as the novel emerged to
tell the story of a previous culture and time. As Murray writes, the term emphasizes as well
"the enactment of the story in the particular fictional space of the computer." Inevitably the
term also turns our attention toward those ("dramatic") new media artifacts that resemble
theater, cinema, or television — as we were similarly directed by the title of Murray's seminal
Hamlet on the Holodeck (1997).

Murray's *Hamlet* followed Brenda Laurel's *Computers as Theatre,* which had, six years earlier,
made dramatic experience a central topic of discussion in the new media community. Laurel's
book was itself picking up themes from her 1986 Ph.D. thesis, which focused on forms of
interactive, first person, computer-enabled storytelling. In both works Laurel offered
Aristotelian dramatic experience as the model toward which designers of interactive computer
experiences should aspire.

It is generally agreed that cyberdrama must give human participants an experience of
agency. Usually this has meant that the participant's actions have an appropriate and
understandable impact on the world the computer presents to them (though the term is given
a somewhat different spin by Ken Perlin in his essay included here). Other goals defined by
Murray include *immersion* and *transformation.* To achieve these goals through a combination of
experience design, computer graphics, and artificial intelligence — especially in a form
reminiscent of interactive Shakespearian tragedy — has become a sort of "holy grail" for
cyberdrama.

There are profound difficulties in achieving these goals, but the three authors presented here
continue to work actively on the design and development of cyberdramatic experiences. They
persevere, perhaps, because they and many others believe that a large number of new media's
most successful creations (*Zork, Myst, Everquest, The Sims*) incline toward cyberdrama. Perhaps
also because cyberdrama exists as a powerful force of imagination (on- or off-board the
Enterprise) even if it has not yet been fully realized.

The essayists in this section are theorist-practitioners of cyberdrama, and each addresses a
major question for cyberdramatists (also a primary theme of this volume): Is there a game-
story? Many in the new media field see cyberdrama as an attempt to marry the structures of
games and stories — and many of cyberdrama's harshest critiques come from those who
believe this to be impossible. The first essay here is from Murray herself, who postulates that
the "game-story" question is fundamentally misformulated. Ken Perlin follows, who finds
engaging characters to be the element missing from even the most successful game-story
examples to date. Finally, Michael Mateas offers what may be the "unified field theory" of
Laurel's and Murray's work; giving a definition of neo-Aristotelian interactive drama, as well as
describing the project he and Andrew Stern are creating through its guidance — a project that
may allow them finally to take hold of cyberdrama's grail.

From Game-Story to Cyberdrama
Janet Murray

Is there a game-story? I think this is the wrong question, though an inevitable one for this moment.

In our discussion here, *game-story* means the story-rich new gaming formats that are proliferating in digital formats: the hero-driven video game, the atmospheric first person shooter, the genre-focused role-playing game, the character-focused simulation. All of these are certainly more storylike than, say, checkers. But, as Celia Pearce has pointed out, not more storylike than chess or Monopoly. Games are always stories, even abstract games such as checkers or *Tetris*, which are about winning and losing, casting the player as the opponent-battling or environment-battling hero.

But why are we particularly drawn to discussion of digital games in terms of story? And why is so much storytelling going on in electronic games? First of all, the digital medium is well-suited to gaming because it is procedural (generating behavior based on rules) and participatory (allowing the player as well as creator move things around). This makes for a lot of gaming. Secondly, it is a medium that includes still images, moving images, text, audio, three-dimensional, navigable space — more of the building blocks of storytelling than any single medium has ever offered us. So gamemakers can include more of these elements in the game world.

Furthermore, games and stories have in common two important structures, and so resemble one another whenever they emphasize these structures. The first structure is the contest, the meeting of opponents in pursuit of mutually exclusive aims. This is a structure of human experience, of course, from parenting to courtship to war, and as a cognitive structure it may have evolved as a survival mechanism in the original struggle of predator and prey in the primeval world. Games take this form, enacting this core experience; stories dramatize and narrate this experience. Most stories and most games include some element of the contest between protagonist and antagonist.

The second structure is the puzzle, which can also be seen as a contest between the reader/player and the author/game-designer. In a puzzle story, the challenge is to the mind, and the pacing is often one of open-ended rearranging rather than turn-based moves. Mystery stories are puzzles, and are often evaluated as games in terms of how challenging and fairly constructed they are. In fact, it makes as much sense to talk about the puzzle-contest (Scrabble) as it does to

Response by Bryan Loyall

In her essay, Janet Murray paints a compelling landscape of the varied forms of cyberdrama and presents criteria for their creation. Especially interesting to me is the *replay story*, and its ability to draw attention to the ramifications of the stream of choices each of us takes for granted each day.

One property of Murray's three main examples is that the participant is consciously aware of the story and actively manipulating it. These forms give powerful ways to tell new types of stories, but for me, one of the joys of a story is when I forget about it being a story. I am simply there. The experience is dense and powerful, and I like the characters, or hate the characters, or am disturbed by them.

I would like to extend Murray's landscape with

another form that has this property, and, following her lead, then suggest criteria to guide its creation.

The form I would like to add is one that combines the high interactivity and immersion of many computer games with the strong story and characters of traditional linear stories. Viewers can enter a simulated world with rich interactive characters, be substantially free to continuously do whatever they want, and yet still experience the powerful dramatic story that the author intended. My colleagues and I at Zoesis Studios and the Carnegie Mellon Oz Project call this form *interactive drama*, and we have been working to create it since the late 1980s.

Some have argued that this combination is impossible. As Murray points out, there are those who say that games and stories are opposed, and what

talk about the story-game. Most stories and most games, electronic or otherwise, include some contest elements and some puzzle elements. So perhaps the question should be, is there a story-game? Which comes first, the story or the game? For me, it is always the story that comes first, because storytelling is a core human activity, one we take into every medium of expression, from the oral-formulaic to the digital multimedia.

Stories and games are also both distanced from the real world, although they often include activities that are done "for real" in other domains. The stock market, for example is a betting game, but real world resources are exchanged and people's out-of-game or out-of-trading-floor lives are profoundly changed by events taking place there. Baseball, on the other hand, is run as a business and has economic and emotional impact on the lives of the players and observers, but the hits-and-misses on the field are in themselves only game moves. Similarly, a dramatization of a murder may be problematic in many ways to a community, but it does not directly result in anyone's death. A story is also different from a report of an event, though we are increasingly aware of how much about an event is invented or constructed by the teller, even when the intention is to be purely factual. Stories and games are like one another in their insularity from the real world,

the world of verifiable events and survival-related consequences.

In a postmodern world, however, everyday experience has come to seem increasingly gamelike, and we are aware of the constructed nature of all our narratives. The ordinary categories of experience, such as parent, child, lover, employer, or friend, have come to be described as "roles" and are readily deconstructed into their culturally invented components. Therefore the union of game and story is a vibrant space, open to exploration by high and low culture, and in sustained and incidental engagements by all of us as we negotiate the shifting social arrangements of the global community and the shifting scientific understandings of our inner landscape. The human brain, the map of the earth, the protocols of human relationships, are all elements in an improvised collective story-game, an aggregation of overlapping, conflicting, constantly morphing structures that make up the rules by which we act and interpret our experiences.

We need a new medium to express this story, to practice playing this new game, and we have found it in the computer. The digital medium is the appropriate locus for enacting and exploring the contests and puzzles of the new global community and the postmodern inner life. As I argued in *Hamlet on the Holodeck: The Future of Narrative in Cyberspace* (1997),

makes a good story makes a bad game and vice versa. Yet, we and others working to create interactive drama think this combination is possible. As evidence for our position let me describe a working implementation. (An interesting side note pointed out by this implementation is that interactive drama does not require computers to exist.)

Imagine collecting an acting company whose sole job is to allow a single person to participate in an interactive drama. The actors each have a role to play, and the author writes a story that places the participant directly in the center of the action. The director is able to communicate privately to the actors through radio headsets. The director's job is to watch the flow of action, particularly what the participant does as the central character, and give direction to the

actors to subtly guide the flow of activity toward the author's story.

Interactive dramas such as this have been created. One of best-documented versions gave the participant the experience of witnessing the evolution of a mugging, having the power to stop it, and facing the continually arising questions of how to react in such a situation as it unfolds (Kelso, Weyhrauch, and Bates 1993).

One obvious problem with this implementation, though, is that not everyone can afford their own dedicated acting troupe. The main advantage that computers give us, once we learn how to make simulated interactive characters and interactive directors for specific stories, is the ability to distribute interactive dramas widely, and thereby encourage their

we can see a new kind of storytelling emerging to match the need for expressing our life in the twenty-first century. The first signs of this new storytelling are in the linear media, which seem to be outgrowing the strictures of the novel and movie in the same way that we might imagine a painting outgrowing the frame and morphing into a three-dimensional sculpture. Stories like Borges' "The Garden of Forking Paths" (1962) and films like *Groundhog Day* (1993) are harbingers of the emerging new story form. The term "story-game" is similar to the term "photoplay" that was used of early movies, as if the new format were merely the addition of photography to theater. We need a different term and a different take on the emerging form, one that recognizes it as moving beyond the additive into a shape unique to its medium. Neal Stephenson, in his science fiction novel *The Diamond Age* (1995), proposes the term "'ractive," which is a contraction of "interactive." In *Hamlet on the Holodeck,* I reluctantly coined the term *cyberdrama*, emphasizing the enactment of the story in the particular fictional space of the computer. Espen Aarseth (1997) uses the term "ergodic literature," which he defines as "open, dynamic texts where the reader must perform specific actions to generate a literary sequence, which may vary for every reading." Some such term is needed to mark the change we are experiencing, the invention of a new genre

altogether, which is narrative in shape and that includes elements we associate with games.

The forms of cyberdrama that I described in *Hamlet on the Holodeck* have proliferated since the book was published in 1997. Role-playing games have blossomed into a new genre, the Massively Multiplayer Online Role-Playing Game, starting with *Ultima Online* (1997), reaching a usership of over 400,000 with *Everquest* (1999), and perhaps reaching over a million with *Star Wars Galaxies,* which as of this writing is planned for release in the summer of 2003. Interactive characters have also become wildly popular, starting with the Tamagotchi, which came out in the United States at the same time as my book, and moving to the current most popular game in digital form, Will Wright's imaginative *The Sims* (2000), which is like a novel-generating system. If there is to be a Charles Dickens or Charlotte Brontë of the digital medium, then Will Wright is surely one of his or her key antecedents. In *The Sims,* Wright has created a multivariant world of rich events and complex character interactions that is open to endless exploration and extension. *The Sims* embodies an ambivalent vision of consumerism and suburban life inside a structure that seems simply to celebrate it. It engages players in building up households in a fictional world that has its own momentum and generates its own plot events. Duplicitous neighbors and morbid

creation. (Computers also allow for a wider range of worlds and characters, but this is secondary to the practical enablement of the form in the first place.)

1.response.1. *OttoAndIris.com.* (Zoesis)

We believe widely distributable interactive drama will become a reality, and as it does it will be important to find criteria to guide the work of creators. I would like to describe some of the criteria we have used while trying to create interactive drama, focusing on criteria that illuminate relations to traditional games and stories.

Murray suggests agency as a criterion for all forms of cyberdrama, and it is central to effective interactive dramas as well. It is a core part of the freedom I mentioned earlier — and, like game designers, we focus our interactive dramas on the participant's constraints and options to help enable agency.

Another important property for interactive drama that comes from its definition is one Murray mentions in her book: immersion. Two related criteria apply to

clowns come to visit and destroy the happiness of the household. The time clock pushes relentlessly forward, with every day a workday, with carpools to meet and chores to do for those at home. The world of *The Sims* has its own moral physics: education leads to job success; a bigger house means more friends; too many possessions lead to exhausting labor; neglect of a pet can lead to the death of a child. The losses in *The Sims* are oddly poignant, with neighbors joining in the prolonged and repeated mourning process. Looking back one hundred years from now, *The Sims* may be seen as the breakthrough text of cyberdrama, just as *Don Quixote* (1605) was for the novel or *The Great Train Robbery* (1905) was for the movies.

The Sims offers strong evidence that a new genre title is needed and it persuades me that "cyberdrama" is probably the best one currently proposed. *The Sims* is neither game nor story. It is a simulation world driven by a new kind of synthetic actor, an actor authored by Will Wright, but also (in the case of the protagonists) instantiated by the interactor who sets the parameters of the character's personality. The actions of the world are also a collaborative improvisation, partly generated by the author's coding and partly triggered by the actions the interactor takes within the mechanical world. It is a kind of Rube Goldberg machine in which a whimsical but compelling chain of events can move in

many ways. The story of *The Sims* is the collective story of all its many instantiations, and users share their events in comic strip "albums" — screenshots with captions that narrate the events of the simulated world. They also trade characters and will soon be able to send their characters on dates together. It is a simulation, a story world, opening the possibility of a *David Copperfield* or *Middlemarch* or *War and Peace* emerging some day, built around other compelling experiences of the global community: not just consumerism in the suburbs, but survival struggles among the underclass of the industrialized nations or postcolonial or ethnically divided countries.

Another community of practice that has grown since 1997 is in the domain of interactive video. As television and computing converge, there are increasing experiments in interactive storytelling, including several prototypes sponsored by the Corporation for Public Broadcasting, or emerging from the Hollywood-based Enhanced TV Workshop of the American Film Institute (which has convened yearly since 1998), or from the Habitat program of the Canadian Film Centre. Of course, our assumptions about the hardware for delivering interactive video have also changed significantly since 1997, and the situation is far from resolved. In spring 2001 there were fewer than five million homes in the United States with set-top boxes,

the characters. For immersion to take place, the characters in the world need to seem real to the participant. This means that they need to be believable enough that the participant cares about them (whether that caring is liking them, hating them or being disturbed by them). Further, we have found that they need to be real enough that the participant respects them. If the participant feels that she can do whatever she wants to the characters (as though they are toys to be played with), then the stakes of the experience and the ability of the characters to seem alive are both weakened.

Our most recent system, *OttoAndIris.com*, is an attempt to create a world that has these properties (see figures 1.response.1–4). It is a playful space that one can enter to play games with two characters, Otto and

Iris. Otto and Iris treat you as an equal, as one of them. Even though you are special in the sense that the whole experience is for you as the participant, the characters

1.response.2. *OttoAndIris.com.* (Zoesis)

but as many as sixty million homes in which the television and the computer were in the same room.

Ford Motor Company sponsored a set of interactive commercials in Spring 2000 in which viewers contributed dialog suggestions and voted on branching choices for a four-episode story broadcast live within a single hour of prime-time network television. In the first episode a couple (chosen from among several possible characters over the internet) leave on a blind date for the surprising destination of the laundromat. The audience is invited to submit a flirtatious remark by which the nerdy male can retrieve the situation. Suggestions poured in over the internet and were scanned on the set during the 15-minute interval before the next episode aired. A witticism about "static cling" was selected and credited to a viewer. Audiences were then asked to guess the number of dirty shirts in the trunk, and later to choose whether the hero should use his last quarter to buy his date a trinket from a vending machine or to pay the parking meter. East coast audiences paid the parking meter and west coast audiences opted for the more romantic plotline. The directing of the story by the audience in real time on a mass stage is similar in its way to the sharing of stories from *The Sims*. It offers us a public stage for remotely controlled actors in structured situations. Most of all, it offers us the sense of a world in which things can go

more than one way.

Since *Hamlet on the Holodeck* came out I've also moved personally: from MIT (where I was directing projects aimed at educational uses of the digital medium and teaching a single undergraduate/graduate course in interactive narrative), to Georgia Tech, where I now direct the Information Design and Technology Program (IDT). IDT is the oldest humanities-based graduate program in interactive design in the world — although it is still only ten years old — and welcomes around twenty graduate students a year. Here we are beginning to see a community of practice arise among the students, including considerable work in new storytelling genres. One of the most promising aspects of this practice, which I have been actively encouraging, is a subgenre I have begun to think of as the *replay story*.

Replay is an aspect of gaming, one of the most pleasurable and characteristic structures of computer-based gaming in particular, which is usually accomplished by saving the game state at regular intervals (before and after each major decision point in the game "script"). In a procedural world, the interactor is scripted by the environment as well as acting upon it. In a game, the object can be to master the script, to perform the right actions in the right order. (This is also an aspect of harbinger storytelling — as in *Groundhog Day* or *Back to the Future* or *Run Lola Run*, in

have their own egos. For example, if you spend too long ignoring Iris, Iris will lose interest in you and leave. Similarly, if you are repeatedly mean to Otto by not

letting him play, he will mope, and stop trying to play with you. If you want him to play again, you will have to wait for his sadness to subside, try to cheer him up,

1.response.3. *OttoAndIris.com.*(Zoesis)

1.response.4. *OttoAndIris.com.*(Zoesis)

which the protagonist inexplicably gets the chance of a "do-over" in the real world.) But it also can reflect our sense of the multiple possibilities of a single moment, the "pullulating" moment, as Borges called it, in which all the quantum possibilities of the world are present. A replay story world allows the interactor to experience all the possibilities of a moment, without privileging any one of them as the single choice.

One successful version of such a replay story is Sarah Cooper's *Reliving Last Night,* initially created as a masters project for the IDT program in spring 2001. In Cooper's interactive video, a woman wakes up confused about who is in bed with her. The rest of the story is a flashback of an evening in which an acquaintance comes over for a study date and an almost-ex-boyfriend shows up hoping to reconcile. The interactor can trace the events of the evening, changing three parameters: what she wears, what beverage she serves, what music she chooses. All of the outcomes reflect the personalities and previous experiences of the characters, and taken as a whole they present a fuller understanding of who they are individually and of the intriguingly rich space of possibilities within a seemingly simple encounter. The story works because of the careful segmentation of the drama into parallel moments, and the well-framed navigation, which allows the interactor to change only one parameter at a time.[1]

Figure 1.sidebar.1:
The areas of game and story have both independent and overlapping features, and for our discussion the areas of contest and puzzle are equally relevant.

We could call *Reliving Last Night* a game-story or a story-game, because it contains elements of gaming. We could call it "new media," which is an increasingly popular term, although both words are problematic: "new" because it is too vague and ephemeral, and "media" because the computer is a single new medium. Or we could call it "ergodic" or 'ractive or cyberdrama. The important thing, to my mind, is to encourage it. The computer is the most powerful pattern-making medium we have available to us, and it includes the legacy patterns of "old" media, but it is not merely

or try to coax him into playing again.

Informal reactions from participants suggest that such strong egos add to, rather than detract from, participants' feeling of immersion and belief in the life of the characters. In an early version of the system, kids testing it drew pictures afterwards of Otto as a "crybaby," and kept talking about the time he refused to sing. The refusal was a bug that caused part of Otto's mind to completely freeze. We thought the bug had ruined the test, but to the kids it showed Otto's strong will and made him seem more alive.

Another criterion we have found important for interactive dramas is that they have compressed intensity. It is important that the story move at a reasonable pace and never get stuck. This is at odds with many games based on solving puzzles. If the

participant can get stuck, then the story doesn't progress, and the compressed intensity that is a hallmark of many traditional stories suffers.

Compressed intensity can be achieved by sharing the advancement of the story between the participant and the world. In a prototype interactive drama system, *The*

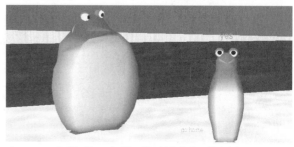

1.response.5. *The Penguin Who Wouldn't Swim.* (Zoesis)

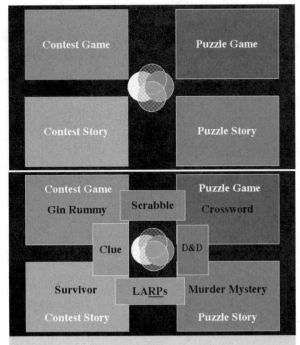

Figures 1.sidebar.2 - 1.sidebar.3. Thinking about nondigital overlap cases, in multiple directions, may be a particularly fruitful activity.

limited to these patterns. It is not merely "new" media or "multimedia" or story-game or game-story. It is redefining the boundaries of storytelling and gameplaying in its own way.

Just as there is no reason to think of mystery novels or role-playing games as merely versions of chess, there is no reason to think of the new forms of story telling as extensions of filmmaking or board games, though they may include elements of all of these. Storytelling and gaming have always been overlapping experiences and will continue to be so. Human experience demands every modality of narration that we can bring to it. The stories we tell reflect and determine how we think about ourselves and one another. A new medium of expression allows us to tell stories we could not tell before, to retell the age-old stories in new ways, to imagine ourselves as creatures of a parameterized world of multiple possibilities, to understand ourselves as authors of rule systems which drive behavior and shape our possibilities.

The computer is a medium in which the puzzle and the game, the instantiated artifact and the performed ritual, both exist (see sidebar). It has its own affordances, which I describe in chapter 3 of *Hamlet on the Holodeck*. The computer is procedural, participatory, encyclopedic, and spatial. This means it can embody rules and execute them; it allows us to manipulate its objects; it can contain more information in more forms than any previous medium; and it can create a world that we can navigate and even inhabit as well as observe. All of these characteristics are appealing for

Penguin Who Wouldn't Swim (1999), the participant is a penguin who is trapped on a chunk of ice with two other penguins, drifting out to a dangerous sea (see figures 1.response.5–7). One of the penguins wants to stay, and the other wants to try to swim back to shore. The participant is always free to do as she wishes in the situation. To adjust the pacing, there is a dramatic guidance system that continuously estimates the

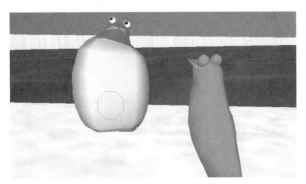

1.response.6. *The Penguin Who Wouldn't Swim*. (Zoesis)

1.response.7. *The Penguin Who Wouldn't Swim*. (Zoesis)

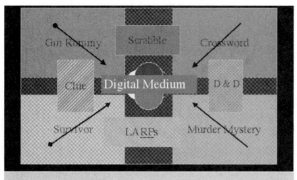

Figure 1.sidebar.4. When we get to the digital medium, we find a medium that can accommodate the features of all these nondigital examples.

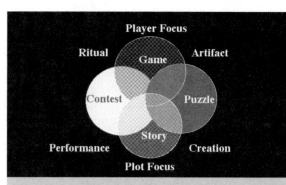

Figure 1.sidebar.5. We can also think of the game/story axis as a player focus/plot focus axis.

Figure 1.sidebar.6. But what if we take a step back, and reconsider the notion that game and story represent two directions of an axis? An interesting territory may open.

gaming; all of these characteristics are appealing for storytelling. Gaming and storytelling have always overlapped. They are both being expanded at this moment as authors take advantage of these new affordances, and they have increased opportunities to develop in their areas of overlap. But there is no reason to limit the resulting form to the dichotomies between story and game, which are more rigidly established in legacy media. We can think instead of matters of degree. A story has greater emphasis on plot; a game has greater emphasis on the actions of the player. But where the player is also the protagonist or the god of the story world, then player action and plot event begin to merge. The task before us, to my mind, is not to

participant's subjective feeling of pacing. If that pacing is good, the system does nothing, leaving space for the participant's actions. When the subjective pacing is bad, the system acts to advance or slow down the story as appropriate, using the characters and other active elements. (As this is going on, the dramatic guidance system is also acting to guide the flow of events toward the author's story.)

All of these criteria are related to those of traditional stories and games, yet many are different in important ways needed for interactive drama. Murray urges us to not be limited by the dichotomy between stories and games, but rather to recombine and reinvent their primitive elements. In working to build these systems we have found that this is not just useful, but necessary. Interactive drama allows us to tell stories that we

couldn't tell before. It combines strengths and elements of stories and games, and is both and yet neither. If we are to reach the potential of expression that it offers, we must work directly in the new medium to explore, experiment and build.

enforce legacy genre boundaries, but to enhance practice within this new medium.

The question that most often arises, in one form or another, in "new media" practice, is how do we tell a good one from a bad one? How do we make it better if we don't know what it is? Too often, the criteria of divergent disciplines or genres are set against one another. We hear, for example, that games and stories are opposed and what makes a good story makes a bad game and vice versa.

But the more useful question is, how do we make a better cyberdrama? One criterion that I have found useful is the concept of dramatic agency. Agency is the term I use to distinguish the pleasure of interactivity, which arises from the two properties of the procedural and the participatory. When the world responds expressively and coherently to our engagement with it, then we experience agency. Agency requires that we script the interactor as well as the world, so that we know how to engage the world, and so that we build up the appropriate expectations. We can experience agency in using a word processing program, when our direct manipulation of the text makes it appropriately change to italics or boldface, for example. In an interactive story world, the experience of agency can be intensified by dramatic effect. If changing what a character is wearing makes for a change in mood within the scene,

if navigating to a different point of view reveals a startling change in physical or emotional perspective, then we experience dramatic agency. Dramatic agency can arise from a losing game move, as when we wind up imprisoned at the end of *Myst*. It is the fittingness of the result to the action taken that makes it satisfying.

Critique of the game-story or story-game or ergodic-'ractive-cyberdrama will be most useful when it helps us to identify what works, especially what works in new ways. A new genre grows from a community of practice elaborating expressive conventions. I would argue that we stop trying to assimilate the new artifacts to the old categories of print- or cinema-based story and board- or player-based game. We should instead think of the characteristics of stories and games and how these separable characteristics are being recombined and reinvented within the astonishingly plastic world of cyberspace.

From Espen Aarseth's Online Response

That the problematic, largely unreplayable, story-game hybrid will dominate the future of digital entertainment seems no more likely than a future with only one kind of sport. While there might be a future for narrative and new forms of storytelling in this cornucopia of new digital and cultural formats, the largest potential seems to be in new types of games, forms that blend the social and the aesthetic in creative ways and on an unprecedented scale. As a new generation of gamers grows up, the word "game" will no longer be as tainted as it is today. Then euphemisms such as "story-puzzles" and "interactors" will no longer be necessary. Games will be games and gamers will be gamers. Storytelling, on the other hand,

still seems eminently suited to sequential formats such as books, films, and e-mails, and might not be in need of structural rejuvenation after all. If it ain't broke, why fix it?

http://www.electronicbookreview.com/thread/firstperson/aarsethr1

Murray Responds

In the end, it does not matter what we call such new artifacts as *The Sims, Façade,* or "Kabul Kaboom": dollhouses, stories, cyberdramas, participatory dramas, interactive cartoons, or even games. The important thing is that we keep producing them.

http://www.electronicbookreview.com/thread/firstperson/murrayr2

Note

1. Parameters can, however, be changed at any time — and the parameter choice controls are always exposed on the interface of *Reliving Last Night*. As Noah Wardrip-Fruin points out, this allows for continual "at-will" switches between alternate versions during the flow of the story. This is different from most game replay, in which seeing another version requires restoring to a previous game state and then making new choices from that point forward. Only by recording several play-throughs of different game options and running these recordings in parallel could the continual, in-flow comparisons of *Reliving Last Night* be achieved.

References: Literature

Aarseth, Espen (1995). "Le Texte de l'Ordinateur est à Moitié Construit: Problèmes de Poétique Automatisée." In *Littérature et Informatique*, edited by Alain Vuillemin and Michel Lenoble. Arras: Artois P Université.

Aarseth, Espen (1997). *Cybertext: Perspectives on Ergodic Literature*. Baltimore: Johns Hopkins University Press.

Borges, Jorge Luis (1962). "The Garden of Forking Paths." In *Ficciones*, edited by Anthony Kerrigan. New York: Grove Press.

Kelso, Margaret Thomas, Peter Weyhrauch, and Joseph Bates (1993). "Dramatic Presence." *Presence: The Journal of Teleoperators and Virtual Environments* 2, no.1 (Winter 1993).

Murray, Janet (1997). *Hamlet on the Holodeck. The Future of Narrative in Cyberspace*. New York: The Free Press.

Stephenson, Neal (1995). *The Diamond Age: or, A Young Lady's Illustrated Primer*. New York: Spectra.

References: Games

Kabul Kaboom. Gonzalo Frasca. 2001.
<http://www.ludology.org/games/kabulkaboom.html>.

New York Defender. Uzinagaz. 2001.
<http://www.uzinagaz.com/index.php?entry_point=wtc>.

The Penguin Who Wouldn't Swim. Zoesis. 1999.

Can There Be a Form between a Game and a Story?
Ken Perlin

Why does a character in a book or movie seem more "real" to us than a character in a computer game? And what would it take to make an interactive character on our computer screen seem real to us the way that a character on the page or silver screen does? In other words, is there something intermediate between a story character and a game character? As I write this I'm looking at my computer screen, where an interactively animated character that I've created appears to be looking back at me. In what sense can that character be considered "real"? Obviously it's all relative; there's no actual person in my computer, any more than a character in a movie is an actual person. We're talking about a test of "dramatic" reality. But what sort of dramatic reality?

If I'm seeing a movie and the protagonist gets hurt, I feel bad because I've grown to identify with that character. The filmmakers have (with my consent) manipulated my emotions so as to make me view the world from that character's point of view for 100 minutes or so. I implicitly consent to this transference process; I "willingly suspend my disbelief." As I watch the movie, I am continually testing the protagonist's apparent inner moral choices against my own inner moral measuring stick, looking for affirmation of higher goals and ideals, or for betrayal of those ideals. That transference is why a character such as Tony Soprano, for example, is so gripping: the narrative and point of view lead us forcefully into his vulnerable inner landscape, into the way, for example, that he finds connection with his own need for family by nurturing a family of wild ducklings. And then we are led to scenes of him being a brutal mob boss, hurting or maiming adversaries who get in his way. The power of the work lies in pulling us into the point of view of a character who makes moral choices wildly at odds with the choices that most of us would make. In some strange sense we "become" Tony Soprano for a time, a very novel and unsettling experience for most of us.

This transference can be effected in such a focused and powerful way only because we agree (when we start watching) to give over our choice-making power, and to passively allow the narrative to lead us where it will. When this is done well, then we are drawn inside the head of one character (or in some cases several characters). In that mode we are taken to places that we

Response by Will Wright

Ken Perlin raises some very good points in his article. I think the question of "agency" is particularly relevant (who's in control) but first I would like to step back a bit and look at a somewhat larger view.

Since the dawn of computer games (a mere 20 years ago) there has always been this underlying assumption that they would one day merge somehow with the more predominant media forms (books, movies, TV). A strong, compelling (but still interactive) story seems to be the thing that people feel is missing from games. I agree that the believable, virtual actors that Ken envisions would be a major step towards this goal.

However, I've always had a hard time accepting the idea that games should aspire to tell better stories.

There seems to be this expectation that new media forms will evolve smoothly from older forms (Books → Radio → Movies → TV) and then go on to find their niche. The jump from linear media to nonlinear is in many ways a much more fundamental shift, though.

From a design viewpoint the dramatic arc (and its associated character development) is the central scaffolding around which story is built. The characters that we become immersed in as an audience are inextricably moving through a linear sequence of events that are designed to evoke maximum emotional involvement. Everything else (setting, mood, world) is free to be molded around this scaffolding. They are subservient to it. The story is free to dictate the design of the world in which it occurs.

might never reach in our actual lives.

The form I have just described, of course, arises from what I will call "The Novel," which has for some time been the dominant literary form of Western civilization. Whether it is in the form of oral storytelling, written text, dramatic staging, or cinema, the basic premise is the same. A trusted storyteller says to us, "Let me tell you a story. There was a guy (or gal), and one day the following conflict happened, and then this other thing happened, and then. . .," and by some transference process we become that guy or gal for the duration of the story. His conflict becomes our conflict, his choices our choices, and his fictional changes of character seem, oddly, like a sort of personal journey for our own souls. My focus here will be more on those variants of the novel in which the narrative is literally played out by embodied actors, such as staged theater, cinema and figurative animation, because those are the narrative media with the closest connection to modern computer games.

There's an odd sort of alchemy at work in the way that the transference process by which viewer identifies with the protagonist succeeds precisely because it is not literal. For example, imagine a novel in which countless millions of innocent people die a senseless and brutal death, with much of the world's population being wiped out, yet in which the protagonists, when faced with

difficult moral choices, acquit themselves admirably and stay true to their ideals. This will probably result in an uplifting story. (This is precisely the recipe, for example, of the films *When Worlds Collide* and *Independence Day*.) In such a story, the protagonist doesn't even need to survive — as long as he dies nobly, exiting with a suitably stirring speech on his tongue or a grim gleam of stoic heroism in his steely eye.

On the other hand, imagine another novel in which nobody is killed or even hurt, but in which the sympathetic protagonist betrays his inner ideals. This is inevitably a tragic tale, and reading or viewing it will fill us with despair. *The Bicycle Thief* is a classic example.

Note that there are certainly other art forms that convey personality, soul, and character without following the paradigm of linear narrative. Figurative sculpture, for example, does not impose a narrative on us, although it certainly can transport us to a different emotional state or psychological point of view. There is no fixed viewpoint from which we are expected to look at a sculpture. There isn't even a recommended sequence of successive viewpoints. And yet sculpture, without narrative, can powerfully convey emotions, personality, struggle.

So, there is something very particular about the way the novel, in all its many variants, goes about its business. By telling us a story, it asks us to set aside

A game is structured quite differently. The paramount constructs here are the constraints on the player. As a game designer I try to envision an interesting landscape of possibilities to drop the player into and then design the constraints of the world to keep them there. Within this space the landscape of possibilities (and challenges) need to be interesting, varied, and plausible (imagine a well-crafted botanical garden). It is within this defined space that the player will move, and hence define *their own* story arc.

My aspirations for this new form are not about telling better stories but about allowing players to "play" better stories within these artificial worlds. The role of the designer becomes trying to best leverage the agency of the player in finding dramatic and

interesting paths through this space. Likewise, I think that placing character design and development in the player's hands rather than the designer's will lead to a much richer future for this new medium.

Back to Ken's points, I do agree that there is a strong linkage between the believability of the characters and the dramatic potential of the work. This has been perhaps the most technically limiting factor to dramatic game design. In *The Sims* we fell back on abstraction to address this issue. By purposely making the Sims fairly low-detail and keeping a certain distance from them we forced the players to fill in the representational blanks with their imaginations (an amazingly effective process which is well-covered in Scott McCloud's (1993) *Understanding Comics*).

2.sidebar.1. A promotional image of Lara Croft. (Eidos Interactive, Core Design)

our right to make choices — our agency. Instead, the agency of a protagonist takes over, and we are swept up in observation of his struggle, more or less from his point of view, as though we were some invisible spirit or angel perched upon his shoulder, watching but

never interfering.

By way of contrast, look at games. A game does not force us to relinquish our agency. In fact, the game depends on it.

When you play *Tomb Raider* you don't actually think of Lara Croft as a person the same way, say, you think of Harry Potter as a person (see sidebar images). There is a fictional construct in the backstory to the game. But while you're actually playing the game, the very effectiveness of the experience depends on *you* becoming Lara Croft. The humanlike figure you see on your computer screen is really a game token, and every choice she makes, whether to shoot, to leap, to run, to change weapons, is your choice.

When you stop the game play momentarily, there is no sense that the personality of Lara Croft is anywhere to be found. While you're taking inventory, changing weapons, etc., the game figure on the screen stands impassively, and you know that the figure would stand that way forever if you were never to reenter gameplay mode. In other words, even a bare minimum of suspension of disbelief is not attempted. In fact, you are supposed to "become" Lara Croft — it is that immediacy and responsiveness that makes the game so exciting.

So let's compare Harry Potter to Lara Croft. When I am reading one of the Harry Potter books, and I put the

What excites me the most about Ken's work is the idea that I can create a character with a few simple brush strokes (personality, quirks, hidden flaws) and then unleash that character into a world and watch what naturally emerges from those traits. The chaotic interaction of this simple (but plausible and believable) character with its environment has the potential to drive empathy to a much higher level than nonlinear media because I'm not just an observer; I'm her creator. She is not only controlled by me (potentially) but her flaws and quirks were defined by me; she contains a part of me in a way that other media forms can only loosely approximate.

From Victoria Vesna's Online Response

Perlin's discussion of hyper-real responsive characters, that would presumably allow for a real actor with agency to emerge, does not explain the popularity of game formats such as MUDs and MOOs. These simple text-based early game genres (*Multi-User Domain,* and *MUD, Object Oriented,* respectively) were successful in working with the player's imagination, allowing for identification to happen on the basis of world-building and interaction with an online community. MUDs and MOOs are excellent examples of using words and stories that come from conventional literature in such radically different ways that an entirely new form of literature, if it can be called this, emerged.

http://www.electronicbookreview.com/thread/firstperson/vesnar1

book aside for a while, I can easily sustain the pleasant fiction that there is an actual Harry Potter, with a continued set of feelings and goals, living "offstage" somewhere. This is because to read Harry Potter is to experience his agency, as he navigates the various difficult challenges that life presents him. In contrast, when I walk away from my computer screen, I cannot sustain the fiction that an actual Lara Croft continues to exist offstage, because I have not actually experienced her agency. All I have really experienced is *my* agency.

Of course, linear narrative forms and games are intended to serve very different purposes. The traditional goal of a linear narrative is to take you on a vicarious emotional journey, whereas the traditional goal of a game is to provide you with a succession of active challenges to master. A "character" in a game is traditionally merely a convenient vehicle for framing and embodying these challenges. In this sense, a game is traditionally all about player control, since without active control, the player cannot meet the challenges that the game poses.

So how could the two forms, story and game, grow closer together? Well, to start, let's look at narrative structure. Here's a classic story arc: in the beginning, we are introduced to the basic characters, and some introductory conflicts are played out in small scale.

Choices are made early on by the protagonists that have ramifications only much later in the drama (foreshadowing). Over time, the stakes get raised; the conflict becomes stripped to its essentials, culminating in a dramatic climax near the end. When the dust settles, in the release of dramatic tension that inevitably follows climax, there is a clear outcome.

Of course what I've just described is the basic gameplay of both *Monopoly* and chess. One obvious thing that distinguishes these games from narrative literature is that their protagonists are the players. In contrast, the conflicts in a work of narrative literature are played out by fictional characters, and the author's deeper purpose in building the narrative structure is generally to take the reader through the dynamic psychological journey of these characters. It was once said of writing narrative fiction that: "'Plot' is the drugged meat that you throw over the fence to put the guard dog to sleep so you can rob the house." In other words, story is about conveying character. To do that interactively would require some sort of plausible psychological agency on the part of somebody within the interactive narrative.

If we look at "linear narrative" and "interactive game" as a dialectic, how can we really get into intermediate states along this dialectic? In other words, can we create a form in which the wall between "my agency" and "the

Perlin Responds

The main point on which I take issue with Vesna's response is her characterization of what I'm proposing as a sort of "hyper-realism." More accurately, I'm proposing a sort of "hyper-believability," as compared to the game genre in its current form.

http://www.electronicbookreview.com/thread/firstperson/perlinr2

2.sidebar.2. A screenshot from the PDA version of *Tomb Raider*.
(Eidos Interactive, Core Design)

agency of an entity that seems psychologically present and real to me" can be removed or blurred?

But what exactly would intermediate agency look like? A fascinating insight is provided by Philip Pullman's trilogy of novels *His Dark Materials*. These novels take place in an alternate universe in which the soul of a person is an external, embodied entity. In this universe your soul is neither distinctly "self" nor "other," but rather an embodied familiar, or daemon, who always travels with you, who helps you to wrestle with choices, and with whom you can converse. Interestingly, the daemons of two people can converse with each other directly. If one imagines a similar relationship between a player and a character, this dramatic structure could plausibly lead to a form of creative work with is intermediate between "linear narrative" and "game," by enabling a psychologically present entity which is somewhere in between "me" and "other."

There has been some movement in the computer gaming world toward something that one could call "character." But these attempts have been hindered by the fact that characters in games can't act within an interactive scene in any compelling way. Of particular interest are "god-games" — those games, such as Will Wright's *SimCity*, in which the player takes a "God's eye view" of the proceedings. More recently, Wright introduced *The Sims* — a simulated suburban world in which the player nurtures simulated people, sort of as pets (see sidebar image). The player directs these virtual people, who have no knowledge of the existence of the player, to buy things, marry, have children, take care of their physical and psychological needs, and so forth.

In a sense, the player is asked to take on some of the traditional role of an author — *The Sims* itself is more of a simulator toy than a game. By playing with this simulator, the player becomes a sort of author. As in many god-games, the player himself is expected to design much of the dramatic arc of the experience — it is up to him to starve or to feed his Sims characters, to introduce them, encourage them to acquire possessions or children. Given the current state of technology, it would be impossible to sustain the dramatic illusion if these characters were to attempt to speak to each other in clear English. For this reason, Wright has made the clever design decision to have the characters "talk" to each other in a sort of gibberish. This allows us to buy into the illusion that they are engaging each other in substantive conversations about something or other. In this way, *The Sims* replaces some social activity in its simulated world with the *texture* of social activity.

Playing *The Sims* is lots of fun, but one thing conspicuously lacking from the experience is any compelling feeling that the characters are real. Much of this lack comes from *The Sims'* reliance on sequences of linear animation to convey the behavior of its characters. For example, if the player indicates to a Sims character that the character should feed her baby, then the character will run a canned animation to walk over to the baby's bassinet, pick up the baby, and make feeding movements. If the player then tells her to play with the baby, she will put the baby down, return to a previous position, then begin the animation to approach the bassinet, again pick up the baby, and start to play. One result of this mechanical behavior is that there is no real possibility of willing suspension of disbelief on the part of the player as to the reality of the character.

The player ends up thinking of *The Sims* as a sort of probabilistic game, not really as a world inhabited by feeling creatures. A player quickly realizes that anything that happens that is not caused by his own agency is being caused by the equivalent of a set of dice being thrown inside the software, not through the agency of

2.sidebar.3. Caring for baby in *The Sims*. (Electronic Arts, Maxis)

thinking, feeling characters. *The Sims* remains, dramatically, a world-building game, not a psychological narrative in which one believes in the agency of the characters.

In the gaming world, one can also see a small step in the direction of intermediate agency in the game *Black and White*, a god-game in which the player has the use of embodied daemons to do his bidding. Yet the daemons in this game do not seem like interestingly real characters. I believe that one key reason for this is that the key ingredients of successful narrative film are simply not yet available for use in games.

In order to create a psychological suspension of disbelief, a visual narrative medium requires all three of the following elements: writing, directing, and acting. If any of these is missing, then a narrative on stage or film cannot provide observers with the essential framework they need to suspend their disbelief.

Of these elements, in computer games to date, acting has been conspicuously missing. Even in the most badly executed films (e.g., the films of Ed Wood) the essential humanity of the actors playing the characters somehow manages to come through. We *believe* the actor is attempting to convey a specific character within a specific scene, and we respond by agreeing to pretend that the actor has become that character, responding to the psychological challenges of the moment.

Yet imagine that film or theater did not have acting as we know it — but that instead all cast members

were constrained to act in the most rotely mechanical way, repeating lines of dialogue and movements without any feeling that was specific to the scene (think of the mother putting down the baby only to pick it up again, in *The Sims*).

This is precisely the situation that game designers are faced with today when they foray into more narrative-based forms. If, as a creator, you have a nonlinear, interactive narrative structure, but it is embodied in such a way that acting is essentially nonexistent, then there is no way to create emotional buy-in for that character — the willing suspension of disbelief by the audience in that character's existence. *Myst* cleverly got around this by creating an interactive narrative in which there were no people (they were all gone before the observer shows up). But when the sequel *Riven* introduced actual fictional characters, the results were far less compelling, because it became immediately apparent that these were mere precanned game characters — windup toys — about whom the player could not really suspend disbelief.

A number of people have been working very hard over the years on "nonlinear" or interactive narrative. It is my contention that these efforts cannot move forward to merge film and games, and that we will not

2.sidebar.4. A promotional image of Lara Croft. (Eidos Interactive, Core Design)

1.1: NYU's Responsive Face.

number of emotional primitives. You can see to the right of the face the basic elements of facial expression. Just above those are some example "presets" — complex facial expressions that are simply linear combinations of the lower-level primitives. Above that are some tools to let the user string together sequences of expressions to tell an emotional story.

Tools such as this one can help us to learn what works (or doesn't work) to make an effective interactive actor. With any luck (and some hard work), we will have good interactive acting on our computer screens by the time the next edition of this book comes out. And that capability will, in turn, provide one of the key tools needed to properly explore the space of an interactive narrative form intermediate between story and game.

be able to find a way to create an intermediate agency that will allow the viewer to find their way into caring about characters, until we provide a way that characters can act well enough to embody an interactive narrative.

For this reason, and to lay the groundwork for interactive media that are intermediate in the "agency" dialectic, a number of us have been working on various techniques for "better interactive acting ability" by computer-based virtual actors. This work involves body language, facial expression, rhythm of conversational response, varieties of ways to convey focus and attention between actors, and various ways to convey internal emotional states and awareness while playing a scene.

Right now, we're all in a learning stage, trying to figure out what works to make effective emotionally interactive actors. For example, presented here (figure 2.1) is the control panel for an interactive applet we made at NYU that teaches its user how to build a large vocabulary of facial expressions by combining a small

Reference

McCloud, Scott (1993). *Understanding Comics: The Invisible Art.* Lettering by Bob Lappan. Northampton, MA: Tundra.

A Preliminary Poetics for Interactive Drama and Games

Michael Mateas

Introduction

Interactive drama has been discussed for a number of years as a new AI-based interactive experience (Laurel 1986; Bates 1992). While there has been substantial technical progress in building believable agents (Bates, Loyall, and Reilly 1992; Blumberg 1996, Hayes-Roth, van Gent, and Huber 1996), and some technical progress in interactive plot (Weyhrauch 1997), no work has yet been completed that combines plot and character into a full-fledged dramatic experience. The game industry has been producing plot-based interactive experiences (adventure games) since the beginning of the industry, but only a few of them (such as *The Last Express*) begin to approach the status of interactive drama. Part of the difficulty in achieving interactive drama is due to the lack of a theoretical framework guiding the exploration of the technological and design issues surrounding interactive drama. This paper proposes a theory of interactive drama based on Aristotle's dramatic theory, but modified to address the interactivity added by player agency. This theory both provides design guidance for interactive dramatic experiences that attempt to maximize player agency (answering the question "What should I build?") and technical direction for the AI work necessary to build the system (answering the question "How should I build it?"). In addition to clarifying notions of interactive drama, the model developed in this essay also provides general framework for analyzing player agency in any interactive experience (e.g., interactive games).

This neo-Aristotelian theory integrates Murray's (1998) proposed aesthetic categories for interactive stories and Aristotle's structural categories for drama. The theory borrows from Laurel's treatment of Aristotle in an interactive context (Laurel 1986, 1991) but extends it by situating Murray's category of agency within the model; the new model provides specific design guidelines for maximizing user agency. First, I present the definition of interactive drama motivating this theory and situate this definition with respect to other notions of interactive story. Next, I present Murray's three categories of immersion, agency, and transformation. Then, I present a model of Aristotle's categories relating them in terms of formal and material causation. Within this model, agency will be

---

Response by Brenda Laurel

Michael Mateas begins by noting that AI has, so far, failed to produce a viable example of interactive dramatic experience. Ain't it a horrible disappointment? But this author brings a fresh approach to AI that may save the day after all. In any case, it is far nobler to go for the grail than simply admire all the different ways you can look at the stained-glass windows.

I agree with Mateas that agency is essential to robust interaction. In my dissertation research, I learned that "significance" was a key aspect of agency — that is, that the effect that a player's actions has on the plot needs to be substantial. I used the example of changing the color of the flowers in the King's garden — an early example of interactivity that we built into an interactive fairy tale at Cybervision (1977). We couldn't imagine significant interaction, probably because it wasn't possible with only 2K of RAM and programs being loaded from cassette tape. Later in my experience with virtual reality (VR), I learned that immersion and agency are deeply related. Without agency, we are simply looking at absorbing images, or, as in the case of motion-platform rides, having ourselves shaken around by some other agency. Mateas's formulation of the "primacy of agency" is an excellent translation of Aristotle's "primacy of action" to a first-person, interactive context.

An experiential or phenomenological analysis of dramatic experience is not new. Aristotle addressed the emotional effects of drama in terms of empathy — the ability to "feel with" characters — and catharsis, the release of emotion when the outcome of an action

situated as two new causal chains inserted at the level of character. Finally, I use the resulting model to clarify conceptual and technical issues involved in building interactive dramatic worlds, and briefly describe a current project informed by this model.

Defining Interactive Drama

Many game designers, writers, and theorists have wrestled with the vexing question, "What is interactive story?" This paper continues a specific thread of discussion with respect to this question, the thread begun by Laurel's adoption of an Aristotelian framework first for interactive drama (Laurel 1986) and then more generally for interactive experiences (Laurel 1991) and continued by Murray's description of the experiential pleasures and properties of interactive stories (Murray 1998). Whereas Murray explores a variety of interactive story types, this essay focuses explicitly on the notion of interactive drama as defined in Laurel's thesis (Laurel 1986) and pursued by the Oz Project at Carnegie Mellon University (Bates, Loyall, and Reilly 1992; Weyhrauch 1997).

MUD stands for Multi-User Dungeon, Multi-User Dimension, or Multi-User Dialogue. MOO stands for MUD, Object-Oriented.

In this conception of interactive drama, the player assumes the role of a first-person character in a dramatic story.

The player does not sit above the story, watching it as in a simulation, but is immersed *in* the story.

Following Laurel, dramatic (Aristotelian) stories are distinguished from narrative stories by the following properties:

> Enactment vs. Description
>
> Intensification vs. Extensification
>
> Unity of Action vs. Episodic Structure

Enactment refers to action. Dramas utilize action rather than description to tell a story. Intensification is achieved by arranging incidents so as to intensify emotion and condense time. In contrast, narrative forms often "explode" incidents by offering many interpretations of the same incident, examining the incident from multiple perspectives, and expanding time. Unity of action refers to the arrangement of incidents such that they are all causally related to a central action. One central theme organizes all the incidents that occur in the story. Narratives tend to employ episodic structure, in which the story consists of a collection of causally unrelated incidents.

Certainly not all interactive story experiences must have the properties of Aristotelian drama. In fact, most interactive story experiences built to date have either been highly episodic (generally those narrative

becomes clear. These can be seen as transformative experiences. Empathy might be seen as a weak form of masquerade, using Murray's terms, in the sense that an audience member "tries on" the inner experiences of a character. Catharsis can be seen as "personal transformation" — indeed, in Greek tragedy, this personal transformation was the end cause. The idea of variety is inherent in the very nature of drama itself, which represents actions that are other than "reality."

Mateas states that "the formal cause is the authorial view of the play." Actually, in Aristotelean terms, the author's intent and work are the efficient, not the formal, cause (*Physics, Metaphysics*). The idea of theme does not appear in the *Poetics*. A more purist definition would be that the author has constructed a plot in order to represent a whole action. A theme would,

however, fall in the category of efficient cause, along with the author and the tools used.

Mateas also asserts that "the material cause is the audience view of the play." Again, to be a purist about it, Aristotle does not couch material causality in terms of the audience, but rather as the materials that are successively formulated by the playwright into the plot. Interestingly enough, the audience's "a-ha" experience may be thought of as the end cause of a play rather than its formal cause; that is, the form of drama is deployed to the end of providing catharsis or understanding for the audience.

Mateas's new causal chains (as represented in his Figure 3.2) are based on a very interesting analysis and a good inversion. Speaking in Aristotelean terms, however, the player does not provide formal causality.

experiences built by the game industry, e.g., adventure games), have employed a hypertextual logic of association rather than a logic of dramatic probability and causality (generally those experiences built by fine artists and writers), or have focused on story not as a highly structured experience created by an author for consumption by an audience, but rather as a shared social construction facilitating human communication (e.g., multiuser worlds such as MUDs, MOOs, and avatar spaces; massive multiplayer games such as *Everquest* and *Ultima Online*; and games such as Purple Moon's *Rocket* series or Will Wright's *The Sims*). Additionally, the interaction in an interactive story does not necessarily have to be first-person interaction as a character within the story. The neo-Aristotelian poetics developed here informs a specific niche within the space of interactive narrative and provides a principled way of distinguishing this niche from other interactive narrative experiences.

Murray's Aesthetic Categories

Murray (1998) proposes three aesthetic categories for the analysis of interactive story experiences: immersion, agency, and transformation.

Immersion is the feeling of being present in another place and engaged in the action therein. Immersion is related to Coleridge's "willing suspension of disbelief"

— when a participant is immersed in an experience, they are willing to accept the internal logic of the experience, even though this logic deviates from the logic of the real world. A species of immersion is telepresence, the feeling of being physically present (from a first-person point of view) in a remote environment.

Agency is the feeling of empowerment that comes from being able to take actions in the world whose effects relate to the player's intention. This is not mere interface activity. If there are many buttons and knobs for the player to twiddle, but all this twiddling has little effect on the experience, there is no agency. Furthermore, the effect must relate to the player intention. If, in manipulating the interface elements, the player does have an effect on the world, but they are not the effects that the player intended (perhaps the player was randomly trying things because they didn't know what to do, or perhaps the player thought that an action would have one effect, but it instead had another), then there is no agency.

Transformation is the most problematic of Murray's three categories. Transformation has at least three distinct meanings.

Transformation as masquerade. The game experience allows the player to transform

but contributes efficient causality to the extent that she shares authorship of the plot, and also contributes materially to the plot by presenting thought and character (patterns of choice) that can influence the shape of the particular plot. Later, Mateas correctly implies that knowledge (or intuition) about the form can act as a constraint on the player's actions. Mateas's key contribution, in my view, is his novel and extremely useful observation that "in order to invoke a sense of agency, an interactive experience must strike a balance between the material and formal constraints."

I think it's brilliant to place "the mechanism of interaction" (as an affordance) at the level of spectacle, referring specifically what the interface presents to the player as the possible modes of interaction. It is consistent with Aristotelean spectacle in that it must be

available to the senses. We should add that a player may be enabled to impinge on the evolving plot at various levels, and that this may suggest some new criteria for judging the robustness of interactivity. An interface that enables language or symbolic communication enables a player to contribute material at the level of diction. How far-ranging the player's choices may be (from predetermined one-button responses to inventive solutions) can be seen as the range available at the level of thought. But thought counts for naught (rhyme intended) unless it can be expressed in action, and action doesn't count unless it is consequential at the level of plot. This means that enabling blathering, hand-wringing, and random smiting does not constitute robust interaction design, unless these behaviors change the course of the plot itself.

themselves into someone else for the duration of the experience.

Transformation as variety. The game experience offers a multitude of variations on a theme. The player is able to exhaustively explore these variations and thus gain an understanding of the theme.

Personal transformation. The game experience takes the player on a journey of personal transformation.

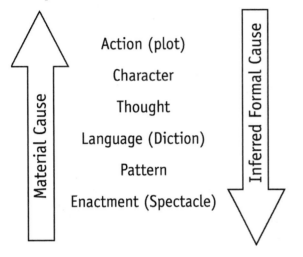

Action (plot)

Character

Thought

Language (Diction)

Pattern

Enactment (Spectacle)

Material Cause

Inferred Formal Cause

3.1 Aristotelian theory of drama

Transformation as masquerade and variety can be seen as means to effect personal transformation.

Integrating Agency into Aristotle

Murray's categories are phenomenological categories of the interactive story experience, that is, categories describing what it *feels* like to participate in an interactive story. Aristotle's categories (described later) are structural categories for the analysis of drama, that is, categories describing what *parts* a dramatic story is made out of. The trick in developing a theoretical framework for interactive drama is integrating the phenomenological (that is, what it feels like) aspect of first-person experiences with the structural aspects of carefully crafted stories. In attempting this integration, I first discuss the primacy of the category of agency. Second, I briefly present an interpretation of the Aristotelian categories in terms of material and formal cause. Finally, agency is integrated into this model.

Primacy of Agency

From an interactive dramatic perspective, agency is the most fundamental of Murray's three categories. Immersion, in the form of engagement, is already implied in the Aristotelian model. Engagement and identification with the protagonist are necessary in order for an audience to experience catharsis.

Immersion is a tricky subject. Certainly, it enhances empathy and the experience of flow. Just as Aristotle identified enactment as a key differentiator of drama from other forms of narrative, so sensory immersion may be seen to distinguish interactive drama from interactive fiction. I agree with Mateas and Murray that immersion also requires agency.

Regarding transformation, the sort of "transformation as variety" that Murray suggests ("a kaleidoscopic narrative that refuses closure") strikes me as an exercise that would be pleasurable primarily for postmodern literary theorists. The rest of us probably prefer a more muscular form of interaction. Mateas reinforces this point when he says that the dramatic world "must provide agency *and* transformation as variety." I would merely emphasize (again) that the

agency must have real significance at the level of plot.

Mateas emphasizes the role of replayability with noticeable differences in plot as an essential characteristic of IF. Murray's analysis seems not to address the appeal of the idea that one can reenter the world and personally (as a character) shove the plot in a different direction. Certainly, the mutability of plot as a direct result of player interaction makes re-playing a game intrinsically different than re-reading a novel or re-viewing a film. As Mateas correctly observes, within the space of a dramatic world's potential, an interactor should be able to influence how the possible is formulated into the probably and ultimately the necessary. (For a visual representation of this, see figure 3.2 of *Computers as Theatre*).

I am delighted by Mateas and Stern's technical

Transformation, in the form of change in the protagonist, also already exists in the Aristotelian model. Murray's discussion of transformation as variety, particularly in the form of the kaleidoscopic narrative that refuses closure, is contrary to the Aristotelian ideals of unity and intensification. To the extent that we want a model of interactive *drama*, as opposed to interactive narrative, much of Murray's discussion of transformation falls outside the scope of such a model. While immersion and transformation exist in some form in noninteractive drama, the audience's sense of having agency within the story is a genuinely new experience enabled by interactivity. For these reasons, agency will be the category integrated with Aristotle.

Aristotelian Drama

Following Laurel (1991), Aristotle's theory of drama is represented in figure 3.1. Aristotle analyzed plays in terms of six hierarchical categories, corresponding to different "parts" of a play. These categories are related via material cause and formal cause. The material cause of something is the material out of which the thing is created. For example, the material cause of a building is the building materials of which it is constructed. The formal cause of something is the abstract plan, goal, or ideal towards which something is heading. For example,

the formal cause of a building is the architectural blueprints.

In drama, the formal cause is the authorial view of the play. The author has constructed a plot that attempts to explicate some theme. The characters required in the play are determined by the plot; the plot is the formal cause of the characters. A character's thought processes are determined by the kind of character they are. The language spoken by the characters is determined by their thought. The patterns (song) present in the play are determined, to a large extent, by the characters' language (more generally, their actions). The spectacle, the sensory display presented to the audience, is determined by the patterns enacted by the characters.

In drama, the material cause is the audience's view of the play. The audience experiences a spectacle, a sensory display. In this display, the audience detects patterns. These patterns are understood as character actions (including language). Based on the character's actions and spoken utterances, the audience infers the characters' thought processes. Based on this understanding of the characters' thought processes, the audience develops an understanding of the characters, the characters' traits and propensities. Based on all this information, the audience understands the plot structure and the theme. In a successful play, the

---

agenda. The element of "beats" in their proposed architecture sounds very promising, and their goals are right on the money. Mateas states, "We are interested in interactive experiences that appeal to the adult, non-computer-geek, movie-and-theater-going public." I can't help observing that the emphasis on relationships and narrative would be extremely appealing to women. Now wouldn't that be nice? The insistence that the player perform as protagonist will yield the most satisfying experience. It will also be the hardest to accomplish, but damn the torpedoes, as they say. I am personally elated that Mateas and Stern continue the work on the problem of IF and carry it in an interesting new direction.

From Gonzalo Frasca's Online Response

If, as Mateas affirms, players "should not be over-constrained by a role" and they should be encouraged "to be themselves" then they will expect a degree of freedom of action that is incompatible with Mateas' goals. Imagine, as game designer Tim Schafer once suggested to me, that you wanted to create a game where you play the role of Gandhi. How would you give agency to players while preventing them from turning peace-loving Gandhi into a *Quake*-like killing machine? The traditional solution would be to put authorial constraints and, for example, prevent the player from using potential weapons. Of course, you can try to fool the player by tricking him into doing what the author wants her to do. But, as Mateas admits, this option fails after the software is used a couple of times. I can only

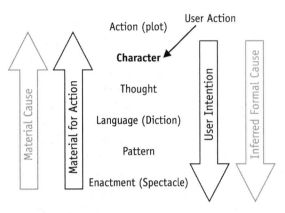

3.2 Neo-Aristotelian theory of drama

audience is then able to recapitulate the chain of formal causation. When the plot is understood, there should be an "a-ha" experience in which the audience is now able to understand how the characters relate to the plot (and why they must be the characters they are), why those types of characters think the way they do, why they took the actions they did and said what they did, how their speech and actions created patterns of activity, and how those patterns of activity resulted in the spectacle that the audience saw. By a process of interpretation, the audience works up the chain of material cause in order to recapitulate the chain of formal cause.

Interactive Drama

Adding interaction to the Aristotelian model can be considered the addition of two new causal chains at the level of character.

In figure 3.2, the gray arrows are the traditional chains of material and formal causation. The player has been added to the model as a character who can choose his or her own actions. This has the consequence of introducing two new causal chains. The player's intentions become a new source of formal causation. By taking action in the experience, the player's intentions become the formal cause of activity happening at the levels from language down to spectacle. But this ability to take action is not completely free; it is constrained from below by material resources and from above by authorial formal causation from the level of plot.

The elements present below the level of character provide the player with the material resources (material cause) for taking action. The only actions available are the actions supported by the material resources present in the game. The notion of affordance (Norman 1988) from interface design is useful here. In interface design, affordances are the opportunities for action made available by an object or interface. But affordance is even stronger than implied by the phrase "made available"; in order for an interface to be said to afford a certain action, the interface must in some sense "cry

---

envision two possible solutions to this dilemma. You could either kill replayability by creating disposable software that could only be experienced once (Frasca 2001) or you could build a nonimmersive — and therefore non-Aristotelian — environment where players would not "be themselves" but rather encouraged to become aware of their own performances while trying to perform coherently to their character's personality, as some professional role-playing game (RPG) players do.

Mateas Responds

If an interactive Gandhi story left weapons and power-ups lying about, but used some heavy-handed interaction constraint (like the cursor turning red and beeping) to prevent the player from picking them up, then the experience would certainly be offering material affordances ("here's a gun for you to pick up — oops, not really") not balanced by the formal affordances (the dramatic probabilities of the Gandhi story), resulting in a decrease in the feeling of user agency. If, however, the Gandhi world never provided access to such weapons, and given the plot it never made sense to think of using such weapons, the player would still experience agency, even in the absence of access to plasma cannons.

out" for the action to be taken. There should be a naturalness to the afforded action that makes it the obvious thing to do. For example, the handle on a teapot affords picking up the teapot with your hand. The handle cries out to be grasped. In a similar manner, the material resources in an interactive drama afford action. Thus these resources not only limit what actions can be taken (the negative form of constraint) but cry out to make certain actions obvious (the positive form of constraint). Several examples of the material affordances in interactive drama are provided later.

The characters in an interactive drama should be rich enough that the player can infer a consistent model of the characters' thoughts. If the characters' thoughts can be understood (e.g., goals, motivations, desires), then these thoughts become a material resource for player action. By reasoning about the other characters' thoughts, the player can take actions to influence these characters, either to change their thoughts, or actively help or hinder them in their goals and plans.

The dialogue (language) spoken by the characters and the opportunities for the player to engage in dialogue are other material resources for action. Dialogue is a powerful means for characters to express their thoughts, thus instrumental for helping the player to infer a model of the characters' thoughts. Conversely, dialogue is a powerful means to influence character behavior. If the experience makes dialogue available to the player (and most contemporary interactive experiences do not), this becomes a powerful resource for expressing player intention.

The objects available in the experience (I place the presence of interactive objects somewhere between spectacle and pattern) are yet another resource for player action.

Finally, the mechanics of interaction (spectacle) provide the low-level resources for player actions. The mechanics provide the interface conventions for taking action.

In addition to the material affordances (constraints) from below, the player experiences formal constraints from above. Of course, these constraints are not directly perceived by the player, but, just as in noninteractive drama, are understood by recapitulating the author's chain of formal causation by making inferences along the chain of material causation. In noninteractive drama, understanding the formal chain of causation allows the audience to appreciate how all the action of the play stems from the dramatic necessity of the plot and theme. In interactive drama, the understanding of the formal causation from the level of plot to character additionally helps the player to have an understanding of what to do, that is, why they should take action within the story world at all. Just as the material constraints can be considered as affording action from the levels of spectacle through thought, the formal constraints afford motivation from the level of plot. This motivation is conveyed as dramatic probability. By understanding what actions are dramatically probable, the player understands what actions are worth considering.

Agency

We are now ready to propose a prescriptive, structural model for agency. *A player will experience agency when there is a balance between the material and formal constraints.* When the actions motivated by the formal constraints (affordances) via dramatic probability in the plot are commensurate with the material constraints (affordances) made available from the levels of spectacle, pattern, language, and thought, then the player will experience agency. An imbalance results in a decrease in agency. This will be made clearer by considering several examples.

Many puzzle-based adventures suffer from the imbalance of providing more material affordances than formal affordances. This results in the feeling of having many things to do (places to go, objects to fiddle with) without having any sense of why any one action would be preferable to another. For example, *Zork Grand Inquisitor* offers a rich world to navigate and many objects to collect and manipulate. Yet, since there is no unity of action, there is no way to relate current actions to the eventual goal of defeating the Grand Inquisitor. This leaves the player in the position of randomly wandering about trying strange juxtapositions of objects. This detracts from the sense of agency — though the player can take action, this action is often not tied to a high-level player intention. Notice that adding more material opportunities for action would not help the matter. The problem is not a lack of options of things to do, the problem is having insufficient formal constraint to decide between choices.

Quake (and its ilk) induce agency by providing a nice balance between material and formal constraints. The proto-plot establishes the following formal constraints (dramatic probabilities):

> Everything that moves will try to kill you.
>
> You should try to kill everything.
>
> You should try to move through as many levels as possible.

From these three principles, all the rest of the action follows. The material affordances perfectly balance these formal affordances. The player can run swiftly and smoothly through the space. The player can pick up a wide array of lethal weapons. The player can fire these weapons at monsters and produce satisfying, gory deaths. The monsters' behavior is completely consistent with the "kill or be killed" ethos. Everything that one would want to try and do given the formal constraints is doable. There are no extraneous actions available (for example, being able to strike up a conversation with a monster) that are not dictated by the formal constraints.

Note that though these example games are not specifically interactive drama, the model can still be used to analyze player agency within these games. Though the model is motivated by interactive drama, it can be used to analyze the sense of agency in any interactive experience by analyzing the experience in *terms of the dramatic categories* offered by the model. For example, though *Quake* has neither plot nor characters in the strict sense, there are top-down player expectations established by a "proto-plot." This "proto-plot" is communicated by the general design of the spectacle (e.g., the design of the creepy industrial mazes) as well as the actions of the characters, even if these characters do have primitive diction and thought.

Again, in order to invoke a sense of agency, an interactive experience must strike a balance between the material and formal constraints. An experience that successfully invokes a sense of agency inhabits a "sweet spot" in design space. Trying to add additional formal constraints (more plot) or additional material constraints (more actions) to a balanced experience will likely move it out of the sweet spot.

Relationship to Immersion and Transformation

In the previous section, agency was taken as the fundamental Murray category to integrate with Aristotle. In this section, I examine what the new, integrated model has to say about immersion and transformation.

Immersion

Murray suggests three ways of inducing immersion: structuring participation with a mask (an avatar), structuring participation as a visit, and making the interaction conventions (the interface mechanics) seamless. These three mechanisms can be viewed, in turn, as a way to provide material and formal constraints, as a design suggestion for balancing the constraints, or as a design suggestion for providing effective material constraints at the level of spectacle. Agency is a necessary condition for immersion.

An avatar can provide both material and formal constraints on a player's actions. The avatar can provide character exposition through such traits as physical mannerisms and speech patterns. This character exposition helps the player to recapitulate the formal, plot constraints. Through both input and output filtering (e.g., the characters in *Everquest*, or Mateas 1997), the avatar can provide material constraints (affordances) for action.

A visit is one metaphor for balancing material and formal constraints when the material opportunities for action are limited. From the formal side, the conventions of a visit tell the player that they won't be able to do much. Visits are about just looking around, possibly being guided through a space. Given the limited expectations for action communicated by the formal constraints, the designer can get away with (and in fact, must only) provide limited material means for action.

The mechanics provide the material resources for action at the level of spectacle (the interface can be considered part of the spectacle). Providing a clean, transparent interface insures that agency (and thus immersion) will not be disrupted.

Transformation

Most of Murray's discussion of transformation examines transformation as variety, particularly in the form of kaleidoscopic narratives that can be reentered multiple times so as to experience different aspects of the story. Agency, however, requires that a plot structure be present to provide formal constraints. An open-ended story without a clear point of view may disrupt the plot structure too much, thus disrupting agency. However, transformation as variety is necessary to make interaction really matter. If, every time a player enters the dramatic world, roughly the same story events occur regardless of the actions taken by the player, the player's interaction will seem inconsequential; the player will actually have no real effect on the story.

One way to resolve the apparent conflict between transformation and agency is to note that agency is a first-person experience induced by making moment-by-moment decisions within a balanced (materially and formally) interactive system, while transformation as variety is a third-person experience induced by observing and reflecting on a number of interactive experiences. Imagine an interactive drama system that guides the player through a fixed plot. As the player interacts in the world, the system, through a number of clever and subtle devices, moves the fixed plot forward. Given that these devices are clever and subtle, the player never experiences them as coercive; the player is fully engaged in the story, forming intentions, acting on them, and experiencing agency. Imagine an observer who watches many players interact with this system. The observer notices that no matter what the players do, the same plot happens (meaning that roughly the same story events occur in the same order, leading to the same climax).

By watching many players interact with the system, the observer has begun to discern the devices that control the plot in the face of player interaction. This observer will conclude that the player has no true agency, that the player is not able to form any intentions within the dramatic world that actually matter. But the first-time player within the world is experiencing agency. The designer of the dramatic world could conclude — because they are designing the world for the player, not for the observer — that as long as the player experiences a true sense of interactive freedom (that is, agency) transformation as variety is not an important design consideration.

The problem with this solution to the agency vs. transformation dilemma becomes apparent as the player interacts with the world a second time. On subsequent replays of the world, the player and the observer become the same person. The total interactive experience consists of both first-person engagement within the dramatic world and third-person reflection across multiple experiences in the world. In order to support the total experience, the dramatic world must support both first-person engagement and third-person reflection; must provide agency and transformation as variety.

A dramatic world supporting this total experience could provide agency (and the concomitant need to have a plot structure providing formal constraints) *and* transformation by actively constructing the player experience such that each run-through of the story has a clean, unitary plot structure, but multiple run-throughs have different, unitary plot structures. Small changes in the player's choices early on result in experiencing a different unfolding plot. The trick is to design the experience such that, once the end occurs, any particular run-through has the force of dramatic necessity.

The story should have the dramatic probabilities smoothly narrowing to a necessary end. Early choices may result in different necessary ends — later choices can have less effect on changing the whole story, since the set of dramatically probable events has already significantly narrowed. Change in the plot should not be traceable to distinct branch points; the player will not be offered an occasional small number of obvious choices that force the plot in a different direction. Rather, the plot should be smoothly mutable, varying in response to some global state that is itself a function of the many small actions performed by the player throughout the experience.

The Type of Experience Informed by the Model

This neo-Aristotelian poetics clarifies a specific conceptual experiment in the space of interactive stories. Specifically, the experiment consists of creating an interactive dramatic experience with the experiential properties of traditional drama, namely enactment, intensity, catharsis, unity, and closure. The Aristotelian analytic categories describe the structure (parts and relationships) of a story experience that induces these experiential properties. The way in which interaction has been incorporated into this model clarifies what is meant by interactive dramatic experience. Here, interaction means first-person interaction as a character within the story. Further, the essential experiential property of interactivity is taken to be agency. The interactive dramatic experience should be structured in such a way as to maximize the player's sense of agency within the story. The model provides prescriptive structural guidance for maximizing agency, namely, to balance material and formal constraints. So the conceptual experiment informed by this model can be more precisely stated as follows: build a first-person, interactive dramatic world that, in addition to the classical experiential properties of Aristotelian drama, also provides the player with a strong sense of agency.

Technical Agenda

In addition to clarifying conceptual and design issues in interactive drama, the neo-Aristotelian model informs a technical agenda of AI research necessary to enable this kind of experience.

The primary heuristic offered by the model is, again, that to maintain a sense of player agency in an interactive experience, material and formal constraints must be balanced. As the sophistication of the theme and plot of an experience increases, maintaining this

balance will require characters whose motivations and desires are inferable from their actions. In addition, these characters will have to respond to the player's actions. Believable agents, that is, computer-controlled characters with rich personalities and emotions, will be necessary. Additionally, in many cases (e.g., domestic dramas in which the plot centers around relationships, trust, betrayal, infidelity, and self-deception), language is necessary to communicate the plot.

In order to convey the formal constraints provided by the plot, the characters must have a rich repertoire of dialogue available. In addition, the player must be able to talk back. One can imagine a system in which the characters can engage in complex dialogue but the player can only select actions from menus or click on hotspots on the screen; this is, in fact, the strategy employed by character-based multimedia artwork and contemporary adventure games. But this strategy diminishes agency precisely by unbalancing material and formal constraints. The characters are able to express complex thoughts through language. However, the player is not able to influence their thoughts except at the coarse level provided by the mouse-click interactivity. Thus maximizing player agency requires providing at least a limited form of natural language dialogue.

The function of interactive characters is primarily to communicate material and formal constraints. That is, the player should be able to understand why characters take the actions they do, and how these actions relate to the plot. Sengers (this volume, 1998a) provides a nice analysis of how an audience-based focus on agents as communication requires changes in agent architectures. When the focus changes from "doing the right thing" (action selection) to "doing the thing right" (action expression), the technical research agenda changes (Sengers 1998b). The neo-Aristotelian model indicates that action expression is exactly what is needed. In addition, an interactive drama system must communicate dramatic probability (likely activity given the plot) while smoothly narrowing the space of dramatic probability over time. This means that story action must be coordinated in such a way as to communicate these plot-level constraints. Thus it is not enough for an individual character's actions to be "readable" by an observer. Multiple characters must be coordinated in such a way that their joint activity communicates both formal and material (plot and character level) affordances. This requires a technical solution that blurs the firm plot/character distinction usually made in AI architectures for interactive drama (Blumberg and Galyean 1995; Weyhrauch 1997).

Façade: An Interactive Drama Guided by the Model

The author is currently engaged in a three-year collaboration with Andrew Stern to build *Façade* (Mateas and Stern 2000, Stern this volume), an interactive story world that seeks to carry out the conceptual and technical experiment informed by the neo-Aristotelian poetics. Together we will:

>	Create a compelling, well-written story that obeys dramatic principles, designed with many potential ways to play out.

>	Build artificial intelligence (AI) that can control the behavior of real-time-animated computer characters, to be used for performing the roles of all but one of the characters in the story.

>	Create a user interface that allows the player to move easily within the world, and converse and gesture with the computer characters.

>	Build AI that can understand a natural language and gestural input within the context of the story.

>	Build AI that can integrate the user's interactions into the space of potential plot directions and character behaviors in the story.

>	Collaborate with voice actors and animators to author spoken dialogue, character behavior and story events within the engine, to construct the finished story world.

Story Requirements

The story requirements describe the properties we wish our story to have. These are not intended to be absolute requirements; that is, this is not a description of the properties that all interactive stories must have. Rather, these requirements are the set of assumptions grounding the design of the particular interactive story we intend to build.

Short One-Act Play. Any one run of the scenario should take the player 15 to 20 minutes to complete. We focus on the short story for a couple of reasons. Building an interactive story has all the difficulties of writing and producing a noninteractive story (film or play) plus all the difficulty of supporting true player agency in the story. In exploring this new interactive art form it makes sense to first work with a distilled form of the problem, exploring scenarios with the minimum structure required to support dramatically interesting interaction. In addition, a short one-act play is an extreme, contrarian response to the many hours of gameplay celebrated in the design of contemporary computer games. Instead of providing the player with 40 to 60 hours of episodic action and endless wandering in a huge world, we want to design an experience that provides the player with 15 to 20 minutes of emotionally intense, tightly unified, dramatic action. The story should have the intensity, economy, and catharsis of traditional drama.

Relationships. Rather than being about manipulating magical objects, fighting monsters, and rescuing princesses, the story should be about the emotional entanglements of human relationships. We are interested in interactive experiences that appeal to the adult, non-computer-geek, movie-and-theater-going public.

Three Characters. The story should have three characters, two controlled by the computer and one controlled by the player. Three is the minimum number of characters needed to support complex social interaction without placing the responsibility on the player to continually move the story forward. If the player is shy or confused about interacting, the two computer controlled characters can conspire to set up dramatic situations, all the while trying to get the player involved.

Player as Protagonist. Ideally the player should experience the change in the protagonist as a personal journey. The player should be more than an "interactive observer," not simply poking at the two computer-controlled characters to see how they change.

Embodied Interaction Matters. Though dialogue should be a significant (perhaps the primary) mechanism for character interaction, it should not be the sole mechanism. Embodied interaction, such as moving from one location to another, picking up an object, or touching a character, should play a role in the action. These physical actions should carry emotional and symbolic weight, and should have a real influence on the characters and their evolving interaction. The physical representation of the characters and their environment should support action significant to the plot.

Action in a Single Location. This provides unity of space and forces a focus on plot and character interaction.

Player's Role not Over-constrained. The amount of noninteractive exposition describing the player's role should be minimal. The player should not have the feeling of playing a role, of actively having to think about how the character they are playing would react. Rather, the player should be able to be themselves as they explore the dramatic situation. Any role-related scripting of the interactor (Murray 1998) should occur as a natural by-product of their interaction in the world. The player should "ease into" their role; the role should be the "natural" way to act in the environment, given the dramatic situation.

Story

Our story, which satisfies these story requirements, is a domestic drama in which a married couple has invited the player over for dinner. (Assume for the moment that the player's character is male.) Grace and Trip are apparently a model couple, socially and financial successful, well-liked by all. Grace and Trip both know the player from work. Trip and the player are friends; Grace and the player have gotten to know each other fairly recently. Shortly after arriving at their house for

dinner, Grace confesses to the player that she has fallen in love with him. Throughout the rest of the evening, the player discovers that Grace and Trip's marriage is actually falling apart. Their marriage has been sour for years; deep differences, buried frustrations, and unspoken infidelities have killed their love for each other. How the façade of their marriage cracks, what is revealed, and the final disposition of Grace and Trip's marriage, and Grace and the player's relationship, depends on the actions of the player. The story's controlling idea: to be happy you must be true to yourself.

Interface

The story world is presented to the player as an animated, three-dimensional environment. The environment and characters within the environment are rendered in an illustrative style reminiscent of graphic novels. The player is able to move about this environment from a first-person point of view, gesture and pick up objects, and converse with the other characters by typing. The computer-controlled characters look directly out of the screen to gesture and talk to the player. The conversation discourse is real-time; that is, if the player is typing, it is as if they are speaking those words in (pseudo) real-time.

Story Structure

The story is structured as a classic Aristotelian plot arc. The AI plot system explicitly attempts to change dramatic values (e.g., the love between Trip and Grace, the trust between the player and Trip) in such a way as to make a well-formed plot arc happen. In the theory of (classical) dramatic writing, the smallest unit of value change is the beat (McKee 1997). Roughly, a beat consists of an action/reaction pair between characters. Beats are sequenced to make scenes, scenes to make acts, acts to make stories. The AI plot system contains a library of beats appropriate for our story. The system dynamically sequences beats in such a way as to respond to player activity and yet maintain a well-formed plot arc. For the player, each run-through of the story should have the force of dramatic necessity.

Explicit decision points, which would highlight the nonlinearity of the story, should not be visible. However, in multiple run-throughs of the story, the player's actions have a significant influence on what events occur in the plot, which are left out, and how the story ends. Only after playing the experience six or seven times should the player begin to feel they have "exhausted" the interactive story. In fact, full appreciation of the experience requires that the story be played multiple times. In *Façade*, our goal is to create an interactive story experience that provides the player with the agency to have an effect on the trajectory of the story, yet has the feel of a traditional, linear, dramatic experience.

AI Architecture

The architecture for *Façade* is informed by the neo-Aristotelian poetics of interactive drama, specifically by the technical agenda following from the poetics to:

> Support the coordination of multiple characters' actions to communicate material and formal affordances; that is, the coordination of multiple characters in carrying out dramatic action, and

> Support natural language dialogue so as to maintain player agency in an interactive story with a complex theme.

> Again, the architectural basis for providing each of these capabilities is the smallest unit of dramatic value change, the beat.

Beats

In *Façade*, beats are architectural entities. A beat consists of: preconditions, a description of the values changed by the beat, success and failure conditions, and joint behaviors, to coordinate the characters in order to carry out the specific beat. Scenes have a similar structure, except that instead of having joint behaviors, a scene has a collection of beats it can use to try and make the scene happen. Preconditions and effects are used to first select a scene, and then, within the scene, beats. When a beat is selected, the joint behaviors

associated with this beat are activated in the characters. These joint behaviors extend the reactive behaviors of Hap (Loyall and Bates 1991; Loyall 1997) to include explicit support for multi-agent (in our case, multicharacter) coordination in a manner similar to the STEAM architecture (Tambe 1997). As the player interacts within the beat, she will influence the specific performance of the beat. Because the beat is trying to cause specific value changes, it may turn out that there is no performance of the beat that believably incorporates player interaction while appropriately changing the values. In this case the beat is aborted and another beat is selected.

Multicharacter Coordination

Most approaches to computer-controlled characters have been driven by a notion of strong autonomy; that is, by the idea that the character independently chooses moment-by-moment what action to take next, based on local state (what has recently happened in the world). But interactive drama requires that character action make sense globally as well as locally; all of a character's actions must "add up" to a consistent set of material and formal affordances, while still providing immediate response to player interaction. Rather than putting all the "character-ness" in the characters and all the "story-ness" in a drama manager, the architectural construct of the beat tightly binds character-specific and story-specific knowledge, just as character and plot are tightly related in the neo-Aristotelian poetics. Character behavior is now organized around the dramatic functions that the behavior serves, rather than organized around a conception of the character as independent of the dramatic action.

Natural Language Dialogue

Natural language understanding is a notoriously difficult AI problem; it is commonly agreed that building a system that is as good as a human being at participating in dialogue would be tantamount to modeling all of human intelligence. Thus, on first blush, our desire to have the player engage in unrestricted dialogue with the characters seems ludicrous. But here the fact that what we really want is dramatic dialogue within a specific story context comes to the rescue. The player's dialogue and actions are additional material causes in the story (a contribution to the material out of which the story is being built), while the player's intentions are additional formal causes in the story.

Of course these material and formal contributions must be consonant with the author-provided chains of material and formal causation. So for natural language understanding, we don't need something that can glean the open-ended meaning out of arbitrary utterances, but rather something that interprets dialogue as contributions within a specific dramatic context. This is accomplished as follows: template rules map from surface text to a small number of discourse acts (things like "praise Grace," or "praise Trip," or "mention-topic marriage"). This is a many-to-few mapping, in which a huge number of surface productions get turned into a few discourse acts out of a small set of possible acts. Forward chaining rules then map the initial discourse acts to final discourse acts in a context-specific way. Discourse context is maintained by beats; the current active beat is the current active discourse context. Associated with beats are the beat-specific mapping rules that get added to the general rules when the beat is activated. When an utterance is not understood (no mapping rule is activated), recovery mechanisms try to mask the failure to understand while moving the story forward.

Conclusion

In this essay, Murray's concept of agency was integrated into Laurel's Aristotelian structural model to yield a proposed Aristotelian interactive poetics. This model illuminates the general conditions under which a user will experience agency in any interactive experience and provides design and technology guidance for the particular case of building interactive dramatic experiences. The design of *Façade*, an interactive dramatic world being built by the author and Andrew Stern, is informed by this interactive poetics.

References

Aaarseth, Espen (1997). *Cybertext: Perspectives on Ergodic Literature*. Baltimore: Johns Hopkins University Press.

Aristotle (1997). *The Poetics*. Mineola, NY: Dover.

Avedon, Elliot M. and Brian Sutton-Smith (1971). *The Study of Games*. New York: Wiley.

Bates, J. (1992). "Virtual Reality, Art, and Entertainment." *Presence: The Journal of Teleoperators and Virtual Environments* 1, no.1 (1992): 133–138.

Bates, J., A.B. Loyall, and W.S. Reilly (1992). "Integrating Reactivity, Goals and Emotion in a Broad Agent." Technical Report (CMU-CS-92-142), Department of Computer Science, Carnegie Mellon University, Pittsburg, Pennsylvania.

Blumberg, B. (1996). "Old Tricks, New Dogs: Ethology and Interactive Creatures." Ph.D. Thesis, MIT Media Lab. Cambridge, Massachusetts.

Blumberg, B., and T. Galyean (1995). "Multi-level Direction of Autonomous Creatures for Real-Time Virtual Environments." In Proceedings of SIGGRAPH 95, (1995): 47–54.

Eskelinen, Markku (2001). "The Gaming Situation." *Game Studies* 1, no.1 (July 2001). <http://www.gamestudies.org/0101/eskelinen/>.

Frasca, Gonzalo (2001). "Ephemeral Games: Is it Barbaric to Design Videogames after Auschwitz?" In *Cybertext Yearbook 2001*, edited by Markku Eskelinen and Raine Koskimaa. Jyväskylä: Research Centre for Contemporary Culture, University of Jyväskylä. <http://www.jacaranda.org/frasca/ephemeralFRASCA.pdf>.

Hayes-Roth, B., R. van Gent, and D. Huber (1996). "Acting in Character." In *Creating Personalities for Synthetic Actors*, edited by R. Trappl and P. Petta. Berlin and New York: Springer. Also available as Stanford Knowledge Systems Laboratory Report KSL-96-13 (1996).

Kelso, M.T., P. Weyhrauch, and J. Bates (1999). "Dramatic Presence." *Presence: The Journal of Teleoperators and Virtual Environments* 2, no. 1 (Winter 1993): 1–15. <http://www2.cs.cmu.edu/afs/cs.cmu.edu/project/oz/web/papers/CMU-CS-92-195.ps>.

Laurel, Brenda (1986). "Towards the Design of a Computer-Based Interactive Fantasy System." Ph.D. Thesis, Ohio State University, Columbus, Ohio.

Laurel, Brenda (1991). *Computers as Theatre*. Reading, MA: Addison-Wesley.

Loyall, A.B. (1997). "Believable Agents." Ph.D. Thesis (Tech report CMU-CS-97-123), Carnegie Mellon University, Pittsburgh, Pennsylvania.

Loyall, A.B., and J. Bates (1991). "Hap: A Reactive, Adaptive Architecture for Agents." Technical Report CMU-CS-91-147, Department of Computer Science, Carnegie Mellon University Pittsburgh, Pennsylvania.

Mateas, Michael (1997). "Computational Subjectivity in Virtual World Avatars." In *Working Notes of the Socially Intelligent Agents Symposium, 1997 AAAI Fall Symposium Series*. Menlo Park, CA: AAAI Press.

Mateas, Michael, and Andrew Stern (2000). "Towards Integrating Plot and Character for Interactive Drama." In *Working Notes of the Socially Intelligent Agents: Human in the Loop Symposium, 2000 AAAI Fall Symposium Series*. Menlo Park, CA: AAAI Press.

McKee, Robert (1997). *Story: Substance, Structure, Style and the Principles of Screenwriting*. New York: Harper Collins.

Murray, Janet (1998). *Hamlet on the Holodeck*. Cambridge, MA: MIT Press.

Norman, Don (1988). *The Design of Everyday Things*. New York: Doubleday.

Sengers, Phoebe (1998a). "Anti-Boxology: Agent Design in Cultural Context." Ph.D. Thesis (Technical Report CMU-CS-98-151), School of Computer Science, Carnegie Mellon University, Pittsburgh, Pennsylvania.

Sengers, Phoebe (1998b). "Do the Thing Right: An Architecture for Action Expression." In Proceedings of the Second International Conference on Autonomous Agents, 24-31. May, 1998

Tambe, Milind (1997). "Towards Flexible Teamwork." *Journal of Artificial Intelligence Research* 7, (1997): 83–124.

Weyhrauch, P. (1997). "Guiding Interactive Drama." Ph.D. Thesis (Technical Report CMU-CS-97-109), School of Computer Science, Carnegie Mellon University, Pittsburgh, Pennsylvania.

Ludology

To a ludologist, cyberdramatic perspectives can seem exceedingly strange. Ludologists ask, why expend so much theoretical and technical effort on subjects like neo-Aristotelian interactive drama? Why focus on things that do not exist, are arguably impossible, and, should they ever be created, might turn out to be of only marginal interest? Instead, they say, let's focus on computer games, which do exist, are clearly a vibrant aesthetic and commercial force, and seem only likely to increase in importance.

Ludologists are not alone in realizing the importance of computer games, but their image of the field of computer game studies is significantly different from that found in literature or film departments, the popular press, or media industry conferences. Ludologists believe much of current game theory to be founded on a series of ill-advised analogies between computer games and the individual theorists' fields of study — rather than a specific analysis of the "gaming situation" itself.

In seeking a new approach, ludologists follow the function-oriented modus operandi of Espen Aarseth, whose *Cybertext* (1997) addressed "ergodic texts" (ranging from print works to hypertexts to games) without confining its scope to any one media form. In fact, the term *ludology* was introduced to computer game studies in the *Cybertext Yearbook*[1] — named for Aarseth's term — and has been partly popularized by the community around the journal *Game Studies*, of which Aarseth is the general editor.

Aarseth's theoretical positions were influenced by those of Stuart Moulthrop, whose work as a critic and artist (which rose to prominence with the dual 1991 publications of the essay, "You Say You Want a Revolution?" and the hypertext novel, *Victory Garden*) works toward an understanding of new media text on its own terms, rather than as a reflection of the already-understood. However, Aarseth's *Cybertext* was focused primarily on the texts themselves, whereas Moulthrop was equally concerned with the texts' larger social, political and economic contexts. Now that both Aarseth and Moulthrop have increasingly turned their attention to computer games, this distinction between their perspectives persists.

It is a distinction made explicit in the essays by Aarseth and Moulthrop included here. Their contributions follow an essay from Markku Eskelinen — perhaps ludology's most outspoken and controversial proponent. These three essays each work to define ludology or game studies. By exposing the limits of other approaches to computer games, they demonstrate the necessity of such work. They also begin to nominate areas of focus for the emerging discipline. (Many of these — such as the function of time in games, the primacy of simulation, and the meaning of Lara Croft's breasts — are also explored in other sections of this volume.) Although there is certainly no consensus among these three authors, in this section we can see the outlines of a discipline beginning to emerge.

1. According to Gonzalo Frasca, who is credited with introducing ludology and operates <ludology.org>. Markku Eskelinen is coeditor of the *Cybertext Yearbook,* with Raine Koskimaa.

References

Aarseth, Espen (1997). *Cybertext: Perspectives on Ergodic Literature.* Baltimore: Johns Hopkins University Press.

Moulthrop, Stuart (1991a). "You Say You Want a Revolution?" *Postmodern Culture* 1, no.3 (May 1991).

Moulthrop, Stuart (1991b). *Victory Garden.* Watertown MA, Eastgate Systems.

Towards Computer Game Studies
Markku Eskelinen

Introduction: Ludology[1] and Narratology

It is relatively stress-free to write about computer games, as nothing too much has been said yet, and almost anything goes. The situation is pretty much the same in what comes to writing about games and gaming in general. The sad fact, with alarming cumulative consequences, is that they are under-theorized; there are Huizinga (1950), Caillois (1979), Ehrmann (1969), and Sutton-Smith (1997, Avedon and Sutton-Smith 1971) of course, and libraries full of board-game studies, in addition to game theory and bits and pieces of philosophy — most notably Wittgenstein's — but they won't get us very far with computer games. So if there already is or soon will be a legitimate field for computer game studies, this field is also very open to intrusions and colonisations from the already organized scholarly tribes. Resisting and beating them is the goal of our first survival game in this paper, as what these emerging studies need is independence, or at least relative independence.

It should be self-evident that we can't apply print narratology, hypertext theory, film or theater and drama studies directly to computer games, but it isn't. Therefore the majority of the random notes and power-ups that follow will be spent modifying the presuppositions firmly based on the academic denial of helplessness. Obviously I need a strategy, and fortunately I have one: to use the theories of those would-be-colonizers against themselves. For example, as we shall soon see, if you actually know your narrative theory[2] (instead of resorting to outdated notions of Aristotle, Propp, or Victorian novels) you won't argue that games are (interactive or procedural) narratives or anything even remotely similar. Luckily, outside theory, people are usually excellent at distinguishing between narrative situations and gaming situations: if I throw a ball at you, I don't expect you to drop it and wait until it starts telling stories.

It's good we don't have to start from scratch, as there have been attempts to locate, describe, and analyze the basic components and aspects of the gaming situation, which are essentially different from the basic constituents of narrative and dramatic situations. I'm thinking here of Chris Crawford's early classic *The Art of Computer Game Design* (1982) (and its comparison of games and computer games in particular), Gonzalo Frasca's (Frasca 1998, 2001) and Jesper Juul's (Juul

---

Response by J. Yellowlees Douglas

Eskelinen makes some compelling points in "Towards Computer Game Studies" that traverse ground that has remained virtually untrammeled. Surprisingly so, given the recent, explosive growth of PC and videogames — in 2001, Americans began to lay out more cash for interactive games than for evenings at the cinema. And Markku's uses of both Genette and Aarseth help make games like *Tetris* and *Civilization III* intelligible in theoretical terms. In the end, treating all computer games as if they fell tidily into a single genre is a heroic gesture, intended to lay the foundation for a sound critical understanding of what transpires when a user picks up the phone and hears a threatening message from *Majestic* on the other end of the line, as well as for what's going on during the forty hours you've just

spent with *Grim Fandango*.

But while *The Sims* and *Black and White* are closer to, say, a game of chess than to an episode of *ER*, a growing number of games use narratives as affective hooks to draw readers in and hold their interest, and to appeal to a wider audience (see the Douglas and Hargadon chapter for online surveys calling strongly for more backstory), an audience not necessarily interested in the gratifications offered by shoot-'em-up skill-based games or by strategy-based simulations. *X-Files: The Game*, for example, like *The Last Express*, derives its entire intelligibility and appeal from blending the trappings and satisfactions of traditional narratives with the exploratory and agency-based pleasures of interactivity. In both *X-Files* and *Last Express*, as well as Sega's *Shenmue*, virtually none of the action represents

Ludology> Eskelinen   **Douglas Schechner**
       Aarseth   Crawford Moulthrop
       Moulthrop   Gromala Cayley   **II. Ludology**

37

1999, 2000) papers and theses on ludology, and most of all Espen Aarseth's articles on computer games and cybertext theory (Aarseth 1994, 1997, 1998a, 1998b, 2001a, 2001b).

To begin, I'd like to demonstrate or test a safe and painless passage from narratives to games by trying to "exhaust" classic narratology (Chatman 1978, 1990; Genette 1980, 1988; Prince 1982, 1987; Bordwell 1984). Most naïve comparisons between narratives and games usually result from too narrow, broad or feeble definitions of the former: usually it comes down to discovering "plots" and "characters" in both modes — games and narratives. However, we should know that's not good enough, as we can find those events and existents in drama as well, which is clearly its own mode. The minimal definition of narrative derived from Gerald Prince and Gérard Genette states basically that there must be two things or components to constitute a narrative: a temporal sequence of events (a plot, if you want to water down the concept) and a narrative situation (with both narrators and narratees for starters). I think we can safely say we can't find narrative situations within games. (Or if we sometimes do, most probably in *Myst* or *The Last Express*, the narrative components are then at the service of an ergodic dominant).

In short: a story, a backstory or a plot is not enough.

A sequence of events enacted constitutes a drama, a sequence of events taking place a performance, a sequence of events recounted a narrative, and perhaps a sequence of events produced by manipulating equipment and following formal rules constitutes a game. This is really very trivial but crucial; there are series and sequences of events that do not become or form stories (in *Tetris*, for example). The reason for this is equally simple.[3] In games, the dominant temporal relation is the one between user time and event time and not the narrative one between story time and discourse time.

Regarding the fallacy of recognizing similar characters or existents in games, drama, and narratives, the situation is similar. In computer games you can operate your character, if there is one in the first place,[4] perhaps also discuss with other characters or voices; and the characters can be dynamic and developing (not only in an interpretative sense), such as by changing themselves with level points and power-ups. Such "characters" are entirely functional and combinatorial (a means to an end); instead of any intrinsic values, they have only use and exchange values to them. These entities are definitely not acting or behaving like traditional narrators, characters, directors, and actors, their supposed counterparts in literature, film, and the stage.

---

a test of any kind of skill, dexterity, or problem-solving. In fact, unlike all other games, your ability to remain within the other-world of the interactive depends mostly on your continued willing suspension of disbelief and not on your ability to out-maneuver, out-serve, out-gun, or out-run your opponents.

Ultimately, looking to either narratology or to games for our understanding of interactives will offer only a highly limited return, since we're looking at, essentially, a still-developing range of genres in a new medium. Just as film is more than the sum of image, mise-en-scene, sound, and narrative, interactives can be both more than the sum of game or narrative. In *Shenmue*, for example, players can track Ryo's search for his father's killer, but they can also elect to live in Ryo's world and simply interact with its constituents — 332 characters

(including several animals) — hang out at the local arcade, visit the family shrine, work, browse the contents of your fridge, and care for your ailing kitten. Is this a game? A narrative? Or something else altogether?

Regarding Richard Schechner's Response
Richard Schechner's response to Douglas and Hargadon's essay (which also responds to Markku Eskelinen's essay) is found on p. 192.

Eskelinen Responds
I don't think Richard Schechner's "I don't think" carries the intellectual weight it was perhaps intended to carry. In fact I don't think it even qualifies as a commentary.

http://www.electronicbookreview.com/thread/firstperson/eskelinenr2

To summarize: different existents, different event structures, and different situations. On the other hand, narratology is not completely useless, if its key concepts and distinctions are not taken for granted but traced back to their roots. In the following pages that is exactly what we try to do.[5] The elementary categories of classic narratology are transformed into an open series of ludological components, if for no any other reason than to further specify the features inherent to games.

Before going into the finer points of ludology, the more or less peaceful coexistence of local traditions and global technologies should also be acknowledged. There's no guarantee whatsoever that the aesthetic traditions of the West are relevant to game studies in general and computer game studies in particular. It's tempting to assume that one reason for the never-ending series of unsuccessful game definitions and disciplines is the need or urge to make clear-cut distinctions and compartmentalize aesthetics. To take an obvious counterexample: according to the *Natyasastra* every art contains parts of other arts.[6] It would be almost equally sensible to speculate on Japanese aesthetics (after Keene 1995) and claim that a tradition that emphasizes the values of perishability, suggestion, irregularity, incompleteness, and simplicity, is perhaps better suited to approach computer games than its Western counterpart.[7]

The Gaming Situation[8]

According to David Parlett, formal games are systems of ends and means (Parlett 1999, 3). The latter part consists of specific procedural rules of how to manipulate the equipment (pieces or tokens or whatever). In computer games there are events and existents, the relations and properties of which the player has to manipulate or configure in order to progress in the game or just to be able to continue it. Events, existents, and the relations between them can be described at least in spatial, temporal, causal, and functional terms. It's equally self-evident that the importance of these dimensions varies from game to game and sometimes also within the phases and levels of an individual game.

A quick look at Espen Aarseth's typology of cybertexts (Aarseth 1997, 62–65) should make us see that the dominant user function in literature, theater and film is interpretative, but in games it is the configurative one. To generalize: in art we might have to configure in order to be able to interpret, whereas in games we have to interpret in order to be able to configure, and proceed from the beginning to the winning or some other situation. Consequently, gaming is seen here as configurative practice, and the gaming situation as a combination of ends, means, rules, equipment, and manipulative action.

Jacques Ehrmann understood games as economy, articulation, and communication, and the player as both the subject and the object of the game (Ehrmann 1969, 55–57). The levels of articulation as specified by Warren Motte — the relations of player-to-game, player-to-player and game-to-world (Motte 1995, 25) — give important clues concerning the elementary differences between games and narratives. To take only one example: in multiplayer games the positions of players constantly affect each other. Such an arrangement would be very unusual but not impossible to execute in narrative fiction. The way I read *The Idiot* (Dostoevsky 1955) would then change other people's *Idiot*s, or their readers' possibilities when reading them, and vice versa. That wouldn't make much sense, but in games such a practice has always already been in existence, and the current massive multiplayer games may very well be the most important change in audience structure since the invention of the choir, as Espen Aarseth (2001b) recently suggested.

Accordingly, we can distinguish the static user positions of literature, film, and average drama from the dynamic ones of games and certain installations and performances. We should also mention mobile positions in the wake of mobile gaming and games such as the recent *Nokia Game*[9] that contacts the player through multiple channels (text messages, television, the web etc.) and demands action.

As we already stated, games have other than mere interpretative goals. These goals can be reached by traversing, negotiating, or otherwise overcoming a series of obstacles and gaps. When studying narratives

Ludology>Eskelinen   Douglas Schechner   **II. Ludology**
Aarseth   Crawford Moulthrop
Moulthrop   Gromala Cayley

39

as systems of gaps, Meir Sternberg (1978) made three heuristic distinctions: gaps are either permanent or temporary, focused or diffused, and either flaunted or suppressed.[10]

I think computer games can also be described that way, with the all-important exception that these gaps are not static and interpretative but ergodic (Aarseth 1997, 1) and dynamic: they need action to be encountered, closed, and dealt with. Aarseth's four user functions (interpretative, explorative, configurative, and textonic (Aarseth 1997, 60–62)) are useful in specifying what kind of action is required from the player. In practical terms this means options such as finding paths, completing prefabricated relations, or adding new game elements for the other players to struggle with. The resulting typology of 32 possibilities could then be used to map out both qualitative and quantitative differences in the information given to the player in different stages and phases and levels of the game.

Focalization is one of the key elements of the narrative situation in classic narratology. In its most abstract sense, it's a channel for narrative information and is ultimately based on the assumption of the uneven distribution of knowledge. Focalization is accompanied by the category of distance that regulates the amount (too much or too little) of information distributed through the channel, or two channels (audio and visual), as in film. This is exactly the level where I would like to draw a few parallels between this ludology-in-progress and narratology. One could argue that information is distributed and regulated very differently in games than in narratives, as in the former it's also invested in formal rules. In some cases the knowledge of these rules is all that's needed to succeed in the game (in *Tetris* for example). It's important to understand that rules are not conventions. One can by all means change between conventions while reading a narrative, but one cannot change the rules of the game while playing.[11] The situation is more complex however, since it is common that the player has all the information needed but lacks skills.

In Genette's (1980, 215) narratology there are three main categories — narrative level, person, and time of the narrating — that specify the narrator's position or the coordinates of narrative acts. Parallels are pretty obvious, or at least easy to draw, as it would be only sensible to note the arrangement of levels in a game, and whether or not the player is represented by a character in a game as well as the player's possibilities to time her action.

Aspects of Time in Computer Games

According to the famous statement of Christian Metz, "one of the functions of narrative is to invent one time scheme in terms of another time scheme" (Metz 1974, 18). Contrary to this, in games there's only one necessary time scheme, the one already noted: the movement from the beginning to the winning or some other situation. In cases where another time scheme is invented, it is not as important as the first one.

Still, we could split this progression into two interplaying registers and argue that the dominant temporal relation in (computer) games is the one between user time (the actions of the player) and event time (the happenings of the game), whereas in narratives it is situated between story time (the time of the events told) and discourse time (the time of the telling). The key concept here is the dominant.[12] As we all know, narratives such as Stuart Moulthrop's *Hegirascope* (1995) and *Reagan Library* (1999)[13] can utilize both user and event times for narrative purposes, and games like *The Last Express*[14] can use story and discourse times for gaming purposes (see sidebar). Despite these possible hybrids, the underlying restriction remains the same: there's no narrative without story and discourse times and no game without user and event times – everything else is optional.

In the course of a game the player encounters temporal phenomena or events with different durations, speeds, orders, and frequencies — and some of these must be manipulated or configured to move from the beginning to the winning or some other situation. Even though game time doesn't have much in common with narrative time, this does not prevent us from observing similar temporal categories in both modes, as order, repetition or speed are not narrative or gamelike in themselves.

I, Emily Saint Cloud, bequeath to certain of the ways my garden of first-class <u>objects</u>.

Do you <u>really</u> want to know? Surely this can't <u>go on</u>. Is 'what?' a question?

Now you see them, blue, green, and gold, laid out on the big wheel. This world has a basic circularity.

Varnish... Monorail...

This is the world I made, a garden of remembering.

The Tale Is The Traveler

<u>How this might look</u>

<u>Hold the mirror lower</u>

Where have you been in the Net today?

<u>Having ten million links</u>

<u>Hypertext more or less</u>

The Traveler Is The Tale

4.sidebar.1–2. Screenshots from Stuart Moulthrop's *Reagan Library* (1999) and *Hegirascope* (1995).

In formal narratology,[15] events are divided into actions and happenings based on their agency, and into kernels and satellites based on their relative importance. There's also a difference between punctual acts and more durational actions (Chatman 1978, 32-56). Events can, of course, be more or less separate or connected, and we can borrow the three elementary possibilities of combination from Claude Bremond: embedding, enchaining, and joining (Bremond 1980).

In our case, games can be differentiated from each other on the basis of which events can or cannot be manipulated, which parts and dimensions of events can be manipulated, and for how long and how deeply. An almost ready-made set of temporal relations can be derived from print and film narratologies — this act gives us six categories to study: order, speed, duration, frequency, simultaneity, and the time of action. It's very probable there exist other noteworthy temporal relations, but I'll begin with these.[16]

Let me note in passing that the manipulation or completion of multiple relations takes place in time — a kind of general economy of games — but here we are dealing only with the restricted economy of manipulating temporal relations. The importance of mutable temporalities varies from game-to-game, and there are games that are more dependent on other kinds of variables. For example, turn-based strategy games such as *Civilization* seem to favor causal relations over temporal ones to create event structures that have remarkable similarities to complex board games. We are talking here about quantitative differences: at one extreme there are multiple and highly interdependent chains of events with a complex tactical and strategic calculus, and at the other end looser chains of completed action episodes or stimulus-response cycles with no or minimal cumulative consequences. Taking into account the demands of gameplay (a well-balanced combination of tempo and cognitive tasks) it makes sense that the former games utilize intransient time and the latter transient time.

Order. In computer games this is the relation between user events and system events, or the actions of the player and their interaction with the event structure (happenings) of the game. In some cases there's only one sequence of events, and the player has to act accordingly, in the sense of keeping up with it for as long as is humanly possible. *Tetris* (like many of its arcade relatives) best exemplifies this type of game. In other cases, commonly in exploration games such as *Doom*, order is a tripartite combination of events, negotiation, and progression (Aarseth 1997, 97–128); in these cases the player must find and test possible event sequences until the right one is found and the

Ludology> Eskelinen   Douglas Schechner   **II. Ludology**
          Aarseth   Crawford Moulthrop
          Moulthrop Gromala Cayley

game can continue. So you either follow the order or spend your time finding it. In cases where the player cannot affect the order of events there is still the difference between variable and invariable sequences of events. In *Tetris*, where those objects just keep falling, the player can't know in what exact order they'll follow each other. This is also one of the simplest ways to limit or prevent anticipation.

Frequency. This factor concerns the repetitive capacities of the game. Basically, both events and actions (or to be precise, the player's chances for taking action) may happen only once or an unlimited number of times. There may also be a limit to these recurrences, a kind of a middle ground between those two extremes. In some computer games, especially in role-playing games such as *Ultima Online*, at least some actions are irreversible and one cannot go back to a previous situation and undo the changes. In other kinds of games, the player can by all means keep banging his head against the wall until a break occurs somewhere. Sometimes it is even advisable. We could also describe recurring events in terms of their determination (the span of time in which an event or set of events recurs), specification (the rhythm of recurrence of the event or set of events), and extension (the duration of the recurring event or set of events) (Genette 1980, 127–140).

Speed. This aspect concerns pace. As we know, one of the great gifts computers brought to gaming is their superb ability to keep pace. To once again borrow a concept or two from Espen Aarseth, we can say that the main difference here is between transient and intransient games. In the former, the computer controls the pace and in the latter the player controls the pace. On the other hand, this concerns only the agent of speed. There are at least two other relevant dimensions of speed: its steadiness (for some reason the obvious alternative to this is almost always acceleration, not deceleration), and its importance as a goal in itself (as in some sports games).

Duration. This variable contains at least three aspects. First, Richard Schechner distinguishes between event time and set time (Schechner 1988, 6–7). In the former case, the game is over after all the

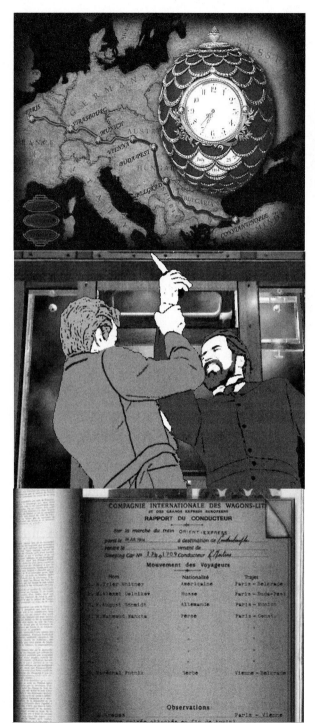

4.sidebar.3–5. Screenshots from *The Last Express,* designed by Jordan Mechner (1997). (Jordan Mechner, Phoenix Licensing)

42

events are properly traversed, and in the latter there's a temporal limit to all this and the winner is the one who's in the better position when the set time is up. Second, temporal limitations can either affect the whole game in its entirety, or only some parts of it that should be traversed within the set time. *The Last Express* is an intriguing combination of these possibilities. In games such as *Doom* the players should usually try to reduce the time span or duration allotted to any odd monster. If such an entity is allowed to live life to its full extent, the game is over. Third, the reverse options may be equally valid depending on the situation — to reduce the duration of an event by cheating or getting out of the situation, or to prolong the duration of an event (letting it happen) by avoiding any confrontation, as in *Thief*.

The time of action concerns the player's possibilities for action. Basically, the player can act before, after, during (or in between) events. Not all games allow all these possibilities, and not all of these possibilities are equally important in any one game or in any one situation in a game. This is just one aspect of the type or the modality of action. It also corresponds in some degree to the difference between turn-based and real-time strategy games.

Simultaneity. The player may have to increase or decrease the number of simultaneous or parallel events, generate, or initiate such events. A typical example would be *Command and Conquer* and its multiple pieces. Events may have to be alternated, embedded, or linked to each other, or such prefabricated connections and arrangements may have to be reversed and dismantled.

We could easily go into greater detail here by introducing various subdivisions to the temporal categories discussed previously; or by taking more rigorously into account temporal requirements (in terms of speed, order, duration, etc.) set for the player's possible and necessary actions, and mapping them onto the temporal dimensions of game events. So, after all, there's still much nontrivial work to be done, as ludology, like the games it studies, is not about story and discourse at all but about actions and events, the relations of which are not completely fixed.[17]

Notes:

1. A concept introduced to computer game studies by Gonzalo Frasca in 1998.

2. Those who see and wish to see narratives everywhere (to me, a serious disorder in aesthetic pattern recognition) should at least know their narratology, which is usually not the case. Narrative is a contested concept for sure, but it still doesn't make sense that comparisons between narratives and games, as well as those between print and hypertext narratives, are and were based on seriously outdated and unsophisticated theories of narrative. In order to make any reliable claims for novelties or similarities between modes and media, one should (at least) first gather the most sophisticated knowledge there is; let's say combining formal narratology (Genette, Prince) with the narrative tricks and treats of postmodernist fiction that once again reconfigured the relations between narrative and textual designs (see McHale 1987, 1992), and the tradition of procedural writing (especially various poetics of the OuLiPo; see Bénabou 1998) — and then transform that knowledge into the digital realm, perhaps through Aarseth's cybertext theory (Aarseth 1997) and its functional and heuristic map of the textual medium (a seriously understudied dimension of traditional literary studies). It's painfully obvious this is not the case, and narrative is just another marketing tool used to sell us everything else except narratives. To complete the irony, it could be observed that various poetries and poetic practices (such as John Cayley's programmatology, Eduardo Kac's holopoetry, and Loss Pequeno Glazier's kinetic works) which give their strings of signs different durational values are much "closer" to games than print and classic hypertext narratives with their static (permanent) scriptons and intransient time.

3. There are plenty of reasons, of course. The main thing is that any element can be turned into a game element, and a single element is enough to constitute a game if it allows manipulation, and this fact alone allows combinations not witnessed in narratives or drama. Consequently, both the number of game elements and the relations between them can be different in specific ways that are typical of (computer) games and only of them.

4. This is crucial too, as from chess and soccer to *Tetris*, games have managed quite well without characters.

5. We'll discuss the gaming situation and game time in separate sections; this division mimics Genette's presentation of tense, mood and voice in *Narrative Discourse* (1980).

6. This Sanskrit classic is then about remediation some 1,500 years before Bolter and Grusin (1999). There are important differences of course. The fact that dance theatre contains elements of music doesn't turn the latter to the former in the *Natyasastra*. But for Bolter and Grusin, computer games are audiovisual narratives, because they seem to contain cinematic components.

7. Of course this is a broad generalisation, but an educated one.

8. This section is kind of a footnote to Eskelinen (2001b), where the gaming situation and its spatial, causal, functional, and temporal parameters are studied and articulated more fully.

9. *Nokia Game* <http://www.nokiagame.com> is interesting in how

it makes use of the immediate media environment of the player, as the following excerpt from its rules makes clear:

> The player must complete various kinds of challenges and puzzles based on the given clues in order to proceed to the next stage of the Game. A time period for completing a task in question may be limited for some tasks (e.g. for couple of hours or the clue might be given at an exact time). This time limit will be informed to the player with the task or clue in question. The player may find clues via received short messages to his or her mobile phone or via other various kind of media, such as e-mail, Internet, TV, radio, magazines or newspapers. At most stages of the Game the player has only one chance to complete the task in question. At some stage of the Game some players will be excluded from the Game based on a wrong answer or action, or based on not being among the announced number of best players that performed the task in question.

The game continues for a month for the winner, and a little less for the other players.

10. Sternberg's gaps are not to be confused with the inevitable overdetermination and ambiguity of meaning in Wolfgang Iser's phenomenology of reading (Iser 1978) and literary anthropology (Iser 1989). Instead, they are regulating the flow of information, and what readers can and cannot know. So even though we might guess it was the butler who did it, the appropriate information will be released at a specific point in the text.

11. Or if one does, then it is another game. Conventions usually change over time but rules don't (or not necessarily). This means games can be played by their original rules (if they are known) whereas writing is always already an orphan that can't be reduced to its original context (and conventions long gone).

12. Dominant, or to put the same idea in a politically correct way: "textual service" (see Chatman 1990, 10). Throughout this essay I invoke the heritage of Russian formalism on purpose, as it may well be that computer game studies need to go through formalistic phases similar to the ones that film and theater studies went through in the first half of the twentieth century, to gain their relative independence.

13. *Hegirascope*, a web fiction by Stuart Moulthrop, limits the reaction time of its readers to 30 seconds per node. Within that period of time the reader must decide which narrative thread to follow and choose a link; otherwise the program makes that decision for the player. In *Reagan Library*, also by Moulthrop, the content of the nodes change when they are revisited for the first three times (there's more text available for the persistent reader). This affects or at least has the capacity to affect and alter the temporal relations between story time and discourse time (see Eskelinen 2001a).

14. *The Last Express* is an adventure game (a murder mystery) happening in the real-time of the game world. The player must find the culprit in time; that is, he may run out of time to solve the crime, as there's a temporal limit to the duration of the

exploration. In other words, the wasted time also counts, and the player has to manipulate "discourse time" and condense it to contain the relevant story events.

15. Genette distinguishes between formal and thematic narratology (Genette 1988, 16). The latter is content-oriented, and interested in stories and themes (i.e., things like plot configuration and characters, in general, the "narrated"), and the former focuses on the specifics of narrative as a mode. To the detriment of thematic narratology (best exemplified by Marie-Laure Ryan's approach to games (Ryan 2001)), there are no specific "narrative contents."

16. For possible "new" categories, see Eskelinen and Koskimaa (2001).

17. Here's a preliminary example of how to apply some of the key concepts utilized in this paper to *Tetris*, probably the most successful abstract computer game ever:

story time	< narratives >	discourse time/event time	< games >	user time
order	......			X (random)
speed	......			X (accelerating)
frequency (repetition)	......			0
duration	......			0
simultaneity	......			X (no simultaneity)
time of narration/ action	......			X (during and after)

Explanation: Dotted line = non-existent relation, X = non-manipulatable relation, 0 = manipulatable relation.

Discourse time in narratology is somewhat similar to event time in ludology. The former could be seen as a series or a combination of individual event times, either fixed (or semifixed) as in print or hypertext narratives, or variable as in games. Still, as the time needed to complete a game usually varies considerably from player to player, I prefer event time to discourse time. One should also note that in computer games there's always a conceptual difference between events as they exist in the game and as they are presented to or generated for the player (very much like textons and scriptons in cybertext theory; see Aarseth 1997, 62). In less abstract games there might be a fictive timeline into which the events are situated (in *Civilization*, it is the continuum between 3000 B.C. and 2020); it could be called content time (because we are not dealing with stories here).

References

Aarseth, Espen (1994). "Nonlinearity and Literary Theory." In *Hyper/text/theory*, edited by George P. Landow. Baltimore: Johns Hopkins University Press.

Aarseth, Espen (1997). *Cybertext: Perspectives on Ergodic Literature*. Baltimore: Johns Hopkins University Press.

Aarseth, Espen (1998a). "Dataspillets Diskurs." In *Digitalkultur og Nettverkskommunikasjon*, edited by Espen Aarseth. Bergen: Espen Aarseth.

44

Aarseth, Espen (1998b). "Aporia and Epiphany in *Doom* and *The Speaking Clock*: Temporality in Ergodic Art." In *Cyberspace Textuality*, edited by Marie-Laure Ryan. Bloomington: University of Indiana Press.

Aarseth, Espen (2001a). "Allegories of Space." In *Cybertext Yearbook 2000*, edited by Markku Eskelinen and Raine Koskimaa. Saarijärvi: Publications of the Research Centre for Contemporary Culture, University of Jyväskylä.

Aarseth, Espen (2001b). "Computer Game Studies, Year One." *Game Studies* 1, no.1 (July 2001). <http://www.gamestudies.org/0101/editorial.html>.

Avedon, Elliott M., and Brian Sutton-Smith (1971). *The Study of Games*. New York: Wiley.

Bénabou, Marcel (1998). "Rule and Constraint." In *Oulipo: A Primer of Potential Literature*, edited by Warren J. Motte, Jr. Normal, IL: Dalkey Archive Press.

Bolter, Jay David, and Richard Grusin (1999). *Remediation: Understanding New Media*. Cambridge, MA: MIT Press.

Bordwell, David (1984). *Narration in the Fiction Film*. Madison: University of Wisconsin Press.

Bremond, Claude (1980). "The Logic of Narrative Possibilities." *New Literary History* 11 (1980): 398–411.

Caillois, Roger (translated by Meyer Barash) (1979). *Man, Play, Games*. New York: Schocken Books.

Chatman, Seymour (1978). *Story and Discourse*. Ithaca: Cornell University Press.

Chatman, Seymour (1990). *Coming to Terms*. Ithaca: Cornell University Press.

Crawford, Chris (1982). *The Art of Computer Game Design*. <http://www.vancouver.wsu.edu/fac/peabody/game-book/Coverpage.html>.

Dostoevsky, Fyodor (translated by David Magarshack) (1955). *The Idiot*. Penguin: London.

Jacques Ehrmann, "Homo Ludens Revisited." *Yale French Studies* 41, 38-57 (1969).

Eskelinen, Markku (2001a). "Introduction to Cybertext Narratology." In *Cybertext Yearbook 2000*, edited by Markku Eskelinen and Raine Koskimaa. Saarijärvi: Publications of the Research Centre for Contemporary Culture, University of Jyväskylä.

Eskelinen, Markku (2001b). "The Gaming Situation." *Game Studies* 1, no.1 (July 2001). <http://www.gamestudies.org/0101/eskelinen/>.

Eskelinen, Markku, and Raine Koskimaa (2001). "Discourse Timer: Towards Temporally Dynamic Texts." *Dichtung Digital* 17 (2001). <http://www.dichtung-digital.de/2001/05/29-Esk-Kosk>.

Frasca, Gonzalo (1998). "Ludology Meets Narratology." <http://www.ludology.org/articles/ludology.html>.

Frasca, Gonzalo (2001). "Videogames of the Oppressed." M.A. Thesis: School of Literature, Communication and Culture, Georgia Institute of Technology, Atlanta, Georgia. <http://www.ludology.org/articles/thesis/>.

Genette, Gerard (1980). *Narrative Discourse*. Ithaca: Cornell University Press.

Genette, Gerard (1988). *Narrative Discourse Revisited*. Ithaca: Cornell University Press.

Huizinga, Johan (1950). *Homo Ludens: A Study of the Play Element in Culture*. New York: Roy Publishers.

Iser, Wolfgang (1978). *The Act of Reading: A Theory of Aesthetic Response*. Baltimore: Johns Hopkins University Press.

Iser, Wolfgang (1989). *Prospecting: From Reader Response to Literary Anthropology*. Baltimore: Johns Hopkins University Press.

Juul, Jesper (1999). "A Clash Between Game and Narrative." M.A. Thesis, University of Copenhagen, Denmark. <http://www.jesperjuul.dk/thesis>.

Juul, Jesper (2000). "What Computer Games Can and Can't Do." Paper presented at the Digital Arts and Culture, Bergen, August 2-4, 2000. <http://www.jesperjuul.dk/text/WCGCACD.html>.

Keene, Donald (1995). "Japanese Aesthetics." In *Japanese Aesthetics and Culture*, edited by Nancy G. Hume. Albany: State University of New York.

McHale, Brian (1987). *Postmodernist Fiction*. New York: Methuen.

McHale, Brian (1992). *Constructing Postmodernism*. London: Routledge.

Metz, Christian (1974). *Film Language. A Semiotics of Cinema*. New York: Oxford University Press

Motte, Warren (1995). *Playtexts*. Lincoln: University of Nebraska Press.

Moulthrop, Stuart (1995). *Hegirascope*. <http://iat.ubalt.edu/moulthrop/hypertexts/hgs/>.

Moulthrop, Stuart (1990). *Reagan Library*. <http://iat.ubalt.edu/moulthrop/hypertexts/rl/>.

Parlett, David (1999). *The Oxford History of Board Games*. Oxford: Oxford University Press.

Prince, Gerald (1982). *Narratology*. Berlin: Walter de Gruyter.

Prince, Gerald (1987). *The Dictionary of Narratology*. Lincoln: University of Nebraska Press.

Ryan, Marie-Laure (2001). "Beyond Myth and Metaphor: The Case of Narrative in Digital Media." *Game Studies* 1, no.1 (July 2001). <http://www.gamestudies.org/0101/ryan/>.

Schechner, Richard (1988). *Performance Theory*. London: Routledge.

Sternberg, Meir (1978). *Expositional Modes and Temporal Ordering in Fiction*. Baltimore: Johns Hopkins University Press.

Sutton-Smith, Brian (1997). *The Ambiguity of Play*. Cambridge: Harvard University Press.

Vatsyayan, Kapila (1996). *Bharata: The Natyasastra*. Delhi: Sahitya Akademi.

Genre Trouble: Narrativism and the Art of Simulation

Espen Aarseth

Introduction: Stories and Games

Currently in game and digital culture studies, a controversy rages over the relevance of narratology for game aesthetics. One side argues that computer games are media for telling stories, while the opposing side claims that stories and games are different structures that are in effect doing opposite things. One crucial aspect of this debate is whether games can be said to be "texts," and thereby subject to a textual-hermeneutic approach. Here we find the political question of genre at play: the fight over the games' generic categorization is a fight for academic influence over what is perhaps the dominant contemporary form of cultural expression. After forty years of fairly quiet evolution, the cultural genre of computer games is finally recognized as a large-scale social and aesthetic phenomenon to be taken seriously. In the last few years, games have gone from *media non grata* to a recognized field of great scholarly potential, a place for academic expansion and recognition.

The great stake-claiming race is on, and academics from neighboring fields, such as literature and film studies, are eagerly grasping "the chance to begin again, in a golden land of opportunity and adventure" (to quote from the ad in *Blade Runner*). As with any land rush, the respect for local culture and history is minimal, while the belief in one's own tradition, tools and competence is unfailing. Computer game studies is virgin soil, ready to be plotted and plowed by the machineries of cultural and textual studies. What better way to map the territory than by using the trusty, dominant paradigm of stories and storytelling? The story perspective has many benefits: it is safe, trendy, and flexible. In a (Western) world troubled by addiction, attention deficiency, and random violence, stories are morally and aesthetically acceptable. In stories, meaning can be controlled (despite what those deconstructionists may have claimed). Storytelling is a valuable skill, the main mode of successful communication. And theories of storytelling are (seemingly) universal: they can be applied to and explain any medium, phenomenon, or culture. So why should not games also be a type of story?

In the context of computer games (and in most other contexts as well) stories and storytelling appear to be extremely old phenomena, spanning all of media

Response by Chris Crawford

Three elements of Espen Aarseth's paper dominate my attentions. First is the assumed conflict between interactivity and narrative. This assumption is certainly widely shared, and seems justified by our complete failure to produce a truly interactive storytelling product. However, one need only contemplate the process by which a grandparent might tell a child a bedtime story to realize that interactive storytelling has been with us a long time. Our task is to design algorithms that capture the dramatic rules used in such practices. Such algorithms are certainly beyond our grasp just yet, but we should not be too hasty to assume them ungraspable. Give us some time; we can do it.

A second point that caught my attention was Aarseth's apparent dismissal of interactivity:

The hidden structure behind these, and most, computer games is not narrative — or that silly and abused term, "interactivity" — but *simulation*.

While I certainly agree that the poor term has been much abused, I still believe that it remains the very essence of the entire computing experience. The computer is not at heart an audiovideo device: videocassette recorders handle that task better. Nor is it a data storage device: paper provides a cheaper and more capacious means of storing data. While computers before 1980 had batch input, processing, and output, the computer revolution that began twenty years ago arose from the ability to close the loop with the user, so that input, processing, and output were

history, and numerous media technologies. Show me a medium not suited to storytelling: it is probably a completely useless one. Computer games, with scarcely forty years of history, represent a mere last few seconds in the long evolutionary history of storytelling. Clearly, when we compare stories to computer games, stories hold a much stronger position, which games cannot dream of reaching in the near future. Well, that is the optimistic version. Some see it in pessimistic terms; in the words of a prominent Scandinavian literary theorist, computer games are a sign of cultural decay. Perhaps they need a new name – how about "interactive narratives"?

There are many types of comparativism. It can be dangerous, especially when one object is cherished and well-known, and the other is marginal and suspect. And in the context of this general story/game discussion, we have the danger of generic criticism. You know the kind that goes: "Traditional music is much better than jazz," or "Novels are a higher art form than movies." If we judge individual works on the basis of their genre, we may have lost already.

But what about stories and games? To address computer games as a consistent genre or medium is highly problematic. From *Tetris* on a mobile phone to *Super Mario* on a Gameboy to *Everquest* on a Midi-tower Windows machine there is a rather large span of

different genres, social contexts, and media technologies. It cannot be repeated often enough that the computer is not a medium, but a flexible material technology that will accomodate many very different media. Hence, there is no "computer medium" with one set of fixed capabilities, not is there "the medium of the computer game." Games are, at best, a somewhat definable cultural genre.

No doubt the same can be said for stories. However, if we compare them as cultural traditions, their positions become more equal. How can that be? Well, computer games are games, and games are not new, but very old, probably older than stories. It could even be argued that games are older than human culture, since even animals play games. You don't see cats or dogs tell each other stories, but they will play. And games are interspecies communication: you can't tell your dog a story, but the two of you can play together.

So, rather than being a newcomer, computer games are games in a new material technology, just as print novels were literature in a new technology 500 years ago. Yet, it seems, "we" only discovered games as cultural artifacts a few years ago. Before that, games were not an object for aesthetic study, but relegated to the study of children and primitive cultures, with a very few notable exceptions, such as Brian Sutton-Smith (Sutton-Smith 1997). However, games are not camera-

---

part of a continuous interaction. Pre-personal computers could handle budget calculations, but the spreadsheet (an interactive budget) caught fire. Pre-personal computers had text-formatting programs allowing users to print out documents, but it was the advent of the interactive word processor that made PCs so compelling.

Last, I would agree with Aarseth's recommendation that we pursue simulation — if we expand the notion of simulation somewhat. Traditionally, simulation has been gauged by its technical accuracy. For the purposes of entertainment, we need to expand the notion of accuracy to include the expectations and thought processes of our audience. I sometimes use the phrase *dramatic laws of physics* to express this notion. Just as a

flight simulator must be true to the laws of physics, so too must an entertainment product be true to the laws of drama. For example, most games use spatial algorithms that correspond to geometric laws but violate dramatic laws. Characters cannot travel from point A to point B without traversing all the terrain between those two points, no matter how boring that terrain might be. In drama, a character who must travel between two points simply disappears from one location (stage) and reappears at the other. This conforms to dramatic standards, but completely defies all conventions of what we normally think of as simulation.

5.sidebar.1–2. Two screenshots from the PDA version of *Tomb Raider*. (Eidos Interactive, Core Design)

ready pieces of art either. Because games are not one form, but many, they cannot be one art form. And why would aesthetics be the most relevant perspective? Some games may have artistic ambitions, others do not. Games are games, a rich and extremely diverse family of practices, and share qualities with performance arts (play, dance, music, sports) material arts, (sculpture, painting, architecture, gardening) and the verbal arts (drama, narrative, the epos). But fundamentally, they are games. The artistic elements are merely supports for what the Finnish avant garde writer and game

theorist Markku Eskelinen calls "the gaming situation," the gameplay (Eskelinen 2001).

Are games texts? The best reason I can think of why one would ask such a crude question is because one is a literary or semiotic theorist and wants to believe in the relevance of one's training.

Games are not "textual" or at least not primarily textual: where is the text in chess? We might say that the *rules* of chess constitute its "text," but there is no recitation of the rules during gameplay, so that would reduce the textuality of chess to a subtextuality or a paratextuality. A central "text" does not exist — merely context. Any game consists of three aspects: (1) rules,

From Stuart Moulthrop's Online Response

With a rigor perhaps born of militancy, Aarseth insists that games "are self-contained," insulated from any intertextuality. "Unlike in music, where a national anthem played on electric guitar takes on a whole new meaning," he writes, "the value system of a game is strictly internal, determined unambivalently by the rules." Seeking to exclude narrativist contraband, Aarseth embargoes all cultural implications. We are not to understand the game of chess as an allegory of feudalism or *Tomb Raider* as misogynist–masochist fantasy. By his reasoning, chess would be the same game even if the pieces were replaced with bottle caps and called minks, warts, and chevrolets instead of bishops, knights, and pawns. Likewise, Aarseth claims,

the pneumatic Lara Croft could be traded for a less salacious anatomy, leaving the game intact. In each case the player's engagement with the rule system — the "gaming situation" — matters far more than incidental details of the "gameworld."

If these claims seem indisputable at face value it is only because they are alarmingly narrow. *Mink takes chevrolet* may contain no reference to chivalric hierarchy but it does assert a logic of territorial domination and unequal privilege. No doubt one can play the game without connecting this logic to European history, but such an approach reduces chess to a series of abstract transactions, which may work well enough for mathematics but seems far too narrow for any serious cultural critique. *Tomb Raider* shows even more clearly

(2) a material/semiotic system (a gameworld), and (3) gameplay (the events resulting from application of the rules to the gameworld). Of these three, the semiotic system is the most coincidental to the game. As the Danish theorist and game designer Jesper Juul has pointed out (Juul 2001b), games are eminently themeable: you can play chess with some rocks in the mud, or with pieces that look like the Simpson family rather than kings and queens. It would still be the same game. The "royal" theme of the traditional pieces is all but irrelevant to our understanding of chess. Likewise, the dimensions of Lara Croft's body, already analyzed to death by film theorists, are irrelevant to me as a player, because a different-looking body would not make me play differently (see sidebar). When I play, I don't even see her body, but see through it and past it. In addition to these three components, there is the player's active knowledge of the game, in the form of strategies and performance techniques, and mental topographies, as well as written guides and other paratextual information about the games.

It follows that games are not intertextual either; games are self-contained. You don't need to have played poker or ludo to understand chess, and knowledge of roulette will not help you to understand Russian roulette. (Neither will cultural knowledge of Russia. On the other hand, *Tetris* is also a dangerous Russian game...) Knowing *Star Wars: The Phantom Menace* will not make you better at playing *Pod Racer* (Juul 2001a). Unlike in music, where a national anthem played on electric guitar takes on a whole new meaning, the value system of a game is strictly internal, determined unambivalently by the rules. Among the many differences between games and stories, one of the most obvious is that of ambiguity. In *Tetris*, I do not stop to ponder what those bricks are really supposed to be made of. In *Doom*, there is no moral dilemma resulting from the killing of probably innocent monsters. The pleasure of games is quite different from the pleasures of the novel: for a chess or *Tetris* player, replaying is the norm, while most novels are read only once. You can be an expert chess player without playing any other game, but to understand even a single novel you will need to have studied numerous others.

Certainly many — indeed most — games, use texts much the same way food products do ("boil the spaghetti for seven minutes"), but it seems unreasonable therefore to claim that food is textual. And in driving your car, you are constantly reading the traffic signs and the meters on your dashboard, but we still don't consider driving cars as a subgenre of reading.

However, the (academic) discovery of computer games over the last two decades is accompanied by the most smothering form of generic criticism: the attempt

this artificial restriction of focus. Certainly one could swap Lara Croft for a digitized Rowan Atkinson without technically changing the feedback loop between player and program. It seems unlikely, though, that *Mr. Bean: Tomb Raider* would sell nearly as well to its primary audience. Lara Croft's physique may consist of raw data but it cannot be treated as such for critical purposes (see figure 5.response.1). While one may look past or through the avatar body during play, the significance of games as cultural forms goes beyond the player's time in the loop.

http://www.electronicbookreview.com/thread/firstperson/moulthropr1

5.response.1. A promotional image of Lara Croft. (Eidos Interactive, Core Design.)

to reform games into a more acceptable form of art, literature or film; i.e., as narratives. Shakespeare's *Hamlet* was pretty good, but soon we can have something even better: Hamlet the Game. This idea, termed the "Holodeck myth" by Marie-Laure Ryan (2001) with reference to Janet Murray's book *Hamlet on the Holodeck* (1997), was first proposed by Brenda Laurel (1986; 1991) as a form of computer-controlled real-time participant drama, and attempted by research projects such as Joseph Bates' Oz project at Carnegie Mellon University. As a theory, this narrativistic colonialism might seem aesthetically problematic (Aarseth 1997, chapter six), as well as technologically unachievable (Bringsjord 2001), but there are many versions of it, and some are more sophisticated than others.

The Story-Game Ideology

Underlying the drive to reform games as "interactive narratives," as they are sometimes called, lies a complex web of motives, from economic ("games need narratives to become better products"), elitist and eschatological ("games are a base, low-cultural form; let's try to escape the humble origins and achieve 'literary' qualities"), to academic colonialism ("computer games *are* narratives, we only need to redefine narratives in such a way that these new narrative forms are included"). At a recent game conference, it was stated that the difference between films and games was simply the "interactivity" of the games.

This latter motive, the only one of the three mentioned before to concern us here, seems to me to spring out of a certain ideology, much practiced by humanists, and also well beyond our ivory towers; an ideology that we might call "narrativism." This is the notion that everything is a story, and that story-telling is our primary, perhaps only, mode of understanding, our cognitive perspective on the world. Life is a story, this discussion is a story, and the building that I work in is also a story, or better, an architectural narrative. Ironically, most proper narratologists, who actually have to think about and define narratives in a scholarly responsible and accurate way, are not guilty of this overgeneralization.

Yet among anthropologists, business people, technologists, visual artists, media theorists, and other laypersons, this ideology — or what Alan Rauch once fittingly called *story fetishism* — is strong and uncontested. And to us humanists, the (let's face it) lowest caste of the academic world, it is nice to feel important again, for once. Finally, our expertise matters! We don't know much about technology, or biology, but we do know stories and storytelling. So why be critical when we can be important instead?

Aarseth Responds

To paraphrase Moulthrop, the polygonal significance of Lara Croft's physique goes beyond the gameplay. But that doesn't mean it tells us much, if anything, about the gameplay, does it?

http://www.electronicbookreview.com/thread/firstperson/aarsethr2

So, then, is storytelling the solution to all the world's problems, from business strategies to computer game design? If rhetoric is indeed our game, then we should be able to see through this one. But it *is* a very nice dream.

And this is of course not an attack on the importance of stories. Storytelling has been, and still is, the dominant form of cultural expression. But it is not the only game in town, the only mode of discourse. It is quite possible, not to mention necessary, to identify other modes, games among them, as alternatives to storytelling.

But what exactly is the relationship between games and stories? Is it a dichotomy? A rivalry? Or perhaps a continuum? As Eskelinen has pointed out, both stories and games are medium-independent. A story can be translated from novel to comic book, to movie, to TV series, to opera, etc. A game can be translated from board and dice, to a live role-play out in the woods, to numbers and letters on a screen, to a three-dimensional virtual world. From *SpaceWar* (1961) to *Star Raiders* (1979), *Elite* (1984), *to X – Beyond the Frontier* (1999), not much has happened in the rules and gameplay: the games have increasingly better 3D graphics, but the theme and objectives remain the same. *Rogue* (1980) and *Diablo* (1997) are basically the same game (see sidebar).

What is lost in translation? In the various versions of a story, key events and relationships remain; in the versions of a game, the rules remain.[1] But when we try to translate a game into a story, what happens to the rules? What happens to the gameplay? And a story into a game: what happens to the plot? And, to use Marie-

Laure Ryan's example (2001), what player, in the game version of *Anna Karenina*, playing the main character, Holodeck style, would actually commit suicide, even virtually? Novels are very good at relating the inner lives of characters (films perhaps less so); games are awful at that, or, wisely, they don't even try. We might say that, unlike literature, games are not about the Other, they are about the Self. Games focus on self-mastery and exploration of the external world, not exploration of interpersonal relationships (except for multiplayer games). Or when they try to, like the recent bestselling games *The Sims* or *Black and White*, it is from a godlike, Asmodean perspective.

The aim of *The Sims* is to control and shape the interactions and daily life of your characters, not take human form yourself. Nevertheless, games like *The Sims* are sometimes (not often) used as storytelling machines, when particularly memorable moments in the game are retold by the player/god. But this is not translation from game to story, this is simply good, old after-the-fact narration, like the football column in the Monday sports section, the lab experiment report, or the slide show of one's Carribean vacation. Something interesting happened, and we want to tell others about it. Ontologically, the capacity for generating memorable moments is something games have in common with real life, as well as with stories. A story-generating system does not have to be a story itself. In fact, while life and games are primary, real-time phenomena, consisting of real or virtual events, stories are secondary phenomena, a revision of the primary event, or a revision of a revision, etc.

And yet, we do have games inspired by films and novels, and vice versa: *The Hobbit*, *The Hitchhiker's Guide to the Galaxy*, *Super Mario Brothers*, *Tomb Raider*, *Goldeneye*, *Blade Runner*; the list is nearly endless. Are they not translations?

Genre theory can help us describe what goes on here: John Cawelti's (1976) distinction between "underlying form" and "specific cultural conventions" would tell us that the underlying form (narrative structure or game rules) remains untranslatable, but the cultural conventions, such as the setting and character types of, say, *Star Wars*, are translated. While, as Jesper Juul has

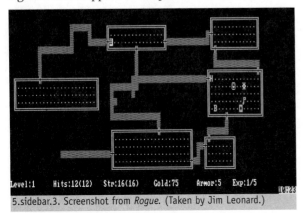

5.sidebar.3. Screenshot from *Rogue*. (Taken by Jim Leonard.)

pointed out (Juul 2001a), the story of *Star Wars* is unextractable from the game of the same name, the setting, atmosphere and characters can be deduced. So, although nonnarrative and nonludic elements can be translated, the key elements, the narration and the gameplay, like oil and water, are not easily mixed.

Story-Game Hybrids:
The Adventure Game Genre

And yet, there is a game genre that may also be called narrative. This is the so-called adventure game, a computer game genre that was born in 1976, when Donald Woods turned William Crowther's text-based cave simulation into a fantasy game. This game, *Adventure*, which consists of moving through a labyrinthine cave by solving puzzles ("how to get past the snake," etc.), has a storylike, episodic structure, where the player/hero progresses in a linear fashion through the maze. For a while very popular, this textual genre died out commercially in the late 1980s when graphical computer games took over the market.

Structurally, however, it lives on in graphical computer games such as *Myst* (1993) and *Half-Life* (1997), where the same deterministic linearity and rule system dominate the play. By looking at sales figures, it could be claimed that these games successfully demonstrate the potential for combining stories and games. However, sales figures are not a reliable measure of artistic success, or — dare we say — quality. And according to one of the successful designer brothers of *Myst*, Robyn Miller, artistically *Myst* was a frustrating project. Miller, arguably one of the most successful game designers ever, later stopped making games and turned to animated movies, because he felt the game format in conflict with storytelling and character development. And there was this annoying intervening person, the player, to put up with. Most critics agree that the Miller brothers succeeded eminently in making a fascinating visual landscape, a haunting and beautiful gameworld, but to experienced gamers, the gameplay was boring and derivative, with the same linear structure that was introduced by the first *Adventure* game sixteen years earlier. Nice video graphics, shame about the game.

The greatest aesthetic problem for the adventure story-game seems to be believable characters. In the first adventure game there were just animals and monsters, and hardly any dialogue, and in *Myst* there were no characters at all, except for in a few static video sequences. In more dramatic adventure games, the characters' behavior is totally prescripted, with a few lines repeated endlessly and brainlessly. The dramatic ambitions of these games remain unfulfilled and seem as unreachable as ever. What keeps the genre alive is increasingly more photorealistic, detailed three-dimensional graphical environments, but apart from that, it is mostly the same story-game over and over again. Unlike other games, but like most novels, these games are normally only played once, and typically not completed. This makes them very different from other games. Players are often stuck on one of the puzzles, and have no choice but either to buy the solutions book, download a "walkthrough" guide from the internet, or give up. Perhaps we could say that this genre is really only one and the same game, the same rule system repeated over and over with variable cultural conventions and increasingly better technology.

As Robyn Miller suggested, the aesthetic problem in these games is a conflict between the opposing goals of gameplay and storytelling. Adventure games seldom, if at all, contain good stories. Even the most entertaining of these games, like Warren Spector's *Deus Ex* (1999), contains a cliched storyline that would make a B-movie writer blush, and characters so wooden that they make The Flintstones look like Strindberg. The gameplay is constrained by the story in unrealistic ways (in *Deus Ex*, if you try to kill the secretary, it is simply not possible, because it does not fit the storyline). What makes such games playable at all, and indeed attractive, is the sequence of shifting, exotic, often fascinating settings (levels), where you explore the topography and master the virtual environment. The gameworld is its own reward, and the end, if and when it comes, does not offer dramatic satisfaction, but a feeling of limbo. There is no turning back, and no going forward. You are no longer employed by the game. Time to buy another.

The Art of Simulation

Other game genres may also employ storylines. In god-games such as *Civilization*, history itself plays the role of storyline. In strategy games such as *Heroes of Might and Magic, Command and Conquer, Warcraft,* or role-playing games such as *Ultima Underworld* or *Diablo*, the story is often an episodic progression between levels, with each level constituting a self-enclosed episode, like the individual matches in a football cup. True to their war-oriented themes, these series of levels are often called campaigns. A successful game such as *Heroes of Might and Magic* will offer both multilevel campaigns and stand-alone levels or "maps" (gameworlds), sometimes generated randomly by the game software. A randomly generated map can be just as satisfying to play as a human-authored gameworld or campaign, and this tells us that the real aesthetic quality of these games is in the design of the rule system, rather than in the design of the gameworld.

The pleasures of video games, as James Newman (2001) has pointed out, comparing *Tomb Raider* to the cartoonish-looking *Super Mario Kart*, are not primarily visual, but kinaesthetic, functional and cognitive. Your skills are rewarded, your mistakes punished, quite literally. The game gaze is not the same as the cinema gaze, although I fear it will be a long time before film critics studying computer games will understand the difference. (Alongside narrativism, there is the equally problematic *visualism*.) But pleasure follows function, we might say. When it is there at all, the story in these games is superficial, like a bored taxi driver whose only function is to take us on to the next ludic event. In the case of *Heroes of Might and Magic*, story fragments pop up at specific times in a level. They are completely superfluous, like illustrations in a storybook, and ignoring them will not affect the gameplay at all.

The hidden structure behind these, and most, computer games is not narrative — or that silly and abused term, "interactivity" — but *simulation*. Simulation is the key concept, a bottom-up hermeneutic strategy that forms the basis of so many cognitive activities: all sorts of training, from learning to pilot a plane to learning to command troops, but also the use of spreadsheets, urban planning, architectural design and CAD, scientific experiments, reconstructive surgery, and generative linguistics. And in entertainment: computer games. If you want to understand a phenomenon, it is not enough to be a good storyteller, you need to understand how the parts work together, and the best way to do that is to build a simulation. Through the hermeneutic circle of simulation/construction, testing, modification, more testing, and so forth, the model is moved closer to the simulated phenomenon.

The computer game is the art of simulation. A subgenre of simulation, in other words. Strategy games are sometimes misleadingly called "simulation" games, but all computer games contain simulation. Indeed, it is the dynamic aspect of the game that creates a consistent gameworld. Simulation is the hermeneutic Other of narratives; the alternative mode of discourse, bottom up and emergent where stories are top-down and preplanned. In simulations, knowledge and experience is created by the player's actions and strategies, rather than recreated by a writer or moviemaker.

Culturally, especially in "high culture," stories dominate still, but are currently losing ground to the new simulation-based discourse-types, e.g., in the entertainment market, where movies are being outsold by computer games. Stories and simulations are not totally incompatible, but the simulation, as a primary phenomenon, must form the basis of any combination of the two, and not vice versa, just as with stories and life. When you have built a simulation, such as a rule-based gameworld, you may use it to tell stories in (or for other purposes); but stories, on the other hand, can only contain simulations in a metaphorical sense, such as the movie *Groundhog Day*, or Tad Williams' *Otherland* novels.

In the adventure games where there is a conflict between narrative and ludic aesthetics, it is typically the simulation that, on its own, allows actions that the story prohibits, or which make the story break down. Players exploit this to invent strategies that make a mockery of the author's intentions. Dead or not, the authors of these games are little more than ghosts in the machine, and hardly *auteurs*. When you put a story on top of a simulation, the simulation (or the player) will always have the last word.

Ludology> Aarseth
Moulthrop
Eskelinen
Douglas Schechner
Crawford Moulthrop
Gromala Cayley

II. Ludology

53

It is time to recognize simulation and the need to simulate as a major new hermeneutic discourse mode, coinciding with the rise of computer technology, and with roots in games and playing.

But What about Literature?

But what about that other type of hybrid: not games with narrative ambitions, but narratives with game elements? Why don't we look at texts that play games?, you may well ask. There is a long tradition of playful texts, from *Tristram Shandy* via detective stories and the OuLiPo, to experimental texts that happen to be digital; and some of these are of course very worthy of critical attention. John McDaid's *Uncle Buddy's Phantom Funhouse* (1991) springs to mind. But here I wanted to address the structure of gaming in its nonmetaphorical form. When we try to guess the murderer in a Poirot novel, we are adding a coincidental game to the story. The guessing game is not necessary, and the narrator doesn't care whether we play or not. If we happen to guess correctly early on, nothing different happens in the novel. Worse, we may even stop reading prematurely, since the ending has become obvious and boring. These novels are games only in a metaphorical sense; they tease us, but we are not real players. In the case of hypertext fictions, we are explorers, but without recognizable rules, there is no real game. To equalize these metaphorical games with a real game is to marginalize an already (academically) marginal phenomenon, to privilege the *illusion* of play over real play. And for game scholars, that is a poor strategy.

Literary experiments are either interesting or they are not. What medium they take place in should have little or nothing to do with it. In a world where practically all the arts use digital technology, it is only natural that literature also should do so, but hardly revolutionary. Generic criticism is a problem, whether it favors or marginalizes digital literature. Either way it is a kind of discrimination.

Katherine Hayles, the influential U.S. theorist of science and literature, recently rose to defend electronic literature as the endangered hybrid species produced by computer games and literature:

While it is understandable that scholars fighting for critical turf want to claim all of the territory for themselves, the nature of the beast called electronic literature cannot be adequately understood if it is orphaned on either side of the family tree. From computer games come interactivity, major tropes such as searching for keys to a central mystery, and multiple narrative pathways chosen by interactors; from literary traditions come devices developed over millennia of experimentation and criticism such as point of view, narrative voice and literary allusions. To omit either of these resources would be to reduce electronic literature to something beyond our recognition. (Hayles 2001)

While I share Hayles' concern that electronic literature should not be killed off in the border wars between game scholars and narrativists, I think her paternity case is rather weak. The real father of electronic literature is not computer games, but the computer interface itself. And the result, in the form of hypernovels such as Michael Joyce's *afternoon* (1991), or generative poetry such as John Cayley's *The Speaking Clock* (1995), is no hybrid, it is literature. The real game-literature hybrid, the textual adventure game, still lives on in the prolific amateur groups such as <rec.arts.int-fiction> on the internet, but seems to have little influence on either game culture or literary culture in general.

Digital literature is still literature, pure, if not simple. When I can read a Harry Potter novel on my Palm Pilot, paper is no longer an integral part of literature's material or ideological foundations. Digital literature, whether experimental like Talan Memmott's "Lexia to Perplexia" (2000) or strictly mainstream like Stephen King's "Riding the Bullet" (2000), is still literature, not a hybrid. Like our ATM cards, which are just as real (and just as symbolic) as paper money, digital literature is real literature.

Conclusion: From Multiplayers to Players

The aesthetics and hermeneutics of games and simulations and their relations to stories (and also to knowledge production) pose a rich problem, of which I have only scratched the surface here. This is the kind of problem that makes aesthetic research meaningful and gratifying. Games and stories have distinct teleologies and artistic potentials, and it is analytically useful (for those of us genuinely interested in games as games, at least) to maintain a conceptual terminology that distinguishes between them. As I have argued here, the traditional hermeneutic paradigms of text, narrative and semiotics are not well-suited to the problems of a simulational hermeneutic. Games (as games) might be the best empirical entry point to this new mode of discourse, at least if we continue the humanist tradition of privileging artistic genres in our hermeneutic research.

My warnings about narrativism and theoretical colonialism might seem unduly harsh and even militant. Why not let the matter resolve itself, through scholarly, logical dialogue? The reason for this vigilance, however, is based on numbers. The sheer number of students trained in film and literary studies will ensure that the slanted and crude misapplication of "narrative" theory to games will continue and probably overwhelm game scholarship for a long time to come. As long as vast numbers of journals and supervisors from traditional narrative studies continue to sanction dissertations and papers that take the narrativity of games for granted and confuse the story-game hybrids with games in general, good, critical scholarship on games will be outnumbered by incompetence, and this is a problem for all involved. Hopefully this is just a short-lived phase, but it certainly is a phase that we are in right now. As more scholars from other disciplines, such as sociology, linguistics, history, economics, and geography, start to do research on games, perhaps the narrativist camp (and the *visualist* camp) will realize more of the many differences between games and narratives, and even contribute valuable analyses using (and not abusing) narratology, but until then the narrativist paradigm will but slowly melt.

The weak and repetitive tradition of adventure story-games such as *Myst* and *Half-Life* should not be given our privileged, undivided attention, just because they remind us more of the movies and novels we used to study. Compared to replayable games such as *Warcraft* and *Counter-Strike*, the story-games do not pose a very interesting theoretical challenge for game studies, once we have identified their dual heritage. There are so many more important aesthetic questions to ask of better and more successful games, in particular multiplayer games. What kind of socioaesthetic exchange goes on in the South Korean multiplayer game *Lineage*, with two million active players? These games are not only the future of gaming, they are huge social experiments that will affect and shape the future of human communication. They will probably use stories, too; not as the overarching design principle, but as rhetorical, interplayer communication strategies, like we all do in our ordinary lives. Ever more advanced online, multiplayer games, with real instead of artificial intelligences, and ever more sophisticated simulation-worlds, will set the agenda for game studies in the coming years. But they probably won't be called online, multiplayer games for much longer. Or "interactive narratives."

Just games, once again.

Notes

An earlier version of this article was presented at the "Problems of Genre" conference of the *Nordic Society for Comparative Literature*, in Gothenburg, 26 August, 2001.

1. The following discussion builds on Juul (2001a).

References

Aarseth, Espen (1997). *Cybertext: Perspectives on Ergodic Literature*. Baltimore: Johns Hopkins University Press.

Bringsjord, Selmer (2001). "Is It Possible to Build Dramatically Compelling Interactive Digital Entertainment?" *Game Studies* 1, no. 1 (2001). <http://gamestudies.org/0101/bringsjord/>.

Cawelti, John (1976). *Adventure, Mystery, and Romance. Formula Stories as Art and Popular Culture*. Chicago: University of Chicago Press.

Cayley, John (1995). *Speaking Clock*. <http://www.shadoof.net/in/incat.html#CLOCK>.

Eskelinen, Markku (2001). "The Gaming Situation." *Game Studies* 1, no. 1 (July 2001). <http://gamestudies.org/0101/eskelinen/>.

Hayles, N. Katherine (2001). "Cyber|literature and Multicourses: Rescuing Electronic Literature from Infanticide." *Electronic Book Review* 11 (2001). <http://altx.com/ebr/riposte/rip11/rip11hay.htm>.

Joyce, Michael (1991). *afternoon*. Watertown, MA: Eastgate Systems.

Juul, Jesper (2001a). "Games Telling Stories? A Brief Note on Games and Narratives." *Game Studies* 1, no. 1 (2001). <http://gamestudies.org/0101/juul-gts/>.

Juul, Jesper (2001b). "Game Time, Event Time, Themability." Presented at the CGDT Conference, Copenhagen, March 1, 2001.

Laurel, Brenda (1986). "Toward the Design of a Computer-Based Interactive Fantasy System." Ph.D. Thesis, Ohio State University, Columbus, Ohio.

Laurel, Brenda (1991). *Computers as Theatre*. Reading, MA: Addison–Wesley.

Memmott, Talan (2000). *Lexia to Perplexia. Electronic Book Review* 11. <http://www.altx.com/ebr/ebr11/>.

Murray, Janet (1997). *Hamlet on the Holodeck: The Future of Narrative in Cyberspace*. New York: The Free Press.

King, Stephen (2000). *Riding the Bullet*. New York: Scribner eBook.

Newman, James (2001). "Reconfiguring the Videogame Player." Games Cultures Conference, Bristol, June 30, 2001.

Ryan, Marie-Laure (2001). "Beyond Myth and Metaphor – The Case of Narrative in Digital Media." *Game Studies* 1, no. 1 (2001). <http://gamestudies.org/0101/ryan/>.

Sutton-Smith, Brian (1997). *The Ambiguity of Play*. Cambridge, MA: Harvard University Press.

From Work to Play: Molecular Culture in the Time of Deadly Games

Stuart Moulthrop

Play Suspended

This essay got its start in my keynote remarks for the Digital Arts and Culture Conference in the spring of 2001 and took its present form during the summer and fall of that unforgettable year. Those were not easy months in which to think about changes in media and culture, however momentous. With the implosion of the internet bubble, the future that had recently looked so glorious tumbled suddenly from promise to delusion. A popular song from those days sardonically recalls "the time when new media / was the big idea," suggesting that even nostalgia had come to work on internet time. Or had that sort of time run out? As the digital generation's ecstatic orbit swung through the dark side of the business cycle, some wondered if the abrupt end of the boom might send the American economy into the same dismal straits as the Japanese (Krugman

2001). To make matters vastly worse, September saw the infamous terror attacks that killed thousands in the U.S. and touched off a conflict of indefinite scope and duration. Much indeed has changed.

With troops on the ground and war talk in the air it has become difficult to give much space to art, literature, and other forms of cultural production, let alone their critical controversies. The going gets even harder if one's concerns run less to the polite than the popular, not to novels or plays but to games and simulations. The subject of play is inherently troublesome in a postindustrial or neo-Taylorist regime, even without economic troubles or terrorist threats. Yet games and play demand serious attention even in such times as these, and perhaps especially now. As Donna Haraway observed in 1985, "we are living through a movement from an organic, industrial society to a polymorphous, information system — from all work to all play, a deadly game" (Haraway 1991, 161). Some might describe this shift as decline or decadence, a falling away from moral certitude into confusion or relativism — a weakness hardly to be tolerated in wartime. But such dismissals obscure the primary significance of the change.

As people explore the affordances of digital communications networks, social institutions and practices take on different characters, moving from

Response by Diane Gromala

Stuart Moulthrop is always the most trustworthy guide to understanding the vicissitudes of cultural and technological change, even as these seemingly incomprehensible waves wash over us with relentless regularity. He grapples here with important issues through characteristic good sense, scrupulous argumentation, and unerring judgment.

How do we understand games in deep and meaningful ways? At the present, the major contributors to the emerging field of ludology (the study of games, or, more precisely, of play), are those from literary backgrounds. They not only offer a rich intellectual tradition in understanding narrative forms of literature, drama, and cinema, but contribute to our

larger understanding of language and culture. In this context, Moulthrop outlines the contentious debate between (particularly neo-Aristotelian) narratology and ergodics. That is, between understanding games as a form of storytelling versus a cultural form in their own right. Deftly unraveling the strands of this debate, Moulthrop offers a crucial turn. By extending Eskalinen's definition of "configurative practice" to include "a way of engaging not just immediate game elements, but also the game's social and material conditions — and by extension, the conditions of other rule-systems such as work and citizenship," he lays opens the ground for what is likely to be the most promising and productive next direction in ludology.

By pursuing Moulthrop's proposition, the crucial

what Pierre Lévy calls the "molar" or mass form of industrial society toward a more intimately networked "molecular" state (Lévy 1997, 40–42). This transition affects all modes and sectors of the social, from commerce and politics to language and culture; and it continues despite the exigencies of geopolitics. The developments discussed in this chapter — a shift from narrative to ludic engagement with texts and from interpretation to configuration as a dominant approach to information systems — are in fact inevitably implicated in the current upheavals of society. This is true enough in the general sense that terror victimizes whole nations; also in the sense that the world's current divisions reflect what Haraway calls an "informatics of domination" (Haraway 1991, 161) that increasingly polarizes the liberal and the fundamentalist. However, there may also be more specific links between the emerging culture of serious play and the crises of the new century.

In the turn from consumption to participation, from interpretative to configurative practices, we find ourselves in a new relationship to media. Since configuration requires active awareness of systems and their structures of control, this turn allows us to resist the assertion of invisibility or transparency in communications systems — a danger that seems particularly pronounced in these new wars of the 24-

hour news cycle. It may happen that in refusing the transparency of media we make ourselves better able to interrogate the nature of the conflict, perhaps even to understand more clearly what we mean when we talk about war and other deadly games. This is to cast the discussion in very broad terms, however, taking up large social concerns, including what in an age of writing came to be called literacy. That term may no longer apply without significant alteration, but it still seems true that a general understanding of media, the prevailing logic of production and reception in our modes of communication, is conditioned by local instances and practices. Or to put this in Lévy's terms, the emergence of molecular society involves scalar similarities: what holds in large holds also in little. Thus even apparently parochial and academic controversies, such as those to which we now turn, may reflect a more significant process.

Let the Games be Games

There is a consensus for change growing among some of those concerned with creative work in digital media. This sentiment can be seen increasingly in interactive art pieces, conference papers, manifesti, web logs, and journals such as the newly launched *Game Studies*. Like all so-called movements, the partisans of digital game theory or *ludology* comprise a loose and fractious

distinction of work and play, along with the very meaning of play, can be examined. In this realm, a more robust and nuanced understanding of varied intensities of interaction and play can be developed and understood. What foregrounds the legitimacy of such study can be carefully explored in Moulthrop's more expansive definition, to provide a measure of awareness necessary to the viability of a proposed new field. It is in this extended realm that the status of play, agency, immersion, subjectivity, pleasure, and sensual response can be more thoroughly questioned. And it is here that what I would argue are the complex relations of immersion, transparency, and critical awareness can be teased apart and reconfigured.

To further explore Moulthrop's proposition, I would

ask him to expand on the idea and felt experience of immersion. Can immersion be redefined in more productive ways? Are there forms of immersion that can be critical? Is immersion necessarily dependent on transparency?

Allow me the indulgence of using my own work as a foil (see figure 6.response.1). Using biofeedback interfaces in virtual and augmented reality pieces, I explore sensory immersion and subjectivity in ways that I hope disturb our tendency to continually reinscribe the mind/body split. Sensorial immersion, I argue, can also be a form of critical awareness. Such complex experiences in simulations may not be games in the strict sense, but are certainly configurative practices, and configurative practices that engage our

community, but most share at least one premise. We feel that narrative in certain conventional senses — mainly defined by the theater, the novel, and cinema — no longer animates the work we find most interesting as creators and/or critics. Some will insist we reached the turning point long ago, at a time when people such as Jay Bolter, Michael Joyce, George Landow, and myself were content with primarily literary models. More radical thinkers, such as Espen Aarseth, began to discard such approaches long ago, even before his landmark study of "cybertext." However we date the change, though, we should be able to agree on what Aarseth would call the "ergodics" or pathwork of the moment: we have reached a fork in the road. Beyond this point the traditional narrative interest leads one way, while a second track diverges. We do not yet have a very good name for this other path, though we can associate some concepts with it: *play*, *simulation*, and more generally, *game*.

This parting does not spell the end of electronic literature. Poets, for whom narrative has perhaps always been more affordance than obsession, have turned very playful indeed where the digital interface is concerned, as witness the work of Talan Memmott <http://memmott.org/talan/works.html>, or Megan Sapnar and Ingrid Ankerson in *PoemsThatGo* <http://www.poemsthatgo.com>. We will no doubt

continue to see important projects that call themselves cybertext or hypermedia but retain a deep investment in words, along with a rich sense of symbolism and nuance. Some of these projects may even have major narrative elements, as in the *Myst* saga or Nick Montfort's interactive fiction, *Winchester's Nightmare*. Yet it seems clear that some people involved with digital media will be much more strongly drawn to ludic forms, from complex ecological simulations and virtual cosmogonies down to first-person shooting contests. For a few the shift may mark a strong departure from previous work and training. For others it may seem no choice at all, but the only logical response to contemporary media and culture.

In some cases this stance may entail a certain opposition. Markku Eskelinen notes elsewhere in this volume: "If I throw a ball at you I don't expect you to drop it and wait until it starts telling stories." Yet as Eskelinen and others believe, many followers of digital culture do drop the theoretical ball, insisting that so-called interactive forms be engaged in a general project of storytelling. Among Eskelinen's favorite opponents is Janet Murray, whose remarkable insights about digital art come mixed with an oddly antique strain of narrative theory that seems bound to annoy even lapsed poststructuralists. In Murray's view, digital productions, from adventure games to multiuser

---

bodies in very direct ways — and in ways that question the social and material conditions of our felt experience. Yet this strategy is reliant on a sense of immersion. What then is the relation of such a form of immersion to the notion of transparency?

It would be easy to dismiss "immersive" virtual reality (VR) as simply an example of transparency par excellence. To assume the position of the devil's advocate, by provoking the sensory responses characteristic of VR, we are both playing on our well-worn fears and denigration of the body, as well as engaging in the pleasures of sensorial stimulation. In the first instance, by provoking sensory immersion, we are foreclosing the possibility of critical awareness. Why? Because in our intellectual tradition, we routinely deny the body as the very site of knowledge.

A body shimmering with sensory awareness cannot also be a body capable of critical awareness, or so the story goes. In the second instance, indulging in sensory pleasures is merely just consuming an opiate that distracts us from serious, critical thinking, no? No. My work is part of a much larger tradition in art that disputes these assumptions. If the body is the very ground of knowledge and awareness, and if a form of immersion can also be critical, what then is the relation of transparency to immersion? What is the relation of felt experience and sensorial provocation to immersion? To transparency?

While these questions arise from artistic pursuit — where forms of bodily knowledge are regularly explored, practiced, embodied, and performed — the issues are of

Eskelinen   Douglas Schechner
Aarseth   Crawford Moulthrop
Ludology> Moulthrop   Gromala Cayley

II. Ludology

59

environments, are all formally deficient because they refuse to sanction singular outcomes. While such texts may provide a type of closure, Murray considers this effect a counterfeit:

> ...electronic closure occurs when a work's structure, though not its plot, is understood. This closure involves a cognitive activity at one remove from the usual pleasures of hearing a story.... There is no emotional release or perception of fittingness, just a sense of going from the unknown to the known. This is very different from and far less pleasurable than our more traditional expectations of closure, as arising from the plot of the story and marking the end point of an action. (Murray 1997, 174)

The full extent of the debate between ludologists such as Eskelinen and neo-Aristotelians such as Murray has many dimensions, but few seem as definitive as the insistence on catharsis as the proper source of narrative pleasure. Murray's position does seem debatable on theoretical grounds. Murray's critics complain that she shows little interest in either the modernist agenda of formal experiment or the postmodern critique of literary ideology.

Indeed, any theory based on "hearing a story" seems notably backward after the deconstruction of language as presence. Yet, however controversial, Murray's critical apostasy is really a side issue. In the final analysis the objections to Murray by Eskelinen and company are not theoretical but practical.

At least in the kind of narrative Murray champions, the reader's primary "cognitive activity" consists of interpretation. Our ritual release of pity and fear arrives when we fully understand the relationships among characters and the pattern of causes that constitute a plot; or to expand beyond narrative terms, when we grasp the structure of metaphor and memory that informs a lyric, meditation, or confession. Our engagement with the text is driven by the desire to apprehend the structure in its entirety. As Eskelinen points out, we expect readers to study every word of a literary work, but web surfers, Multi-User Domain dwellers, game players, and others involved with ergodic texts come under no such obligation. Indeed, game play often involves limiting engagement with the work, avoiding irrelevant or distracting details. One observer of digital culture, Steven Johnson, describes "information filtering" as a primary concern of all electronic discourse (1997, 32). Murray seems not to be interested in such strategies, however. Her notion of

course relevant to games and play, as any user of a joystick or Gameboy could attest. Yet in literary forms, to examine the relation of felt experience, immersion, and transparency is to write about it, as we would expect. How does this limit our ability to think and theorize? No matter how extensively interactive media affects our culture, we still legitimize knowledge — particularly forms of knowledge that we call theory — primarily in texts and in books. Thus, literary scholars, perhaps, are in a better position to offer more to emerging discourses such as ludology. Although few literary scholars depart from this tradition, Moulthrop does, and does so in bold ways. His oeuvre, which extends into forms that are interactive and include visuals, tweaks my throbbing interest, as does his rare

6.response.1. *Dancing with the Virtual Dervish: Virtual Bodies.*

"electronic closure," the moment at which the reader of an interactive text understands the rationale of its design and likely limits of its productive capacity, reasserts the regime of interpretation. As Murray sees it, configuration serves interpretation.

Yet the story of gaming may not be so simple even when games are mistaken for stories. Murray herself recognizes that those engaged with electronic texts sometimes fail to read for the plot; indeed, sometimes they cease to be readers and turn into players. *Hamlet on the Holodeck* begins with an account of Captain Janeway from the *Star Trek: Voyager* television series, who logs many hours in a simulation called *Lucy Davenport*, a concoction that resembles the novel *Jane Eyre* (a kind of *Jane Away* or *Eyre in Space*). Janeway's character in the simulation serves as governess to the children of a Rochester-like figure, with all the familiar erotic tensions. Yet as Murray notes, Janeway seems less engaged with the cathartic "moral physics" of the plot than with tending to her simulated charges and maintaining the imaginary household. She subverts the closural design of the "holonovel" by sticking perversely to the middle of things, a behavior Murray finds more intriguing than problematic (Murray 1997, 16). This interesting subtlety surfaces at other points in her study as well. In a later section discussing the adventure game *Myst*, Murray makes a point I would later echo

with respect to its sequel, *Riven*: namely, that the authorized, successful solutions to the game are less interesting than the more numerous losing outcomes (Murray 1997, 142). Murray argues that the game's main charm lies in protracted exploration rather than end-directed questing, a practice I call *misadventure* (Moulthrop 1999).

These partial recognitions do not much impress the game theorists. From Eskelinen's perspective, neither Murray nor I saw very far into the matter because we thought about games as distorted or perverse narratives, not as cultural forms in their own right. We therefore missed a crucial distinction. In games the primary cognitive activity is not interpretation but *configuration*, the capacity to transform certain aspects of the virtual environment with potentially significant consequences for the system as a whole. As Eskelinen says, expanding upon Aarseth, "the dominant user function in literature, theater, and film is interpretative, but in games it is the configurative.... in art we might have to configure in order to be able to interpret, whereas in games we have to interpret in order to be able to configure, and proceed from the beginning to the winning or some other situation." As will be apparent, the difference between "winning" and "other" situations requires further scrutiny; but for the moment it is sufficient to recognize that ludologists set

ability to look far beyond his discipline of origin. So, I ask Moulthrop a final set of questions, although they may be unfairly beyond the purview of his essay. The literary tradition offers us profound ways to question games and play. Narrative forms can also be sensorially provocative, although this area remains relatively unexamined. What, then, are the implications of more literally sensory immersion to the literary tradition and to practices of theorizing? Is it a radical proposition to suggest that forms of reading and writing can be immersive in realms like virtual reality, where our bodies are more directly provoked? How does his own interactive work affect his thinking about the sticky issue of theory and practice? To what degree does ludology require the confluence of disciplines as diverse as anthropology, computer science, and art?

From John Cayley's Online Response: Playing with Play

The formulation: *configuration for the sake of interpretation = art/work; interpretation for the sake of configuration = game/play* is highly suggestive and useful as an articulation of distinct practices. However, the formulation itself implies and necessitates both an interplay of these overarching "user functions" (as they are called in the Aarseth/Eskelinen schemes) and the possibility of continuously varying admixtures of these same functions, such that, for example, culture objects (even single objects over time) might differ in their degree of determination by one or other function. This, thankfully, does not bode well for a breakaway, psuedo-autonomous ludology, and I am entirely in agreement with Moulthrop in hoping that ludology will continue

aside narrative because they wish to focus on "configurative practice," as Eskelinen calls it. This shift could be profoundly important for the future of digital culture.

Go Configure

In those classic Infocom games of the 1980s, unparsable commands would sometimes elicit something like this from the program: "I'm sorry, you have used the words *profoundly important* in a way I don't understand. Please try again." As perhaps we should. The claims made here for digital game culture may seem at odds with the state of the art. In the popular mind and marketplace, the terms *video game* or *computer game* suggest products such as *Mortal Kombat*, *Tomb Raider*, *Half-Life*, *Evil Dead*, *Quake*, *Doom*, and *Unreal*. To be sure, the game business has also delivered better fare: the epic adventures of Infocom and Cyan, the attempts to reinvent game culture by Brenda Laurel's Purple Moon, complex entertainments such as *Bad Day on the Midway* or *Grim Fandango*, and triumphs of simulation including *Black and White* and *The Sims*. By the same token, the best work in older media depends on vast quantities of disposable output which somehow never come to mind when we use the word *literature*. We can have no serious drama like *Copenhagen* without a dozen recycled *Producers*, no

Summer of Sam without a handful of *Lethal Weapons*, no short stack of Annie Proulx absent mounds of Jack Welch.

Nonetheless, a different standard seems to apply where play is involved. For complicated reasons, computer games seem more keenly exposed to cultural critique than most older forms. This has partly to do with every adult's natural phobic response to teenagers, a complex that stems as much from memory and self-contempt as from fear of the other. It may also proceed from industrial culture's deep distrust of configurative practices. Whatever the reason, many people, especially in the United States, find games at least vaguely antisocial. Noting their capacity to debase and desensitize, the mavens of morality particularly deplore violent games, and perhaps with some reason. As Simon Penny points out in this volume, specialists in military training believe that simulated killing quite literally makes the real thing easier.

Murray registers the need "to find substitutes for shooting off a gun that will offer the same immediacy of effect but allow for more complex and engaging story content" (Murray 1997, 147). Eskelinen and the ludologists may disclaim Murray's concern for story, but it seems very hard these days to defend digital gunplay, even in overtly antiterrorist scenarios like *Counter-Strike*. Less militant offerings come under

---

to take itself seriously and allow itself to be considered as serious cultural practice, on a level playing field with literature, just as I expect writing in networked and programmable media to continue to play havoc with traditional literary work and value. My own direct experience of games in networked and programmable media isn't great, but the development of the *Sims* games is suggestive for me, since I understand that, for example, *Sim Theme Park* builds in facilities for the publication of successful parks, which have, at the point of publication, been configured for the sake of interpretation without ceasing to be part of game play.

Moulthrop Responds: Second Thoughts

In my defense I can only suggest that process and implementation will ultimately count more than polemics and theory. We do not yet know in material, social terms how work in configurative media can best contribute to molecular culture and the reformation of the social bond.

http://www.electronicbookreview.com/thread/firstperson/cayleyr1

http://www.electronicbookreview.com/thread/firstperson/moulthropr2

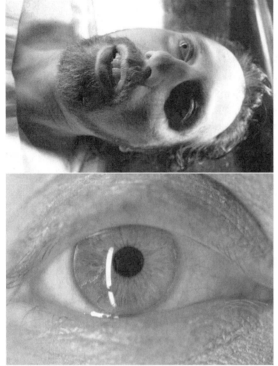

6.sidebar.1–2. A puzzle from *The Beast,* the promotional game for *A.I.* Players located an autopsy report for a deceased character. They were interested in the last message received on the character's PDA but the screen was blank. Closer examination of the character's eyes revealed something that looked like a shattered green lens over his iris. (Microsoft)

suspicion as well, for instance when we learn that earlier versions of Microsoft's *Flight Simulator* could be used to reenact the attacks on the World Trade Center. Perhaps a proper study of play might lead to Murray's pacifist alternative, but just as arguably any account of game culture must begin with what the market offers, including its worst celebrations of carnage. Thus the attempt to find social significance in games requires a certain intellectual courage — or at least that is one name for it.

What some call courage, others may consider opportunistic chutzpah; what is ludology if not a professional stratagem? Games of all sorts, not just those invented since the microprocessor, have yet to receive careful academic attention. Cinema has had its Eisenstein, de Lauretis, and Deleuze, literature its Derrida, Foucault, and Cixous, but with a few notable exceptions, the study of games as a cultural form has yet to begin. Games thus comprise an untheorized frontier whose blankness seems very attractive for those who would rather set than follow precedent. Ludologists often characterize the relationship of narrative and games in terms of colonization, casting narrative in the role of cultural empire; but such critiques may ricochet, for as western history demonstrates, rebellious colonies are sometimes empires in embryo.

For those of cynical disposition, the turn from narrative to gaming may seem just another power play in the modern academy's Beirut-of-the-mind. This observation may appear crass, but practical matters often do. Much as we try to separate the work of theory from squabbles over cultural funding, faculty salaries, and tenure decisions, political realities must be acknowledged. Declaring the independence of digital game studies from narratology may mean seceding from literature departments, film studies programs, and perhaps even arts faculties. It could mean forging new alliances both inside and outside the academic community. If such speculations seem rash, consider that profits from computer games surpassed those of popular film before the turn of the century. As Espen Aarseth points out in his introduction to the *Game Studies* journal, game development is a billion-dollar industry with no clear research agenda (Aarseth 2001).

Cynicism has its uses, but also its limits. A billion-dollar industry is as much a cultural as an economic phenomenon. Or to put this another way, what seems merely a professorial turf war may in fact embody a more profound generational conflict. The turn from narrative forms such as plays, novels, and films to ludic forms such as games and simulations marks the emergence of a younger cohort who acquired their orientation to language as much from dynamic systems as from Aristotelian or even modernist genres. Those who find this group's concerns childish, shallow, or improperly pleasurable may need to examine their premises lest they find themselves on the wrong side of O.B. Hardison's "horizon of invisibility" (Hardison 1989, 5). Of this barrier Hardison notes: "Those who have passed through it cannot put their experience into

BIO-OPTIC FILTERING ENABLED

```
CORONER'S REPORT ADDENDUM
RECORD ID #: OPT-0-3-PS
 COMMENT: DATA RETRIEVED FROM PDA SYSTEM
 BELONGING TO THE DECEASED. LAST ITEM
 RECOVERED PRIOR TO OPERATING SYSTEM FAILURE.
 SYSTEM TRANSFERRED TO LAW ENFORCEMENT
 AUTHORITIES.
 STATUS: NON-FUNCTIONAL
```

Tok free bird
2 DC nxt
4 nu fns,
UV dip, eras,
hmd of Z
enjNr 4 ?
rashini hdr 4 dox

Rmembr yr memrz!

6.sidebar.3–4. (Continued from 6.sidebar.1–2.) Players realized that if they applied the green filter found in the character's eyes to the PDA screen, a hidden message could be read (above). Cutting through the techno-babble on the screen led the players to <http://www.rationalhatter.com/>. (Microsoft)

familiar words and images because the languages they have inherited are inadequate to the new worlds they inhabit." What we have here may indeed be a failure to communicate, with much to learn from the breakdown.

Turmoil in the academy often mirrors fundamental social shifts. Games are profitable because they are broadly popular, and this popularity does not depend entirely on simulated violence or other crude wish fulfillments. Just as there are more generic possibilities than first-person shooters, so there is more to game culture than simple aggression. Consider the case of the promotional game produced in the summer of 2001 to publicize Steven Spielberg's *A.I.* (see sidebar). Consisting of an elaborate system of puzzles distributed over numerous web sites, the game was only tenuously connected to the content of Spielberg's film, and while its main premise was narrative and interpretive (a murder mystery), its primary appeal was procedural. Players had to decipher obscure references and codes, in some cases involving messages buried in the

infrastructure of web pages. Many participants in the game found it considerably more interesting than its cinematic pretext. As one put it: "The game is great. The movie is garbage" (Gallagher 2001).

While this development may seem highly salient, it should not be surprising. Games — computer games in particular — appeal because they are configurative, offering the chance to manipulate complex systems within continuous loops of intervention, observation, and response. Interest in such activities grows as more people exchange e-mail, surf the world wide web, post to newsgroups, build web logs, engage in chat and instant messaging, and trade media files through peer-to-peer networks. As in various sorts of gaming, these are all in some degree configurative practices, involving manipulation of dynamic systems that develop in unpredictable or emergent ways. More importantly, as Aarseth says, they may only be fully understood as active enterprises: in order to know what they are truly about, we must become involved in production or play (Aarseth 2001).

It might be absurd to suggest that all interactive media are species of game, but games do seem to offer a useful way of thinking about such media. Games model or inculcate a crucial set of cognitive practices. In the older cultures of print and broadcasting, the term *literacy* came to represent the fundamental capacity to process information — that is, primarily to interpret. It may be possible to expand the concept of literacy to cover digital systems, as in Nancy Kaplan's argument for hypertextual "E-Literacies" (Kaplan 1995). On the other hand, the shift from interpretation to configuration may require something more than revision, perhaps even a fresh conceptual start, as in Greg Ulmer's "electracy" (Memmott 2001). By looking at cyberspace through the lens of game play, scholars may find it easier to resolve this question, modifying or supplementing the old concept of literacy. Or as one particularly astute critic sums up: "The more we see life in terms of systems, the more we need a system-modeling medium to represent it — and the less we can dismiss such organized rule systems as mere games."

Play Nicely

The source of this quotation should give us pause. It comes not from Aarseth, Eskelinen, Jesper Juul, Marie-Laure Ryan, Gonzalo Frasca, or some other master of digital games. It was written by the eminent Aristotelian herself, Janet Murray (Murray 1997, 93).

This confluence of sentiments, if not of doctrine, suggests that ludology and narratology may not be absolutely antithetical. In some respects, Murray seems to value configurative practice quite highly. She defends aesthetics of the "multiform story" against critics who find such work simply incoherent (89); she points out that the computer is an "engine," not a broadcast receiver (72) and holds that the key to future artwork lies in "procedural composition" (275); she argues that interactive design must find "formats" appropriate to

digital technologies, rejecting those inherited from earlier media (64). In her work following *Hamlet on the Holodeck* Murray emphasizes the uniqueness of digital forms, insisting that "[w]e do not need designers who can produce more-attractive interfaces with the same formats of communications. We need designers who can re-think the processes of communication, exploiting the capacity of the digital environment to be more responsive to human needs" (Murray 1999, 4).

We might wonder how Murray can square these quite sophisticated views with an apparently naïve classicism. If we need new formats, why re-impose the traditional architectures of fiction and drama? If digital technologies take us so far from writing, print, and broadcasting, how can we resort to the ostensible simplicity of the *Poetics*? Eskelinen charges that Murray lacks interest in theoretical insights developed since the Second World War, but it would be unfair to accuse her of simple negligence. In fact Murray's positions represent an American cybernetic pragmatism whose serious engagement with technological realities deserves a measure of respect, even if one takes issue with some of its implications.

Murray adopts her Aristotelianism at least in part from Brenda Laurel, a figure whose theoretical contributions are deeply informed by her experience as a commercial software developer (Laurel 2001). Murray herself designed groundbreaking simulations at MIT, pioneering educational multimedia. Her apparent lack of regard for contemporary theory may reflect a countervailing emphasis on practice which perhaps fulfills George Landow's prediction that emerging media will provide an empirical testing ground for textual theories (Laurel 2001, 11). In other words, Murray's approach to theory comes via application rather than contemplation — making her, in Aarseth's terms, a legitimate player. She knows better than most that in the so-called new media it is not enough simply to describe or postulate differences: they must be produced in a marketplace of objects as well as ideas. She thus declares that the future of digital creativity depends on popular as well as elite efforts:

...the shape of narrative art and

entertainment in the next few decades will be determined by the interplay of these two forces, that is, the more nimble, independent experimenters, who are comfortable with hypertext, procedural thinking, and virtual environments, and the giant conglomerates of the entertainment industry, who have vast resources and an established connection to mass audiences. (Murray 1997, 252)

With a few modifications — say, striking "narrative" and substituting "cybertext" for "hypertext" — this forecast might pass among the ludologists without strong objection. Certainly their focus on popular entertainment suggests they might see themselves in Murray's equation of forces, no doubt among the iconoclasts and pioneers. But while this analysis may narrow the division between games and narrative, the separation cannot be entirely erased. At least one salient issue remains. Although Murray and the game theorists might agree that the future depends on a contest of established and emergent interests, they probably do not see the same outcome for this struggle. Indeed they should not, if game studies have any critical value.

Do Not Immerse

Murray's approach to new media seems both culturally and technically conservative; for some indeed this may be its main virtue. Like the design theorists she most admires, Laurel and her mentor Donald Norman, Murray assumes that new media should provide highly efficient, minimally obtrusive tools. She seems to agree with Norman that the best computer is an invisible computer, at least where narrative is concerned:

> Eventually all successful storytelling technologies become "transparent": we lose consciousness of the medium and see neither print nor film but only the power of the story itself. If digital art reaches the same level of expressiveness as these older media, we will no longer concern ourselves

with how we are receiving the information. We will only think about what truth it has told us about our lives. (Murray 1997, 26)

Murray's claims about "immersive" technologies seem accurate enough. Whether we are considering a fantasized holodeck or an actual computer game, interactive media tend to envelop the player in consistent rule systems, if not virtual realities. Indeed, this immersiveness or "holding power" is a major aspect of game experience, as Sherry Turkle pointed out long ago (Turkle, 64). Murray's theory might thus be useful even to game studies, at least up to a point. However, it remains to be seen whether configurative media such as games will necessarily follow the same logic of disappearance that has governed print and film. Configuration after all differs fundamentally from interpretation. Although their behavior may be constrained by the arbitrary construct of a game, players are obliged to know the rules and repeatedly to consider a range of possible interventions, which leads to Murray's controversial distinction between "electronic closure" and catharsis. Arguably the immersiveness of games differs crucially from that of narratives, and much may depend on this difference.

Reducing any medium to transparency confines it to a fixed and usually limited range of function. Consider an example from recent history. We have heard many times that the U.S. craze for citizen's band (CB) radio died out at the end of the 1970s when users found nothing of importance to say on the air. This version of the story appears to confirm Murray's assumptions about media. Ostensibly, people stopped taking an active part in their audio entertainment and went back simply to listening. After briefly dropping its cloak of invisibility, radio reverted to its transparent state, a commercial, one-to-many technology under stable corporate control. The CB fad thus apparently reconfirms the general rule that media are private properties, not civic services. Never mind that commercial radio began to switch to talk formats even as CB faded, squeezing some of the upstart's crude popularity into more narrow and profitable channels.

Disregard the very plausible connections from CB through internet relay chat to instant messaging, where a popular form of communication has once again been devoured by oligopolies. Ignore the suggestion that private control of media may be an aberration, not the natural order of things. Transparent media may not bear much scrutiny, but happily for business elites, they do not present themselves for inspection.

If Murray's process of disappearance is truly inevitable, it seems clear that the turbulent "interplay" of forces she posits must eventually subside into the steady state of mass markets dominated by a few major interests. An invisible computer is most likely a monopolist's best friend — a dictum that seems as true at Sun Microsystems, home of the NetPC, as in any precinct of the Redmond campus. Molecular society emerges in a paradoxical moment, as great transformations always do. The irruption of popular empowerment coincides with the climax phase in the evolution of oligopolies, a final division of very great spoils.

One can address this double logic more or less dialectically, as does Jay Bolter in his theory of remediation (Bolter and Grusin 2000), or one can learn from the story of Napster and other recent popular assaults on traditional profit centers that the major interests are less likely to seek compromise than continued dominance. The development of media in this century seems inevitably fraught with controversy, and as citizens of intensively informed societies we have great stakes in these oppositions, even when they appear to concern mere entertainment or play. Therefore if narrative forms play any role in the process by which "we lose consciousness of the medium," there may be good reason to turn away from storytelling as the prime agenda of art.

This schism could have significant consequences. Eskelinen defines "configurative practice" rather narrowly as the player's strategic operation upon the elements of a game, but it is possible to broaden this term significantly. If we conceive of configuration as a way of engaging not just immediate game elements, but also the game's social and material conditions — and by extension, the conditions of other rule-systems such

as work and citizenship — then it may be very important to insist upon the difference between play and interpretation, the better to resist immersion. Any analogue of literacy for interactive media would probably need to encompass such resistance.

It remains to be seen, though, whether game theory will help in this social and cognitive undertaking. As promised, we return to Eskelinen's assertion that game players must "proceed from the beginning to the winning *or some other* situation." If digital game theory concerns itself primarily with choices that lead to winning situations — solutions circumscribed within a narrow calculus of outcomes — then it may be just as inimical as any narratology to a proper understanding of configurative practice. Limiting the definition of games to systems with simple distinctions between winning and losing could restrict this study to zero-sum antagonism, a domain that seems every bit as constrained and potentially obscuring as narrative. It might also lead the study of digital games into uncritical acceptance of existing genres. To be blunt, if we tie configuration inflexibly to some duelistic protocol, we might produce a game theory whose insights are limited by its gunsights.

In fact, Eskelinen complains at length about the limited conceptions of mass-market games, asking why they insist on simpleminded visual realism and leave so little room for strategic variation even within competitive contexts. He has proposed hypothetical games where players manipulate data gathered from external reality, or where game elements intrude into real space. In one of these scenarios, "[t]he Pokémons on the screen and in your living room... team up and steal your credit card numbers to order reinforcements" (Eskelinen 2001).

Although this last example is oppositional if not militant, Eskelinen's probes seem generally to lead away from simple contests toward the sort of complex, open-ended play that is more often called simulation than game.

Improvisations and simulations seem even further removed from teleological narrative than agons, whose general principle might still be confused with cathartic closure. Moreover, the kind of configurative practice involved in these activities offers an excellent countermeasure against the transparency of media. Eskelinen's hypothetical Pokémon uprising, for instance, nicely reverses Murray's disappearing act. While the experience would no doubt teach some "truth about our lives," that truth concerns the autonomy we grant to increasingly dynamic media. It might remind us that cyberspace is not a storybook or a moving picture but a complex virtual environment that should never be allowed to become second nature — or which, at any rate, ought never to be given free access to our charge accounts.

Molecular Society and the State of War

This chapter began, however, by alluding to a different sort of credit or credibility: our need for information and perspective in a continuing crisis, a theme to which we must now return. It is one thing to dream up mischievous invasions by surrealist software, but what can such fantasies tell us about a world where terribly real attacks have murdered thousands? The events of late 2001 have been variously described as the end of postmodernism, the death of irony, and a very bad time for comedians. No doubt they must also overshadow any attempt to speak seriously about games; however, that shadow need not become a total eclipse.

At this point we might want to think beyond games in their most literal sense, or rather to see them as elements of a larger process, Lévy's transition from "molar" to "molecular" social orders. Molar technologies "manage objects in bulk, in the mass, blindly, and entropically" (Lévy, 40), whereas molecular technologies embody both a miniaturization of control (literally down to the molecular level in nanotechnology) and a devolution of that control throughout the human community. This pattern manifests itself as much in media and culture as it does in manufacturing or material technologies. Lévy notes:

> Information technology is molecular because it does not simply reproduce and distribute messages... but enables us to create and modify them at will, provide them with a finely graduated capability of

reaction through total control of their microstructure.... Thus digitization reestablishes sensibility within the context of somatic technologies while preserving the media's power of recording and distribution. (Lévy, 48–49)

Lévy's allusion to the "somatic" here is particularly important. The term means for him the embodied, the personal, that which requires particular human intervention or presence. Molecular media do not simply invite configurative practice, they require it. At their best they do not vanish into perfect transparency but present themselves as "a system-modeling medium," to borrow Murray's phrase, in which we must place configuration before interpretation. Increasingly, ordinary life requires us to apprehend these systems, to understand their rules and develop effective strategies for managing their effects and affordances. Thus, in their capacity to teach what Aarseth calls "ergodics" or multidimensional pathfinding, games represent an enormously powerful, perhaps a fundamental form of molecular culture. Games may be our surest route from the old world of "molar" literacy into electracy, ergodics, e-literacy, or whatever we finally call the new regime.

But how does this regime square with the latest new world order, with Mr. Bush's "first war of the 21st century," or as skeptics have it, the First Crusade? Since we have set aside Murray's values of transparency and immersion, we can assume that molecular media will not lend themselves readily to any general mobilization. On the contrary, cultivating more conscious, active engagement with information systems implies at least the possibility of opposition. Indeed, as we have already suggested, the political economy of media in the 21st century seems to demand dissent and intervention. The declaration (or acclamation) of war may distract attention from preexisting conflicts inherent in information culture.

The legal scholar Lawrence Lessig explains that "[w]e can build, or architect, cyberspace to protect values that we believe are fundamental, or we can build, or architect, or code cyberspace to allow those values to disappear. There is no middle ground" (Lessig 1999, 6).

As Lessig sees it, a confluence of government and commercial interests must severely impede any movement toward Lévy's molecular society unless a constituency develops to oppose them. This resistance must be active and deliberate. Lessig insists that "[t]here is no choice that does not include some kind of *building*. Code is never found; it is only ever made, and only ever made by us" (Lessig 1999, 6).

It is tempting to compare Lessig's semi-utopian "us" to Lévy's equally hypothetical notion of "the just," the quiet minority of believers in human potential who embody "both the necessary condition of the universe and the superfluity that makes it worthwhile" (Lévy 1997, 39). To the extent that a culture of digital play increases the reach of this always dubious pronoun — producing more people who refuse to play the accepted storylines, or who know enough about the *techne* of code to rewrite it — then it may set a limit on the power of purely interpretive media. Such may be the dream.

No limit once set, though, ever escapes testing. Writing back in the old century, before the present terror war boiled up, Lessig worries primarily about efforts to foreclose on the development of open-source software. Access to source code, he rightly notes, allows users to gain control of system architecture, the most powerful regulating factor in cyberspace. Indeed, the ability to intervene at that architectural level must be another key component of molecular, configurative culture. He might see it as the most serious practical opposition that can come from the ethos of games and simulations; but its status remains very much in doubt.

Unlike Lévy, Lessig is a most reluctant utopian. He points out that the communitarian ethic of the early internet has been largely eroded by dot-com profiteering, even as government and press have systematically demonized autonomous code writers as outlaw "hackers" (Lessig 1999, 8). These observations are sobering. No doubt the struggle over open code will become a major battlefront when the full implications of the war on terrorism present themselves. As government defines its concept of extended, perhaps unlimited conflict, controversies seem sure to erupt over privacy of communications, access to effective

encryption, freedom of association and speech. If terror attacks recur or escalate, decision makers may move toward more rigid, unconfigurable architectures — in effect locking down the terms of the national security state. Such developments would push back toward a more centrally managed, homogeneous, "molar" organization of media and society.

As one considers the possibilities for repression, the attraction of the old zero-sum game becomes strong, especially if one is among the majority of U.S. citizens who voted for someone other than George Bush in 2000. Yet if a configurative approach to media teaches anything, it is an appreciation of complex and multiple situations. As Thomas Pynchon noted, They-systems tend to breed We-systems; but to place absolute faith in either is to embrace delusion (Pynchon 1973, 638). The best kind of game culture must teach us when to jump outside the game. The contest of suits-versus-hackers, libertarian idealists against the military-infotainment state, is only part of a larger, and in Haraway's words a "deadly" interplay.

As Lévy notes, the climax of automation renders unto machines the machinic and leaves to us the unavoidable work of human beings: "the production of the social bond" (Lévy 1997, 21). The current state of war — whatever anyone means by that term — results not from one but many ruptures of this bond. Emergence of Lévy's molecular society is threatened just as desperately by international terror as it is by reactionary instincts of the new world order. Indeed, our culture's very capacity for change, its headlong rush into new forms of experience, seems a major cause of our enemies' resentment. These facts demand consideration no matter what sort of ballot one cast in recent elections. Production of a new, more just social bond goes far beyond the reinvention of media, or of literacy and its sequelae. We know that this task involves blood and anger as much as stories and games: all the more reason to be very, very serious about the subject of digital play.

References

Aarseth, Espen (1997). *Cybertext: Perspectives on Ergodic Literature*
Baltimore: Johns Hopkins University Press.

Aarseth, Espen (2001). "Game Studies Year One." *Game Studies* 1,
no.1 (2001). <http://www.gamestudies.org/0101/editorial.html>.

Bolter, Jay David, and Richard Grusin (2000). *Remediation:
Understanding New Media*. Cambridge, MA: The MIT Press.

Eskelinen, Markku (2001). "The Gaming Situation." *Game Studies* 1,
no.1 (2001). <http://www.gamestudies.org/0101/eskelinen>.

Gallagher, David F. (2001). "Online Tie-In Outshines Film It Was
Pushing, Fans Say." *New York Times*, July 9, 2001, C1, C6.

Haraway, Donna J. (1991). *Simians, Cyborgs, and Women: The
Reinvention of Nature*. New York: Routledge.

Hardison, O.B. (1989). *Disappearing through the Skylight: Culture
and Technology in the Twentieth Century*. New York: Viking.

Johnson, Steven (1997). *Interface Culture: How New Technology
Transforms the Way We Create and Communicate*. San Francisco:
Harper Edge.

Kaplan, Nancy (1995). "E-Literacies: Politexts, Hypertexts, and
Other Cultural Formations in the Late Age of Print."
<http://iat.ubalt.edu/kaplan/lit/>

Krugman, Paul (2001). "The Fear Economy." *New York Times
Magazine*, September 30, 2001, 38-41, 54-55, 84-85.

Landow, George P. (1992). *Hypertext: The Convergence of
Contemporary Theory and Technology*. Baltimore: Johns Hopkins
University Press.

Laurel, Brenda (2001). *Utopian Entrepreneur*. Cambridge, MA: The
MIT Press.

Lessig, Lawrence (1999). *Code and Other Laws of Cyberspace*. New
York: Basic Books.

Lévy, Pierre (1997). *Collective Intelligence: Mankind's Emerging
World in Cyberspace*. New York: Plenum.

Memmott, Talan (2001). "Toward Electracy: A Conversation with
Gregory Ulmer." *Beehive* 4, no.2 (June 2001).
<http://beehive.temporalimage.com/content_apps34/app_a.html>

Moulthrop, Stuart (1999). "Misadventure: Future Fiction and the
New Networks." *Style* 33, no.2 (1999): 184-203.

Murray, Janet (1997). *Hamlet on the Holodeck: The Future of
Narrative in Cyberspace*. Cambridge, MA: The MIT Press.

Murray, Janet (1999). "Interactive Design: a Profession in Search of
Professional Education." *The Chronicle of Higher Education* 45,
no.33 (1999): 4-6.

Pynchon, Thomas (1973). *Gravity's Rainbow*. New York: Viking.

Turkle, Sherry (1984). *The Second Self: Computers and the Human
Spirit*. New York: Simon and Schuster.

Critical Simulation

In earlier sections of this volume, contributors have touched on the importance of simulation as a framework for understanding new forms of computer media. This section develops a critical consideration of simulation as it is practiced in computer media (from videogames to interactive art to the "agents" of artificial intelligence); each author presenting a framework in which simulations can become more meaningfully socially situated.

The history of computer simulation media (both graphical, as in flight simulation, and artificially intelligent, as in battlefield simulation) includes an extended intimate connection to the military. As well though, this history's highest profile elements have arisen through a connection to the entertainment industries, via film special effects and computer games. Neither of these connections have provided a suitable foundation for the types of critical practices advocated by this section's contributors. Perhaps for this reason, each essayist draws into their discussion of simulation critical perspectives rarely heard in this context — ranging from interactive political theater, to theories of physical training, to narrative psychology.

Although the most famous theorist of simulation is the French thinker Jean Baudrillard, the simulation discussed by him is a cultural phenomenon, not a computational one — and as such is fully existent in old media as well as new. More germane to the discussion here are the works of Bill Nichols and Lev Manovich. Both Nichols and Manovich outline ways in which simulation differs from other formal traditions, especially from the film/video tradition from which their work arises. Nichols's widely reprinted "The Work of Culture in the Age of Cybernetic Systems" (1988) set out to update Walter Benjamin's famous 1935 essay "The Work of Art in the Age of Mechanical Reproduction" (1969) for the world of computation, intellectual property law, genetics, space weaponry, and *Pac-Man* — connecting simulation to the wider social world of multinational capitalism. Manovich's *The Language of New Media* (2001) outlined a history of simulation, with the word considered in two senses. In the first sense, simulation is seen to be continuous with the artistic traditions of frescoes, dioramas, and the Baroque – an immersion in a virtual universe. In another sense, simulation's history is a series of attempts to model other orders of reality beyond the visual: physics, economics, psychology. In either sense, simulation must be understood using different terms than those developed for other media.

But even post-Nichols and Manovich, some theorists continue to operate from the assumption that simulation media (such as games) are best understood through analogy with representation media (such as film) — that *Counter-Strike* can be approached via *Delta Force*. Simon Penny opens this section with a position on this argument, which initially dovetails with Espen Aarseth's in this volume. But Penny soon diverges fundamentally from Aarseth, as well as from Nichols and Manovich, as he focuses on the consequences of simulative enaction — consequences ethically different from those of traditional media consumption. This focus on ethics, and on the potential impact of simulative action on real-world action, continues with Gonzalo Frasca's essay. Frasca proposes that the political simulations of playwright/theorist Augusto Boal might guide the creation of computer game simulations that engage the sociopolitical circumstances of their designer and players.

Gonzalo Frasca, in his essay here, discusses player alteration of game mechanics — a practice common with tabletop games, if not computer ones.

Dice-and-paper roleplayers often continue to play the same gaming system because they like the setting or genre, while finding much to criticize about the rules; most roleplayers create their own homebrew rules to fix these perceived problems. Conversely, certain rules systems can support many different settings: Chaosium's Basic Role Playing, Steve Jackson's *GURPS*, and Wizard of the Coast's Open Gaming License/d20 system.

Tabletop game mechanics, if flexible enough, can also drive more than one game. The mechanics of the James Ernest-designed *Xxxenophile* collectible card game were later recycled by him for the non-collectible *Girl Genius: The Works*. Tabletop games are also re-themed for different markets. Reiner Knizia's *Maginor* was first released in Europe as *Vegas*. For the U.S. market the game was redesigned, transforming from a gambling simulation to a game of Harry Potter-esque wizardly competition. But the basic game mechanics were left unchanged. We might ask, is story just an afterthought added to a game's underlying formal structure? Maybe, but Bruno Faidutti and Serge Laget's *Mystery of the Abbey* was designed to model the investigative structure of Umberto Eco's novel *The Name of the Rose;* here, story seems to dictate the rules of the game.

Penny's and Frasca's approaches could be characterized as Critical Technical Practices (CTP) – procedures incorporating the working methods of both technical research and cultural critique — though neither essayist uses the term.

Phoebe Sengers, in this section's final essay, characterizes her work explicitly as CTP. Sengers attempts to formulate new designs for AI agents; such agents, although central to much AI practice (and to many cyberdramatic visions), have customarily engaged in intricate internal behavior that can be difficult for an observer to interpret. Sengers's solution to this problem may be viewed as the inverse of the earlier concern: while theorists trained on film and literature may see simulation too much in terms of narrative, it may be that computer scientists see it too little in these terms.

References: Literature

Benjamin, Walter (translated by Harry Zohn) (1969). "The Work of Art in the Age of Mechanical Reproduction." In *Illuminations*. New York: Schocken Books.

Eco, Umberto (translated by William Weaver) (1983). *The Name of the Rose*. Orlando; Harcourt Books.

Manovich, Lev (2001). *The Language of New Media*. Cambridge, MA: The MIT Press.

Nichols, Bill (1988). "The Work of Culture in the Age of Cybernetic Systems," *Screen* 21, no.1 (Winter 1988): 22-46.

Wizards of the Coast (2000). "Open Game License Version 1.0a." <http://www.opengamingfoundation.org/ogl.html>.

References: Games

Basic Role Playing: The Chaosium System. Greg Stafford and Lynn Willis; Chaosium. 2002.

Girl Genius: The Works. James Ernest; Cheapass Games/James Ernest Games. 2001.

GURPS. Steve Jackson et al.; Steve Jackson Games. 1986.

Maginor. Reiner Knizia; Fantasy Flight Games. 2001.

Mystery of the Abbey. Bruno Faidutti and Serge Laget; Days of Wonder. 2003.

Vegas. Reiner Knizia; Ravensburger Germany. 1996.

Xxxenophile. James Ernest; Slag-Blah Entertainment. 1996

Critical Simulation> Penny   Thacker Hayles
Frasca   Ito Zimmerman
Sengers   Suchman Mateas

III. Critical Simulation

Representation, Enaction, and the Ethics of Simulation
Simon Penny

The goal of this essay is twofold, academic and activist. The academic goal is to attempt to enhance critical discussion of interactive media practice and interactive media cultural practice by introducing a consideration of the implications of embodied involvement in the process. The activist dimension arises from this, and raises a question of ethical responsibility regarding cultural objects that might function as training environments to build behaviors that will ultimately be expressed in the real world.

While sociologists and anthropologists have examined virtual communities, gaming culture, and related cyberspatial phenomena, interest has centered upon issues of identity, subjectivity, and community. The evaluation of the psychological and sociological aspects of interactive entertainment has, to my mind, been limited. The embodied, enacted dimension of interactive entertainment has not been adequately considered. In particular, embodied interaction with a representation, where bodily action changes the

representation in a way which is analogous to, and is designed to be analogous to, human action in the world of physical objects and forces, raises scenarios which conventional critiques of representation, and those aspects of art theory that remain influenced by traditional psychology of visual perception, are not well equipped to deal with.

The core of this conversation then is in the space between pictorial representation and simulation, or rather, in the gray and murky area where they overlap. We need a new way to think about the relation between user behavior and digital representations in interactive entertainment. The embodied aspects of simulation feed back onto representation, make representation not inert but interactive. In order to gain some purchase on this territory, I want to juxtapose three aspects of human activity: interactive entertainment, professional simulator training, and the not-technologically-facilitated learning of bodily disciplines and regimes of behavior.

Body Training

One need go no further that Foucault for persuasive argument and evidence that bodily training is a powerful tool in the formation of citizens (Foucault 1977, 3–8). Repetitive physical actions have been an integral part of education and socialization since

73

Response by Eugene Thacker

Technologies of simulation, and the concept of simulation itself, have become one of those delirious cultural forms that seem to endlessly spiral into themselves. In VR, videogames, and computer graphics in film, the threshold between realism and hyper-realism becomes ever more blurred, and, to paraphrase Jean Baudrillard, the simulation increasingly becomes the alibi for the real: if it's Memorex, then it must have been live.

Simon Penny's essay on the aesthetics and ethics of simulation raises such issues, especially as they relate to the links between video games, social–cognitive behavior, and military technology. As Penny argues, technologies of simulation are also social technologies

because they are hardware and software systems that model, induce, and articulate particular types of actions and behaviors.

For instance, one common assumption in current uses of VR is that a single, unitary, and consistent "body" operates across two different ontological worlds. The measure of success of simulation would be, presumably, the ease with which an individual can cross the border between virtual and real. But we might also ask: is there any reason to assume that "the body" in a VR environment is the same as "the body" in the real world? For current uses of VR in the military, the answer is yes: what counts is the resultant effect, the physical inscribing of sets of actions, and not the qualitative changes brought by technological mediation preliterate times. Anthropological observations by Marcel Mauss (and others) attest to the unacknowledged but pervasive power of physical behaviors in social and cultural formation. Indeed, physical imitation is a key component in social development. The establishment of gender roles, for instance, through such emulation, voluntary or coerced, is well documented.

Pierre Bordieu (1977) and others have established that social behaviors are often learned without conscious intellectual understanding. The way someone rationalizes or explains an activity on an intellectual level, and the behaviors that have been learned and are enacted can be different, even diametrically opposed.[1] There is a small industry of corporate training in the reading and deployment of body language. Legion are the training and rehabilitation systems which rely on repetitive physical action, even to exhaustion. From this perspective, military boot camp, football training, some forms of yoga and other spiritual training, ballet lessons and some schools of drug, juvenile delinquency and other psychosocial rehabilitation are almost indistinguishable, except on the level of academicization of the particular techniques.

One quality common to sports training, martial arts training and military training is anti-intellectuality. Whether an activity is introduced verbally and

methodically or is instilled by discipline and repetition, it is universally acknowledged by both teacher and (successful) student that the training it is only really effective when it becomes automatic, reflex. It becomes *not* conscious. The unsuccessful student is told, "You think too much."

The Military-Entertainment Complex

Computer simulated immersive environments are clearly an effective tool for bodily training, demonstrated by their use in civil aviation and in the military. Over the last decade, applications have broadened; VR simulations have even been applied to psychotherapy. Such simulations create a useful environment for desensitizing phobic patients who transfer what they've learned in the "simulated" world to the "real" world, allowing them to ride elevators and cross high bridges. So, while the electronic game industry vehemently counters claims that interactive electronic games have any real-life consequences, psychotherapists employ simulation technologies precisely because they have effect in people's lives.

Early simulator systems focused on training human users of machine systems whose behavior was relatively easy to simulate. "Psychological tracking and targeting research [of the early 1940s] became an ergonomic discipline aimed at the construction of

(the introduction of wearable technological gadgetry, the use of multiple screens, the use of audio, the architecture of the training room itself).

The example of military VR is especially instructive because, as Penny suggests, it does not make a clear-cut distinction between virtual and real worlds. Unlike psychotherapeutic applications of VR, one does not first use VR in military training, and then go out into the battlefield to "apply" what has been learned. The virtual environment is layered onto the real (we might be tempted to say "material") environment. As military technology today makes clear, the VR, videogame interface *is* the "real world" of navigation, combat and warfare. This situation is akin to Orson Scott Card's (1985) popular story *Ender's Game*, in which young

pilots trained by the military on futuristic video games unknowingly wipe out an alien race in an intergalactic war/video game.

Penny asks: what are video game users being trained to do? One answer might be: they are being trained to act instinctually — that is "naturally" — through information and computer technologies. Part of what this means is developing new modes of navigating real world spaces, through the lens of simulation technologies (an upgraded version of Kant's notion of the senses as "spectacles" that could never be taken off). And because those simulations — be they first-person shooter games or military VR training — have a common logic to them, their modes of navigating the world will necessarily be enframed by a process that

integrated human-machine cyborgs. Among its most fertile offshoots were military experimental training simulators similar to modern videogames, complete with joystick controls" (Edwards 1996, 199). This technology trickled down from the military and found particular application in the many generations of flight simulators, from the "link trainer" on.[2] In general, simulators find application anywhere where the cost of the simulator is less than the cost of the real item, as is clearly the case with commercial aircraft.

Training simulation and interactive entertainment were born joined at the hip. There is no better place to examine that join than SIGGRAPH, the Special Interest Group in Computer Graphics and Interactive Techniques of the Association for Computing Machinery (ACM).[3] Here the military simulator development community, the academic computer science community and the high-end civilian computer graphics and animation community blend. For in truth, there is substantial overlap, and personnel movements between the communities is constant and smooth.

During the 1980s, DARPA (the Defense Advanced Research Projects Agency) and the U.S. Army developed simulators for tanks and vehicles that were integrated in a local network, a multiuser virtual environment. About the same time that Simnet became public in the early 1990s, a high-end immersive multiuser battle

simulation game called *Battletech* opened in Chicago. In the early 1990s, Simnet became integrated into STOW, the military-wide "Synthetic Theater of War." STOW is a "synthetic battlespace" in which "Computer Generated Forces" are integrated with live military exercises and manned SIMNET simulators, with all data integrated allowing for overall Command and Control. In late 1999, the University of Southern California received a five-year contract from the U.S. Army to establish the Institute For Creative Technologies (ICT). The ICT's mandate is: "to enlist the resources and talents of the entertainment and game development industries and work collaboratively with computer scientists to advance the state of immersive training simulation."[4] The fact that the U.S. military have invested millions in Simnet, STOW and other simulation training systems is proof enough that simulation is an effective tool for such training. It is clear that immersive simulation environments are effective in producing such training, and that such training transfers usefully to the "real world."

In the mid-90s, it was revealed that the U.S. Marines had licensed *Doom* from Id Software and built "Marine Doom," to use as a tactical training tool. The U.S. Army MARKS military training device is manufactured by Nintendo. It is highly reminiscent of *Duck Hunt* except the gun is a plastic M-16, and the targets are images of

---

naturalizes a kind of "seek-and-destroy" strategy. The problem, ethically speaking, with the link between video games and violence is less a desensitizing to the real world, and more of a resensitizing to the dematerialized and totally malleable world of simulation.

When Penny states that "the interactive image cannot be spoken of in the terms of traditional passive images because it is procedural," he is asking us to rethink virtuality beyond representation. In one sense this means thinking about agency and ethics in simulated environments beyond a traditional active/passive model. If simulated environments are, or can be, "intelligent" and adaptive, then the individuals acting in those environments are accountable not only

for other individuals, but for the system dynamics as well. In calling for a "procedural aesthetics" or an aesthetics of interactivity, Penny seems to be opening the door to building systems that would generate reflexive behavior in real time. Not just the physical inscription of actions and behaviors, but environments that occasion reflexive thought, though that is inseparable from ethical acting. From one perspective, the basis of this is to treat ethics as intertwined with technology, where this does not imply a disembodiedness.

From Katherine Hayles's Online Response

What implications are generated by the reading practices required by electronic environments,

people, not ducks. More recently the Navy has been using *The Sims* to model the organisation of terrorist cells (Kaplan 2001). So, in the spirit of "what's good for the goose is good for the gander," we are drawn to the conclusion that what separates the first person shooter from the high-end battle simulator is the location of one in an adolescent bedroom and the other in a military base. And having accepted that simulators are effective environments for training, we must accept that so too are the desktop shooter games. The question is: what exactly is the user being trained to do?

David Grossman, a retired Lieutenant-Colonel and expert at desensitizing soldiers to increase their killing efficiency is well known (1996) for his opposition to violent video-games on the basis that the entertainment industry conditions the young in exactly the same way the military does: they hardwire young people for shooting at humans.[5] On the other hand, advocates for game culture do their best to downplay such associations.

Game designers and theorists Frank Lantz and Eric Zimmerman (1999), in an apologia for *Quake*, argue:

> In single player mode, and especially in multiplayer "deathmatch" mode, *Quake*'s blend of lightspeed tactics and hand-eye coordination has more

in common with the cerebral athletics of tennis than the spectacular violence of Rambo. *Quake* and games like it have succeeded in creating meaningful spaces for play where the extravagant promises of virtual reality have failed. They have focused design on what participants are actually doing from moment to moment in the game, rather than on just the visual and kinetic sensations of moving through an immersive space.[6]

In their choice of tennis as a comparison, Lantz and Zimmerman may be suspected of a little tactical disingenuousness. War and combat are clearly present in games such as rugby, chess and *Quake*, metaphorized to varying degrees. But in tennis one does not claim territory, there is no body contact; it is even difficult to regard the ball as a metaphorized projectile. The narrative logic of the game seems to map more clearly the strategic exchange of a token (a metaphorization of commerce) or debate (a metaphorization of diplomacy),[7] whereas *Quake* is mired in images of gobs of steaming bloody flesh and graphic depictions of death of the most violent kind.

compared to print? With print, the reader's physical activity is limited to the relatively trivial action of turning pages. Regardless of how fast or slow the page is turned, the words remain durably inscribed, immune to the reader's manipulations (short of such drastic actions as cutting or folding the pages). With electronic hypertext, however, the reader absorbs new assumptions about the nature of textuality through physical engagement with the electronic text — assumptions all the more powerful because they are absorbed through physical actions rather than conscious reflection. These assumptions I will call cognitive entailments, because they constitute a form of bodily cognition with powerful implications for what the text means. In recognition of these cognitive

entailments, I will henceforth refer to the reader as an "interactor," a term that more accurately captures the nature of reading in electronic environments.

http://www.electronicbookreview.com/thread/firstperson/haylesr1

Penny Responds

Procedural works are designed systems that exhibit behavior with which we might be engaged. The design occurs substantially at a meta-level, designing the qualities of behavior which human users can recognize and to which they will respond. This meta-literature is where the new aesthethic operates.

http://www.electronicbookreview.com/thread/firstperson/pennyr2

Lantz and Zimmerman continue:

> *Quake* is an undeniably elaborate and ritualized spectacle of violence. But what is the best way to frame this violence? As culture, *Quake* is serious hardcore pulp, a self-consciously adolescent blood and gore frenzy. But should we consider *Quake* as the ultimate embodiment of male computerdom's phallocentric obsessions? Or as the refusal of the mess and blood of the body to be excluded from the clean and infinite perspectives of cyberspace? As the ironic product of a generation of young men with no war to fight?

Or, one is tempted to continue: as the cultural/psychological backwash of two generations of Cold War mentality, of the militarization of education and entertainment, or possibly as an enactment, in the most graphic way, of the reigning dog-eat-dog ethic of the business world?

Is it unfair to blame such atrocities as the Columbine and Jonesboro school massacres purely on such products? Clearly most people, even most *Quake* players, have a reasonable grasp of the difference between simulation and real life. But equally clearly, these games would not find a market if a larger cultural formation had not prepared the ground. It is in this context that we must ask: what behaviors do these games train? While Zimmerman and Lantz remain equivocal on the issue of whether such game play anesthetizes players to the horrors of real-world violence, others, such as Grossman, are explicit, not just about their desensitizing role but about their ability to efficiently build killing skills:

> Whatever you train to do, under stress, is coming out the other end. That's why we do fire drills. That's why we do flight simulators... Well, when the children play the violent video games, they're drilling, drilling, drilling — not two times a year — every night, to kill every living creature in front of you, until you run out of targets or you run out of bullets... we're reasonably confident that in Pearl, Mississippi, and in Paducah, Kentucky, and in Jonesboro, Arkansas, these juvenile, adolescent killers set out to shoot just one person: usually their girlfriend... maybe a teacher. But, then, they kept on going! And, they gunned down every living creature in front of them, until they ran out of targets or ran out of bullets...! [A]fterwards, the police asked them... "Okay. You shot the person you were mad at. Why did you shoot all these others? Some of 'em were your friends!" And the kids don't know. (Steinberg, 2000)[8]

Grossman argues that not only do such games train children to "to kill every living creature in front of you," but as with real training simulators, the children become excellent shots.

Simulation and Metaphorization

Between the full force-feedback VR suit fantasy of the early 1990s (or even the direct neural jack) and the "choose-your-own-adventure" book lies a vast range of technologies of simulation in which bodily action is more or less metaphorized. Often, interactive interfaces depend on complex layers of metaphorization of bodily behavior. The notion of "navigation," in graphically rendered virtual spaces is a good case example, whether we're talking about *Quake*, about immersive VR or navigable three-dimensional web environments. Even in immersive stereoscopic environments (such as the CAVE) the user is navigating not a real space, but a pictorial representation of a space, according to certain culturally established pictorial conventions of spatial representation (such as perspective) established centuries ago for static images. One is not navigating

7.1. *The Legible City* (1988). (Jeffrey Shaw)

space, but projecting, in the imagination, the implications of manipulating an interactive image medium in a way that will generate a presumed logical next step in a stream of images that represent a space perspectivally from a sequence of points of view.

Little of the proprioceptive or perceptuo-motor correlation characteristic of bodily movement in real space is simulated or accommodated. In the case of the CAVE, for instance, such correlation is utterly scrambled in paradigmatically mechanistic style by the disconnection of forward movement from turning, of "drive" from "steering." One can bodily turn, but one cannot bodily walk, lest one rend the screen or wrench the gear off your head. The illusion of forward movement is achieved by dragging the world under

one's feet using codified button clicks. This is a laughable example of the way that such systems often inhere awkward and paradoxical user constraints as a result of hardware limitations. More surprising is that this inconsistency seems not to have been found problematic, even in the professional literature.

"Spatial navigation" on the desktop is achieved by the utilization of streams of perspectively rendered images which correspond to the movement of an avatar in a virtual world, combined with arbitrary combinations of mouse movements and keystrokes which correspond to movement on several degrees of freedom (DOF). The notion of "navigation" in a highly metaphorical "space" of data is several degrees more abstracted. At this point the notion of "navigation" is so highly metaphorized that a substantial amount of cultural background is necessary to make the use of the term comprehensible. Web "navigation," like many computer applications, leverages and metaphorizes human skills in spatial location and spatial navigation to facilitate information searches.[9]

The degree of literalness of simulation depends substantially upon the precision with which bodily behaviors germane to that task in the real world can be accommodated and measured in a simulator environment. Commercial simulators and many interactive artworks make the assumption that a close and accurate accommodation of bodily behaviors results in a more persuasive simulation. *The Legible City*, Jeffrey Shaw's paradigmatic immersive artwork of 1988, provides a good case example (figure 7.1). The interface for *The Legible City* was a stationery bicycle, instrumented so that the speed of pedaling and angle of steering could be extracted. These data directly drove the projection of streetlike imagery on a large projection screen in front of the user. The effect was a fairly complete and persuasive simulation of riding a bicycle through a city.

In a similar vein, Janet Murray relates that her immersion in the *Mad Dog McRee* arcade game "depended heavily on the heft and six shooter shape of the laser gun controller and on the way it was placed in a hip height holster ready for quick draw contests. As soon as I picked up that gun, I was transported back to my childhood and to the world of TV Westerns" (Murray 1997, 146). She notes that her son needed no such tangible interface to enjoy the desktop version of the game. The interface hardware stimulated a bodily memory in Murray, which itself was connected with voluminous cultural background from her childhood, experiences not shared by her son.

If you play *Quake* on a standard desktop PC, there is no gun-sized, gun-shaped input device. There is a QWERTY keyboard. It must be acknowledged that, as the pen is mightier than the sword, so in the post-Gulf War era, such a device is regularly the interface to machines which kill, maim and destroy, at distances greater than the flight of most projectiles. All that notwithstanding, a keyboard is not like a gun. And this is often the (naïve) argument made to adduce that first-person shooters do not induce violent behavior. But the user's relation to the system is not that simplistic. The user of a first-person shooter sees the front end of a weapon on the screen. She can point that weapon in various directions. She can press a key with an index finger to see and hear a plume of fire emanate from the weapon and incinerate some alien beast who writhes in agony in a rewarding fashion before collapsing into a steaming heap.

Many "mouse/keyboard" games can be played with joysticks, which are essentially a pistol grip complete with a trigger. More recent joystick peripherals provides force feedback: the user feels a recoil jolt in the hand when the trigger is pulled. And of course, more elaborate arcade game interfaces simulate such effects more completely. Janet Murray notes: "The most compelling aspect of the fighting game is the tight visceral match between the game controller and the screen action. A palpable click on the mouse or joystick results in an explosion. It requires very little imaginative effort to enter such a world because the sense of agency is so direct" (Murray 1997, 146). This statement demonstrates the way that conventional critiques of representation are rendered inadequate in this fusing of bodily action and real-time effect in modeled 3D worlds. The weapon is no longer just a picture. The representation is controlled, driven. In this space between mere pictures and the "real world" the

embodied aspects of simulation influence representation in real time.

Why Theories of Visual Representation Are Inadequate

In the postwar years, theories of visual perception based in gestalt psychology, by such authors as Rudolf Arnheim, Ernst Gombrich, and R. L. Gregory, had a significant effect in art theory and criticism.[10] From a contemporary point of view, this work, especially when it considered art, was characterized by a conception of vision and visual perception as a one-way process of information inflow, through the eyes into the brain.[11] This conception of the detached observer eye, the disembodied mindlike eye, the eye as extension of mind, is dualist and objectivist. The shortcoming of such approaches is that they disregard the dynamic perceptuo-motoric nature of visual learning. In a classic experiment by Held and Hein (1958), a group of kittens were reared in total darkness. The kittens were fitted in a gantry arrangement with two baskets. One basket had holes for the legs such that the physical movements of one kitten would drive both animals through roughly similar spatial experiences. In each case, after a few weeks the kitten that walked and could associate visual information with its own physical movement developed effective vision. The rider in the basket remained functionally blind.

We could never interpret an image of a domestic space, had we not actually moved about in such spaces. Physical experience does not simply disambiguate, it is the key by which images are understood. A baby learns about its visual system via physical exploration and hand-eye experiments. Such experiments might be said to "calibrate" the baby's visual system but in fact they build it, they build a correlation between visual signals and a kinesthetic/tactile nature of the world. Vision is remote sensing but it is grounded on touch and proprioception, on reaching and grasping, stumbling and falling.

In interactive media a user is not simply exposed to images that may contain representations of things and actions. The user is trained in the enaction of behaviors in response to images, and images appear in response to behaviors in the same way that a pilot is trained in a flight simulator. Passive observation may be shown to have some effect on the beliefs or even the actions of an observer, but an enacted training regime must be a more powerful technique. So critiques of representation derived from painting, photography, film and video are inadequate for discussing the power of interactive experience.

Much debate has occurred on the correlation between pornographic images and sex-crime. Conversations about representations of violence typically conflate movies and computer games, as if they were in the same category. Whatever the power of images, interactive media is more. Not "just a picture," it is an interactive picture that responds to my actions. Our analysis of interactive media must therefore go beyond theories of representation in images. The image is just the target, the surface. The interactive image cannot be spoken of in the terms of traditional passive images because it is procedural. The content is as much in the routine that runs the image as it is in the image itself. Interactive applications are not pictures, they are machines which generate pictures.

Interactive Art and Antisocial Behavior

In late 2000, I visited an interactive installation that in my opinion was unfortunate and ill-conceived. I mention it here only because in a rather extreme way it raises these issues in a fine art context. The work, *Kan Xuan* by Alexander Brandt, consisted of a full-length image of a naked Asian woman lying face up projected, life-size, on a crumpled cloth on the cold stone floor in a dark corner. The only way to interact with this work was to stomp on the woman, and the only reward was that she recoiled in pain. If you stomped a lot she faded away. But after a few seconds she returned, like the repressed. The figure never objected or defended herself, but neither did she encourage such treatment. It was simply the only possible mode of engagement presented to the user. Inescapably: the audience is invited to enact violence against a naked, prone woman of color. Here is a case study of the potential of electronic representations to encourage or reinforce behaviors in the real world, in this case racist and/or

misogynist behaviors.

There was no explanatory text or any other device to encourage a reflexive reading of the work.[12] Beyond the projected image and the sheet, the only other element was the soundtrack of a plaintive, wailing song sung by an Asian woman that added to the air of misery. It bears emphasizing the figure was not a fashionably fetishized object of S&M porn, she was not wearing high heels or makeup, there was nothing about her pose contrived to induce desire. Her flesh tones were grayed out and pale, her eyes were closed, abject. While its subject matter was, to my mind, deeply unfortunate, the work was quite proficient technically and formally. Its interface was well-designed, self-explanatory with excellent economy.[13]

What is immediately relevant to this and other interactive work, is the (to my knowledge, unremarked) gap between "representation" and "enactment." In the area of digital media practice that is attached to the visual arts, theories of visual representation have been a powerful critical force. But, as I have been arguing, an interactive "representation" is more than a representation. In desktop computer-based interactives, there are additional levels of metaphorization (i.e., of mouse clicks for body movement) but "embodied interactives" are in a kinesthetically different and more literal territory. Although a mouse-click on an HTML document may "represent," in a manner similar to a picture, the action of turning a page, it is still in the realm of the symbolic. But actually lifting one's leg and stomping down on a face moves the action several steps toward the literal. It was not a flesh-and-blood face, nor a rubber model of a face, but on the continuum, a responding photo-real interactive image is definitely more "real" than a block of text or a diagrammatic pistol-shooting target.

When soldiers shoot at targets shaped like people, this trains them to shoot real people. When pilots work in flight simulators, the skills they develop transfer to the real world. When children play "first-person shooters," they develop skills of marksmanship. So we must accept that there is something that qualitatively separates a work like the one discussed above from a static image of a misogynistic beating, or even a movie

Critical Simulation> Penny   Thacker Hayles
Frasca   Ito Zimmerman
Sengers   Suchman Mateas

III. Critical Simulation

of the same subject. That something is the potential to build behaviors that can exist without or separate from, and possibly contrary to, rational argument or ideology.

Why Doesn't the Army Teach Acting?

I have proposed that interactive entertainments must be assumed to have the same pedagogical power as training simulators, and we must therefore consider their ramifications in this light. I have argued that use of such technologies, both for entertainment and for training, is a bodily training and thus its techniques and effects can be related to nontechnological techniques of body training. Yet, a counterexample is sometimes proposed, which appears to problematize the entire argument. It might be phrased this way: If training in simulated worlds is productive of real-world skills, then why don't actors who play serial killers usually go on to be serial killers? By introducing another term into the equation, that of the theater, such an objection allows us to explore in more detail the relation between the various parts of my argument.

The counterargument assumes that the theater is a virtual world and that acting is a bodily training. This begs certain other questions: What is the difference between acting and simulation? Why doesn't the army teach acting? What is the difference between, say, battle simulation training and *Macbeth*, in terms of its residual effect on the psyche of the enactant?

In order to disentangle these questions, we must first decide whether we are considering the actor or the audience. Given that the audience's relation with the spectacle is not significantly interactive, we must assume we are talking about the actor. Yet the environment of the (conventional) play is not in any substantial sense interactive. The illusion has been built up, painstakingly, by actor and director, piece by piece, over weeks or months. Every movement is known. The complete illusion, with all the characters, costumes, props, lighting, and sound effects is usually only assembled at a late stage in the process. The illusion is not, it must be remembered, for the actor, but for the audience.

Theater is reflexive and double. A world is conjured but it is a world open on one side to the audience, who are not in that world, but are keen to engage in the illusion that they are. People cry over deaths in the theater, knowing full well that the same actor will die the same way the next night. The actor plays to the audience and gauges their reactions; this is the measure of her success. The audience knows she is the character, and also the actor. The stage is colored lights and painted cardboard, but it is also High Dunsinane. The actor learns the part to help produce a persuasive illusion for the audience. The soldier indulges in a persuasive illusion in order to become better at fighting a war, killing and surviving: a distinctly nonillusory experience.

In simulation, in VR, one is encouraged to believe there is no "outside." The desire is for complete enveloping illusion. The soldier or the student pilot is not encouraged to look reflexively at the artifice but is encouraged to make no distinction between the simulation and the simulated. But cultural experience rides on the celebration of artifice, the manipulation of the threshold of illusion, where it simultaneously is and isn't. The holy grail of total immersion is ultimately either psychotic or hallucinogenic. No surprise then that Timothy Leary was enlisted as an early booster for VR, which he referred to as "electronic acid." Much art, on the other hand, enlists the active intelligence of the viewer to discern fugitive patterns on a perceptual, conceptual or narrative level.

Serious Play

My conclusion is that the objection concerning acting and serial killing does not significantly destabilize my basic argument. It may be proposed that engagement with interactive work, or gaming for that matter, is "just a game," is "play," and therefore doesn't matter. This turn of phrase obscures the fact that the truth is the opposite: "play" is a powerful training tool. To return to the key question: what behaviors do these games train?[14] In the case of *Quake*, a simplistic response would be that they improve hand-eye coordination at the computer console. This would be true to their cybernetic human-machine interaction roots. Yet this would be to ignore any interaction between the physical action and the imagery and narrative of the game.

We know that simulators do train effectively. Skills learned in simulation are elicited in the world. A pilot responds, "instinctually" to a situation familiar from training. No reasoning is necessary; indeed, that is exactly the point: this training, like football training, is about making responses rapid, reflexive. Any *Quake*-playing kid knows how to blow away approaching enemies — knows, in fact, according to the logic of the game, that any approaching stranger is an enemy and must therefore be blown away immediately. We must assume that these "learned responses" can also transfer to the real world, if triggered. Such a bodily training may not correlate with any considered political position. Indeed, one might contend that the power of interactive experience is to inculcate behaviors, and these behaviors do not require any ideological correlation. In fact they might work best without such correlation. Such learned behaviors are triggered, without conscious decision making, when the current context matches the conditions of the training context.[15] There is the possibility that such behaviors might be expressed in situations which resemble the visual context or emotional tenor of the gameplay. Which is to say, games and interactive media in general can be powerful inculcators of behaviors, and these learned behaviors can be expressed outside the realm of the game. And if this is true, then it is hard to escape the conclusion that an interactive artwork might encourage misogynistic violence or that first person shooters actively contribute to an increase in gun violence among kids.

Coda: The Aesthetics of Interactivity

The emerging range of digital social practices calls for a new range of sociological studies, among them a consideration of the implications of interactive technologies, the "cyber-social." In the arts, the same technologies demand the development of new areas of aesthetics. The "aesthetics of interactivity" can be divided into two mirroring aspects.[16] The machine-centric aspect is concerned with semi-autonomous programs and systems which generate variations of

output in response to real-time inputs, with behaviors defined by algorithmic procedures. The second aspect is user-centric and is concerned with the users' behavior and experience.

Part of the machine-centric aspect concerns the temporal modeling of lifelike systems, with Grey Walter's "turtles" being early examples. A generation later, Craig Reynolds's *Boids* system, of 1987, generated the temporal behavior of a flock of birds in a highly abstracted 3D environment. The Boids are the paradigmatic example of "procedural modeling," a set of techniques that transformed computer animation. No longer was animation a matter of successions of images, but of computational entities that exhibited temporal behaviors. Reynolds's work was highly suggestive for the group of researchers who, about that time, claimed the title of "Artificial Life" for their field. Out of this group emerged a new paradigm of semi-autonomous systems premised on genetic and evolutionary metaphors, of which Tom Ray's *Tierra* attained early notoriety. Around the same time, some robotics researchers were working with emergent paradigms of robot behavior; many of these were grouped around Luc Steels in Belgium and Rodney Brooks at MIT. Since the late 1980s, the notion of semi-autonomous software entities has proven a rich catalyst for experimentation in both the fine and the applied ends of the electronic arts.

In recent years, complex autonomous entities called agents have been a subject of much excitement, and subgenres of research such as "socially intelligent agents" have arisen.[17] Here procedural systems are combined with real-time response to both digital and real-world entities. One of the applications for such agents is in the field of interactive drama. This area of work has affinities with hypertextual writing, which itself must be regarded as "procedural literature." In hypertext, the aesthetic work is as much in the design of the system that will present text according to the user's behavior, as it is in the construction of the textual elements themselves. In this spirit, Joseph Weizenbaum's *Eliza* program of 1965, which modeled the behavior of a nondirective psychotherapist, must be acknowledged as the first procedural "portrait" or

Critical Simulation> Penny
Frasca
Sengers

Thacker Hayles
Ito Zimmerman
Suchman Mateas

III. Critical Simulation

character study, the first "socially intelligent agent."

Viewed as a class, the common aspect of these projects is their "procedurality." The systems generate behavior on the fly, in the real world or a simulated physical or social context. This phenomenon of computational entities responding to their environments implies a new aesthetic field that we might call "procedural aesthetics" or an "aesthetics of automated behavior."

It is the second aspect of the aesthetics of interactivity that has concerned me most in this paper: the design of (a context for) user behavior. Each work affords, accommodates, or permits only certain types of behavior. So, the behavior of the user is constrained and in a sense, modeled. The quality of this behavior becomes a key component of the user's experience. Many works, both at the desktop and as installations such as *The Legible City*, encourage a calm contemplative manner. Some, such as *Quake*, elicit rapid reactions and adrenaline rushes, but little physical movement. Others encourage large athletic movement, like my own work, *Fugitive*.[18]

Yet, consciousness of the bodily action of the user per se is only part of this complex. It is necessary that we begin to be able to discuss with some precision the relationship between user behavior and system behavior, or system expression: graphics, text, sound and mechanical events. As I have argued in this paper, the persuasiveness of interactivity is not in the images per se, but in the fact that bodily behavior is intertwined with the formation of representations. It is the ongoing interaction between these representations and the embodied behavior of the user that makes such images more than images. This interaction renders conventional critiques of representation inadequate, and calls for the theoretical and aesthetic study of embodied interaction.

Notes

1. Maria Fernandez has (at the Performative Sites Symposium 2000: Intersecting Art, Technology and the Body, Oct. 24–28, Penn State) argued that racist behavior exhibits both ideological and bodily dimensions. Alarmingly, she observes that racist bodily behaviors can be in place and expressed, even while a subject believes she is not racist, and believes that she is not behaving in a racist manner. Such training exists below the level of consciousness,

verbalizations and rationalization.

A version of this paper will appear in a forthcoming anthology of papers from the conference edited by Charles Garoian and Yvonne Gaudelius. The paper is also found at: <http://on1.zkm.de/zkm/magazin/rascism_embodiment>.

2. The Link flight trainer was designed in the U.S. by Edwin Link, primarily as an amusement park flying simulator. However, with the developments in aviation in the 1930s, it was adapted as an instrument flying trainer.

3. SIGGRAPH holds a vast annual conference that is attended by academic computer scientists, the computer industry, the entertainment industry and military personnel.

4. <http://www.ict.usc.edu/>.

5. David Grossman is an expert on the psychology of killing. Retired from the U.S. Army, he now teaches psychology at Arkansas State University, directs the Killology Research Group in Jonesboro, Arkansas. See David Grossman (1996), *On Killing: The Psychological Cost of Learning to Kill in War and Society*; and David Grossman and Gloria DeGaetano (1999), *Stop Teaching Our Kids to Kill: A Call To Action Against TV, Movie & Video Game Violence*.

6. This discussion of first-person shooters should not be regarded as a tirade against gaming and game culture per se. I am strongly sympathetic to the open source, hackivist sentiments adduced by Lantz and Zimmerman, and the rejection of sterile corporate product in favor of the vigor of anarchic street culture. I believe that gaming and its offshoots are perhaps the most vibrant and novel cultural forms to have arisen in digital media. Perhaps the most extraordinary of these offshoots is the "machinimation" (my term) community who make synthetic movies using game engines.

7. In the 11th or 12th centuries a simple handball game called *jeu de paume* ("game of the hand") was played in French monasteries. Later it was adopted by the nobility and moved indoors, where it became known as tennis. It seems to have been devoid of militaristic narratives.

8. In the same interview, Grossman continues: "I guess the classic example was in Paducah, Kentucky. In Paducah, a 14-year-old boy stole a 22-caliber pistol from a neighbor's house. Now, prior to stealing that gun, he had never fired a pistol before in his life. He fired a few shots, on a couple of nights before the killings, with the neighbor boy. And, then he brought that gun into school, and he fired eight shots.

"Now, the FBI says that the average officer in the average engagement hits with one bullet in five. In the Amadou Diallo shooting, they fired 41 shots at point-blank range, against an unarmed man: They hit 19 times. The guy that went into the Jewish daycare center in Los Angeles last summer, fired 70 shots, and hit five of those helpless children. So, this boy fires eight shots. How many hits does he get? Eight shots, eight hits, on eight different children. Five of them are head shots. The other three are upper torso. This is stunning."

9. Without doubt, a substantial part of our capability as humans is our enormously rich sensory-motor coordination that allows us to move and work so well in the 2.1-dimensional space we live in. (I use the fractal nomenclature of fractional dimension to emphasize the fact that we do not really live in three dimensions, as birds and fish do. Whereas manually, on a small scale, we work in three dimensions, on the larger scale we exist in just over two, even if that 'thick plane' is folded and crumpled into architecture and landscape.) But whether that spatial sensibility (developed to varying degrees and in various ways in different individuals and probably cultures) can be usefully exploited in computational systems depends entirely on what sort of data is being represented and what the desired mode of interaction might be, and most importantly the affordances of each particular interface technology and hardware platform.

84

10. See Rudolf Arnheim (1954), *Art and Visual Perception: A Psychology of the Creative Eye*; Rudolf Arnheim (1966), *Toward a Psychology of Art*; E.H. Gombrich (1960), *Art and Illusion: A Study in the Psychology of Pictorial Representation*; and R L. Gregory (1990), *Eye and Brain: The Psychology of Seeing*.

11. Gregory's reporting of Helds and Hein's research (cited later) notwithstanding.

12. It might be argued that the work was blackly ironic: that is, by presenting an extreme image, the work promotes in the viewer a powerfully negative response, and has therefore triggered critical thought. Whereas this argument sometimes has merits, it falls into a double trap of double coding. First, there is always a sector of the population for whom the work is not ironic, and in such cases it serves to reinforce the values it (ostensibly) works against. Second, ironic double coding allows the speaker or maker equivocality, to be simultaneously for and against.

13. *Kan Xuan* by Alexander Brandt was included in the "Beyond the Screen" exhibition of ISEA 2000 in Paris, at the Ecole Normale Superieur de Beaux Arts.

14. For certainly they do train. Some game production companies are known to implement so-called "reinforcement schedules" based on the long-standing psychological knowledge that intermittent reinforcement is a more effective training technique that consistent reinforcement.

15. How does the subject know, unconsciously, to produce a specific trained behavior in a specific context? Subtle codes and emotional tenor must play key roles in such triggering.

16. A deeper analysis of these two aspects of the aesthetics of interactivity, and the theoretical background relevant to them is the subject of a more substantial forthcoming study.

17. In my presentation at one such gathering, the 1997 AAAI Fall workshop on Socially Intelligent Agents at MIT, I coined the term "culturally intelligent agents" to describe my own work. See Simon Penny (2000), "Agents as Artworks and Agent Design as Artistic Practice."

18. <http://www.art.cfa.cmu.edu/Penny/works/fugitive/fugitive.html>.

References

Arnheim, Rudolf (1954). *Art and Visual Perception: A Psychology of the Creative Eye*. Berkeley: University of California Press.

Arnheim, Rudolf (1966). *Toward a Psychology of Art*. Berkeley: University of California Press.

Bordieu, Pierre (1977). *Outline of a Theory of Practice*. New York: Cambridge University Press.

Card, Orson Scott (1985). *Ender's Game*. New York: Tor Books.

Connerton, Paul (1989). *How Societies Remember (Themes in the Social Sciences)*. Cambridge, UK: Cambridge University Press.

Edwards, Paul N. (1996). *The Closed World: Computers and the Politics of Discourse in Cold War America*. Cambridge, MA: The MIT Press.

Fernandez, Maria (2000). Presentation at Performative Sites Symposium 2000, Intersecting Art, Technology and the Body, October 24-28, Pennsylvania State University, State College, Pennsylvania. <http://on1.zkm.de/zkm/magazin/rascism_embodiment>.

Foucault, Michel (translated by Alan Sheridan) (1977). *Discipline and Punish: The Birth of the Prison*. New York: Vintage.

Gombrich, E.H. (1960). *Art and Illusion: A Study in the Psychology of Pictorial Representation*. Princeton: Princeton University Press.

Gregory, R.L. (1990). *Eye and Brain: The Psychology of Seeing*. Princeton: Princeton University Press.

Grossman, David (1996). *On Killing: The Psychological Cost of Learning to Kill in War and Society*. Boston: Little, Brown and Co.

Grossman, David, and Gloria DeGaetano (1999). *Stop Teaching Our Kids to Kill: A Call To Action Against TV, Movie & Video Game Violence*. New York: Random House.

Held, R., and A. Hein (1958). "Adaption of Disarranged Hand-Eye Coordination Contingent upon Re-afferent Stimulation," *Perceptual-Motor Skills* 8 (1958): 87-97.

Kaplan, Karen (2001). "The Sims Take on Al Qaeda." *The Los Angeles Times* Record edition (Nov 2, 2001): A1.

Lantz, Frank, and Eric Zimmerman (1999). "Rules, Play, and Culture: Checkmate." *Merge Magazine* 1, no.5 (Summer 1999): 41-43.

Maus, Marcel (translated by Ben Brewster) (1973). "Techniques of the Body." *Economy and Society* 2.1 (1973). Original in *Journal de Psychologie Normal et Pathologique*, Paris Année xxxii (1935): 271-93.

Murray, Janet (1997). *Hamlet on the Holodeck: The Future of Narrative in Cyberspace*. New York: Free Press.

Penny, Simon (2000). "Agents as Artworks and Agent Design as Artistic Practice." In *Human Cognition and Social Agent Technology*, edited by Kerstin Dautenhahn. Amsterdam: John Benjamins.

Steinberg, Jeffrey (2000). "Interview with David Grossman: Giving Children the Skill and the Will To Kill." *The Executive Intelligence Review*, March 17, 2000. <http://members.tripod.com/~american_almanac/grossint.htm>.

Videogames of the Oppressed: Critical Thinking, Education, Tolerance, and Other Trivial Issues

Gonzalo Frasca

Is it possible to design videogames that deal with social and political issues? Could videogames be used as a tool for encouraging critical thinking? Do videogames offer an alternative way of understanding reality? Although videogames are now about three decades old, these questions remain unanswered. It seems that even if the medium has reached incredible popularity, it is still far away from becoming a mature communication form that could deal with such things as human relationships, or political and social issues. Or maybe it can never become such thing. After all, as many may say, these are simply games and games have been considered trivial entertainment for ages. Nevertheless, I claim that videogames could indeed deal with human relationships and social issues, while encouraging

critical thinking. In this essay, I explore the possibilities of non-Aristotelian game design, mainly based on the work of drama theorist Augusto Boal.

Simulation and Representation

The design of consciousness-raising videogames is not as simple as replacing Nintendo's Mario and Luigi with Sacco and Vanzetti. According to Brenda Laurel's now-classic *Computers as Theater* (1991), computer software and videogames can be understood through the same rules that Aristotle described in his *Poetics*. The "interactive drama/storytelling/narrative" paradigm has been the leading design guide in most current videogame design, supported both by such theorists as Laurel and Janet Murray (Murray 1997) and by the videogame industry. It seems that the current tendency is to explain the computer (and videogames) as an extension of a previously existent medium: Laurel did it with drama, Murray with storytelling and, more recently, Lev Manovich (Manovich 2001) based his approach on film studies. The main advantage of these perspectives is that they depict the similitude between so-called "new" and "old" media.

It would be extremely naïve to think that videogames are a brand new cultural manifestation that does not draw upon any previous tradition. However, even if it sounds obvious, videogames are, before anything else,

Response by Mizuko Ito

Gonzalo Frasca's essay urges us to consider what it would take to make videogames a tool for critical engagement with social and political issues. I applaud this move to expand the scope of videogames' role in our social worlds, both in terms of broadening analytic frameworks for understanding games, as well as extending the ways games could be designed and mobilized. From the idiosyncratic vantage point of a cultural anthropologist of computing, currently researching children's media in Japan, I would like to offer a complementary but somewhat different angle on some of the topics that Frasca addresses.

Frasca points out how the unique characteristics of simulation and digital media open up possibilities for active participation, critical engagement, and

experimentation which are less available to audiences of traditional narrative forms. This seems to me to be mostly right, and I too have been intrigued and excited by the opportunities that users of digital media have to appropriate, reshape, and subvert centrally-produced content, particularly with the advent of the web and greater mobilization of user communities.

At the same time, I feel it is important to consider not only the differences between videogames and narrative forms but also the connections and overlaps. I am not necessarily pointing to the use of narrative form and theory in game design, but rather how our engagements with popular culture embed us in a hybrid media ecology as print, movies, games, and television increasingly reference one another. Looking at the media mix around children's content in Japan,

games. Sadly, good formal research on games is scarce. It seems that it is easier to use already popular theories rather than exploring the field from a fresh perspective. If we want to understand videogames, we first need to understand games. We need a *ludology* (Frasca, 1999), a formal discipline that focuses on games, both traditional and electronic.

If videogames are not narratives, what are they? I am not denying that games and narrative do share many elements, but as Espen Aarseth argues (Aarseth 1997), it is necessary to study games through a cybernetic approach. Unlike narrative, which is constituted by a fixed series of actions and descriptions, videogames need the active participation of the user not just for interpretational matters, but also for accessing its content. Narrative is based on semiotic representation, while videogames also rely on simulation,[1] understood as the modeling of a dynamic system through another system. A narrative film about a dog gives us information about the dog itself (description) and the sequence of events that this particular dog endured (action). A virtual pet, such as a *Tamagotchi*, is not about description or action, but rather about how it conducts itself in relationship with the player and the environment (behavior). In temporal terms, narrative is about what already happened while simulation is about what could happen.

Because of its static essence, narrative has been used by our culture to make statements. We explain, understand and deal with reality through narrative. Our religious and moral values have been historically shaped in this way through different sacred books (Bible, Koran, Popol Vuh). Although the interpretation of sacred texts has always been open, the written words and the stories themselves have mainly remained fixed. On the other hand, simulation is dynamic and its essence is change: it produces different outcomes. This makes simulations not such a good choice for sacred moral codes since you may not want to have your holy scripts alternately read, "Thou shall not kill," and "Thou shall kill." This also explains why videogames are not a good realm for historic events or characters or for making moral statements. A videogame about Anne Frank would be perceived as immoral, since the fact that she could survive or die depending on the player's performance would trivialize the value of human life. We all know that Anne Frank died and the reasons for her death; her story serves to convey a particular set of values.

The potential of simulation is not as a conveyor of values, but as a way to explore the mechanics of dynamic systems. *SimCity*™, Will Wright's urban simulator, is not about Paris or Rome, but about potential cities. Of course, it is possible to learn a lot

---

the hybridization between different media types is one of the most interesting sites of action. The narrative strengths of television, movies, and comic books furnish compelling characters, backstory, and setting for the more interactively intense and personalized formats of card games, videogames, and digital pets.

Thus, more than the distinction between narrative and simulation, I find myself galvanized by Frasca's distinguishing between different stances of engagement: critical versus immersed, actor versus spectator, or producer versus consumer. I am just back from Comiket, the largest convention in Japan, which is devoted to buying and selling comics and computer games created by fans. Content ranges from genre mixing, to pornographic renderings of mainstream characters, to exploring alternative narratives and

character qualities. This material would not be taken up by mainstream publishers, and often embeds a critical stance toward mainstream media. "Biohazard Pikachu" is mostly about humor, pleasure, and play, but is also a critical commentary on Nintendo's production of sanitized cuteness. This kind of appropriation and remaking seems to be at the heart of what Frasca envisions for the videogame community, and is something that cross-cuts media genres, as studies of fan communities have amply demonstrated (Penley 1991; Jenkins 1992; Tulloch and Jenkins 1995).

The productions of fan culture are just one piece of the dead serious economic and social negotiations around popular culture, and the ongoing political struggles between producers and consumers. For example, adult action entertainment is in a politically

about a big city such as Paris — or any other — through *SimCity*, but that kind of knowledge is different from what we can read in a Hemingway or Balzac book. It would be possible to create a model of Paris in *SimCity* and use it for experimentation: "What would happen if I removed the Seine River? What if I built narrow streets rather than large avenues?" Novels usually take a concrete set of characters, in a particular setting, enduring a particular set of events. Simulations also have particularities and referents, but their main characteristic is that they allow tweaking and changing the original model. Certainly, a reader can extrapolate the characteristics of the characters and settings of a novel to model its ideological rules. Although this is an exception in narrative reserved for sophisticated readers, it is a requirement in simulations. Simulation is an ideal medium for exposing rules rather than particular events.

Resurfacing from Immersion

Laurel's approach to software design and part of Murray's — particularly her concept of immersion as one of the three key providers of pleasure in interactive environments — are heavily influenced by Aristotelian poetics. The fact is that, while Aristotle's ideas are definitively popular in our culture, other approaches exist. One of the biggest problems of Aristotelian

poetics, as explained by such theorists as Bertolt Brecht, is that spectators get immersed in the stories and lose their critical distance from what is happening on the stage or screen. Of course, this effect is seen as narcotic only by authors whose intentions go further than simple entertainment and want to trigger critical thinking in their audience — for educational, social, and/or political reasons. The current tendency of the videogame industry is definitively Aristotelian: immersion needs to be increased by creating more realistic graphics and sounds.

In *Life on the Screen* (1995), a brilliant study in how people deal with computers and simulations, Sherry Turkle envisioned the possibility of using simulations for players to analyze and question their ideological assumptions:

> But one can imagine a third response. This would take the cultural pervasiveness of simulation as a challenge to develop a more sophisticated social criticism. This new criticism would not lump all simulations together, but would discriminate among them. It would take as its goal the development of simulations that actually help players challenge the model's built-in assumptions. This new

87

antagonistic relationship with educational children's media, both at the institutional level (capitalist/private versus nonprofit/public), and at the level of explicit representational content. This antagonism is a force in everyday negotiations about play versus homework, what software makes it into the schools, or whether a game should be marketed as an entertainment, kids, or educational title. In other words, videogames function as political actors in a wide range of settings that extend beyond moments of game play.

At the end of his paper, Frasca ruminates on the difficulties of getting people to engage deeply with the videogaming medium in the form of programming. Clearly this is a key barrier to the types of social engagements that Frasca envisions. Again Comiket strikes a hopeful note. The content at Comiket spans

gender categories and a broad range of genres such as Action, Romance, and Fantasy, and the technical sophistication of the productions is often on par with professional comic production. My hope, my belief even, is that if people identify with the content, have a compelling investment, and a degree of organization, they will overcome substantial technical obstacles.

As Frasca reminds us, it is not just the design of games that creates new social possibilities, but the ways in which this content gets mobilized by players. Frasca's proposals are perhaps most radical as a call for changing the social and economic conditions in which games get produced and played, even more than as a call for different sorts of game content. His example of critical engagement with *The Sims* importantly relies on an open-source model. In addition to considering how

criticism would try to use simulation as a means of consciousness-raising. (71)

These alternative simulations imagined by Turkle are not yet available on the computer. Interestingly, they are available somewhere else. For more than three decades, Brazilian playwright and drama theorist Augusto Boal has developed the "Theater of the Oppressed," an original form of theater that combines theater and simulation in order to produce social and political simulations. He built his techniques based on the Marxist theater tradition developed by Bertolt Brecht, as well as on Paulo Freire's *Pedagogy of the Oppressed* (1970).

Bertolt Brecht's drama challenged Aristotle's ideas; as mentioned previously, he argued that Aristotelian theater keeps the audience immersed without giving them a chance to take a step back and critically think about what is happening on the stage. Brecht created several techniques in order to alienate what is familiar in the play, constantly reminding the spectators that they were experiencing a representation and stimulating them to think about what they were watching. Brecht's techniques, however, were not exclusively targeted at the audience. He also encouraged performers to be completely aware of their actions. Instead of being "inside the skin" of the character, he

encouraged having a critical distance that would let them understand their role.

Brazilian dramatist Augusto Boal (1971) took Brecht's ideas even further by creating a set of techniques, known as the "Theater of the Oppressed" (TO), that tear down the stage's "fourth wall." Boal's main goal is to foster critical thinking and break the actor/spectator dichotomy by creating the "spect-actor," a new category that integrates both by giving them active participation in the play. The repertoire of techniques of TO is extremely large and includes, among others, the "invisible theater" — where actors work "undercover" in public spaces — and the "Forum Theater."

Forums are created around a short play (five to 10 minutes long), usually scripted on-site, and based on the suggestions of the participants. The scene always enacts an oppressive situation, where the protagonist has to deal with powerful characters that do not let her achieve her goals. For example, the play could be about a housewife whose husband forbids her to go out with her friends. The scene is enacted without showing a solution to the problem. After one representation, anybody in the audience can take over the role of the protagonist and suggest, through her acting, a solution that she thinks would break the oppression. Since the problems are complex, the solutions are generally

---

game design can support player tinkering, we could also consider the political, social, and economic arrangements necessary for such activity. What kinds of economic and institutional arrangements can support critical player engagement? How could we fund open-source game design and game communities? How can we make videogame hacking an accessible and legitimate enterprise outside of the core game community?

Yes, there is much to be done, and it is encouraging to see Gonzalo Frasca is working in this space.

From Eric Zimmerman's Online Response

If, as I believe, existing digital games are riddled with ideological baggage, why not use one of the many open-game creation systems commercially available? *Zillions of Games* <http://www.zillions-of-games.com> is a software package that lets users design the art and create the rulesets of turn-based multiplayer games. *Adventure Game Engine* <http://www.twilightsoftware.com> lets players script complex multimedia adventure games. *Game Maker* <http://www.cs.uu.nl/people/markov/gmaker/> is a free software package that lets players create action games. Similar nondigital game exercises exist as well, such as *STARPOWER*, a classroom exercise that explores power, economics, and society though the

incomplete. This is why the process is repeated several times, always offering a new perspective on the subject. In Boal's (1992) own words: "It is more important to achieve a good debate than a good solution." It is central to stress that Boal uses theater as a tool, not as a goal per se. In other words, the ultimate objective of Forum Theater plays is not to produce beautiful or enjoyable performances, but rather to promote critical discussions among the participants. Unlike traditional theater that offers just one complete, closed sequence of actions, Forum Theater sessions show multiple perspectives on a particular problem. They do not show "what happened" but rather "what could happen." It is a theater that stresses the possibility of change, at both social and personal levels.

For these reasons, TO is a perfect model for creating non-Aristotelian, nonimmersive videogames. Earlier in this essay, I criticized other authors that explain games through narrative and theater, and here I am proposing a drama model for videogames! However, while Boal certainly uses theater techniques, his work is closer to games and simulation than to theater. As performance theorist Philip Auslander argues, Boal had to give up performance altogether in order to bridge the gap between performers and spectators (Auslander, 1999). Forum Theater is nothing but a game, with specific rules, that uses theater to simulate certain events and behaviors. Without a single line of computer code, Boal created a Third World, non-Aristotelian version of the Holodeck. And the best thing about it is that it actually works.

The Search for a Social and Political Logo
Certainly, the idea of using simulation and videogames for educational purposes is far from new and was already extensively explored by constructionism. The idea was developed by Seymour Papert through *Mindstorms* (1985) and Logo, and it was continued by such authors as Yasmin Kafai (Kafai 1995), whose students learned mathematics through videogame design. The main problem with constructionism is that it was not designed for dealing with social and humanities education. This can be easily explained by many factors, including Papert's own background as a mathematician and the election of the computer as their main tool. Certainly, Kafai's students had to research Greek mythology to create their videogames, but this was mainly a side effect, because their focus was on mathematics. In fact constructionism's main success stories are in the field of science education, and it does not seem to be the ideal environment for critically discussing human and social matters.

Paulo Freire's pedagogy was developed about the same time as constructionism. In fact, they share many

programmed breakdown of social game rules (Ellington, Addinal, Percival, 1982). [. . .]

In his second proposal, Frasca seems to exhibit a fundamental misunderstanding of the way that games function. Near the beginning of presenting his *Sims*-based "videogame of the oppressed," he laments the many "constraints" of *The Sims*. Actually, constraints are the raw material out of which games are made. This misstep leads to other problems.

http://www.electronicbookreview.com/thread/firstperson/zimmermanr1

Frasca Responds

Mods and hacks certainly could help to develop "videogames of the oppressed" but the top-down approach is also needed. We will not see critical videogames until major games are developed by biased authors that understand that fun is not the only thing that could be conveyed through this medium.

http://www.electronicbookreview.com/thread/firstperson/frascar2

characteristics. However, Freire had different goals (mainly adult literacy and the development of critical attitudes towards reality in order to attain social change) and settings (the Brazilian Nordeste, one of the poorest places of the world). Unlike constructionism, his pedagogy offers great tools for critical discussion and social awareness — but it is not as well suited for science education.

What I am proposing here is to use Boalian techniques to develop a complementary approach to constructionism that would allow the use of videogames as tools for education and sociopolitical awareness. To create a simile with Logo, I argue that we need an engaged, political Logo. We need an environment that engages children in questioning the ideological assumptions of videogames. We need a political microworld where it would matter if the turtle turns left or right. In the next sections, I introduce two examples on how Boalian techniques could be brought to the computer. Please note that both systems are hypothetical and serve only as an illustration of the potential of non-Aristotelian videogames.

Forum Videogames

The following technique is a computer-based equivalent of Boal's Forum Theater that uses videogame rather than drama. Instead of performing on a stage, participants would discuss real-life situations by creating videogames and then modifying them in order to reflect their personal points of view.

Forum Videogames could work as a feature available inside a bigger "Videogames of the Oppressed" online community. It would be targeted to a homogenous small group — for example, a class of high school teenagers — coordinated by a moderator. Any participant — who will be referred as the "protagonist" — would be able to start a forum. The protagonist would be able to design one or a series of videogames where she would try to simulate a problematic situation that she is trying to deal with. The process of videogame design would be done by modifying preexistent templates based on classic videogames (*Space Invaders*, *Street Fighter*, *Pac-Man*, etc.).

Once the game is ready, the protagonist would post it online, allowing the rest of the group to play with it. Players would be able to post their written comments and even submit a modified version of the game that reflects their personal position towards the protagonist's problem. The modified version could be a variant of the protagonist's original game, or a brand new game based on a different template. The process would repeat many times, just as it happens in Forum Theater, triggering new designs and discussions.

For example, let's imagine that the protagonist's problem is that he is being bullied at school and he doesn't know how to deal with this. In order to simulate his problem, he could use a *Pac-Man* template and modify the original game. He would replace the Pac-Man with a cartoon version of himself and replace the ghosts with images of his harassers. In addition to this, he could also take away the score feature and the pills, leaving nothing but a labyrinth where he is being constantly chased. Once that game is posted online, the other members of the group could respond by creating variants. One of them could be to modify the structure of the labyrinth to create a small space where the protagonist could live isolated, safe from the bullies. But other players could say that this means giving up his freedom and, therefore, that it is not a good solution. Then, another player could suggest using violence, by introducing weapons on the environment. Another may suggest introducing more players (several Pac-Mans) who would stick together and defend themselves as a group of virtual vigilantes. Of course, somebody may argue that it is technically impossible to be all the time surrounded by your friends: the bullies will find you alone sooner or later.

Again, the goal of these games is not to find appropriate solutions, but rather serve to trigger discussions — which could take place in person or through online chat. It would not matter if the games could not simulate the situation with realistic accuracy. Instead, these games would work as metonyms that could guide discussions and serve to explore alternative ways of dealing with real life issues.

Simulating Characters in The Sims

The Sims represents a breakthrough in videogame design. For the first time, a best-selling game is not about trolls and wizards. This simulation is about regular people — known as Sims — in everyday situations in an American, suburban environment.

In my opinion, *The Sims*'s biggest achievement was that it fully opened the Pandora's box of simulating human life. Although structurally *The Sims* is similar to other resource management simulations, the fact that it portrays people, and not aliens, results in players asking questions about the game's ideology. Is it okay to let a Sim starve to death? Is it possible to have same-sex Sims relationships? What about threesomes? Will I spoil my Sim child if I buy her too many toys? All these questions would have probably never been asked if the game had been about monsters or aliens. The fact that the best-selling game of the year 2000 was about people is a clear sign that videogames are on their way towards maturity.

For ages, our civilization has been learning to deal with the issues of representation, including concerns about its accuracy and its limits. Videogames like *The Sims* are introducing to the masses a different form of representation — simulation — which has always been present in our culture through games, but that now can dare to start modeling more complex systems, such as human life. Even if *The Sims* is a very limited model of human relationships, it is a harbinger of videogames as a mature communicational and artistic form.

The Sims's constraints are many. For example, Sims cannot communicate in a verbal language and their personal relationships are not described with depth. In addition, the consumerist ideology that drives the simulation is nothing short of disturbing: the amount of friends that you have literally depends on the number of goods that you own and the size of your house. Nevertheless, simulation is an extremely complex task and, despite its shortcomings, *The Sims* succeeds at delivering an enjoyable game involving human characters.

The game allows players to create their own skins and designs and then share them online. However, the designers did not create an open environment where players could modify the rules of the simulation by coding new behaviors and objects. This is understandable from a marketing perspective: software companies want both to retain authorial control over their productions and to prevent players from creating controversial materials.

What follows is a description of how a hypothetical, open-source, modified version of *The Sims* could serve as an environment for players to distance themselves from the representation and engage in critical discussions. My intention is to show that Boal's ideas could also be used in mainstream videogame design. Although my previous example was better suited for small groups, educational or therapeutic environments, this one could appeal to a larger community of players.

In traditional videogames, the player "is" the character. In *The Sims* the player can control the character in a less direct way. However, *The Sims*'s characters are generally flat, because most of their differences are based either on their moods, or on visual traits that do not affect their behavior. This would be solved if players had more control over character creation by deciding their behavioral rules instead of just selecting their clothes. In order to encourage critical debate, the modified version of *The Sims* that I propose would allow players to modify the internal rules of the characters. The basic gameplay would be similar to the current game but, in addition to downloadable objects and skins, it would also be possible to get user-designed characters with different personalities and particular sets of actions. These characters would be created with a special tool that would require programming. Players would be able to rate the different characters and even create their own versions, based on behavioral details that they think need improvement in order to attain a higher level of realism. Both behaviors and comments would be available online in a "Character Exchange" site.

A Sample Scenario

The following is a sample scenario of a particular session, based on the rules that I am proposing:

Agnes has been playing with the simulation for many days. She knows its basic dynamics and enjoys it. Nevertheless, she feels that it would be better if family relationships were more realistic. So, she goes to the "Character Exchange" web site and browses through different characters. She finds one that looks interesting. It is called "Dave's Alcoholic Mother version 0.9," and it has the following description:

> This mother spends a lot of time working, and she is very tired when she gets back home. Still, every night she has to fix dinner and do some housecleaning. She can get very annoyed by children and pets and may become violent. In order to escape from her reality, she drinks a lot of bourbon.

Agnes considers giving it a try and downloads it into one of the houses with which she has been playing. Agnes's virtual household is composed of a couple, three children, and a cat. After the download, her original mother character is replaced by "Dave's Alcoholic Mother version 0.9." Agnes finds the character quite interesting. After playing with it for a while, she realizes that when the mother reaches a certain degree of fatigue, she starts drinking. The more she drinks, the less she will care about her family. She remains calm unless her husband insists on cuddling or giving her a back rub.

Although Agnes thinks that the character is pretty well-depicted, there are details that she does not agree with. For example, the character always gets her drinks from the little bar in the living room. Agnes knows from personal experience that, in general, alcoholics hide their bottles around the house and try not to drink in public. So, she goes back to the "Character Exchange" and writes a public critique of Dave's creation. After doing this, she tries alternative alcoholic-mother behaviors. If the available characters do not satisfy her, she can modify one of the available versions and introduce a new behavior that makes the mother hide her alcohol bottles. She can then post this new character online and make it available to other players.

Some weeks later, Agnes gets a little tired of playing with her character and wants to give her some more personality. So, she decides that it would be great if she could add some extra behavioral code to it. Agnes downloads a character described as "Peter's Radical Greenpeace Activist version 9.1." After some editing and modifications, Agnes introduces this behavior to her alcoholic-mother character. The new character would still be an alcoholic, but she would take more care of plants, recycle everything and would never kick her cat while drunk.

The Problems of Simulation Building

As I previously said, the biggest obstacle for building Boalian videogames lies in the fact that programming simulated behaviors is an extremely difficult and time-consuming task. Even with a design tool that involved templates or some kind of visual object-oriented programming, it is likely that the average player would consider the task overwhelming. Still, as Amy Bruckman's (1998) work on *MOOSE Crossing* — an object-oriented, multi-user dungeon where participants can modify the environment by creating new objects — suggests, players can become really involved with programming simulated features and will exchange tips and help with others who are less skilled programmers.

Although it is possible that certain players could deal with the programming of new behaviors, it is likely that most participants would only be able to download behaviors made by others. I think that even if most players would not be able to code their own features, they could at least tinker with preexisting behaviors. The fact that a single behavior such as alcoholism could be available in so many different versions from players from different social and cultural backgrounds would encourage players to think about issues such as social construction of reality — but also about defending their points of view and listening to alternative opinions.

Of course, the lack of programming proficiency is not the only problem that Boalian videogame designers

Critical Simulation>
Penny
Frasca
Sengers
Thacker Hayles
Ito Zimmerman
Suchman Mateas

III. Critical Simulation

would face. However, the popularity of simulators such as *The Sims* or *SimCity* may serve as a tool for transforming the perception of videogames from interactive narratives into simulated models. As the public becomes more familiar with manipulating and modifying simulations, the concept of designing their own may become more appealing.

Conclusion: Videogames of Tolerance

The two examples that I just gave should be considered more as illustrations of the paths that could be taken in order to design Boalian videogames than as blueprints for actual systems. The main goal of these examples is to show that videogames could be used as tools for better understanding reality and raising critical awareness among players. Current Aristotelian videogame design paradigms such as immersion should not be taken for granted, since questioning the values and mechanics of videogames could also be a source of engagement for players.

The main problem with these examples is that they require players to be very good programmers, a prerequisite that might be impossible to attain. Nevertheless, there may be some possible solutions to this problem. Further details on these techniques can be found in "Videogames of the Oppressed," a thesis (Frasca 2001) developed at the Georgia Institute of Technology and on which this article is based (available at <www.ludology.org>).

When I describe these ideas to fellow researchers or game designers, they usually ask me if I really believe that social and personal change is possible through videogames. My answer is always a straight "no." Neither art not games can change reality, but I do believe that they can encourage people to question it and to envision possible changes.

Unlike narrative, simulations are a kaleidoscopic form of representation that can provide us with multiple and alternative points of view. By accepting this paradigm, players can realize that there are many possible ways to deal with their personal and social reality. Hopefully, this might lead to the development of a tolerant attitude that accepts multiplicity as the rule and not the exception.

Note

1. I am often criticized for using the term "simulation" in a very broad sense, particularly by colleagues with a computer science background. Traditionally, simulations model real systems and connote an intention of scientific understanding. When I use the term it is in order to describe a different form of representation and, as in modern semiotics, I do not see the need for a real referent. Just as the word "unicorn" lacks a real referent, I say that *Mario Brothers* simulates an imaginary dynamic system (the Mario world).

References: Literature

Aarseth, Espen (1997). *Cybertext: Perspectives on Ergodic Literature*. Baltimore: John Hopkins, 1997.

Aristotle, *Poetics* (1967). Ann Arbor: University of Michigan Press.

Auslander, Philip (1999). "Boal, Blau, Brecht: the Body." In *Playing Boal*, edited by Mady Schutzman and Jan Cohen-Cruz. London: Routledge.

Boal, Augusto (1992). *Games for Actors and Non-Actors*. London: Routledge.

Boal, Augusto (1985). *Theatre of the Oppressed*. New York: TCG.

Bruckman, Amy (1998). *Community Support for Constructionist Learning*. <http://www.cc.gatech.edu/fac/Amy.Bruckman/papers/cscw.html>.

Ellington, Henry, Eric Addinal, and Fred Percival (1982). *A Handbook of Game Design*. London: Kogan Page Limited.

Eskelinen, Markku (2001). "The Gaming Situation." *Game Studies* 1, no.1 (July 2001). <http://cmc.uib.no/gamestudies/0101/eskelinen/>

Eskelinen, Markku, and Raine Koskimaa, editors (2001). *Cybertext Yearbook 2000*. Saarijärvi: Publications of the Research Centre for Contemporary Culture, University of Jyväskylä.

Frasca, Gonzalo (1998). "Don't play it again, Sam: One-session games of Narration." <http://cmc.uib.no/dac98/papers/frasca.html>.

Frasca, Gonzalo (2001). "Videogames of the Oppressed." M.A. Thesis: School of Literature, Communication and Culture, Georgia Institute of Technology, Atlanta (2001). <http://www.jacaranda.org/frasca/thesis/>.

Frasca, Gonzalo (1999). "Narratology meets Ludology: Similitude and Differences Between (Video)games and Narrative." *Parnasso* 3: 365-371. <http://www.jacaranda.org/frasca/ludology.htm>.

Freire, Paulo (2000). *Pedagogy of the Oppressed*. New York: Continuum.

Jenkins, Henry (1992). *Textual Poachers: Television Fans and Paricipatory Culture*. New York: Routledge.

Kafai, Yasmin (1995). *Minds in Play: Computer Game Design as a Context for Children's Learning*. Mahwah, NJ: Lawrence Erlbaum Associates, Inc.

Laurel, Brenda (1991). *Computers as Theatr*e. London: Addison Wesley.

Manovich, Lev (2001). *The Language of New Media*. Cambridge: The MIT Press.

Murray, Janet (1997). *Hamlet on the Holodeck*. New York: Free Press.

Papert, Seymour (1985). *Mindstorms: Children, Computers, and Powerful Ideas*. New York: Basic Books.

Penley, Constance (1991). "Brownian Motion: Women, Tactics, and Technology." In *Technoculture*, edited by Constance Penley and Alex Ross. Minneapolis: University of Minnesota Press.

Spiegelman, Art (1993). *Maus: A Survivor's Tale*. New York: Pantheon Books.

Tulloch, John, and Henry Jenkins (1995). *Science Fiction Audiences: Watching* Doctor Who *and* Star Trek. New York: Routledge, 1995.

Turkle, Sherry (1995). *Life on the Screen: Identity in the Age of the Internet*. New York: Simon and Schuster.

Willet, John, editor (1995). *Brecht on Theatre: The Development of an Aesthetic*. New York: Hill and Wang.

References: Games

The Sims. Will Wright; Electronic Arts. 2000.
<http://thesims.ea.com>.

SimCity 2000. Will Wright; Electronic Arts. 1995.

94

Schizophrenia and Narrative in Artificial Agents
Phoebe Sengers

Introduction

In recent years, computer graphics has turned to AI techniques in order to simplify the problem of determining the movements of objects for rendering (Blumberg and Galyean 1995; Perlin and Goldberg 1996; Reynolds 1999). By modeling the minds of graphically represented creatures, their movements can be determined automatically through AI algorithms, and need not be directly controlled by the designer. But what kind of baggage do these AI algorithms bring with them? Here I argue that predominant AI approaches to modeling agents result in behavior that is fragmented, depersonalized, lifeless, and incomprehensible. Drawing inspiration from narrative psychology and antipsychiatry, I argue that agent behavior should be narratively understandable, and present an agent architecture that structures behavior to be comprehensible as narrative.

The approach I take in this essay is a hybrid of critical theory and AI agent technology. It is one example of a *critical technical practice* (Agre 1997), instantiating a cultural critique of AI practice in a technological innovation. In the final section of this essay, I describe the theoretical and practical foundations of the critical technical practice pursued here, which I term *socially situated AI*.

The premise of this work is that there is something deeply missing from AI, or more specifically, from the currently dominant ways of building artificial agents. This uncomfortable intuition has been with me for a long time, perhaps from my start as an AI researcher, although for most of that time I was not able to articulate it clearly. Artificial agents seem to be lacking a primeval awareness, a coherence of action over time, something one might — for lack of a better metaphor — term "soul."

Roboticist Rodney Brooks expresses this worry eloquently:

> Perhaps it is the case that all the approaches to building intelligent systems are just completely off-base, and are doomed to fail.... [C]ertainly it is the case that all biological systems.... [b]ehave in a way which just simply seems *life-like* in a way that our robots never do.

Response by Lucy Suchman:
Methods and Madness

Just-so stories, Harold Garfinkel has argued, are the stuff of which the professional social and behavioral sciences are made. As a genre, these narratives contrast with detailed investigations of the specificities of in situ, ordinary activities, organized through what Garfinkel names "ethno," or members' "methods" (Garfinkel 1996). The latter are the contingent practices through which the mundane intelligibility, or mutual accountability, of everyday life is (more and less successfully) achieved. In "Schizophrenia and Narrative in Artificial Agents," Phoebe Sengers sets out to deepen our understanding of ethnomethods as the shared subject matter of (anti)psychiatry and of AI. Inspired by Phil Agre's project of "instantiating a cultural critique of AI practice in a technological innovation," Sengers takes on the fascinating and potentially illuminating strategy of reading across the literatures of narrative psychology and agent systems, trying to draw out their mutual relevances. More specifically, she draws an analogy between the antipsychiatry movement's argument to the effect that institutional psychiatric practices in fact reproduce rather than relieve the symptoms of "schizophrenia," and a critique of mainstream AI as effectively creating an artificially "lifeless" and incomprehensible form of agency. The alternative for both, she proposes, is an approach that takes "narrative" as the foundation of personal and social integration.

Perhaps we have all missed some organizing principle of biological systems, or some general truth about them. Perhaps there is a way of looking at biological systems which will illuminate an inherent necessity in some aspect of the interactions of their parts that is completely missing from our artificial systems.... [P]erhaps at this point we simply do not *get it*, and... there is some fundamental change necessary in our thinking... [P]erhaps we are currently missing the *juice* of life.
(Brooks 1997, 299–300)

Here, I argue that the "juice" we are missing is *narrative*. The divide-and-conquer methodologies currently used to design artificial agents result in fragmented, depersonalized behavior, which mimics the fragmentation and depersonalization of schizophrenia in institutional psychiatry. Antipsychiatry and narrative psychology suggest that the fundamental problem for both schizophrenic patients and artificial agents is that observers have difficulty understanding them narratively. This motivates my narrative agent architecture, the *Expressivator*, which structures agent behavior to support narrative, thereby creating agents that are intentionally comprehensible.

The Problem

Building complex, integrated artificial agents is one of the dreams of AI. Classically, complex agents are constructed by identifying functional components — natural language processing, vision, planning, etc. — designing and building each separately, then integrating them into an agent. More recently, some practitioners have argued that the various components of an agent strongly constrain one another, and that the complex functionalities classical AI could come up with could not easily be coordinated into a whole system. They offer other construction methodologies instead. In particular, behavior-based AI proposes that the agent should be split up, not into disparate cognitive functionalities, but into behaviors, each of which integrates all of the agent's functions for a particular behavior in which the agent engages. Examples of such behaviors include foraging, sleeping, and hunting.

Even such systems, however, have not been entirely successful in building agents that integrate a wide range of behaviors. Rod Brooks, for example, has stated that one of the challenges of the field is to find a way to build an agent that can integrate many behaviors, where he defines many to be more than a dozen (Brooks 1990). Programmers can create robust, subtle, effective, and expressive behaviors, but the agent's overall behavior tends to gradually fall apart as more

---

There follows a brilliant interweaving of the projects of psychiatry and of AI, along with suggestions for how the critique of one might shed light on the other. But as the narrative unfolds, I find myself experiencing a deepening sense of disorientation. It's not only that the figure of a "discarded lamp" in an Industrial Graveyard takes on the persona of "the Patient," and finds its/her/himself in a relation of codependent sado-masochism with an unspecified figure named "the Overseer." It's that I am now positioned, without warning or transition, as a kind of "user"-voyeur for whom the Patient's life is written, by an equally omniscient and regulatory "designer"-creator. "Behaviors," which have earlier been problematized for their overly stabilized, fragmented and insular properties, are increasingly animated until they are

engaged in an uneasy collective of their own. Their ability to "kill other behaviors that are not appropriate" makes it possible for them to be aligned, through the device of "metalevel controls," into the aggregate entity of the Patient performing as a rationally accountable actor. "Narrative" as a term that referred to the ongoing achievement of intelligibility in the course of action and interaction slides into "narrative" in the sense of the animated theater, and "agents" slip, without transition, from the subjects of psychological and (anti)psychiatric discourse to the cartoon creations of an unseen master's artful and authoritative hand.

Extraordinarily, in the process, Phoebe Senger's paper reenacts the very experience that it describes. Like the psychiatrist facing the schizophrenic patient, the multiple narratives that the paper presents pose

and more behaviors are combined. For small numbers of behaviors, this disintegration can be managed by the programmer, but as more and more behaviors are combined, their interactions become so complex that they become at least time-consuming and at worst impossible to manage.

In both cases, divide-and-conquer methodologies lead to integration problems. With classical agents, who are split up by functionality, there are often problems with a functional underintegration. This underintegration manifests itself in various kinds of inconsistency between the different functions, such as not being able to use knowledge for one function that is available for another. For example, the agent may speak a word it cannot understand or visibly register aspects of the world that do not affect its subsequent behavior. In behavior-based agents, underintegration manifests itself on the behavioral level. These agents generally have a set of black-boxed behaviors. Following the action-selection paradigm, agents continuously redecide which behavior is most appropriate. As a consequence, they tend to jump around from behavior-to-behavior according to which one is currently the best.[1]

What this means is that the overall character of behavior of the agent ends up being deficient; generally speaking, its behavior consists of short dalliances in individual, shallow high-level behaviors with abrupt

changes between behaviors. It is this overall defective nature of agent behavior, caused by underintegration of behavioral units, that I term *schizophrenia* and propose to address here.

Schizophrenia is a loaded term. I use it here to draw attention to important connections between current approaches to agent-building and the experience of being schizophrenic in institutional psychiatry. In the next two sections, I draw out those connections, then show how an alternative approach to psychiatric schizophrenia can motivate changes in AI practice. These changes form the basis for narrative agent architecture.

Schizophrenia

Schizophrenia's connection to AI is grounded in one of its more baffling symptoms — the *sentimente d'automatisme*, or subjective experience of being a machine (Janet 1889). This feeling is the flip side of AI's hoped-for machinic experience of being subjective, and is described by one patient this way: "`I am unable to give an account of what I really do, everything is mechanical in me and is done unconsciously. I am nothing but a machine'" (an anonymous schizophrenic patient; Ronell 1989, 118).

R. D. Laing describes how some schizophrenic patients experience or fear experiencing themselves as

97

increasingly insurmountable problems of integration for me as reader. Two larger fragments — a critical project and the account of an agent system — sit side-by-side in uneasy (dis)association. As a reader I find myself following with growing interest the unfolding narrative of schizophrenia and its implications for AI, when I'm suddenly thrown without warning, like Alice through the looking-glass, into a world of agent systems-building, motivated by that world's characters, problems, projects, and prospects.

The latter narrative becomes increasingly incomprehensible until I realize that this is not a story that can be resolved into any single, familiar frame. What if, I find myself asking at the end, Phoebe Sengers' story were renarrated not as the design of an agent system, but along the lines that she herself

recommends at the close of her paper; that is, as the design of a new genre of computationally dynamic, communicative animation? What would be lost, and what would be gained, and how might the story be a different one? And how might I, at least, be able to follow it more successfully?

And what, to return to where we started, might the prospects be for working together the insights of narrative psychology/antipsychiatry and AI? A first step, I believe, is to recognize the profound difference between a textual (or even dynamically graphical) narrative, designed to support comprehension, and the coproduction of mutual intelligibility. As Sengers points out, for most of us there is no invisible hand stipulating our "intentions" or "reasons" for action, or setting the parameters of behavioral "simplicity," or assessing things, as "its," instead of as people (Laing 1960). Schizophrenia is, for some, a frightening feeling of being drained of life, of being reduced to a robot or automaton.

This feeling of mechanicity is correlated with a fragmentation of the affected patient's being; sometimes, a schizophrenic patient's very subjectivity seems to be split apart.

> In listening to Julie, it was often as though one were doing group psychotherapy with the one patient. Thus I was confronted with a babble or jumble of quite disparate attitudes, feelings, expressions of impulse. The patient's intonations, gestures, mannerisms, changed their character from moment to moment. One may begin to recognize patches of speech, or fragments of behaviour cropping up at different times, which seem to belong together by reason of similarities of the intonation, the vocabulary, syntax, the preoccupations in the utterance or to cohere as behaviour by reason of certain stereotyped gestures or mannerisms. It seemed therefore that one was in the presence of various fragments, or incomplete elements, of

different 'personalities' in operation at the one time. Her 'word-salad' seemed to be the result of a number of quasi-autonomous partial systems striving to give expression to themselves out of the same mouth at the same time. (Laing 1960, 195–196)

Laing goes on to describe Julie's existence in ways that are eerily similar to the problems with autonomous agents we discussed in the last section: "Julie's being as a chronic schizophrenic was... characterized by lack of unity and by division into what might variously be called partial 'assemblies,' complexes, partial systems, or 'internal objects.' Each of these partial systems had recognizable features and distinctive ways of its own" (Laing 1960, 197). Like the parts of behavior-based agents, each subsystem exists independently, with its own perception and action. Subsystems communicate, in Brooks's phraseology, "through the world," not by being integrated as a unified whole:

> Each partial system seemed to have within it its own focus or centre of awareness: it had its own very limited memory schemata and limited ways of structuring percepts; its own quasi-autonomous drives

whether our intentions have been "properly communicated." Nor can what has been communicated be definitively tracked and managed. Rather, as the case of the "schizophrenic" so clearly shows, our stories are always provisional and ultimately extremely fragile. Life is only metaphorically a story.

From Michael Mateas's Online Response

Sengers provides three postulates for SS-AI:

> An agent can only be evaluated with respect to its environment, which includes not only the objects with which it interacts, but also the creators and observers of the agent.

> An agent's design should focus, not on the agent itself, but on the dynamics of that agent with respect to its physical and social environments.

> An agent is a representation. [. . .]

or component drives; its own tendency to preserve its autonomy, and special dangers which threatened its autonomy. She would refer to these diverse aspects as "he," or "she," or address them as "you." That is, instead of having a reflective awareness of those aspects of herself, "she" would *perceive* the operation of a partial system as though it was not of "her", but belonged outside. (Laing 1960, 198)[2]

In this sense, there is a direct link between schizophrenia and behavior-based methodology — and symptomatology.

Depersonalization

While we can presume that artificial systems do not particularly care about being fragmented, for schizophrenic patients this feeling of coming apart, of losing life, of being reduced to a machine, is intensely painful. It is therefore ironic that, as a number of critics have argued, psychiatric institutions themselves reinforce this feeling of mechanicity and lack of autonomous self. For example, Erving Goffman, in his ground-breaking anthropological study *Asylums*, argues that a major feature of psychiatric institutions is the "programming" of each inmate "into an object that can

be fed into the administrative machinery of the establishment, to be worked on smoothly by routine operations." (Goffman, 16)

One of the signs of this mechanization is the reduction of patient to symptomatology. Patients are constantly monitored, their behavior continuously being examined for and interpreted as signs of illness. The patient's actions only function insofar as they are informational — they only *act* as ciphers, which it is then the responsibility and right of the doctor to decode. Rather than being taken seriously as such, a patient's words are used to place the patient in the narrative of the doctor's diagnosis. "When you spoke, they judged your words as a delusion to confirm their concepts." (Robear 1991, 19)

Understood symptomatically, the patient's subjective experience is ignored. Susan Baur describes this limitation of the institutional approach to mental illness:

> I... believe that the medical model of mental illness excludes too much of the patient. Using this model, only parts of the patient are considered, and even when these parts are assembled by a multidisciplinary team into a manikin of a schizophrenic or of a manic-depressive, the

99

How fundamental is SS-AI's focus on agency and the associated critique of autonomy to SS-AI as a practice? What would it mean to extend SS-AI to other metaphor clusters within AI? In the three postulates of SS-AI, if one just replaced the word "agent" with the phrase "AI system," what would this change? Do the three postulates summarize the results of the analysis of autonomy (i.e., schizoanalysis, the analysis of institutionalization, the application of narrative psychology) or do they serve as a framework within which many humanistic interventions (perhaps not organized around the notion of agent) can be made, with the analysis of autonomy as a concrete instance?

http://www.electronicbookreview.com/thread/firstperson/mateasr1

Sengers Responds

Yes, life is not a story, and therefore, by extension, the Patient is not alive. The lesson from the critique from anti-psychiatry and narrative psychology for Artificial Intelligence is the danger of assuming that life can be cleanly understood and implemented, represented, as Lucy Suchman says, by an "omniscient and regulatory 'designer'-creator."

http://www.electronicbookreview.com/thread/firstperson/sengersr2

spirit that animates the real person gets lost. Especially in chronic cases where mental illness and the desperately clever adaptations it inspires have become central to an individual's personality, the patient's own story and explanations — his delusions and imaginary worlds — must be included. (Baur 1991, 105–106)

The patient is formalized, reduced to a set of somewhat arbitrarily connected symptoms. The patient is no longer a living, unique, complex individual, but fragmented into a pile of signs: "she is autistic," "she shows signs of depersonalization," or "she lacks affect."

This fragmentation into symptoms, Laing argues, actually reinforces, rather than treats, schizophrenia. When mechanistic explanations reduce the patient to a bundle of pathological processes, the patient as human is rendered incomprehensible. Laing argues that institutional psychiatric practice cannot fully understand schizophrenia because it actually mimics schizophrenic ways of thinking, depersonalizing and fragmenting patients.

> The most serious objection to the technical vocabulary currently used to describe psychiatric patients is that it consists of words which split man up verbally in a way which is analogous to the existential splits we have to describe here.... [W]e are (then) condemned to start our study of schizoid and schizophrenic people with a verbal and conceptual splitting that matches the split up of the totality of the schizoid being-in-the-world. Moreover, the secondary verbal and conceptual task of reintegrating the various bits and pieces will parallel the despairing efforts of the schizophrenic to put his disintegrated self and world together again. (Laing 1960, 19–20)

By studying schizophrenics in isolation and in parts, psychiatry threatens to itself become schizophrenic,

and schizophrenics become incomprehensible.

This problem of conceptual splitting parallels closely the problem of AI, suggesting that mechanistic explanations of the sort necessary to build agents are also responsible for their de-intentionalized appearance. The symptomatology of institutional psychiatry is reflected in behavioral black-boxing in behavior-based AI. In the next section, we will explore alternatives to this fragmentation in psychiatry, searching for clues for dealing with the problem of schizophrenia in AI.

Antipsychiatry

In the 1960s and 1970s, Laing and other sympathetic colleagues, termed *antipsychiatrists* for their opposition to mainstream psychiatry, suggested that the schizophrenizing aspects of institutional psychiatry can be avoided by changing our viewpoint on patients: instead of thinking of schizophrenics as self-contained clusters of symptoms, we should try to understand them phenomenologically, as complex humans whose behavior is meaningful. The schizophrenizing clinical approach reifies the patient's behavior into a cluster of pathological symptoms, with no apparent relation to each other or the patient's broader life experience:

> [S]he had auditory hallucinations and was depersonalized; showed signs of catatonia; exhibited affective impoverishment and autistic withdrawal. Occasionally she was held to be "impulsive." (Laing and Esterson 1970, 32)

The phenomenological approach, on the other hand, tries to understand the patient's experience of herself as a person:

> [S]he experienced herself as a machine, rather than as a person: she lacked a sense of her motives, agency and intentions belonging together: she was very confused about her autonomous identity. She felt it necessary to move and speak with studious and scrupulous correctness. She sometimes felt that her thoughts were

controlled by others, and she said that not she but her "voices" often did her thinking. (*ibid.*)

Antipsychiatrists believe that statistics and symptomatology, the foundations of institutional psychiatry, are misleading because they reduce the patient to a mass of unrelated signs. Instead of leading to a greater understanding of the patient, the patient's subjective experiences are lost under a pile of unconnected data.

> It is just possible to have a thorough knowledge of what has been discovered about the hereditary or familial incidence of manic-depressive psychosis or schizophrenia, to have a facility in recognizing schizoid "ego distortion" and schizophrenic ego defects, plus the various "disorders" of thought, memory, perceptions, etc., to know, in fact, just about everything that can be known about the psychopathology of schizophrenia or of schizophrenia as a disease without being able to understand one single schizophrenic. Such data are all ways of *not* understanding him. (Laing and Esterson 1970, 33)

Instead of trying to extract objectively verifiable data about the patient, antipsychiatrists believe psychiatry should be based on *hermeneutics*, a subjective process of interpretation which aims for a better understanding of the way in which the schizophrenic patient experiences life. Laing finds that when schizophrenic patients are treated "subjectively" — that is to say, when attempts are made, not to catalog their symptoms, but to understand their phenomenological viewpoints, even when they include such apparently alien components as delusions or hallucinations — schizophrenia can be made much more comprehensible. In *Sanity, Madness, and the Family*, Laing and Esterson (1970) give eleven case studies of schizophrenic patients whose behavior, initially incomprehensible and

even frightening, is made understandable by putting it in the context of the patient's family life. For example, a patient with a delusion that other people are controlling her thoughts is found to live in a family where her parents undermine every expression of independent thought, telling her that they know better than her what she thinks.

This focus on hermeneutic interpretation rather than data extraction as a way of understanding intentional behavior can be applied to agent design. From this perspective, when we focus largely on the decomposition of agents' behavior into individually designed units, we will necessarily end up with fragmented and depersonalized agents. On the other hand, if we take an interpretive, holistic perspective to agents, we may be able to build agents without undermining their intentionality.

In solving the problem of schizophrenic agents, this is a lead — but only that. In order to make concrete changes in agent technology, we need to have a more exact understanding of what this change in "intentional stance" (Dennett 1987) means. We will use narrative psychology to specify the change in understanding suggested by antipsychiatry; this, it turns out, will give us a toehold in agent design.

Narrative Psychology

Narrative psychology, an area of study developed by Jerome Bruner (1986, 1990), focuses on how people interpret specifically intentional behavior. Narrative psychology shows that, whereas people tend to understand inanimate objects in terms of cause-effect rules and by using logical reasoning, intentional behavior is made comprehensible by structuring it into narrative or "stories." Narrative psychology suggests that this process of creating narrative is the fundamental difference between the way people understand intentional beings and mechanical artifacts.

That is to say, if I want to understand and build an inanimate object, I may decompose it, try to understand what different pieces are for, replicate how they work, and figure out the rules underlying its behavior. On the other hand, if I want to understand a person's behavior, I am interested in such things as what motivates him or her, the reasons he or she engages in particular activity, and how their behavior reflects on his or her whole personality.

This contrast between narrative explanations that explore the meaning of living activity and atomistic explanations that allow for the understanding and construction of mechanical artifacts provides a theoretical basis for the criticisms of antipsychiatry. Antipsychiatrists, after all, complain that the difficulty with institutional psychiatry is that it reduces the patient to a pile of data, thereby making a machine of a living person. The antipsychiatric solution of interpretation uses narrative understanding to "repersonalize" patients: structuring and relating the "data" of a patient's life into the semicoherent story of a meaningful, though painful, existence; focusing on the patient not as an instance of a disease but as a particular individual and how that person feels about his or her life experience; and relating the doctor's narrative to its background conditions and the life context in which it is created and understood. It is only through this process of narrative interpretation that antipsychiatry feels the psychiatrist can fully respect and understand the patient's subjective experience as a human being.

In AI, this distinction between mechanism and intentional being becomes problematic. AI agents should ideally be understandable both as well-specified physical objects and as sentient creatures. In order to understand intentional behavior, users attempt to construct narrative explanations of what the presumed intentional being is doing; but this approach conflicts with the mechanistic explanations designers themselves need to use in order to identify, structure, and replicate behavior. The resulting abrupt behavioral breaks create the (often correct) impression that there is no relationship between the agent's behaviors; rather than focusing on understanding the agent as a whole, the user is left to wonder how individually recognizable behaviors are related to each other and the agent's personality. Behaviors are designed in isolation and interleaved according to opportunity — but users, like it or not, attempt to interpret behaviors in sequence

and in relationship to each other. The result of this mismatch between agent design and agent interpretation is confusion and frustration on the part of the user and the destruction of apparent agent intentionality.

At this point, there seems to be a basic and unsolvable mismatch between fragmentation and intentionality. But narrative psychology suggests that the fundamental problem with current agent-building techniques is not simply recognizable fragmentation in and of itself, but rather that fragmented agents do not provide proper support for narrative interpretation. From this follows the major insight of this paper: *if humans understand intentional behavior by organizing it into narrative, then our agents will be more "intentionally comprehensible" if they provide narrative cues.* That is to say, rather than simply presenting intelligent actions, agents should give visible cues that support users in their ongoing mission to generate narrative explanation of an agent's activity. We can do this by organizing our agents so that their behavior provides the visible markers of narrative.

Narrative Agent Architecture

What does it mean for agents to support narrative comprehension? The properties of narrative are complex (Bruner 1991); elsewhere I have discussed in detail how they can apply to AI (Sengers 1998, 2000). For the sake of brevity, I will here limit discussion to the following properties:

Context-Sensitivity and Negotiability
In behavior-based systems, the "meaning" of a behavior is thought of as always the same: the name the designer gives the internally defined behavior. But in narrative comprehension, meaning is not a matter of identifying already-given symbols, but comes out of a complex process of negotiation between the interpreter and the events being interpreted. The meaning of the same event can change radically based on the context in which it occurs, as well as on the background, assumptions, knowledge, and perspective of the interpreter. In order to design narratively expressive

agents, designers must respect (rather than attempt to override) the context- and audience-dependency of narrative comprehension.

Intentional State Entailment
In most behavior-based systems, the reason a behavior is run is implicit in its action-selection mechanism. The behavior is then necessarily communicated to the user on a "just the facts, ma'am" basis: it is usually easy to see *what* an agent is doing, but hard to tell *why*. But in narrative, the reasons or motivations behind actions are just as important as — if not more so than — what is done. People do not want to know just the events that occur in the narrative, but also the motivations, thoughts, and feelings behind them. Supporting narrative comprehension means communicating clearly not just what the agent does, but its reason for doing it.

Diachronicity
Behavior-based agents jump from behavior to behavior according to what is currently optimal. Each of these behaviors is designed independently, with minimal interaction. But a fundamental property of narrative is its diachronicity; it relates events over time. In a narrative, events do not happen randomly and independently; they are connected to and affect one another. Narrative support in a behavior-based agent requires normally independent behaviors to be able to influence each other, to present a coherent picture of narrative development to the user over time.

These properties are the motivation for the Expressivator, an agent architecture that focuses on the narrative expression of agent behavior. The Expressivator is an extension of Bryan Loyall's Hap (Loyall 1997; Loyall and Bates 1991), a behavior-based language designed for believable agents. The Expressivator has been tested in the *Industrial Graveyard*, a virtual environment in which the Patient, a discarded lamp character implemented with the Expressivator, attempts to eke out a miserable existence while being bullied about by the Overseer, an agent implemented in Hap.

Generally, the Expressivator supports narrative comprehension using the following heuristic:

> Behaviors should be *as simple as possible*. The agent's life comes from thinking out the *connections* between behaviors and *displaying* them to the user.

Simpler behaviors are essential because complex processing is lost on the user. Most of the time, the user has a hard time picking up on the subtle differences in behavior that bring such pleasure to the heart of the computer programmer. But the properties of narrative interpretation mean that simpler behaviors are also enough. Because the user is very good at interpretation, minimal behavioral cues suffice.

More specifically, the Expressivator provides systematic support for narrative comprehensibility through the following mechanisms:

Context-sensitivity and negotiability
Rather than building an agent from conventional context- and communication-independent actions and behaviors, a designer builds agents from context-dependent *signs* and *signifiers* that are to be communicated to the user.

Intentional state entailment
Transitions are added between signifiers to explain why the agent's observed behavior is changing.

Diachronicity
Signifiers can use *metalevel controls* to influence one another, presenting a coherent behavioral picture over time.

Signs, Signifiers, and Sign Management
Typical behavior-based agents are designed for correctness, not for user comprehensibility. The first step the Expressivator takes in creating narratively understandable agents is to open the architecture up for communication. Agent design is based, not on the functions the agent must fulfill, but on its intended, context-dependent interpretation by the user. In the Expressivator, signs and signifiers support the

construction of clearly communicated behavior; sign management allows the agent itself to keep track of what has been communicated, so it can tailor subsequent behavioral communication to the user's current interpretation.

Signs and Signifiers
Current behavior-based approaches are based on an internal, problem-solving approach, and generally divide an agent into activities in which the agent likes to, or needs to, engage. Typical behavior-based systems divide an agent into three parts: (1) physical actions in which the agent engages; (2) low-level behaviors, which are the agent's simple activities; and (3) high-level behaviors, which combine low-level behaviors into high-level activities using more complex reasoning. Because these activities are implemented according to what makes sense from the agent's internal point of view, there is no necessary correlation between the agent's behaviors and the behaviors we would like the user to see in our agent.

But if the agent is to be narratively comprehensible, it may make more sense to design the agent according to the desired user interpretation, i.e. making the internal behaviors exactly those behaviors we want to communicate to the user. Then, communicating what the agent does reduces to the problem of making sure that each of these behaviors is properly communicated. For this reason, the Expressivator structures an agent not into physical actions and problem-solving behaviors, but into signs and signifiers, or units of action that are likely to be meaningful to the user. This structure involves three levels, roughly corresponding to those of generic behavior-based AI: (1) *signs*, which are small sets of physical actions that are likely to be interpreted in a particular way by the user; (2) *low-level signifiers*, which combine signs, physical actions, and mental actions to communicate particular immediate physical activities to the user; and (3) *high-level signifiers*, which combine low-level signifiers to communicate the agent's high-level activities.

There are several differences between these structural units and the default behavior-based ones.

Unlike physical actions and behaviors, signs and signifiers focus on what the user is likely to interpret, rather than what the agent is "actually" (i.e., internally) doing. In addition, signs and signifiers are context-dependent, the same physical movements may lead to different signs or signifiers, depending on the context in which the actions are interpreted. Most importantly, signs and signifiers carry an explicit commitment to communication; they require the agent designer to think about how the agent should be interpreted and to provide visual cues to support that interpretation.

Signs and signifiers are not simply design constructs; they also have technical manifestations. Formally, a sign is a token the system produces after having engaged in physical behavior that is likely to be interpreted in a particular way. This token consists of an arbitrary label and an optional set of arguments. The label, such as "noticed possible insult," is meaningful to the designer, and represents how the designer expects that physical behavior to be interpreted. The arguments (such as "would-be insulter is Wilma") give more information about the sign. This token is stored by the sign-management system described next, so that the agent can use it to influence its subsequent behavioral decisions. A low-level signifier is a behavior that is annotated with the special form "(with low_level_signifying...)"; a high-level signifier is similarly annotated "(with high_level_signifying...)". Signifiers can also generate tokens for the sign-management system, as described next.

Sign Management
Once a designer has structured an agent according to what it needs to communicate, agents can reason about what has been communicated in order to fine-tune the presentation of subsequent signs and signifiers. That is, by noting which signifiers have been communicated, agents can reason about the user's likely current interpretation of their actions and use this as a basis for deciding how to communicate subsequent activity.

The most obvious way for the agent to keep track of what the user thinks is for it simply to notice which signs and signifiers are currently running. After all, signifiers represent what is being communicated to the user. But it turns out in practice that this is not correct because the user's interpretation of signs and signifiers lags behind the agent's engagement in them. For example, if the agent is currently running a "head-banging" signifier, the user will need to see the agent smack its head a few times before realizing that the agent is doing it.

The sign-management system deals with this problem by having the agent *post* signs and signifiers when it believes the user must have seen them. A behavior can post a sign each time it has engaged in some physical actions that express that sign, using the "post_sign" language mechanism. Similarly, once signs have been posted that express a low-level signifier, behaviors use "post_low_level" to post that that low-level signifier has been successfully expressed. Once the right low-level signifiers have been posted to express a high-level signifier, "post_high_level" is used to post that high-level signifier.

Each of these commands causes a token to be stored in the agent's memory listing the current sign, low-level signifier, or high-level signifier, respectively, along with a time stamp. Once signs and signifiers have been posted, other behaviors can check to see what has been posted recently before they decide what to do. The result is that the signs and signifiers the agent has expressed can be used just like environmental stimuli and internal drives to affect subsequent behavioral presentation, tuning the agent's behavior to the user's interpretation.

Transitions

The second requirement of narrative comprehensibility is that the user should be able to tell why the agent is doing what it is doing. In behavior-based terms, every time an agent selects a particular behavior, it should express to the user the reason it is changing from the old behavior to the new one. This is difficult to do in most behavior-based systems because behaviors are designed and run independently; when a behavior is chosen, it has no idea who it succeeds, let alone why.

In the Expressivator, behavioral *transitions* are used to express the agent's reasoning. Transitions are special

behaviors that act to "glue" two signifying behaviors together. When a transition notices that it is time to switch between two signifiers, it takes over from the old signifier. Instead of switching abruptly to the new signifier, it takes a moment to express to the user the reason for the behavioral change.

Transitions are implemented in two parts, each of which is a full-fledged behavior: (1) *transition triggers*, that determine when it is appropriate to switch to another behavior for a particular reason, and (2) *transition daemons*, that implement the transition sequence that expresses that reason to the user. Transition triggers run in the background, generally checking which behaviors are running (e.g., ~exploring the world), and combining this information with sensory input about current conditions (e.g., ~the Overseer is approaching). When its conditions are fulfilled, the transition trigger adds a special token to memory, noting the behavior that should terminate, the behavior that should replace it, and a label that represents the reason for the replacement (e.g., "afraid_of_overseer").

Transition daemons monitor memory, waiting for a transition for a particular reason to be triggered. They then choose an appropriate behavioral expression for the reason for change, according to the current likely user interpretation and conditions in the virtual environment. Expressing the reasoning behind behavioral change often requires changes to subsequent behaviors; for example, if the Patient starts doing some odious task because it is forced to by the Overseer, it should include some annoyed glances at the Overseer as part of the task-fulfilling behavior. Transitions are able to express these kinds of interbehavioral influences using the metalevel controls described next.

Metalevel Controls

The third requirement of narrative comprehensibility is that behaviors should be structured into a coherent sequence. Instead of jumping around between apparently independent actions, the agent's activities should express some common threads. But these relationships between behaviors are difficult to express in most behavior-based systems because they treat individual behaviors as distinct entities that do not have access to each other. Conflicts and influences between behaviors are not handled by behaviors themselves but by underlying mechanisms within the architecture. Because the mechanisms that handle relationships between behaviors are part of the implicit architecture of the agent, they are not directly expressible to the user.

The Expressivator deals with this problem by giving behaviors *metalevel controls*, special powers to sense and influence each other. Because metalevel controls are explicitly intended for communication and coordination between behaviors, they are in some sense a violation of the behavior-based principle of minimal behavioral interaction. Nevertheless, metalevel controls are so useful for coordinating behavior that several have already found a home in behavior-based architectures. An example is Hamsterdam's meta-level commands, which allow nonactive behaviors to suggest actions for the currently dominant behavior to do on the side (Blumberg 1996). In the Expressivator, behaviors can (1) *query* which other behaviors have recently happened or are currently active; (2) *delete* other behaviors; (3) *add* new behaviors, not as sub-behaviors, but at the top level of the agent; (4) *add new subbehaviors* to *other* behaviors; (5) *change the internal variables* that affect the way in which other behaviors are processed; (6) *turn off* a behavior's ability to send motor commands; and 7) *move running subbehaviors* from one behavior to another.

The most important function for these metalevel controls in the Expressivator is to allow for the implementation of transitions. Transitions, at a minimum, need to be able to find out when an old behavior needs to be terminated, delete the old behavior, engage in some action, and then start a new behavior. This means that transition behaviors need to have all the abilities of a regular behavior, and a few more: (1) they need to be able to know what other behaviors are running; (2) they need to be able to delete an old behavior; and (3) they need to be able to begin a new behavior. Ideally, they should also be able to alter the new behavior's processing to reflect how it relates to what the agent was doing before. In the

Expressivator, transitions can do all these things with metalevel controls.

More generally, metalevel controls make the relationships between behaviors explicit, as much a part of the agent design as behaviors themselves. They allow behaviors to affect one another directly when necessary, rather than making interbehavioral effects subtle side-effects of the agent design. Metalevel controls give agent builders more power to expose the inner workings of agents by letting them access and then express aspects of behavior processing that other systems leave implicit.

Putting It All Together

Narrative psychology suggests that narrative comprehension is context-sensitive, focuses on agent motivation, and seeks connections between events over time. The Expressivator supports comprehensibility by expressing the agent's actions with signs and signifiers, the reasons for agent activity with transitions, and the coherent threads through activities with metalevel controls.

These architectural mechanisms are described separately, but used together in the agent design process, changing the way in which agents are designed. In a typical behavior-based system, an agent is defined in three major steps: (1) deciding on the high-level behaviors in which the agent will engage; (2) implementing each high-level behavior, generally in terms of a number of low-level behaviors and some miscellaneous behavior to knit them together; (3) using environmental triggers, conflicts, and other design strategies to know when each behavior is appropriate for the creature to engage in. With the Expressivator, the choice and expression of these structural "units" for the agent is not enough; in order to support the user's comprehension, the designer must also give careful consideration to expressing the reasons for and connections between those units. These connections are designed and implemented with transitions, which alter the signifiers they connect into a narrative sequence. In practice, transitions are the keystone of the architecture, combining signifiers in meaningful ways through the use of metalevel controls.

Results

The best way to see how the Expressivator changes the quality of agent behavior is to look at how its transitions work in detail. Here, I review one point where the agent switches behaviors, and explain how transitions make this switch more narratively comprehensible. One example does not a full proof make, but it does take up a lot of space; the skeptical reader can find more in my (1998) essay, "Anti-Boxology: Agent Design in Cultural Context."

As our excerpt begins, the Patient notices the schedule of daily activities that is posted on the fence, and goes over to read the schedule. The Overseer, noticing that the Patient is at the schedule and that the user is watching the Patient, goes over to the schedule, changes the time to 10:00, and forces the Patient to engage in the activity for that hour: exercising.

The goal of this part of the plot is to communicate to the user the daily regime into which the Patient is strapped. The Patient does not have autonomy over its actions; it can be forced by the Overseer to engage in activities completely independently of its desires. The specific behavioral change from reading the schedule to exercising, then, should show the user that the agent changes its activity because (1) it notices the Overseer; (2) the Overseer enforces the scheduled activities; (3) the activity that is currently scheduled is exercising.

Without transitions, the Patient's response to the Overseer is basically stimulus-response (figure 9.1). The Patient starts out reading the schedule. As soon as the Patient senses the Overseer, it immediately starts exercising. This reaction is both correct and instantaneous; the Patient is doing an excellent job of problem solving and rapidly selecting optimal behavior. But this behavioral sequence is also perplexing; the chain of logic that connects the Overseer's presence and the various environmental props to the Patient's actions is not displayed to the user, being jumped over in the instantaneous change from one behavior to another.

With transitions, attempts are made to make the reasons behind the behavioral change clearer (figure

9.2). Again, the behavior starts with the Patient reading the schedule. This time, when the Overseer approaches, the Patient just glances at the Overseer and returns to reading. Because the Patient normally has a strongly fearful reaction to the Overseer (and by this time the Overseer's enthusiasm for punishing the Patient has already generally aroused sympathy in the user's mind), the user has a good chance of understanding that this simple glance without further reaction means that the Patient has not really processed that the Overseer is standing behind it.

Suddenly, the Patient becomes startled and quickly looks back at the Overseer again. Now, the user can get the impression that the Patient has registered the Overseer's presence. Whatever happens next must be a reaction to that presence. Next, the Patient checks the time and the schedule of activities to determine that it is time to exercise. Then the Patient whirls to face the Overseer and frantically and energetically begins exercising, tapering off in enthusiasm as the Overseer departs. This transition narrativizes the agent's behavior in the following ways:

> The agent design is predicated on the user's context-dependent interpretation, e.g., that the user will interpret the agent's short glance at the Overseer differently now than earlier in the story;

> The transition communicates that the change in behavior is connected to several factors: the presence of the Overseer, the clock, and the schedule. This is in contrast with the transition-less sequence, in which there is no clear connection between any of the environmental factors and the Patient's behavioral change;

> The subsequent exercising behavior is altered to fit into a narrative sequence by making it more frantic in response to the agent's panic during the transition.

107

9.1 Response without transitions

Evaluation

How good is the Expressivator? The kind of detailed transition analysis given here suggests that, with the Expressivator, the agent's behavior is designed for context, provides more information about the reasons for agent behavior, and makes for a smoother narrative sequence. This is certainly a basis for improved narrative understanding, but does not necessarily imply actual improvement. In particular, the quality of the animation is not up to snuff, which means users sometimes have trouble interpreting the simple movements of the agent. All the innovations the Expressivator introduces are worthless if individual signs are not clearly animated; everything rests on the substantial animation problem of getting a sigh to look like a sigh and not like a cough or a snort. This problem is exacerbated when, as in Hap, there is a mind-body split, with the mind generating actions that are implemented autonomously by the body. The resulting divide between command and execution makes accurate timing and therefore effective control of animation impossible. This problem of generating expressive animation, although not a straightforward "AI problem," must be addressed by any architecture that is going to implement graphically presented, comprehensible agents.

The *Industrial Graveyard* is an entertainment application, but the constructs of the Expressivator are not limited to believable agents. The concept of a narrative structure for behavior can be just as important for tele-autonomous robots, semi-autonomous avatars, or pedagogical agents. However, the Expressivator's focus on visible behavior and concrete action probably does not adequately support systems like automatic theorem provers that engage in complex, abstract reasoning.

The greatest conceptual problem with the Expressivator is the potential explosion of the number of transitions needed between signifiers; but this turned out not to be a problem in practice. For the Patient's eight high-level signifiers there were only 15 transitions, and for the Patient's 16 low-level signifiers, there were only 25 transitions. This is for several reasons. First of all, transitions are only needed between high-level signifiers, and between low-level signifiers that share the same high-level signifier — *not* between low-level signifiers in different high-level signifiers.[3] I also cut out many transitions by writing several generic transitions, that could go from any behavior to a particular behavior. Most importantly, I found in practice that many of the possible transitions did not make practical sense because of the semantics of the behaviors involved.

The greatest advantage of the Expressivator for the behavior programmer is that it makes it much easier to handle interbehavioral effects. The coordination of multiple high-level behaviors is one of the major stumbling blocks of behavior-based architectures (Brooks 1990); since interbehavioral factors are implicit in the architecture they are hard to control, leading to multiple behaviors battling it out over the agent's body, and hours of tweaking to get each

108

9.2 Response with transitions

behavior to happen when and only when it is supposed to. This is much easier to handle when behaviors can simply kill other behaviors that are not appropriate, and when the trigger conditions for each behavior can be explicitly set.

Introduction to Socially Situated AI

So far, I have argued that there is a fundamental lack in autonomous agents' behavior, which reduces their apparent intentionality. By being constructed in a fragmented manner, agents suffer a kind of schizophrenia, a schizophrenia that can be addressed, in analogy to antipsychiatry, by making agents narratively understandable. In order to do this, I have built an agent architecture that combines (1) redefinition of behaviors as signifiers and their reorganization in terms of audience interpretation; (2) the use of transitions to explain agent motivation, structuring user-recognized behaviors into narrative sequences; and (3) the use of metalevel controls to strategically undermine fragmentation of the agent's behaviors. Preliminary results are encouraging, but further work, preferably involving the development of support for graphical presentation, will be necessary in order to fully evaluate the implications of and possibilities for the architecture.

More generally, if black-box behaviorism involves thinking of human life mechanically, reducing it to a matter of cause-effect, whereas narrative allows for the full elucidation of meaningful intentional existence, then it seems likely that narrative — and by extension the humanities, for whom narrative is a modus operandi — can address meaningful human life in a way that an atomizing science simply cannot. If humans comprehend intentional behavior by structuring it into narrative, then AI must respect and address that way of knowing in order to create artifacts that stimulate interpretation as meaningful, living beings. This suggests that the schizophrenia we see in autonomous agents is the symptomatology of an overzealous commitment to mechanistic explanation in AI, a commitment that is not necessarily unhelpful (as it forms the foundation for building mechanical artifacts), but needs to be balanced by an equal commitment to narrative as the wellspring of intentionality.

In this final section, I show that the focus on narrative communication to generate artificial beings that appear lifelike is part of a broader shift in view that comes about when AI is looked at from a cultural perspective. The resulting perspective I call *socially situated AI*, and it shares close affinity to culturally-oriented approaches taken by other AI researchers, notably Michael Mateas, Simon Penny, and Warren Sack (Penny 1997; Sack 1999; Mateas 2000).

To recap, the analysis in the first sections of this paper suggests that AI and institutionalization share properties that lead to schizophrenia. Both AI and institutionalization take objective views of living beings. By "objective," I mean that they are taken out of their sociocultural context and reduced to a set of data.[4] Because these data are not related to one another or the context from which they sprung, the result is the fragmentation of experience that cultural theorists term schizophrenia.

The conclusion of this argument is that, in order to address schizophrenia, we can take the opposite approach. Rather than seeing patients as objects to be manipulated or diagnosed, we could see them subjectively. This means turning objectivity as defined above on its head: studying people in their life context and relating the things we notice about them to their existence as a whole.

If you are a technical researcher, it is quite possible

that the early sections of this essay left you with lingering doubts about the accuracy or validity of the cultural theory argument. But however you feel about the understandability or truth-value of that argument, the perspective cultural theory brings can be understood as a kind of heuristic which could be tried out in AI. At this level, cultural theory suggests the following: if your agents are schizophrenic, perhaps you need to put them in their sociocultural context.

In this section, we'll explore what it means for an agent to be designed and built with respect to a sociocultural environment — which, again, I term *socially situated AI*. I differentiate socially situated AI from the approaches taken in classical and alternative AI, and then discuss the impact this methodological framework has on the way AI problems are defined and understood. This different way of approaching AI was, in retrospect, the key to solving schizophrenia by suggesting the redefinition of the problem of schizophrenia as a difficulty of agent communication rather than of internal agent structure.

AI in Context

The heuristic suggested by cultural theory — that agents should be considered with respect to their context — should have a familiar ring to technical researchers. The contextualization of agents, i.e., their definition and design with respect to their environment is, after all, one of the major bones alternativists like to pick with classicists. Alternative AI argues that agents can or should only be understood with respect to the environment in which they operate. The complexity or "intelligence" of behavior is said to be a function of an agent within a particular environment, not the agent understood in isolation as a brain-in-a-box.

But the contextualization that is so promoted in alternative AI is actually limited, in particular by the following implicit caveat to its methodology: the agent is generally understood purely in terms of its physical environment — not in terms of the sociocultural environment in which it is embedded. Generally speaking, alternativists examine the dynamics of the agent's activity with respect to the objects with which the agent interacts, the forces placed upon it, and the opportunities its physical locale affords. Some alternativists have also done interesting work examining the dynamics of agent activity in *social* environments, where "social" is defined as interaction with other agents. They generally do not, however, consider the sociocultural aspects of that environment: the unconscious background of metaphors upon which researchers draw in order to try to understand agents, the social structures of funding and prestige that encourage particular avenues of agent construction, the cultural expectations that users — as well as scientific peers — maintain about intentional beings and that influence the way in which the agent comes to be used and judged.

In fact, when such aspects of the agent's environment are considered at all, many alternativists abandon their previous championing of contextualization. They see these not-so-quantifiable aspects of agent existence not as part-and-parcel of what it means to be an agent in the world, but as mere sources of noise or confusion that obscure the actual agent. They may say things like this: "The term 'agent' is, of course, a favourite of the folk psychological ontology. It consequently carries with it notions of intentionality and purposefulness that we wish to avoid. Here we use the term divested of such associated baggage" (Smithers 1992, 33) — as though the social and cultural environment of the agent, unlike its physical environment, is simply so much baggage to be discarded.

In this respect, the alternativist view of agents-in-context is not so different from the Taylorist view of worker-in-context or the institutional view of patient-in-context. After all, Taylorists certainly look at human workers in context; in the terminology of situated action, they analyze and optimize the ongoing dynamics of worker-and-equipment within the situation of a concrete task, rather than the action of the worker alone and in general. Similarly, institutional psychiatrists look at human patients in context; they are happy to observe and analyze the dynamics of patient interaction with other people and objects in the world, as long as in those observations and analyses they do not need to include themselves. In each of these

cases, contextualization is stopping at the same point: where the social dynamics between the expert and the object of expertise, as well as its cultural foundation, would be examined.

I do not believe that the elision of sociocultural aspects from the environment as understood by alternative AI is due to any nefarious attempt to hide social relations, to push cultural issues under the rug, to intentionally mislead the public about the nature of agents, and so on. Rather, I believe that because AI is part of the scientific and engineering traditions, most alternativists simply do not have the training to include these aspects in their work. Science values simplification through separation, and one of the key ways in which this is done is by separating the object of study from the complex and rich life background in which it exists. This strategy lets researchers focus on and hopefully solve the technical problems involved without getting bogged down in all kinds of interconnected and complex issues that may not have direct bearing on the task at hand.

The Return of the Repressed

The problem, though, is that even from a straightforward technical point of view, excluding the sociocultural context is sometimes unhelpful. At its most basic, ignoring this context does not make it go away. What ends up happening is that, by insisting that cultural influences are not at work, those influences often come back through the back door in ways that are harder to understand and utilize.

As an example, consider programming through the use of symbols. Symbolic programming involves the use of tokens, often with names such as "reason," "belief," or "feeling" that are loaded with cultural meaning to the agent designer. Critics point out that the meaningfulness of these terms to humans can obscure the vacuousness of their actual use in the program. So a programmer who writes a piece of code that manipulates tokens called "thoughts" may unintentionally lead him- or herself into believing that this program must be thinking.

Alternative AI, generally speaking, involves a rejection of these sorts of symbols as tokens in programs. This rejection is often based on a recognition that symbolic programming of the kind classical AI engages in is grounded in culture, and that symbols carry a load of cultural baggage that affects the way programs are understood. Some of them believe that by abandoning symbolic programming they, unlike classicists, have also abandoned the problem of cultural presuppositions creeping into their work. And, in fact, it is true that many alternative AI programs do use such symbols sparingly, if at all, in their internal representations.

Nevertheless, it would be fair to say that the architecture of such agents involves symbols to the extent that the engineer of the agent must think of the world and agent in a symbolic way in order to build the creature. For example, the creature may have more or less continuous sensors of the world, but each of those sensors may be interpreted in a way that yields, once again, symbols — even when those symbols are not represented explicitly as a written token in an agent's program. For example, a visual image may be processed to output one of two control signals, one of which triggers a walking style appropriate when on carpets, and one of which triggers a walking style appropriate when not on carpets. Although a variable named "on-carpet" may not appear in the agent's code, it would be fair to predicate an "on-carpet" symbol in the designer's thinking as s/he constructed the agent — a symbol that is as informed by the designer's cultural background as the identifiable "on-carpet" symbol in a classical AI program.

The behaviors into which the agent is split are similarly fundamentally symbolic ("play fetch," "sleep," "beg," etc.) and are influenced by cultural notions of what behaviors can plausibly be. Although alternative AI has gotten away from symbolic representations within the agent when seen in isolation, it has not gotten away from symbolic representations when the agent is seen in its full context. Once you look at the entire environment of the agent, including its creator, it is clear that despite the rhetoric that surrounds alternative AI, these symbols — and their accompanying sociocultural baggage — still play a large role.

Leaving out the social context, then, is both epistemologically inadequate and obfuscating. By not looking at the subjective aspects of agent design, the very nature of alternative AI programming, as well as the origin of various technical problems, becomes obscured. This is particularly problematic because not being able to see what causes technical problems may make them hard, if not impossible, to solve. This is exactly what happens with schizophrenia — and by taking the opposite tack a path to solution becomes much more straightforward.

Socially Situated AI

What should AI do instead? Alternativists believe that situating agents in their physical context often provides insight into otherwise obscure technical problems. I propose that we build on this line of thinking by taking seriously the idea that the social and cultural environment of the agent can also be, not just a distracting factor in the design and analysis of agents, but a valuable resource for it (figure 9.3). I coined the term "socially situated AI" for this method of agent research.

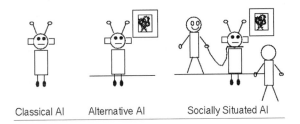

9.3 The increased context from classical through alternative to socially situated AI.

Here, I first describe at a philosophical level the postulates of socially situated AI. This lays out the broad framework within which technical work can proceed. I then discuss at a more concrete level what it means to design and build agents with respect to their sociocultural context.

Postulates of Socially Situated AI

Like other methodological frameworks, including classical and alternative AI, socially situated AI involves, not just a kind of technology, but a way of understanding how to define problems and likely avenues of success. I represent this changed way of thinking here through an enumeration of postulates of socially situated AI. These are propositions that form the framework for how research is done and evaluated. Specifically, socially situated AI distinguishes itself from other forms of AI through explicit commitment to the following principles:

1. *An agent can only be evaluated with respect to its environment, which includes not only the objects with which it interacts, but also the creators and observers of the agent.* Autonomous agents are not "intelligent" in and of themselves, but rather with reference to a particular system of constitution and evaluation, which includes the explicit and implicit goals of the project creating it, the group dynamics of that project, and the sources of funding that both facilitate and circumscribe the directions in which the project can be taken. An agent's construction is not limited to the lines of code that form its program but involves a whole social network, which must be analyzed in order to get a complete picture of what that agent is, without which agents cannot be meaningfully judged.

2. *An agent's design should focus, not on the agent itself, but on the dynamics of that agent with respect to its physical and social environments.* In classical AI, an agent is designed alone; in alternative AI, it is designed for a physical environment; in socially situated AI, an agent is designed for a physical, cultural, and social environment, which includes the designer of its architecture, the creator of the agent, and the audience that interacts with and judges the agent, including both the people who engage it and the intellectual peers who judge its epistemological status. The goals of all these people must be explicitly taken into account in deciding what kind of agent to build and how to build it.

3. *An agent is a representation.* Artificial agents are a mirror of their creators' understanding of what it means to be at once mechanical and human, intelligent, alive — what cultural theorists call a *subject*. Rather

than being a pristine testing-ground for theories of mind, agents come overcoded with cultural values, a rich crossroads where culture and technology intersect and reveal their coarticulation. This means in a fundamental sense that, in our agents, we are not creating life but representing it, in ways that make sense to us, given our specific cultural backgrounds.

Socially Situated AI as Technical Methodology

These philosophical principles do not necessarily give technical researchers much to go on in their day-to-day work. Concretely speaking, socially situated AI can be understood in the following way. Rather than seeing an agent as a being in a social vacuum, we can see it as represented in figure 9.4: as a kind of *communication* between a human *designer* who is using it to embody a conception of an agent and a human *audience* trying to understand it.

9.4 Agents as communication.

After all, for many applications it is not enough for an agent to function correctly in a technical sense. Many times, the agent should also be understandable. For example, when an agent researcher designs an artificial cat, s/he will have some ideas about the kinds of behaviors the cat should have and the kind of motivations behind the cat's selection of various behaviors — ideas which, optimally and sometimes crucially, the viewers of the agent should also pick up on. In this sense the agent as program is a kind of vehicle for a conception of a particular agent, which is communicated from the agent-builder through the technical artifact to the observers of or interactors with the agent.

This way of understanding socially situated AI can be thought of as a change in metaphor. Many current approaches to AI are based on the metaphor of *agent-as-autonomous*: the fundamental property of such an agent is its basic independence from its creator or users. Lenny Foner, for example, defines autonomy as one of the most basic aspects of being an agent:

> Any agent should have a measure of autonomy from its user. Otherwise, it's just a glorified front-end, irrevocably fixed, lock-step, to the actions of its user. A more autonomous agent can pursue agenda independently of its user. This requires aspects of periodic action, spontaneous execution, and initiative, in that the agent must be able to take preemptive or independent actions that will eventually benefit the user. (Foner 1993, 35)

This autonomy implies that the agent's fundamental being is as a thing-for-itself, rather than what it actually is: a human construction, usually a tool. AI researchers are far from believing that agents magically spring from nowhere, and autonomy can certainly be a useful notion. Nevertheless, the focus on autonomy — separation from designer and user — as a defining factor for agents can unwittingly hide the degree to which both designers and users are involved in the agent's construction and use.

As an alternative to this metaphor, socially situated AI suggests the metaphor of *agent-as-communication*. Socially situated AI sees agents not as beings in a vacuum, but as representations that are to be communicated from an agent-builder to an audience. This point of view is deeply informed by recent work in believable agents such as that of Reilly (1996), Loyall (1997), Wavish and Graham (1996), and Blumberg and Galyean (1995) — which focus more and more on the

audience's perception of agents, rather than on an agent's correctness per se. This conception of agents is also very like contemporary conventional conceptions of artwork, as vehicles through which ideas can be transmitted from a designer to his or her audience.

But the concept of agent-as-communication is not limited to believability or other "artsy" applications. This is because proper perception of agents matters not only when we want to communicate a particular personality through our agents. It matters in any situation where the design of the agent — including its purpose, methods, functions, or limitations — should be understood by the people with which the agent interacts.

Thinking of agents as communication has several advantages. The notion of an agent as communication is clearly a more accurate description of how agents function culturally than the notion of an agent in an autonomous vacuum. It also brings advantages from a purely technical point of view. By making the commitment that "agentiness" is meant to be communicated, we can explicitly communicate to the audience what the agent is about, rather than assuming (often incorrectly) that this will happen as a side effect of the agent "doing the right thing." And by building agents with an eye to their reception, builders can tailor their agents to maximize their effectiveness for their target audience. In this sense, agents built for social contexts can be not only more engaging but more correct than purely rational, problem-solving agents, in the following sense: they may actually get across the message for which they have been designed.

Notes

1. A similar observation is made by Luc Steels.

2. This splitting into subsystems is not the same thing as multiple personality. They are not experienced as completely separate individuals. In addition, Laing posits the subsystems as an explanatory mechanism that makes Julie's utterances more understandable; no one can directly know Julie's subjective experience, and she is not in a position to articulate it.

3. This would be implemented instead with a transition between the respective high-level signifiers.

4. The notion of what exactly objectivity means in various fields and usages is a quagmire in which, at the moment, I prefer not to be morassed. Please accept this usage of objectivity as a definitional statement of what I mean by "objectivity" here, as opposed to a pronouncement of what anyone would mean by it.

References

Agre, Philip E. (1997). *Computation and Human Experience*. Cambridge, UK: Cambridge University Press.

Baur, Susan (1991). *The Dinosaur Man: Tales of Madness and Enchantment from the Back Ward*. New York: Edward Burlingame Books.

Blumberg, Bruce (1996). "Old Tricks, New Dogs: Ethology and Interactive Creatures." PhD Thesis, MIT Media Lab, Cambridge, MA.

Blumberg, Bruce, and Tinsley A. Galyean (1995). "Multi-level Direction of Autonomous Creatures for Real-time Virtual Environments." Proceedings of SIGGRAPH 1995.

Boehlen, M., and Michael Mateas (1998). "Office Plant #1: Intimate Space and Contemplative Entertainment." *Leonardo* 31, no. 5 (1998): 345-348.

Brooks, Rodney A. (1990). "Elephants Don't Play Chess." In *Designing Autonomous Agents*, edited by Pattie Maes. Cambridge, MA: The MIT Press.

Brooks, Rodney A. (1997). "From Earwigs to Humans." *Robotics and Autonomous Systems* 20 (2-4) (June 1997): 291-304.

Bruner, Jerome (1986). *Actual Minds, Possible Worlds*. Cambridge, MA: Harvard University Press.

Bruner, Jerome (1990). *Acts of Meaning*. Cambridge, MA: Harvard University Press.

Bruner, Jerome (1991). "The Narrative Construction of Reality." *Critical Inquiry* 18, no.1: 1-21.

Dennett, Daniel (1987). *The Intentional Stance*. Cambridge, MA: The MIT Press.

Foner, Lenny (1993). "What's an agent, anyway?" <http://foner.www.media.mit.edu/people/foner/Julia/Julia.html>. Published in a revised version in The Proceedings of the First International Conference on Autonomous Agents (AA 1997).

Garfinkel, Harold (1996). "Ethnomethodology's Program." *Social Psychology Quarterly* 59, no. 1 (1996): 5-20.

Goffman, Erving (1961). *Asylums: Essays on the Social Situation of Mental Patients and Other Inmates*. Garden City, NY: Anchor Books.

Janet, Pierre (1889). *L'Automatisme Psychologique: Essai de Psychologie Experimentale sur les Formes Inferieures de l'Activite Humaine*, edited by Felix Alcan. Paris: Ancienne Librairie Germer Bailliere et Cie.

Laing, R.D. (1960). *The Divided Self: An Existential Study in Sanity and Madness*. Middlesex: Penguin Books.

Laing, R.D., and A. Esterson (1970). *Sanity, Madness, and the Family*. Middlesex: Penguin Books, Ltd.

Loyall, A. Bryan (1997). "Believable Agents: Building Interactive Personalities." Ph.D. Thesis (CMU-CS-97-123), Carnegie Mellon University, Pittsburgh, Pennsylvania.

Loyall, A. Bryan, and Joseph Bates (1991). "Hap: A Reactive, Adaptive Architecture for Agents,." Technical Report (CMU-CS-91-147), Carnegie Mellon University, Pittsburgh, Pennsylvania.

Mateas, Michael (2000). "Expressive AI." SIGGRAPH Art and Culture Papers, Proceedings of SIGGRAPH 2000.

Mateas, Michael, P. Vanouse, and S. Domike (2000). "Generation of Ideologically-Biased Historical Documentaries." Proceedings of AAAI 2000, Austin, Texas.

Penny, Simon (1997). "Embodied Cultural Agents at the Intersection of Robotics, Cognitive Science, and Interactive Art." In *Socially Intelligent Agents: Papers from the 1997 Fall Symposium*, edited by Kerstin Dautenhahn. Menlo Park: AAAI Press.

Penny, Simon (2000). "Agents as Artworks and Agent Design as Artistic Practice." In *Human Cognition and Social Agent Technology*, edited by Kerstin Dautenhahn. Amsterdam: John Benjamins Publishing Company.

Penny, Simon, Jeffrey Smith, Phoebe Sengers, Andre Bernhardt and Jamieson Schulte (2001). "Traces: Embodied Immersive Interaction with Semi-Autonomous Avatars." *Convergence* 7, no. 2 (2001).

Perlin, Ken, and Athomas Goldberg (1996). "Improv: A System for Scripting Interactive Actors in Virtual Worlds." *Computer Graphics* 29, no.3 (1996).

Reilly, W. Scott Neal (1996). "Believable Social and Emotional Agents." Ph.D. Thesis (CMU-CS-96-138), Carnegie Mellon University, Pittsburgh, Pennsylvania.

Reynolds, Craig (1999). "Steering Behaviors for Autonomous Characters." 1999 Game Developers Conference, San Jose, CA, March 1999.

Robear, Jr., James Walter (1991). "Reality Check." In *In the Realms of the Unreal: "Insane" Writings*, edited by John G.H. Oakes. New York: Four Walls Eight Windows.

Ronell, Avital (1989). *The Telephone Book: Technology, Schizophrenia, Electric Speech*. Lincoln: University of Nebraska Press.

Russell, S., and P. Norvig (1995). *Artificial Intelligence: A Modern Approach*. Upper Saddle River, NJ: Prentice Hall.

Sack, Warren (1999). "Stories and Social Networks." *1999 AAAI*

115

Symposium on Narrative Intelligence. Menlo Park, AAAI Press.

Sengers, Phoebe (1995). "Madness and Automation: On Institutionalization." *Postmodern Culture* 5, no.3 (May 1995).

Sengers, Phoebe (1998). "Anti-Boxology: Agent Design in Cultural Context." Ph.D. Thesis, Carnegie Mellon University Department of Computer Science and Program in Literary and Cultural Theory, Pittsburgh, Pennsylvania.

Sengers, Phoebe (2000). "Narrative Intelligence." In *Human Cognition and Social Agent Technology (Advances in Consciousness vol. 19)*, edited by Kerstin Dautenhahn. Amsterdam: John Benjamins.

Smithers, Tim (1992). "Taking Eliminative Materialism Seriously: A Methodology for Autonomous Systems Research." In *Towards a Practice of Autonomous Systems: Proceedings of the First European Conference on Artificial Life*, edited by Francisco J. Varela and Paul Bourgine. Cambridge, MA: The MIT Press.

Steels, Luc (1994). "The Artificial Life Roots of Artificial Intelligence." *Artificial Life* 1 nos. 1-2 (1994): 75-110.

Wardrip-Fruin, Noah, and Brion Moss (2002). "The Impermanence Agent: Project and Context." In *Cybertext Yearbook 2001*, edited by Markku Eskelinen and Raine Koskimaa. Saarijärvi: Publications of the Research Centre for Contemporary Culture, University of Jyväskylä.

Wavish, Peter and Michael Graham (1996). "A Situated Action Approach to Implementing Characters in Computer Games." *AAI* 10.

116

Game Theories

In his 1974 *Computer Lib/Dream Machines*, Ted Nelson argued that human-computer interaction design was more properly viewed as a analogue of moviemaking than of engineering. A year later, the first personal computer kit became available for purchase, and it was not long before computers conceived of as entertainment devices — rather than as work tools — began appearing in U.S. homes and local arcades.

Now, like moviemaking before it, computer-based entertainment — even the oft-maligned computer game — is beginning to receive scholarly attention and to be viewed as something other than a public nuisance. At the same time, computer games are themselves in a period of considerable development and redefinition. Identifiable genres (first-person shooters, god-games, massively multiplayer online role-playing games [MMORPGs]) are emerging and entering the public awareness; the channels of game interaction (PCs, consoles, handhelds, cell phones, PDAs) are multiplying; and as new artistic and marketing methods arise and the first generations of computer gamers come of age, games are reaching and being developed for an ever-broadening demographic.

Although the four authors presented here emerge from different backgrounds and are at home in different communities, all of their work is grounded in the specifics of actual games (rather than theories of games-in-the-abstract) and each author opens discussion with both scholars and game developers. Further, a point of focus for each essayist is the game/story question that runs through this volume.

MIT professor Henry Jenkins directly addresses the game/story formulation. Well-known for his work with comparative media studies, Jenkins describes a middle ground between narratologists and ludologists, while also focusing attention on the dynamics of space, which he believes neither camp fully appreciates. Jesper Juul, on the other hand, is identified with ludology. His topic here, the operation of time in games, is one that he has previously utilized to differentiate between games and narratives. This essay moves further than the basic distinction, beginning to lay the groundwork for a comprehensive understanding of game time. Celia Pearce, a familiar figure in the game development and location-based entertainment communities, furthers the argument for a native discipline of game theory, while also introducing six "operators" for understanding the role of narrative in games. These operators structure her analysis of the author/audience dynamics that emerge in game forms like MMORPGs and user-modifiable simulations. Finally, Eric Zimmerman, a game designer and theorist, takes to task four terms that unacceptably run amok in the new media field (not to mention this volume!): narrative, interactivity, play, and games. In disciplining these terms, he reformulates the game/story discussion as well, opening up new areas of investigation for those interested in progressive game design and game theory.

Reference

Nelson, Ted (1974). *Computer Lib / Dream Machines*. 1st edition: self-published, 1974. 2nd edition: Redmond, WA: Tempus Books/Microsoft Press, 1987.

Game Design as Narrative Architecture

Henry Jenkins

The relationship between games and story remains a divisive question among game fans, designers, and scholars alike. At a recent academic Games Studies conference, for example, a blood feud threatened to erupt between the self-proclaimed ludologists, who wanted to see the focus shift onto the mechanics of game play, and the narratologists, who were interested in studying games alongside other storytelling media.[1] Consider some recent statements made on this issue:

> Interactivity is almost the opposite of narrative; narrative flows under the direction of the author, while interactivity depends on the player for motive power. (Adams 1999)

> There is a direct, immediate conflict between the demands of a story and the demands of a game. Divergence from a story's path is likely to make for a less satisfying story; restricting a player's freedom of action is likely to make for a less satisfying game. (Costikyan 2000, 44–53)

> Computer games are not narratives.... Rather the narrative tends to be isolated from or even work against the computer-game-ness of the game. (Juul 1998)[2]

> Outside academic theory people are usually excellent at making distinctions between narrative, drama and games. If I throw a ball at you I don't expect you to drop it and wait until it starts telling stories. (Eskelinen 2001)

I find myself responding to this perspective with mixed feelings. On the one hand, I understand what these writers are arguing against — various attempts to map traditional narrative structures ("hypertext," "Interactive Cinema," "nonlinear narrative") onto games at the expense of an attention to their specificity as an emerging mode of entertainment. You say "narrative" to the average gamer and what they are apt to imagine is something on the order of a choose-your-own

Response by Jon McKenzie

The model of creativity often associated with digital media is not that of originality and uniqueness but recombination and multiplicity, a model hardwired to the computer's uncanny ability to copy and combine images, sounds, texts, and other materials from an endless array of sources. Indeed, in different though related ways, both digital media and poststructuralist theory teach us that it is impossible to create and study the new without drawing at times on forms and processes taken from what is already around us. From this perspective, no genre, work, or field is unique and self-contained: each is a specific yet fuzzy combination of other things that are themselves diverse and nonunique. In short, what makes something "unique" is not so much its make-up but its "mix-up."

For practical, conceptual, and institutional reasons, any formation of a field of "ludology" may inevitably involve arguing for that field's uniqueness and originality, its clear-cut distinction from other fields: thus, "games are not narratives, not films, not plays, etc." Yet I'm willing to gamble that if a formal discipline of ludology ever does emerge, it will sooner or later discover what other disciplines have learned: discoveries are triggered by the oddest (and oldest) of sources.

As Henry Jenkins suggests, games are indeed not narratives, not films, not plays — but they're also not-not-narratives, not-not-films, not-not-plays. Games share traits with other forms of cultural production,

adventure book, a form noted for its lifelessness and mechanical exposition rather than enthralling entertainment, thematic sophistication, or character complexity. And game industry executives are perhaps justly skeptical that they have much to learn from the resolutely unpopular (and often overtly antipopular) aesthetics promoted by hypertext theorists. The application of film theory to games can seem heavy-handed and literal-minded, often failing to recognize the profound differences between the two media. Yet, at the same time, there is a tremendous amount that game designers and critics could learn through making meaningful comparisons with other storytelling media. One gets rid of narrative as a framework for thinking about games only at one's own risk. In this short piece, I hope to offer a middle-ground position between the ludologists and the narratologists, one that respects the particularity of this emerging medium — examining games less as stories than as spaces ripe with narrative possibility.

Let's start at some points where we might all agree:

1. Not all games tell stories. Games may be an abstract, expressive, and experiential form, closer to music or modern dance than to cinema. Some ballets (*The Nutcracker* for example) tell stories, but storytelling isn't

an intrinsic or defining feature of dance. Similarly, many of my own favorite games — *Tetris, Blix, Snood* — are simple graphic games that do not lend themselves very well to narrative exposition.[3] To understand such games, we need other terms and concepts beyond narrative, including interface design and expressive movement for starters. The last thing we want to do is to reign in the creative experimentation that needs to occur in the earlier years of a medium's development.

2. Many games *do* have narrative aspirations. Minimally, they want to tap the emotional residue of previous narrative experiences. Often, they depend on our familiarity with the roles and goals of genre entertainment to orient us to the action, and in many cases, game designers want to create a series of narrative experiences for the player. Given those narrative aspirations, it seems reasonable to suggest that some understanding of how games relate to narrative is necessary before we understand the aesthetics of game design or the nature of contemporary game culture.

3. Narrative analysis need not be prescriptive, even if some narratologists — Janet Murray is the most oft-cited example — do seem to be advocating for games to pursue particular narrative forms. There is not one

although reducing them to any one of these comes at a certain cost. Jenkins rightly contends that game designers should therefore seek to expand the forms and processes from which to draw, rather than reduce them. He is also right to point out that some ludologists are themselves much too quick to reduce narrative to overly simplistic models (e.g., strictly linear structures). Most importantly, his exploration of spatially oriented narrative forms provides provocative approaches to contemporary game design. At the same time, however, Jenkins's stated goal to offer a "middle ground" between ludologists and narratologists remains slanted toward the narratological end of things. This is indicated in his essay's title, "Game Design as Narrative Architecture." A more playful

ludologist might have offered a response titled "Narrative Architecture as Game Design." Johan Huizinga, after all, analyzed law, war, poetry, and philosophy "as" play, and across diverse cultural traditions storytelling has complex agonistic dimensions.

Another middle ground for ludology might be "experience design," a notion and practice that runs in different ways from Brenda Laurel to Donald Norman to Eric Zimmerman. Experience design refers to the generation and shaping of actions, emotions, and thoughts. How one operates a kitchen appliance, takes in a sophisticated science exhibition, or becomes enmeshed in a role-playing game — or for that matter shops in a store, reads a novel, or visits a polling booth — all this

future of games. The goal should be to foster diversification of genres, aesthetics, and audiences, to open gamers to the broadest possible range of experiences. The past few years have been ones of enormous creative experimentation and innovation within the games industry, as might be represented by a list of some of the groundbreaking titles. *The Sims, Black and White, Majestic, Shenmue*; each represents profoundly different concepts of what makes for compelling game play. A discussion of the narrative potentials of games need not imply a privileging of storytelling over all the other possible things games can do, even if we might suggest that if game designers are going to tell stories, they should tell them well. In order to do that, game designers, who are most often schooled in computer science or graphic design, need to be retooled in the basic vocabulary of narrative theory.

4. The experience of playing games can never be simply reduced to the experience of a story. Many other factors that have little or nothing to do with storytelling per se contribute to the development of great games and we need to significantly broaden our critical vocabulary for talking about games to deal more fully with those other topics. Here, the ludologist's insistence that game scholars focus more attention on the mechanics of game play seems totally in order.

5. If some games tell stories, they are unlikely to tell them in the same ways that other media tell stories. Stories are not empty content that can be ported from one media pipeline to another. One would be hard-pressed, for example, to translate the internal dialogue of Proust's *Remembrance of Things Past* into a compelling cinematic experience, and the tight control over viewer experience that Hitchcock achieves in his suspense films would be directly antithetical to the aesthetics of good game design. We must, therefore, be attentive to the particularity of games as a medium, specifically what distinguishes them from other narrative traditions. Yet, in order to do so requires precise comparisons — not the mapping of old models onto games but a testing of those models against existing games to determine what features they share with other media and how they differ.

Much of the writing in the ludologist tradition is unduly polemical: they are so busy trying to pull game designers out of their "cinema envy" or define a field where no hypertext theorist dares to venture that they are prematurely dismissing the use value of narrative for understanding their desired object of study. For my money, a series of conceptual blind spots prevent them from developing a full understanding of the interplay between narrative and games.

First, the discussion operates with too narrow a

can be approached in terms of experience design. How are interactions organized and solicited? How does one event flow into another? How does the overall experience "hang together"? Although Laurel theorizes experience design using the model of Aristotelian theater (arguing that it has been shaping audiences' experience for centuries), there are in practice an almost unlimited set of performative models to draw upon: sports, rituals, sagas, popular entertainments, novels, jokes, and so on.

Perhaps what's really at stake in ludology is less the right model and more a sense of tone and attitude — a willingness to mix it up, to entertain many possibilities, to play with lots of different models.

From Markku Eskelinen's Online Response

For some reason Henry Jenkins doesn't define the contested concepts (narratives, stories, and games) so central to his argumentation. That's certainly an effective way of building a middle ground (or a periphery), but perhaps not the most convincing one. [. . .]

Jenkins also misrepresents a dispute (on the usefulness of narratology), important parts of which he seems to be unaware of. It has its roots both in Espen Aarseth's *Cybertext* (which deals extensively with the relationship between stories and games, showing elementary differences in communicative structures of narratives and adventure games) and Gonzalo Frasca's introduction of *ludology* to computer game studies. A model of narrative, one preoccupied with the rules and conventions of classical linear storytelling at the expense of consideration of other kinds of narratives, not only the modernist and postmodernist experimentation that inspired the hypertext theorists, but also popular traditions that emphasize spatial exploration over causal event chains or which seek to balance the competing demands of narrative and spectacle.[4]

Second, the discussion operates with too limited an understanding of narration, focusing more on the activities and aspirations of the storyteller and too little on the process of narrative comprehension.[5]

Third, the discussion deals only with the question of whether whole games tell stories and not whether narrative elements might enter games at a more localized level. Finally, the discussion assumes that narratives must be self-contained rather than understanding games as serving some specific functions within a new transmedia storytelling environment. Rethinking each of these issues might lead us to a new understanding of the relationship between games and stories. Specifically, I want to introduce an important third term into this discussion — spatiality — and argue for an understanding of game designers less as storytellers and more as narrative architects.

Spatial Stories and Environmental Storytelling

Game designers don't simply tell stories; they design worlds and sculpt spaces. It is no accident, for example, that game design documents have historically been more interested in issues of level design than on plotting or character motivation. A prehistory of video and computer games might take us through the evolution of paper mazes or board games, both preoccupied with the design of spaces, even where they also provided some narrative context. Monopoly, for example, may tell a narrative about how fortunes are won and lost; the individual Chance cards may provide some story pretext for our gaining or losing a certain number of places; but ultimately, what we remember is the experience of moving around the board and landing on someone's real estate. Performance theorists have described role-playing games (RPGs) as a mode of collaborative storytelling, but the Dungeon Master's activities start with designing the space — the dungeon — where the players' quest will take place. Even many of the early text-based games, such as *Zork,* which could have told a wide array of different kinds of stories, centered around enabling players to move through narratively compelling spaces: "You are facing the north side of a white house. There is no door here, and all of the windows are boarded up. To the north a

discussion of the present topic, which ignores these works, cannot hope to break new ground. A few facts of cultural history wouldn't hurt either: as the oldest astragals (forerunners of dice) date back to prehistory, I'm not so sure "games fit within a much older tradition of spatial stories."

Jenkins Responds

I feel a bit like Travis Bickle when I ask Eskelinen, "Are you talking to me?" For starters, I don't consider myself to be a narratologist at all.

10.1. *Civilization 3*. (Atari)

narrow path winds through the trees." The early Nintendo games have simple narrative hooks — rescue Princess Toadstool — but what gamers found astonishing when they first played them were their complex and imaginative graphic realms, which were so much more sophisticated than the simple grids that *Pong* or *Pac-Man* had offered us a decade earlier.

When we refer to such influential early works as Shigeru Miyamoto's *Super Mario Bros.* as "scroll games," we situate them alongside a much older tradition of spatial storytelling: many Japanese scroll paintings map, for example, the passing of the seasons onto an unfolding space. When you adapt a film into a game, the process typically involves translating events in the film into environments within the game. When gamer magazines want to describe the experience of gameplay, they are more likely to reproduce maps of the game world than to recount their narratives.[6] Before we can talk about game narratives, then, we need to talk about game spaces. Across a series of essays, I have made the case that game consoles should be regarded as machines for generating compelling spaces, that their virtual playspaces have helped to compensate for the declining place of the traditional backyard in contemporary boy culture, and that the core narratives behind many games center around the struggle to explore, map, and master contested spaces (Fuller and Jenkins 1994; Jenkins 1998). Here, I want to broaden that discussion further to consider in what ways the structuring of game space

facilitates different kinds of narrative experiences.

As such, games fit within a much older tradition of spatial stories, which have often taken the form of hero's odysseys, quest myths, or travel narratives.[7] The best works of J.R.R. Tolkien, Jules Verne, Homer, L. Frank Baum, or Jack London fall loosely within this tradition, as does, for example, the sequence in *War and Peace* that describes Pierre's aimless wanderings across the battlefield at Borodino. Often, such works exist on the outer borders of literature. They are much loved by readers, to be sure, and passed down from one generation to another, but they rarely figure in the canon of great literary works. How often, for example, has science fiction been criticized for being preoccupied with world-making at the expense of character psychology or plot development?

These writers seem constantly to be pushing against the limits of what can be accomplished in a printed text and thus their works fare badly against aesthetic standards defined around classically constructed novels. In many cases, the characters — our guides through these richly developed worlds — are stripped down to the bare bones, description displaces exposition, and plots fragment into a series of episodes and encounters. When game designers draw story elements from existing film or literary genres, they are most apt to tap those genres — fantasy, adventure, science fiction, horror, war — which are most invested in world-making and spatial storytelling. Games, in turn, may more fully realize the spatiality of these stories, giving a much more immersive and compelling representation of their narrative worlds. Anyone who doubts that Tolstoy might have achieved his true calling as a game designer should reread the final segment of *War and Peace* where he works through how a series of alternative choices might have reversed the outcome of Napoleon's Russian campaign. The passage is dead weight in the context of a novel, yet it outlines ideas that could be easily communicated in god-games such as those in the *Civilization* series (figure 10.1).

Don Carson, who worked as a Senior Show Designer for Walt Disney Imagineering, has argued that game designers can learn a great deal by studying techniques of "environmental storytelling," which Disney employs in designing amusement park attractions. Carson explains,

> The story element is infused into the physical space a guest walks or rides through. It is the physical space that does much of the work of conveying the story the designers are trying to tell.... Armed only with their own knowledge of the world, and those visions collected from movies and books, the audience is ripe to be dropped into your adventure. The trick is to play on those memories and expectations to heighten the thrill of venturing into your created universe. (Carson 2000)

The amusement park attraction doesn't so much reproduce the story of a literary work, such as *The Wind in the Willows*, as it evokes its atmosphere; the original story provides "a set of rules that will guide the design and project team to a common goal" and that will help give structure and meaning to the visitor's experience. If, for example, the attraction centers around pirates, Carson writes, "every texture you use, every sound you play, every turn in the road should reinforce the concept of pirates," while any contradictory element may shatter the sense of immersion into this narrative universe. The same might be said for a game such as *Sea Dogs*, which, no less than *Pirates of the Caribbean*, depends on its ability to map our preexisting pirate fantasies. The most significant difference is that amusement park designers count on visitors keeping their hands and arms in the car at all times and thus have a greater control in shaping our total experience, whereas game designers have to develop worlds where we can touch, grab, and fling things about at will.

Environmental storytelling creates the preconditions for an immersive narrative experience in at least one of four ways: spatial stories can evoke pre-existing narrative associations; they can provide a staging ground where narrative events are enacted; they may embed narrative information within their mise-en-scene; or they provide resources for emergent narratives.

10.2. American McGee's Alice (Rogue Entertainment, Electronic Arts)

Evocative Spaces

The most compelling amusement park attractions build upon stories or genre traditions already well-known to visitors, allowing them to enter physically into spaces they have visited many times before in their fantasies. These attractions may either remediate a preexisting story (*Back to the Future*) or draw upon a broadly shared genre tradition (Disney's Haunted Mansion). Such works do not so much tell self-contained stories as draw upon our previously existing narrative competencies. They can paint their worlds in fairly broad outlines and count on the visitor/player to do the rest. Something similar might be said of many games. For example, *American McGee's Alice*™ is an original interpretation of Lewis Carroll's *Alice in Wonderland* (figure 10.2). Alice has been pushed into madness after years of living with uncertainty about whether her

123

Wonderland experiences were real or hallucinations; now, she's come back into this world and is looking for blood. McGee's wonderland is not a whimsical dreamscape but a dark nightmare realm. McGee can safely assume that players start the game with a pretty well-developed mental map of the spaces, characters, and situations associated with Carroll's fictional universe and that they will read his distorted and often monstrous images against the background of mental images formed from previous encounters with storybook illustrations and Disney movies. McGee rewrites Alice's story in large part by redesigning Alice's spaces.

Arguing against games as stories, Jesper Juul suggests that, "you clearly can't deduct the story of *Star Wars* from *Star Wars* the game," whereas a film version of a novel will give you at least the broad outlines of the plot (Juul 1998). This is a pretty old-fashioned model of the process of adaptation. Increasingly, we inhabit a world of transmedia storytelling, one that depends less on each individual work being self-sufficient than on each work contributing to a larger narrative economy. The *Star Wars* game may not simply retell the story of *Star Wars*, but it doesn't have to in order to enrich or expand our experience of the *Star Wars* saga.

We already know the story before we even buy the game and would be frustrated if all it offered us was a regurgitation of the original film experience. Rather, the *Star Wars* game exists in dialogue with the films, conveying new narrative experiences through its creative manipulation of environmental details. One can imagine games taking their place within a larger narrative system with story information communicated through books, film, television, comics, and other media, each doing what it does best, each a relatively autonomous experience, but the richest understanding of the story world coming to those who follow the narrative across the various channels. In such a system, what games do best will almost certainly center around their ability to give concrete shape to our memories and imaginings of the storyworld, creating an immersive environment we can wander through and interact with.

Enacting Stories

Most often, when we discuss games as stories, we are referring to games that either enable players to perform or witness narrative events — for example, to grab a light-saber and dispatch Darth Maul in a *Star Wars* game. Narrative enters such games on two levels — in terms of broadly defined goals or conflicts and on the level of localized incidents.

Many game critics assume that all stories must be classically constructed with each element tightly integrated into the overall plot trajectory. Costikyan (2000) writes, for example, that "a story is a controlled experience; the author consciously crafts it, choosing certain events precisely, in a certain order, to create a story with maximum impact."[8]

Adams (1999) claims, "a good story hangs together the way a good jigsaw puzzle hangs together. When you pick it up, every piece is locked tightly in place next to its neighbors."

Spatial stories, on the other hand, are often dismissed as episodic — that is, each episode (or set piece) can become compelling on its own terms without contributing significantly to the plot development, and often the episodes could be reordered without significantly impacting our experience as a whole. There may be broad movements or series of stages within the story, as Troy Dunniway suggests when he draws parallels between the stages in the Hero's journey (as outlined by Joseph Campbell) and the levels of a classic adventure game, but within each stage, the sequencing of actions may be quite loose. Spatial stories are not badly constructed stories; rather, they are stories that respond to alternative aesthetic principles, privileging spatial exploration over plot development. Spatial stories are held together by broadly defined goals and conflicts and pushed forward by the character's movement across the map. Their resolution often hinges on the player reaching his or her final destination, though, as Mary Fuller notes, not all travel narratives end successfully or resolve the narrative enigmas that set them into motion. Once again, we are back to principles of "environmental storytelling." The organization of the plot becomes a matter of designing the geography of imaginary worlds,

Game Theories > Jenkins   McKenzie Eskelinen
                      Juul   Ito Pearce
                      Pearce   Flanagan Bernstein
                      Zimmerman Crawford Juul

IV. Game Theories

125

so that obstacles thwart and affordances facilitate the protagonist's forward movement towards resolution. Over the past several decades, game designers have become more and more adept at setting and varying the rhythm of game play through features of the game space.

Narrative can also enter games on the level of localized incident, or what I am calling micronarratives. We might understand how micronarratives work by thinking about the Odessa Steps sequence in Sergei Eisenstein's *Battleship Potemkin*. First, recognize that, whatever its serious moral tone, the scene basically deals with the same kind of material as most games — the steps are a contested space with one group (the peasants) trying to advance up and another (the Cossacks) moving down.

Eisenstein intensifies our emotional engagement with this large-scale conflict through a series of short narrative units. The woman with the baby carriage is perhaps the best known of those micronarratives. Each of these units builds upon stock characters or situations drawn from the repertoire of melodrama. None of them last more than a few seconds, though Eisenstein prolongs them (and intensifies their emotional impact) through cross-cutting between multiple incidents. Eisenstein used the term "attraction" to describe such emotionally packed elements in his work; contemporary game designers might call them "memorable moments." Just as some memorable moments in games depend on sensations (the sense of speed in a racing game) or perceptions (the sudden expanse of sky in a snowboarding game) as well as narrative hooks, Eisenstein used the word "attractions" broadly to describe any element within a work that produces a profound emotional impact, and theorized that the themes of the work could be communicated across and through these discrete elements. Even games that do not create large-scale plot trajectories may well depend on these micronarratives to shape the player's emotional experience. Micronarratives may be cut-scenes, but they don't have to be. One can imagine a simple sequence of preprogrammed actions through which an opposing player responds to your successful touchdown in a football game as a micronarrative.

Game critics often note that the player's participation poses a potential threat to the narrative construction, whereas the hard rails of the plotting can overly constrain the "freedom, power, and self-expression" associated with interactivity (Adams 1999). The tension between performance (or game play) and exposition (or story) is far from unique to games. The pleasures of popular culture often center on spectacular performance numbers and self-contained set pieces. It makes no sense to describe musical numbers or gag sequences or action scenes as disruptions of the film's plots: the reason we go to see a kung fu movie is to see Jackie Chan show his stuff.[9] Yet, few films consist simply of such moments, typically falling back on some broad narrative exposition to create a framework within which localized actions become meaningful.[10]

We might describe musicals, action films, or slapstick comedies as having accordion-like structures. Certain plot points are fixed, whereas other moments can be expanded or contracted in response to audience feedback without serious consequences to the overall plot. The introduction needs to establish the character's goals or explain the basic conflict; the conclusion needs to show the successful completion of those goals or the final defeat of the antagonist. In *commedia dell'arte*, for example, the masks define the relationships between the characters and give us some sense of their goals and desires.[11]

The masks set limits on the action, even though the performance as a whole is created through improvisation. The actors have mastered the possible moves, or *lazzi*, associated with each character, much as a game player has mastered the combination of buttons that must be pushed to enable certain character actions. No author prescribes what the actors do once they get on the stage, but the shape of the story emerges from this basic vocabulary of possible actions and from the broad parameters set by this theatrical tradition. Some of the *lazzi* can contribute to the plot development, but many of them are simple restagings of the basic oppositions (the knave tricks the master or gets beaten).

These performance or spectacle-centered genres often display a pleasure in process — in the experiences along the road — that can overwhelm any strong sense of goal or resolution, while exposition can be experienced as an unwelcome interruption to the pleasure of performance. Game designers struggle with this same balancing act — trying to determine how much plot will create a compelling framework and how much freedom players can enjoy at a local level without totally derailing the larger narrative trajectory. As inexperienced storytellers, they often fall back on rather mechanical exposition through cut scenes, much as early filmmakers were sometimes overly reliant on intertitles rather than learning the skills of visual storytelling. Yet, as with any other aesthetic tradition, game designers are apt to develop craft through a process of experimentation and refinement of basic narrative devices, becoming better at shaping narrative experiences without unduly constraining the space for improvisation within the game.

Embedded Narratives

Russian formalist critics make a useful distinction between plot (or syuzhet) that refers to, in Kristen Thompson's (1988) terms, "the structured set of all causal events as we see and hear them presented in the film itself," and story (or fabula), which refers to the viewer's mental construction of the chronology of those events (Thompson 1988, 39–40). Few films or novels are absolutely linear; most make use of some forms of backstory that is revealed gradually as we move through the narrative action. The detective story is the classic illustration of this principle, telling two stories — one more or less chronological (the story of the investigation itself) and the other told radically out of sequence (the events motivating and leading up to the murder).

According to this model, narrative comprehension is an active process by which viewers assemble and make hypotheses about likely narrative developments on the basis of information drawn from textual cues and clues.[12] As they move through the film, spectators test and reformulate their mental maps of the narrative action and the story space. In games, players are forced to act upon those mental maps, to literally test them against the game world itself. If you are wrong about

whether the bad guys lurk behind the next door, you will find out soon enough — perhaps by being blown away and having to start the game over. The heavy-handed exposition that opens many games serves a useful function in orienting spectators to the core premises so that they are less likely to make stupid and costly errors as they first enter into the game world. Some games create a space for rehearsal, as well, so that we can make sure we understand our character's potential moves before we come up against the challenges of navigating narrational space.

Read in this light, a story is less a temporal structure than a body of information. The author of a film or a book has a high degree of control over when and if we receive specific bits of information, but a game designer can somewhat control the narrational process by distributing the information across the game space. Within an open-ended and exploratory narrative structure like a game, essential narrative information must be presented redundantly across a range of spaces and artifacts, because one cannot assume the player will necessarily locate or recognize the significance of any given element. Game designers have developed a variety of kludges that allow them to prompt players or steer them towards narratively salient spaces. Yet, this is no different from the ways that redundancy is built into a television soap opera, where the assumption is that a certain number of viewers are apt to miss any given episode, or even in classical Hollywood narrative, where the law of three suggests that any essential plot point needs to be communicated in at least three ways.

To continue with the detective example, then, one can imagine the game designer as developing two kinds of narratives — one relatively unstructured and controlled by the player as they explore the game space and unlock its secrets; the other prestructured but embedded within the mise-en-scene awaiting discovery. The game world becomes a kind of information space, a memory palace. *Myst* is a highly successful example of this kind of embedded narrative, but embedded narrative does not necessarily require an emptying of the space of contemporary narrative activities, as a game such as *Half-Life* might suggest. Embedded narrative can and often does occur within contested spaces. We may have to battle our way past antagonists, navigate through mazes, or figure out how to pick locks in order to move through the narratively impregnated mise-en-scene. Such a mixture of enacted and embedded narrative elements can allow for a balance between the flexibility of interactivity and the coherence of a pre-authored narrative.

Using *Quake* as an example, Jesper Juul argues that flashbacks are impossible within games, because the game play always occurs in real-time (Juul 1998). Yet, this is to confuse story and plot. Games are no more locked into an eternal present than films are always linear. Many games contain moments of revelation or artifacts that shed light on past actions. Carson (2000) suggests that part of the art of game design comes in finding artful ways of embedding narrative information into the environment without destroying its immersiveness and without giving the player a sensation of being drug around by the neck:

> Staged areas... [can] lead the game player to come to their own conclusions about a previous event or to suggest a potential danger just ahead. Some examples include... doors that have been broken open, traces of a recent explosion, a crashed vehicle, a piano dropped from a great height, charred remains of a fire.

Players, he argues, can return to a familiar space later in the game and discover it has been transformed by subsequent (off-screen) events. *Clive Barker's Undying*, for example, creates a powerful sense of backstory in precisely this manner. It is a story of sibling rivalry that has taken on supernatural dimensions. As we visit each character's space, we have a sense of the human they once were and the demon they have become. In Peter Molyneux's *Black and White*, the player's ethical choices within the game leave traces on the landscape or reconfigure the physical appearances of their characters. Here, we might read narrative consequences off mise-en-scene the same way we read Dorian Gray's debauchery off of his portrait. Carson describes such narrative devices as "following Saknussemm," referring

to the ways that the protagonists of Jules Verne's *Journey to The Center of the Earth* keep stumbling across clues and artifacts left behind by the sixteenth-century Icelandic scientist/explorer Arne Saknussemm, and readers become fascinated to see what they can learn about his ultimate fate as the travelers come closer to reaching their intended destination.

Game designers might study melodrama for a better understanding of how artifacts or spaces can contain affective potential or communicate significant narrative information. Melodrama depends on the external projection of internal states, often through costume design, art direction, or lighting choices. As we enter spaces, we may become overwhelmed with powerful feelings of loss or nostalgia, especially in those instances where the space has been transformed by narrative events. Consider, for example, the moment in *Doctor Zhivago* when the characters return to the mansion, now completely deserted and encased in ice, or when Scarlett O'Hara travels across the scorched remains of her family estate in *Gone With the Wind* following the burning of Atlanta. In Alfred Hitchcock's *Rebecca*, the title character never appears, but she exerts a powerful influence over the other characters — especially the second Mrs. DeWinter, who must inhabit a space where every artifact recalls her predecessor. Hitchcock creates a number of scenes of his protagonist wandering through Rebecca's space, passing through locked doors, staring at her overwhelming portrait on the wall, touching her things in drawers, or feeling the texture of fabrics and curtains. No matter where she goes in the house, she cannot escape Rebecca's memory.

A game such as Neil Young's *Majestic* pushes this notion of embedded narrative to its logical extreme. Here, the embedded narrative is no longer contained within the console but rather flows across multiple information channels. The player's activity consists of sorting through documents, deciphering codes, making sense of garbled transmissions, moving step-by-step towards a fuller understanding of the conspiracy that is the game's primary narrative focus. We follow links between web sites; we get information through webcasts, faxes, e-mails, and phone calls. Such an embedded narrative doesn't require a branching story

127

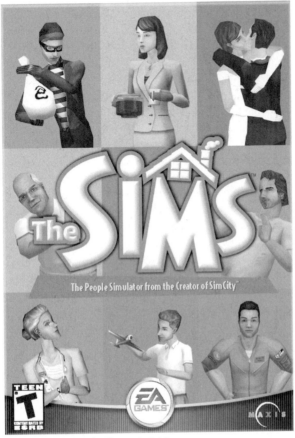

10.3 *The Sims*. (Maxis, Electronic Arts)

Emergent Narratives

The Sims represents a fourth model of how narrative possibilities might get mapped onto game space (figure 10.3). Emergent narratives are not prestructured or preprogrammed, taking shape through the game play, yet they are not as unstructured, chaotic, and frustrating as life itself. Game worlds, ultimately, are not real worlds, even those as densely developed as *Shenmue* or as geographically expansive as *Everquest*. Will Wright frequently describes *The Sims* as a sandbox or dollhouse game, suggesting that it should be understood as a kind of authoring environment within which players can define their own goals and write their own stories. Yet, unlike Microsoft Word, the game doesn't open on a blank screen. Most players come away from spending time with *The Sims* with some degree of narrative satisfaction. Wright has created a world ripe with narrative possibilities, where each design decision has been made with an eye towards increasing the prospects of interpersonal romance or conflict.

The ability to design our own "skins" encourages players to create characters who are emotionally significant to them, to rehearse their own relationships with friends, family, or coworkers or to map characters from other fictional universes onto *The Sims*. A glance at the various scrapbooks players have posted on the web suggests that they have been quick to take advantage of its relatively open-ended structure. Yet, let's not underestimate the designers' contributions. The characters have a will of their own, not always submitting easily to the player's control, as when a depressed protagonist refuses to seek employment, preferring to spend hour upon hour soaking in their bath or moping on the front porch.

Characters are given desires, urges, and needs, which can come into conflict with each other, and thus produce dramatically compelling encounters. Characters respond emotionally to events in their environment, as when characters mourn the loss of a loved one. Our choices have consequences, as when we spend all of our money and have nothing left to buy them food. The gibberish language and flashing symbols allow us to map our own meanings onto the conversations, yet the

structure but rather depends on scrambling the pieces of a linear story and allowing us to reconstruct the plot through our acts of detection, speculation, exploration, and decryption. Not surprisingly, most embedded narratives, at present, take the form of detective or conspiracy stories, since these genres help to motivate the player's active examination of clues and exploration of spaces and provide a rationale for our efforts to reconstruct the narrative of past events. Yet, as the preceding examples suggest, melodrama provides another — and as yet largely unexplored — model for how an embedded story might work, as we read letters and diaries, snoop around in bedroom drawers and closets, in search of secrets that might shed light on the relationships between characters.

128

tone of voice and body language can powerfully express specific emotional states, which encourage us to understand those interactions within familiar plot situations. The designers have made choices about what kinds of actions are and are not possible in this world, such as allowing for same-sex kisses, but limiting the degree of explicit sexual activity that can occur. (Good programmers may be able to get around such restrictions, but most players probably work within the limitations of the system as given.)

Janet Murray's *Hamlet on the Holodeck* might describe some of what Wright accomplishes here as procedural authorship. Yet, I would argue that his choices go deeper than this, working not simply through the programming, but also through the design of the game space. For example, just as a dollhouse offers a streamlined representation that cuts out much of the clutter of an actual domestic space, the Sims' houses are stripped down to only a small number of artifacts, each of which perform specific kinds of narrative functions. Newspapers, for example, communicate job information. Characters sleep in beds. Bookcases can make you smarter. Bottles are for spinning and thus motivating lots of kissing. Such choices result in a highly legible narrative space. In his classic study *The Image of The City*, Kevin Lynch made the case that urban designers needed to be more sensitive to the narrative potentials of city spaces, describing city planning as "the deliberate manipulation of the world for sensuous ends" (Lynch 1960, 116).

Urban designers exert even less control than game designers over how people use the spaces they create or what kinds of scenes they stage there. Yet, some kinds of space lend themselves more readily to narratively memorable or emotionally meaningful experiences than others. Lynch suggested that urban planners should not attempt to totally predetermine the uses and meanings of the spaces they create: "a landscape whose every rock tells a story may make difficult the creation of fresh stories" (Lynch 1960, 6). Rather, he proposes an aesthetic of urban design that endows each space with "poetic and symbolic" potential: "Such a sense of place in itself enhances every human activity that occurs there, and encourages the deposit of a

memory trace" (Lynch 1960, 119). Game designers would do well to study Lynch's book, especially as they move into the production of game platforms which support player-generated narratives.

In each of these cases, choices about the design and organization of game spaces have narratological consequences. In the case of evoked narratives, spatial design can either enhance our sense of immersion within a familiar world or communicate a fresh perspective on that story through the altering of established details. In the case of enacted narratives, the story itself may be structured around the character's movement through space and the features of the environment may retard or accelerate that plot trajectory. In the case of embedded narratives, the game space becomes a memory palace whose contents must be deciphered as the player tries to reconstruct the plot. And in the case of emergent narratives, game spaces are designed to be rich with narrative potential, enabling the story-constructing activity of players. In each case, it makes sense to think of game designers less as storytellers than as narrative architects.

Notes

1. The term "ludology" was coined by Espen Aarseth, who advocates the emergence of a new field of study, specifically focused on the study of games and game play, rather than framed through the concerns of pre-existing disciplines or other media. (Editors' note: Markku Eskelinen, in his response to this essay, points out that the term was introduced to computer game studies by Gonzalo Frasca. This introduction, according to Frasca, was in the *Cybertext Yearbook* — a publication coedited by Eskelinen and named for Aarseth's *Cybertext* [1997].)

2. For a more recent formulation of this same argument, see Jesper Juul (2001), "Games Telling Stories?"

3. Eskelinen (2001) takes Janet Murray to task for her narrative analysis of *Tetris* as "a perfect enactment of the overtasked lives of Americans in the 1990s — of the constant bombardment of tasks that demand our attention and that we must somehow fit into our overcrowded schedules and clear off our desks in order to make room for the next onslaught." Eskelinen is correct to note that the abstraction of *Tetris* would seem to defy narrative interpretation, but that is not the same thing as insisting that no meaningful analysis can be made of the game and its fit within contemporary culture. *Tetris* might well express something of the frenzied pace of modern life, just as modern dances might, without being a story.

4. "A story is a collection of facts in a time-sequenced order that suggest a cause and effect relationship" (Crawford 1982). "The story is the antithesis of game. The best way to tell a story is in linear form. The best way to create a game is to provide a structure within which the player has freedom of action" (Costikyan, 2000).

129

5. "In its richest form, storytelling — narrative — means the reader's surrender to the author. The author takes the reader by the hand and leads him into the world of his imagination. The reader has a role to play, but it's a fairly passive role: to pay attention, to understand, perhaps to think... but not to act" (Adams 1999).

6. As I have noted elsewhere, these maps take a distinctive form — not objective or abstract top-down views but composites of screenshots that represent the game world as we will encounter it in our travels through its space. Game space never exists in abstract, but always experientially.

7. My concept of spatial stories is strongly influenced by Michel de Certeau (1988) *The Practice of Everyday Life* and Henri LeFebvre (1991), *The Production of Space*.

8. For a fuller discussion of the norms of classically constructed narrative, see Bordwell, Staiger, and Thompson (1985), *The Classical Hollywood Cinema*.

9. For useful discussion of this issue in film theory, see Donald Crafton (1995), "Pie and Chase: Gag, Spectacle and Narrative in Slapstick Comedy," in Kristine Brunovska Karnick and Henry Jenkins (eds.), *Classical Hollywood Comedy*; Henry Jenkins (1991), *What Made Pistachio Nuts?: Early Sound Comedy and The Vaudeville Aesthetic*; Rick Altman (1999), *The American Film Musical*; Tom Gunning (1990), "The Cinema of Attractions: Early Film, Its Spectator and the Avant Garde" in Thomas Elsaesser with Adam Barker (eds.), *Early Cinema: Space, Frame, Narrative*; Linda Williams (1999), *Hard Core: Power, Pleasure and "The Frenzy of the Visible."*

10. "Games that just have nonstop action are fun for a while but often get boring. This is because of the lack of intrigue, suspense, and drama. How many action movies have you seen where the hero of the story shoots his gun every few seconds and is always on the run? People lose interest watching this kind of movie. Playing a game is a bit different, but the fact is the brain becomes over stimulated after too much nonstop action" (Dunniway 2000).

11. See, for example, John Rudlin (1994), *Commedia Dell'Arte: An Actor's Handbook* for a detailed inventory of the masks and *lazzi* of this tradition.

12. See, for example, David Bordwell (1989), *Narration in the Fiction Film*, and Edward Branigan (1992), *Narrative Comprehension and Film*.

References

Aarseth, Espen (1997). *Cybertext: Perspectives on Ergodic Literature*. Baltimore: Johns Hopkins University Press.

Adams, Ernest (1999). "Three Problems For Interactive Storytellers." *Gamasutra*, December 29, 1999.

Altman, Rick (1999). *The American Film Musical*. Bloomington: Indiana University Press.

Bordwell, David, Janet Staiger, and Kristen Thompson (1985). *The Classical Hollywood Cinema*. New York: Columbia University Press.

Bordwell, David (1989). *Narration in the Fiction Film*. Madison: University of Wisconsin.

Branigan, Edward (1992). *Narrative Comprehension and Film*. New York: Routledge.

Carson, Don (2000). "Environmental Storytelling: Creating Immersive 3D Worlds Using Lessons Learned From the Theme Park Industry." *Gamasutra*, March 1, 2000. <http://www.gamasutra.com/features/20000301/carson_pfv.htm>.

Costikyan, Greg (2000). "Where Stories End and Games Begin." *Game Developer*, September 2000.

Crafton, Donald (1995). "Pie and Chase: Gag, Spectacle and Narrative in Slapstick Comedy." In *Classical Hollywood Comedy*, edited by Kristine Brunovska Karnick and Henry Jenkins. New York: Routledge/American Film Institute.

Crawford, Chris (1982). *The Art of Computer Game Design*. <http://www.vancouver.wsu.edu/fac/peabody/game-book/Coverpage.html>.

de Certeau, Michel (1988). *The Practice of Everyday Life*. Berkeley: University of California Press.

Dunniway, Troy (2000). "Using the Hero's Journey in Games." *Gamasutra*, November 27, 2000. <http://www.gamasutra.com/features/20001127/dunniway_pfv.htm>.

Eskelinen, Markku (2001). "The Gaming Situation." *Game Studies* 1, no.1 (July 2001). <http://cmc.uib.no/gamestudies/0101/eskelinen>.

Frasca, Gonzalo (1999). "Ludology Meets Narratology: Similitude and Differences between (Video) Games and Narrative." <http://www.jacaranda.org/frasca/ludology.htm>.

Fuller, Mary, and Henry Jenkins (1994). "Nintendo and New World Narrative." In *Communications in Cyberspace*, edited by Steve Jones. New York: Sage.

Gunning, Tom (1990). "The Cinema of Attractions: Early Film, Its Spectator and the Avant Garde." In *Early Cinema: Space, Frame, Narrative*, edited by Thomas Elsaesser with Adam Barker. London: British Film Institute.

Jenkins, Henry (1991). *What Made Pistachio Nuts?: Early Sound Comedy and The Vaudeville Aesthetic*. New York: Columbia University Press.

Jenkins, Henry (1993). "x Logic: Placing Nintendo in Children's Lives." *Quarterly Review of Film and Video*, August 1993.

Jenkins, Henry (1998). 'Complete Freedom of Movement': Video Games as Gendered Playspace." In *From Barbie to Mortal Kombat: Gender and Computer Games*," edited by Justine Cassell and Henry Jenkins. Cambridge: The MIT Press.

Juul, Jesper (1998). "A Clash Between Games and Narrative." Paper presented at the Digital Arts and Culture Conference, Bergen, November 1998. <http://www.jesperjuul.dk/text/DAC%20Paper%201998.html>.

Juul, Jesper (2001). "Games Telling Stories?" *Game Studies* 1, no.1 (July 2001). <http://cmc.uib.no/gamestudies/0101/juul-gts>.

LeFebvre, Henri (1991). *The Production of Space*. London: Blackwell.

Lynch, Kevin (1960). *The Image of the City*. Cambridge: The MIT Press.

Murray, Janet (1997). *Hamlet on the Holodeck: The Future of Narrative in Cyberspace*. Cambridge: The MIT Press.

Ritvo, Harriet (1998). *The Platypus and the Mermaid, and Other Figments of the Classifying Imagination*. Cambridge: Harvard University Press.

Rudlin, John (1994). *Commedia Dell'Arte: An Actor's Handbook*. New York: Routledge.

Thompson, Kristen (1988). *Breaking the Glass Armor: Neoformalist Film Analysis*. Princeton: Princeton University Press.

Williams, Linda (1999). *Hard Core: Power, Pleasure and "The Frenzy of the Visible."* Berkeley: University of California Press.

Introduction to Game Time

Jesper Juul

The following sketches a theory of time in games. This is motivated by: (1) plain curiosity; (2) theoretical lack: much work has been done on time in other cultural forms, but there is very little theory of time in games; and (3) the hope that a theory of game time may help us examine specific games, help trace the historical development of games, connect to the big question of how a game feeds player experiences, and generally serve as an analytical tool for opening other discussions in game studies and game design.

Most computer games project a game world, and to play them is therefore to engage in a kind of pretense-play: you are both "yourself," and you have another role in the game world. This duality is reflected in the *game time*, which can be described as a basic duality of *play time* (the time the player takes to play) and *event time* (the time taken in the game world). The relationship between play time and event time is, as we shall see, highly variable between games and game genres: action games tend to proceed in real time, but strategy and simulation games often feature sped-up time or even the possibility of manually speeding or slowing the game. Running counter to this, abstract games do not project a game world at all, and therefore do not have a separate event time.

The play-element of games is reflected in the way we discuss them: if we utter the sentence "Brian is a pig," this is usually considered a metaphor and an insult. A metaphor, since we would propose a transfer of our ideas of a pig to Brian as a person, and an insult, since this would cast Brian in a negative light. But as Ana Marjanovic-Shane describes, to say, "Brian is a pig" while playing a game does not describe Brian as person; it only says that in this play context, Brian assumes the role of a pig. Marjanovic-Shane describes this as a proposition about a fictive plane, rather than a proposition about reality. So, computer games are much like the pretense-play of children (and adults); if we play the World War II game *Axis and Allies*, all our actions have a double meaning. We move a piece around a board, but this also means invading Scandinavia with our troops. We click the keys on the keyboard, but we are also moving Lara Croft.[1] The harmless statement "Brian is a pig" can obviously also be said of an actor in a play, but not of the audience: if Brian is watching the movie *Babe*, we don't say, "Brian is a pig." This means that when we talk about games, we assume a much more direct connection between the game and the

---

Response by Mizuko Ito

Time has received little attention in comparison to related discussions of identity and place in virtual worlds, and Jesper Juul's discussion opens up intriguing analytic territory. Juul draws continuities with issues of identity, place, and pretense-play; just as games enable players to try on different identities and teleport to fantastic worlds, they also enable players to experience time in ways not available in real life: time warps, time lapse, time travel, frozen time. At the same time, there are also interesting peculiarities in how to account and coordinate between "real" and "virtual"[1] time, or Juul's play time and event time, and these issues resonate with and diverge from parallel conversations about identity and place in interesting ways. Juul's essay brings these peculiarities up with careful and thought-provoking detail.

The question of representational realism and fidelity in the case of time is particularly intriguing. What are the trade-offs for particular game genres? In the case of objects, people, and places, certain game genres demand higher degrees of realism with regard to real life, such as flight and sport simulations, but most games take advantage of the opportunity for fantasy characters, settings, and physics. In the case of time, pauses, warps, and replays are all player-accessible technical capabilities. Current game design seems to support these options for time play at the expense of temporal realism and consistency in part to manage the balance between flow and dead time that Juul points

player than we would in movies or novels, because games map the player into the game world.

My inquiry therefore proceeds from the belief that a game theory is best built not so much by plainly importing assumptions from other cultural forms, as by examining actual games.[2] The primary focus here is on computer games (in a broad sense, including arcade and console games), but nonelectronic games are also included for an historical perspective.

The theory primarily describes linear, measurable time in games. An obvious objection to this would be that since the playing of a game is a subjective experience, objective time is of secondary importance. But as we shall see, the subjective experience of time is strongly affected by objective time structured by the game: game design and game rules work with objective time in order to create the player's subjective experiences. So examining objective time in games is, paradoxically, a way of understanding how the formal structure of a game feeds the more elusive player experience. The aesthetic problems surrounding "save games" are a prime example.

Finally, game time can be used for examining game history; the development of time in computer games can be seen as the interaction of two different base models: the adventure game that creates coherent worlds that the player must explore in a coherent time,

and the action game that favors unexplained jumps in world and time by way of unconnected levels and rounds.

Abstract Games and the State Machine

To play a game takes time. A game begins and it ends. I'd like to call this time *play time*. Play time denotes the time span taken to play a game. As a first example, we may look at checkers. In abstract games such as checkers or *Tetris*, it would seem that this was all there was to it: that we play games, that everything in the game happens now, while we play. In soccer — which is really just a physical abstract game — the same thing would be true. To draw a diagram of time in such a game is rather trivial:

Play time

Time in abstract games

When playing checkers, tennis, or *Tetris* it does not make sense to say that you are immersed in a world: they do not contain play-pretense. The more fundamental part of games is a change of state, the movement from the initial state (the outcome has not been decided) to another state (the outcome has been decided). To help understand this, we may take a cue

---

out, but also to coordinate between real life rhythms and play time.

This leads to another intriguing question embedded in the essay. Given fantasy time and time play as a parallel to fantasy worlds and identity play, how do we coordinate between real and virtual time? When players are essentially in two places at the same time, as two different personas, and in two different points in time, something has to give. Event and play time ideally track along the neat railroad diagrams in Juul's paper, as player and software engage in coordinated exchanges, but in reality, the contingencies of our real lives constantly intrude and put brakes on our play time. How do you answer the door to get a pizza to nourish your flesh-and-blood body when you are in the

middle of life and death online combat? If your opponent is a home computer, you probably have the luxury of freezing both event and play time, but if you are playing an online multi-user game, event time marches relentlessly on unless you can somehow convince your opponent to take into account your real-life circumstances.

Quickly completed games like *Tetris* or turn-based games have appeal because they can easily fit in temporal interstices. For games that demand real-time interaction and extended play, it seems crucial to lean on the capabilities of fantasy time and time play to smooth the coordination task. And Juul notes how players take nonrealist conventions of saves, replays, cut scenes, warps, level changes, and loading pauses in

Game Theories >
Jenkins   McKenzie Eskelinen
Juul   **Ito Pearce**
Pearce   Flanagan Bernstein
Zimmerman Crawford Juul

IV. Game Theories

from computer science, saying that a game is actually a *state machine*: it is a system that can be in different states; it contains input and output functions, and definitions of what state and what input will lead to what following state. You can move the piece from E2 to E4, but not to E5; if you are hit by the rocket launcher, you lose energy; if your base is taken, you have lost; etc. When you play a game, you are interacting with the state machine that is the game. In a board game, this state is stored in the position of the pieces on the board; in sports, the game state *is* the players; in computer games, the state is stored as variables and then represented on screen.[3] In the rest of this article, I will be referring to the state of a game as the *game state*. When you play a game, you are simply interacting with the game state:

Player

Game state

To play a game is to interact with the game state.
(Zoom on play time)

If you cannot influence the game state in any way (as opposed to being unable to influence it in the right way), you are not playing a game. The difference between a real-time abstract game and a turn-based abstract game is simply that in the latter case the game

state only changes when the player takes a turn. In a real-time game, not doing anything also has consequences. Additionally, turn-based games do not specify the amount of play time that the player can use on a specific move. (Although this may be specified by tournament rules or social pressure.)

Real-Time Games with Worlds

If we then play a real-time game like *Quake III* or *Unreal Tournament* we experience the duality described in the play section above: you are both "yourself," and a character in the game world. I propose the term "event time" to denominate the time of the events happening in the game world. In most action games and in the traditional arcade game, the play time/event time relation is presented as being 1:1. The frenetic *Quake III* is a good example of the urgency and immediacy provided by a real-time game.

Pressing the fire key or moving the mouse immediately affects the world inside the game. So the game presents a parallel world, happening in real time:

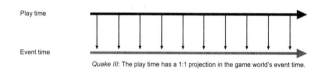

Play time

Event time

Quake III: The play time has a 1:1 projection in the game world's event time.

133

---

stride as easily as they assume the identity of Lara Croft. Now if only we could pause real-life time to get on with the work of gaming.

From Celia Pearce's Online Response

Juul talks about player manipulation of time (speeding up, slowing down, saving) to adjust for skill level. However, player-manipulated time schemes can also be used as a game strategy. For example, in *The Sims*, I frequently load the characters up with "dead" actions, such as chores, then run the game on double-speed until they're done. This is a time-efficiency strategy so that I can focus on more interesting game events, such as socializing. [. . .]

Juul's in-depth discussion of "saving" is incredibly

useful, but I was surprised that he made no mention of conventions of reincarnation and the role of death in game time. In many first-person shooter games, it is possible to die and rise again; whereas games such as *EverQuest* employ the convention of "perma-death." I think these approaches to and metaphors of death and reincarnation are very important, especially in terms of fictive time schemes, and should be addressed further.

http://www.electronicbookreview.com/thread/firstperson/pearcer1

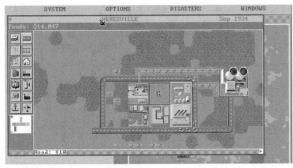

11.1. *SimCity*. (Maxis, Electronic Arts)

In *SimCity* we also find play time and event time. But what *happens* in the game — investing in infrastructure, building houses — happens faster than we would expect it to, were these real-life events. The event time depends on either explicit marks such as dates or on cultural assumptions about the duration of the game events. *SimCity* has both: we know that building a power plant

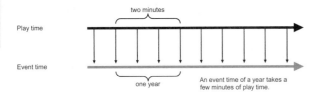

takes more than a few seconds, and the interface displays the current date in the event time. Playing for two minutes makes a year pass in the event time/game world.

Mapping

The relationship between play time and event time can be described as *mapping*. Mapping means that the player's time and actions are projected into a game world. This is the play-element of games; you click with your mouse, but you are also the mayor of a fictive city.

In this way, there is a basic sense of *now* when you play a game; the events in a game, be they ever so strange and unlike the player's situation, have a basic link to the player. Games require at least one instance of the player interacting with the game state; so games that are not abstract also require at least one instance of mapping — one instance where the player performs some act, such as moving a piece on a board or pressing a key on a keyboard, that is projected as having a specific meaning in the game world. The moment of mapping is one that has a basic sense of happening *now*, when you play. Pressing a key influences the game world, which then logically (and intuitively) has to be happening in the same *now*.

As described, action games tend to have a 1:1 mapping of the play time to the event time. In some games such as *Shogun: Total War*, or *The Sims*, the player

Juul responds

My point is not that real-time games are inherently better or ultimately more compelling than turn-based games, but we can observe that non-paced computer games have all but disappeared: the strategy game has become real-time strategy; the adventure game is often pronounced dead (and is perhaps being replaced by games like *Alice* or *Half-Life*); the commercial puzzle games are real-time.

http://www.electronicbookreview.com/thread/firstperson/juulr2

Game Theories > Jenkins
Juul
Pearce
Zimmerman

McKenzie Eskelinen
Ito Pearce
Flanagan Bernstein
Crawford Juul

IV. Game Theories

11.2 Navigating the game world in search of a potion to make Alice small. (Rogue Entertainment, Electronic Arts)

11.3. Having completed a task, you are rewarded with a cut-scene which gives you information about the next task. (Rogue Entertainment, Electronic Arts)

135

can select the game speed, thus specifying the relation between play time and event time.[4] So the play time can be mapped to event time with a specific *speed*; the player decides how long a period in play time will map to in event time.

There is one extra point about the mapping itself; many games claim to depict historical events: *Axis and Allies* (about World War II) may be a good example, as may the computer game *Age of Empires*. In these games, the event time is assigned to a specific historical period. It is thus perfectly possible to play a real-time game that takes place in 15th Century France or in space in the 32nd. This can be indicated by something as simple as the text on the box ("The year is 3133"), or it can be something the player deduces from the game setting. The year specification in *SimCity* serves the same purpose: so the play time can be mapped to event time with a specific speed and it can be fixated historically.

Modern Games with Cut-Scenes

But not all event time is mapped from play time; it is quite common for the computer games of today to contain intro-sequences and cut-scenes. As an example we can look at the game *American McGee's Alice*.

The single-player game in *Alice* is a mission-based real-time game where each mission is framed by *cut-scenes*. Cut-scenes depict events in the event time (in the game world). Cut-scenes are not a parallel time or

11.4 Navigating the game world in search of the promised concoction. (Rogue Entertainment, Electronic Arts)

an extra level, but a different way of creating the event time. They do not by themselves modify the game state — this is why they can usually be skipped, and why the user can't do anything during a cut-scene. Whereas action sequences have play time mapped to event time, cut-scenes disconnect play time from event time:

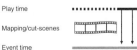
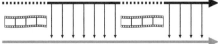

Play time

Mapping/cut-scenes

Event time

Alternation between play time mapping to event time and event time being narrated by cut-scenes.

Interestingly, there is something of a convention that the play sequences use the full screen, while the cut-scenes are "letterbox," i.e., black bars are added at top and bottom. This presumably signifies "cinema," and also indicates the absence of interactivity. The letterbox presentation cues the player to interpret the graphics using cinematic conventions rather than game conventions.

The Chronology of Time in Games

Regardless of inspirations from cinema, time in games is almost always chronological, and there are several reasons for this. Flash-forwards are highly problematic, since describing events-to-come means that the player's actions do not really matter.[5] Using cut-scenes or in-game artifacts, it is possible to describe events that lead to the current event time, but doing an interactive flashback leads to the classical time machine problem: the player's actions in the past may suddenly render the present impossible, and what then?[6] So time in games is almost always chronological.[7]

But one of the more interesting developments in recent years is that game designers have become better at creating games where things in the game's event time point to past events. Modern adventure games tend to contain not only cut-scenes, but also artifacts in the game world (event time) that tell the player what happened at a previous point in event time. This is the basic detective game model. In *Myst*, books in the game world will also tell you of events that happened prior to the time of the playing, or at least outside the time that you can interact.

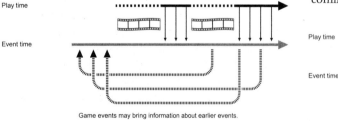

Game events may bring information about earlier events.

Adventure and *Pong*: Coherent Time vs. Level Time

Many, especially newer, games are careful to craft the event time as being continuous, creating a believable world. In *Half-Life*, the entire game world is presented as coherent (even if it features teleports). When loading, this is indicated by the word "loading": the event time is described as continuous, but the play time is on pause while loading:

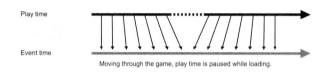

Moving through the game, play time is paused while loading.

But on the other hand, many games are quite imprecise with event time. In the classical arcade game, the changing of levels is usually not described as making any sense in the game world; in fact arcade games tend to present several ontologically separate worlds that simply replace one another with no indication of any connection. One way to soothe the passage between two levels is, of course, to use cut-scenes. One of the earliest examples of this, from 1982, is *Pengo*:[8]

This cut-scene does not actually make any kind of temporal sense; it does not mean that something happens in the game world, but rather presents a break between two separate worlds in the game; the timeline of both play time and game time are broken. Play time is not mapped to event time; there is no connection between the event time of the previous level and the coming level:

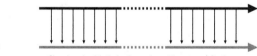

Changing a level, both play time and event time are undefined.

Game Theories > | Jenkins | McKenzie Eskelinen
Juul | Ito **Pearce**
Pearce | Flanagan Bernstein
Zimmerman | Crawford Juul

IV. Game Theories

137

```
1P  7160  HI 20000  2P        0

    GAME TIME      MIN.35 SEC.

    FROM 00 TO 19 .5000 PTS.
    FROM 20 TO 29 .2000 PTS.
    FROM 30 TO 39 .1000 PTS.
    FROM 40 TO 49 ..500 PTS.
    FROM 50 TO 59 ...10 PTS.
    60 AND OVER      NO BONUS.




ACT 2                © SEGA 1982
```

11.5. *Pengo*. After level 2, penguins dance to Beethoven's *An Die Freude*. (Sega)

Similarly, in newer games like *Quake III* or *Counter-Strike*, the jump between different levels is not explained, and the display refers to the materiality of the game ("loading"/"awaiting gamestate") rather than to the game world.

If we think of games as fiction or stories, these kind of abrupt jumps seem unwarranted and esoteric. So why these series of separate worlds without sensible connection? Tracing this historically, we can look at the 1977 game *Space Invaders*, since this game also features several levels: having destroyed all the advancing aliens, the player is simply presented with a new wave of aliens without any explanation. There is no clear relation between these levels. The popularity of this kind of incoherent time can be explained by way of 1971's *Pong*: *Pong* is presented as a kind of tennis, and each session is played with several balls. Pong is structured like a meta-game consisting of separate

rounds, but it makes sense here — this is, in fact, just like tennis. *Space Invaders* borrows the concept of rounds *and* projects a game world. So levels seem connected to the rounds found in sports and other pre-electronic games. This makes sense as an activity (in play time), but not when the game projects a world (in event time). But players do not seem to have any problems with such discontinuities.

Standard Violations of Game Time

In addition to the lack of connection between levels in some games, there are also some standard violations of the play time/event time relationship. Since the play time is projected into the event time, pausing the play time is supposed to pause the event time, bringing the game world to a standstill. The most common violation of this principle regards sound; in *Black and White*, the environmental sounds continue playing when the game is paused. In *The Sims*, the CD player you've purchased for your Sims continues playing when the game is paused. *Space Quest* has a rare but serious violation: *Space Quest* has several speed settings which then influence the play time/event time relation, making the player move faster on higher speeds. In one scene, acid drops falling from a ceiling have a constant speed regardless of the speed setting, and it is thus much easier to outrun the dangerous drops on the high-speed setting (example from Rau 2001).[9]

Save Games

So far, this discussion has been about time in individual game sessions, but adventure games and action-based exploratory games such as *Half-Life* require many game sessions and many saves to complete. In fact, the author's playing of *Half-Life* included literally hundreds of saves and reloads. The same save games were reloaded many times until progress had been made.

Save games are manipulations of game time. They obviously allow the player to store the game state at a moment in play time and then later continue playing from that position. In retrospect, my playing of *Half-Life* is a combination of a multitude of small play sessions that moved the protagonist from the game's beginning to the end. A reconstruction of all the time used on the game would yield a giant tree with numerous forks (the save games), numerous dead ends, and only one path through.

There are several arguments against save games, and all relate to the fact that save games allow the player to chop up the game time. First of all, save games are accused of decreasing the dramatic tension of the game, since the player simply reloads if something goes wrong. Another argument is that saves make the game easier or too easy. Both arguments could apply to my experience with *Half-Life*, since a large part of the game was played in a slightly disinterested save-try-reload routine. Although save games make *Half-Life* much easier, it nevertheless appears humanly impossible to complete the game without them. And another counter to these two arguments is the immense frustration to be had if you are forced to replay an entire game level simply because you made a mistake at the very end.[10] For example, the recent games *Hitman: Codename 47* and *Giants: Citizen Kabuto* have been blasted for lacking an in-level save function (see Osborne 2000). A third argument is that the possibility of saving destroys the player's sense of immersion. The fourth is Chris Crawford's uncompromising position, that the need for save games is a symptom of design flaws:

> Experienced gamers have come to regard the save-die-reload cycle as a normal component of the total gaming experience... Any game that requires reloading as a normal part of the player's progress through the system is fundamentally flawed. On the very first playing, even a below-average player should be able to successfully traverse the game sequence. As the player grows more skilled, he may become faster or experience other challenges, but he should never have to start over after dying.
> (Crawford; in Rollings and Morris 2001, 5)

It seems that Crawford is thinking mostly about fairly replayable games rather than exploratory and adventure games, and in fact there are hardly any

games that fit Crawford's description of being completable in the first go and being replayable and interesting afterwards. Save games are probably not an evil to be avoided at all costs.

But save games are mostly tied to single-player games[11], and mostly to exploratory and adventure games. Persistent games such as MUDs or *EverQuest* only have one play time/event time, and the players do not have an option of saving the game state and going back in play time (i.e., they can't save time, only things).

The Experience of Time

What I haven't touched on so far is the question of subjective time: how the player experiences time in games. The objective, linear time described in the game time model feeds subjective time experiences. The experience is a product of both the play time/event time relation and of the tasks and choices presented to the player. Games are supposed to be, if not fun, at least enjoyable experiences, but this is obviously not always the case: I'd like to invoke the concept of *dead time* — when you have to perform unchallenging activities for the sake of a higher goal. One example is that to progress in *EverQuest* or *Ultima Online*, you must spend hours or days doing mundane tasks such as walking, waiting for monsters to respawn, or even fishing or chopping wood. It makes perfect sense within the context of the game world but it is a dull experience — this is the dead time. You have to perform a specific task to advance in the game, but the task in itself holds no interest.[12]

What makes a game interesting? In *Game Architecture and Design*, Rollings and Morris (2001) (referring to Sid Meier) describe a good game as being a series of interesting choices. This means that for every choice the player faces, there must be no single obviously best option; neither may all options be equally good; and finally the player needs to be able to make some kind of qualified choice within the time allocated to the task. Obvious choices make for uninteresting gameplay. The counterargument to the idea of games as interesting choices is that in the author's experience, some sequences bear repetition even though they contain no interesting choices. Repetition of a trivial task can even be hugely enjoyable — such as getting a perfect 100% score on the challenge stage in *Galaga*.

The concept of *flow* described by Mihaly Csikszentmihalyi can be used for shedding some light on this: Csikszentmihalyi claims that flow is a mental state of enjoyment shared by people in a variety of situations, such as rock-climbing, chess-playing, and composing music. Flow has eight key traits, two of which are clear goals and feedback (very gamelike!). The flow experience also alters the sense of duration: "Hours pass by in minutes, and minutes can stretch out to seem like hours." (Csikszentmihalyi 1991, 49) To reach a state of flow, a game must be neither too hard (which leads to anxiety) nor too easy (which leads to boredom). This means that the experience of time is tied not only to the play time/event time relation and to the challenges provided by the game, but also to the relation between game difficulty and player ability. This creates some design problems by itself since players have varying skills. There are then a variety of ways to deal with this such as skill settings, training missions, handicaps (in multiplayer games), and secret areas to explore (letting the good player experience more). The player's options of changing game speed on the fly in the aforementioned *Sims* and *Shogun* also affects the difficulty (and thereby the cognitive effort needed), allowing the player to select a game that matches his or her skills.

According to the flow framework, the player will only enjoy playing if the challenges match the player's abilities and thereby lead to a state of *flow* (the player loses the sense of objective time — time will fly). If the game is too hard, the player will experience anxiety or frustration. If the game is too easy, repetition or triviality of choice will make time be experienced as unimportant, *dead* time (time will drag).

Flow is a compelling angle on games, but it does not explain everything: David Myers has noted that the fascination of mechanically repeating trivial tasks in some games contradicts flow — repetition should lead to boredom but doesn't always. It also seems to me that frustration is a more *positive* factor than in Csikszentmihalyi's description, because frustration may actually motivate the player to improve in order to

escape frustration. Finally, flow can only explain games as a challenging activity in play time but ignores the projected world, the event time.

A Model of Time in Games

Game state: The state of the game at a given time.

Play time: The time used by the player to play the game.

Event time: The time of the events in the game.

Mapping: The process of claiming that what the player does is also something in event time; a projection of the play time onto event time.

Speed: The relation between the play time and the event time.

Fixation: The historical time of the event time, if any.

Cut-scenes: When the event time is constructed through narration (i.e. told rather than played).

A History of Game Time

Time in games has become increasingly complex and varied during the history of the computer game, but it is a development that moves in two directions. The root of games in play time allows them to define their worlds much more loosely and less coherently than we would accept in most other cultural forms. At the same time, the continued developments in processing power and data storage make it possible to craft event time with increasing detail and precision. These two directions can be traced to two original computer games: the round-based, sports-like game of *Pong* (the action game) and the world-creating, explorative game of *Adventure* (the adventure game).[13]

One of the biggest changes in computer game history is the movement from being primarily played in arcades to being primarily played at home. One of the selling points of the original Pong machine was actually "Ball serves automatically" — the economics of publicly available arcade games demanded that arcade game designers create extremely short (real-time) game sessions in order to have more players insert coins. The home game has made possible games of longer duration, save games, slow games... in fact, more varied game time.

On a historical note, traditional board-, sports-, and card games tend to be quite abstract, whereas computer games mostly project worlds. Though card games in some sense present a third option since the cards are, at

139

least historically, assigned symbolic meanings and are therefore neither abstract, nor world-projecting. Chess is, depending on your interpretation, probably symbolic and somewhere between abstract games and nonabstract games: it *is* possible to see chess as two societies at war (even if it isn't "realistic"), but it would be very hard to interpret chess as specifying event time; that the moving of a rook would "really" take three hours in event time. This is because event time needs to be created by textual and visual cues, and chess is very low on these.

The main difference between the computer game and its nonelectronic precursors is that computer games add automation and complexity — they can uphold and calculate game rules on their own, thereby allowing for richer game worlds; this also lets them keep pace. So computer games create more worlds, more real time, and more single player games than nonelectronic games. (The combination of automation and pace essentially paved the way for the real-time strategy game.) Games with pace seem to be more compelling, or at least more immediately appealing, than turn-based or nonpacing games.

But as always, new forms do not simply annihilate the older ones. Some of the strangest play time/event time mappings can be found in modern pinball games, whose basic rule continues to be "hit all the flashing things," but this is now augmented by a small display sending the player on "missions." The 1993 *Star Trek: Next Generation* contains (among others) a "destroy the asteroid" mission, where an asteroid threatens "the ship," and it is the player's job to destroy the asteroid... by hitting a flashing thing with the ball. There is no way that we can believe in a connection between the player's shooting the ball around and the story happening on the display, but it does not seem to matter.

Conclusion

This essay has described some fundamentals of time in games. The duality of play time and event time appears basic because it is a basic play relation. As shown, the time model proposed here can be used for examining variations in the worlds constructed by different games; it connects to the player's relation to the game, and it can be used for thinking more broadly about game aesthetics. It is also a strong genre indicator, and an essential part of game history. A further step would be more detailed examinations of how game time is constructed through manuals, visual and acoustic cues, and gameplay. Much work is also needed to understand how game time and gameplay create player experiences.

When playing a game that projects a world, the player is (or the player's actions are) projected into the game world in a very direct way — this is the play element of computer games. A more open question is whether this means that we long for the virtual reality dream of being completely immersed in games. Many of the games mentioned here work against the idea of immersion, because their discontinuous times and worlds point strongly to themselves as being games rather then believable fictional environments. This, however, does not make them any less enjoyable. Games do not need to make sense to be fun.

Looking at the terms and diagrams in the text above should not make us forget how incredibly quickly we grasp the complexities of game time when playing. The question "When was the power plant built?" has two answers: July 2001 and September 1934. Doing several things at the same time, acting both here and in a fictive world, comes naturally to most people. As such, there is a lot of work to be done in bringing out the tacit knowledge we use when playing games.

Juul Notes

1. In the play perspective, computer games have several unique traits, one being that play works by projecting actual objects into a fictive plane (such as saying, "This mouse is a spaceship.") A common problem when playing is that the real objects do not have the properties to simulate what they are supposed to represent, i.e., the mouse does not actually fly. It may not matter that much, as it is then possible to say, "The spaceship is flying," but the objects used (the props) are unable to simulate this on their own. In other words, play is good at producing any kind of world, but has problem with consistency. (Computer) games are much better at providing consistency, but they cannot easily create the worlds that play can: the subject matter of a game has to be formalized and created as rules before the game can start.

2. See Juul (2001) for a discussion of the problems of using narrative theory in the study of games.

3. On a technical note, most games are discrete, finite state machines; meaning that the ball is objectively either in or out, and that there is a limitation to the number of possible positions (this is in games such as tic-tac-toe, chess, or *Quake*). Sports are basically analog, infinite state machines; meaning that the ball may be in any number of positions between in and out, and that there is no limit to the possible soccer matches that can be played. Sports tend to have an umpire to decide in doubtful cases, since there may be argument about whether the ball was in or out. This doesn't happen in chess. For the sake of completeness, I must add that some variations of four-in-a-row allow the playing board to be expanded indefinitely; and as such they are discrete, infinite state machines.

4. The play time/event time relation depends somewhat on the familiarity of the game events. The real-time strategy game *StarCraft* (1998) is set in space, and the player doesn't have strong expectation for the speed of the units of the Zergs or the Protoss: the speed selection is consequently not described in relation to the play time (such as "twice as fast"), but simply named "normal," "faster," etc.

5. Flash-forwards *can* be included as indicating something either outside the player's influence or something that the player has to fight to reach. (This then ceases to make sense as a flash-forward, if the player doesn't reach it.)

6. This kind of paradox can be found in *Max Payne* (2001) where the game simply restarts the flashback level if the player fails.

7. The prevalence of unchronological time in traditional narratives is afforded by the fixed nature of the events. Because the story in a sense has already happened, the events can easily be presented in nonchronological order for aesthetic effect.

8. *Donkey Kong* is a year earlier (1981) and features cut-scenes that actually make sense in the game world.

9. Rau's interpretation is that this incident in *Space Quest* destabilizes the notion of event time; I think it has the appearance of a mistake and so rather confirms the idea. Although I think it is perfectly possible to deliberately create such clashes and illogic, I do not think it is the case here.

10. And then again, the joy of winning correlates positively to the amount of frustration experienced on the way, but the general trend from the 1980s till now is to make games easier or at least more tuned towards giving the player many small victories and fewer long stretches of frustration.

11. *Age of Empires II* (1999) is one of the few multiplayer games to contain a save function. This obviously requires a bit of cooperation and communication between players.

12. In an interview, game designer Starr Long comments on the dead time in such games:

Up until now, we've been building these big, giant virtual worlds. And we like to brag about, "Oh, it takes four hours to walk from one end of the continent to the other." Somewhere along the line we lost that it's not really fun to walk for four hours. That's why people don't do it a lot. Imagine if I could go from doing one fun thing to another fun thing without this big dead time in between, where I was either getting lost because it's hard to find my way around, or I get killed on my way and have to start back over. [MacIsaac 2001]

13. This is a simplistic description of computer game history, but the 1980s term "action adventure" captured the marriage of action with exploration. The third major influence on computer games is probably board games, particularly strategy games. Card games do not seem to have had a significant impact on computer games. (Most likely because they are the only major nonspatial game genre, whereas computer games are almost exclusively spatial.)

Ito Response Note

1. I use "real" and "virtual," hereafter not in quotes, as a shorthand to refer to computationally and otherwise embodied phenomenon, not to refer to an ontological distinction.

References: Literature

Csikszentmihalyi, Mihaly (1991). *Flow: The Psychology of Optimal Experience*. New York: Harper Perennial.

Juul, Jesper (2001). "Games Telling Stories?" *Game Studies* 1, No.1 (2001). <http://www.gamestudies.org/0101/juul-gts/>.

Marjanovic-Shane, Ana (1989). "'You Are a Pig': For Real or Just Pretend? — Different Orientations in Play and Metaphor." *Play and Culture* 2, yr. 3 (1989): 225-234.

Myers, David (1992). "Time, Symbol Transformations, and Computer Games." *Play and Culture* 5 (1992): 441-457.

Osborne, Scott (2000). *"Hitman: Codename 47* review." *Gamespot* (2000). <http://gamespot.com/gamespot/stories/reviews/0,10867,2658770 ,00.html>.

Osborne, Scott (2000). *"Giants: Citizen Kabuto* review." *Gamespot* (2000). <http://gamespot.com/gamespot/stories/reviews/0,10867,2664536 ,00.html>.

Rau, Anja (2001). "Reload — Yes/No. Clashing Times in Graphic Adventure Games." Paper Presentation at Computer Games and Digital Textualities, Copenhagen, March 1-2, 2001.

Rollings, Andrew, and Dave Morris (2000). *Game Architecture and Design*. Scottsdale, Arizona: Coriolis.

Rouse III, Richard (2001). *Game Design: Theory & Practice*. Plano, Texas: Wordware.

Selic, Bran, Garth Gullekson, and Paul T. Ward (1994). *Real-Time Object-Oriented Modeling*. New York: John Wiley & Sons.

References: Games

Adventure. Willie Crowther and Don Woods. 1976.

Age of Empires II. Ensemble Studios; Microsoft. 1999.

American McGee's Alice. Rogue Entertainment, Electronic Arts. 2000.

Axis and Allies. Nova Game Design; Milton Bradley. 1984.

Black and White. Lionhead Studios; EA Games. 2001.

Counter-Strike. The Counter-Strike Team. 2000.

Donkey Kong. Nintendo. 1981.

EverQuest. Verant Interactive; Sony Online Entertainment. 1999.

Galaga. Namco. 1981.

Half-Life. Valve Software; Sierra. 1998.

Hitman: Codename 47. IO Interactive; Eidos Interactive. 2000.

Max Payne. Remedy; Take 2 Interactive. 2001.

Myst, Cyan; Brøderbund. 1993.

Pengo. Sega. 1982.

Pong. Atari. 1973.

Quake III Arena. ID Software; Electronic Arts. 1999.

Shogun: Total War. Creative Assembly; Electronic Arts. 2000.

The Sims. Maxis. 2000.

SimCity. Maxis. 1989.

Space Quest I: The Sarien Encounter. Sierra Online; Sierra. 1987.

StarCraft. Blizzard Entertainment. 1998.

Star Trek: The Next Generation. Williams. 1993.

Tetris. Alexey Pazhitnov; Spectrum Holobyte. 1985.

Ultima Online. Origin Systems. 1997.

Unreal Tournament. GT Interactive. 1999.

Game Theories > Pearce

Jenkins   McKenzie Eskelinen
Juul   Ito Pearce
Pearce   Flanagan Bernstein
Zimmerman Crawford Juul

IV. Game Theories

Towards a Game Theory of Game

Celia Pearce

Introduction: Why Game Theory

In mapping the trajectory of popular media, we can see a clear corollary between theory and practice. Literature, film, even popular music all began to a certain extent as "folk" genres that, once their cultural relevance had been proven lasting, caught the attention of theorists and entered into academic discourse.

Such a cycle is currently underway vis-à-vis computer games. This medium is still erroneously considered to be in its "infancy." (In fact, it is just coming of legal drinking age in some states.) The evolution of a body of theory on computer games is an exciting prospect. As with other media, it promises to broaden and deepen the discourse of the medium (we can start talking about something beyond violence, for example). In addition, if history is any indicator, it will also have a positive influence on the practice of creating games, just as the development of film theory in the sixties and seventies did on film craft. It is ironic that academia, the birthplace of games, has mostly shunned them until recently. It is also quite appropriate that

MIT, where the first computer game — *SpaceWar* — was created as an independent hack by computer science Ph.D. students, was one of the first places to embrace game design and game culture as a subject of academic study. Here I will invoke MIT's own Henry Jenkins, who stated in his January 2001 presentation at "Entertainment in the Interactive Age," at the University of Southern California, that the most significant evolutionary leap in the film craft occurred when people started writing about it.

Repurposing Theory

Because computer game theory is a relatively new discipline, much of what has emerged thus far has come out of theorists from other disciplines absorbing game theory into their purview. It seems axiomatic that there must always be a phase where established media seek to "repurpose" their existing "assets" for use in the new medium. Most notably, film and literary theorists have begun to discuss game theory within their own idiosyncratic frameworks. These disciplines have much to add to the discourse on games, particularly when the discussion is centered on narrative. However, they are missing a fundamental understanding of what games are about. Because of this, they continue to struggle to "fit a square peg into a round hole," so to speak, by attempting to force games into their own notions of

143

Response by Mary Flanagan

Celia Pearce's wake-up call for new ways of thinking about games in her article "Towards a Game Theory of Game" is well-timed. Computer games, at least those of a commercial genre, long ago reached their "adulthood." As a capitalist affirmation of "digital culture," the gaming industry is now more profitable than box office sales in the film industry (ticket sales were just 7.7 billion in 2000; Associated Press, 2001). In 2001, games represented a $10.5 billion dollar industry, growing 15 % per year from 1997 [IDSA]. Gaming is a social and technological phenomenon that has worldwide influence.

But. . . what will theories of and for gaming actually look like?

Pearce follows in the steps of cybertext theorist Espen Aarseth, who has argued against "applying one's favorite theory" such as literary, film, or television studies to emerging forms. In effect, Aarseth argues, this combination of theories reduces new media phenomena to broad conceptual terms such as "interactive," "labyrinthine," and "worlds." The textuality of a computer game whose materials are entirely computer-based needs to be addressed in a way that brings the experiential, social, and material aspects of such work to the forefront.

Although the application of old theories to new forms can result in such linguistic muddling, to argue that we must define game studies *devoid* of knowledge of other art and entertainment forms is not

narrative and "text." To quote the old adage, "If you have a hammer, everything looks like a nail." The result is a kind of theoretical imperialism which those in the gaming world are scarcely aware of, let alone involved with. A small handful of significant theorists, such as Henry Jenkins, J.C. Herz, and Janet Murray, have moved game theory into its own realm by helping to define and articulate what is unique to games and game culture, even while comparing games to other media.

A number of debates have been raging about the definition and role of "narrative" in games. It seems only natural that people who have considerable expertise in other narrative media would seek to bring their own knowledge to bear in this argument. However, it is very important to understand that narrative has a profoundly different function in games than it does in other narrative-based media. In games, narrative structures operate in a comparable but at the same time diametrically opposed way to that of traditional narratives. And although there is much to be learned from traditional narratives, and a great value in drawing comparisons between the two, without understanding the fundamental differences, the discourse becomes ultimately irrelevant because it entirely misses the fundamental point of what games are about.

A Play-Centric Approach

The first and most important thing to know about games is that they center on PLAY. Unlike literature and film, which center on STORY, in games, everything revolves around play and the player experience. Game designers are much less interested in telling a story than in creating a compelling framework for play.

If we begin with this fundamental fact, it enables us to look at narrative in a play-centric context, rather than a "storytelling" context. At its highest level, the function of narrative in games is to engender compelling, interesting play. The reason that narrative games have gained such popularity is because they borrow what is engaging and interesting about other forms of narrative and use it to enhance the play experience. Where interactive narrative tends to fail is where the model is based on interacting with a linear narrative genre, such as interactive movies. Interactive "novels" have been slightly more effective from a critical perspective, but they have made virtually no impact on the mainstream of interactive media.

Narrative, again, operates at a fundamentally different level in games than it does in other media. A game is most simply described as framework for structured play. In most cases, this structure will include some type of goal, obstacles to that goal, and resources to help you achieve the goal, as well as

---

constructive. We must recognize historical contexts of gaming against the torrent of "novelty" rhetoric in "new" media by looking around us at our own human history. Games have been important throughout time: the *Royal Game of Ur* may be 5,000 years old, *Weiqi (Go)* is said to have a 4,000-year history, and various sports have fascinated participants and observers since before the Greeks. "Modern" (or as Pearce notes, postindustrial) computer-based games utilize traditional sport and board game elements, dimensional spaces, aspects of narrative, and other aspects that each have historical contexts, bringing to the forefront the concept of play and fun over all other principles.

Gaming brings elements of other media forms into

play, but to develop a cohesive study of computer gaming, scholars must look at a very wide range of disciplines and histories, some extremely popular and "lowbrow." Cultural studies as a theoretical discipline has thankfully paved the way for the academic study of popular culture, so that activities from kitsch refrigerator magnets to Barbie collecting can be studied with intellectual ferocity. Those who look at games need to draw upon studies of communities in sociology and other areas, cognitive psychology, and studies of interaction and use patterns in fields such as industrial design and architecture (areas that have long considered "the user/participant," and have made multiple tracts/multiple motivations of users and a consideration of space essential parts of good design).

consequences, in the form of penalties and rewards (which can often translate into obstacles and resources). At its simplest level, these elements create a generic deconstructed narrative structure of sorts. The author has identified six different narrative "operators" that can exist within a game; the first is clearly a component of all games, by definition. The second through fourth can exist in various combinations, or not at all:

Experiential: The emergent narrative that develops out of the inherent "conflict" of the game as it is played, as experienced by the players themselves.

Performative: The emergent narrative as seen by spectators watching and/or interpreting the game underway.

Augmentary: Layers of information, interpretation, backstory, and contextual frameworks around the game that enhance other narrative operators.

Descriptive: The retelling of description of game events to third parties, and the culture that emerges out of that.

Metastory: A specific narrative "overlay" that creates a context or framework for the game conflict.

Story System: A rule-based story system or kit of generic narrative parts that allows the player to create their own narrative content; story systems can exist independent of or in conjunction with a metastory.

A good game, even one without an obvious "storyline" (or *metastory*), while being played, will tend to follow something that resembles the emotional curve of a dramatic arc. A great example of this would be basketball. At its heart is the dynamic "conflict" between the teams, and subconflicts among the individual players, including players within a team. This is the *experiential* aspect, the narrative that *emerges* as a product of the play itself, between the players. To the spectator, this translates into a *performative* drama which the viewer experiences in the third person, but which also has an equal amount of dramatic impact. This aspect of the narrative is enhanced by the *augmentary* content of journalistic reportage that the spectator has access to before, during and after the game. This content takes the forms of the numerous

145

Unfortunately, calling for new language and methodologies with which to consider computer games is not the same thing as writing them. Now we begin the "dirty work" to articulate exactly what types of intersections of theories we can use to explore games. Certainly questions concerning authorship, individual and collective action, game world time, perception, and positions in between audience and participant need to be better articulated — perhaps even new words invented to develop and enhance these sites and positions. Just to be troublesome, I'll end this response with a quote from Barthes. "A text's unity lies not in its origin but in its destination" (Barthes 1988, 171). In other words, the best games are the ones tightly woven around the user's desires, seamless, catering, which

seem to be filled with options for those who need to break the levels. Participatory, skill-based, emotional, addictive, often competitive, instinctual, frequently violent, yet at the same time, immersive, creative, sharing, rewarding, empowering, and frequently community-building, gaming occupies a critical cultural niche. We must learn how to talk about it.

From Mark Bernstein's Online Response: "And Back Again"

To assume that games cannot hold a mirror up to nature, that they cannot move us or change us, is almost to assume that they are hardly worth discussing. Children play games, but the games we study are not

subplots that are layered over the game itself, such as conflicts between teammates, personal narratives of players, city rivalries, etc. The *descriptive* aspect of basketball, which is captured primary through postgame sports coverage, operates in the retelling of the game afterward. Some games, while rife with narrative suspense during game play, may tend to lose something in the translation. As J. C. Herz has pointed out, golf may be fun to play, but it doesn't make much of a story after the fact. In basketball, the descriptive element is almost always accompanied by augmentary elements, which tend to carry through before, during and after the game itself. These capture the personal, behind-the-scenes narrative, "the thrill of victory and the agony of defeat."

Although basketball provides an excellent example of the first four narrative operators described previously, it includes neither a metastory nor a story system. It's important to realize that in many games, particularly precomputer games, narrative operates on a much more abstract level than it does in other narrative media. In board games, for example, the metanarrative generally functions as a metaphorical overlay for a mathematical or logical structure. Thus, a game can be deconstructed for its "pure" structure, as well as its narrative overlay or metastory. They key to game narrative is that it is, by definition, incomplete. It must be in order to leave

room for the player to bring it to fruition. This is one of the primary flaws of applying literary or film theory to games; the authorial control, which is implicit in other genres, tends to undermine the quality of the user experience.

Some games are pure structure with no metastory. For example, Tic-Tac-Toe is a simple game that has a clear structure that results in a very compressed narrative arc on the experiential level. Needless to say, both its performative and descriptive properties are somewhat thin. And it has no metastory whatever. *Battleship,* on the other hand, can be deconstructed in terms of its pure logical construction (the positioning and targeting of objects in a grid), as well as its metastory, a battle between two seafaring fleets. Note the level of abstraction of the narrative in *Battleship.* Also note that there are no characters. In typical narrative texts, both literary and cinematic, characters are central to the conflict. You cannot really imagine a story without characters. In a game, on the other hand, it is quite possible, and often desirable, to have a narrative with no "characters" whatsoever. And in fact, well-developed characters often get in the way. Games tend to favor abstracted personas over "developed" characters with clear personalities and motivations. More abstracted characters leave more room for the player, and are therefore better suited to support a play-centric model.

---

child's play (and child's play, to children, is deadly serious). Children like to dress up as kings and to undress, but drama is not merely playing house or playing doctor.

Tolkien does indeed hold an important place in the development of computer games, but Pearce utterly misunderstands *The Lord of the Rings*. Tolkien's importance has little to do with the maps that adorn his endpapers. Yes, Tolkien spoke of writing as a journey through imagined worlds, but this perception is not uncommon. Neither is it necessarily helpful in understanding either Middle Earth or interactive art. Yes, he kept elaborate notebooks. This is not uncommon, either: we know many of the War Poets through their notebooks. (Tolkien on The Somme was

24, and if no poppies bloom in the Dead Marshes, we still recognize the muck and thirst of Flanders refracted through the memory of the Burma Road and Stalingrad and That Fucking Island, the land even Marines would not name.)

Game designers who see only Sherlock Holmes's puzzle solving are missing the point, just as game designers who think the story of war is the struggle between two generals have forgotten the lessons of last two centuries. They have forgotten *The Naked and the Dead* and *Catch-22*, or, for that matter, *Run Silent, Run Deep* and *Apocalypse Now...*

http://www.electronicbookreview.com/thread/firstperson/bernsteinr1

Jenkins   McKenzie Eskelinen
Juul   Ito Pearce
Game Theories > Pearce   **Flanagan Bernstein**
Zimmerman Crawford Juul

IV. Game Theories

Perhaps the best example of the ways narrative operates in a noncomputer game can be demonstrated by chess. Chess has a brilliant mathematical and logical structure that we can look at purely for its structural elegance. It has a clear experiential and performative arc. In addition, it has a metastory of two battling kings and their armies and minions (figure 12.1). To understand the narrative of chess, it might be helpful to compare it to a traditional narrative with a similar plot: Shakespeare's *Macbeth*. Although both have a similar "storyline," the comparison clearly highlights the profound difference in how narrative operates in each genre.

In chess, the drama of the experience resides in the strategic conflict between the players, not in empathizing with characters, as in *Macbeth*. The metanarrative operates at a highly abstracted level, creating a context for this intellectual contest. It is interesting to note that this conflict between the players is played out entirely without the benefit of dialogue. Conversation often has a role in games, but in chess it is minimal. It is hard to imagine *Macbeth* without dialogue. Chess replaces the classic Aristotelian techniques of mimesis and empathy with the game-specific technique of agency by giving the player "avatars" that serve as representatives for his or her own actions.

12.1. The chess set of King Edward II, Tower of London. (Photo by Celia Pearce)

As you can see, the distinction has profound implications in terms of narrative. Although both techniques involve projection of the player/audience into a character space, they do this in profoundly different ways. Empathy/mimesis requires the development of highly constructed and authored characters with which viewers develop an empathic bond. Agency creates a container for players to inhabit. Avatars must by definition have a certain level of ambiguity in their characters in order to allow the players to transpose or project themselves into them. Part of the technique of game design is making

147

Pearce Responds

Games do not ask the player to construct or interpret what the author is trying to "tell" them. Rather they function as a kit of parts that allows the player to construct their own story or variation thereof.

strategic decisions about how much and what sort of room to leave for the player.

In addition, chess has an ambiguous ideology or morality. There is no clear "good guy" or "bad guy." *Macbeth* too employs a technique of ambiguous morality: although we know that Macbeth is someone we would not necessarily aspire to be like, we empathize with his struggle nonetheless. But the way these ambiguities are conveyed is very different. Chess has a sort of "Zen" quality of symmetry, equality and fair play. It is interesting that more recent games of military strategy, such as *Risk*, and its computer relatives such as *Age of Empires* and *Civilization*, utilize an asymmetrical structure in which all players do not start with equal assets. This technique can tend to enhance the drama, as well as the potential variations in the emergent narrative.

Recent Examples

To illustrate my points in terms of contemporary computer games, I would like to highlight two game genres in particular that I think have been successful because they are based on a play-centric model of narrative. Before doing so, however, I want to take a few moments to ponder the drawbacks of narrative within games.

Whereas narrative theorists, academics, and those engaged in a critique of games are obsessed with narrative, many game players find narrative quite problematic. The largest controversy has to do with the use of "cut-scenes," also known as "cinematics." These are linear segments within a game that are used to create a narrative context, or "reward" the player for having completed a mission or achieved a subgoal in the game. While often beautifully rendered (since typically they are not rendered in real time, they have the luxury of higher graphical quality), many players find cut-scenes to be egregiously interruptive to their play experience. It seems counterintuitive to use passivity as a reward for play. Many game players associate the idea of "narrative" with this type of enforced linearity, which is a throwback to cinema.

What are much more interesting, and I think are proving to be the so-called "killer apps" of narrative in

gaming, are various procedural forms of narrative, which combine various levels of metastory and story systems. I am going to look at two genres in particular which have caused considerable groundswell, and by looking at them from a play-centric point of view, gain some perspective as to why they have been both critical and popular successes.

The first genre I'd like to look at is the massively multiplayer online role-playing game, or, in game culture parlance "MMORPG." The two most popular of these are *Ultima Online* and *EverQuest,* and second-tier games include *Baldur's Gate, Asheron's Call,* and *Diablo.* Although they differ in some significant ways, what all these games have in common is that they create fantasy story worlds in which players improvise narratives in real time. These games, all of which share the common theme of medieval fantasy, represent the evolution of about forty years of popular culture converging on the computer. They can be traced back to J.R.R. Tolkien's *The Hobbit,* and its sequels, which caused what can only be called a pop culture phenomenon starting in the 1960s. This highly elaborate imaginary world was tailor-made for interaction because, in Tolkien's own words, the stories were developed as a means to explore the worlds. From this emerged the analog role-playing game *Dungeons and Dragons,* first introduced by TSR, Inc. in the mid-1970s, and its online text-based descendents, MUDs (Multi-User Dungeons).

In many respects, the medieval fantasy genre MMORPG is a graphical MUD, and most of them still rely heavily on text for dialogue, although what used to be handled through textual descriptions (e.g., "You are stranding outside the castle, facing north"), is now done visually. This hybrid visual/text form has developed a small but adamant following, and although by game sales standards they are something of a niche market, these games have a great enough audience that they manage to at the very least support themselves as commercial endeavors.

The MMORPG combines a metastory, primarily in the form of a predesigned story world and various plots within it, with a story system that allows players to evolve their own narratives within the game's story framework. The central play mechanic of the

Jenkins   McKenzie Eskelinen
Juul   Ito Pearce
Game Theories > Pearce   Flanagan Bernstein
Zimmerman Crawford Juul

IV. Game Theories

149

12.2. Screenshot from *EverQuest: The Shadows of Luclin*.
(Verant, Sony Online Entertainment)

MMORPG is what I refer to as social storytelling, or collaborative fiction. The idea is that the story emerges as a direct result of social interaction. As with the Renaissance Faire (also a huge commercial success throughout the U.S.), players enter a fully constructed three-dimensional world. Rather than selecting fixed characters, they select particular character roles. These are somewhat generic, but allow players to configure unique characters composed of various traits, which they can then evolve over time into a fully developed persona through a system of improvisational collaborative narrative (figure 12.2).

In traditional narrative, a classic view of character development is that characters are what they do. It is the actions of the characters that not only tell us who they are, but also determine who they are. The choices they make in a sense configure their personalities. In the MMORPG genre, this dynamic is put in the hands of the player. Players take actions that construct their characters on the fly. For example, depending on your role, you may be endowed with certain innate traits or talents, such as strength or intelligence or magical powers. You also have the opportunity to acquire skills. In games like *EverQuest* and *Ultima Online*, the game is structured in such a way as to make it beneficial for players to join forces and form spontaneous teams. As your team develops over time, your role on the team will cause your character, originally a generic kit of skills, to evolve distinctive personality traits. The

strategies you choose in enacting your innate talents and acquired skills engage you in a process of real-time character creation. In addition, you can acquire property, including weapons, tools, magic amulets, and even real estate, which will all become part of your character's unique personality. Some players choose to act out in an antisocial way. In many cases, these players are penalized by game operators, but just as often, they are penalized socially. For in these worlds, reputation is the most valuable currency.

These games, because they are highly improvisational in nature, require constant attention from their operators. *EverQuest*, for example, has a Command Central at its San Diego headquarters where its customer service staff wanders about the virtual game world assisting players, and creating narrative events, conflicts and missions for players to engage in. They carefully watch what players are doing and constantly evolve the game, the game rules, and the game narrative accordingly. Again, a play-centric model, in which the player is revered and constantly accommodated.

The result is an emergent narrative, a story that evolves over time as a result of an interplay between rules and players. In addition, there is the emergent infrastructure that is constantly reformulating itself, evolving, and adapting, much like an ecosystem, to the player behavior. Most of these games work on a product-plus-subscription economic formula: you purchase a CD at the software store, then pay a nominal monthly fee (seldom more than $20) for unlimited play. Although at present the audience for these games is relatively small compared to the mainstream, their fan base is extremely committed. MMORGs require a large time investment because they are strongly skills — and relationship-based. It requires a commitment of at least ten hours a week to maintain ongoing engagement in these games, and many players put in well above that. Interestingly, most of the original MMORPGs' meta-stories focus on medieval fantasy/*Dungeons and Dragons* style themes, although more mainstream themes are forthcoming, which will most likely expand the audience for this genre.

The second game genre we are going to look at, currently represented by one game and its various sequels and enhancements, is *The Sims,* designed by Will Wright of Maxis. *The Sims* evolved out of an entirely different tradition and genre in games, that of the simulation game. I want to note that there are two distinctly different types of games that are referred to as simulations. One is the training-based simulator, which comes out of the military world, and puts the player into a first-person role centering on mechanical control of a vehicle, e.g., a flight or tank simulator. The other is a simulation that dynamically models an entire system. This tradition comes from a variety of sources, but was used extensively in paper-and-pencil form in the social sciences, history, and economics in the 1960s and 1970s. *SimCity* was one of first computer games to employ techniques of this type of simulation in a game context, and at the time it was released (1989), it revolutionized the game experience and business. Since then, this genre has been expanded into a range of metastory contexts, including Maxis' *SimEarth, SimAnt,* as well as *Roller Coaster Tycoon* by Microprose.

The Sims has been described as a human behavior or psychological simulator. Rather than employing purely player-inhabited characters or purely autonomous characters, the game puts players in the role of influencing semi-autonomous characters. They are semi-autonomous because while they have their own innate behaviors, they depend on player influence to dictate their actions. The viewpoint is isometric rather than first person, allowing players to have a god-like view over the game terrain.

The Sims is a story system described as a kind of narrative Lego. Designer Will Wright himself describes it as a sort of virtual dollhouse. The original prototype was created as a physical model using model railroad materials. *The Sims* uses the emergent narrative model, but leaves the metastory relatively open-ended. The original *Sims* Game, which has now spun off into a variety of add-ons and enhancements, is basically a domestic drama, or a sitcom, depending on how you play. You create a family and place them in a house that you can then enhance and occupy with a variety of items to better the Sims' lifestyle and comfort level. There is a strong anticonsumerist satirical subtext to the game. I refer to it as the IKEA game, because a

major feature is the catalogue of humorously described household items and enhancements (figure 12.3). The subtext is that characters need things to make them happy, but over time, the things begin to own them. A larger house requires more cleaning time. You can hire a maid, but the higher expenses require that you maintain a certain earning power. As your characters evolve, they form various relationships with each other. Some can even fall in love and form domestic partnerships, even same-sex partnerships.

The Sims is a cross between a dollhouse, a Tamagotchi, and the television program *Big Brother*. In *Big Brother,* contestants inhabit an enclosed house for eighty days, eliminated one-by-one by audience vote until only one roommate is left standing. As in *Big Brother,* the *Sims* player is a voyeur with an all-seeing eye and definite influence on the characters, even though they also have their own "free will," so to speak. You must maintain a constant vigil over them or calamity might result. Characters without adequate cooking skills can perish in kitchen fires, and children can be taken from negligent parents by social services.

Sims characters are built from a kit of character parts that includes various physical (mostly having to do with appearance), as well as personal traits. The emphasis here is more on personality than skills, however (figure 12.4). You can construct your own configuration of such traits as neatness, friendliness, etc., or you can select an astrological sign that will automatically configure a personality for you. Based on this, the character will have certain natural qualities and aptitudes. Your characters can also acquire skills that will enable them to avoid things such as kitchen fires, or improve their job performance, thereby earning promotions at work.

Sims are very moody and when they aren't getting their needs meant, they will throw tantrums, shaking their fists and calling to you in "Sim-ish," a combination of verbal gibberish and symbols that appear in comic book bubbles over their heads. Images such as food, kissing, and recreational activities provide indicators of what Sims want or what they are conversing about.

The Sims has taken a radically different approach to narrative than most of the games that preceded it. In

Game Theories > Pearce

Jenkins   McKenzie Eskelinen
Juul   Ito Pearce
Pearce   Flanagan Bernstein
Zimmerman Crawford Juul

IV. Game Theories

addition to a story system that results in an experiential narrative, *The Sims* has a built-in descriptive component (a feature it shares with some of the MMORPGs) in the form of a "Family Album" feature that allows players to take snapshots of their game underway. They can then make descriptive storyboards and post them on *The Sims* web site for others to view. As a result, a new play trend has emerged, in which players have transformed the game into a storyboard authoring tool (figure 12.5). Players have used it to recreate autobiographical or even news stories.

In addition, players can upload their games onto the site so that other players can continue the gameplay. In other words, if you create a family, you can put it up on *The Sims* web site, and another player can pick it up where you left off. Thus, there might be multiple versions of your family, having been taken in different directions by different players.

The game also allows for skinning, which the MMORPGs sometimes (but not always) allow for. Skinning is the practice of pulling your own assets into the game. Most of the time, it consists of placing new texture maps on game environments or characters. Maxis encourages this sort of thing and has even created a trading post within the web site where players can exchange skins and other custom-built game features.

Part of why it is interesting to look at the *The Sims* in terms of narrative fiction overall is that it represents an abdication of authorial control, or, perhaps more

accurately, a shift in the definition of "author." The creation of meta-stories and story systems has become a new form of authorship that is a sort of author/nonauthor role. It is somewhat ironic in light of the "death of the author" debate that has raged in poststructuralist literary theory, from Barthes to Foucault to L'Dieaux, that it is games, rather than literature, that have been able to finally dispense or at least significantly reframe the author's role as creator of content.

The Sims is a story system that lets the player drive the story experience within a set of carefully crafted rules, processes, and constraints. It blurs the line between audience and author in the same way the MMORPGs do, but with a more open-ended story framework. Furthermore, Maxis is developing even more interesting ways to blur that line. In his keynote address at "Entertainment in the Interactive Age," Will Wright presented a diagram showing the role of players in content creation. His "pyramid" content scheme states that if the 10% of players who occupy the top level of the pyramid are defined as expert storytellers, then for every million players there are 100,000 people creating high-level game content. The idea here is that the "author" shifts into a role as facilitator, and the audience now takes over the role of storytelling.

Maxis is currently looking at ways to reward this top 10% of player/creators, either financially or with free game subscriptions, updates, etc. At this writing, Maxis is in development with *The Sims Online*, a massively

12.3. Build mode in *The Sims,* aka The IKEA Game.
(Maxis, Electronic Arts)

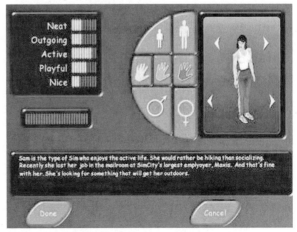

12.4. Character kit in *The Sims*.
(Maxis, Electronic Arts)

Pete the Lawn Gnome makes an "anonymous" call to report the death of Bob, his lonely but devoted owner.

The first of several failed attempts at killing Bob's drunken son, Tony, who has inherited the house.

With the help of an army of plastic pink flamingos, Pete succeeds in incinerating Tony.

Tony is destined to spend the rest of his days as a lawn ornament.

12.5. Scenes from "A Lawn Gnomes Revenge" [sic], a player-created story using *The Sims*.(Maxis, Electronic Arts)

multiplayer *Sims* world that players can co-inhabit. Here players will be able to start their own businesses and devise their own entertainment for other *Sims* characters.

This notion of authorial abdication is essential to understanding where game narrative diverges from other narrative media. Other narrative media focus on "text," and text as a signifier of authorial authority. The text is fixed, and it has a single authoritative source. In some cases, that authoritative source might be a community, but nonetheless, the text is fixed. It may be open to a range of interpretation, and I will here take exception to those who say that all narrative is interactive. If we use the term as defined in the dictionary, interactive is by definition responsive. In other words, it must have a visibly different manifestation with each user's individual input. A nonlinear book may arguably fall into this definition by virtue of the fact that the reader assembles its sequence as he or she reads. But a linear story does not allow for any variable manifestations, and therefore, by definition, it cannot be interactive.

Looking at the differentiations between game-based and other forms of narratives can give us some vital clues as to the pitfalls of transitioning between the two. Repeatedly, filmmakers have attempted to leverage the popularity of video and computer games. But if we review some of the points made above, we can easily see why the game-to-movie adaptation has repeatedly failed.

The number one reason is that the function of character in each medium is diametrically opposed. The contrast between Macbeth and the chess king sheds light on why *Mario Brothers*, *Dungeons and Dragons*, and *Tomb Raider* have made disappointing films. One only has to imagine chess as a stage play to understand why these transitions consistently fail. In the game *Tomb Raider*, Lara Croft is a partially formed character; she is in essence a cartoon who serves as an avatar onto which the player is meant to project her — or more often, his — own interpretation. It is important that the character is incomplete, because if the character is too developed there is nothing compelling for the player to contribute. I frequently liken game design to having a good conversation: in order for it to work, you have to listen, which means leaving gaps for the other person to fill. Taking a caricature that has been created as a vehicle for player projection and trying to develop it into a full-blown cinematic character is a dangerous game to play, so to speak.

Reverse adaptations have been slightly more successful, but it's important to understand why. Generally a game version of a film character will need to be streamlined. Some characters, such as Indiana Jones, are cartoony-enough that they can easily transition into game characters. In *Blade Runner*, the designers at Westwood Studios chose not to use the main character in the movie, but developed a new character broadly based on the film. Because the *Blade Runner* character is mysterious and ambiguous to begin with, this was an easier stunt to pull than taking a highly articulated, nuanced character and trying to develop it for a game. On the other hand, it may simply be that all characters played by Harrison Ford are particularly well-suited for game narratives.

In fact, a deeper analysis reveals that certain story genres are more innately gamelike to begin with. These include mysteries, mission or goal-based adventures, or combat scenarios. James Bond and *Mission: Impossible* are two examples of gamelike film genres that have transitioned into critically and popularly successful games. In any case, it seems that games are weaker at character development, whereas they excel at adventure, mystery, and action. Even non-movie-based games based on these themes, such as *Thief* and *Deus Ex*, have been the more popular among games that employ a more literal metanarrative.

The other sort of narrative genre that does well in a game framework is the world-based narrative. *The Hobbit* was an example cited earlier. In fact, Tolkien himself spent many years developing the world, its cultures and languages, and the story was really just a way to describe and explore the world. Any book that has a map in it is likely to be good material for a game, because it is clear that the game is about the relationship between the characters and the world.

Star Wars is a great example of a story world that is tailor-made for gaming. The first movie is much more of a game than a film. As is the case in all the *Star Wars* films, the characters tend to be archetypal and somewhat cartoon-like (Harrison Ford again!), which makes them perfect building blocks for game narrative. George Lucas's strengths as a world-builder have resulted in story contexts that have proven to be endlessly fascinating to at least two generations thus far. At this writing, Verant, the creators of *EverQuest*, are developing *Star Wars: Galaxies*, a MMORPG based on the *Star Wars* worlds. Based on sneak previews at E3, most game industry pundits are predicting a slam dunk. This is a case where the world will be complete, deeply developed and highly dynamic, but the story will be open-ended, to allow players to create their own narrative within this familiar imaginary space.

The most compelling thing about these trends is that they are changing the distinction between producers and consumers. In film, television, theater and literary forms, there is generally a very clear line between producer and consumer. However, in these new forms of interactive narrative, particularly those that employ story systems, this line has become blurred. The consumer is now becoming a producer/consumer.

Computer games are really the first medium that blurs this boundary between author and audience so completely. As such, it undermines some of the fundamental tenets of postindustrial (e.g., printing press, film projector, television) narrative, which is based on a mass-production, one-to-many "broadcast" model. With the computer as a two-way, dynamic medium, those engaged in game design are creating an entirely and radically new ideology about narrative. They are not so much storytellers as context creators, and what they are doing is nothing short of revolutionary. As such, I believe that they have earned their own unique and indigenous theoretical discourse.

References: Literature

Aarseth, Espen (1997). *Cybertext: Perspectives on Ergodic Literature*. Baltimore: Johns Hopkins University Press.

Associated Press (2001), "Video Game Industry Reports Growth." *The Times of India Online*, May 1, 2001. <http://www.timesofindia.com/020501/02info6.htm>.

Barthes, Roland (translated by Steven Heath) (1968). "The Death of the Author." In *Modern Criticism and Theory: A Reader*, edited by David Lodge. London and New York: Longman. First published as "La mort de l'auteur." *Manteia* 5 (1968).

Interactive Digital Software Association (2001). "New Research Commissioned by the IDSA Shows Major Impact of Computer and Video Game Industries on the US Economy." IDSA web site, May 2001. <http://www.idsa.com>.

Jenkins, Henry (2001). Presentation at "Entertainment in the Interactive Age," at the University of Southern California, January 2001.

References: Games

EverQuest. Verant Interactive; Sony Online Entertainment. 1999.

The Sims. Will Wright; Maxis; Electronic Arts. 2000.

Star Wars: Galaxies. LucasArts; Sony Interactive; Verant. 2002.

Narrative, Interactivity, Play, and Games: Four Naughty Concepts in Need of Discipline

Eric Zimmerman

Discipline?

Yes, discipline. On one level, this essay is about identifying a desperate need for discipline and the delivery of that discipline to its well-deserved targets. A kind of disciplinary spanking, if you will.

On another level, this essay is about games and stories. Undoubtedly, there is a tremendous amount of interest in the intersection of games and stories these days. Academic journals, conferences, and courses about computer-based storytelling, digital interactivity, and gaming culture have flourished like a species of virulent weed in the manicured garden of the university. On the commercial end of things, game developers increasingly rely on filmic story techniques in the design of their products, turning present-day computer and video games into a kind of mutant cinema. Meanwhile, shelves of books like this one are being written and published, tossed out like stepping stones into the emerging terrain where design, technology, art, entertainment, and academia meet.

Curiously, so much of this interest is driven by a kind of love/hate relationship with the medium. For as much as we seem enamored by the possibilities of digital media, we seem just as soundly dissatisfied with its current state. Lurking just below the surface of most of the chapters in this volume is one sort of frustration or another: frustration with the lack of cultural sophistication in the gaming industry; frustration with the limitations of current technology; frustration with a lack of critical theory for properly understanding the medium. Perhaps frustration is a necessary part of the process. But perhaps we can relieve some of that frustration with some good old-fashioned discipline.

Looking Closer

Compared to the more robust fields that cluster about the theory and practice of other media, it's clear that the "game-story" as a form remains largely unexplored. Terms and concepts run amuck like naughty schoolchildren. And a more disciplined look would indeed seem to be in order. But what would it mean to take a closer look at games and stories?

Response by Chris Crawford

Thank you, Eric Zimmerman, for taking the time and energy to nail down four central terms that have suffered much abuse in recent years. Those four terms have been stretched to fit everybody's pet theories, so becoming shapeless blobs. We are past due for a housecleaning of these words, a "back to basics" movement, a tightening-up of the terminology.

Zimmerman does justice to the task. Eschewing the conceit of formal definition, he concentrates on utility rather than form. The sole test of his success then lies in the answer to the question: how useful are Zimmerman's definitions? To what extent do they bring us closer to understanding the concoction of game and narrative? Unfortunately, the concluding suggestions he offers don't seem to get us very far; no grand answers leap from the page. Perhaps this is too harsh a standard by which to judge the chapter. Perhaps we should settle for a more lenient standard of judgment, to wit: had these ideas been widely accepted ten years ago, would we have been spared some of the many disastrous marriages of narrative and interactivity we have seen?

Consider branching stories on the computer. After many years and hundreds of attempts, most with dismal results, many old pros have abandoned this design concept (although it retains a hard core of followers). If we apply these definitions to branching stories, will we unearth a fatal flaw? I think not. Branching stories don't violate any of the terms of

Jenkins   McKenzie Eskelinen
Juul   Ito Pearce
Pearce   Flanagan Bernstein
Game Theories > Zimmerman Crawford Juul

IV. Game Theories

Does it mean figuring out how to make games more like stories? Or how to make stories more gamelike? Does it mean documenting and typologizing new forms of game/story culture? Integrating games into learning? Mapping relationships between digital media and other media? Inventing programming strategies for storytelling? Understanding the ways that digital media operate in culture at large? There are as many approaches to the question of "games and stories" as there are designers, artists, technologists, and academics asking the questions.

The truth, of course, is that there are no right or wrong approaches. It all depends on the field in which a particular inquiry is operating and exactly what the inquiry itself is trying to accomplish. However, there is common ground. What everyone investigating the "game-story" would share are in fact those two strange terms: "games" and "stories."

Concepts and terms do seem to be at the heart of the matter. This essay tackles the terminological knot of the "game-story" by prying apart and recombining the two concepts into four: narrative, interactivity, play, and games. Each concept is considered in relationship to each other as well as to the larger question of "games and stories." My goal is to frame these concepts in ways that bring insight to their interrelations, with the larger aim of providing critical tools for others who are

attempting to create or study the conundrum of the game-story.

Four Naughty Terms

Play. Games. Narrative. Interactivity. What a motley bunch. Honestly, have you ever seen such a suspicious set of slippery and ambiguous, overused, and ill-defined terms? Indeed, they are all four in need of some discipline, just to make them sit still and behave. Before I roll up my sleeves and get to work on them, however, allow me to lay some of my cards on the table, in the form of a series of disclaimers.

Disclaimer 1: Concepts, Not Categories
In presenting these four terms (games, play, narrative, and interactivity), I'm not creating a typology. The four terms are not mutually exclusive, nor do they represent four categories, with each category containing a different kind of phenomena. They are four concepts, each concept overlapping and intersecting the others in complex and unique ways. In other words, the four words are not the four quadrants of a grid or the four levels of a building. They are "things to think with"; they are signs for clusters of concepts; they are frames and schemas for understanding; they are dynamic conceptual tools; they represent a network of ideas that flow into and through each other.

these definitions, nor do they run against the grain of the further elucidations Zimmerman offers.

This troubles me; the primary value of these definitions should lie in their utility, but they seem useless in exposing an already-known failure. How can we trust them to guide us to something that works when they can't guide us away from something that doesn't work? Nevertheless, I don't dismiss these definitions. They aren't wrong or misleading; they just don't go far enough. They require tightening and polishing, not disposal. Indeed, I suspect that Zimmerman has already captured all the fundamental truths he needs to take us further, but is restrained by a politic recognition of the sensibilities of other workers in the field. It is my hope that this chapter will nudge us

all towards a closer convergence that will permit an even tighter set of definitions in future.

From Jesper Juul's Online Response: Unruly Games

Perhaps the problem is that my relation to games is rather unambiguous, and so I fall outside the love/hate relations described in the essay: I am happy about the games I have played in the past 15 to 20 years, and I am pretty happy about the games I get to play these days. As such I am not especially dissatisfied with the gaming industry, except in the sense that the increasingly large budgets are leaving less room for experimental games. With this perspective, the marriage of storytelling and gaming may be more of a problem than a solution. I can

Disclaimer 2: Forget the Computer
While digital media is certainly a primary vector in the momentum of interest that has led to this book, the phenomena we call games and stories — as well as play, narrative, and interactivity — predate computers by millennia. Computer media is one context for understanding them, but I'm going to try to avoid typical technological myopia by examining these concepts in a broad spectrum of digital and nondigital manifestations.

Disclaimer 3: Defining Definitions
For each of the four key terms, I do present a "definition." The value of a definition in this essay is not its scientific accuracy but instead its conceptual utility. I give definitions not in order to explain phenomena, but in order to understand them.

Disclaimer 4: Why I'm Doing This
Why does it matter to me to better understand "games and stories"? Because I'm a designer of game-stories, and a closet Modernist to boot. I'm looking to better understand the medium in which I work, in order to create new and meaningful things that no one has ever experienced before. It's certainly not the only kind of stance to take. But now you know where I'm coming from.

Narrative

First term: narrative. I'm going to begin with this close cousin to the "stories" of the "games and stories" equation. My strategy of discipline for the term narrative is to present a broad and expansive understanding of the concept, to think beyond the normal limits of what we might consider narrative, to help uncover the common turf of stories and games.

The Definition
I draw my definition from an essay by J. Hillis Miller: "Narrative," from the book *Critical Terms for Literary Study* (1995). Miller's definition of the term "narrative," grossly paraphrased, has three parts:

1. A narrative has an initial state, a change in that state, and insight brought about by that change. You might call this process the "events" of a narrative.

2. A narrative is not merely a series of events, but a personification of events though a medium such as language. This component of the definition references the representational aspect of narrative.

3. And last, this representation is

13.response.1.
Wing Commander 4: The Price of Freedom raised the production values bar again, featuring actors such as Mark Hamill (Origin, Electronic Arts)

follow Chris Crawford, who has actually attributed what he sees as the sorry state of the industry to the "cinematic game" *Wing Commander*™ (13.response.1), blaming it for radically raising the expectations for production value, thereby leading to the death of experiment.

Zimmerman's pragmatic idea of stories as one specific way of framing games is quite liberating, but I want to emphasize that such framings always carry a large amount of ideology and historical baggage. The obvious critique would be that the game-story angle is a lens that emphasizes character, graphical production value, and retrospection — and hides player activity, gameplay, and replayability. As Zimmerman states, games are good at things that other media are bad at

constituted by patterning and repetition. This is true for every level of a narrative, whether it is the material form of the narrative itself or its conceptual thematics.

It's quite a general definition. Let's see what might be considered narrative according to these three criteria. A book is certainly a narrative by this definition, whether it is a straightforward linear novel or a choose-your-own-adventure interactive book, in which each page ends with a choice that can bring the reader to different sections of the book. Both kinds of books contain events which are represented through text and through the patterned experience of the book and its language.

A game of chess could also be considered a narrative by this scheme. How? Chess certainly has a beginning state (the setup of the game), changes to that state (the gameplay), and a resulting insight (the outcome of the game). It is a representation — a stylized representation of war, complete with a cast of colorful characters. And the game takes place in highly patterned structures of time (turns), and space (the checkerboard grid).

Many other kinds of things fall into the wide net Miller casts as well — some of them activities or objects we wouldn't normally think of as narrative. A

marriage ceremony. A meal. A conversation. The cleverness of Miller's definition is that it is in fact so inclusive, while still rigorously defining exactly what a narrative is.

Because, what I wish to ask is NOT the overused question:

> Is this thing (such as a game) a "narrative thing" or not?

Instead, the question I'd like to pose is:

> In what ways might we consider this thing (such as a game) a "narrative thing"?

What am I after? If I'm intersecting games and stories to create something new out of the synthesis of both, my aim with the concept of narrative should not be to replicate existing narrative forms but to invent new ones. The commercial game industry is suffering from a peculiar case of cinema envy at the moment, trying to recreate the pleasures of another media. What would a game-story be like that wouldn't be so beholden to preexisting linear media? Good question. But I'm getting ahead of myself. We're still two full terms away from games. Next victim: interactivity.

157

— and vice versa. My basic worry is then that the story angle is asking games to focus on their weaknesses rather than their strengths.

Zimmerman Responds:

Are "grandiose claims" really what we need? Possibly. But for me the questions that cluster about the game-story are so complex that there can't be just a single set of answers.

Interactivity

Interactivity is one of those words which can mean everything and nothing at once. So in corralling this naughty concept, my aim is to try to understand it in its most general sense, but also to identify those very particular aspects of interactivity which are relevant to "games and stories."

The Definition
Try this on for size, from <dictionary.com>:

> *interactive*: reciprocally active; acting upon or influencing each other; allowing a two-way flow of information between a device and a user, responding to the user's input

OK. So there's an adequate common-sense definition. But if we're triangulating our concept of narrative with this concept of interactivity, the problem is that by this definition all forms of narrative end up being interactive. For example, take this book you're holding. Can you really say that the experience of reading it isn't interactive? Aren't you holding the book and physically turning the pages? Aren't you emotionally and psychologically immersed? Aren't you cognitively engaging with language itself to decode the signs of the text? And doesn't the physical form of the book and your understanding of its contents evolve as you interact with it? Yes and no.

If what we're after is relationships between our terms, it's important to find the terrain of overlap between narrative and interactivity. But we don't want the two terms to be identical. It seems important to be able to say that some narratives are interactive and some are not — or rather, that perhaps all narratives can be interactive, but they can be interactive in different ways.

Intuitively, there is in fact some kind of difference between a typical linear book and a choose-your-own-adventure book. And it seems that the difference in some way is that naughty concept of interactivity. Here's one solution. Instead of understanding "interactivity" as a singular phenomenon, let's subdivide it into the various ways it can be paired up with a

narrative experience. Four modes of narrative interactivity are presented:

Mode 1: Cognitive Interactivity; or Interpretive Participation with a Text
This is the psychological, emotional, hermeneutic, semiotic, reader-response, Rashomon-effect-ish, etc. kind of interactions that a participant can have with the so-called "content" of a text. Example: you reread a book after several years have passed and you find it's completely different than the book you remember.

Mode 2: Functional Interactivity; or Utilitarian Participation with a Text
Included here: functional, structural interactions with the material textual apparatus. That book you reread: did it have a table of contents? An index? What was the graphic design of the pages? How thick was the paper stock? How large was the book? How heavy? All of these characteristics are part of the total experience of reading interaction.

Mode 3: Explicit Interactivity; or Participation with Designed Choices and Procedures in a Text
This is "interaction" in the obvious sense of the word: overt participation such as clicking the nonlinear links of a hypertext novel, following the rules of a Surrealist language game, rearranging the clothing on a set of paper dolls. Included here: choices, random events, dynamic simulations, and other procedures programmed into the interactive experience.

Mode 4: Meta-interactivity; or Cultural Participation with a Text
This is interaction outside the experience of a single text. The clearest examples come from fan culture, in which readers appropriate, deconstruct, and reconstruct linear media, participating in and propagating massive communal narrative worlds. These four modes of narrative interactivity (cognitive, functional, explicit, and cultural) are not four distinct categories, but four overlapping flavors of participation that occur to varying degrees in all media experience. Most interactive activities incorporate some or all of

158

them simultaneously.

So, what we normally think of as "interactive," what separates the book from the choose-your-own-adventure, is category number three: explicit interactivity. As we hone in on our four terms, note that we've made enough progress to already identify those phenomena we might call "interactive narratives." The newspaper as a whole is not explicitly interactive, but the letters-to-the-editor section is. Are games interactive narratives in this sense? Absolutely. The choices and decisions that game players make certainly constitute very explicit interactivity. We're getting closer to games. But first: *play*.

Play

Perhaps more than any other one of the four concepts, play is used in so many contexts and in so many different ways that it's going to be a real struggle to make it play nice with our other terms. We play games. We play with toys. We play musical instruments and we play the radio. We can make a play on words, be playful during sex, or simply be in a playful state of mind.

What do all of those meanings have to do with narrative and interactivity? Before jumping into a definition of play, first let's try to categorize all of these diverse play phenomena. We can put them into three general categories.

Category 1: Game Play, or the Formal Play of Games
This is the focused kind of play that occurs when one or more players plays a game, whether it is a board game, card game, sport, computer game, etc. What exactly is a game? We're getting to that soon.

Category 2: Ludic Activities, or Informal Play
This category includes all of those nongame behaviors that we also think of as "playing:" dogs chasing each other, two college students tossing a frisbee back and forth, a circle of children playing ring-around-the-rosy, etc. Ludic activities are quite similar to games, but generally less formalized.

Category 3: Being Playful, or Being in a Play State of Mind
This broad category includes all of the ways we can "be

playful" in the context of other activities. Being in a play state of mind does not necessarily mean that you are playing — but rather that you are injecting a spirit of play into some other action. For example, it is one thing to insult a friend's appearance, but it is another thing entirely if the insult is delivered playfully.

A quick structural note — the latter categories contain the earlier ones. Game play (1) is a particular kind of ludic activity (2) and ludic activities (2) are a particular way of being playful (3). But what overarching definition could we possibly give to the word "play" that would address all of these uses?

The Definition
How about:

> Play is the free space of movement within a more rigid structure. Play exists both because of and also despite the more rigid structures of a system.

That sounds quite abstract and obtuse for a fun-loving word like "play," doesn't it? But it is actually quite handy. This definition of play is about relationships between the elements of a system. Think about the use of the word "play" when we talk about the "free play" of a steering wheel. The free play is the amount of movement that the steering wheel can turn before it begins to affect the tires of the car. The play itself exists only because of the more utilitarian structures of the driving-system: the drive shaft, axles, wheels, etc.

But even though the play only occurs because of these structures, the play is also exactly that thing that exists despite the system, the free movement within it, in the interstitial spaces between and among its components. Play exists in opposition to the structures it inhabits, at odds with the utilitarian functioning of the system. Yet play is at the same time an expression of a system, and intrinsically a part of it.

This definition of play does in fact cover all three kinds that we mentioned previously. Playing *Chutes and Ladders* occurs only because of the rigid rules of the game — but the gameplay itself is a kind of dance of fate which occurs somewhere among the dice, pieces, board, and game players. Playing a musical instrument means manipulating within the free space of audio possibilities that the structure of the instrument was designed to engender. Being playful in a conversation means playing in and among the linguistic and social structures that constitute the conversational context. Play can manifest in a dizzying variety of forms, from intellectual and physical play to semiotic and cultural play.

One way to link this understanding of play to narrative and interactivity is to consider the play of an explicitly interactive narrative. The challenge for the creator of an interactive narrative is to design the potential for play into the structure of the experience, whether that experience is a physical object, a computer program, an inhabited space, or a set of behaviors.

And the real trick is that the designed structure can guide and engender play, but never completely script it in advance. If the interaction is completely predetermined, there's no room for play in the system. The author of a choose-your-own-adventure creates the structure that the reader inhabits, but the play emerges out of that system as the reader navigates through it. Even if the reader breaks the structure by cheating and skipping ahead, that is merely another form of play within the designed system.

Games

We have arrived at our fourth and final term: games. With this concept, we have a new kind of naughtiness. Play, interactivity, and narrative threatened us with overinclusion. "Games," on the other hand, needs some discipline because it's difficult to understand exactly and precisely what a game is. My approach with this concept is to define it as narrowly as possible so that we can understand what separates the play of games from other kinds of ludic activities. We are, after all, looking at *games* and stories, not *play* and stories.

The Definition

The fact that games are a formal kind of play was referenced before. But how exactly is that formality manifest? Here is a definition that separates games from other forms of play:

A game is a voluntary interactive activity, in which one or more players follow rules that constrain their behavior, enacting an artificial conflict that ends in a quantifiable outcome.

It is a bit dense. Here are the primary elements of the definition, teased out for your perusal:

Voluntary
If you're forced against your will to play a game, you're not really playing. Games are voluntary activities.

Interactive
Remember this word? It's referencing our third mode of interactivity: explicit participation.

Behavior-Constraining Rules
All games have rules. These rules provide the structure out of which the play emerges. It's also important to realize that rules are essentially restrictive and limit what the player can do.

Artificiality
Games maintain a boundary from so-called "real life" in both time and space. Although games obviously do occur within the real world, artificiality is one of their defining features. Consider, for example, the formal limits of time and space that are necessary to define even a casual game of street hoops.

Conflict
All games embody a contest of powers. It might be a conflict between two players as in chess; it might be a contest between several teams, as in a track meet; a game might be a conflict between a single player and the forces of luck and skill embodied in solitaire; or even a group of players competing together against the clock on a game show.

Quantifiable Outcome
The conflict of a game has an end result, and this is the quantifiable outcome. At the conclusion of a game, the participants either won or lost (they might all win or

lose together) or they received a numerical score, as in a videogame. This idea of a quantifiable outcome is what often distinguishes a bona fide game from other less formal play activities.

Games embody the same structure-play relationship of other ludic activities, where play emerges as the free space of movement within more rigid structures. But the fact that games are so formalized gives them a special status in this regard. To create a game is to design a set of game rules (as well as game materials, which are an extension of the rules).

The rules of a game serve to limit players' behaviors. In a game of Parcheesi, for example, players interact with the dice in extremely particular ways. You don't eat them, hide them from other players, or make jewelry out of them. When it is your turn, you roll the dice, and translate the numerical results into the movement of your pieces. To take part in a game is to submit your behavior to the restrictions of the rules.

Rules might not seem like much fun. But once players set the system of a game into motion, play emerges. And play is the opposite of rules. Rules are fixed, rigid, closed, and unambiguous. Play, on the other hand, is uncertain, creative, improvisational, and open-ended. The strange coupling of rules and play is one of the fascinating paradoxes of games.

Mixing and Matching
We've arrived at a relatively clear understanding of exactly what constitutes a game. So how do games intersect with the other three concepts at hand?

Narrative: As we observed with chess, games are in fact narrative systems. They aren't the only form that narrative can take, but every game can be considered a narrative system.

Interactivity: Games are interactive too. They generally embody all four modes of interactivity outlined in this essay, but they are particularly good examples of the third kind: explicit interactivity.

Play: Games are among the many and diverse forms of play. The formal quality of games distinguishes them from other ludic play-activities.

What does this mean? It is possible to frame games as narrative systems, or as interactive systems, or as systems of play. Whereas this seems like an obvious set of conclusions to draw, remember that the goal wasn't to place the concept of games inside some categories and keep it out of others. Armed with very particular understandings of narrative, play, and interactivity, these three concepts become frames or schemas that we can use to tease out particular qualities of the complex phenomena of games.

And it goes without saying that there are innumerable other terms we might bring to bear on the concept of games as well: games as mathematical systems, ideological systems, semiotic systems, systems of desire. It's an endless list. I chose play, narrative, and interactivity in order to shed light on the game-story. So let's get back to that important question.

Stories and Games
So. We've disciplined our four naughty terms until they've finally behaved and we've come full circle, back to the original question of games and stories. This essay began by observing a general dissatisfaction with the current state of game-story theory and practice. Perhaps it can end with some suggestions for future work.

A story is the experience of a narrative. And the dissatisfaction with game-stories is a dissatisfaction with the way that games function as storytelling systems. Remembering the concept of narrative, story-systems function by representing changes of events though pattern and repetition. This act of representation — or, we might say, signification — is how narrative operates.

So one relevant question to ask is: How can games represent narrative meaning? Or rather: How can games signify? Remember, it's not a question of whether or not games are narrative, but instead how they are narrative. And if my agenda with this investigation of the "game-story" is to inculcate genuinely new forms of experience, then we need to ask not just how games can be narrative systems, but we need to ask how games can be narrative systems in ways that other media cannot.

It's clear that games can signify in ways that other narrative forms have already established: through sound and image, material and text, representations of movement and space. But perhaps there are ways that only games can signify, drawing on their unique status as explicitly interactive narrative systems of formal play.

Example: Ms. Pac-Man

This much we know: one way of framing games is to frame them as game-stories. So let's take a well-known example — the arcade game *Ms. Pac-Man* (figure 13.1) — and look closely at the diverse ways that it signifies narrative.

First observation: there are many story elements to *Ms. Pac-Man* that are not directly related to the gameplay. For instance, the large-scale characters on the physical arcade game cabinet establish a graphical story about the chase between Ms. Pac-Man and the ghosts. There are also brief noninteractive animations inside the game, which appear between every few levels. These simple cartoons chronicle events in the life of Ms. Pac-Man: meeting her beau Pac-Man, outwitting the ever-pursuing ghosts, etc.

But while these story-components are important parts of the larger *Ms. Pac-Man* experience, they are not at the heart of what distinguishes *Ms. Pac-Man* as a

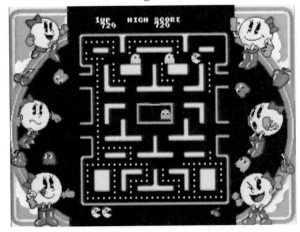

13.1. *Ms. Pac-Man*. (Namco)

game-story. The arcade cabinet graphics and linear cartoon animations sit adjacent to the actual gameplay itself, where a different kind of narrative awaits. As the player participates with the system, playing the game, exploring its rule-structures, finding the patterns of free play that will let the game continue, a narrative unfolds in real time.

What kind of story is it? It's a narrative about life and death, about consumption and power. It's a narrative about strategic pursuit through a constrained space, about dramatic reversals of fortune where the hunter becomes the hunted. It's a narrative about relationships, in which every character on the screen, every munchable dot and empty corridor, are meaningful parts of a larger system. It's a narrative that always has the same elements, yet unfolds differently each time it is experienced. And it's also a kind of journey, where the player and protagonist are mapped onto each other in complicated and subtle ways. This is a narrative in which procedures, relationships, and complex systems dynamically signify. It is the kind of narrative that only a game could tell.

Quick reminder: although I may have focused on the gameplay elements of the *Ms. Pac-Man* narrative, ultimately the player's experience of the game-story is composed of the entire arcade game. This includes not just the gameplay itself but the cabinet graphics and the cartoon animations, the sound of a quarter dropping and the texture of the joystick, the social and architectural dynamics of the arcade itself, the gender ideologies of the game and its historical relationship to the original *Pac-Man*, the marketing of the character and its penetration into pop culture at large.

But at the center of this expansive game experience is the *game* of *Ms. Pac-Man* — that artificial conflict with a quantifiable outcome. The gameplay of *Ms. Pac-Man* is in some sense the kernel at the center of the machine, the engine that drives all of the other elements, putting the *game* in the game-story.

And as a story, it is compelling enough to have found *Ms. Pac-Man* a worldwide audience of dedicated players. It's important to note that the "story" of the *Ms. Pac-Man* game-story certainly does not provide the same pleasures of a novel or film. But why should we expect

Jenkins   McKenzie Eskelinen
Juul   Ito Pearce
Pearce   Flanagan Bernstein

Game Theories > Zimmerman Crawford Juul

IV. Game Theories

it to? The question is, what pleasures can it provide that books or film cannot?

Wrap-up and Send-off

Because games are always already narrative systems, the question that weaves through this book — the question "Is there a game-story?" — is ultimately moot. Recognizing that narrative is one of many ways to frame a game experience, for me a more important question is: How can we capitalize on the unique qualities of games in order to create new kinds of game-stories? What if dynamic play procedures were used as the very building blocks of storytelling?

There are already many wonderful examples of this kind of thinking. The children's board game *Up the River* by Ravensburger uses a modular game board to procedurally recreate the rhythmic flow of a stream. And *The Sims*, a computer game mentioned often in this volume, is a game-story too. Instead of presenting a prescripted narrative like most digital "interactive narratives," *The Sims* functions as a kind of story-machine, generating unexpected narrative events out of complex and playful simulation.

But much more needs to be done. Any observation made about games, play, narrative, and interactivity could be used as the starting point for a new kind of game-story. Here are some examples that cannibalize statements I made earlier in this essay:

The concept of "narrative" casts a wide net. Many experiences can be considered narrative experiences, like a meal or a marriage ceremony. How would we make a game-story about these kinds of subjects?

Interactivity can occur on a cultural level. How could a game-story be designed with meta-interactivity in mind, so that the narrative emerged as the sum of many different player experiences in otherwise unrelated games?

Mischief is a form of play. What would a game be like that encouraged players to break the existing rules in order to form new ones?

Games are about conflict. OK, so we're drowning in fighting games. What about a game that told a story of the feints, bluffing, trickery, and intimidation of a good argument?

Yes, these are difficult kinds of challenges. But if we're going to move through our collective dissatisfaction with the current state of the game-story, it's time to rethink the terms of the debate and arrive at new ways of understanding game-stories, and new strategies for creating them.

This essay attempted to re-present some of those terms. In this painfully brief space, I have been able to do no more than gesture towards some of these new avenues. There are many more concepts in need of discipline. And the rest is up to you.

Notes

Many of the ideas in this essay were generated in collaboration with Frank Lantz, with whom I have taught Game Design and Interactive Narrative Design for many years. Many ideas also stem from my collaborations with Katie Salen, with whom I am currently co-authoring a Game Design textbook for MIT Press.

The four categories of Narrative Interactivity first appeared in print in an essay called, "Against Hypertext," for *American Letters & Commentary*.

The definition of games presented here is loosely inspired by a definition of games presented by Elliott Avedon & Brian Sutton-Smith in *The Study of Games*. However, elements are also borrowed from Roger Callois's *Man, Play, and Games,* as well as Johannes Huizinga's *Homo Ludens: A Study of the Play Element in Culture* and Bernard Suit's *Grasshopper: Games, Life, and Utopia*.

Lastly: despite my extensive and gratuitous use of the disciplinary metaphor, I do not advocate spanking children in any context. Disciplinary activity that occurs between two consenting adults is another matter entirely. In any case don't let the bad pun distract you — the "discipline" I am talking about in this essay is a discipline: the field of game design.

References

Avedon, Elliott, and Brian Sutton-Smith (1971). *The Study of Games*. New York: John Wiley & Sons.

Callois, Roger (1961). *Man, Play, and Games*. New York: Free Press.

Huizinga, Johannes (1955). *Homo Ludens: A Study of the Play Element in Culture*. Boston: Beacon Press.

Miller, J. Hillis (1995). "Narrative." In *Critical Terms for Literary Study*, edited by Thomas McLaughlin and Frank Lentriccia. Chicago: University of Chicago Press.

Suit, Bernard (1990). *Grasshopper: Games, Life, and Utopia*. Boston: David R. Godine.

Zimmerman, Eric (2000). "Against Hypertext." *American Letters & Commentary* no.12 (2000).

Hypertexts & Interactives

In the range of perspectives on new media, that of the hypertext tradition is distinguished by its focus on authored rather than emergent experiences. To put it another way: the hypertext project's focus is antithetical to that of artificial intelligence. While Nicholas Negroponte, prior to founding the MIT Media Lab, dreamed of an intelligent machine that could learn to be an ideal — hyperpersonalized — architect's assistant, hypertext figures such as Ted Nelson and Doug Engelbart dreamed of systems no more "intelligent" than power tools or movie cameras — and just as effective when placed in trained, talented hands.

More recently, some thinkers have attempted to bridge these perspectives. (*First Person* contributors Phoebe Sengers, Michael Mateas, and Warren Sack combine approaches from both groups.) Yet in general AI and hypertext theorists do not simply diverge, but in fact begin their practices from radically different points.

For the authors in this section, Nelson and Engelbart's hypertext concepts are not simply an unspoken background; these essayists are well-known for their engagement with hypertext, and have directly addressed Nelson and Engelbart's work, as well as that of hypertexts both preceding and outside of the web.

Thus we have our hypertexts. We find "interactives" in this section's third essay, by J. Yellowlees Douglas and Andrew Hargadon. *Interactive* is a candidate term for what we might otherwise call interactive narratives, hypertext fictions, or videogames. Like most such terms ("cyberdrama" comes to mind), its use implies a focus on certain types of examples and a general approach to their interpretation.

One might ask, do we require a term like "interactive"? This is a more interesting question in this case than it is for most neologisms because, as Mark Bernstein and Diane Greco demonstrate in their essay, systems that might at first seem beyond the bounds of hypertext, which might seem to cry out for the label "interactives," may prove on closer examination to be hypertexts. *Thespis*, one of the systems Bernstein and Greco discuss, is an example of this phenomenon which also upsets a number of common assumptions about writing and play. While many forms of language play (from *Scrabble* to the "exquisite corpse") are rule-bounded, multiplayer games, we do not generally think of preauthored texts as being such. Yet this is what *Thespis* creates — a multiplayer performance in which an absent author's text becomes crafted, through gameplay, into a narrative.

Arguments such as this operate against the unfortunately narrow popular conception of hypertext. Still, it may yet prove to be the case that this constricted idea of hypertext is now too well-cemented — and that a neologism such as Douglas and Hargadon's "interactive" is required to explain to audiences that the systems under discussion are not limited to web-based hypertexts.

Textually and theoretically, hypertext poet Stephanie Strickland is situated somewhere between our two other essays. She turns our attention to the experience of writing and reading hypertexts, particularly hypertext poetry. Strickland's examples further extend what types of systems and artifacts might be included in our categories of hypertexts or interactives: from systems that emphasize the performance of direct configurative practice by the reader, to texts one explores and reconfigures with the eye and mind (and not with a mouse, keyboard, or console controller). Understanding the experience and pleasure of interacting with these new forms — seen through schemas related to authorship rather than

165

emergence — is also the explicit topic of Douglas and Hargadon's essay. And the opening of Bernstein and Greco's essay is designed to correct what they perceive as the major critical misunderstandings of the reader's experience of hypertext literature.

It could be argued that this focus on understanding the reading experience is a natural outgrowth of creating new media from a hypertext perspective. Freed from worrying whether system intelligence has been achieved, those who work in hypertext can instead focus on developing new formal crafts, on new methods of creating pleasure and meaning.

Card Shark and *Thespis:* Exotic Tools for Hypertext Narrative

Mark Bernstein and Diane Greco

Hypertext Fiction and Its Critics

Although games, visual art, and textual experiments had long been areas of academic research, the first artistically convincing explorations of literary computing appeared in the late 1980s. It was only in these years that computers became sufficiently commonplace that a computational creation could realistically hope to find an audience. Of equal importance was the gradual acceptance of Ted Nelson's thesis (Nelson 1976) that computers could be tools for artistic expression, for even in 1982 the title of Nelson's *Literary Machines* was meant to shock and surprise.

The final and critical step, first taken by an informal workshop of American writers who called themselves TINAC, was to recognize that hypertext links need not be merely annotations (as in Yankelovich, Meyrowitz, and van Dam 1985) or plot points (as in *Adventure*). Links, they realized, could serve as exquisite literary connections, explicitly opening the text to the readerly interactions and interventions that are explicitly (albeit tacitly) part of all serious reading. Links could change point of view, enact a time shift, or hold contradictory elements in suspension. Links could suggest new formalisms, new structure, a new large-scale punctuation. Indeed, even the absence of an expected link, or the readerly effort require to decode the gap between the point of departure and the point of arrival, could prove as eloquent as a dramatic musical rest (Bolter and Joyce 1987; Joyce 1988; Harpold 1991).

Although the TINAC group agreed on these principles, they differed strikingly in execution, giving rise to three quite distinct approaches to literary hypertext that continue to shape the literature today. Michael Joyce (1990), in *afternoon*, built dense, lyrical explorations of reality and memory. Stuart Moulthrop (1991), in *Victory Garden*, uses links in an ironic, less purely evocative mode; Joyce speaks of links as "words that yield," but Moulthrop's witty (and, often, bitterly sarcastic) links yield nothing to anyone. Where Joyce's work is overtly metafictional, Moulthrop and J. Yellowlees Douglas (1993; "I Have Said Nothing") use links as *hyperbaton* (Bolter 1997). That is, where in

167

Response by Andrew Stern

Bernstein and Greco's proposed systems, *Card Shark* and *Thespis,* push interactive narrative in a direction similar to the design goals of Façade, my current collaboration with Michael Mateas (see Mateas this volume). This convergence is exciting and interesting to me because Bernstein and Greco's jumping-off point is hypertext literature (Bernstein 1998b), whereas I am building upon work on AI-based animated virtual characters (Stern 1999, 2001). Although Bernstein and Greco push strongly against the vision of the Holodeck and its reliance on "unlimited computing power," I believe their approach shares something with AI-based approaches to interactive story. Likewise, aspects of my practice have fundamental similarity to that of hypertext authors, even though I use AI-based tools.

Façade is an interactive drama in which a single user, playing the Guest character, and two real-time animated virtual characters, Grace and Trip, perform a story about a married couple about to split up (figure 14.response.1). From a first-person point-of-view the player types text to speak and gesture, and uses the arrow keys and mouse to navigate and use objects in a three-dimensional world. The virtual characters speak with digital voices and express emotion and personality through animation (Mateas and Stern 2000).

Both *Thespis* and *Façade* are making unexpected, "exotic" departures from their respective fields. On the spectrum between hypertext and the Holodeck, *Thespis* offers hypertext rich in character; *Façade* offers an

rhetoric we might depart from idiomatic word order to achieve a dramatic effect, so in hypertext we may contrive to reveal an underlying narrative that gradually emerges as the reader interprets scenes traversed in a sequence outside the writer's immediate control. Finally, in *Uncle Buddy's Phantom Funhouse*, John McDaid (1992) devises an artifactual hypertext, literally a literary machine, simulated on the reader's computer, which the reader must learn to operate and decode.

All three approaches received substantial critical applause, a lasting following, and (perhaps most importantly) have inspired numbers of subsequent hypertext artists. Joyce's lyrical hypertextuality finds recent echoes, for example, in Chapman's (2001) *Turning In*, Strickland's (1998) *True North*, as well as Arnold and Derby's (1999) *Kokura*. Moulthrop's hyperbaton is key to Coverly's (2000) *Califia*, Cramer's (1993) "In Small & Large Pieces," Eisen's (2001) "What Fits," and Amerika's (1997) *Grammatron*. McDaid's artifactual approach, dormant for some years, finds recent expression in Bly's *We Descend*, Malloy and Marshall's (1996) *Forward Anywhere*, and in Sondheim's executable poems. Many combine several approaches, as when Shelley Jackson's (1996) *Patchwork Girl* masterfully shifts among all three.

A substantial critical literature has grown up around these works, as scholars and critics have sought to understand and appreciate them more fully. Robert Coover's early essay (Coover 1992) and his comprehensive, thoughtful review of the entire body of early hypertext fiction (Coover 1993), helped situate hypertext fiction near the center of the contemporary literary landscape. Bolter's (1991) *Writing Space* situated hypermedia in the continuing development of writing, and Landow's (1992) *Hypertext: The Convergence of Contemporary Critical Theory and Technology* called attention to the theoretical complexity of reading and criticism. Lanham (1993), Gaggi (1997), Murray (1997), Douglas (2000; in *The End of Books – or Books without End?*, a revision of her 1992 dissertation), and Aarseth (1997) each contributed monographs with important early readings of key hypertexts.

Despite the ahistorical claim that early hypertext critics were blindly supportive (Eskelinen and Koskimaa 2000), hypertext fiction has always attracted stern criticism as well as praise. Much of the early critique centered on the apparent similarity of the computer to the television, expressing the fear that images, mixed media, and luminosity will of necessity subvert literary values (Birkerts 1994). Others, perceiving the relationship between hypertext and postmodernism and finding postmodern theory distasteful, sought to ridicule postmodern theory by

14.response.1. Grace and Trip from Façade.

animated virtual world rich in dialog and introspection. Just as Bernstein and Greco are careful to point out

about *Thespis*, *Façade* is not a game, it is not about realism. It is drama. The goal is not to "win" but to experience a compelling story, which in *Façade*'s case does not have a happy ending. And although we employ AI techniques, we too are only after the *appearance* of intentionality and individuality — the core tenet of the believable agent approach to artificial intelligence (Bates, Loyall, and Reilly 1992). *Façade*'s simple models of psychology, emotion, and language understanding are customized to the requirements of our story; they are no more than sophisticated ways of keeping track of the story state that matters theatrically. That is, we are using AI techniques for artistic purposes; we are not creating realistic cognitive models.

With any interactive work, the author shares control

denouncing hypertext (Miller 1998). Inevitably, individual works received both praise and blame, and it is not uncommon to read of critics who, after the passage of months or years, found great merit in work they had previously disliked (Walker 1999).

Narrative and the Nature of Hypermedia

An important and common perception among literary critics with scant experience of hypertext is that hypertext is necessarily incoherent, and that its incoherence is due to its technological substrate. They assume that, although even nontraditional print narratives convincingly and pleasurably mimic the apparent linearity of temporal experience, the technological qualities of hypermedia limit it to a particularly intolerable nonlinearity in which narrative is necessarily fractured, unsatisfying, and unpleasurable.

Whereas recalling the obvious fact that print is itself a technology with a long history of change and development would be enough to refute this flimsy argument, there is also much positive evidence that satisfying narratives are indeed produced in hypermedia. For instance, one may point to the continued popularity of early hypertext fictions (e.g., *afternoon*, *Victory Garden*), to the appearance of new fictions (e.g., *Turning In*, Holeton's (2001) *Figurski At*

Findhorn on Acid), to the myriad university courses in hypertext fiction, writing and criticism, or to the flourishing secondary literature on the subject (such as that by Nelson award winners Walker (1999), Tosca (2000), and Miles (2001)). Moreover, the importance of narrative in the craft of hypertext writing has been recognized from the beginning (Bolter and Joyce 1987), for narrative is central not only to works of imagination but also to myriad other forms of human expression, including technical (Bernstein 1991) and scholarly writing (Kolb 1997).

Hypertexts are not structureless, and to call them "nonlinear" is too general to be informative. After fifteen years of hypertext publishing, it is clear that once writers reject the idea that the linear narrative typical of print is the only acceptable model for storytelling, there is no theoretical limit on the varieties of structure that an author may develop. Nonetheless, we require a working vocabulary. In "Patterns of Hypertext," Bernstein (1998b) catalogs some common patterns in observed hypermedia narratives and argues that patterning and narrative coherence are tightly coupled when dealing (as one often does in hypermedia) with stories that unfold according to organizations of composites and aggregates. Just as tapping a glassful of supersaturated solution can precipitate entire crystals, traversing a link can reorder

of the narrative sequencing with the reader/player. An important feature of *Thespis* is that the author additionally shares control of the narrative sequencing with the system itself, *Card Shark*. That is, instead of carefully placed links the author can be assured the reader will see and choose from, there is now a much larger "tangle" of links that the author must trust *Card Shark* (with her guidance) to pick among and offer the reader. I found it interesting to discover that the rules that *Card Shark* uses to make its decisions and the particular way its story nodes are structured and annotated are akin to the AI system that controls the story sequencing in *Façade*.

In our attempt to make a story interactive, we've found the devil is in the details of exactly how you

deconstruct the story's content into pieces (or more specifically, a hierarchy of pieces), and how to build a system that integrates the player's interactions into the reconstruction — the performance — of those pieces.

Bernstein and Greco propose cards, each containing a brief, focused passage of text and annotated with constraints on the context in which they can be used and modifications they make to the reading context. The cards are played out using a simple set of rules by a single reader (*Card Shark*) or potentially by multiple readers (*Social Shark*). They say, "Rather than create complex actors, we create simple automata that say interesting things about important matters."

We've found that an effective way to create complex actors is in fact to carefully combine layers of simple events in a whole narrative. If a narrative contains more than one link (and most hypertexts do), ordering events is a complex task indeed. Patterns allow coherence to emerge when a narrative supports many different possible orderings of events.[1]

Do the patterns we observe in hypertext fiction arise directly from hypertextuality, or are they artifacts arising from the mediation of the system?

The nature of hypertext is best discerned by studying actual hypertexts, which at this early point in the history of hypermedia, cannot yet be separated from the tools of their production, presentation, and increasingly, distribution. Over the past decade, the descendants of three systems — HyperCard, Storyspace, and Mosaic — have been the tools most frequently selected by hypertext fiction writers.[2] Different writers use the same system in drastically different ways,[3] but systems inevitably shape hypertexts. Are the properties of hypertext fiction, such as those observed in Bernstein's "Patterns of Hypertext," and deplored by Miller (1998) in "www.claptrap.com," intrinsic to hypertext, or do they arise from the idiosyncrasies of specific systems?

This paper reviews two exotic hypertext systems, tools suitable for hypertext narrative but dramatically unlike the tools currently in use. Our motivation for describing these tools is also unusual. The customary

170

reason for building a new system is to build a *better* system; here, we wanted to build a *strange* system, a hypertext environment that might let us step back from Storyspace and the web in order to gain a better perspective. We do not wish to argue that these systems are better than, say, Storyspace: Storyspace is simpler, more elegant, more flexible, more widely available. We do not suggest that hypertexts written with the new system will be better than those written with other tools. For our purposes, we need not be better, we need only be different.

In the remainder of this paper, we first explore a language or notation, *Card Shark*, that describes *sculptural hypertexts. Shark* is small, simple, and appears not to be very expressive, but it can readily describe complex hypertext structures. Next, we embed *Shark* in a dramatic context: we create a simple theatrical environment that represents characters moving through space, a space through which the reader moves to witness and perhaps to participate in the action. The nature of this participation, though superficially similar to interactive fiction, may avoid internal contradictions that confront conventional immersive fictions. Finally, we conclude with some thoughts on how this approach might be evaluated.

automata. *Façade's* architecture is a hierarchy of layers of automata, each representing a subset of the story content at different granularities. Each layer runs in parallel and can modulate the performance of the layers below. (Hierarchy of representation is a powerful technique commonly used in AI.) At the bottom-most level are short animated *actions* with pieces such as hand motions, facial expressions and walk steps. The next level up contains *behaviors* with pieces such as walking from place to place, acting nervous, and crying. The next level up contains story *beats*, which are clusters of dialogue akin to the cards in *Card Shark*. Finally, the top most level contains *scenes*, which are large collections of beats.

Like *Card Shark* cards, *Façade's* story beats are

annotated with preconditions and effects. The *Façade* beat manager runs a set of rules that decides which beat to play next, by searching for authored story beats with preconditions that match the player's current interactions and the story memory (what has happened so far). When multiple beats are available to play at any one time, the system may look at the effects of each beat and choose the one that best matches the dramatic arc the author is trying to achieve.

In systems such as *Card Shark* and *Façade* the author starts with a large partial ordering of story nodes, a tangle. We've been discovering and struggling with how to author in this way. For our story we want the partial ordering to be as loose as possible to give the player as much agency as we can, while maintaining "coherence,

Hypertexts & Interactives> **Bernstein & Greco**
Strickland
Douglas & Hargadon

Stern Perlin
Raley Utterback
Schechner Jenkins

V. Hypertexts & Interactives

Sculptural Hypertext and *Card Shark*

Conventional hypertexts take a set of unconnected nodes (or pages, or lexia) and link them together. *Card Shark* begins with a set of lexia, all of which are connected to each other, and builds structure by removing unwanted connections. We call this initial set a *tangle*. We call *Card Shark sculptural* because we create structure by removing unwanted connections, much as a sculptor may create form by removing unwanted stone. Traditional hypertext tools, in this sense, are *calligraphic*; we create structure by adding lines until we have added exactly the necessary degree of connection.

Where a sculptural strategy has been employed in the past — most notably, perhaps, in Malloy's (1993) *its name was Penelope* and in Malloy and Marshall's (1996) *Forward Anywhere* — it has been chosen in part to deemphasize temporal sequence and narrative structure (Golovchinsky and Marshall 2000). *Card Shark*, as we shall see, foregrounds sequence and emphasizes structure.

A *Card Shark* node (or card) contains some text, typically a brief, focused passage. Each card may also specify constraints on the context in which it may appear. For example, AFTER 10 requires that the node may be visited only after ten other nodes have been seen. A node that appears BEFORE 25 may only be visited early in the reading; if it is not seen early, it will

"I cannot help you. Perhaps Rick has the necessary influence with the underground... I, alas, do not.

"Ilsa thought back to days long forgotten. Days with Rick, nights with Rick, before the war..."

14.1. *Card Shark* nodes establish conditions that subsequent nodes must satisfy

not be seen at all. A variety of constraints may be applied to a node; as in a conventional hypertext, it is likely that some nodes will never appear in any given reading.

Each card may also specify modifications it makes to the reading context, chiefly by posting assertions on a blackboard. A passage that serves to introduce a new character, for example, could ASSERT WENDY. Other cards that REQUIRE WENDY can be visited only after this introduction. Later, a passage may remove WENDY from the scene and RETRACT WENDY.

Given a collection of cards, we read them by following a simple set of rules[4]:

---

causality and closure," allowing us achieve the design goal of a quasi-Aristotelian story (Mateas and Stern 2001). The tighter we make the partial ordering by "sculpting" the tangle, by using stricter preconditions on beats — that is, the more we, as authors, take control of the sequencing — the less freedom the system has to make its own decisions, and the closer to a hard-link hypertext structure the story becomes.

Bernstein and Greco are quick to make important distinctions between *Thespis* (player-as-minor-character) and traditional interactive fiction (player-as-protagonist). Perhaps there is a middle-ground between the two. Although not the central character, the interactor in *Façade* plays *herself*, using her own name, gender and ideally any backstory she wishes to bring to

the experience. In order to ensure a high-quality dramatic experience, the computer characters are intended to be the most active and important characters. But we aspire for the player to become a major character. The system is designed to regularly offer her opportunities to significantly affect the progression of the story. She is a catalyst for affecting the other characters, with the potential for an internal progression of her own through her subjective experience of playing the story.

"Illusions that place the reader on stage necessarily founder when promised freedom of action is contradicted by the limitations of the simulated environment." This is hard to accept. Is it hopeless to give the player the freedom to say whatever she wishes,

1. The collection of cards is shuffled and the blackboard is wiped clean.

2. The reader receives seven cards from the deck.

3. The constraints for each of the player's cards are evaluated. Cards whose conditions are not satisfied are disabled; the reader sees at most a brief title and an indication of what conditions need to be satisfied for the card to be seen.

4. From among the cards whose constraints are met, the player selects a node to visit next.

5. The selected node is visited. Its full text appears (or is performed) on the screen. If the node makes assertions or modifies the environment, those actions are performed. The card remains "on the table"; we may look at it again whenever we like, but it will never be "played" again.

6. The player receives a new card, and repeats until the reading is over.

If the granularity of the lexia — the size of the "card" — is large, *Card Shark*'s constraints describe the episodic architecture of the narrative. If the granularity is very small — individual words or phrases — the constraints describe a text generation engine. If the lexia were lines of iambic pentameter, the constraints could describe a rhyme scheme.

We can easily envision other variations. In particular, we might use one deck but maintain two separate blackboards (perhaps called Plot and Subplot). The two blackboards provide separate contexts in which cards could appear, offering the reader and the writer greater flexibility.

In conventional hypertext tools, connecting nodes in a sequence is easy but connecting nodes in a dense tangle requires effort. Indeed, despite a priori concerns that hypertext disorientation would lead to confusion, incoherence, or inattention, the variety of expedients authors adopt to deliberately disrupt the reading line clearly suggests that disorientation is hard to achieve (Landow 1990; Bernstein 1991). In *Grammatron*, we see time stress and fluid links (Zellweger et al. 2001); in Guyer's (1992) *Quibbling* we observe dense links that refuse to signify their intent; in Rosenberg's *Intergrams*, lexia are superimposed and links are dynamically entwined. If disorientation followed naturally from the nature of hypertext, would such expedients be

to freely express herself? I feel it is too soon to answer this as definitively and devastatingly as Bernstein and Greco do. Certainly this kind of freedom is the dream for many players and authors. Bernstein and Greco seem to think that because we cannot fully deliver on this expectation, that we should discard the approach altogether. That's their choice, and their proposals are excellent alternatives. However this dream should not be abandoned because it is technically and artistically challenging to achieve. Instead let's try to work within the limitations of the technology, push on them, use them as artistic constraints. The player's expectations must be set at the appropriate level so she avoids struggling against a "necessarily recalcitrant world-model." Some of us believe that today's computational

environment *can* in fact match at least *some* of our aspirations, and as technology inevitably improves over time, it will be able to match even more.

With *Façade* we are experimenting, walking up closely to this edge. By carefully choosing the context of our story, an apartment, we implicitly limit the interface to a finite number of objects and gestures. But, because we leave language wide open — the player can type any dialogue they want — we are putting a lot of effort into "recovery" from situations where the system does not understand or have a specific authored response for what the player is saying. (Characters will *never* literally say, "I don't understand.") We feel there is a lot of room to experiment with scripting the interactor (Murray 1997) to allow for the experience of

necessary or useful?

Card Shark inverts the situation; making a tangle is easy, but making a strict sequence takes work. The tangle, not the link, is a *Card Shark* primitive.

Liveness, *Card Shark*, and Transitions

When writing for *Card Shark*, we are naturally concerned with *liveness* — with avoiding premature termination or inadvertent closure (Douglas 2000). Consider a reader in the midst of reading a *Card Shark* hypertext. A time may come when the reader examines her seven options and finds that none of the preconditions are met. The position is dead, the reader is stuck.[5] Sooner or later, this is inevitable: we will run out of cards and the story must eventually end. But the story should have a chance to play out first; we must take care to let the story begin before it ends, to avoid stranding the reader at the start.

Imagine, for example, a *Card Shark* hypertext that describes a twilight encounter in the garden on Tuesday night, and its dénouement in the nearby bedroom the following morning. Some actions REQUIRE NIGHT; others REQUIRE MORNING. If our current context is the night and our available actions require that it be morning, we need a transition that moves from night to morning. Conversely, if we have been reading about events in the dawn-lit bedroom and

there is more to learn about last night's unexpected encounter in the garden, we require a transition that moves from the morning to the previous night, from the bedroom to the garden. Indeed, if readers are not to constantly encounter dead positions, we need to provide a rich assortment of transitions to facilitate movement, to shift between times, and to get characters on and off stage.

Multivalence is not a vice, of course (Bernstein 2000). That is, these transitions need not limit themselves to their immediate business. It is important to observe that the text of a *Shark* node need not describe the change it accomplishes. The text might, for example, proceed from the consequence of the asserted change without describing the transition. Some transitions may not need to be expressed, either because the reader will understand them or because we want to startle the unwary. At other times, the transition may itself be the crucial expressive element.

Transitional nodes, when used naturally, can help maintain coherence and causality. But, as noted in the literature on hypertext fiction, apprehension of pattern can itself lend coherence (Harpold 1991; Hayles 2000). Some patterns are more natural to sculptural hypertext than others. For instance, although cycles are the central structural motif observed in most successful calligraphic hypertexts (Joyce 1997; Bernstein 1998b),

173

---

freedom for the player, when the actual number of responses is necessarily finite. "I don't understand" is an inevitable position for the system to be in, but not an inevitable response.

"Even if we could experience *Hamlet* on the holodeck, it wouldn't work. Tragedy requires that the characters be blind..." I agree, it seems likely that certain types of stories such as traditional tragedy may not work as an interactive story, for the reasons Bernstein and Greco describe. Instead authors will need to tell the kinds of stories that do work interactively. *Façade* is a more open-ended, explorative, psychological situation. Is this drama anymore? We hope to understand this better once we get a chance to play with the finished work.

"*Card Shark* avoids this contradiction by

foregrounding the familiar convention of reading and drama: we may *want* our favorite characters to prosper, but as spectators, we cannot choose the outcome. *Thespis* gives us a greater range of action and might offer us a chance to take a role, but that role is not central and our limitations are evident." That is both its strength and its weakness.

From Ken Perlin's Online Response

I'm particularly intrigued by the notion posited in *Card Shark* of starting with an overabundance of possible paths, and creating the experience as a careful pruning away of potential paths, mainly through the use of ordering-condition constraints, as the primary way of authoring an experience for the reader/player. This

cycles prove rare in *Card Shark*. To permit recurrence, the same passage must occur on two or more different cards.

Incoherence, oscillation, repetition, and cycles are sometimes seen as inherent to hypertext, especially by those who don't like the hypertexts they've read (Birkerts 1994; Miller 1998). These patterns, however, may inhere more closely to the inclinations of the artist and the propensities of the tools the artist chose, rather than to the nature of the medium itself.

Social Shark

Reading is often considered a solitary activity, but we might also enjoy *Card Shark* hypertexts with company. Extending *Card Shark* for collaborative reading creates *Social Shark,* and with it some interesting opportunities.

Consider two readers, Mr. Green and Ms. Blue, who meet (perhaps over the net) to read a *Social Shark* hypertext together. The computer unwraps a fresh deck, shuffles the cards, and deals seven cards apiece to Green and to Blue. The two readers take turns, following the rules of *Card Shark*; the reading continues until neither reader can continue.

Each card, in addition to its text, its preconditions, and its assertions, is labeled with a green number and a blue number. Whenever a card is played, Mr. Green receives a number of points specified in green, and Blue receives the number of points specified in blue. At the end of the reading, when neither player can continue, the player with the highest score wins.

Extensions to additional participants are easily envisioned by adding additional score numbers. Alternatively, a third player might seek to maximize the combined blue and green score, a fourth player might seek to minimize it, and so on. Indeed, the game need not be competitive: Green and Blue might conspire toward a shared goal, perhaps in a common struggle against some quality inherent to the fictive universe. In that case, the gameworld itself would constitute a third character.

How might writers assign these values to cards? One simple approach identifies each player with a goal: Green is rewarded whenever Love grows between two characters, while Blue is rewarded when complications or misunderstandings separate them. The goal may extend to plot and subplot, where Green is rewarded whenever anyone falls in love. But the goals of Green and Blue need not be orthogonal: Green might be rewarded when Love advances while Blue is rewarded by anarchy and chaos. In this case, Green's triumph is a romantic comedy — *Pretty Woman* or *The Tempest* — while Blue's triumph is hilarity — *Horse Feathers* or *The Importance of Being Earnest*.

---

approach makes very clear the sense that nonlinear hypertext narrative is a sort of interactive sculpture or garden, a negative space carved by pruning away from a universe of possibilities.

Unfortunately, it is somewhat difficult for me to get a strong handle on this essay, because it describes an enabling mechanism, without any real and specific content built on that mechanism. I can't ask myself the sorts of questions that would tell me whether what is being described is a truly effective medium (and therefore truly interesting).

http://www.electronicbookreview.com/thread/firstperson/perlinr1

Bernstein and Greco Respond

The difference between our *Thespis* and Stern's *Façade* lies, in the end, in two questions: whether computational representation of the internal psychic life of characters is feasible, and whether it is useful.

http://www.electronicbookreview.com/thread/firstperson/bernsteingrecor2

Thespis

Thespis, our second exotic tool, extends the core idea of *Card Shark* by allowing many agents to participate in a single hypertext. Each agent or *actor* receives cards that describe possible actions, and each in turn selects an action to take. One actor represents the reader; the reader chooses actions as she wishes. The other agents are computational structures; they choose according to their design.

Each actor has a name and a simple internal state. Each actor also has its unique function Happiness (state), modeled as a linear combination of state values. Actors select available actions that are likely to improve their happiness. Faced with the same options, different character may choose different actions. One character may value money more than another; one may crave excitement while another avoids it. These crude behaviors are not meant to model psychology, but merely to provide the *appearance* of intentionality and individuality. We are not making (Mateas and Stern 2001); we're making theater (Laurel 1991).

Each actor moves across the bounded, two-dimensional space that represents the *stage*. The reader sees and hears things that happen nearby; more distant actions may be unnoticed. This spatial component neatly reifies the hypertextuality of Thespian space; rather than following *this* link and not *that* one, we are standing *here*, not elsewhere. Perhaps we are sitting at the bar and talking with Hugh, Cathy, and Kaj. Across the room, we might see Randy and Stuart arguing with Susana, but if we want to hear them we'll have to walk over there — and then we'll miss the action now unfolding before us.

We may constrain actions in *Thespis* by reference to the environment and to the context.

> *It's getting dark. Winter is coming. I tried to remember winter — the last winter before the war. It seems so long ago.*

Without constraint, any actor might say this. But we can easily impose constraints, choosing who may say this, or to whom it may be said. We could specify when and where it can be spoken. A variety of partial constraints are provided; for example, an action that is OnlyExcited can only be performed if the actor is unusually agitated, and a Private action can only be performed if the participants don't know they're being observed.

Actors and actions are simple. Rather than create complex actors, we create simple automata that say interesting things about important matters. Actors can move (to a landmark or to another actor), they can use props (eating, for example, if they feel like it), and they can talk. The point of this computational mechanism is merely to keep the actor-automaton from breaking the theatrical illusion. We enforce a naïve physics of the stage, decreeing, for example, that actors should never walk through walls. Simple logic can give rise to complex emergent behavior (Resnick 1997), and this aggregate behavior can be convincingly organic.

Perhaps more important, though, is the recruitment of the reader as a dramatic coconspirator. If simple automata are well-written, if they are engaging and convincing, readers will want to attribute agency, intentionality, and emotional depth to them (Reeves and Nass 1996).

A Thespian Example

What would it be like to read a hypertext written for *Thespis*? Let's imagine one.[6] We'll call it *The Trojan Kids*, an experimental adaptation of Euripides' *Trojan Women*, in modern dress. It's set in a large, open, metal-roofed shed, a community center for a small village that has fallen recently to the conquering invaders. It's the night of the big school dance; life goes on. It could be France in 1940, it could be a village in Rwanda or Kosovo or Chechnya.

The reader is ALICE, uncertain, unsure, unimportant.

She is met at the doorway by EMILY, a plain and unpopular student who has done most of the work of arranging the dance, setting out the refreshments, getting permits from the Provisional Government. She greets us warmly:

> Emily: *Come in, come in. I'm so glad you're here. Everybody's here. Come in, let's all be together, together again. Let's celebrate the*

blessings of peace.

Alice: *But, Emily, we lost! After ten years, our gates lie in ruins, Greek soldiers patrol the streets, smoke rises from the palace. What blessing is this?*

Emily: *Defeat is bitter, sure. But now we have peace! At last! With honor! And in our time. Now we can have our party. It's our tradition, and the Greeks gave us a permit.*

Go on in. Try the shrimp — I hear the dip is really spicy!

Emily is a Pollyanna, an accommodator, a collaborationist in embryo, and the stink of a dark future hangs over her irritating cheeriness. Can she be saved?

Inside, there's a crowd. They're kids; most of them have simple motivations. Some hope to get drunk. Some hope for a memorable moment of basketball or Nintendo. Some hope to get lucky. Some of these kids were conceived in the secluded dunes out back, at a party very much like this, just five or six years before the war began.

Others have more to say. CASSIE (Cassandra) is dark, sexy, strange. She knows stuff. She's seen Emily, for example, a few years from now, her head shaved, hounded through the street. Cassie knows that some of her friends here tonight will be in the cheering crowd. She knows that others won't make it that far. While Cassie isn't popular, and nobody pays attention to her stories, she's hard to ignore; she draws boys like a flame and those boys draw girls. She's rarely alone.

POLLY (Polixena) is the old king's niece. She shouldn't be here; she doesn't know this crowd; she goes to private school. She was away from the palace when the soldiers came. She's on the run. She's escaped the patrols so far, but she's running out of options. Perhaps, if she can blend in, nobody will notice that there's a member of the royal family still at large. Perhaps she can stay free, perhaps she can live a little longer.

FRANK and BILL are drinking from a hip flask and debating the relevance of class struggle to the war. They've been having this debate since 7th grade. Bill has just realized that he is in love with Polly, that her radiant smile makes the bare 60-watt bulbs burn brighter. He thinks he's never seen her before, that she's a new kid. In fact, he's seen her on TV a thousand times, but not in jeans and a t-shirt. Frank has known for years that he's in love with Bill, and he sees this immediately and knows that it cannot come to good.

We always begin at the entrance, with Emily, but after that our experience depends on our choices. Perhaps Cassie and her coterie are hovering near the refreshments; we might join them. Cassie has plenty to say (and she can say it, because she's a prophet and prophets aren't bound by temporal constraints). Or we might first wander over to Polly. Perhaps we stand off a little ways and eavesdrop as Bill tries to chat up Polly while visions of sand dunes dance in his head. Perhaps Emily rushes up with cups of punch, urging Polly to cheer up and have a great time and get out and dance!

Each of the characters has things to say. They're kids, they'll talk about insights and philosophies to anyone who will listen. They move in clusters (as kids at a party do), and sometimes individuals or couples will spin off or two groups will coalesce. Topics of conversation are introduced, old topics are exhausted or discreetly abandoned. Questions and conflicts abound — each individual and unique, but each also connected to the others and to us.

Patterns in *Thespis*

Is this a hypertext? *The Trojan Kids* has no links, no blue underlined text, no map view. But these are mere externals. *Thespis* discloses a chunk of text and then offers the reader a set of choices, and the choice selected determines what is seen next. In *Thespis*, a reader selects among seven potential options at any moment, although some might, in this specific context, be unavailable. This sounds like a hypertext.

Hypertext, Joyce observed, requires rereading (Joyce 1994; Rau 2000). *Thespis* can be enjoyed on first reading, but its gamelike qualities encourage rereading and experimentation. In the *Trojan Kids*, Alice isn't assigned a mission — there are no captive princesses to be saved — but there are lots of things she could do differently, and many consequences can be imagined. Nothing Alice does can operate by brute force. She can't protect Polly by fighting off the Army of Occupation with her superpowers; she has no spell to redeem Emily nor elixir to cheer Cassandra. But if she had taken Polly for a midnight walk on the beach, perhaps the police would have missed them in the dark? It's worth a try. Ineptly done, this is mere puzzle play. Done well, it's the expression of the tension between tragedy, where fate is inexorable, and comedy, where our effort[7] can perhaps be rewarded with triumph.

Coherence, causality, and closure — those suspect qualities whose (supposed) absence bedevils the reputation of hyperfiction — can be achieved easily in *Thespis* if we want them. Assertions form a convenient shorthand for episodes, so explicit temporal contingencies are not difficult to maintain. Overlapping dialogue and episodic collision (Kushner 1993), conversely, provide opportunity for cinematic montage (Miles 2001). We can create Thespian tales that use multiple decks, one after another: a set of characters and actions becomes a scene or an act of a larger drama. Closure, too, can be achieved in all the conventional dramatic ways.

What becomes of the hypertext patterns with which we have become so familiar? Some flourish unchanged; an assertion that opens up a new topic for discussion introduces a *split*, and the retraction then becomes the balancing *join*. Indeed, because assertions are easy to retract, *split/joins* may be more common, larger, and more elaborate in Thespian hypertexts. *Basements* or *mirrorworlds* can be constructed in Thespian space; one room contains the theme, another room the counterpoint, with access between the two restricted by a *bottleneck*. *Feints* are at once more problematic (we have no maps) and less (characters lie). And tangles, obviously, are *Thespis*'s natural pattern.

Other familiar patterns may be less common in Thespian hypertext. For instance, recurrence in *Thespis* tends to be rare, brief, and deliberate. Writers who like recurrence (a pattern of *cycles*) can easily provide duplicate actions, but this is neither as effortless nor as obvious as cycles are in calligraphic hypertext systems.

The more elaborate cycles that are the staple of many Storyspace hyperfictions are harder to reproduce in *Thespis*. Douglas's cycle, in which repetition signals closure, is difficult to implement, and Joyce's cycle appears infeasible.

Other Directions

Thespis is a sketch, a prototype. A host of design decisions are arbitrary. Why does the player choose from *seven* alternatives? Should assertions remain on the blackboard forever, or should they fade over time? When the player sees or hears something, the current *Thespis* prototype adds the description to the end of a long scroll; would it be better to display the text in a large, dynamic collage (Bernstein 2000)? Or in lots of separate windows? *Thespis* is a chunky hypertext system that generates a smooth (and linear) text; perhaps it should be generating a smooth hypertext, or a chunky one?

It is also interesting to observe that we can add new actions — indeed, entire new characters — to an existing scene. This could give rise to several intriguing possibilities. Not only might we reread a familiar Thespian play, but we might attempt a reading in the presence of a new, supplemental character. We could envision extensible, recombinant fictions, dramas to which readers could add or remove some of the characters. Or we could let several different people control several characters within the same scene, perhaps through the network; notably, *Thespis*'s constraints on actions averts the worst faults of the graffiti problem, the tendency for open, collaborative writing spaces to be defaced by nonsensical, obscene, or territorial pronouncements.

My Friend Hamlet:
Immersion, Games, Interaction

Thespis shares some characteristics with Interactive Fiction (IF) — adventure games, MUDs, and MOOs (Murray 1997). The resemblance, however, is superficial. Unlike IF, the unimportance of the reader's proxy may be essential to Thespian hypertext.

In IF, the reader is the player, the protagonist, the central character. The reader-protagonist's actions shape the course of events. In contrast, the reader-protagonist in *Thespis* is a minor character inhabiting the periphery of the action, a witness to events that unfold. The reader's choices may indeed alter what happens, but the reader is neither the most interesting nor the most active character on stage.

In most IF, the reader commands a hero protagonist, which naturally leads the reader to test the limits of the possible. That's what heroes do. The drama rapidly devolves into a negotiation between the reader and the world model: the reader asks to do the unexpected, and the system typically responds with incomprehension. Illusions that place the reader on stage necessarily founder when promised freedom of action is contradicted by the limitations of the simulated environment. Although IF asks us to find a creative, imaginative, and successful resolution to the dramatic problem, the imaginative reader is bound to think of things the creator never envisioned, and the reader's best thinking inevitably generates the dullest response: "I don't understand."

Ironic detachment — the witty, improbable remarks of a Leisure Suit Larry or a Boris Urquhart — makes things worse, not better. If the reader-protagonist still needs to test the rules, any struggle against fate in the narrative reduces, thematically and experientially, to the reader-protagonist's struggle against the system. This reduction to a gamer's-picaresque impoverishes interactive narrative, implying that the story of the player's developing virtuosity is the only story worth attending to. Because the Thespian protagonist is patently unimportant, unheroic, and obviously constrained *within* the frame of the narrative, dramatic necessity need not continually draw the reader's attention to the limits of the possible (and hence to the shortcomings of the system).

The computational environment can never match our aspirations. Another way to say this is: we are always more creative than our systems (and that is the good news). Allusions to unlimited computing power of the future (the Starship Holodeck) can't rectify the fundamental problem: readers will always want to do things nobody (and no computer) could anticipate. That, after all, is why people are interesting, and why

we enjoy fiction.

Even if we could experience *Hamlet* on the Holodeck, it wouldn't work. Tragedy requires that the characters be blind (as we ourselves, at times, are blind). If you let a sane and sensible reader–protagonist into the room, everything is bound to collapse. Take Hamlet: it's absolutely obvious that he should go back to school, get roaring drunk, get laid, and await his opportunity. He knows this. Horatio knows this. Ophelia knows this. Even Claudius and Gertrude know — why else send for his college pals? Nobody can bring themselves to say the words — that's the tragedy. But, if you're the sane and sensible character with Hamlet on the Holodeck, what's to stop *you*? Only brute force and error messages ("You can't do that") that call attention to the arbitrary boundaries of the world. If you make *Hamlet* a game, it has to be rigged so that actions taken by a reasonable and sane reader-protagonist — not to mention a wildly inventive one — do not derail the train of events that must ensue if this is to be *Hamlet* and not, say, *Timon of Athens* or *A Midsummer Night's Dream*.

It's not just Hamlet. Oedipus needs to get out of town and change his name, to enter the Foreign Legion or the Witness Protection Program. Antigone needs a long talk with her rabbi. Juliet needs to tell her parents exactly what she did last night. She can't, of course, but what's to stop you?

This game is rigged and, more importantly, the game constantly calls our attention to the fact that it is rigged. Whenever we struggle against the bonds of fate (and the boundaries of the system), we're told, "I don't understand." The more we struggle — the more conviction and intelligence be bring to the action — the greater the likelihood that the system will find no appropriate response. The artist's struggle to convey difficult truths is inevitably superceded by the reader-protagonist's struggle to do difficult or at least interesting things with a necessarily recalcitrant world-model.

Card Shark avoids this contradiction by foregrounding the familiar convention of reading and drama: we may *want* our favorite characters to prosper, but as spectators, we cannot choose the outcome. *Thespis* gives us a greater range of action and might offer us a chance to take a role, but that role is not central and our limitations are evident.

In contrast to the more ambitious interactive fiction projects (Mateas and Stern 2001), *Thespis* makes no attempt to model character, emotions, or cognitive state. A trivial mechanism lets the actors choose among possible actions. What really matters is what is said, and everything that can be said in *Thespis* is written in advance. Authorial control retains its customary (if ambiguous) place.

Interactive fictions tend to be spatial; the implicit narrative of *Adventure* and *Myst* is one of travel and discovery (Jenkins and Fully 1994). *Thespis* is performed in imaginative space, too, but Thespian spaces tend to differ in scale and design from adventure-game spaces. IF spaces tend to be numerous, small, varied, and thinly populated. *Thespis*, on the other hand, uses space chiefly as a place in which actors move; Thespian spaces tend to be large, bland, and crowded. There may be interesting settings and props in a Thespian world, but these are static and durable. The actors, on the other hand, are moving and speaking; if we don't listen to them now, we may never hear what they say.

Towards Evaluation

Card Shark and *Thespis* present alternative approaches to hypertext. They stand far afield from Storyspace and the web, but share the core values of literary hypertext.

A difficult question, of course, concerns utility: are *Shark* and *Thespis* good for anything?

First, as formal experiments, their simplicity is inherently desirable. Neither system requires elaborate infrastructure. Indeed, *Shark* was readily prototyped in Flash, while *Thespis* was a matter of a few weeks' programming. Variants of either system can easily be implemented and explored without extraordinary technological or financial investment.

Thespis was designed for works of the imagination. Can it be used for argumentation, pedagogy, or technical documentation? Clearly sequential presentation is invaluable for mathematical proofs and for some kinds of schoolwork. Information retrieval is clearly ideal for answering specific, well-posed

questions. If Thespian hypertext has a place outside the world of imagination, that place most probably lies in exploring multifaceted topics for an expert, engaged audience.

One can readily envision, for example, a lively Thespian discussion about areas of professional and scholarly controversy. Was Captain Cook considered a deity, or merely an unwelcome dinner guest? Should Web site design emphasize familiarity and ease of use, or unique identity and value? Argumentative strategies, personified as characters, could inhabit a discursive space through which the reader might wander, witnessing debate and pursuing the most interesting parts of the discussion, but simultaneously aware that these discussions necessarily impinge on a wider range of questions.

We might also envision Thespian explorations of naturally discursive subjects — the aesthetics of algorithms, the beauty of chemical synthetic pathways, or the experience of life in London in 1680. Here, the weight of the argument lies in the accumulation of detail and in allowing readers to discover the specific details that speak most powerfully to them. If you want to argue that algorithms or sculpture are beautiful, you'd best be prepared with a variety of examples and let the audience tell you what they like. While this approach to the art of persuasion differs markedly from an argument that proceeds in lockstep from proposition to lemma to conclusion, intellectual history is rife with examples of precisely this more capacious rhetorical artistry, from Burton's *Anatomy of Melancholy* to Kolb's *Socrates in the Labyrinth*.

Wandering through Thespian spaces lets the reader see what she wants, yet *Thespis* also indicates unobtrusively that there is more to see, and sketches where she might go next.

Acknowledgments

Eric A. Cohen, Mary Cavill, and Charles S. Bennett read early drafts of this paper and made many valuable suggestions. Portions of this paper originally appeared, in somewhat different form, in *Proceedings of the Twelfth ACM Conference on Hypertext and Hypermedia*, Hugh Davis, Yellowlees Douglas, and David G. Durand, eds.

Notes:

1. Unless otherwise noted, the words "structure" and "pattern" are used interchangeably in this paper to refer to ways in which hypermedia narratives can be said to cohere (though see Alexander, Ishikawa, *et al.*). For detailed discussion see Mark Bernstein, "Patterns of Hypertext" and "Hypertext Gardens."

2. The dominance of these particular systems among fiction writers need not be ascribed to any inherent virtue or suitability to the task. Accessibility plays a crucial role, as do the accidents of history. If Guide, Trellis, or NoteCards had survived to develop a literary following, our current impressions of the nature of hypertext narrative might be quite different.

3. Compare, for example, Joyce's *afternoon*, Arnold's *Lust*, Landow and Lanestedt's *The In Memoriam Web*, and Strickland's *True North*. All were written with Storyspace, but their use of links varies tremendously.

4. The details of these performance rules are often arbitrary and the reader may easily envision alternatives. These procedural details affect pacing and rhythm during performance, but effective writing is far more important to the performance than the details of these performance rules.

5. The situation is directly analogous to reaching a conventional hypertext node with no outbound links, or to an short, inescapable cycle that signals closure [Bernstein 1998b]. Early hypertext writers worried about deadness almost as much as they worried about disorientation [Bernstein 1991]; today, we press the Back button and wonder what the fuss was about.

6. We beg the reader's indulgence for this lengthy exposition of the plot of an unimportant, incomplete prototype. Demonstrating narrative is a vexing problem; the only way to understand a work is to experience it, and even then the illustration may founder on accidents of taste, interest, or understanding. The intent of this section is to establish the example in sufficient detail to permit the reader to construct a similar hypertext in her own laboratory. The alternative — presenting a formalization of *Thespis* — seems futile.

7. Or, in romance, our inherent virtue, our intrinsic wonderfulness [Mamet 1998].

References: Literature

Aarseth, Espen (1993). "Nonlinearity and Literary Theory." In *Hypertext and Literary Theory*, edited by P. Delany and G.P. Landow. Baltimore: Johns Hopkins University Press.

Alexander, C., S. Ishikawa, M. Silverstein, M. Jacobson, I. Fiksdahl-King and S. Angel (1977). *A Pattern Language: Towns, Buildings, Construction*. New York: Oxford University Press.

Amerika, Mark (1997). *Grammatron*. <http://www.grammatron.com/>.

Arnold, Mary-Kim (1993). "Lust." In *Eastgate Quarterly Review of Hypertext* 1, no. 2. Watertown, MA: Eastgate Systems.

Arnold, Mary-Kim, and Matthew Derby (1999). *Kokura*. Watertown, MA: Eastgate Reading Room. <http://www.eastgate.com/Kokura/>.

Bates, J., A.B. Loyall and W.S. Reilly (1992). "Integrating Reactivity, Goals, and Emotion in a Broad Agent." In Proceedings of the Fourteenth Annual Conference of the Cognitive Science Society, Bloomington, Indiana, July 1992.

Bernstein, Mark (1991). "Deeply Intertwingled Hypertext: The Navigation Problem Reconsidered." Technical Communication.

Bernstein, Mark (1998a). "Hypertext Gardens." <http://www.eastgate.com/garden/>.

Bernstein, Mark (1998b). "Patterns of Hypertext." In Proceedings of Hypertext 1998, Pittsburgh, PA.

Bernstein, Mark (2000). "More Than Legible: On Links that Readers Don't Want to Follow." In Proceedings of Hypertext 2000, San Antonio, TX.

Bernstein, Mark (2001). "Card Shark and Thespis: Exotic Tools for Hypertext Narrative." In *Proceedings of the Twelfth ACM Conference on Hypertext and Hypermedia,* edited by Hugh Davis, Yellowlees Douglas, and David G. Durand. New York: ACM Press.

Birkerts, Sven (1994). *The Gutenberg Elegies*. Boston: Faber and Faber.

Bly, Bill (1997). *We Descend*. Watertown, MA: Eastgate Systems, Inc.

Bolter, Jay David (1991). *Writing Space*. Lawrence Erlbaum Associates.

Bolter, Jay David (1997). "The Rhetoric of Interactive Fiction." In *Texts and Textuality*, edited by P. Cohen. New York: Garland.

Bolter, Jay David, and Michael Joyce (1987). "Hypertext and Creative Writing." In Proceedings of Hypertext 1987, Chapel Hill, NC.

Chapman, Wes (2001). *Turning In*. Watertown, MA: Eastgate Systems, Inc.

Coover, Robert (1992). "The End of Books." *The New York Times Book Review*, June 21, 1992: 23-25.

Coover, Robert (1993). "Hyperfiction: Novels for Computer." *The New York Times Book Review*, August 29, 1993: 1-12.

Coverly, M.D. (2000). *Califia*. Watertown, MA: Eastgate Systems, Inc.

Cramer, Kathryn (1993). "In Small & Large Pieces." *Eastgate Quarterly Review of Hypertext* 1, no.3.

Douglas, J. Yellowlees (1993). "I Have Said Nothing." *Eastgate Quarterly Review of Hypertext* 1, no.2.

Douglas, J. Yellowlees (2000). *The End of Books — or Books Without End?* Ann Arbor: University of Michigan Press.

Eisen, Adrienne (2001). *What Fits*. Watertown, MA: Eastgate Systems, Inc. <http://www.eastgate.com/ReadingRoom/WhatFits/>.

Eskilinen, Markku, and Raine Koskimaa (2000). *Cybertext Yearbook 2000*. Jyvaskylä: University of Jyvaskylä, Research Centre for Contemporary Culture.

Gaggi, Silvio (1997). "From Text To Hypertext: Decentering the

Hypertexts & Interactives> Bernstein & Greco
Strickland
Douglas & Hargadon
Stern Perlin
Raley Utterback
Schechner Jenkins

V. Hypertexts & Interactives

Subject." In *Fiction, Film, the Visual Arts, and Electronic Media*. Philadelphia: University of Pennsylvania Press.

Golovchinsky, Gene, and Catherine C. Marshall (2000). "Hypertext Interaction Revisited." In Proceedings of Hypertext 2000, San Antonio, TX.

Guyer, Carolyn (1992). *Quibbling*. Watertown, MA: Eastgate Systems, Inc.

Harpold, Terry (1991). "Threnody: Psychoanalytic Digressions on the Subject of Hypertexts." In *Hypermedia and Literary Criticism*, edited by P. Delany and G.P. Landow. Cambridge, MA: The MIT Press.

Hayles, N. Katherine (2000). "Flickering Connectivities in Shelley Jackson's *Patchwork Girl*: The Importance of Media-Specific Analysis." *Postmodern Culture* 10, no.2.

Holeton, Richard (2001). *Figurski At Findhorn on Acid*. Watertown, MA: Eastgate Systems, Inc.

Jackson, Shelley (1996). *Patchwork Girl: by Mary/Shelley/and Herself*. Watertown, MA: Eastgate Systems, Inc.

Jenkins, Henry, and Mary Fully (1994). "Nintendo and New World Narrative." In *Communications in Cyberspace*, edited by Steve Jones. Los Angeles: Sage.

Joyce, Michael (1988). "Siren Shapes: Exploratory and Constructive Hypertexts." *Academic Computing* 3 (1988): 10-14, 37-42.

Joyce, Michael (1990). *afternoon, a story*. Watertown, MA: Eastgate Systems, Inc.

Joyce, Michael (1994). *Of Two Minds: Hypertext Pedagogy and Poetics*. Ann Arbor: University of Michigan Press.

Joyce, Michael (1997). "Nonce Upon Some Times: Rereading Hypertext Fiction." *Modern Fiction Studies* 43, no.3 (1997): 579-597.

Kolb, David (1997). "Scholarly Hypertext: Self-Represented Complexity." In Proceedings of Hypertext 1997, Southampton, UK.

Kushner, Tony (1993). *Angels in America: Millennium Approaches*. New York: Theater Communications Group.

Landow, George P. (1990). "Popular Fallacies about Hypertext." In *Designing Hypertext/Hypermedia for Learning*, edited by D.J.J.a.H. Mandl. Heidelberg: Springer-Verlag.

Landow, George P. (1992). *Hypertext: The Convergence of Contemporary Critical Theory and Technology*. Baltimore: Johns Hopkins Press.

Lanham, Richard A. (1993). *The Electronic Word: Democracy, Technology, and the Arts*. Chicago: University of Chicago Press.

Laurel, Brenda (1991). *Computers as Theatre*. Reading, MA: Addison-Wesley.

Malloy, Judy (1993). *Its Name was Penelope*. Watertown, MA: Eastgate Systems, Inc. First shown at The Richmond Art Center in the exhibition "Revealing Conversations," (1989) curated by Zlata Baum.

Malloy, Judy, and Cathy Marshall (1996). *Forward Anywhere*.

Watertown, MA: Eastgate Systems, Inc.

Mamet, David (1999). *True and False: Heresy and Common Sense for the Actor*. New York: Vintage.

Mamet, David (1998). *Three Uses Of The Knife: On the Nature and Purpose of Drama*. New York, Columbia University Press.

Mateas, Michael, and Andrew Stern (2000). "Towards Integrating Plot and Character for Interactive Drama." Working notes of *Socially Intelligent Agents: Human in the Loop — 2000 AAAI Fall Symposium Series*. Menlo Park, CA: AAAI Press.

Mateas, Michael, and Andrew Stern (2001). "Towards Building a Fully-Realized Interactive Drama." In Proceedings of Digital Arts and Culture, Providence, RI, April 2001.

McDaid, John (1992). *Uncle Buddy's Phantom Funhouse*. Watertown, MA: Eastgate Systems, Inc.

Miles, Adrian (2001). "Hypertext Structure as the Event of Connection." In Proceedings of the 12th ACM Conference on Hypertext and Hypermedia, Århus, Denmark.

Miller, Laura (1998). "www.claptrap.com." *The New York Times Book Review*, March 15, 1998: 43. <http://www.nytimes.com/books/98/03/15/bookend/bookend.html>.

Moulthrop, Stuart (1991). *Victory Garden*. Watertown, MA: Eastgate Systems, Inc.

Murray, Janet (1997). *Hamlet On The Holodeck: The Future of Narrative in Cyberspace*. New York: Free Press.

Nelson, Theodor Holm (1982). *Literary Machines*. <http://www.sfc.keio.ac.jp/~ted/TN/PUBS/LM/LMpage.html>.

Nelson, Theodor Holm (1987). *Computer Lib / Dream Machines*. 1st edition: self-published, 1974. 2nd edition: Redmond, WA: Tempus Books/Microsoft Press.

Rau, Anja (2000). "Wreader's Digest: How To Appreciate Hyperfiction." *Journal of Digital Information* 1, no.7 (2000).

Reeves, B., and C. Nass (1996). *The Media Equation — How People Treat Computers, Television, and New Media Like Real People and Places*. Cambridge, MA: Cambridge University Press.

Resnick, Mitchell (1997). *Turtles, Termites, and Traffic Jams: Explorations in Massively Parallel Microworlds*. Cambridge, MA: The MIT Press.

Rosenberg, Jim (1993). "Intergrams." *Eastgate Quarterly Review of Hypertext* 1, no.1 (1993).

Sondheim, Alan (2001). "Codework." *American Book Review* 22, no.6 (2001).

Stern, Andrew (1999). "Virtual Babyz: Believable Agents with Narrative Intelligence." Working notes of *Narrative Intelligence — 1999 AAAI Fall Symposium Series*. Menlo Park, CA: AAAI Press.

Stern, Andrew (2001). "Creating Emotional Relationships with Virtual Characters." In *Emotions in Humans and Artifacts*, edited by R. Trappl. Cambridge, MA: The MIT Press.

Strickland, Stephanie (1998). *True North*. Watertown, MA: Eastgate Systems, Inc.

Tolkien, J.R.R. (1984). "On Fairy Stories." In *The Monsters and the Critics, and Other Essays*, edited by Christopher Tolkein. Boston: Houghton Mifflin.

Tosca, Susana Pajares (2000). "A Pragmatics of Links." In Proceedings of Hypertext 2000, San Antonio, TX.

Walker, Jill (1999). "Piecing Together and Tearing Apart: Finding the Story in *afternoon*." In Proceedings of Hypertext 1999, Darmstadt, Germany.

Yankelovich, N., N. Meyrowitz, and A. van Dam (1985). "Reading and Writing the Electronic Book." *IEEE Computer* 18, no. 10 (October 1985).

Zellweger, Polle T. (2001). "Fluid Annotations in an Open World." In Proceedings of the 12th ACM Conference on Hypertext and Hypermedia, Århus, Denmark.

Reference: Games

Adventure. Will Crowther and Don Woods (1972-1976).

Hypertexts & Interactives> Bernstein & Greco
Strickland
Douglas & Hargadon

Stern Perlin
Raley Utterback
Schechner Jenkins

V. Hypertexts & Interactives

Moving Through Me as I Move: A Paradigm for Interaction
Stephanie Strickland

Vannevar Bush wanted his Memex to intercept and capture the neural circuits of the stenographer who could reduce his words to a phonetic code on the fly, whose encoding practice was encompassed by her body. As an electronic poet, I want to do the same thing, not from the position of Bush, outside the device, but from the position of the stenographer, attached to it. In her body, words moved through her as she moved, a fluent circuit of meaning that she hosted, instigated, permitted, understood, explored, and enjoyed.

Bush exhibited some justified fear as to whether her practice would be complete and accurate according to his standards:

> A girl strokes [the stenotype's] keys languidly and looks about the room and sometimes at the speaker with a

disquieting gaze. From it emerges a typed strip which records in a phonetically simplified language a record of what the speaker is *supposed* to have said. Later this strip is retyped into ordinary language, for in its nascent form it is intelligible only to the initiated. (Bush 1994, section 3, paragraph 3 [emphasis added])

He also wanted to capture the neural knowledge she attained by intervening in the production of the text:

> The impulses which flow in the arm nerves of a typist convey to her fingers the translated information which reaches her eye, in order that the fingers may be caused to strike the proper keys. Might not these currents be intercepted, either in the original form in which information is conveyed to the brain, or in the marvelously metamorphosed form in which they then proceed to the hand? (Bush 1994, section 8, paragraph 6)

Hers is a somatic practice that deflects not only the threat of analytic dispersal, into "simplified language. . . nascent form. . . intelligible only to the initiated," as

Response by Rita Raley

Stephanie Strickland wants her electronic poetry to generate a somatic practice of reading appropriate to its medium. Specifically, she codes her poetry, and the field of new media writing of which it is a part, in terms of a physically engaged practice of reading that goes beyond affective response and hermeneutic activity and additionally depends upon mechanized operations, the "nontrivial" movement of reader-user, and a mode of cognitive processing that we continue to learn. It is not simply that her poetry thematically concerns itself with information culture, its own technological and material substrate, and the mechanism of its own production (as does much new media writing, including Strickland's (1998) own Storyspace hypertext *True North*, the *Vispo*

of Jim Andrews (2001), and the more recent codework of Talan Memmott (2000) and Mez (2000)). Rather, her poetry and her criticism outlines a practice and paradigm of reading that tells us something about both the distinctive properties of digital textuality and the defining features of an evolving mode of interactivity. The properties of the text and of a "new" interactivity and reader engagement are not only simultaneously thought, but inextricably connected.

Strickland's articulation of this new paradigm of interactivity opens with a reading of the figure of the stenographer — really a stenotypist — in Vannevar Bush's essay. While Bush raises the possibility of intercepting and diverting the currents of information that pass from eye to brain to hand as the stenotypist

Bush characterizes her code, but also the threat of obsessive recombination and confusion, the multiple overlapping streams of speech she is asked to transcribe.

The notion of "moving through me as I move," as a paradigm for interaction, intends to install the stenographer, and not her employer, as the crucial creative/receptive presence in digital art. Hers is an egalitarian position that can be stated of, and by, each element in a dynamic network. "Move through me as I move" is as much the "voice" of a hypertext as it is of the writer/encoder. It is also the voice of the network addressing all those hosting it and served by it. In the case of work open to multiple authoring, or to synchronous reading and performance, the command "move through me as I move" represents the utterance of each of the performers and participants speaking to all the others. In this mutual command there is an implicit promise of fluent mutual adjustment to whatever comes.

The stenographer, however, is more than a writer/reader/monitor; she is also the operator of an appliance. This position is described by Talan Memmott (2001), here explicating his theory/fiction hybrid, *Lexia to Perplexia,* winner of the 2000 trAce/altx New Media Writing competition:

With a document that is acted upon, unfolded, revealed, opened rather than read, full of holes to elsewhere, hiding secret inScriptions, filled with links like mines and traps and triggers — we are no longer talking page or screen, but appliance. Navigating the Lexia of *Lexia to Perplexia* is kind of like getting a new device and trying to figure out how the heck it works... (Memmott 2001)

The stenographer moves within an unforeseeable context. Communicating by "strokes" in an energized yet languid atmosphere, she is absorbed, alert, and somehow also free to gaze about the room — the aspect that most disquieted Bush. She participates in a form of dancing in which the lead changes many times a minute, her moments of apprehending/encoding activity giving way to deep moments of passive reception in a regular alternation or oscillation.

An oscillating, or flickering, pattern has often been invoked with regard to electronic art. Katherine Hayles has said, "We have only begun to construct a semiotics that takes into account the different functions signifiers perform when they cease to be flat marks and become instead layers of code correlated through correspondence rules" (Hayles 2000). In recognition of

transcribes a speech, what draws Strickland to this scene is the stenotypist's movement between active apprehension and passive reception, between attention and inattention. The stenotypist, then, is a writing machine that embodies the data streams that pass through her, with the potential for disruption and interruption always present. Updated for our current moment, this figure's visual and cognitive orientation vis-à-vis the text can best be understood in terms of multiple oscillations. What emerges in Strickland's review of such poets as Jim Rosenberg and Mez is the sense that new media writing literally commands an oscillation between cognitive and machinic processing, between blur and focus, between legibility and visuality, between signification and noise. In these terms, the concept of interactivity speaks to a

cyborgian interplay between the body and the machine as the new media reader-user intermittently captures, processes, transmits, and even introduces data streams, all of which may themselves have different rhythms and tempos. When our hands change the scale, visual orientation, and dimension of a digital poem and cause it to fluctuate between states of legibility and illegibility, we have shifted from one mode of reading to a more varied and complex mode of interaction with the divergent and convergent currents of information within a new media environment. (The "I" in Strickland's title is not singular, encompassing as it does the reader, hypertext system, programmer, and network alike.)

Although not exactly new, Strickland's absorbing articulation of interactivity contributes to its poetics.

the layered dynamic interactions between text and code, she proposed the term "flickering signifiers" for text onscreen. Both Richard Lanham (1993) in *The Electronic Word* and Bolter and Grusin (1999) in *Remediation* have remarked the importance of an oscillation between the viewer positions of "looking at" and "looking through"; that is, between experiencing works primarily as heavily mediated and "windowed," in the software sense, or primarily immediate and immersive, as in looking through transparent glass. I would like to propose a third kind of flickering or oscillation, the oscillation that occurs between the processing of alphabetic text and the processing of image in works that use both. A digital writer who uses image and text is in fact writing a score for their shifting interrelation.

Flickering or oscillating poems differ from pure sound and pure image work in the following respect: whereas sound layered on sound creates new sound, and image on image makes a new image, alphabetic text, superimposed on alphabetic text *or* on image, does not reliably yield legible text. In the poems that explore this truth, one flickers between seeing the viewable and reading the legible. Jim Rosenberg (1996) and Mez (Mary-Anne Breeze 2000) are poets who approach this movement very differently.

Rosenberg (figure 15.1) works with the words and

15.1. Jim Rosenberg, *The Barrier Frames*. (Eastgate Systems)

phrases of a standard vocabulary but overlays them in a dense blur of self-interfering micro-information. A presenting image of tangle is literally drawn apart by hand into legible text, but no sooner do words come into focus than the slightest mouse movement dissolves them back into blur. These texts thus move through the reader, as she moves, at exactly the pace her hand/brain browses — and superimposed on that oscillation, one experiences a constant trembling across the view/read cusp.

Mez, on the other hand, in a practice she calls "M[ez]ang.elle.ing," leads us to confront the legible with strategies ordinarily reserved for the viewable. A good characterization of her work comes from a source that,

185

Further, her articulation of new media writing in terms of an interrelation of data elements shifts the critical terrain away from the less-productive discussions of the ontology of text, image, and sound (here she echoes previous accounts of text and image as different manifestations of code). Her claims about adaptive cognitive responses, however, do at times leave the legitimate and apposite area of phenomenology and its account of the reading-viewing experience, for the only partially charted area of neurobiology. This is perhaps appropriate in that interactivity for her has an "unforeseeable context" and unforeseeable results; nevertheless it remains the case that the complexity of cognitive processing is as yet unknown even to science. Strickland can be applauded for both her poetic and critical gestures toward a mode of perception that still

awaits a future realization. Her genre here, after all, is precisely that of the cyborg manifesto, which orients its vision toward the future.

From Camille Utterback's Online Response

Mark-making is not an essential element of an interactive work, but it seems a necessary component for a stenographic model of interactivity. The marks left by a real stenographer are, in fact, the main purpose of her toils. She makes marks so that information can be conveyed between individuals, so that information can be passed on and communicated. The stenographer may also leave unintentional marks — the smudge of the ink on her tape, the accidental drip of coffee. Both the intentional and accidental mark-making abilities of the real stenographer contrast the purely navigational

Re][stuttered][[sutured][: not][net][.art
Date:
Wed, 21 Feb 2001 10:56:26 +1100

][the x.press][ed 4 time,
4 the answer,
4 the dreamic caul 2 a][r][mories][][

][jumper lead.ing 2 a p][asse][o][mo][lished
cliff-curve][

.drain the cu][s]p n datadrown.

....+
.............+[not.art is][net][a rutting corpse-
knot]+
....+

+please stop+

+++ please l][ectro][][gl][isten +++

15.2. Excerpts from Mez's email writing.

Creative orthography frees words from
traditional. . . constraints, allowing textual
re-presentation of multidimensional
concepts by projecting multilayered
structure into linear text. Extended
electronic typography. . . provides
additional parsing cues. . . (Cohen 1992,
449)

on the face of it, has nothing to do with poetry. Michael
Cohen's (1992) "*Blush* and *Zebrackets:* Two Schemes for
Typographic Representation of Nested Associativity"
describes two tools that treat words and documents as
pictures, in order to create denser data without loss of
legibility. Cohen has understood that one can intensify
both the density of picture data and the legibility of
read data at the same time. He says of these tools:

If we add the idea of both packing and unpacking
compound symbols, we have an excellent description of
Mez's practice, excerpted sentences of which, from her
e-mail writing, appear in figure 15.2. What Mez attains,
that Cohen, in his search for greater legibility, does not
attempt, is the feat of keeping us in motion from one
view/read cusp to the next, seeding the screen with
many cues for reading backwards, up and down, and
slantwise, as well as forward. Indeed, we are often
stopped in our tracks, caught in a kind of pleasurable
stutter and thrown back to rescan the whole field, a
perceptual act more often associated with image. Mez's
text/image pictures allow for multiple, plural, and
contradictory readings of her text. In her article, "The
Art of M[ez]ang.elle.ing," Mez (2000) lists fourteen
goals or techniques, which include:

2 phone.tic[k-tock]aulli m-bellish a tract ov

186

role of the user in most hyperlinked journeys through
digital media.

Intentional mark-making is often an active product
of creativity, but unintentional mark-making is at the
very least a sign of our human presence. Our presence
in the real world leaves scuff marks and wears down
edges. When our interactions with digital space provide
us neither a way to make marks, nor to leave casual
evidence of our passing, how can our travels affect the
experience of others that come after us? How does one
find the well-trodden paths? Where are the grease
stains on the most loved pages? Even our casual marks
communicate meaning. The lack of these marks in the
digital realm informs much of what feels sterile about
our travels there. Part of what catches the

stenographer's attention is precisely the unintentional.

http://www.electronicbookreview.com/thread/firstperson/utterbackr1

Strickland Responds

I believe it is misleading to contrast "navigational" with
"up out of her chair" movement. These are differences
of scale. If I move my feet on an electronically triggered
floor, my arms before a video camera, my finger on a
mouse, or my eyelash at some newly-sensitive monitor,
in all cases my response is moving in real time into a
responding situation.

http://www.electronicbookreview.com/thread/firstperson/stricklandr2

Hypertexts & Interactives> Bernstein & Greco
Strickland
Douglas & Hargadon
Stern Perlin
Raley Utterback
Schechner Jenkins

V. Hypertexts & Interactives

text in2 a neo.logistic maze;

2 network 2 the hilt N create
de[e]pen.den[ting]cies on email lizts for
the wurkz dis.purse.all;

2 uze computer kode kon.[e]vent.ionz
spliced with irc emoticons and
ab[scess]breviations.

She says, in an e-mail to the Webartery list
[December 20, "Visual Minds" thread (2001a)]: "I
personally tend 2 b drawn 2wards the fragment, the
smaller echos/works, and I think this reflects my
n.herent need 2 m.ulate the network
packet/communication mentality. . . ." She is drawn,
that is, to emulate her partner, the network, to follow
its lead even as she leads it through her constructions.

By contrast, Jim Andrews (2001a), who gives us the
term "langu(im)age," works with individual letters
which he can animate and overlay with sequences of
sound loops in his *Nio* (figure 15.3) engine. He is not
primarily, or at all, concerned with providing a reading
experience. He says:

> Much of my work is lettristic in the sense
> that rather than working with words and
> extended texts, I work with individual
> letters. Part of my attraction to working
> this way is philosophical and sonical. . . but
> part of it is also out of interest in treating
> literary objects/material, and individual
> letters are quite well suited to such
> treatment. Individual letters are graphically
> more interesting than whole words. . .
> [they] take up less memory, and are thereby
> manipulated more quickly. And they spin
> nicer than words do, for instance, because
> of their shapes. There is more variety in
> their shapes than there is in words. And
> they are quite mysterious to me. Geometry
> and basic architectures of language. (E-mail
> to Webartery list, February 10, 2001, on
> thread "re: teaser 2" [2001b])

15.3. Jim Andrews, *Nio*.

Later, he says: ". . . it's really when you get down to the
word and the letter, rather than the paragraph, that
language cracks open and code spills out" [Webartery
list, February 24, on thread "checkout counter"]. One
feels the difference from the stenographic model, a
model of accommodation rather than breaking and
entering. But one also feels, and can sympathize with,
an attraction to a different arena, the world of the
purely sonic and visual, where compounds stay
themselves and are thereby experienced more fluidly.
However, oscillation does occur in Andrews's *Nio*,
between the visual and the sonic elements, and this
oscillation is elegant, playful, and deeply pleasing.

My own work investigates oscillation between image,
text, sound, and animation, both within and between
linked units. In this way, several states or layers of
oscillation, a set of cross-rhythms, come into being.

In 1995, I translated my book-length poem *True
North* to Storyspace. The *True North* themes of
navigation and embeddedness moved from being print
concepts, refracted in language, to being the steering
mechanism and constitutive *structure* of the hypertext.
The Storyspace software provides many ways to
operate the poem, but they are not intuitive: to move
fluidly one must spend time learning the rich interface.
For this textually driven work about navigation, I
designed the two most important orienting elements
to be visual. The first of these is a set of mouse-drawn
Storyspace maps. Figure 15.4 shows two of them, "The

187

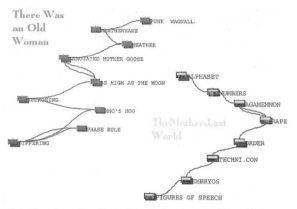

15.4. Maps from *True North*: "The Mother–Lost World" and "There Was an Old Woman." (Eastgate Systems)

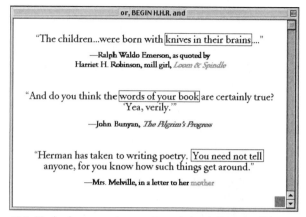

15.6. Word colors suggest connections, but not places to click.

Mother–Lost World" and "There Was an Old Woman." Figure 15.5 shows two others, maps of the sections called "Language Is a Cast of the Human Mind" and "Numbers Nesting in Numbers-Nesting-In Numbers."

The emblematic map shapes, with their legends of node names, can be read by themselves. These sitemaps, functioning as pattern poems, give a very fair idea or sampling of *True North* — a mode of understanding that may supplement, *or* substitute for, following links and reading text. Such a displacement of text by image, that also functions recursively as a guide to text, is itself a distinct mode of oscillation — one which coexists with the familiar reference oscillation between a map and what it maps.

The coloring of a few words on each page is the second orienting device (figure 15.6). Since Storyspace

does not use color to signify text-links, instead requiring the reader to press a key to reveal boxes around link words, each color operates visually to suggest a connection between similarly colored words: each color is an embedded link, but one traceable only by human memory, not by software.

A different kind and rate of oscillation occurs in *To Be Here as Stone Is* (1999), a digital poem written collaboratively with M. D. Coverley. This poem is composed of two very different sorts of screens: six highly visual ones with sound that use complex Anfy Java applets (figure 15.7) and thirteen primarily textual ones where lines of verse are overlaid on a visual background (figures 15.8a and 15.8b) itself layered with a text ribbon. The links between these promote a rapid exchange between two kinds of attention, between primary viewing/listening and primary reading/searching, for the links must be sought for, by cursor scanning, on the textual pages. The experience

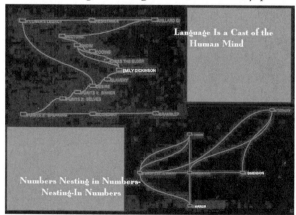

15.5. Maps from *True North*: "Language Is a Cast of the Human Mind" and "Numbers Nesting in Numbers-Nesting-In Numbers."

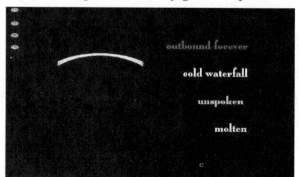

15.7. A Java applet screen in *To Be Here as Stone Is*.

Hypertexts & Interactives> **Strickland**
Bernstein & Greco
Douglas & Hargadon
Stern Perlin
Raley Utterback
Schechner Jenkins

V. Hypertexts & Interactives

of strongly discernable shift resonates with the text of this poem that shifts the reader from photons to cosmos and back.

In the Flash poem, *Errand Upon Which We Came,* Coverley and I (2000/2001) choreographed animation for the alphabetic text as well as for accompanying images and sound. The reader/operator of this text may press the silver butterfly to the screen if she wishes to read with complete accuracy, but she may prefer to oscillate between sampled reading and periods of viewing. The words of *Errand* address the reader, speak to her of fragmented mobile text; speak to her, in fact, of the very act of reading she has undertaken: in response, she may actively intervene in the poem to read or redirect it, or she may attend to it as a movie.

In figure 15.9, we see a moment in the life of the Flash stanza that begins with the question "space?" floating down from the top of the screen, followed by a second question about knowledge-mining. A flock of butterflies flies in from upper right and circles around toward screen center. A third and fourth question, about "go(o)ds" refusing to go to market, appear onscreen. They imitate the butterflies' circling motion. At the end of the Flash movie we see two dimnesses in the central far distance, one, the almost out-of-sight V of butterflies; the other, the lines of the last two questions, now collapsed to one extremely faint line poised at the butterflies like a lance. The question is posed visually as to whether the image and text must attack each other, or may perhaps exist in oscillating accommodation.

The Ballad of Sand and Harry Soot (Strickland 1999), coded with the help of Janet Holmes, creates a seeming disjunction of image and text on each of its 33 similarly designed pages. The pages are highly visual, but their unmoving text asks to be read. Images from Jean-Pierre Hébert's (1999) *Sisyphus* — a device shown at SIGGRAPH 1999 that inscribes algorithmic patterns in sand with a steel ball — are the ones most prevalent in the *Ballad*. In figure 15.10 both *Sisyphus* and a *Sisyphus* pattern can be seen. Other images suggestive of digital or mathematical culture, such as a Metro card, webcam photos, a core dump, or an animated fractal, accompany the text of a love poem, a ballad of love gone wrong or

15.8a and 15.8b. Primarily textual screens in *To Be Here as Stone Is.*

at least not entirely right, between two characters called Sand and Soot. At one level, the disjunction of image and text mirrors the difficulties of this pair; however, the particular discordance, or nonreference, that seems to exist *between* image and text will, at some point, spring into resonant oscillation for the reader who either sees, or reads, an avatar of carbon-based chemistry in Harry Soot and one of silicon life in Sand.

space? Where do we mine that knowledge of what cannot be *precipitous,* nor yet delayed?

What if the go (o)ds refuse to go to market? What then?

< 00000 00>

15.9. Moment of *Errand Upon Which We Came.*

15.10. *Sisyphus* (above) and a *Sisyphus* pattern (below).

cohered there as "naturally" as they do in the stenographer's body. But a change in scale is a change of context: the view/read cusp will shift differently for zoomed text than it will for text that is panned. In fact, this kind of zoom or scale-changing cusp may be a particularly important one in a world where we are asked to process simultaneously scales from the nano to the cosmic.

Delivered to and through new media, we find new understandings. Delivered to and through new media, the bitstream displays varying modalities that our bodies and brains have long been used to processing differently. We shift differently, we censor differently, we move differently, to sound, to text, to image, and to animation. Today, perforce, we are learning to oscillate differently, in new "ratios," as Blake or McLuhan would say. The stenographer at her stenotype was an early pioneer of this environment. Her continual active choice to attend or to blur her focus, to remain poised or to flow within the moving stream, is a task we take up. We will not all take it up the same way. We bring many biophysical and cultural heritages to the task. It is for this reason that my collaborators and I choose to make work that can be operated, and thus read, across many modalities at many rates and rhythms of oscillation.

Four key images in the *Ballad* were created by Alex Heilner and shown at the Sixth Annual Digital Salon. On his contributor page within the *Ballad*, Heilner (Strickland 1999) explains: "This series of 'microbe' images. . . seeks to invert traditional understanding of our internal and external environments. Large, orthogonal, built objects. . . have been re-imagined here to represent the most basic organic living beings. . . ."

Thus, in figure 15.11, we see that Heilner has represented the island of Manhattan so that it reads as a collection of floating microbes. Scale is elided on the Web, as it is in the stenographer's practice, where events in the conference room, in her brain, in her hand, and on her code-filled writing machine are nearly simultaneous. Many different scales can be present to the same screen, as if they belonged together, as if they

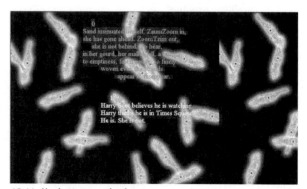

15.11. Manhattan as microbes.

Hypertexts & Interactives> **Strickland**
Douglas & Hargadon

Bernstein & Greco
Stern Perlin
Raley Utterback
Schechner Jenkins

V. Hypertexts & Interactives

References:

Andrews, Jim (2001a). *Nio*.
<http://www.turbulence.org/Works/Nio/>.

Andrews, Jim (2001b). E-mail to Webartery list, February 10, 2001, on thread "re: teaser 2."
<http://www.egroups.com/community/webartery>.

Andrews, Jim (2001c). E-mail to Webartery list, February 24, 2001, on thread "check out counter."
<http://www.egroups.com/community/webartery>.

Bolter, Jay David, and Richard Grusin (1999). *Remediation: Understanding New Media*. Cambridge, MA: The MIT Press.

Bush, Vannevar (prepared by Deny Duchier) (1994). "As We May Think." <http://www.isg.sfu.ca/~duchier/misc/vbush/>.

Coverley, M.D., and Stephanie Strickland (1999). "To Be Here As Stone Is." *Riding the Meridian* 1, no. 2 (1999).
<http://califia.hispeed.com/SI/stone1.htm>.

Coverley, M.D., and Stephanie Strickland (2000/2001). "Errand Upon Which We Came." *Cauldron & Net* 3 (Winter/Spring 2000/2001). <http://califia.hispeed.com/Errand/title1a.htm>.

Cohen, Michael (1992). "*Blush* and *Zebrackets:* Two Schemes for Typographical Representation of Nested Associativity." *Visible Language* 26, no.3/4 (1992): 436-449.

Hayles, N. Katherine (2000). Commentary section of "The Dinner Party." *Riding the Meridian* 2, no. 1 (Spring 2000).
<http://www.heelstone.com/meridian/templates/Dinner/hayles.htm>.

Hébert, Jean-Pierre (1999). *Sisyphus*.
<http://www.solo.com/sand/sand.html>.

Joyce, Michael (2000). *Othermindedness: The Emergence of Network Culture*. Ann Arbor: University of Michigan Press.

Lanham, Richard A. (1993). *The Electronic Word: Democracy, Technology, and the Arts*. Chicago: University of Chicago Press.

Memmott, Talan (2000). "Lexia to Perplexia." *The Iowa Review Web* (September 2000).
<http://www.uiowa.edu/~iareview/tirweb/hypermedia/talan_memmott/index.html>.

Memmott, Talan (2001). Interview, *Rhizome*, January 16, 2001.
<http://rhizome.org/object.rhiz?2145>.

Mez (Mary Anne Breeze) (2000a). E-mail to Webartery list, December 20, 2000, on thread "Visual Mind."
<http://www.egroups.com/community/webartery>.

Mez (Mary Anne Breeze) (2000b). "The Art of M[ez]ang.elle.ing: Constructing Polysemic & Neology Fic/Factions Online." *Beehive* 3, no. 4 (December 2000). <http://beehive.temporalimage.com>.

Rosenberg, Jim (1996). "Barrier Frames." *Eastgate Quarterly Review of Hypertext* 2, no. 3 (1996).
<http://www.well.com/user/jer/j/barrier_frames_4.html>.

Strickland, Stephanie (1999). *Ballad of Sand and Harry Soot*. WordCircuits. <http://wordcircuits.com/gallery/sandsoot/>.

Strickland, Stephanie (1999). "To Be Both in Touch and in Control," *ebr* 9 (Spring 1999).
<http://www.altx.com/ebr/ebr9/9strick.htm>.

Strickland, Stephanie (1998). *True North*. Watertown, MA: Eastgate Systems.

191

The Pleasures of Immersion and Interaction: Schemas, Scripts, and the Fifth Business

J. Yellowlees Douglas and Andrew Hargadon

It must be granted that there is some value in mystification, labyrinth, or surprise in the environment... This is so, however, only under two conditions. First, there must be no danger of losing basic form or orientation, of never coming out. The surprise must occur in an over-all framework; the confusions must be small regions in a visible whole. Furthermore, the labyrinth or mystery must in itself have some form that can be explored and

in time apprehended. Complete chaos without hint of connection is never pleasurable.
—Kevin Lynch (1960), *The Image of the City*

Those roles which, being neither those of Hero nor Heroine, Confidante nor Villain, but which were nonetheless essential to bring about the recognition or the dénouement, were called the Fifth Business in drama and opera companies organized according to the old style; the player who acted these parts was often referred to as Fifth Business.
—Robertson Davies (1983), *The Deptford Trilogy: The Fifth Business*

Introduction: Schemas and the Pleasure Principle

Oddly enough, after decades of theorizing about texts, their authors (or lack thereof), and their relationship to readers, economics, and culture, we know comparatively little about the affective pleasures of reading. Why do we read for pleasure? What keeps us turning the pages between an author's name on the title page and a novel's last gasp on its very last page? How are we able

---

Response by Richard Schechner

[Editors' note: Richard Schechner is responding simultaneously to Markku Eskelinen's essay in this volume (p. 36) and to that of J. Yellowlees Douglas and Andrew Hargadon.]

What about the "pleasures of reading" and the "pleasures of interactive video games"? And what about the relationship between traditional narration and interactive computer/videogames? One measure of pleasure is the surplus of affect over effort. This works for most pleasurable activities in most circumstances, including most interactives. In this economy, fantasy is

excellent currency. Relatively little effort is expended, nor is there much physical danger. Reading and interactive video deal in fantasy arousal and satisfaction. Interactives yield an additional dividend of apparent individual action and choice. The player leaves the voyeur chair and makes decisions that affect the outcome. Gaming is more complex than simple receiving. However, even in simple receiving — watching a movie, reading a novel — the receiver often puts herself into the action, becomes a player: identifies with the characters. Interactive video games are just that: "games." They are not narratively revolutionary but deeply traditional. They use electronic technology to involve players in the kinds of choices that gamers have always made. However, they do combine

to turn a sprinkling of abstract symbols on a white page into scenarios and vignettes so arresting that we can shut out turbulence and the roar of aircraft engines on a red-eye merely by reading a flimsy paperback book? Few critics have dared tackle the affective aspects of reading, although many critics have pointed out the importance of pleasure to the act of reading itself [de Beaugrande and Colby (1979); Bruner (1986); Harpold (1991); Murray (1997); States (1993)]. Moreover, few critics would have thought the topic worthy of scrutiny, since the conventions shaping the acts of writing and reading print narratives alike are so well-established and so familiar that we can function perfectly well without the faintest inkling of how the whole enterprise works — just as we do with so much of the technology that surrounds us.

Enter interactive narratives, hypertext fiction, and videogames that offer scenarios, tools, plots, and characters that demand input from their users. Writers and designers of interactives must work in relatively uncharted territory. First, we do not entirely understand where precisely interactives fall on the continuum of pleasurable — or ludic — pursuits. Second, we must also grapple with a paucity of conventions, fixed genres, and precedents that tell us the sorts of interactions users expect, how to flag meaningful options or tools, or even how to signal closure.

At every turn, we're dogged by unresolved, sticky questions. On the continuum of ludic pleasures do interactives fall somewhere, say, between a game of chess and watching *The Sixth Sense*? Or do they, too, occupy a range of positions on that continuum, each interactive offering an affective pleasure as distinctive from one another as chess itself is from watching films? How much freedom do users want when it comes to plotting strategy or getting acquainted with characters? And is a cut-scene that signifies closure a reward for working your way through a videogame's myriad of firefights, kung fu contests, and puzzles? Or do cut-scenes nullify the openness of both narrative and plot seemingly promised by the entire concept of interactivity? If we can understand our audiences' affective experiences in reading hypertext fiction or playing interactive games, we can begin to determine the types of stories, tools, and even interfaces that lend pleasure to the act of reading and interacting with hypertext and hypermedia.

To date, most studies of reading and hypertext have focused almost entirely on readers' physical and cognitive encounters with texts (Bernstein 1997, 2001a, 2001b; Douglas 1991, 1999; Rosenberg 1996), not on the affective pleasures readers derive from their encounters. Yet we can explore the affective dimension of interactive narratives without invoking arguments

---

narrational elements that previously belonged to fiction, then to "news" as a kind of "docu-fiction," and now to the very blurred boundaries between entertainment and image-made so-called current events. While traditional sports — ball games, strategy games such as chess, games of chance like dice, and so on — created their own distinct worlds, video interactives feed on everyday life rendered melodramatically (as some of the relatively newer sports such as auto racing do). This may be read as an impoverishment: while traditional sports created relatively independent worlds with their own rules and realities, video interactives feed off ordinary life as rendered dramatic by television.

Then there are the pleasures of effort — mountain

climbing, strenuous sports, for example; and the pleasures of pain — ranging from a "good cry" to what sado-masochists crave. Here clearly the effort/pleasure economy is turned upside down. The great effort is the pleasure, the experience of the pain is what feels good. And finally there are the pleasures of what I have called "dark play," play in which the rules are murky or always changing, the players hard to identify, and the risks high. I mean a wide range of activities from con games and stings to Russian roulette. Exactly why many persons find pleasure in these kinds of experiences can't be generalized. Freudians have one explanation, cognitive psychologists another. Anthropologists would insist on culture-specific explanations.

As for "hypertext," how much really do the

about either hard-wired or socially engendered aesthetics by using schema theory to analyze hypertexts and exploring how these frustrate or play off readers' schemas of other texts. Long employed by linguists (de Beaugrande 1980; Schank and Abelson 1997), cognitive psychologists (Bruner 1986), art historians (Gombrich 1956), and AI researchers (Bolter and Grusin 1999; Schank 1982, 1990), schema theory charts how information processes can shape perception and action alike, focusing our expectations and even determining the fine grain of our interactions with objects (de Beaugrande and Colby 1979). Defined simply, schemas are the building blocks of information-processing, a cognitive framework that determines what we know about the world, the objects it contains, the tasks we perform within it — even what we see (Schank 1990).

Schemas enable us to perceive objects and occurrences around us and to make sense of them efficiently by consulting our ready-made store of similar occurrences and understandings, which we gain from reading, personal experience, and even advice we receive from others (Basalla 1988). Schemas may be as simple as the series of understandings and actions that enable us to both recognize what a car is and how to drive one — or as complex as our understanding of the specific roles characters play in, say, teen slasher flicks,

where we expect basements to be hotbeds of horror or peril and teenagers having sex to become victims. Schemas also entail scripts, sets of tasks or actions appropriate to certain schemas. In Schank's famous "restaurant script," people entering restaurants understand, seemingly automatically, what to do with a menu, how to order, and how to behave throughout the restaurant experience (Schank and Abelson 1977). Scripts, moreover, are flexible, as we can rapidly and easily modify existing scripts to accommodate new scenarios. A single restaurant script easily covers a visit to McDonald's, Le Cirque, a sushi bar, even a Roman *antipasti* restaurant, where you merely help yourself to whatever dish is being handed around.

Once we have identified a single schema, we begin calling on relevant scripts that shape our perception, navigation and interaction within a scenario — whether it exists in life, on a page, or in a stroll on the decks of Titanic in the interactive game *Titanic: Adventure Out of Time*. We watch the trials and travails of a couple in a romantic comedy with considerably less trepidation than we would the eponymous couple in the likes of *Romeo and Juliet*, which we know to be a tragedy, because our schemas for romantic comedies tell us that, in the end, the obstacles exist merely to make the final union all the more satisfying. We know we must treat all clues as potentially relevant when we

---

participants contribute? They participate for the most part in games that are fixed, making choices that are extremely limited: they agree, that is, to be manipulated. Again, this may replicate the daily experience of most people. How many really believe the myths of democracy? Do the "people rule" or is it a matter of molding so-called public opinion? At the deepest philosophical level of whether or not "free choice" actually exists in life, these games seem to indicate that it does not. Choice is a selection from a "menu," and whether that menu is handed to a player by a waiter or pops up on a screen, the contents of the menu itself, and the programming of the reality that gives rise to the menu, are not controlled by the client or player. The game, like the menu, gives choice within

a strictly defined and tightly limited field. The job of the restaurateur and the programmer is to make it appear as if the client or player is free. The better the data manager, the more convincing the illusion.

Douglas makes a point that traditional games are clock limited or event determined, while interactives are more openly structured. But so are soap operas and the nightly news. These go on as long as one pays attention to them. The question is open concerning the amount of positive feedback linking interactives to soaps and news. This chicken-and-egg dilemma is not worth resolving. That is because the interactives, the soaps, and the news are all products of an underlying actuality: a craving for immortality in a world where many people no longer believe in an afterlife. The flow

Bernstein & Greco
Strickland

Stern Perlin
Raley Utterback

V. Hypertexts & Interactives

Schechner Jenkins

Hypertexts & Interactives> Douglas & Hargadon

read a Patricia Cornwell mystery, just as our schemas for mysteries also tell us that the author will dangle as many false leads, innocent suspects, and red herrings as she possibly can before us — all tactics to delay our resolving the mystery's central puzzle until the book's ultimate pages.

Schemas are, moreover, such vital perceptual tools that, when objects or works violate long-held conventions, we become frustrated and fail to understand them. Films such as *Jacob's Ladder* become box office bombs because they begin by inviting viewers to latch onto a single schema — initially, a thriller involving war games in the Mekong Delta and psychotropic drugs — then rapidly deploy elements from contradictory schemas. The film, by turns, shuttles through a series of schemas, becoming a horror film complete with the requisite demons and aliens in nurses' uniforms, a thriller about a government conspiracy, and a horror film about madness. Throughout, the film remains too slippery for readers to understand it through a single schema. Not surprisingly, its resolution could never prove satisfying to any audience. The film ultimately can resolve the dilemma posed by only a single schema — which turns out, unfortunately, to belong to a fifth schema that is not revealed until the film's final scene. *Jacob's Ladder* ends with an "oh-it-*was*-all-a-dream" schema that

accounts for the illogical and fantastic nature of events by situating them inside a dream or, in this case, a dying man's last hallucinations.

Pleasure: Immersion and Engagement

When aesthetic objects invite us to rely on certain schemas, they are not, however, necessarily guaranteeing us an entirely predictable experience. Schemas may enhance our pleasure in, say, reading a John Grisham paperback, because they provide a detailed framework that frees us to focus intently on the minutiae of the narrative by providing us information about what, roughly, to expect from the characters, events, and plot generally, as well as, of course, its eventual outcome (de Beaugrande and Colby 1979). The presence and nature of schemas in a work, moreover, dictate not only the type of genre the work belongs to, but also both the sort of audience the work attracts and the kind of affective experience that audiences may expect. Genre fiction generally hews tightly to highly normative schemas, while postmodern novels tend to invert narrative conventions and rupture the stock developments and resolutions of mainstream fiction. Not surprisingly, the predictability afforded by genre schemas makes them ideal fodder for the trance-like reading cognitive psychologists such as Victor Nell note is the hallmark

195

of experience is our collective afterlife, ironically lived "right now." The afterlife of postmodernity is dramatized current events in a positive feedback loop with open-ended games.

Eskelinen wants to drive a wedge between ordinary narration and what happens in a game. I don't think the categories are so easily separable. Of course in a novel or a play, etc., there are "characters" and the story is predetermined for the most part (though in theater, the precise way of playing the story — of staging, line reading, and the rest — varies enormously from production to production and even performance to performance); but also in apparently open games various kinds of narrations are involved. And the tight kind of narration that Eskelinen is criticizing

comprises a small portion of the storymaking that goes on in pop life.

It's not for nothing that great achievers in sports are called "heroes," that matches build to specific and resolvable climaxes, that accident and destiny, skill and unforeseen circumstance are continuously interacting. Fans identify with their heroes, boo their villains, and in other ways wholly dramatize what happens in sports. But what about interactive video? I think these figures are generally less lively than actual living gamers. The interactive figures don't really commit crimes, mix with gangsters, get blow jobs in upscale Atlanta strip clubs, lead complex private lives, delight or disappoint their fans on the field and off, during press conferences or in unguarded moments in the locker

of the immersive reading experience.

Of course, as we might expect, immersive affective experiences also tend to garner the largest audiences, as readers pursue immersion to temporarily escape the stresses of everyday life, or vicariously enjoy the exploits of fictional characters as an antidote to the mundanity of their own lives (States 1993). Contrary to expectations, however, our immersion in what some critics might scoff at as "light reading" (Nell 1988) stems from the steady, unbroken rhythm of our reading, which fully occupies our cognitive capacities (Britton, Piha, Davis, and Wehausen 1978). Conversely, readers plowing through more demanding texts, works by what Robert Coover has dubbed "difficult" writers, enjoy no such spell, as the cognitive demands of grappling with the text tend to be discontinuous, involving shuttling between competing schemas, prospecting and retrospecting through the text, and pausing over obscure passages (Britton et al. 1992; Nell 1988).

Highly normative schemas enable readers to "lose" themselves in the text in what we might call an "immersive" affective experience. When immersed in a text, readers' perceptions, reactions, and interactions all take place within the text's frame, which itself usually suggests a single schema and a few definite scripts for highly directed interaction. Conversely, in what we might term the "engaged" affective experience,

contradictory schemas or elements that defy conventional schemas tend to disrupt readers' immersion in the text, obliging them to assume an extratextual perspective on the text itself, as well as on the schemas that have shaped it and the scripts operating within it.

Immersive Interactives:
Beyond Shootouts and Hunt-quests

> [T]oday's most successful interactive artists ultimately see interactivity as an evolutionary (rather than revolutionary) step for storytelling.
> —Brent Hurtig (1998), "The Plot Thickens"

Not surprisingly, the earliest digital interactives, videogames, drew their cues heavily from a singular schema, turning the early commercial computer games into jazzed-up versions of video arcade games. Whether by accident or design, early game developers had hit digital paydirt by founding their first ventures on the bedrock of two essentials: a recipe for interaction that all but guaranteed a deeply immersive experience and strong, normative schemas borrowed from already familiar forms of entertainment. The history of

room. All of these "off the field" activities are part-and-parcel of the live sports scene, the raw material for the soap opera component that is every bit as important as the limited on-the-field competition. No computer game has that kind of complexity.

What we don't know about the "real life" of computer games are the social circumstances that surrounds, and to a large degree guides, their playing. That is, what "other" stories are the players enacting? Fans of sports or movies engage with other like-minded people. They not only follow and collect the lives of their heroes, they enact their own lives in some kind of dependence on the lives of those they adore and follow. How can computer games do likewise? Virtual heroes don't have "real lives" to screw up. They can't really get stoned,

overdose, die, murder, or in other ways find themselves acting out real-life dramas. Gamers can hang out with each other, visit chat rooms, interact, and create the aura of fandom. But they don't have an actually living Star with her or his own life at the center of their interactions. Granted that stars are also media creations, but these creations often get out of hand. This predictable unpredictability is part of their charm. Comparatively speaking, interactives, videogames, and hypertext are relatively hollow. That is because, ultimately, the most interesting part of gaming — any kind of gaming — is the narration created by the players, not the figures or characters. Actors are always more interesting than characters.

196

invention is, after all, littered with dazzling innovations that either withered rapidly into obscurity or, at best, hibernated for decades before their eventual adoption, mostly due to the object's very newness (Basalla 1988). Inventions that are discontinuous with earlier devices and tools tend to offer users few familiar schemas.

The fax, phonograph, answering machine, tape player, and VCR all languished for decades before becoming household fixtures, largely because each of these inventions required users to develop new schemas to accommodate them. Conversely, technologies like Edison's incandescent light were adopted at the technological equivalent of light-speed, despite potentially crippling problems with the limitations of wiring and distribution of centralized electricity, almost entirely because the new innovations essentially invited users to rely on long-familiar, comfortable schemas and scripts (Hargadon and Douglas unpublished) derived from the very forms of technology the innovations were designed to replace.

Ironically, innovations seem to adopted most rapidly when their newness is domesticated, so to speak, by design features that invite us to treat the new object as if it were merely an extension — albeit an improved one — of a familiar object or device. Early video games such as *Pong* stuck to the simple, rigid schema of a ball game with the ball batted between players or against walls. Later successful videogames drew off arcade staples that involved escaping through mazes — itself drawn loosely from the pinball schema — or raining bullets on would-be protagonists, a schema drawn from that staple of county fairs everywhere, the shooting gallery. The result: a game which imposed rigid rules, drawn from already familiar games which could thus be immediately grasped by users, a game featuring fresh local details like gobbling mouths or souped-up weapons, requiring a steady rhythm of interaction. Ironically, the reader paging through Balzac or Dickens, or, for that matter, Judith Krantz, has entered into roughly the same immersive state, enjoying the same high, continuous cognitive load, as the runty kid firing fixedly away at *Space Invaders*.

Later generations of video games have colonized the same turf with notable success — both *Sonic the Hedgehog* and *Super Mario Brothers*, for example, drew off familiar arcade schemas. Yet video and PC game designers have encountered difficulty whenever they have attempted to stray into territory where no dominant schemas reign. Chief among any designer's difficulties is how to invite users to interact with the text itself. While the shoot-out is always immediately comprehensible, that particular schema doesn't easily offer designers sufficient local details to completely

197

From Henry Jenkins's Online Response

Most contemporary genre theory suggests that popular works rarely follow a single genre formula but most often, balance competing formulas against each other. For every *Jacob's Ladder* that fails to achieve an appropriate balance, there is a *Matrix* or *Blade Runner* that demonstrates the popular potential of hybrid genre construction. Contemporary film style is more elliptical and rapid-fire than the classical continuity system precisely because a generation that spends many hours per day consuming media demands cognitive challenges and perceptual puzzles rather than straightforward exposition. Similarly, television narrative has moved towards longer story arcs, denser plot structures, and ensemble casts because fans demand novel structures for expressing familiar plots.

Game players do depend upon formulaic elements to provide their initial orientation. Yet, they would be frustrated, rather than satisfied, if the game unfolded in an altogether predictable fashion. The most compelling games present challenges, albeit challenges the player can reasonably hope to master. Such a process is unlikely to sustain anything as simple as the immersive experience they describe. Rather, it makes more sense to think of game players as fluctuating between states of immersion and engagement, much as film critics can sustain an analytic relationship to cinematic technique and an immersive relationship to narrative content.

http://www.electronicbookreview.com/thread/firstperson/jenkinsr1

differentiate their latest game from the droves of other shoot-outs that have preceded it. Perhaps not terribly surprisingly, game designers have mostly mined only a single other schema: the treasure-hunt-cum-grail-quest, familiar to users of *Myst*, *Titanic: Adventure Out of Time*, *Grim Fandango*, and for that matter, any other interactive that doesn't require users to shoot anything that moves. Yet the hunt-quest remains a remarkably hardy genre, as its schema, unlike the shoot-out, permits a wealth of local detail, sufficiently rich that its users can become immersed in grappling with both its intricacies and what to do with it.

Scripts, Voice-overs, and the Fifth Business

In immersive interactives such as *Myst* or Shannon Gilligan's *Virtual Murder* series, our pleasure stems from our ability to discern a single schema and the several scripts it offers us for both interpretation and directed action. Before we so much as glimpse the title screens of your typical hunt-quest, we already know we need to listen intently, collect everything we can lay our mitts on, and put together our tools and clues to solve the local challenges that confront us, which, in turn, will enable us to solve the interactive's grand challenge — usually something on the order of liberating a prisoner (*Grim Fandango*, *Myst*), altering the course of history

(*Titanic*) or saving the planet (*Obsidian*). Still, designers have no such clear choice of scripts for interaction. We all understand that guns or knives are essential to shoot-outs, but no clear script exists for actions during the hunt-quest.

Furthermore, how do you indicate readiness for action or differentiate the items your protagonist must collect from the normal detritus that makes an environment look convincingly realistic? Contrary to some theorists' beliefs (Laurel 1991; Murray 1997), the existence of tools intra-frame or extra-frame does little to disrupt the user's immersion in the interactive. For example, solving a puzzle, pursuing a clue, or surviving a knife fight involves action that can potentially spill outside the narrative's frame — as in the multiple choice replies *Titanic* offers as responses to characters' conversations with you or the inventory of items protagonist Robert Cath possesses in *The Last Express*. But the aesthetic remains largely immersive as long as the story, setting, and interface adhere to a single schema.

Users face further interface challenges from narratives like *Last Express* that attempt to stray from reliable gaming conventions governing the user's actions, mostly decoding puzzles and dismembering enemies — all of which may frustrate more than engage users expecting well-defined scripts and a tight

Douglas and Hargadon Respond

Our primary point in analyzing the aesthetic pleasures of interactives: we're awaiting the eventual redefinition of entertainment itself, in terms of our schemas and scripts. Before the advent of interactives, you needed a detailed script for pure engagement but only a simple, austere script for pure immersion.

http://www.electronicbookreview.com/thread/firstperson/douglash argadonr2

Bernstein & Greco   Stern Perlin   **V. Hypertexts & Interactives**
Strickland   Raley Utterback
Hypertexts & Interactives> Douglas & Hargadon Schechner Jenkins

framework for directed action. In *Titanic*, for example, if you fail to keep an assignation or meander through the ship, the narrative's clock-time halts abruptly, and all characters vanish, save your steward, who appears periodically to throw you out of the First Class Smoking Lounge or Verandah Café. No agents, frames, or tools exist to jump-start the narrative again once you neglect to pick up the right clues. Even with its highly normative hunt-quest schema, *Myst* frustrated users searching vainly for clues into acts of desperate, random thrashing with the cursor on shrubbery, sundials, library walls — anything that looked like a candidate for the next puzzle-challenge. But even with better indicators for interaction, like *The Longest Journey's* palette of annotated cursor and potential actions (eye, mouth, hand) that flag your potential actions with solid or broken lines and a variety of colors, users are simply left with more elegant weapons to thrash the simulated environment with (figure 16.1). If the environment seems particularly bereft of clues or you don't happen to hit on the ingenious and incredibly improbable notion of using a twig and dinosaur scale to create a funnel, as in *The Longest Journey*, immersion evaporates, and you're left trying to vainly intuit what on earth the designers had in mind when they created the particular scene you're presently trapped in.

If anything, videogame designers, more than their PC counterparts, have even thornier dilemmas awaiting them in interface design during their forays into territory outside the shoot- and hunt-quest genres. With *Sydney 2000*, Dreamcast users can train athletes, expose them to some extra coaching, test them in qualifying trials, and, finally direct them to compete in the Olympics. The problem for users and designers alike: how to provide the means for a potentially complex series of interactions using the same controller originally created for shoot-outs. The solution: users must toggle manically between the former "shoot" switches to provide athletes with the strength, say, to complete a 170 Kg clean and jerk. The greater problem still: to toss the javelin, shoot skeet, triple jump, kayak, or dive, you're left frenetically toggling between the same switches you've just used to provide a sprinter with speed in the 100 meters and to give your weight

16.1. *The Longest Journey*. (Funcom)

lifter, at least theoretically, enough gas to complete a dead lift. The script for interaction shifts with every event and sometimes, even between training mode and trial/competition modes, leaving users in what promises to be the most immersive of interactive experiences — videogames, after all, are direct descendants of the immersive arcade shoot-outs — paging angrily through the slender instruction pamphlet, trying to figure out what functions the "A" and "B" buttons will signify for the next ten minutes.

For our affective experience to remain immersive, both narrative and interface alike need to overtly guide or curtail our possibilities for action. Interactive games fulfill their promise as immersive when they offer us an obvious schema for narrative structure and interface, and when they offer us predictable, tightly scripted interactions enabling us to enjoy virtual experiences either unattractively risky or denied to us in everyday life (States 1993). In *Gadget*, if an informant in the Museum train station has instructions for you to turn your quest around, the train idles helpfully in the station until you venture out of the car, stroll up to one or two likely looking characters, and receive the vital clue. In the *Virtual Murder* series (*Who Killed Sam Rupert?*; *The Magic Death*; *Who Killed Brett Penance? The Environmental Surfer*; *Who Killed Taylor French? The Case of the Undressed Reporter*), Shannon Gilligan provides a detective sidekick who summarizes the crime scene, provides thumbnail sketches on suspects, or weighs in

16.2. In Shannon Gilligan's *Who Killed Taylor French?* (above) the sidekick character, played by Sheryl Lee, offers thoughts on the case. In the interface for Gilligan's *Who Killed Brett Penance?* (below) the sidekick's button becomes active when she has something to say — here, an ironic comment on the suspects.

200

with an opinion when queried (figure 16.2). The series also includes the occasional voice-over by a police superior who harangues you with the work remaining to be completed and the time remaining on your "game" clock.

Both the voice-over and agent are fortuitous additions to Gilligan's series of interactives and, not coincidentally, both are drawn explicitly from film and stage. Beginning with the Greek chorus — itself an early form of voice-over — dramatists and directors have used voice-overs to guide their audiences through scenes, ensuring audiences understood the significance of an action, the true nature of a cloaked villain, or the mental state of some characters. In cinema, writers and directors traditionally use voice-overs to establish conditions at the outset of a narrative or during substantial changes in location or time, or to voice

interior monologues. But some directors have also used voice-overs to make entire narratives intelligible, a vital function in films that rely on a pastiche of images without heavy sequential continuity or on narratives that defy conventions or logic. Famously, Francis Ford Coppola was troubled by the 1.5 million feet of film shot for *Apocalypse Now*, believing he had only "about a twenty percent chance" of assembling the elements intelligibly into a successful feature. Furthermore, sneak preview audiences remained puzzled by the logic and significance of several of the film's key scenes: most troublingly, the film's conclusion. When Coppola, however, commissioned writer Michael Herr to create a voice-over interior monologue for the protagonist — a voice-over narrative that spanned virtually the entire film — audiences immediately understood the film's events, and *Apocalypse Now* reaped over $100 million at the box office (Cowie 1990). Remarkably, voice-overs have been all but unused in interactives: in *The Last Express*, you understand Robert Cath's feelings via the occasional voice-over, and both April Ryan in *Longest Journey* and *Grim Fandango's* Manny Calavera use voice-overs. But both Ryan's and Calavera's voice-overs exist simply to inform you what their characters *cannot* do. When you point either character toward an item that doesn't function as a tool or potential clue, both essentially tell you, "I wouldn't do that," or "I don't think that will work." Game designers, by eschewing the use of anything approximating a voice-over, are forcing users to face challenges akin to understanding the events in a narrative without benefit of either first-, third-person or omniscient narration (which is achieved in cinema via first- or omniscient point-of-view camera), which would prove a challenge even in the comparative cozy familiarity of the print novel.

Gilligan's sidekick, a nameless helpmate portrayed initially by Gilligan herself and, in later additions to the *Virtual Murder* series (*Who Killed Brett Penance?*; *Who Killed Taylor French?*), by actress Sheryl Lee, is also an apt throwback to earlier narrative forms. While her cropping up in a police procedural is, perhaps, unremarkable, she remains the lone example in interactives of what Robertson Davies termed "the Fifth Business," or the agent who exists solely to chivvy

Bernstein & Greco
Strickland
Hypertexts & Interactives> Douglas & Hargadon

Stern Perlin
Raley Utterback
Schechner Jenkins

V. Hypertexts & Interactives

201

the characters and plot toward its conclusion. In police procedurals, detective novels, and mysteries of all stripes, of course, the Fifth Business is usually the protagonist's sidekick. Sherlock Holmes, famously, had Watson to bounce ideas off and to help him unravel clues often unwittingly, and even Inspector Morse had the much-put-upon Sergeant Lewis.

Both Watson and Lewis performed, like every good agent, the function of sniffing down false leads and interviewing suspects while their respective bosses got down to the real detective work and eventually solved the case — significantly, never without some intervention from their sidekicks. Of course, both agents also function as narrative foils to their bosses. Watson and Lewis are famously dim where their superiors are quick-witted, badly read, and poorly mannered where Holmes and Morse are educated, cultured men of the world. Yet the agent is also the mystery's unsung catalyst, a force who can usher the plot along efficiently precisely because he or she is an unobtrusive character never quite in the spotlight. Perhaps, given the paucity of scripts drawn from earlier media, the absence of agents from interactives should seem unremarkable. Yet the agent is such a potent tool, one that can clarify interface elements and possible actions, that we can only wonder why agents remain so strangely unused — apart from Microsoft's brief, mid-nineties foray into plugging an obnoxious agent named Bob into its desktop interface. An agent in *The Longest Journey* could make suggestions about what April Ryan ought to do with the dinosaur scale and twig, saving you from scrabbling for the cheat-sheet walkthrough — decidedly an immersion-busting experience. Similarly, an agent or voice-over could tell you how to position *Grim Fandango's* forklift in the elevator before you embark on your fortieth attempt at halting the elevator or risk losing any remaining vestiges of sanity. Or you could enlist an agent or toggle the voice-over mode on during the early stages of the interactive, when you're still determining the conventions and constraints governing the plot, characters' actions, and environmental cues, only to leave both these guides behind once you've fully grasped the details and immersed yourself in the narrative.

Pleasures of Immersion, Pleasures of Engagement

The pleasure of immersion in interactives stems from our ability to take guided action and see the outcomes from our choice of one or more scripts within a single schema. In contrast, the pleasure of engagement with hypertext fiction comes from users' access to a wide repertoire of schemas and scripts, our attempts to discover congruences between the hypertext and an array of often mutually exclusive schemas, and, ultimately, our ability to make sense of the work as a whole. Even though Janet Murray's list of plots as symbolic actions include sensemaking and assembling fragments into a coherent whole, Murray's objection to what she calls "structured literary hypertext" reveals a criterion for aesthetic pleasure clearly founded only on immersion: "navigation unfold[s] a story that flows from our own meaningful choices."

Yet, readers of modernist works such as *Mrs. Dalloway*, *The Good Soldier*, *In the Labyrinth*, and *Ulysses* must actively wrestle with wandering narrative perspectives, tortuous representations of time, and deliberate disruptions in space, time, and causation, as well as the requirement that they ultimately understand the entire work relative to its spatial form. Anyone who confuses Great Works with an aesthetic of immersion should remember Joseph Frank's famous declaration about *Ulysses*, which, he claimed "could not be read, only reread." These texts engage readers deeply because do not follow schemas for which readers can unthinkingly apply ready-made scripts (Rapoport and Chammah 1965). Instead, they violate existing conventions, switch schemas, and, in the case of works like *In the Labyrinth*, violate even our assumptions about continuity from one paragraph or even sentence to the next.

Not surprisingly, engagement tends to be pursued and enjoyed by those who are widely read, since they have access to a vast array of schemas and scripts. Readers who enjoy engagement also tend to enjoy confronting situations for which they lack scripts, as these provide opportunities for learning, as opposed to merely performing one of a series of scripts within a conventional framework. With a hefty repertoire of scripts to call upon, the well-read are also more likely to recognize when — and to guess how or why — narratives violate long-familiar conventions and patterns. The reactions of even well-intentioned critics — witness Murray's "privileging confusion" — to hypertext fiction grows from confusing engagement with immersion, as well as from the fluid, still-evolving nature of schemas and scripts in hypertext narratives.

Yet even the earliest readers (Douglas 1991) of the first published hypertext narrative, *afternoon*, experienced a kind of engagement that would have seemed familiar to readers of *Ulysses* or "The Wasteland." First, readers bring to new media their schemas and scripts from older media (McLuhan 1964), just as hypertext fiction itself draws on conventions inherited from print for plot, character, intention, and tropes (Bolter and Grusin 1999). Second, published criticism that, in the cases of Joyce and Eliot, included symbolic "keys" to their work, aided readers in developing schemas to fit the new material. Joyce circulated notes that mapped Stephen's and Leopold Bloom's day in Dublin onto the adventures of Odysseus (Groden 1977), while Eliot extensively footnoted his own poem (Eliot 1964; Paul 1995). Readers of hypertext fiction, like Joyce's and Eliot's audiences, are more likely to seek out secondary sources to supplement their array of schemas for understanding the text. These "engaged" readers are also more likely to employ these schemas as simply part of a repertoire, rather than as sources for controlling scripts that determine singular interpretations of a work. Such secondary sources include Michael Joyce's own extensive criticism on hypertext aesthetics (Joyce 1988, 1995, 1997a), as well as a growing body of criticism on the narrative significance of navigational mechanisms in hypertext (Bernstein 1991; Bernstein, Joyce, and Levine; Douglas 1999; Murray 1997). Third, even in a relatively new genre, some of its newly minted "grammar" and tropes are accessible to early audiences: cross-cutting, special effects, and the shot-reaction shot sequence all appeared during cinema's nickelodeon era (Gianetti 1990). In complex hypertexts, immanent structures include proximity signifying causal or relational connections between lexias in spatialized text

(Marshall and Shipman 1993), as well as recurrence to remind readers of previously encountered lexias or to situate already encountered lexias in new contexts where they take on new meanings (Bernstein, Joyce, and Levine 1992; Douglas 1989]. Mark Bernstein (1997, 2001a) has also identified cyclical repetition broken to signify closure (Douglas 1991; Joyce 1990), contour, where cycles coalesce or collide (Bernstein, Joyce and Levine; Joyce 1997b), and montage that establishes connections across the boundaries of nodes or links, as used by George Landow (1992), Shelly Jackson (1996) and Christiane Paul (1995).[1] Readers engaged with hypertext fictions such as *Victory Garden* or *Twelve Blue* (Joyce 1997b) make hypotheses about the relationships between lexias and the significance of links, layering onto the print reader's engagement with character, continuity, time, and space, further interpretations of the significance of spatial relationships and links between lexias, of link types and their conditions. Long-term engagement with the texts, the necessary rereading Michael Joyce describes (1997a) makes some relations immanent, nullifies some hypotheses, thwarts some navigational strategies, and generally enables readers to enlarge their repertoire of textual aesthetics still further.

Immersion into Engagement into Flow

The "episode vortex," as Jim Rosenberg (1996) notes, however, can just as easily frustrate readers, launching them into "foraging" for the next episode. While immersion may easily lure readers into interactive narratives and organize their initial engagement, replacing promised immersion with engagement can also frustrate readers, even when they can develop a script that situates their frustrated immersion as strictly intentional, a deliberate effect designed by the author (Bernstein 1991).

Even in the throes of engagement, disorientation in hypertexts is potentially more disconcerting than the momentary discomforts we experience in other media — notwithstanding our budding repertoire of effects and gambits that signify. The dreaded "lost in hyperspace" (Edward and Hardman 1990) problem is due partly to our awareness that hypertexts exist in virtual, three-dimensional space (which may or may not be represented to readers via maps or spatial navigational tools), partly to our awareness that links often involve recursion and complex conditionals, making visiting every lexia or link once seldom the equivalent of having experienced the entire work. When we consider the affective dimension, however, the absence of guides for the length of time occupied by our engagement or immersion may be still more significant. When we sit down with a novel, settle ourselves into a Broadway theatre or our local cinema, we know approximately how long our immersion or engagement will last.

Book chapters, like film running times, often owe as much to the length of time writers require to develop stories and episodes as they do to publishers' and producers' perceptions of the attention span and disposable time common to contemporary audiences. Although audiences can prove equally adroit at immersing or engaging themselves in lengthy narratives fanning out over weeks and even years in radio and television serials (Bernstein 2001b; Douglas 1999) as well as in professional sports (Bernstein 2001a, 2001b), they require clear-cut guides on the duration of each local session. Football, basketball, and hockey are clock-determined; baseball has nine regular innings; plays have either three or five acts; serials occupy thirty or sixty minutes of airtime. Time can also increase the signifying power of narrative developments and tropes: cues about a character's impending mortality that may not seem particularly significant in Act III acquire dramatic significance when revealed to us in the final moments of Act V.

Not coincidentally, designers of interactives frequently build into games central metaphors or tools that rely on time. All the *Virtual Murder* interactives use a conceit about the seven hours that generally elapse between the discovery of a crime and the swearing out of a warrant for the suspected perpetrator's arrest. Both *Titanic* and *Last Express* unfold against time constraints imposed by, respectively, the sinking of the liner and the onset of World War I. Further, in both the *Virtual Murder* series and *Titanic*, agents periodically surface both to remind you of time passing and to nag you to

keep assignations, ensuring your immersion doesn't shade quickly into frustration.

Other interactives rely on stages that signal readers' progression through the text: "ages" for *Myst*, "realms" for *Obsidian*. Hypertext fictions, however, lack such clear signals to readers, making it difficult for readers to determine if their script-acquiring and -developing have been successful in helping them understand the hypertext as a structure of narrative possibilities, or if they need to accommodate, modify, and generate still more scripts. Some writers have built forms of closure into hypertexts that enable readers to pause in their reading or leave it completely (Douglas 1999; Joyce 1990; Larsen 1994; Moulthrop 1991b). But link conditions in complex hypertexts can yield different juxtapositions of lexia and fresh narrative possibilities, just as a familiar episode may branch in several unexpected directions the next time out, mitigating the cues potentially offered by these approximations of closure.

Finally, while immersion may shade into engagement — now an imminent development with recent calls in the interactive game industry for more backstory and narrative (Brown-Martin 1999; Sierra Studios 1999) — and engagement into immersion, neither of these affective dimensions maps all that tidily onto most definitions of interaction (Brand 1987). As Joyce (1997a) and Aarseth have noted, readers of most hypertext fiction are merely exploring the narrative, not constructing its links and rearranging its structure, or even generating lexia and links themselves. While the advent of the world wide web and collaborative structures such as Brown's Hypertext Hotel (1994) suggest that hypermedia's contribution to aesthetics may be a blurring of the line between reception and creation, the relatively limited interactions of immersive or engaging interactives should not likewise limit our quest for features, metaphors, and conventions that enhance our affective experiences.

Given the enhanced immersive possibilities of full-motion video, not to mention virtual reality, coupled with hypertext fiction's complex possibilities for engagement, future interactives could easily enable casual readers to experience what Mihaly

Csikszentmihalyi (1990) calls "flow," a condition where self-consciousness disappears, perceptions of time become distorted, and concentration becomes so intense that the game or task at hand completely absorbs us. Since flow involves extending our skills to cope with challenges, a sense that we are performing both well and effortlessly, this state hovers on the continuum between immersion and engagement, drawing on the characteristics of both simultaneously.

Presciently in the early eighties, Sherry Turkle (1984) noted something like flow states in teenagers grappling with computer games. Where immersion involves identification with characters and narrative elements — the local details that keep us involved even when we know the plot's trappings intimately — engagement involves deciphering the author's or game designers' intentions. During a flow state, Turkle noticed, teenagers both identified utterly with the objects they were manipulating — the equivalent of "becoming the pinball," unthinkable to the player of the analogue arcade game — just as they also were deeply involved in determining the constraints built into the game. Most vitally, however, she witnessed player after player obliged to keep up with a rhythm dictated by the game itself, a "relentless... demand that all other time stop... and that players take full responsibility for every act." The combination of all three conditions, she realized, when she interviewed inveterate game players from teenaged social misfits to stressed-out banking executives, enabled players to experience the same characteristics of flow first identified by Csikszentmihalyi. All players attested to a sense of stepping outside both the real world and its time, while at the same time retaining an acute perception of the constraints of the game-world and game-time and an ability to play strategically within its constraints.

Flow is, however, elusive, fleeting, and intensely problematic. The social misfits and uptight executives Turkle interviewed most likely achieved flow states during gameplay at least as much due to their desires to achieve mastery over something, however brief and fictive, and not necessarily because they identified intensely with the all-but-nonexistent characters or environment in the videogames they played. Artists,

writers, professional athletes, and musicians can experience flow states during practice or performance — as can connoisseurs of music, film, dance, or sports. For example, film critics may notice how deep focus, changes in film stock, and oblique angles frame a sequence or allude to other films — an extratextual perspective on the film that is characteristic of engagement — even as they remain deeply immersed in the characters and plot developments of the narrative playing before them. Further, since engagement tends to focus our attention on the frame and materials themselves, texts such as *Ulysses* or *afternoon* tend to immerse us only for short periods before demanding our engagement. As interactives, however, begin offering us worlds that increasingly resemble the one outside the text (Brown-Martin 1999; *Shenmue*), and writers begin introducing into them complex plots, characters, and orienting devices like voice-overs or agents, even casual readers may one day experience the flow that today only a privileged few enjoy when watching or creating narratives.

Note

1. Other devices Bernstein notes [Bernstein 1997; Bernstein 2001b] include the missing link [Harpold; Joyce 1990; Moulthrop 1989] and the cognitive maps in hypertexts like Stephanie Strickland's *True North* and J. Yellowlees Douglas's "I Have Said Nothing," that represent the relationships between narrative lexias and sequences and serve as tropes for the narratives themselves. Finally, when hypertext episodes [Miller 1998; Moulthrop 1997] also represent causally linked lexias that generate narrative tension, readers may become immersed in the narrative. Even when immersion gives way to engagement, the immersive lexias or episodes can still act as a centripetal force that compels us to become engaged with the narrative [Douglas 1989].

References: Literature

Aarseth, Espen (1997). *Cybertext: Perspectives on Ergodic Literature.* Baltimore: Johns Hopkins University Press.

Basalla, George (1988). *The Evolution of Technology.* New York: Cambridge University Press.

de Beaugrande, Robert (1980). *Text, Discourse, and Process: Toward a Multidisciplinary Science of Texts.* Norwood, NJ: Ablex.

de Beaugrande, Robert, and Benjamin N. Colby (1979). "Narrative Models of Action and Interaction." *Cognitive Science* no.3 (1979): 43-66.

Bernstein, Mark (1991). "The Navigation Problem Reconsidered." In *Hypertext/Hypermedia Handbook*, edited by Emily Berk and Joseph Devlin. New York: McGraw-Hill.

Bernstein, Mark (1997). *Chasing Our Tails.*

Bernstein & Greco
Strickland

Stern Perlin
Raley Utterback

V. Hypertexts & Interactives

Hypertexts & Interactives> Douglas & Hargadon Schechner Jenkins

<http://www.eastgate.com/tails/Welcome.html>.

Bernstein, Mark, Michael Joyce and David B. Levine (1992). "Contours of Constructive Hypertext." In Proceedings of the European Conference on Hypermedia Technology. Milano: Association for Computing Machinery.

Bernstein, Mark (2001)a. "Hypertext Narrative and Baseball." *HypertextNow* (2001).
<http://www.eastgate.com/HypertextNow/archives/Baseball.html>.

Bernstein, Mark (2001b). "Span of Attention." *HypertextNow* (2001).
<http://www.eastgate.com/HypertextNow//archives/Attention.html>.

Birkerts, Sven (1994). *The Gutenberg Elegies: The Fate of Reading in an Electronic Age*. Boston: Faber & Faber.

Bolter, Jay, and Richard Grusin (1999). *Remediation: Understanding New Media*. Cambridge, MA: The MIT Press.

Brand, Stewart (1987). *The Media Lab: Inventing the Future at MIT*. New York: Viking.

Britton, B.K., A. Piha, J. Davis and E. Wehausen (1978). "Reading and Cognitive Capacity Usage: Adjunct Question Effects." *Memory and Cognition* no.6 (1978): 266-273.

Brown-Martin, Graham (1999). "Hooray for Hollywood." *NextGen* 2, no.2 (1999): 94-101.

Bruner, Jerome (1986). *Actual Minds, Possible Worlds*. Cambridge, MA: Harvard University Press.

Coleridge, Samuel Taylor (1971). "Biographia Literaria." In *Critical Theory Since Plato*, edited by Hazard Adama. New York: Harcourt Brace.

Coover, Robert (1969). *Pricksongs and Descants*. New York: Plume.

Coover, Robert (1992). "The End of Books." *New York Times Book Review*, June 21, 1992: 23-24.

Coover, Robert (editor) (1994). *The Hypertext Hotel*.
<http://duke.cs.brown.edu:8888/>.

Cowie, Peter (1990). *Coppola*. London: Faber and Faber.

Csikszentmihalyi, Mihaly (1990). *Flow: The Psychology of Optimal Experience*. New York: Harper.

Davies, Robertson (1983). *The Deptford Trilogy: Fifth Business*. New York: Penguin.

Douglas, J. Yellowlees (1989). "Wandering through the Labyrinth: Encountering Interactive Fiction." *Computers and Composition* 6, no.3 (1989): 93-103.

Douglas, J. Yellowlees (1991). "Understanding the Act of Reading: The WOE Beginner's Guide to Dissection." *Writing on the Edge* 2, no.2 (1991): 112-126.

Douglas, J. Yellowlees (1994). "I Have Said Nothing." *Eastgate Quarterly Review* 1, no.2 (1994).

Douglas, J. Yellowlees (1999). *The End of Books — or Books Without End? Reading Interactive Narratives*. Ann Arbor: University of Michigan Press.

Edward, Deborah M., and Lynda Hardman (1990). "'Lost in Hyperspace': Cognitive Mapping and Navigation in a Hypertext Environment." In *Hypertext: Theory into Practice*, edited by Ray

McAleese. Oxford: Intellect Books.

Eliot, T.S. (1964). "The Wasteland." In *Selected Poems*. New York: Harcourt Brace Jovanovich.

Ford, Ford Madox (1990). *The Good Soldier: A Tale of Passion*. Oxford: Oxford University Press.

Frank, Joseph (1988). "Spatial Form in Modern Literature." In *Essentials of the Theory of Fiction*, edited by Michael Hoffman and Patrick Murphey. Durham: Duke University Press.

Gianetti, Louis (1990). *Understanding Movies*, 5th edition. Englewood Cliffs, NJ: Prentice Hall.

Gombrich, E.H. (1956). *Art and Illusion: A Study in the Psychology of Pictorial Representation*. Princeton: Princeton University Press.

Groden, Michael (1977). *Ulysses in Progress*. Princeton: Princeton University Press.

Harpold, Terry (1991). "Threnody: Psychoanalytic Digressions on the Subject of Hypertexts." In *Hypermedia and Literary Criticism*, edited by Paul Delany and George Landow. Cambridge, MA: The MIT Press.

Hargadon, Andrew, and J. Yellowlees Douglas (unpublished). "When Innovations Meet Institutions: Edison and the Design of the Electric Light."

Hurtig, Brett (1998). "The Plot Thickens." *New Media*, January 13, 1998.

Iser, Wolfgang (1978). *The Act of Reading: A Theory of Response*. Baltimore: Johns Hopkins University Press.

Jackson, Shelley (1996). *Patchwork Girl: by Mary/Shelley/and Herself*. Watertown, MA: Eastgate Systems.

Joyce, James (1960). *Anna Livia Plurabelle: The Making of a Chapter*, edited by Fred H. Higginson. Minneapolis: University of Minnesota Press.

Joyce, James (1980). *Ulysses*. New York: Vintage.

Joyce, Michael (1988). "Siren Shapes: Exploratory and Constructive Hypertexts." *Academic Computing* 3, no.4 (November 1988): 37-42.

Joyce, Michael (1990). *afternoon: a story*. Watertown, MA: Eastgate Systems.

Joyce, Michael (1995). *Of Two Minds: Hypertext Pedagogy and Poetics*. Ann Arbor: University of Michigan Press.

Joyce, Michael (1997a). "Nonce Upon Some Times: ReReading Hypertext Fiction." *Modern Fiction Studies* 43, no.3 (1997): 579-597.

Joyce, Michael (1997b). *Twelve Blue*.
<http://www.eastgate.com/TwelveBlue/>.

Landow, George P. (1992). *The Dickens Web*. Watertown, MA: Eastgate Systems.

Landow, George P. (1997). *Hypertext 2.0: The Convergence of Contemporary Critical Theory and Technology*, 2nd edition. Baltimore: Johns Hopkins University Press.

Langer, Suzanne (1953). *Feeling and Form*. New York: Scribner.

Larsen, Deena (1994). *Marble Springs*. Watertown, MA: Eastgate Systems.

Laurel, Brenda (1991). *Computers as Theatre*. New York: Addison-Wesley.

Lynch, Kevin (1960). *The Image of the City*. Cambridge, MA: The MIT Press.

Marshall, Catherine C., and Frank M. Shipman (1993). "Searching for the Missing Link: Discovering Implicit Structure in Spatial Hypertext." In Proceedings of Hypertext 1993. <http://www.csdl.tamu.edu/~shipman/ht93-paper/ht93-paper.html>.

McDaid, John (1992). *Uncle Buddy's Phantom Funhouse*. Watertown, MA: Eastgate Systems.

McLuhan, Marshall (1964). *Understanding Media: The Extensions of Man*. New York: Signet.

Miller, Laura (1998). "www.claptrap.com." *New York Times Book Review*, August 29, 1998: 43.

Moulthrop, Stuart (1989). "Hypertext and 'the Hyperreal.'" In Proceedings of Hypertext 1989, Baltimore.

Moulthrop, Stuart (1991a). "Toward a Paradigm for Reading Hypertexts: Making Nothing Happen in Hypermedia Fiction." In *Hypertext/Hypermedia Handbook*, edited by Emily Berk and Joseph Devlin. New York: McGraw-Hill.

Moulthrop, Stuart (1991b). *Victory Garden*. Watertown, MA: Eastgate Systems.

Moulthrop, Stuart (1997). "Where to? A Review of Forward Anywhere by Cathy Marshall and Judy Malloy." *Convergence: The Journal of Research into New Media Technologies* 3, no. 3 (Fall 1997): 132-38.

Murray, Janet (1997). *Hamlet on the Holodeck: The Future of Narrative in Cyberspace*. New York: Free Press.

Nell, Victor (1988). *Lost in a Book: The Psychology of Reading for Pleasure*. New Haven: Yale University Press.

Paul, Christiane (1995). *Unreal City: A Reader's Companion to "The Wasteland."* Watertown, MA: Eastgate Systems.

Rapoport, Anatole, and Albert M. Chammah (1965). *Prisoner's Dilemma*. Ann Arbor: University of Michigan Press.

Robbe-Grillet, Alain (translated by Christine Brooke-Rose) (1959). *In the Labyrinth*. London: John Calder.

Rosenberg, Jim (1996). "The Structure of Hypertext Activity." In Proceedings of Hypertext 1996. <http://www.cs.unc.edu/~barman/HT96/P17/SHA_out.html>.

Schank, Roger C. (1982). *Dynamic Memory: A Theory of Reminding and Learning in Computers and People*. Cambridge: Cambridge University Press.

Schank, Roger C. (1990). *Tell Me a Story: A New Look at Real and Artificial Memory*. New York: Scribners.

Schank, Roger C., and Robert P. Abelson (1977). *Scripts, Plans, Goals and Understanding: An Inquiry into Human Knowledge Structures*. Hillsdale, NJ: Lawrence Erlbaum Associates.

Sierra Studios (1999). Online Survey, August 25, 1999.

States, Bert O. (1993). *Dreaming and Storytelling*. Ithaca: Cornell University Press.

Strickland, Stephanie (1997). *True North*. Watertown, MA: Eastgate Systems.

Turkle, Sherry (1984). *The Second Self: Computers and the Human Spirit*. New York: Simon & Schuster.

van Dijk, Teun (1980). *Macrostructures: An Interdisciplinary Study of Global Structures in Discourse, Interaction, and Cognition*. Hillsdale, NJ: Lawrence Erlbaum Associates.

Woolf, Virginia (1976). *Mrs. Dalloway*. London: Grafton Books.

References: Games

Gadget: Invention, Travel, and Adventure. Haruhiko Shono; Synergy, 1994.

Grim Fandango. Tim Schafer; LucasArts Entertainment, 1998.

The Last Express. Jordan Mechner; Brøderbund, 1997.

The Longest Journey. Funcom, 2000.

Myst. Robyn Miller and Rand Miller; Brøderbund, 1993.

Obsidian. Adam Wolff, Howard Cushnir and Scott Kim; Segasoft, 1996.

Shenmue. Yu Suzuki; Sega Dreamcast, 2001.

Sydney 2000. Eidos, 2000.

Titanic: Adventure out of Time. Cyberflix, 1996.

Who Killed Sam Rupert? Virtual Murder 1. Shannon Gilligan; Creative Multimedia Corporation, 1993.

The Magic Death: Virtual Murder 2. Shannon Gilligan; Creative Multimedia Corporation, 1993.

Who Killed Brett Penance? The Environmental Surfer: Murder Mystery 3. Shannon Gilligan; Creative Multimedia Corporation, 1995.

Who Killed Taylor French? The Case of the Undressed Reporter: Murder Mystery 4. Shannon Gilligan; Creative Multimedia Corporation, 1995.

The Pixel/The Line

Most text that appears on computer screens acts little different from text on paper. It sits on a virtual "page," perhaps reflowing if the page's dimensions are altered. It goes away if we "scroll" beyond it, or if we perform one of the established analogues for page-turning (usually a button-click of some sort). More exotically, our mouse clicks may animate screen text, or we may select pages by typing commands rather than pressing buttons.

This paperlike behavior calls into question claims for electronic writing's newness. Although it is a commonplace to say that electronic writing can exhibit structures and processes that could not plausibly be expressed in traditional media, the pagelike structure of most electronic texts still provokes neophytes into asking, "How is this different from a choose-your-own-adventure book?" And when selections of electronic text are constructed "on the fly" from smaller bits of text, we still might ask, "How is this different from 'A Hundred Thousand Billion Poems'?"[1]

The three artist/theorists presented in this section take our conceptions of textual interaction further. In their work, and in the work by others described herein, text is presented in manners impossible to sensibly understand through the metaphor of the page. Here texts (sentences, words, even letters) alter algorithmically over time. Here our whole bodies engage with texts that take interaction beyond "one finger and one eye." An argument is made that the combinatory possibilities of language — of the "literal" — provide more appropriate guidance for work with digital media objects than the ascendant "image."

In the environments described by these essayists, writing has become very different from most previous electronic writing. As noted above, the atomic unit is no longer the paragraph or the line, but the word or letter. Writing becomes as much about the design of the interaction and textual recombination processes (which will determine the units that appear, and what relation they have to the reader's body) as it is about the composition of the units fed into the system.

Yet it might be argued that these systems represent no more than an extension of the approach of "A Hundred Thousand Billion Poems" — moving beyond the combinatory possibilities of paperspace to video pixels and simple computation. This may be — but this is a significant movement, and its consequences are only beginning to be explored.

1. "A Hundred Thousand Billion Poems" is the text with which Raymond Queneau and François Le Lionnais founded the Oulipo in the early 1960s. It consists of ten printed sonnets: beginning with the first line of any sonnet, one may choose the second line of any of the ten sonnets, and so with the third, and on through the 14th — yielding 10^{14} poems. Today the Oulipo continues its investigation of new structures and frameworks for writing.

207

Reference

Queneau, Raymond (translated by Stanley Chapman) (1961). "100,000,000,000,000 Poems." In *Oulipo Compendium*, edited by Harry Mathews and Alastair Brotchie. London: Atlas Press. Original French text: *Cent Mille Milliards de poèmes* (1961). Paris: Gallimard.

Literal Art: Neither Lines nor Pixels but Letters

John Cayley

"The Pixel/The Line" was our rubric, a constructive irritant for the statement that follows. It implies, for me, an "and/or," a contrast/linkage, a characteristically

empty	mountain	not	see	human
but	hear	human	language	echo
returning	light	enter	deep	wood
again	shine	green	moss	on

17.sidebar.1. The sequence 'empty2alone' shows the successive stages of a transliteral morph from a word-for-character English translation of a classical Chinese quatrain by Wang Wei to a free adaptation of the same poem by myself.

problematic relationship between graphic art and what I now call literal art. Moreover, since "line" is ambiguous, and "pixel" less so, it inclines toward an equally characteristic and underlying assumption that graphic art is predominant in certain contexts, including this context, that of digital cultural production.[1]

"Pixel" is unambiguously associated with digital graphics. Moreover, on the terminal screens of digital media, pixels are used to build up the images of letters. The "atoms" of one system of digital transcription — graphics — provide, in this context, a preferred delivery medium for the atoms of another — writing. But apart from what is perhaps yet another opportunity for graphic art to patronise applied grammatology, it is not usually understood that there is any great significance or affect that accrues from this "BIOS-level" process of programmatological generation. After all, do constraints that are imposed on the manipulation of pixels in order that they produce the outlines of letters tell us anything about those letters or the words which they, in turn, compose?

Now contrast/link certain circumstances pertaining to the line. Lines may also, of course, be graphic elements; yet here, I assume, we are reading them as "lines" as in "lines of text" or "lines of verse": conventional units of writing, with delineated and

Response by Johanna Drucker

Blindness about the bases on which the daily operations of communication work is necessary to the efficacy of communication itself. If we stopped to consider every letter for its formal properties, every sound uttered for its material form, and every line of every bit of writing for its dimensions, its length, stretch, reach, or grace — then the instrumental effectiveness by which a message gets across would be compromised. We might fall into endless trance states hypnotized by serifs, caught in a face-to-face exchange with the engaging features of our fonts. We don't, for the most part, unless the obvious is called to our attention, even really bother to notice the many material codes that inscribe each language act (written

but also verbal) with its specifics and particularities.

John Cayley knows all this very well, and in this dense, suggestive, perhaps slightly too laconic essay — and even more in the seductively beautiful work of his poetic practice — he shows us constantly that the rewards of paying attention are well worth the effort expended in the task.

To what extent does digitization affect poetics? And how? To answer this question, as well as its wonderful counterpart — How do poetics affect digitization? — he takes the technological basis of digital technology, the binaristic capacity of an electronic signal to be identified within a system of discrete differences, and reads it in relation to the meaning of letters and lines. He examines the "contrast and linkage" between pixels

The Pixel/The Line >Cayley
Utterback
Seaman

Drucker Montfort
Gorbet Wortzel
Gromala Walker

VI. The Pixel/The Line

potentially elaborated sense. A line is a string of letters, and letters are the "atoms" of textual materiality. Letters build words and lines in a manner that allows far greater significance and affect to emerge from modulation in processes of compositional or programmatological generation. By this I mean simply that the way my algorithms and I string letters together to make words and lines generates significance and affect far more quickly and with far greater cultural moment than the way my algorithms and I string pixels together. Like the difference between *changing the style of your font* and chngng th wy y spll or chaynjing thuh way u spehl.

Even this minute example reveals what I believe are profound differences in the way that our culture treats pixel and line. Note that rearranging the pixels of the words above engages considerations which are aesthetic and paratextual, matters of style, taste, mode, and so forth. all of which are undeniably meaningful and inalienably linked to the overall significance of, in this case, a phrase, a line, a fragmentary cultural object: *changing the style of your font.*

By contrast, even rule-governed manipulations of letters in a cultural object of similar form, "size" and "weight," immediately evoke notions of legibility, error, and appropriateness; and any aesthetic effects of this literal programming may be stunned by these considerations, which are, as I suggest, of greater cultural moment.[2]

Paradoxically, or perhaps for these very reasons, the programmatological and, specifically, algorithmic manipulation of pixels — to generate or modulate images as such (including the images of letters) — is undertaken with a far better grasp of the significance of such manipulation.[3] We all know, for example, what is suggested by algorithmic "blurring" as applied to an image, including the image of a word — it doesn't change the word, it

and algorithmical basis of machine language and the letters and lines of natural language in literal (all puns intended in my comments and his source text) terms. He extends this examination into a level of abstraction, seeing these differences as metaphors and tropes. He uses and critiques Frederick Kittler's work on technologies of writing and communication, noting Kittler's tendency to reductionist generalization. And he suggests that ultimately a reading of machines, technologies of production, and formal properties of communicative systems is limited if it doesn't position itself within lived, cultural contexts.

Some questions remain to be posed: How can we read the materiality of binarism (electronic technology IS deeply materialist) — rather than reduce it to mere difference? How do the properties of analog systems persist within the digital domain, not in opposition, but as an aspect of communicative systems? (Here we might consider the work of Donald Knuth as written about by Douglas Hofstadter [1985], in an approach

```
enpty              not    see     human
       moudtain
but        hear   humen   ladguageecho

redurninj  light enter e  deep    wood
       e      e         e
    agaid    shide green    moss      on

         e
       e
           e
```

```
anpty               not see      honen

but      mohearingumen    ladguaecho

redurninj  lighemterea  deep     wood
       a  a    t   a
     agaid     shide jreen    moss      on

       a       e
       a
           a
```

```
adpty             nosaa     honed

but       hear gumen      latgecho
       souddain
redulnanv  liemterai deep     wood
    i ti   d   i
    ajait     shitevreen    moss      on

     ti     a
      i
          i
```

```
adfty          sai     goned

but       hearjumen     laechowe

       soutdaan
redulnanw  light
     o do    nestelio deep     wood
    avait     shi ereen    moss      on

      do  e    i
       o
           o
```

```
atsty          saiot  joned
                e
but      heavumen       echooare


    lenulnadralight
     eu nu   ef alou deep     wood
     iwai     fhieeeen    moss      on
     e
     nu   a    o
      u
           u
```

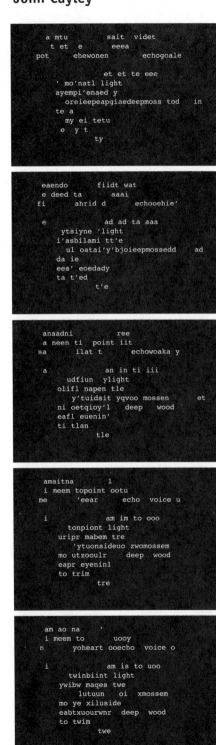

"softens" it, or whatever.[4] With text, there is as yet no accepted repertoire of algorithmic manipulations from, for example, letter to word to line. An important task for writing in programmable media is to address these difficulties and disjunctions. Interaction with text must be founded on its specific materiality, on literal art.[5]

The world of letters has played a crucial role in the development of digital art and culture. Text is indeed "the web's primary and foundational media"[6] and the artists of text are poets. At first "poetic" does not seem promising as a preferred characterisation for a literary or literal art practice that shares in the critical challenges presented by so-called new media. Poets and their poems are the old "geniuses" and "masters" of both Enlightenment and Romance, not to mention High Modernism. But as a matter of recent historical fact, from Mallarmé's "Un Coup de Des" to Jim Rosenberg's "Intergrams" or Brian Kim Stefans' "The Dream Life of Letters," it is in the field of poetry and poetics that we have seen the most consistent and radical critical engagement with literal art. This argues that, in verbal art, if you wish to pursue a practice that might ally with that of contemporary digital art, then you would be wise to take a lead, or at the very least some cognisance, of contemporary poetics. However, I am making a stronger case, suggesting that poetics provides a preferred and even paradigmatic underlying or critical framework for what is currently called digital art, digital cultural production.

•

Literal rather than digital art. Poetic practice informed by the materiality of language has greater power to articulate cultural production than ill-defined digital practice.

quite different from that of Kittler, an approach more deeply embedded within praxis, rather than invented at the distance of theory. My own dissatisfaction with Kittler always comes back to a suspicion that he doesn't really know the tools and practices he writes about, that in fact the problem with his work is precisely that he writes ABOUT technologies of production, not in an intimate, hands-on engagement with them — and I wonder what Cayley thinks about this.) How do we insist on the value of the dialogue between poetics and new technology by asking what the disambiguating demands of computational method require of our poetics — and what poetics may suggest as an affective force in return?

From Nick Montfort's Online Response

Literature certainly shares, as Cayley writes, the "defining qualities of the digital."[1] But although literary production may lead the way for computer art due to its early experience with discrete manipulations, number also

I want to call attention to the bald abstraction and inadequate definition of the term "digital." In general usage, the contrasting "literal" is a fairly flat term, associated either with letters themselves or with minimal, straightforwardly lexical relationships between linguistic signs and their potential significance.[7] By contrast, "digital" seems, shall we say, far more exciting and diverse. Why so? At best, in its literal sense, it pretends to point to the materiality of the media it addresses. In practice, it is usually a placeholder, a way of bringing together a diverse range of work, and then lending that work a gloss of novelty and innovation which is more often an accident of association with the hardware and systems on which the work is played out.

In *The Digital Dialectic*, edited by Peter Lunenfeld (1999), there is, of course, a more concerted attempt to define the digital, in digital systems that "do not use continuously variable representational relationships. Instead, they translate all input into binary structures of 0s and 1s, which can then be stored, transferred, or manipulated at the level of numbers. . ." (Lunenfeld 1999, xv). He then relates this to certain qualities of production in digital culture, exemplified through a contrast with analog photography: the digital is "stepped" (because of pixels) and "crisp." He somewhat fudges the relationship of digital to the overarching project of "new media."

For him the latter term is the placeholder struggling for its paradigm-position with "postmodernism" and others. In terms of media discourse analysis, the telling point in his extended definition is a necessary statement of what seems obvious: "As all manner of representational systems are recast as digital information, they can all be stored, accessed, and controlled *by the same equipment*" (Lunenfeld 1999, xvi [my emphasis]). This is manifestly now the case. All of the recording technologies

provides an intrinsic, not accidental or historical, way of representing text on our mathematically architected computers. Furthermore, even the digit is not the true basis of software. It is "true" and "false," not 0 and 1, that are the fundamental abstractions of computing. Claude Shannon's (1938) joining of Boolean algebra and voltage difference enabled digital computing. So the computer is essentially a logical device upon which arithmetical and then textual symbol-manipulations are implemented; although logical and arithmetical cultural production has been slim,[2] it should be recognized that letters rely on digits and digits on truth-values. I am not suggesting that logic or arithmetic, rather than poetics, will provide a framework for digital art. Rather, I hope the development of a poetic framework will consider the letter's place in computing.

Because letters are built into words to provide great powers of abstraction, they have, following the development of the compiler by Grace Murray Hopper (1952) and others, enabled today's high-level programming

```
am auene  y
i meem to        you'
d     upohearouecho     voice i

i            am is to uou
     tvinqiant light
    'viqv mazes tve
         rotuyn   ia   mosses
   mo 'e cilyside
   eatcyouuvinw  deep wood
   to tvis
              · tve
```

```
am  dyanu
i seom to       youl
t       olhearecho     voice a
     point out
i           as if to you
     tjeanzient light
    ljizj maxes tje
         ritu'n  ae  mossesl
   so le
     eazj erkil'side
     ttk'ouvj       deep wood
         tje
```

```
am  a'one
i seim to      your
        orheecho        voice e
   point out
i           as if to you
     tgeanxient light
   rgixg maces tge
         ratuln  e   mosseslor
   so re
   eaxg ewhillside
   tthloujg        deep wood
         tge
```

```
am i alone
i seem to hear your voice
        or echo

i point out  as if to you
     the ancient light
     which makes the mosses glow

     so we return
     each evening
     to this hillside
     through the deep wood
```

```
Am I alone?
I seem to hear your voice ...
     - or echo?

I point out, as if to you,
     the ancient light
     which makes the mosses glow.

     So we return
     each evening
     to this hillside
     through the deep wood.
```

```
am i alone
i seem to hear your voice
        or echo

i point out  as if to you
      the ancient light
     which makes the mosses glow

     so we return
     each evening
     to this hillside
     through the deep wood
```

```
am  a'one
i seim to      your
      orheecho       voice e
point out
i             as if to you
    tgeanxient light
  rgixg maces tge
         ratuln  e    mosseslor
  so re
  eaxg ewhillside
  tthloujg     deep wood
        tge
```

```
am  ayanu
i seom to      youl
t     olhearecho     voice a
    point out
i             as if to you
    tjeanzient light
  ljizj maxes tje
        ritu'n ae  mossesl
  so le
  eazj erkil'side
  ttk'ouvj      deep wood
        tje
```

```
am auene y
i meem to      you'
d    upohearouecho    voice i

i          am is to uou
    tvinqiant light
  'viqv mazes tve
       rotuyn  ia   mosses
  mo 'e cilyside
  eatcyouwvinw  deep wood
  to tvis
        tve
```

```
am ao na     '
i meem to      uooy
n     yoheart ooecho  voice o

i          am is to uoo
    twinbiint light
  ywibw maqes twe
       lutuun  oi  xmossem
  mo ye xiluside
  eabtxuourwnr  deep  wood
  to twim
        twe
```

discovered and developed since the late 19th century are digitized and therefore mutually transparent at the level of 0s and 1s. But what does this tell us about the *qualities* rather than the *facilities* of digital media?

I have proposed an alternate and more critically-theoretical generative definition of the digital. For me digital characterises any system of transcription with a finite set of agreed identities as its elements.[8] It follows that such a system allows: (1) programmatological manipulation of its constitutive elements (without any threat to their integrity); (2) invisible or seamless editing of cultural objects composed from these elements; and (3) what we now call digital ("perfect") reproduction of such objects.[9]

The point to make here is that literary cultural production in its material manifestation as writing has always already shared these defining qualities of the digital.[10] Although what I call programmatological manipulation of the elements of writing's "digital" system has not often been self-consciously practised prior to the advent of our so-called "digital" age, it was a fully realised potential, as is demonstrated by the existence of, among other things, the *Yi Jing* (or Chinese *Book of Changes*), pattern poetry, acrostics, early universal language systems, the endeavors of the OuLiPo, the language of Joyce in *Ulysses* and *Finnegans Wake*, the work of Emmett Williams, Jackson Mac Low, John Cage, etc. While all poetic writing might properly be seen as characterised by programmatological manipulation of literal materiality, in practice, especially since the Enlightenment and in the West, poeticising has been received as an inspired flow of organic lines recited from voices of genius. It is, rather, an alternative, radically formal tradition of letters projected from Mallarmé, through Dada into the currency of total syntax and post-Concrete visual poetry which nurtures

languages and operating systems — the great-great grandchildren of alphabetization, which first applied an algorithm to letters. Programming languages are used to create software, including pixel-manipulating software. This too is no accident but follows from language's suitability for creating complex algorithms in general, not only when the data to be manipulated is textual. Those graphical programming environments that exist were themselves all ultimately created with textual programming languages.

http://www.electronicbookreview.com/thread/firstperson/montfortr1

programmatological literal art, linking to practitioners in so-called new media: Jim Rosenberg, myself, Brian Stefans, Paul Chan, and an increasing number of poetic practitioners gaining access to new tools.

On the other hand, seamless editing and digital reproduction has been an intrinsic and necessary part of literary culture throughout the entire history of writing, which, as a point of fact, depends (as does speech and all language activity) on "digital" reproduction: the eye must distinguish letters, bracket their accidents and recognise them as identities; the ear does the same with phonemes. Although print technology plays an important role in establishing and propagating these identities and the qualities they carry, please note that these "digital" qualities of writing are already present and persistent in *any* language technology. "Rose is a rose is a rose," no matter how or where or on what it is written or spoken. The materiality of language establishes a poetic institution on the basis of this exchange.

It follows that the so-called digitization of literary phenomena is trivial and that "digital" is a redundant term (in cultural studies at least). It is used for media that would be better characterised as "literal."

This may present itself as a ironic circumstance. I may appear to be proposing that we apply critical tools and criteria from a world of relatively conservative cultural authority, from print culture, from alphabetic minds, and attempting to use them to overdetermine our brave new world of networked and programmable media. However, it should be clear from what I've said so far that I am concerned with addressing the materiality of the media in question, rather than higher-order critical/theoretical structures. I'm trying, as it were, to turn our attention from lines of verse to the letters of literal art and to place the latter in a significant constructive

Cayley Responds

For writers — both in traditional and in networked and programmable media — the problem remains as to why literal abstraction in the context of language art does not have the same cultural sway as, for example, the varieties of abstraction which are familiar to a wide range of viewers and listeners from visual, musical and now new media art. I take this problem to be implicated in the rise of a "digital art" and "new media" practice that ignores or denies its own implicit poetics.

http://www.electronicbookreview.com/thread/firstperson/cayleyr2

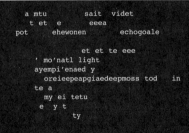

```
    adfty          sai     goned

but      hearjumen      laechowe

       soutdaan        .
 redulnanw  light
   o  do   nestelio deep    wood
  avait    shi ereen   moss    on

     do  e    i
        o

           o
```

```
 adpty .           nosaa     honed

but       hear gumen      latgecho
        souddain         .
                         o
  redulnanv  liemterai deep   wood
    i ti    d     i
   ajait    shitevreen    moss    on

      ti      a
     i
            i            o
  .
          o
```

```
 anpty           not see     honen

but     mohearingumen     ladquaecho
                             o

  redurninj  lighemterea deep   wood
    a   a    t   a
    agaid     shide jreen   moss    on

      a        e
     a
          a
                          .
```

```
 enpty           not  see    human
     moudtain
but      hear   humen    ladguageecho

 redurninj light enter e  deep    wood
    e  e        e
   agaid     shide   green   moss  .  on

      e
   .       e
           e
  o                      .
          o
```

```
empty    mountain   not  . see    human

but     hear    human language  echo

returning light   enter     deep     wood

again    shine    green    moss    on
```

relationship with the pixels of digital graphic art. My argument is that the material manipulation of pixels derives, culturally, from an underlying gasp of the manipulation of letters.

If the materiality of new media is indeed such a familiar and interiorized literal structure, then what is new about it? The answer to this is fairly clear to me. (1) There is genuine historical novelty and cultural innovation which emerges as a function of the discovery and development — at the end of the 19th century — of light and sound recording technologies. (2) More recently, in a related history that is still in train, we have, progressively, the ability to store, edit, manipulate and reproduce the material of art and culture in any and all of the recording and broadcast media available to us *on the same equipment*.

•

> There is no software.
> — Friedrich A. Kittler (1997)

> . . . the unacknowledged programmers of the real . . .

Friedrich A. Kittler (1990, 1999) and other media discourse analysts have suggested that culture may proceed by recasting or downplaying the materiality of language, and reprogramming its agents and subjects in terms of specific technologies and institutions. Such analyses, for example, "flesh out" the deconstruction of print culture as an expression of Romantic logocentrism. Following on from Foucault (1972), mixing in Lacan, and with passing critical acknowledgement of Derrida, Kittler provides us with documentary media history and sophisticated analyses in which, for example, the problematic of the voice and authority of the poet and (great) writer is engaged with media history: McLuhan with all of the advantages of poststructuralism and poststructuralist psychoanalysis.

As such, Kittler shares (with me, for one) in the project of unravelling the (male) mastery of poetic genius. For Kittler, the "age of print" — epitomized for this East German intellectual as the age of Goethe — was (and to an extent still is) a period when, ironically, technologies of writing achieved what he and others see as a perfected, transparent "alphabetisation," which then recited or ventriloquized the concepts of authorship, originality, individuality, intellectual "property," and (male) artistic and intellectual mastery.[11] My first problem with Kittler's analyses arises here. "Alphabetisation" is used paradoxically, and as an abuse term to indicate its opposite. In itself, the term unambiguously refers to the materiality of writing, to a popular conception of writing's constituent structures. However Kittler uses it to refer to a system of inscription (his discourse of 1800) in which this alphabetic materiality has been recast and

The Pixel/The Line >Cayley   Drucker Montfort
  Utterback Gorbet Wortzel
  Seaman Gromala Walker

VI. The Pixel/The Line

downplayed by the institution of the poet's voice. The discrete literal entities of the alphabet have been successfully recited as a "smooth and continuous [analog] flow of personality."[12]

Kittler identifies the moment of radical reconfiguration of the discourse network with the moment of discovery and development of new recording technologies: photography (little discussed), gramophone, film. Undoubtedly it was a crucial moment, a moment "When Old Technologies were New," and surely the jury must still be out over the questions of the significance of this or that technological innovation.[13] However, Kittler allows us to see that it is highly likely that the initial possibilities of: (1) recording and organizing the culture of sound; or of (2) recording and organizing the culture of light; or (3) recording and organizing, as it were, the culture of human time, will prove to be far more significant than the more recent discovery and development of programmable and networked symbol-processing machines. The role of the latter is recast as speed, convenience, manipulation and logistics (and perhaps the final emergence of posthuman culture), whereas the former technologies of 1900 radically altered the phenomenology and practice of so-called human culture.

In the world of language and letters, Kittler (1999) also discovers new writing machines, typified by the typewriter, of which computers are a sort of special case.[14] However, whereas the recording technologies of sound and light lead to entirely new relations with the Real and the Imaginary, the typewriter seems merely to continue to recast or downplay the Symbolic and its materiality, at best further dismantling the voice of the poet by exchanging adoring female recitalists for controlled and controlling machinic female typists.[15] Momentarily, in media history, in *verbal* art and culture, the materiality of the Symbolic is reasserted, but most clearly for Kittler this is as *non*sense, the irrationality of arbitrary alphabetic transcription: Dada. For him, the media of symbolic manipulation, the typewriter/computer, including, perhaps, all programming, all software, is about to become machine and machine only: "the symbolic has, through

17.sidebar.2. 'flesh' is what I call a transliteral register (playing on 'registration' in printing). the successive phases of transliteral morphs from the word 'incarnate' to the words 'to,' 'make,' and 'flesh' are overlayed, then the source words, slightly misregistered, are set in white over the ensuing mass of black letter shapes. 'flesh' was produced for the exhibtion 'Resolute' at the Platform Gallery, London, 1 January, 2000. 'flesh' was a new year's resolution.

Enigma and COLOSSUS, become a world of the machine." (Kittler 1999, 262)

Yet it is hard to see how digitisation — by which I mean the digital transcription of any and all recorded data, sampled from the real — will fit into this current media discourse analysis, Kittler's discourse of 2000. In more than one controversial essay, Kittler seems to show himself as a sort of hardcore reductionist, whose "so-called man" cannot be distinguished from machines that record, store, transfer and process, all with "no software" in the sense that, in the last analysis, there is nothing but "signifiers of voltage differences." "When meanings come down to sentences, and sentences to words, and words to letters, there is no software at all. Rather there would be no software if computer systems were not surrounded by an environment of everyday languages." (Kittler 1997, 150)

I have spent a good deal of time on Kittler not only because I believe that his arguments and contributions require attention, but also because I believe he provides us with one of the most sophisticated arguments explaining the most recent recasting and downplaying of the materiality of language, the subordination of line to pixel, in the context of so-called digital art and culture. How can one justify an engagement with

215

verbal art, with language, when symbolic manipulation may be indistinguishable from the machinic symbolic? It's far too tempting for workers in sound and light to adopt this supposition or to proceed with their work on its basis, in a hypercool posthuman irrational.

Of course, Kittler is concerned not only with media history but questions (after Foucault, 1972) of what, as such, a symbolic system is. If a symbolic system can be a softwareless "so-called man"-less machine, then that is a very significant conclusion. But it is unhelpful to a pragmatics of artistic production. Kittler's statement that there "*would be* no software if computer systems were not surrounded by an environment of everyday languages," (my emphasis) is crucial and telling. They are so surrounded. It is impossible to so-called-humanly conceive of them otherwise, and to work with, against and amongst them. Not only that, but all the other media, of sound and light, are inside them, or *using the same equipment* (in more so-called human terms). Under these conditions, we cannot bracket or stun the materiality of language, the materiality of the symbolic, especially since it is our primary interface to the machine, for more than just historical or contingent reasons. The alternative is to abandon rich literal abstraction for the machinic banal or the machinic unconscious or the machinic real.

Linemakers, poets and writers generally, have long lost all claims to a mastery loaned to them by so-called print culture, by the discourse network of 1800. They must once again serve the literal matter of language, and as such they must serve the machine: typewriter, word processor, programmaton. Its *literal* symbolic materiality should, in turn, be recognised as intrinsically and necessarily, not only historically or momentarily, engaged with the entire gamut of cultural production that emerges from the generalised, networked use of programmable machines. So long as we talk and write over the heads of COLOSSUS, an appreciation of literal art in this sense will enable a more significant and affective analysis of culture than that now accruing from screen-grazing pixelated transcriptions of sound and light in terms of a banal and minimally articulated abstraction: the 0/1 digital.

Cayley Notes

This contribution has been adapted from a paper presentation given at the Digital Arts and Culture Conference 2001, Brown University, Providence RI, 26 April 2001.

1. Graphic art in this context and others allows a continuity with visual art, fine art, and even conceptual and performance art; the relationship of verbal or literal art to these other practices remains problematic.

2. In case the rules are not obvious, they are: (1) spell without vowels and (2) folk-phonetic, or popular-language-guide spelling.

3. Because it is less directly engaged with signification; more a matter of inflecting acts of signification (although necessarily in a meaningful way).

4. Of course, in discussions of rhetoric there is explicit appreciation of language tropes similar to "blurring," for example. In fact, my "or whatever" here is a minute but effective blurring filter.

5. For the materiality of language, of the symbolic, as it is here invoked, I recommend returning to Michel Foucault (1972), *The Archaeology of Knowledge*. Foucault is here working towards a definition of the statement in discourse and, while so doing, he makes clear the necessary difficulties and paradoxes of the materiality of language. Rejecting as its ground both any ideal underlying the statement, and the material of media that delivers statements, he characterises this substance as a "repeatable materiality," one that depends on "possibilities of reinscription and transcription." "The statement cannot be identified with a fragment of matter; but its identity varies with a complex set of material institutions." In a sense the materiality of language arises from the fact of its being *treated as* an object that we "produce, manipulate, use, transform, exchange, combine, decompose and recompose and possibly destroy." I would paraphrase this by saying that the materiality of language is a function of its programmability.

6. From Noah Wardrip-Fruin's introductory remarks to SIGGRAPH 2001, panel AG1000, "The Pixel/The Line: Approaches to interactive text."

7. Note that this is precisely what is disrupted by the rule-governed and entirely construable manipulation of letter arrangements in the tiny example above.

8. More fundamental elements in such a system may of course combine into larger entities and thus generate hierarchies of lower- and higher-order sets of composite elements.

9. You can make a simple test to decide if you are dealing with digital system. Can you perform any of the above three operations? Are you sure that you are dealing with a system composed of quanta? Compare also the fundamental operations of storage, transfer and (conditional) processing in psychoanalytic thinking.

10. See also John Cayley (1998), "Of Programmatology."

11. See especially the chapters "The Mother's Mouth" and "Language Channels" in Kittler, *Discourse Networks*. I am necessarily simplifying complex and rich arguments, which show how—in the discourse network of 1800—the (maternal) voice reconfigured

writing in a process Kittler calls 'alphabetisation,' concealing, for example, its literal, combinatorial materiality. "The Mother's Mouth thus freed children from books. Her voice substituted sounds for letters . . . The educational goal of children in reading is to speak out the written discourses of others . . . Lacan's definition of Woman exactly fits . . . She doesn't speak, she makes others speak." Kittler, *Discourse Networks* 34–35. "The Mother, or source of all discourse, was at the same time into which everything written vanished, only to emerge as pure Spirit and Voice." Kittler, *Discourse Networks* 54.

12. I owe this formulation to the translators' introduction in Friedrich A. Kittler (trans. Geoffrey Winthrop-Young and Michael Wutz), *Gramophone, Film, Typewriter* (Kittler 1999, xxii).

13. The reference is to Carolyn Marvin (1988), *When Old Technologies Were New: Thinking About Electric Communication in the Late Nineteenth Century*.

14. Kittler, 1990. See especially the relevant section pp. 183-263.

15. These are, of course, Lacan's terms which, to grossly simplify, Kittler aligns with media as such: gramophone and the Real, film and the Imaginary, typewriter and the Symbolic. There are rich arguments and lines of thinking here, far beyond the scope of this paper.

Montfort Notes

1. I have registered my agreement on this point already: "a text is a number with typesetting symbols as digits, so it is digital" (Montfort 1995).

2. I do not consider literary work that involves logic, as exemplified by Lewis Carroll's work, to be "logical cultural production," but certain mathematical recreations do count as arithmetical cultural production. John Conway's *Game of Life* is a fine example. It was a direct influence on *SimCity* and the genre of games that followed it.

References

Cayley, John (1998). "Of Programmatology." *Mute* (Fall 1998)": 72-75.

Foucault, Michel (edited by R.D. Laing) (1972). *The Archaeology of Knowledge*. London: Tavistock.

Hofstadter, Douglas R. (1985). *Metamagical Themas: Questing for the Essence of Mind and Pattern*. New York: Basic Books.

Hopper, Grace Murray (1952). "The Education of a Computer." In Proceedings of the Association for Computing Machinery Conference, Pittsburgh, PA. Reprinted in *Annals of the History of Computing* 9, nos. 3-4 (1988): 271.

Kittler, Friedrich A. (1990). *Discourse Networks 1800/1900*. Stanford: Stanford University Press.

Kittler, Friedrich A. (edited by John Johnston (1997). *Literature Media Information Systems: Critical Voices in Art, Theory and Culture*. Amsteldijk: G+B Arts International.

Kittler, Friedrich A. (translated by Geoffrey Winthrop-Young and Michael Wutz) (1999). *Gramophone, Film, Typewriter*. Stanford: Stanford University Press.

Lunenfeld, Peter (editor) (1999). *The Digital Dialectic: New Essays on New Media*. Cambridge: The MIT Press.

Marvin, Carolyn (1988). *When Old Technologies Were New: Thinking About Electric Communication in the Late Nineteenth Century*. Oxford: Oxford University Press.

Montfort, Nick (1995). "Interfacing with Computer Narratives: Literary Possibilities for Interactive Fiction." B.A. Thesis, University of Texas at Austin. <http://www.nickm.com/writing/bathesis/>.

Shannon, Claude (1938). "A Symbolic Analysis of Relay and Switching Circuits." *American Institute of Electrical Engineers* 57 (1938): 713-723.

Unusual Positions — Embodied Interaction with Symbolic Spaces
Camille Utterback

All forms of "interactive text" demand a physical body with which to interact. When we use the now-common interface that consists of a mouse and keyboard as input devices, and the computer screen as display mechanism, it is easy to forget the body whose eyes perceive the screen, and whose hands and fingers manipulate the mouse and keyboard. In her book *How We Became Posthuman*, N. Katherine Hayles (1999) has eloquently explored how "information lost its body." Hayles investigates the theoretical, historical, and literary maneuvers through which modern society has dissociated information from a body or medium. The consequent elevation of abstraction over embodiment is mirrored by a corresponding lack of computer interfaces that meaningfully engage our bodies with the information and codes represented in our machines. The degree to which our physical

interactions with machines is impoverished is illustrated by a common saying in the university department where I teach. The saying describes the "human-computer interface" from the computer's point of view — "when the computer stares back at you, it sees you as one eye and one finger."[1]

With much of my artwork — in both traditional and digital media — I have attempted to draw attention to the connections between human bodies and the symbolic systems our bodies engage with. The digital medium interests me because it is a perfect site to explore the interface between physical bodies and various representational systems, be they language, the linear perspective used in three-dimensional rendering, or the various forms of computer code itself. In my digital works my strategy for this exploration has been to develop interfaces that honor and engage more of the body than just "one eye and one finger." Interfaces, by providing the connective tissue between our bodies and the codes represented in our machines, necessarily engage them both. How and to what extent new interfaces may engage the body, however, is up for grabs.

Practical interfaces are about maintaining the user's sense of control. In this scenario representations on screen must respond to the user in a logical and predictable way. Artists can explore other possibilities.

218

Response by Matt Gorbet

I share Utterback's excitement about the expressive possibilities offered by the new genre of interactive physical interfaces. Meaningfully engaging the body with information can create experiences that are aesthetically and emotionally much more rewarding than the ubiquitous point-and-click, as Utterback shows. However, I question her definition of a "practical" interface as one that is "about maintaining the user's sense of control" and her implication that the "poetic" interfaces she describes in the text do not necessarily need to maintain this control. I suggest, rather, that the success of the works she presents depends precisely on the sense of control afforded by simple and physically familiar interactions. Given this,

the seemingly simple content of these pieces raises interesting questions about the limits of the genre. What is the depth of content that can be expressed, in view of the apparent interaction constraints of such body-centric work?

Early in her essay, Utterback implies that in building interfaces that are "poetic rather than practical," artists can/should create interactions that do not follow logic or are unpredictable. However, all of the pieces she describes succeed in part because of their familiar and consistent physical interfaces: the forms of a ladder, see-saw, bicycle, and (video) mirror are all immediately perceived and well-understood, so these pieces make sense to their users. Contrary to Utterback's implication, these particular interfaces are indeed

In this essay I discuss interactive works by myself and others that incorporate poetic rather than practical interfaces to text or spoken language. In these text-based pieces, the characters function as legible signs, but also take on their own behaviors and responses to the user. These behaviors do not fit the normal obedient role of digital text that is cut, pasted, and clicked. These characters draw attention to themselves through their "misbehavior" as they become active objects, or overstep their bounds in other ingenious ways. Conversely, the pieces that provide unusual interfaces to spoken language question the line between bodies and language by physically putting the user in an unusual "position" with regards to the words. In each case the relationship between the symbolic and the physical is simultaneously thrown into relief and muddled.

In David Small and Tom White's (1997-98) *Stream of Consciousness: An Interactive Poetic Garden* installation, text escapes from the flat screen and spills out into the viewer's physical space (figure 18.1). The installation consists of a garden with rock slabs, plants and water flowing from one level of a multi-tiered fountain to the next. Words and phrases projected down onto the water appear at the top pool of the fountain and swirl and flow with the water as it cascades through the garden, disappearing with the water as it drains out of

18.1. David Small and Tom White's (1997–98) *Stream of Consciousness: An Interactive Poetic Garden*. (Webb Chappell)

219

"about maintaining the users' sense of control." As for the dynamic text in these examples, rather than "misbehaving" as Utterback suggests, the text in each of these pieces follows specific (albeit poetic) rules that are modeled after the physics we know: leaves flowing in a stream, buildings anchored to the roadway, letters falling like snowflakes or raindrops. Because there is no barrier to understanding what is going on, users do maintain control while interacting with the works. It is largely this sense of control that enables the works to impart their meaning; too often, interactive experiences which feature randomness, illogical interactions, or inconsistency result in confused, frustrated visitors who are not able to discern the intent of the piece before moving on to something else. (There are rare

instances, of course, where the artist's intent does involve creating a frustrated user, and these strategies can be very effective for such work.)

Giving the user a sense of control with a simple, body-centric interaction was a primary design goal of another interactive text piece, created by the Research in Experimental Documents group at Xerox PARC. In the context of a museum exhibit on the future of reading (Back, Gold, Balsamo, Chow, Gorbet, Harrison, MacDonald, Minneman, 2001), we designed several installations that engage the body with text and require very little instruction to use. One of the resulting interactive objects is the *Tilty Table* (Xerox 2000) <http://www.theredshift-xfr.com/tilty_tables.html>, a three-foot square surface onto which dynamic text is

the bottom pool. The "physically" modeled behavior of the words produces the convincing illusion that the text is floating on and carried along by the water. The text appears to have entered the viewer's world where forces like gravity and fluid dynamics affect its course. While the text still carries its symbolic weight as words, it also *becomes* the physical objects of leaves or detritus carried along by the water's flow.

The illusion that these characters are somehow objects as well as signs is furthered by one's ability to physically alter the course of the letters as they cascade down the fountain. As viewers press or push their hands on a small pressure-sensitive pad,[2] glowing blue areas appear in corresponding areas of the fountain. The size and shape of the glowing area depends on the size and pressure of your touch. By positioning your "hand" in the path of the letters you can block their flow down the fountain, causing them to swirl in new patterns, and eventually change their meaning as they morph into new words.

The words that Small and White choose to "float" down their fountain hint at the conundrum of the simultaneously virtual, physical, and signifying text in this piece. In one sequence of text the characters are symbols from the periodic table of elements — "Ni," "Ca," etc. These symbols morph into the word for their corresponding element when you stop them

midstream. The boundary between words "standing for" elements that make up the physical world and "standing in" for those elements as a physical object in the fountain is blurred as you push and pull them around in the water, manipulating them with your fingers instead of your mind. The tension between the intangibility of the projected text and its behavior as a tangible object (which you can "touch" via the interface) parallels the tension between the text's position as a signifier for a real object and the real object it represents.

Pressing and sliding one's fingers over the pressure-sensitive pad in this installation provides a more sensual experience than interacting with a mouse, but the interaction is still confined to a relatively narrow channel. The interpenetration between the real and the symbolic in this piece is in fact quite lopsided. While the text seems to have escaped into the physical realm of the fountain almost completely, "you," via the pressure-sensitive pad, are present in the abstract world of these symbols only in the form of a blue glow that changes its position and size.

In *Text Rain*, by myself and Romy Achituv (1999), text again takes on the behaviors of objects that respond to forces in the real world, and also to the physical gestures of viewers (figure 18.2). In *Text Rain* however, the interface of video camera and tracking

18.response.1. *Tilty Table*. (Matt Gorbet)

projected (figure 18.response.1). Visitors can browse the text by gently tilting the surface. The text slides across the surface in response to the tilt, as though it were physically on the table. With this simple interaction, visitors who are new to the exhibit are able to take advantage of their understanding of the physical world to operate the device. As with the interactive pieces Utterback describes, there is very little learning curve, no "right" or "wrong" way to interact, and no instructions need to be given.

Utterback's examples and the *Tilty Table* share another similarity in the nature of the text they present: they employ short forms of text such as poetry, quotations, and symbols. Such texts are effective because they can be quickly grasped and have

The Pixel/The Line > **Utterback**

Cayley
Seaman

Drucker Montfort
Gorbet Wortzel
Gromala Walker

VI. The Pixel/The Line

software allows a viewer's entire body to engage with the text. In the *Text Rain* installation viewers see a mirrored black-and-white video of themselves on a large projection screen. Colored letters in the projection fall down on them from above, like rain or snow. The characters can be caught, lifted, and then let fall again. If a person accumulates enough letters along their outstretched arms, or any other dark object, they can sometimes "catch" an entire word, or even a phrase. The letters are not random, but lines of a poem by Evan Zimroth (1993) about bodies and language.[3]

Similarly to the text in the Poetic Garden, the text here continues to serve its symbolic function as an decipherable code, but also as an "object" viewers can engage with as if it were a real physical entity. In *Stream of Consciousness*, physical interventions cause the text to morph and mutate; in *Text Rain* the physical act of catching letters is necessary in order to read the text at all. The act of reading takes on a physical dimension.

Using a video camera as an input device allows the letters in *Text Rain* to respond to a wide variety of human gestures and motions. There is no "wrong" way to interact with this piece. Because most of one's body is visible in the virtual space of the screen as well as in the physical space in front of the screen, a pleasurable confusion results between the screen space and the real space. Because no complicated apparatus is involved to

18.2 *Text Rain* by Camille Utterback and Romy Achituv (1999).

immediate impact, allowing visitors to start reading anywhere and spend as much or as little time as they like with the piece.

Given these observations about simplicity of interaction and brevity of content, a question presents itself: using a simple, familiar physical interaction which maintains the users' sense of control, how far can the complexity of the content be pushed? Is there a necessary correlation between simple interaction and simple content? Or is it possible to create a body-centric interactive piece with the storytelling capacity of an epic novel or a play? In *Text Rain*, for instance, what would be the appropriate interaction for progressing to a new body of text? How might one "turn the page" or choose a different "chapter"?

This is an issue that we struggled with in the design of the *Tilty Table*, and eventually worked around by building several identical tables with different content on each (a strategy with obvious limitations). Jeffrey Shaw's (1989) bicycle in *The Legible City* (figure 18.4) features a button to select between various cities, which seems like a reasonable concession, but could result in the need for cumbersome instructions and a conceptual separation between "setting up" the piece and actually experiencing it. Of the pieces Utterback describes, perhaps the see-saw has the richest storytelling potential: by presenting the progression of a relationship through two opposing points of view that correspond to the alternating up and down positions of the see-saw, this format can very simply lead the visitor

18.3. *Drawing from Life* by Camille Utterback (2001).

become "immersed" you can easily feel present in both the physical and virtual space simultaneously, or seamlessly shift back and forth between the two.

It is also significant that this interface allows participants to engage not only using their whole bodies, but also with other people's bodies in the installation space. People often cooperate to catch letters — holding hands or stretching coats and scarves

between them. The video interface allows people to be physically engaged with the text, but also to engage with each other while interacting with the text.

In another piece of mine, *Drawing from Life* (2001), the text's behavior is even more tightly coupled to the viewer — it becomes them (figure 18.3). Upon entering the installation space, participants encounter a live video projection of themselves, but their images are completely transformed into the letters "A," "T," "G," and "C" — the letters representing the four proteins of DNA. The letters are color-coded based on the color associated with each protein from computer-analyzed gels scientists use when decoding the genome. The color saturation of any particular letter is based on the brightness of the color in the incoming video, so some amount of detail about each person is visible. It is remarkable how recognizable individuals are even in this abstracted form.

By abstracting live imagery of a viewer's body into the letters that compose DNA, the installation raises questions about our embodiment and the code that is both part of, and helps produce our "selves." As in the previously described installations, here again the boundary between flesh and abstraction is questioned by the content of the interactive text as well as by its behavior.

When viewers recognize that the projected imagery is

through a compelling narrative arc.

All of the works discussed in Utterback's essay create provocatively poetic experiences at the intersection of the body and the symbolic. The physical forms shape the experiences by informing and constraining the interactions. In many ways, the constraints of the pieces described by Utterback are integral to their success and beauty. Like haiku, they have a certain grace and power in their rigid simplicity. If these pieces are the haiku of the genre, how might we go about creating the Homer?

From Adrianne Wortzel's Online Response

Camille Utterback and Romy Achituv's (1999) *Text Rain* is one of my favorite works in the world, in that it acts out the manipulation of text through physical will. In doing so, it not only gives us pleasure but also actualizes the pluralistic significance of words as message, meaning, metaphor, symbol and object. In her writing here, she covers well the story of artists' working with external manipulation by extending ourselves physically. I would like to add some comments on the internalization of these controls by way of attaching computing mechanisms to the body itself and, alternatively, internalizing them.

Stelarc's (1997) performative works are driven by a philosophy that engages the obsolesence of the human

The Pixel/The Line > **Cayley**
Utterback
Seaman

Drucker Montfort
Gorbet Wortzel
Gromala Walker

VI. The Pixel/The Line

a translation of themselves, they "test" the correspondence by moving parts of their body — tilting their head, waving their arms, etc. Once the connection is made, viewers "play" with manipulating their transformed symbolic "self" using their physical body. The ease with which one controls one's video image is comparable to the experience of controlling one's image in a mirror. By distancing this connection through the abstracting of the live image into letters, viewers become more aware of the discrepancy between the abstraction and their bodies. The letters also continually flicker and change between the characters, as if they had a life of their own. Viewers recognize that this abstraction is simultaneously "them" and "not them." The image of DNA characters "stands in" for them, and on some level "stands for" them in the way that genetic code does, and in the way that the letters "stand for" the proteins themselves.

The text in Jeffrey Shaw's (1989) *The Legible City* installation does not respond to user's actions per se, but instead puts the user in the position of acting *within* the space of the text (figure 18.4). *Stream of Consciousness* puts the text into the viewer's physical space. *Text Rain* inserts the viewer's image into a flat abstract space along with the text. *The Legible City* inserts the user's *point of view* via computer-generated linear perspective into a dimensional space made

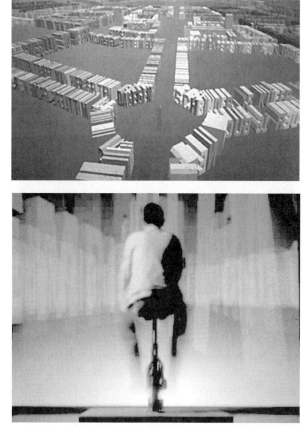

18.4. *The Legible City* by Jeffrey Shaw (1989).

18.response.2. Stelarc's *Exoskeleton*. Cyborg Frictions, Dampfzentrale, Bern, 24 November to 1 December, 1999. (Photo Dominik Landwehr, permission Stelarc)

body and the championing of cyborg development (figure 18.response.2–3). For artists working with extensions of biological functions, in order to express metaphors, they have to work literally, attaching themselves to or ingesting devices. [...]

In *A-positive*, a biobotic work by Eduardo Kac and Ed Bennett (1997), blood was transferred from a human to a robot, dextrose from the robot to the human — man and machine exchanging nutrients in a symbiotic relationship. Alba, the green fluorescent bunny, was created with a synthetic mutation of an existing gene found in a fluorescent jellyfish. Kac describes this work as "a new form of art based on the use of genetic engineering to transfer natural or synthetic genes to an organism, to create unique human beings."

http://www.electronicbookreview.com/thread/firstperson/wortzelr1

entirely of text. In this installation the user sits on a real bicycle and pedals his or her way through a virtual landscape of text. The individual characters of the text in this installation become the architecture. Each letter is monumentally rendered in three dimensions, and takes the place of a building along the city streets of this space. The letters march off into the horizon, defining streets and avenues that correspond to real city maps of New York, Amsterdam, or Karlsruhe, Germany. In two of the cityscapes, the size of each letter in the text actually corresponds to the size of the building it represents. The text from which each city is "created" is also text about that city. The texts vary from contemporary quotes and writing to descriptions of historical events. The *Drawing from Life* installation conflates code with body. In a similar move, *The Legible City* equates descriptions of cities with the city itself.

In *The Legible City*, in order to read the texts stretched along the city streets (similarly to *Text Rain*) one must use one's body. A button on the bicycle interface allows the user to instantaneously switch views between the cities, but to move anywhere within the environment requires real physical exertion. Unlike so many virtual worlds, here distance matters. One's legs are the means of transport, but also an essential part of the equation if one wishes to read. The tension between this symbolic city — both "rendered" by text and virtual —

and the physical exertion required to move through it, is the tension between the material and the abstract that has informed all of the pieces discussed so far.

In Shaw's *The Legible City*, one has the illusion that one's point of view is changing based on the changing imagery on the projection screen. As is often the case with computer interfaces, the viewer sits still while the display simulates motion. Two of my works require that one actually physically change one's point of view to interact with the piece. In the first of these pieces, *Vicissitudes*, a six-foot ladder and a chalk outline on the floor provide the interface for two audio tracks (figure 18.5). One soundtrack consists of interviews of people describing times in their life when they felt "up" or "on top of the world," the other track of times when these same people felt "down" or "low." Climbing the rungs of the ladder raises the volume of the "up" soundtrack, while lying down in the chalk outline raises the volume of the "down" soundtrack. Many of our linguistic constructs rely on physical metaphor, though they have become transparent to us due to their common usage. Through its interface, this piece explores the embodiedness of language itself.

In a recent installation created with Adam Chapman — *See/Saw* — we use a see-saw as the interface to two screens (figure 18.6). One screen is positioned behind each seat of the see-saw across from each other in the

18.response.3. Stelarc's *Handswriting* — writing one word simultaneously with three hands. Maki Gallery, Tokyo, 22 May, 1982. (Photo Keisuke Oki, permission Stelarc)

Utterback Responds

The questions Gorbet's team wrestled with when developing the *Tilty Table* — how to move through content, how to "chose a different chapter" — are important questions when developing a functional form. If one were making art out of a *Tilty Table* however, the question would be instead, what type of emotional content is implied by the tilty-ness of the table, or by the sensation of the text disappearing off the table's edges?

http://www.electronicbookreview.com/thread/firstperson/utterbackr2

The Pixel/The Line >

Cayley
Utterback
Seaman

Drucker Montfort
Gorbet Wortzel
Gromala Walker

VI. The Pixel/The Line

Vicissitudes

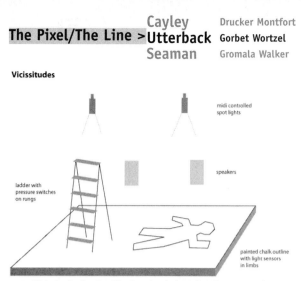

18.5. *Vicissitudes* by Camille Utterback (1998). When a user is completely at the top of the ladder or within the chalk outline, only one soundtrack is audible, but the opposite visual — ladder or outline — is clearly in view. Between either extreme a mix of "up" and "down" is heard. Light levels of spotlights focused on the ladder and chalk outline correspond to the volume levels of the respective soundtracks, providing additional user feedback, and creating a dramatic ambiance.

installation space. As the users operate the see-saw, changing their position from up to down, their motion causes changes in words on the screens behind them. The words or phrases on the opposing screens will always exist in a state of tension or balance corresponding to the dynamic of the people on the see-saw. This installation plays with physical point of view, and the physical relationship of balance and tension between the two users as it relates to language.

Of the pieces described so far in this essay, *Vicissitudes* and *See/Saw* involve the largest-scale motions on the part of the user. While these interfaces engage the viewer's body on a large scale with a symbolic space of language, the language or symbolic space cannot exert a physical force on the viewer. In Orit Kruglanski's (2000) piece *As Much as You Love Me*, the interface allows words to manipulate the user physically as well as emotionally. This interactive poem uses a specially designed force-feedback mouse. As the user uses the mouse to collect icons on the screen she hears the spoken lines of a poem. Each line of the poem is what Kruglanski refers to as a nonapology and starts with the line, "don't forgive me for..." The more nonapologies the user collects and hears, the stronger

18.6. *See/Saw* by Camille Utterback and Adam Chapman (2001).

the magnetic force on the mouse becomes, making it eventually almost impossible for the user to move the mouse. When the last line of the poem is collected ("forgive me this: I can't remember loving you") the force-feedback turns off in a dramatic reversal that mirrors the poem. In Kruglanski's piece the symbolic or emotional weight of words is brought to bear on one's physical freedom of motion. Via the interface of the force-feedback mouse, the symbolic content is viscerally enacted by the interface onto the user's body.

In all the pieces discussed in this essay, the symbolic world of text or language attains presence in the physical world and engagement with viewer's bodies via unusual forms of interface. Creative interfaces that connect our bodies to this digital media allow the line to be transgressed it in new ways. In the Interactive

225

Poetic Garden and *Text Rain*, text becomes objects with seemingly physical properties that the user can engage with using their body. In *Drawing from Life*, characters take the shape of the users' bodies, mirroring their motions and gestures. In *The Legible City*, text forms the architecture one traverses on a physical bicycle. In *Vicissitudes* and *See/Saw*, the body on one side of the interface must "move." In *As Much As You Love Me*, the interface allows the symbolic to reach into the physical world and constrain the user's motions. The flip side of the text's transgression into the physical in these pieces is the manner in which the user's body enters the symbolic space of the texts — as a blue glow, a photographic image, or a point of view. What is at stake in these artistic investigations, more than the creative possibilities for "interactive text," is the position and status of our bodies as they are increasingly represented on screens, or in the virtual space of our machines. As we create new interfaces between our bodies and our symbolic systems we are in a unusual position to rethink and re-embody this relationship.

Notes

1. This saying is originally attributed to Joy Mountford.

2. The pressure-sensitive pad used in this installation has undergone changes through the course of exhibiting the piece. Originally the interface was a liquid-filled bag with a video camera inside that tracked pressure as changes in light. At the installation of the piece in the Ars Electronica Center in Linz, Austria, the liquid bag was replaced by a commercially available pad, which is more responsive and robust.

3. Falling text is excerpted from "Talk, You" by Evan Zimroth, published in *Dead, Dinner, or Naked poems by Evan Zimroth*, TriQuarterly Books, Northwestern University Press, 1993. Used with permission.

226

References

Back, M., R. Gold, A. Balsamo, M. Chow, M. Gorbet, S. Harrison, D. MacDonald, and S. Minneman (2001). "Designing Innovative Reading Experiences for a Museum Exhibition." *IEEE Computer* 34, no. 1 (2001): 80–87.

Hayles, N. Katherine (1999). *How We Became Posthuman*. Chicago: The University of Chicago Press.

Kac, Eduardo (1997). *Time Capsule*. <http://www.ekac.org/timec.html>.

Kac, Eduardo (1997). *A-Positive*. <http://www.ekac.org/apositive.html>.

Kruglanski, Orit (2000). *As Much as You Love Me*. <http://www.ok-centrum.at/ausstellungen/cyberarts00/kruglanski.html>.

Shaw, Jeffrey (1989). *The Legible City*. <http://www.xspace.at/english/shaw.html>.

Small, David and Tom White (1997-98). *Stream of Consciousness: An Interactive Poetic Garden*. <http://acg.media.mit.edu/projects/stream/>.

Stelarc (1997). *Parasite*. <http://www.stelarc.va.com.au/parasite/index.htm>.

Utterback, Camille and Romy Achituv (1999). *Text Rain*. <http://www.camilleutterback.com/textrain.html>.

Utterback, Camille and Adam Chapman (2001). *See/Saw*. <http://www.camilleutterback.com/seesaw.html>.

Utterback, Camille (2001). *Drawing from Life*. <http://www.camilleutterback.com/drawingfromlife.html>.

Xerox PARC (2000). *The Tilty Tables*. <http://www.theredshift-xfr.com/tilty_tables.html>.

Zimroth, Evan (1993). *Dead, Dinner, or Naked*. Evanston, IL: TriQuarterly Books.

Interactive Text and Recombinant Poetics — Media-Element Field Explorations
Bill Seaman

The sensual body finds itself living amidst an expansive set of technologies. In this ever-evolving computational world we encounter texts of varying forms and functionalities — visual, sonic, and code-related. Text may also take physical and/or environmental form. The continuum that bridges distributed bodies with the recombinant communicative and associative functionality of technology is charged with the potential of extending humankind's ability to experience, generate, operate on, store, edit, and disseminate meaningful patterns of experience.[1]

Interwoven with the richness of the workings of our bodies' sensuality, text can not be easily singled out from other media elements or neighboring evocative environmental qualities — nor should it be. Our understanding of text has evolved through a lifelong experience of a cumulative set of environmental patterns. The contemporary mediascape made accessible through the computer takes on an increasing importance in terms of experiencing and coming to know the world. The technologies of the past gave us the power to collect and disseminate specific patterns of usage through letters, words, recordings, and bound volumes. Now, the potential is to address the continuum between the body, the environment and an extended set of language-vehicles that become operative within the highly variable volumes of authored and interauthored physical/computational spaces. Such technological space can also be highly evocative. Charles Sanders Peirce articulates:

> A sign [or representation] stands *for* something *to* the idea which it produces, or modifies. Or, it is a vehicle conveying into the mind something from without. That for which it stands is called its object; that which it conveys, its meaning; and the idea to which it gives rise, its interpretant. (Peirce 1931, 171)

Virtual Worlds and other computer-related media environments have the potential for being authored in such a manner that they can exhibit emergent meaning. These environments can be navigated, and provide

Response by Diane Gromala

Bill Seaman explores the potential of extending our "ability to experience, generate, operate on, store, edit, and disseminate meaningful patterns of experience" through what he terms recombinant poetics. Among other intriguing aspects of his essay, Seaman explores text and extends our understanding of and relationship to text when it becomes interactive, when it can exhibit emergent properties, and when the "body becomes enmeshed experientially." I'd like to explore two major issues of Seaman's essay through four questions concerning text and body. Because my own work is concerned with very similar issues, I will interweave examples in what I hope will prove to be productive engagement with these issues.

First, beginning with text, Seaman seems to refer to it not in the sense of reading for an author's intent, but in the sense of textuality, an open, infinite process that is meaning-generating and subverting. There is much discussion to be had in subsuming "other media elements" and bodily response exclusively within the linguistic domain, but I would like to focus on textual elements of words themselves.

The technological properties of emergence that Seaman alludes to could be a compelling extension of Jacques Derrida's "other" ways of writing and reading, where we take seriously "other" logics of the structure of signification. Akin to Freud's concern with dreams and slips of tongue, Derrida is concerned with the signifying gaps that a standard reading disregards or

evocative forms of experience as well as potentially be modified and/or radically reconfigured. As Peirce suggests, meaning is that which the sign conveys. The volume of virtual space is quantitatively different from that of the bound volume. In terms of text, it has become unhinged — Barthesian[2] anchorage severed (media elements operatively made relative) — flows (Deleuze and Guattari 1987, 21) heightened — potential media-vocabularies enlarged.

In generative virtual environments, meaning is that which the sign conveys in terms of particular media-configurations as well as through the potentials of physical output. Basically this extends the notion that the sign takes on meaning in a particular context — in a generative computer-based environment one can now physically fabricate a new context.

One can witness the advanced potentials of haptics explored by such people as Margaret Minsky[3] as well as the fictional accounts addressed by Stephenson (1995) in *The Diamond Age* — exploring the generative potentials of nanotechnology — where given the appropriate solution environment (with a big nod to Eric Drexler 1986), one can order up furniture, etc. Yet one should take a serious interest in the evocative potentials of both nano-virtual space and that of virtual environments explored through quantum computing. In *Of Grammatology*, Derrida (1977)

describes an extended definition of "writing":

> It is also in this sense that the contemporary biologist speaks of writing and *pro-gram* in relation to the most elementary processes of information within the living cell. And, finally, whether it has essential limits or not, the entire field covered by the cybernetic *program* will be the field of writing.
> (Derrida 1977, 9)

We are teetering at the brink of the development of a physical set of code potentials brought about through nanotechnology,[4] advanced forms of biotechnology,[5] and quantum computing,[6] the ramifications of which one can barely fathom. These new developments explode notions of context. Here, I am particularly interested in the potentials of generative virtual environments functioning in tandem with physical space.[7]

The potential of text, and of code that is currently built of text, is expanding in this era of the physical and the biological, where nature itself is being rethought and redefined. In terms of physical interface, in my textual/musical work "The Poly Field,"[8] I describe a exercise interface that could enable one to move in

represses: discontinuities, contradictions, ambiguities, materiality, silence, space, conflict, margins, and figures. Derrida's concern, of course, relates to parallel concerns in modern and postmodern art. For artists, one instance that can be understood most clearly, perhaps, is in the historical example of Mallarmé's poetry, where the character of the typography and its placement on a page is not transparent to the meaning, but calls attention to itself and to the ways it allows for multiple kinds of readings. Seaman's work with technological emergence, it seems to me, could be a quite compelling part of looking at textuality in this way, because it could make us aware of "other" aspects of text.

My next question concerns an issue of the body. To foreground this question, let me begin by saying that

new technologies undoubtedly do allow us new or at least different ways to "enmesh the body experientially," but they also allow us to overlook the ways in which our cultural practices lead us to repress sensual experience. In my own work in immersive virtual reality (VR), for example, I explored interactive, "immersive" text that was inscribed on surfaces of an MRI of my body. The body itself was of an enormous scale and was the "space" the user was within. The text itself was overtly erotic, and changed as the user "touched" the surfaces of the body.

In VR, the proprioceptive sense of where we are in our bodies, a sense that usually remains under our conscious radar, is easily provoked. I intended to draw upon that sense to disturb and emphasize the more

physical space and do word processing. Currently Ted Krueger is working on an exercise bike[9] to enable astronauts to work and move physically in mixed virtual and physical space (with a nod to Jeffrey Shaw's (1989) *Legible City*). One can also begin to address the poetic spatial relation of text to different positionings of the body, both practical and dance-related. The potential of physical spatial relations to the textual is pivotal — where bodies, entities, objects, sensor data and encoded spatial relations become interoperative is the continuum bridging media-environments with physical environments through sensual interfaces.

Turing's description of the ACE (Automatic Computing Engine) (Turing 1986, 36), the first digital computer, saw the potential for a machine with programmed responsive, "operative" input and output "organs." Yet almost a century before Turing, in her *Notes by The Translator* written to clarify the textual work entitled *Sketch Of the Analytical Engine Invented by Charles Babbage*, Augusta Ada Byron King, the Countess of Lovelace, made some very enlightened remarks:

> The Analytical Engine is an embodying of the science of operations, constructed with particular reference to abstract number as the subject of those operations... Again, it [the Analytical Engine] might act upon

other things beside *number* were objects found whose mutual fundamental relations could be expressed by those of the abstract science of operations and which should be also susceptible of adaptions to the action of the operating notation and mechanism of the engine. Supposing for instance, that the fundamental relations of pitched sounds in the science of harmony and of musical composition were susceptible of such expressions and adaptions, the engine might compose elaborate and scientific pieces of music of any degree of complexity or extent... It may be desirable to explain, that by the word operation, we mean any process which alters the relation of two or more things, be this relation of what kind it may. This is the most general definition and would include all subjects in the universe [this includes text]. (Babbage 1961, 249)

Meaning is now evoked in an environment that potentially implicates multiple senses. We will broaden our potential for knowledge production and exchange by extending our exploration of the biological

sensual relationships we have to text. However, no matter what my artistic claims, it seemed that few users were interested in reading when they could "fly." One might attribute that to the novelty of a VR experience, but I think it also reveals the extent to which we tend to reinscribe the ways we have taught ourself to keep sensual response at bay when it comes to reading. This surely must count as one of Seaman's "meaningful patterns of experience."

To finally arrive at my second question then: how is it that our sensual experience of text is or became less engaging than it could be in the post-Gutenberg print realm, as Roland Barthes (1975) reminded us in *The Pleasure of the Text*? In the print realm, we can and do sensually engage with text, as is most evident with

erotic or pornographic texts. But we are much less aware of the extensive and multiple sensual involvement with other kinds of texts, and have learned not to heed them. We bring this practice into the online realm as well, where we are generally unaware of sensual engagement unless we read overtly erotic texts or we get "flamed." Our sensual distance from text then is both the result of the nature of printed text, as well as the result of the larger cultural and historical practices that involve text, writing, and reading. Although new technologies may provide a momentary opportunity to provoke and create new awareness of sensual response, they do not, in themselves, guarantee that we leave the older cultural practices of disregarding sensual response behind. If

metaphor of bodily relations, learning to parse and become one with multiple streams of machinic sense data. Extended computational environments will also enable us to augment the body in an appurtenant landscape of technological augmentation, enlarging our capacity to produce and experience patterns over time — to come to know. Yet, the complexity and delicacy of the workings of the body will not easily be discarded through the brain-scanning of the mechanisms proposed in a visionary manner by Kurzweil and others. The dangers of such bodily extensions must be continuously reevaluated and articulated in relation to technological change through an ethics of the sensual. An extended discussion of this topic falls outside of the scope of this paper.

Virtual or computational space enables us to explore very new forms of authorship. An expansive distributed set of evocative language-vehicles and computer-based processes become actuated through specified potential interaction or through emergent potentials that arise through use. (See my thesis, where I contrast this notion to Wittgenstein's notion that "the meaning is the use" [Wittgenstein 1958, 20]). Increasingly, one can intentionally reinterpret the potentials of a functionality and thus move outside of the specified programmed probable outcomes of a system and move into the realm of emergent

experience through the recombinance of object-based functionalities. This is a technological heightening of the "illimitable" nature of Derrida's combinatorics of "différance," where he states, "Every sign, linguistic or non-linguistic... can... break with every given context, engendering [and inscribing itself in] an infinity of new contexts in a manner which is absolutely illimitable" (Derrida 1988, 79).[10] From a different perspective we encounter the rhizomatic "flows" and "lines of flight" of Deleuze and Guattari. They articulate a space of electric flows that function in an amorphous continuum, where the flow "enters into a relationship with another flow, such that the first defines a content and the second, an expression. The deterritorialized flows of content and expression are in a state of conjunction or reciprocal precondition that constitutes figures as the ultimate units of both content and expression" (Deleuze and Guattari 1983, 241).

In terms of virtual space, these flows enable the exploration of an advanced recombinance of the word within a mutable context of neighboring media elements, media-processes, physical environments and operative code functionalities. It now makes sense to consider each media element as a field of potential (Seaman 1999). Each field carries an evocative meaning force. Our embodied history of experience of past contexts represents another expansive field that is

230

19.response.1: BioMorphic Typography

that is the case, then how can we use new technologies to provoke us into a more sensually engaged relation to text in ways that don't immediately reinscribe these longstanding practices of repressing sensual response?

Third, to examine this issue more generally, I'd like Seaman to comment on the role of technology and culture. We could read his essay in terms of technological determinism — technology itself drives changes in our perception. How then does he view the relation between cultural contexts and technology?

I ask because I am besotted with similar issues in my own work, particularly in a new form of writing and reading that I term BioMorphic Typography (see figure 19.response.1). The user is hooked up to a biofeedback device that changes the visual character of the font she

brought into this delicate equation. As we encounter virtual or computational spaces we experience an ongoing, time-based summing of meaning forces. Thus text presents one field of meaning force that can only be understood contextually in relation to other "neighboring" meaning forces — other media elements and living processes. The "word" is not valued in a hierarchy over other media elements or processes in such a space. The time-based contextual "figure" or configuration of media elements is in each case weighed in an ongoing process. The participant takes a fluid role in the construction of meaning through different levels and qualities of interaction.

The puny potentials of the text as code provide a hidden plane of operative potential that we as a communicative world are just beginning to come to understand and employ. At this point in time, text should be observed as one media-element within a network of other forms of media elements and processes. The evocative life of words becomes palpable in the quixotic neighborhood of generative virtual environments. As virtual spaces become networked and very different potentialities of use collide or become intentionally conjoined, hybrid functionalities will be both intentionally and unintentionally spawned. To say this in simple language: as computer functionality becomes increasingly object-based, the potential for the

generation of emergent functionality by drawing together distributed media elements and processes is heightened. My work in progress, "The Hybrid Invention Generator," funded by Intel, explores this metaphor. The participant can, in real time, examine a database of past inventions and by choosing two different inventions, engender a hybrid. Yet an underlying textual "conjunction code" suggests the potential of how these hybrid inventions could be built. This metaphor is pointing at the potential of bringing together computer-based functionalities to form hybrid computer-based inventions. Certainly this will become a central metaphor for the open source community.

Our use of recombinant media resources and computer-based functionalities enables the exploration of operational neighboring or interpenetrated configurations of time-based language-vehicles and processes. We can even go so far as to say that the concept of the "Universal Machine," as developed by Turing, is one of the central principles enabling this potential for media-based construction. Andrew Hodges, Turing's biographer, describes certain aspects of the "universal machine":

> ...underneath here lay the same powerful idea that Gödel had used, that there was no essential distinction between

231

is writing with in real time. So, for example, the font "throbs" as the user's heart beats, and grows tendrils and spikes, as the user becomes "excitable." Users can then become aware of their autonomic states of heart rate, respiration, and galvanic skin response as they are writing and as they read what they write. As in VR, users are directly involved in a feedback loop, and in this way, the relation between text and sensual response is both made evident, and is problematized as users are "called back" to an awareness of their body. An interesting component is the role of attention, as it continually seems to shift, oscillate, and buzz among reading the text as it is overtly meant to be read, reading the more covert, visual aspect of text, and reading aspects of one's own body.

However, as the novelty of "reading" one's autonomic states wears, users' attention seem to drift from liminal awareness back to the more general subliminal. Or as Deleuze and Guattari (1987) might put it, the disruptive, liberatory aspects that one gains from making visible the usually imperceptible physical responses (the "molecular") then returns to a "molar" state. That is, the forces or meaningful patterns that we developed to keep those sensual perceptions at bay, though provoked in new ways with new technologies, can again revert, or be reinscribed. The very cause-and-effect that allowed a legibility of autonomic states, a destabilizing move perhaps, seems only temporary.

I address this problem through kinds of coding that intermittently allow the cause-and-effect to "infect" "numbers" and operations on numbers. From a modern mathematical point of view, they were all alike symbols. With this done, it followed that one particular machine could simulate the work done by *any* machine. He [Turing] called it the *universal* machine... It would be a machine to do everything, which was enough to give anyone pause for thought. It was, furthermore, a machine of perfectly definite form. (Hodges 1983, 104)

The varying symbolic properties of computer code become compressed, and function in a pun-like manner, inwardly enabling the functionality of a code-driven conceptual machine within specific hardware environments, while outwardly presenting media and physical process variables. The body becomes enmeshed experientially. A participant exploring such media-spaces becomes structurally coupled with the authored artifacts of computational media elements and processes. Maturana describes this as a linguistic domain. Yet we are just beginning to experience the fruits of how someone uses this potential functionality of computer-based authorship, when they draw upon a cogent field of conveyance potential in the service of expression. Maturana (1970) provides this definition of the linguistic domain:

> The linguistic domain as a domain of orienting behaviour requires at least two interacting organisms with comparable domains of interactions, so that a cooperative system of consensual interactions may be developed in which the emerging conduct of the two organisms is relevant for both... The central feature of human existence is its occurrence in a linguistic cognitive domain. The domain is constitutively social. (Maturana, 1970, p.41, xxiv)

Maturana goes on to say:

> ...I maintain that learned orienting interactions, coupled with some mode of behaviour that allowed for an independent recursive expansion of the domain of interactions of the organism, such as social life (cf. Gardner and Gardner 1969) and/or tool making and use, must have offered a selective basis for the evolution of the orienting behaviour that in hominids led to our present-day language. (31)

more autonomous kinds of response, where the typography seems to have a life of its own, a kind of autonomy that nonetheless issues from direct user feedback, but in unexpected ways (kinds of pictorial and sonic "noise"). If there is no legibility of cause-and-effect, if the interactivity is not legible, I might as well play a videotape. But this intermingling of responsiveness can be a way to sustain awareness and at the same time, to continually provoke different kinds of awareness of autonomic states. Perhaps then a user's awareness may not immediately reorganize itself into "molar" or conventional ways. With these problems in mind, I would like Seaman to address the issue of the role of the legibility of coding and emergence. How can they create meaningful patterns of experience? Do

emergent properties need to be perceived as such?

Fourth, Seaman's reference to "the body" seems to imply that the body is unchanging — it is discussed in singular, monolithic terms. Perhaps this is the result of the necessities imposed by the brevity of an essay. However, much contemporary theory would take issue with that, particularly theorists such as Alice Jardine, Helene Cixous, Luce Irigaray, Susan Bordo, Donna Haraway, and Edward Said, among a long list of others. If technologies that exhibit more literally involved sensual aspects and emergent qualities can allow us to reawaken or extend sensual experience, and if the body is a key site at which culture and cultural identity is articulated, this will be an important question.

My final question goes far beyond the purview of

Cayley   Drucker Montfort
Utterback   Gorbet Wortzel
Gromala Walker

The Pixel/The Line >Seaman

Computer-based tools enable new forms of authorship and interauthorship. The generative virtual environment entitled *The World Generator/The Engine of Desire* (1996–7), by Bill Seaman with Gideon May (programmer), seeks to become a discourse mechanism enabling one to observe operational media elements and processes through interactive exploration of a generative virtual environment (see sidebar). The consensual domain is generated both in networked virtual space, where *vusers* (viewer/users: pronounced view-ser) can coauthor a virtual environment, or when an individual interacts alone within this artistic environment, functioning as an authored, self-organizing organism-like entity, operating through technological agency. Enter the age of the recombinant poetic. The machine functions, in part, as an appurtenant extension of the linguistic intentions of the author (or authors) of the system. All media elements encountered in this generative virtual environment function as operational language-vehicles and can potentially be considered "linguistic" in relation to Maturana's definition. Again, text takes on meaning in an expansive environment of neighboring spatial and temporal relations — generative patterns of use explored over time.

In *Semiotics of Visual Language*, Saint-Martin (1990) speaks about the relevance of "neighboring," which is

19.sidebar.1–2. Examples of *The World Generator* in use.

Seaman to respond to it in a short essay, so I will leave it as a provocative musing: how can these new technologies also enable us to go beyond reinscribing the tendencies that led us to understand body, environment and technology as distinct from one another? Can the very technologies themselves play important roles in the erasure among these boundaries

From Jill Walker's Online Response
Seaman writes of potential and emergence and I think he believes that vusers are free in all this, capable of recombining and reinterpreting objects to create new hybrids. "Increasingly, one can intentionally reinterpret the potentials of a functionality and thus move outside of the specified programmed probable outcomes of a

system and move into the realm of emergent experience through the recombinance of object-based functionalities," he writes. I imagine patterns (combinations, signs, texts, hybrids) that did not exist until being vused and that could not be predicted; meanings that weren't intended by the human(s) who created the machine but that emerge in the meeting between me and it. I feel the seduction of the idea but

I know that I haven't experienced this yet. Digital art (installations, net.art, games, hypertext fiction) seem to me to disempower the vuser more than most previous art forms do. My freedom, my cocreation, is highlighted in the artist's statements I read in the catalogues, or in some of the early theoretical work in the field (Landow 1991, Bolter 1991) but when I actually meet these art

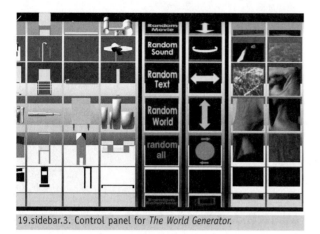

19.sidebar.3. Control panel for *The World Generator*.

central to the production of meaning in a virtual environment:

> The relationship of neighboring is the most important topological notion by which the function of continuity is constructed in any spatial field, whether physical or perceptual. Its importance to physical sciences was underlined by Bachelard when he stated that any force in the continuity of the field "presents itself as determined by the condition of neighboring. The term, vague in everyday

language, acquires all of the desirable conciseness in mathematical expressions." (Saint-Martin 1990, 69)

Thus we enter the nature of the real that enables the virtual — where the evocative nature of media configurations is brought about as a result of recombinant structuring. Instead of printed matter, we have recombinant energy processes or flows. The techno-poetic environment can either be seen in the metaphorical light of waves (an intermingling of fields) or particles (modular-media elements comprised of pixel configurations), depending on how one is observing it.

Interactive Text is one media element culled from a set of media elements that we encounter environmentally. The sensuality of our body becomes engaged. At the core of the research agenda of *Recombinant Poetics* is the holistic transdisciplinary exploration of the evocative potentials of such generative combinatoric environments. Central is the exploration of a continuum that bridges body, environment and technology.

---

works I feel shackled to their rules: sit here, press this button and only this button, move the mouse, follow these links, watch this, move this, walk down these narrow paths. I have to figure out what the computer wants me to do and do it: then it will recombine its bits and pieces and perhaps show me something that no one, not even the author, has seen before. The rules don't emerge in the continuum between me and it. On the contrary. It sets the rules, and I must obey them in order to "interact" at all.

Seaman Responds

The central issue is this — I do not believe we make a text as we perceive, yet we still experience meaning-production. We may choose to make a text later to try to articulate what we have perceived in the form of a text. As we explore more complex experiences under the guise of "authorship," we need to move toward technologies that better enable reflection upon that complexity.

http://www.electronicbookreview.com/thread/firstperson/walkerr1

http://www.electronicbookreview.com/thread/firstperson/seamanr2

Notes

For more on recombinant poetics, see Seaman (1999), "Recombinant Poetics: Emergent Meaning as Examined and Explored Within a Specific Generative Virtual Environment."

1. See Hayles for an in-depth discussion of human/computer relations.

2. See Roland Barthes on anchorage: "Rhetoric of the Image" and *Elements of Semiology*.

3. Sites related to Margaret Minsky's Haptic Research: http://marg.www.media.mit.edu/people/marg/haptics-bibliography.html, http://www.media.mit.edu/people/marg/haptics-pages.html

4. See Eric Drexler, *Engines of Creation* and *Unbounding the Future* and Ed Regis, *Nano: The Emerging Science of Nanotechnology*.

5. See: http://www.ornl.gov/hgmis/publicat/publications.html

6. See David Deutsch, *Machines, Logic and Quantum Physics*: http://xxx.lanl.gov/abs/math.HO/9911150 Also: http://www.qubit.org/

7. See my website for a listing of works and related papers: http://www.cda.ucla.edu/faculty/seaman

8. Produced at ABC Radio in Sydney in 1995 for *The Listening Room*.

9. http://comp.uark.edu/~tkrueger/

10. See also Derrida, *Writing and Difference*.

References

Babbage, Charles (edited by Philip Morrison and Emily Morrison) (1961). *Charles Babbage and his Calculating Engines: Selected Writings by Charles Babbage and Others*. New York: Dover Publications, Inc.

Barthes, Roland (translated by Annette Lavers and Colin Smith) (1967). *Elements of Semiology*. London: Jonathan Cape.

Barthes, Roland (translated by Richard Miller) (1975). *The Pleasure of the Text*. New York: Hill & Wang.

Barthes, Roland (translated by Stephen Heath) (1977). "Rhetoric of the Image." In *Image/Music/Text*. New York: Hill and Wang.

Bolter, J. David (1991). *Writing Space: The Computer, Hypertext and the History of Writing*. Hillsdale, NJ: Lawrence Erlbaum Associates.

Deleuze, Gilles, and Félix Guattari (translated by Robert Hurley, Mark Seem and Helen R. Lane) (1983). *Anti-Oedipus: Capitalism and Schizophrenia*. Minneapolis/London: University of Minnesota Press.

Deleuze, Gilles, and Félix Guattari (translated by Brian Massumi) (1987). *A Thousand Plateaus: Capitalism and Schizophrenia*, vol.2. Minneapolis: University of Minnesota Press.

Derrida, Jacques (translated by Gayatri Spivak) (1977). *Of Grammatology*. Baltimore: Johns Hopkins University Press.

Derrida, Jacques (translated by Alan Bass) (1978). *Writing and Difference*. Chicago: University of Chicago Press.

Derrida, Jacques (translated by Samuel Weber) (1988). *Limited Inc*. Evanston, IL: Northwestern University Press.

Deutsch, David, Artur Ekert and Rossella Lupacchini (1999). "Machines, Logic and Quantum Physics." <http://xxx.lanl.gov/abs/math.HO/9911150>.

Drexler, K. Eric (1986). *Engines of Creation*. New York: Anchor Books. <http://www.foresight.org/EOC/index.html/>.

Drexler, K. Eric (1991). *Unbounding the Future*. New York: William Morrow and Company, Inc. <http://www.foresight.org/UTF/Unbound_LBW/>.

Gardner, R. Allen, and Beatrice T. Gardner (1969). "Teaching Sign Language to a Chimpanzee." *Science* no.165 (1969): 664-672.

Hayles, N. Katherine (1999). *How We Became Posthuman: Virtual Bodies in Cybernetics, Literature and Informatics*. Chicago: University of Chicago Press.

Hodges, Andrew (1983). *Alan Turing: The Enigma*. New York: Simon and Shuster.

Kurtzweil, Ray (2000). *The Age of Spiritual Machines*. New York: Penguin USA. <http://www.penguinputnam.com/static/packages/us/kurzweil/excerpts/exmain.htm>.

Landow, George (1991). *Hypertext: The Convergence of Contemporary Critical Theory and Technology*. Baltimore: Johns Hopkins.

Maturana, Humberto R. (1978). "Biology of Language: The Epistemology of Reality." In *Psychology and Biology of Language and Thought: Essays in Honor of Eric Lenneberg*, edited by George A. Miller and Elizabeth Lenneberg. New York: Academic Press.

Maturana, Humberto R. (1980). Biological Computer Laboratory Research Report BCL 9.0., University of Illinois, 1970. Reprinted in *Autopoiesis and Cognition: The Realization of the Living*. Dordecht: D. Reidel Publishing Co.

Peirce, Charles Sanders (1931). *Collected Papers, Volume I–VIII*. Cambridge: Harvard University Press.

Regis, Ed (1995). *Nano: The Emerging Science of Nanotechnology*. Boston: Little, Brown & Company.

Saint-Martin, Fernande (1990). *Semiotics of Visual Language*. Bloomington: Indiana University Press.

Seaman, Bill (1999). "Recombinant Poetics: Emergent Meaning as Examined and Explored Within a Specific Generative Virtual Environment." <http://www.cda.ucla.edu/faculty/seaman/texts.html>.

Shaw, Jeffrey (edited by Manuela Abel) (1997). *Eine Gebrauchsanweisung: From Expanded Cinema to Virtual Reality*. Ostfildern: Cantz.

Stephenson, Neal (1995). *The Diamond Age*. New York: Bantam.

Turing, Alan (1986). *A. M. Turing's ACE Report of 1946 and Other Papers*, Vol. 10 in the Charles Babbage Institute reprint series for the History of Computing, edited by B.E. Carpenter and R.W. Doran. Cambridge, MA: The MIT Press.

Wittgenstein, Ludwig (translated by G.E.M. Anscomb) (1958). *Philosophical Investigations*. Englewood Cliffs: Prentice-Hall.

Beyond Chat

There are differences between holding a meaningful conversation and simply emitting words in one direction or another. Because of these differences, computers are much better at the latter, and in fact can probably not hold a conversation unassisted. Even chat software doesn't do much to support real conversation — as evidenced by the ease with which bots employ it — though users find ways to use such software toward meaningful conversational ends.

To think through these issues involves considering how we create meaning, how we create technology, and the contexts of our lives in which communication and technology meet. The three essayists collected here consider these issues in depth, not simply for the sake of analysis, but also for intervention. Their interventions include developing new software for understanding online conversations, creating a new community that takes the lack of time for online communication as a topic, and critically examining the forms of offline communication we have with (monologue-prone) voice chips.

These essayists incorporate perspectives from a broad range of disciplines, from artificial intelligence to art, and practice through a variety of theories of communication and cognition. A touchstone for two of the three is the work of theorist/practitioner Lucy Suchman, which has been highly influential in recent discussions of computationally connected objects that speak. Suchman's work helps us understand what we might mean by interaction, either with a computationally driven object or with another person through a computationally supported interface. As she writes in her response to Natalie Jeremijenko (invoking Emanuel Schegloff), interaction is a term for the ongoing contingent coproduction of the sociomaterial world. This is much more than "talking in a conversational manner on different subjects" — this is much more than *chat*.

Warren Sack, this section's first essayist, takes up the challenge of moving beyond chat software for what he calls Very Large-Scale Conversations (VLSCs) — which include Usenet newsgroups and large listservs. His Conversation Map analyzes and visualizes VLSCs, helping users understand what is being produced and how they may wish to participate. He is followed by Victoria Vesna, whose *n0time* is the product of several generations of projects that call into question popular assumptions about the nature of online communities and embodiment. *n0time* extends this work into the boom/bust of millennial angst, dot-com frenzy, and cybernetic hyperfeedback — creating proxy bodies that both collect possibilities for interaction and are destroyed by them. The final essay, by Natalie Jeremijenko, creates an initial typology for understanding our encounters with voice chips — of both speaking and listening varieties — and proposes some insights that may be gained by examining this *reductio ad absurdum* of conversation, this less-than-chat.

What Does a Very Large-Scale Conversation Look Like?

Warren Sack

Introduction

The new electronic spaces that I am interested in have the following characteristics in common:

They are large. Many sites now support interchanges between hundreds and thousands of people. Usenet newsgroups and large listservs are the most common of such sites. I call these usually text-based, usually asynchronous interchanges, *very large-scale conversations.* (Sack 2000c)

They are network-based. More specifically, they support network-based communities. The boundaries of these spaces and the communites they support are not geographic boundaries. Communities of

artists, writers, and scientists are examples of pre-internet, network-based communities; i.e., communities based upon a social network and some shared interests or needs. Network-based communities are of a different kind than geographically based communities such as neighborhoods, cities, and nations. Network-based communities — e.g., the scientific community — have continued to grow with the help of new network technologies, but contemporary technologies have also engendered a variety of new communities; e.g., the open-source community.

They are public. As more and more people gain access to the internet from their home or school rather than from their workplace, the internet increasingly becomes a space for public discussion and exchange. While very large-scale conversations are a common event within the confines of large industry (e.g., the huge number of communications between thousands of people necessary to design and build an airplane or coordinate the

Response by Rebecca Ross

In his 1993 project "Fire Truck," the sculptor Charles Ray scaled a toy fire truck to the size of a "real" fire department engine. Missing the "guts" of an actual fire engine, it took up three parking spots in front of the Whitney. Nostalgia for a childhood toy, when examined at that scale, suddenly became cumbersome and oddly dysfunctional. The proportions of the toy that once offered a God-like scalar relationship with the world had become a broken promise to the mortal adult.

Conversation Map performs an opposing transformation, dynamically scaling down the contents and structure of an internet newsgroup from many screens to a single screen map with immediately legible summaries of the activities of the group. A

combination of its dynamic relationship to the activities of the newsgroup community, the comparative simplicity of newsgroup data and the multi-authorial nature of newsgroups all protect it from the type of breakage that Ray's model embodies.

Conversation Map presents a conflation of interfaces for participation and overview. I think of a sailor consulting a map; I am led to the absurd mental image of a boat cutting through a big paper drawing of the sea — there is nothing really to cross, since the Atlantic is one-third the length of the boat. I want to know more about how we navigate from this position while maintaining some standards of precision. How might conversations be altered if everyone participating did so through the kind of overview that Sack presents?

production of a film), these have a distinctly different character than the very large-scale conversations in which people are participating as individuals rather than as employees. The internet is engendering the production of new public spaces that may offer the means to reinvigorate public discourse. (Tsagarousianou et al. 1998; Hague and Loader 1999)

On the one hand, these electronic spaces — these very large-scale, public conversations — are quite prosaic. Usenet newsgroups, large e-mail lists, and other places on the internet where large volumes of email are exchanged are all good examples of very large-scale conversation. On the other hand, from a different perspective — for example, from the perspective of the history of media — very large-scale conversation is an entirely new and mostly unexplored phenomenon. At no other point in history have we had a medium that supports many-to-many communications between hundreds or thousands of people. VLSC takes place across international borders, often on a daily or hourly basis. Unlike in older media — for instance, telephones — participants in these very large-scale conversations usually do not know the addresses of the others before the start of a conversation.

Reflection on the current social scientific theories and tools we have for understanding and investigating conversations and discourse — for example, the tools and techniques of discourse analysis (Schiffrin 1994) or conversation analysis (Hutchby and Wooffitt 1998) — makes it clear that existing analytic frameworks are inadequate to the task. Existing theories and techniques can handle the analysis of small-scale conversations — e.g., interactions between thirty or fewer people — but it is not a priori obvious how these existing methods can be scaled up to handle the huge, many-to-many interactions that have now become commonplace on the internet. So the challenge is this: how can theories and computational tools be built to help us understand and participate in these very large-scale conversations?

More specifically, the challenge can be posed as a problem from the perspective of a participant in one of these very large-scale conversations. If I want to participate in one of these huge discussions my problem is this: how can I listen to thousands of others; and conversely, how can my words be heard by the thousands of others who might be participating in the same conversation? Phrased as a design problem, the question becomes the following: what software can be designed to help participants navigate these new public spaces?

On the New York City subway, I once exited the N train at City Hall to find a two-way mirror looking into the control room for the entire N line. There were machines with diagrams of the trains' current status as well as microphone radios to issue intervening instructions to train operators. The MTA officials at this location have a lot of good information from which to make a decision. A simple example would be to send more Brooklyn-bound trains out if the majority of the trains are running Queens-bound – drivers themselves have no access to this information. At the same time, as a regular N train rider, I know that these train operators have no concept of how many people are stuffed into the cars at a given moment or even worse, that someone's fallen onto the tracks by Eighth Street.

How does participation in an event or structure, such as a very large conversation, via a map or overview of the structure, alter the nature of the actions we choose to take upon and within that structure? This is an especially important question to consider in the context of some of the phenomena of the very large conversation, which is essentially made of the delicate nuances of social interaction.

From Phoebe Sengers's Online Response

Warren Sack's work on the Conversation Map is an example of what Phil Agre (1997) calls *critical technical practices*. For Agre, this means a practice of technical development in which technical impasses are recognized as philosophical problems, and where

Navigation

Lucy Suchman (1987, citing Gladwin and Berreman) has described how the activity of navigation can be conceived of as a very different practice in different cultures. To illustrate this, she compares the navigation activities of European sailors — which are said to be more plan-directed — with those of the Trukese — whose navigation appears to be more contingent upon an objective rather than a plan. In its current forms, VLSC is usually an intercultural phenomenon since it is usually conducted on the internet between participants from many different countries. To theorize and to design software to browse and navigate VLSCs it is necessary to make explicit the culturally specific assumptions that go into the design work.

Michel Foucault has pointed out that "the comparison between medicine and navigation is a very traditional one (Foucault 2000). Medicine, navigation, and government have to do with guidance, control, and governance. Etymologically, the verb "navigate" comes from the combination of words *navis* (ship) and *agere* (to guide). Thus, in the current case of the navigation of a large, public, information space — like a large archive of Usenet newsgroups — the "ship" has been replaced by a self, and so the point of navigation is self-guidance or self-governance. From this perspective, the right way to evaluate or critique a browser — or any other

piece of navigation software — is with respect to how well it supports self-governance. In the particular case of a VLSC browser it should help us better understand where we are located in a wider network of social and semantic relations. It should also help us consider the existence of a collective, self-organization constructed through the text and talk of a VLSC. I am interested in the larger ethical and philosophical implications of this understanding of navigation.

To better understand the issues of designing software for navigation, I've borrowed a conceptual framework from Paul Dourish and Matthew Chalmers who, in 1994, wrote a paper entitled "Running Out of Space: Models of Information Navigation." In their paper, Dourish and Chalmers assert that there are at least three ways in which large bodies of information can be navigated: socially, semantically, and spatially. I would like to explain my reading of their paper to clarify my position.

> *Social Navigation* First, Dourish and Chalmers claim that software can be designed to support the social navigation of information (Munro, Hook, and Benyon 1999). By social navigation, I understand them to mean, essentially, people helping other people to find information.

---

philosophical and critical methodology is applied to find ways around these impasses. More generally, we may be able to speak of a critical technical practice as a practice of technology development that incorporates as an essential component critical self-reflection. Following this definition, there are many examples of critical technical practitioners represented in this book: Natalie Jeremijenko combines a critical art practice with mechanical and electrical engineering; Michael Mateas combines art and Artificial Intelligence; Simon Penny combines art and robotics; I combine cultural studies and Artificial Intelligence. In Sack's work in particular, questions of algorithms weave together with a philosophical reflection on the place of the technology created in society and on the choice and

design of the technologies involved. An interesting question to ask, therefore, within the very small-scale conversation this book represents, is how Sack's work instantiates a critical technical practice, and what it tells us about what critical technical practices are and what they could be.

http://www.electronicbookreview.com/thread/firstperson/sengersr1

Sack Responds

Ross's question is also a variation on the meta-question that applies to all of us trying to perform a critical technical practice. Namely, how do researchers react or change when they have a representation of the larger discourse within which their work is embedded?

http://www.electronicbookreview.com/thread/firstperson/sackr2

Examples of social navigation software include the mechanisms employed in recommender systems and collaborative filtering (Resnick and Varian 1997). I believe that work done in organizing texts through citation analysis — as is done in the field of science studies — can also be counted as support for social navigation. (Garfield 1979)

Semantic Navigation By semantic navigation, I understand Dourish and Chalmers to mean the sorts of computation we have available to us when we use a search engine on the web. Using techniques from information retrieval and computational linguistics, semantic navigation can be supported through the calculation of some approximation to the meaning of a set of documents.

Spatial Navigation And, finally, by spatial navigation, I understand them to mean the sorts of manipulations often performed in the area of information visualization to convert a large body of data into a two- or three-dimensional image that can then be examined using a graphical interface of some sort. (Card, Mackinlay, and Shneiderman 1999)

My intention is to support all three of these types of information navigation for the domain of very large-scale conversations. My approach, generally speaking, is to use some techniques and tools from sociology to support social navigation; some ideas from linguistics to support semantic navigation; and some aspects of graphical interface design to support spatial navigation of VLSCs. More specifically, the part of sociology that I am interested in borrowing from and extending is that area known as social network analysis (Wasserman and Galaskiewicz 1994). Several researchers have employed the methods of social network analysis to the study of internet discourse (Smith 1997; Wellman 1999). The

subdiscipline of linguistics that I want to use to support semantic navigation of VLSCs is computational, corpus-based linguistics. But, most specifically, what I am interested in is the use and improvement of automatic techniques for the compilation and augmentation of thesauri from large corpora of texts (Hearst 1998; Harabagiu and Moldovan 1999; Grefenstette 1994).

In these pages I am not going to say too much about techniques to support spatial navigation. A more complete description of my approach can be found elsewhere (Sack 2000a, 2000c). However, I will say that it is my goal to provide an interface that — at least in principle — can be used by all of the participants in an online discussion. Thus, graphical interfaces that can be presented as publicly accessible web pages is an important design criterion (and constraint) for me.

Conversation Map

Figure 20.1 is a shot of the main screen of the Conversation Map system. The Conversation Map system accepts a corpus of several thousand messages and analyzes those messages using a set of computational linguistics and sociology techniques in order to generate a summary of the messages that includes who is talking with whom; the themes of discussion that are important to the conversation embodied in the messages; and (what can be understood as) some of the emergent definitions or metaphors of the discussion that are apparent if, in a certain sense, all of the participants' language inscribed in the text — i.e., the content — of the e-mail messages are analyzed and "summed together." In principle, one can use the Conversation Map in a manner akin to the usage of Netscape Messenger, RN, Eudora, or any other conventional news or mail reader. Right now, the text analysis procedures are too slow, but I am reengineering the system to support this usage in the near future. (A complete description of the text analysis procedures developed for the Conversation Map can be found in my thesis [Sack 2000c]; a shorter description of these procedures can also be found in a recent paper [Sack 2000b].) Figure 20.1 was generated by the Conversation Map system after it analyzed about 1,300 messages

What Does a Very Large-Scale Conversation Look Like?
Warren Sack

FIRSTPERSON

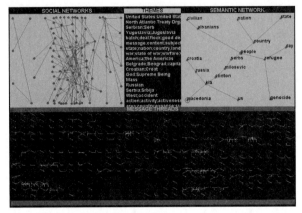

20.1. The Conversation Map interface.

posted to the Usenet newsgroup <soc.culture.Albanian> in Spring 2000, during the war in Kosovo. It is a graphical summary of a large argument that engaged Albanians, Serbs, and others.

Social Networks The upper left quadrant of the interface depicts a set of social networks that record who — within the group of conversational participants — is reciprocating with whom. By "reciprocating" I mean who is mutually responding to and/or quoting from whom. Thus, if I were to post a message to the newsgroup and then you were to respond to it and then, later in the discussion, you were to post to the newsgroup and I replied to — or quoted from — your message, then the two of us would be — according to my definition — said to be reciprocating with one another. Reciprocation is an important property of smaller-scale discussions that has been explored by, for instance, researchers in the field of conversation analysis, and so I believe this may also be an important property of large-scale discussions.

As reciprocating participants of the discussion, you and I will appear as nodes in the graphs representing social networks, and a line will be drawn between us. If we reciprocate many times over the course of the conversation we will be plotted close together. In contrast, those pairs of participants who reciprocate only once will be plotted relatively far apart. Note that posters who spam the group with many messages, but who receive no replies, do not even show up on the graph. Those participants who show up closely

connected are pushed to the middle of the graph and can be understood as virtual mediators of the newsgroup. I say participants in central positions of the social network are "virtual moderators" because most of the analyses I have done have been of unmoderated, public discussion spaces on the Net. To end up in such a position one needs not only to post many messages, but also to have others in the group reply to or quote from many of one's messages. So, the social network display acts both as a filter for spammers and a means to identify some of the main players in a discussion.

"Themes" of Conversation The menu in the upper-middle of the interface lists the "themes" of the conversation. (I put "themes" in quotes because, according to the terms of linguistics, what is being calculated by the system is strictly speaking not the themes, but the *lexical ties* between messages; a necessary, but not sufficient, step in the determination of the themes of discussion.) Let's say I post a message about football, and then you respond with a message that includes some reference to baseball. Then, perhaps later in the discussion, you post a message about skiing and I respond with one concerning skating. Our reciprocation will be represented in the social network, but some approximation to the theme of our exchange will also be listed in the menu of "themes." In this case, because football, baseball, skiing, and skating are all sports, the term "sports" might be listed on the menu of themes. Calculating that these four terms are all sports requires, of course, a machine-readable thesaurus. The thesaurus employed in the Conversation Map system is WordNet, a lexical resource created by George Miller, his colleagues, and students at Princeton University (Fellbaum 1998).

Semantic Network One way to understand the difference between the menu of themes and the graph depicted in the upper right-hand corner of the interface is this: while construction of the menu of themes requires the use of a predefined thesaurus, like WordNet, the calculations performed to create the semantic network in the upper right-hand corner do not use a thesaurus, but, rather, *automatically generate* a rough-draft thesaurus. To create a rough-draft thesaurus, the Conversation Map system does the

Beyond Chat >Sack
Vesna
Jeremijenko

Ross Sengers
Strickland
Suchman Penny

VII. Beyond Chat

following: first, the content of all of the messages exchanged during the conversation is parsed — i.e., subjects, verbs, objects and some other modifying relations are identified between the words of each sentence in the texts of the messages. Next, for each unique noun mentioned in the corpus of messages a profile is built. By "profile" I mean that, for each noun, a vector is created that records all of the verbs for which the subject functioned as a subject; all of the verbs for which the noun functioned as an object; all of the adjectives which modified the noun; etc. Once a profile has been calculated for each noun, the nouns' profiles are compared to one another and each noun's nearest neighbor is identified. An algorithm described by Grefenstette is used to calculate and compare the noun profiles. If two nouns are nearest neighbors then, according to this calculation, they appear in similar contexts. Or, to put it more plainly, if two nouns have similar profiles, then they can be said to have been "talked about" in similar ways by the participants in the discussion. On the semantic network, if two nouns are nearest neighbors, then they are plotted as two nodes connected to one another.

Why, one might ask, is this sort of analysis of interest for the navigation of very large-scale conversations? To answer this question, I compare this sort of analysis with some work done by the cognitive scientists George Lakoff and Mark Johnson (1980). Lakoff and Johnson wrote a book entitled *Metaphors We Live By*. The book is filled with a set of metaphors that Lakoff and Johnson claim are central to our culture. In this book, for instance, they claim that one emergent metaphor of our culture is that "arguments are buildings." As part of their method to argue for the validity of insights like this, they show how two nouns, which might a priori be considered to be completely unalike one another — such as the two terms "argument" and "building" — show up in very similar contexts. For example, one can say, "The building is shaky," but one can also say, "The

argument is shaky." One can say, "The building collapsed," but also, "The argument collapsed." Similarly, both buildings and arguments can be said to have "foundations," "to stand" and "to fall," "to be constructed," "to be supported," "to be buttressed," and so forth. A set of similar sentences of this sort provides an empirical means for thinking about and discovering how definitions and metaphors are produced over the

20.2. An example message thread.

course of a large amount of discussion. Thus, this tool for automatic, rough-draft thesaurus generation can be seen as "training wheels" to allow us, within the context of a specific conversation, to begin to generate the sorts of hypotheses that Lakoff and Johnson explore in their book. So, the Conversation Map gives one some data exploration/navigation tools to start to understand how different conversations differ from one another according to the metaphors and definitions that are produced by the collective efforts of their participants.

Message Archive The lower half of the interface is a graphical representation of all of the messages that have been parsed and analyzed by the Conversation Map system. Messages are organized into threads where a thread is simply defined as an initial post, all of the responses to the initial post, all of the responses to responses, etc. The threads are organized in chronological order from upper left to lower right. The lower half of the screen is divided into a grid and so the first thread posted to the newsgroup appears in the upper left-hand corner and the last thread posted appears in the lower right-hand corner. The specific shapes of the plotted threads will not be explained here. The interested reader can find an explanation in another paper (Sack 2000b). Here, in this essay, I simply want to point out that — if a thread contains many messages — it shows up as an almost completely green

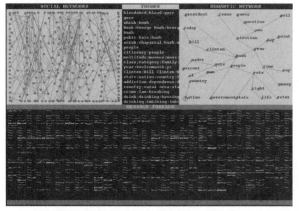

20.3a. Before the election.

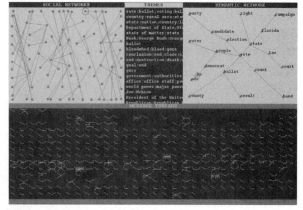

20.3b. After the election.

square on this display. If a thread contains few messages, then it shows up as an almost completely black square. Thus, by reading across and down — from upper left to lower right — the lower half of the screen provides a rough guide to the posting activity in the newsgroup over the period of time spanned by the messages.

Examples

In the following section I show twelve example Conversation Maps that were generated from a wide variety of online public discussions. With these examples, I hope the semiotics of how to read these maps will become understandable. Also I hope that these one page, graphical summaries of hundreds or thousands of e-mail messages will be seen to be a useful thing for gaining a quick glimpse into a very large-scale conversation.

Politics

The map on the left and the map on the right were created about a week apart using messages from the newsgroup alt.politics elections. The map on the left (figure 20.3a) was generated immediately before the 2000 presidential election. Notice how the main themes of discussion center around the candidates: Gore, Bush, and Nader. A week after the election the conversation (as mapped on the right, 20.3b) has moved away from a discussion of the candidates. Now it is a discussion of the technicalities of elections: votes, counts, ballots, laws, and courts are the newly prominent themes of discussion.

Media

This pair of maps (20.4a, 20.4b) show the same newsgroup (a discussion about the television show *The X-Files*) at two different times. Notice how many

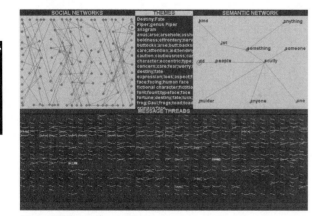

20.4a. Talking to one another.

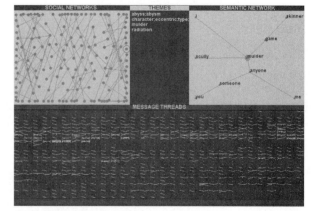

20.4b. Talking at one another.

Beyond Chat >Sack
Vesna
Jeremijenko

Ross Sengers
Strickland
Suchman Penny

VII. Beyond Chat

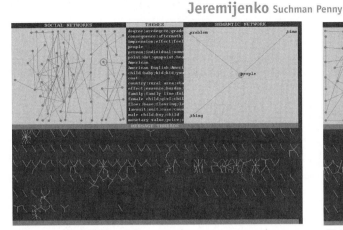

20.5a. People as problems.

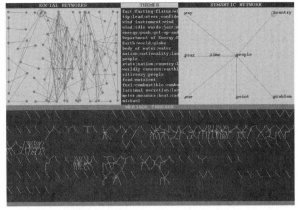

20.5b. And, problems as people.

themes of discussion there are in the map on the left. Now, notice how very few themes of discussion are listed in the map on the right. Because the Conversation Map uses a very generous means of counting the themes of dicussion, it usually lists too many, not too few. What this map tells us is that no one is following up on what other people are saying. The two snapshots in time represented by these two maps demonstrate how an online discussion can change from being one where people talk to one another into one where they just talk at one another. This fact is also represented in the very scattered appearance of the social network.

Environment
The map on the left (20.5a) represents about a month's worth of messages posted to the group <sci.environment>. The map on the right (20.5b)

represents the same newsgroup one month later. By comparing the two maps you can get some idea of how the group has changed over time. One thing that has remained stable between the two maps is the connection in the semantic networks between the terms "people" and "problem." This is a clue that perhaps, in this newsgroup, people are seen to be one of the main causes of environmental problems. But a hypothesis like this that one can come up with by looking at the maps needs further investigation to be confirmed or discarded.

Education
On the left (20.6a) is a map of about 300 messages from the Usenet newsgroup <misc.education>. Note the themes of discussion and compare them to the map on the right. Both maps summarize discussions about education and learning. The map on the right (20.6b)

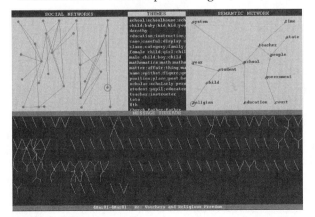

20.6a. A shallow conversation.

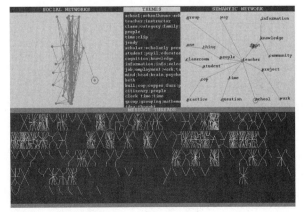

20.6b. A deep conversation.

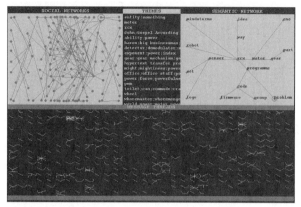

20.7a. Experts as hubs in a social network.

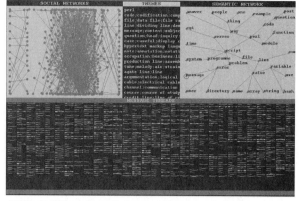

20.7b. A pattern of question-answer pairs.

summarizes a semester's worth of messages posted by a distance learning course taught by Prof. Linda Polin of Pepperdine University. In comparison with the first map, note how much more tightly knit the social network is here: people are responding to one another. Note also the elaborate threads containing many messages as compared to the sparse threads in the first map. These elaborate thread structures show that the participants are repeatedly elaborating on one another's posting. This sort of an exchange is perhaps much deeper than, for example, the quick question-and-answer format of the technology discussions depicted below and the curt exchanges that one can note in the threads of the political discussions above.

Technology

The conversation map on the left (20.7a) was created from about a month's worth of messages posted to a public listserv devoted to the construction of Lego robots. Note how the social network shows that there are multiple hubs: these correspond to an expert in mechanical systems, an expert in programming, and expert in electronics. The second map (20.7b) is an analysis of about 2500 messages from the newsgroup devoted to the Perl programming language: <comp.lang.perl.misc>. Note the dense social network and also compare the thread pattern here with the class-based, education conversation analyzed above. The pattern here is indicative of a series of brief question-answer clusters. The elaborate threads above indicate that participants are repeatedly elaborating on one another's responses.

Health

The conversation depicted in figure 20.8, on the left (20.8a), took place in a public newsgroup devoted to

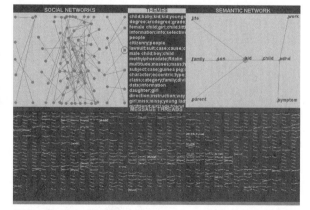

20.8a. Illness and family relations.

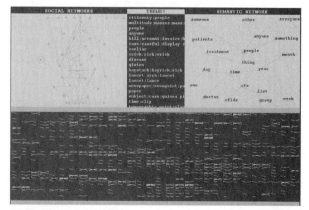

20.8b. Illness and citizens

attention-deficit disorder. However, one can see from the map that the discussion was not just about the illness, but about family members as well. The map on the right (20.8b) is summary of several hundred messages sent to a newsgroup on chronic-fatigue syndrome. As can be seen here too, the discussion focuses — not just on the illness — but on a more general discussion of people and citizenry. The anthropologist of science, Prof. Joseph Dumit of MIT, argues that illness like these (ADD and CFS) are illnesses one has to "fight to get" because they are often not recognized by doctors and insurance companies. Consequently, online discussions can become places where sufferers can meet and illness-based social movements can emerge.

Conclusions

Individuals need a map of the group in order to find their current or desired position in the group. Groups need a map to reflect on their limits and internal structure. This map can be either a metaphorical or a literal map. Maps have historically been very important for geographically circumscribed groups. On a country's map, citizens can find their homes, their proximity to the capital, their range of travel experience, and so forth. Maps usually incorporate several kinds of information; e.g., political boundaries, roads, and elevations might be included on one map of a region. No map can incorporate all kinds of information, but — at least for maps of physical geography — it seems clear that certain kinds of information are essential to all maps. For example, the map of a country needs to include some representation of the country's borders. However, it is not clear what needs to be included in a map of a non-geographically-based group. What, for instance, does a member of a Usenet newsgroup need to see in order to navigate through the VLSC of the newsgroup?

A VLSC is a "space" created through the electronic exchange of words. A map of a VLSC depicts a sea of information in which participants sail through, make waves in, and sometimes beach themselves to become an island or even a continent. Since the map of a VLSC depends upon the words and deeds of the participants,

a participant might use the map to navigate and by so navigating change the map. In this way map construction and navigation of VLSCs can be mutually recursive activities. One might imagine that this relationship between navigation and map-making is specific to information spaces, but in fact it takes only a quick glance at a world map of over ten years ago — before the end of the Cold War — to see that geographically based map-making is predicated on social and political forces and the boundaries of social and political forces are outlined on maps.

Participants in the emergent medium of VLSC will need new technologies to orient themselves in navigating through and interacting with these new public spaces. Moreover, the group of participants involved in a VLSC need a means to recognize themselves as a socially, politically, or economically (in)cohesive entity for purposes of self-governance. The Conversation Map system is an attempt to provide one effort[1] towards building tools for community self-recognition and self-governance.

Note

1. One example among many. See also, for instance, Donath, "The xx of xx," and Smith, "Netscan: Measuring and Mapping the Social Structures of Usenet."

References

Agre, Phil (1997). "Toward a critical technical practice: Lessons learned in trying to reform AI." In *Social Science, Technical Systems and Cooperative Work: Beyond the Great Divide*, edited by Geoffrey C. Bowker, Susan Leigh Star, William Turner, and Les Gasser. Mahwah, NJ: Erlbaum.

Anderson, Benedict (1983). *Imagined Communities: Reflections on the Origin and Spread of Nationalism*. London: Verso.

Berreman, Gerald (1966). "Anemic and Emetic Analyses in Social Anthropology." *American Anthropologist* 68, no.2, part 1 (1966): 346-354.

Card, Stuart K., Jock D. Mackinlay and Ben Shneiderman (editors) (1999). *Readings in Information Visualization: Using Vision to Think*. San Francisco: Morgan Kaufmann Publishers.

Castells, Manuel (1996). *The Rise of the Network Society: Economy, Society and Culture, Vol. I*. Cambridge, MA: Blackwell.

DiBona, Chris, Sam Ockman and Mark Stone (editors) (1999). *Open Sources: Voices from the Open Source Revolution*. Cambridge, MA: O'Reilly.
<http://www.oreilly.com/catalog/opensources/book/toc.html>.

Dourish, Paul, and Matthew Chalmers (1994). "Running Out of

What Does a Very Large-Scale Conversation Look Like?
Warren Sack

FIRSTPERSON

Space: Models of Information Navigation." Presented at HCI 1994, Glasgow.

Fellbaum, Christiane (editor) (1998). *WordNet: An Electronic Lexical Database*. Cambridge, MA: The MIT Press.

Foucault, Michel (2000). "Discourse and Truth: the Problematization of Parrhesia." In *Fearless Speech*, edited by Joseph Pearson. New York and Santa Monica: Semiotext(e)/Smart Art.

Gardner, Howard (1987). *The Mind's New Science: A History of the Cognitive Revolution*. New York : Basic Books.

Garfield, E. (1979). *Citation Indexing: Its Theory and Applications in Science, Technology and Humanities*. New York: John Wiley.

Gladwin, Thomas (1964). "Culture and Logical Process." In *Explorations in Cultural Anthropology: Essays Presented to George Peter Murdock*, edited by W. Goodenough. New York: McGraw-Hill.

Grefenstette, Gregory (1994). *Explorations in Automatic Thesaurus Discovery*. Boston: Kluwer Academic Publishers.

Hague, Barry N., and Brian D. Loader (editors) (1999). *Digital Democracy: Discourse and Decision Making in the Information Age*. New York: Routledge.

Harabagiu, Sanda, and Dan Moldovan (1999). "Enriching the WordNet Taxonomy with Contextual Knowledge Acquired from Text." In *Natural Language Processing and Knowledge Representation: Language for Knowledge and Knowledge for Language* , edited by S. Shapiro and L. Iwanska. Cambridge, MA: AAAI/The MIT Press.

Hearst, Marti (1998). "Automated Discovery of WordNet Relations." In *WordNet: An Electronic Lexical Database*, edited by Christiane Fellbaum. Cambridge, MA: The MIT Press.

Hutchby, Ian, and Robin Wooffitt (1998). *Conversation Analysis: Principles, Practices, and Applications*. Malden, MA: Polity Press.

Johnson, Lewis, and Elliot Soloway (1985). "PROUST: Knowledge-Based Program Understanding." IEEE Transactions on Software Engineering, Vol.SE-11, no.3 (1985): 11-19.

Kuhn, Thomas (1996). *The Structure of Scientific Revolutions*. Chicago, IL : University of Chicago Press.

Lakoff, George, and Mark Johnson (1980). *Metaphors We Live By*. Chicago: University of Chicago Press.

Munro, Alan J., Kristina Hook and David Benyon (editors) (1999). *Social Navigation of Information Space*. London and New York: Springer Verlag.

Resnick, Paul, and Hal R. Varian (1997). "Introduction: Special Section on Recommender Systems." In Communications of the ACM, 40, no.2 (March 1997).

Sack, Warren (1992). "Knowledge Compilation and the Language Design Game." In *Intelligent Tutoring Systems, Second International Conference (Lecture Notes in Computer Science)*, edited by Claude Frasson, Gilles Gauthier, and Gordon McCalla. Berlin: Springer-Verlag.

Sack, Warren (2000a). "Discourse Diagrams: Interface Design for Very Large-Scale Conversations." In Proceedings of the Hawaii

International Conference on System Sciences, Persistent Conversations Track, Maui, January 2000.

Sack, Warren (2000b). "Conversation Map: A Content-based Usenet Newsgroup Browser." In Proceedings of the International Conference on Intelligent User Interfaces, New Orleans, January 2000.

Sack, Warren (2000c). "Design for Very Large-Scale Conversations." Ph.D. Thesis, MIT Media Laboratory, February 2000.

Sack, Warren, and Randy Bennett (1993). *Method and System for Interactive Computer Science Testing, Analysis and Feedback*. Patent number 5,259,766, issued Nov. 9, 1993.

Sack, Warren, and Joseph Dumit (1999). "Very Large-Scale Conversations and Illness-Based Social Movements." Presented at Media in Transition, MIT, October, 1999.

Schiffrin, Deborah (1994). *Approaches to Discourse*. Cambridge, MA: Blackwell, 1994.

Sengers, Phoebe (2001). Critical Technical Practices web page. <http://www-2.cs.cmu.edu/~phoebe/work/critical-technical-practices.html>.

Smith, Marc (1997). "Netscan: Measuring and Mapping the Social Structure of Usenet." Presented at the 17th Annual International Sunbelt Social Network Conference, San Diego, CA: February 13-16, 1997.

Turkle, Sherry (1984). *The Second Self: Computers and the Human Spirit*. New York: Simon and Schuster.

Varian, Hal, and Carl Shapiro (1999). *Information Rules: A Strategic Guide to the Network Economy*. Cambridge, MA: Harvard Business School Press.

Suchman, Lucy (1987). *Plans and Situated Actions: The Problem of Human-Machine Communication*. Cambridge: Cambridge University Press.

Tsagarousianou, Roza, Damian Tambini and Cathy Bryan (editors) (1998). *Cyberdemocracy: Technology, Cities and Civic Networks*. New York: Routledge.

Wardrip-Fruin, Noah, and Brion Moss (2001). "The Impermanence Agent: Project and Context." In *Cybertext Yearbook 2001*, edited by Markku Eskelinen and Raine Koskimaa. Saarijärvi: Publications of the Research Centre for Contemporary Culture, University of Jyväskylä.

Wasserman, Stanley, and Joseph Galaskiewicz (editors) (1994). *Advances in Social Network Analysis: Research in the Social and Behavioral Sciences*. Thousand Oaks, CA: Sage Publications.

Wellman, Barry (1999). "Living Networked in a Wired World." *IEEE Intelligent Systems* 14, no.1 (January/February 1999): 15-17.

Wittgenstein, Ludwig (1958). *The Blue and Brown Books*. New York: Harper and Row.

Community of People with No Time: Collaboration Shifts

Victoria Vesna

Introduction

Although communication networks offer the possibility of a distributed community that can collaborate and exchange vital information, there is little time for these collaborations and exchanges to occur. Ironically, the same technology that makes distributed community a possibility and promised to save us time also prevents us from actually having time to build community. But once one accepts the state of distributed presence, inevitably this means acceptance of a group consciousness, which itself shifts our perception of time and even productivity. This essay uses a large collaborative networked art work *n0time* as an example of how the creative process shifts when working on the networks.

> If the seventeenth and early eighteenth centuries are the age of clocks, and the later eighteenth and the nineteenth

centuries constitute the age of steam engines, the present time is the age of communication and control. (Wiener 1948)

Three qualities are necessary for work on the networks: a need to connect, a willingness to collaborate, and the ability to embrace the fact that the work may change form and be re-appropriated in the process. In other words, this type of work requires letting go of the idea of "control" we inherited from cybernetics and the industrial approach to computing. As we move into the age of bioinformatics, these systems are clearly not working for the advancement of social consciousness or collective intelligence. The internet provides us with a space to address some of these issues, but in order to use this environment effectively, the meaning of "networking" has to be extended beyond the physical computer communication infrastructure. But how does this impact the context that the artist usually works in; i.e., exhibiting the work in cultural institutions, working with the organizers and curators, and most importantly, in relation to the audience?

Although museums and most galleries are not designed to exhibit networked physical installation with all its complexity, and some may even say that they are outmoded as cultural centers, I believe that it is

---

Response by Stephanie Strickland

There is an uncalculated cost to abstracting information patterns from a body, and then again to forming a "data body" from patterns: an energetic cost, a time cost, and a loss that comes from viewing bodies as mere vehicles for pattern, whether that pattern be mathematical, statistical or structural.

Vesna addresses these issues in *n0time*, as she did previously in *Datamining Bodies*. Her solution is to visualize social networks using tetrahedra and tensegrity (Kenneth Snelson, Buckminster Fuller) principles. In other words, a figure that has shown itself to be highly useful at many scales for gravitational architectures — of all polyhedra, the tetrahedron has the greatest resistance to an applied load — is

proposed as equally good for a networked social information architecture; it is hoped that its mathematical beauty — the tetrahedron is its own dual, the tetrahedron is at the root of an omni-symmetrical spacefilling vector matrix — will re-emerge as beautiful human interaction.

Vesna states that her *n0time* project was inspired by 1) a pervasive lack of time "to socialize, to think, to be in a space where there is no constructed time related to efficiency and productivity"; 2) the Y2K moment, in which we became conscious of complex connectivity, of dependence on networks, of our fear of disconnection; and 3) a persistent demand from participants in her earlier *Bodies INC* project, which used graphical human-appearing avatars, for a way to create a community and

important for these very reasons to show the work in these spaces. Traditionally, cultural institutions were designed as social places where people met, viewed art and discussed historical and philosophical issues. This is not a bad tradition to continue, but it certainly warrants some major shifts, and by extending out into the Net, this is bound to happen.

Social networking, on- or off-line, is directly connected to our relationship to time. The project *n0time* is conceived to raise questions about our perception of time and identity as we extend our personal networks through technology. It is designed to address problems most specific to the Western human condition that seems to be entering a crisis because of its particular stress on productivity and efficiency in structuring time. For instance, the year 2000, anticipated with great fear in the West, was year 6236 according to the first Egyptian calendar; 5119 according to the current Mayan Great Cycle; 2753 according to the old Roman calendar; 2749 according to the ancient Babylonian calendar; 2544 according to the Buddhist calendar; 1997 according to Christ's actual birth (*ca.* 4 BC); 1716 according to the Coptic calendar; 1378 according to the Persian calendar; 208 according to the French Revolutionary calendar; and the Year of the Dragon according to the Chinese zodiac.

About Time

"Time Rules Life," the motto of the National Association of Watch and Clock Collectors, is a statement borne out in formal time units that make up our calendar, as well as in the way everyday events in our lives have become organized and packaged. With the expanded influence the Net affords us, our time is becoming increasingly compressed and scarce, thus having a direct effect on how an audience/artist relationship evolves, particularly for artists working online.

As we approached the year 2000, The End of the World as We Know It (TEOWAWKI) was pronounced on the Net. Large discussions were sparked by a small programming glitch. No one imagined that the convention for marking the passage of time used in the 1950s would still be used when 1999 rolled over to 2000. 1999 marked a year of collective anxiety, when people asked: will the phones stop ringing and planes stop flying and money markets start crashing at 12:01, January 1, 2000? Countries mobilized to prevent chaos, shelves in bookstores were dedicated to ever-increasing publications on the subject, legal firms geared up for a profitable year involving the bug. Numerous newsgroups devoted to the subject formed, posting the alarming news that the FAA was hopelessly behind schedule in patching air-traffic control systems;

communicate with each other.

One point muted by this paper is that there are many structures, many mathematics, and many forms of networking that might be played and plied to the human ends Vesna envisions, namely "to move towards embodied information, with all its human qualities. . . ." The very question of whether graphic visualization is the mode for that task, as opposed to a sonic score, a textual environment, scientific visualization, or some combination, has not begun to be comprehensively researched. It will no doubt prove true that no single environment or architecture will prove best for all people or all purposes.

How does *n0time* work? A major interface confusion, for a project whose title and motivation has to do with

time, is the use of the term "interval" which can apply to space or time. People who log in online, or selected members of an installation audience, are invited to "spend a few minutes... determining the length of six intervals," namely the six edges, from which their tetrahedron is built. Though they are given color charts and one-word categories (family, spirituality, finance, etc.) to select from, and may believe they are assigning a length=importance measure to these categories, in fact they are not. In the first place, six edge-lengths for a tetrahedron cannot be determined independently; in the second place, unannounced to the participant, their decisions are being "timed." The amount of time they spend selecting a length, or strength, measure for the categories drives the resulting evolution of the *n0time* economists predicted recessions, and a respected author of computer software books, Ed Yardeni, announced the possible collapse of the U.S. government (Borland 1998).

The millennium bug paranoia was a bit different from the many millennial movements that saw it as yet another sign of the times - it was a tangible problem hardwired into the very fabric of our society (Poulsen 1988, 168). Yet in its fatalistic premise it certainly overlapped with the religious movements, which ironically may be what raised the consciousness of connectivity and the complexity of the global networks we are all part of. It was disappointing to find that most discussion on the subject largely revolved around bug fixes, remedies, and reports, rather than exploring the meaning of that collective fear. This moment that threatened to create havoc by disconnecting parts of the system made many acutely aware of our interdependency on the networks.

Finance systems and the global corporate structures are the most tangibly related to computing networks, and they were particularly worried because of their inherently shaky foundations. It is well known that much of the market's oscillations are based on purely psychological aspects - there are many instances where the market is thrown off-balance in one direction or other by rumors, not fact. Although the fatalistic visions of the millennial bug did not come true, it is quite possible that a collective realization and the resulting fear of being disconnected could ever so slightly have shifted our collective perception of time and networks. Perhaps because so many predictions now seem silly, the discussion around this phenomena has been muted. It is, after all, embarrassing when one considers the stories, rumors and the large amount of resources allocated to "fix" this problem in the West.

To me, it remained an inspiring moment, particularly when conceptualizing a piece that deals with social networks and time. In fact, the core of *n0time* is rooted in this moment in time. How does one approach developing a work that prompts questions of our relation to time in connection to technology and points to how fragile the system is? How does one visualize the fact that one fearful thought, one rumor, one meme,[1] can spark off a ripple of change in our consciousness?

Physicists Per Bak and Kan Chen, of the Santa Fe Institute, wrote a decade ago that systems as large and as complicated as the earth's crust, the stock market, and the ecosystem are not only impacted by the force of a mighty blow but also by a drop of a pin (Bak and Chan 1991, 46). Large interactive systems perpetually organize themselves to a critical state in which a minor event starts a chain reaction that can lead to a catastrophe. Along with their colleague Chao Tang, they

---

tetrahedral body. The data body is further personalized by choosing four memes, one per vertex, with which the participants associate a soundscape, creating "a unique composition for each person."

Whether this unique composition well represents someone for human communication is, I think, open to question. Vesna cites both chaos theory and tensegrity background for her work, but I think the thermodynamic-based thought of Fuller is more prominent than the chaos studies. It would be interesting to test the *n0time* system for sensitive dependence on initial conditions, that human input which has been so abbreviated, and in part unknowing.

The other difficulty, for me, are the memes. The trouble with memes is they can't be thought — they, rather, present themselves as units of thought. As with genes, blasts of energy must be brought to break them up. A project that interrogates the meme "clone," not to propagate it through recombination, but to destroy it, so that a more adequate concept might arise, is Natalie Jeremijenko's (1998–present) *OneTrees*. Jeremijenko's cloned tree/s looked different, even as seedlings within their nursery environment, to the great disappointment of visitors trained by the meme to believe that they should expect perfected identity. The clone tree/s, now planted around San Francisco, continue to diverge in history and appearance, giving the lie to genetic determinism, DNA code as the essence of life, and other implications of the "clone" meme.

The destination of the *n0time* data body is a

251

proposed a theory of self-organized criticality: many composite systems naturally evolve to a critical state in which a minor event starts a chain reaction that can affect a number of elements in the system. Chain reactions are a integral part of a dynamic system. As Buckminster Fuller (1986) proposed with "synergetics" decades before, their approach is holistic - global features of the system cannot be understood by analyzing the parts separately. Y2K, then, was a symptom of such a pin.

Art Time

Mechanical reproduction permitted art to leave the museum, and music to leave the concert hall. Printing, photography, and audio recording made the objects of culture available to anyone interested. In the process, the value and mystery surrounding the original work of art - what Walter Benjamin called its "aura" - was diluted in a sea of similar images. Equally, as the communication networks expand our field of influence much wider than we can handle alone, the aura has by necessity to expand to a group of people rather than a single individual. Shifting from industrial to digital/internet time requires a shift in our consciousness.

Art, traditionally a resort of meditative stillness, became preoccupied with motion early in the twentieth century, and we are inheriting a world that is trying to catch up to the computing speed. In 1912, Marcel Duchamp incited a scandal with his *Nude Descending a Staircase*; Edward Mybridge used the camera to analyze the mysteries of locomotion; cinema speed accelerated; and even architecture is not conceived of as fixed. Through the twentieth century, war, as Paul Virilio (1984) argues, has served as a "speed factory." Einstein explained that the inertia of matter increases with acceleration. Therefore the faster we go, the more damage we do to others and ourselves.

Perhaps the most interesting and ambitious project that addresses the issue of chasing time is "The Clock of the Long Now." Conceived by Danny Hillis, developer of the "massive parallel" architecture of the current generation of supercomputers, the clock was designed to respond to the computer industry's love affair with speed. The clock ticks once a year, bongs once a century, and the cuckoo comes out once every millennium. It is meant to inspire people to think long term, to embody "deep time." The clock project became the Clock/Library - a library of deep future, for the deep future, storing extremely long-term scientific studies, or accumulating a Responsibility Record of policy decisions with long-term consequences. In addition to the physical clock, this idea as a cultural tool is planned to be distributed via the Net, in publications and distributed services.

dramatized, announced implosion which occurs automatically when it reaches a point of information overflow, stated on the web site <http://n0time.arts.ucla.edu/concept/concept_content-int.htm> to consist of 150 intervals. "The overflowing body is archived and accessible only to the owner." Since "[e]ach *n0time* body becomes a chat room where people can meet," it seems the function of the program is to kill and remove the "old body," as occurs on MOOs, but without offering the actual affordances for communication and community present on many MOOs.

How does *n0time* relate to time? A claim Vesna makes in her introduction is that distributed presence shifts our perception of time. I do believe that online experience and distributed presence shift our perception of time, as argued in (Strickland 2000/2001) "Dalí Clocks: Time Dimensions of Hypermedia." Vesna wants to make audiences aware "that one fearful thought, one rumor, one meme can spark a ripple of change in our consciousness," and the perception of a wave effect traveling through a visualization may well do this, creating a sense of that Y2K moment, but neither our lack of time nor our craving for communal communication are relieved.

To the contrary, the *n0time* project, though demanding very little initially from its participants, is very time-intensive thereafter. Participants must individually vet those permitted to interact with their data bodies, even though, somewhat ironically, Vesna's

Internet Time

> Whether communication is by telephone hook-up or by wireless radio, what you and I transmit is only weightless metaphysical information. Metaphysical, information appreciative, you and I are not the telephones nor the wire or wireless means of the metaphysical information transmitting. (Fuller 1975, 326.05)

Computer networks demand efficiency and result in fragmentation and what Innis coined as obsession with present-mindedness (Innis 1951, 87) and what Jeremy Rifkin (1987) calls the new nanosecond culture. As we expand our fields of communication and influence through the Net, so we compress the time we have. In *The Condition of Postmodernity*, social geographer and theorist David Harvey refers frequently to time-space compression: processes that so revolutionize the objective qualities of space and time that we are forced to alter, sometimes in quite radical ways, how we represent the world to ourselves. Harvey finds such compression central to understanding the now commonplace concepts of the world as a global village (Harvey 1989, 240).

Steven Jones argues that: "A particular interest of the internet is its bias towards time, and not space; though the most popular definition of it is cyberspace" (Jones 1997, 12). He believes that the internet does in its way have a bias towards space too, but a laissez-faire bias, not one that structures space, so much as one that entirely obliterates it as a sense-able construct and so renders it absurd. But, if we are to gain an understanding of how networked environments may best be worked with, it is necessary to consider time as not separate from the information space we inhabit with our attention. Cyberspace is seen as a place that is inherently artificial, while time-space is not perceived of as fictitious or imaginary. In fact both are artificial constructs and one cannot exist without other. Information demands time, relationships demand time. If appreciation of art is connected to the premise of helping the audiences transcend the clock time and enter into a non-production-oriented time, the question then is: who has the luxury of such time?

Biological Time

> "Life," materialized as information and signified by the gene, displaces "Nature," preeminently embodied and signified by the old-fashioned organisms. From the point of view of the Gene, a self-replicating

own experience of connecting with her programming collaborator, Gerald de Jong, came not from her personal 500-person network but through that open-ended, time-draining activity, "researching on the Web." Any communication (other than intratetrahedral) occurs as a result of logging in, or navigating onsite at an installation, to check out avatar growth and perhaps engage in chat, devoting "attention and time," as Vesna states.

I would hope that in one of the further phases of *n0time* its interface and visual display would more clearly communicate that a timed profile was being collected. Might it also explore other times and timings — dating of time-sliced structures, variously timed rates of growth and disclosure, filtering for rhythmic

preference? Community according to time available is presently created by listservs and chatrooms, but community sensitive to variations in time-handling is not understood.

Any kind of time/timing system calls for calibration. A lunar calendar must be calibrated with a solar one, and these with an atomic clock. The interrelation of these, or their analogues, could be handled within a digital network — and the experience of "living with" different intervals could be sampled. We know, from written accounts, that a world timed by sun position felt very different to one governed by the ringing of church bells, and that, in turn, very different to one organized into international time zones and transportation schedules. Time online is yet another auto-generator, "the whole is not the sum of its parts, [but] the parts summarize the whole." (Haraway 1998, 183)

In 1944, Erwin Schrödinger, an Austrian physicist who developed the understanding of wave mechanics and received a Nobel prize as a result, wrote a short book entitled *What is Life?* (1992), in which he advanced a hypothesis about the molecular structure of genes. This book stimulated biologists to think about genetics in novel ways and opened a new frontier of science - molecular biology. This new field unraveled the genetic code and ushered us into an age when we began perceiving our own physical architecture as "information." That same year, George R. Stibitz of the Bell Telephone laboratories produced the very first general purpose, relay-operated digital computer. We are now at the threshold of entering an age of biologically driven computers and can only anticipate that this will entail an enormous paradigm shift from industrial-based digital mechanics to ubiquitous computing that could become true extensions of our bodies.

Biologists such as Francesco Varela (1995) and Lynn Margulis (2000) are questioning what relationships our own bodily architecture and our societal organizations have to these underlying biological principles. An entire field of consciousness studies is questioning what we know now about neurons in our brain and their relationship to consciousness. The consideration of silicon chips linked into high-bandwidth channels as the neurons of our culture, looking to how networks have naturally evolved, and comparing this to any network has two ingredients: nodes and connections. How these are designed and what the implications are is a very important question for information architects to ask themselves.

Gene mapping, according to Donna Haraway (1998), is a particular kind of spatialization, she calls "corporealization," which she defines as "the interactions of humans and non-humans in the distributed, heterogeneous work processes of technoscience.... The work processes result in specific material-semiotic bodies - or natural-technical objects of knowledge and practice - such as cells, genes, organisms, viruses and ecosystems" (Haraway 1998, 186). Information topographies are emerging: in the biological sciences, mapping the human body or the genome, and in the computer sciences mapping the information activities on the networks.

In January 1998, Donald E. Ingber published an article in *Scientific American* in which he makes the extraordinary claim that he has recognized a universal set of building principles that guide the design of

time world, one that *n0time* may perhaps explore more specifically. With variations in the representation of visitors and with a greater variety of time paths by which their data-bodies seek others, *n0time* can teach us more about social network creation.

Vesna Responds

Connect the n space to the 0 and understand that the lack of time due to information overflow is an illusion. There is, however, 0 time in n space that we can strive for.

http://www.electronicbookreview.com/thread/firstperson/vesnar2

organic structures, from simple carbon compounds to complex cells and tissues. This article proved to be a major inspiration for n0time and reaffirmed my belief that the architectural principles of which Fuller was a proponent could be of significant importance when considering building information architectures. In his article Ingber states that "identifying and describing the molecular puzzle pieces will do little if we do not understand the rules of their assembly" (Ingber 1998, 30). For two decades he discovered and explored the fundamental aspects of self-assembly. For example, in the human body, large molecules self-assemble into cellular components known as organelles, which self-assemble into cells, which self-assemble into tissues. Ingber discovered that an astoundingly wide variety of natural systems including carbon atoms, water molecules, proteins, viruses, cells, tissues, humans, and other living creatures are constructed by a common form of architecture known as tensegrity (figure 21.1).

Tensegrity takes us back to Black Mountain College in 1948, where Buckminster Fuller taught and worked with Kenneth Snelson, now an internationally renowned sculptor, then a young student who came under his spell along with John Cage and many others. Deeply inspired by Fuller, Snelson came up with a prototype employing discontinuous compression that Fuller later coined "tensegrity." Tensegrity (Tensional Integrity) was at the heart of Fuller's universe. After some time passed, Fuller ceased to credit Snelson for the prototype, causing a deep rift between the two for decades.

Donald Ingber writes: "...in the complex tensegrity structure inside every one of us, bones are the compression struts, and muscles, tendons, and ligaments are the tension-bearing members. At the other end of the scale, proteins and other key molecules in the body also stabilize themselves through the principles of tensegrity" (Ingber 1998, 32). Using a simple tensegrity model of a cell built with dowels and elastic cords, he shows how tensegrity structures mimic the known behavior of living cells. A tensegrity structure, like that of a living cell, flattens itself and its nucleus when it attaches itself to a rigid surface and retracts into a more spherical shape on a flexible

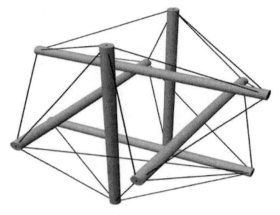

21.1. A tensegrity structure.

substrate. Understanding the mechanics of cellular structures could lead to new approaches to cancer therapy and tissue repair and perhaps even to the creation of artificial tissue replacements (Ingber 1998, 30–39).

Ingber talks about Fuller in his article and about the molecule that was named after him, and indeed has been well-acquainted with the work of Snelson as well as Fuller. In 1983, he wrote a letter to Fuller in which he stated,

> The beauty of life is once again that of geometry with spatial constraints as the only unifying principle. It is of interest to note that, as presented in the accompanying paper, cancer may be then viewed as the opposite of life resulting from a breakdown of this geometric hierarchy of synergetic arrangements. (Edmonson, 257)

In 1962 when chemist Sir Aaron Klug observed geodesic structuring of viruses and wrote to Fuller telling him of his discovery, Fuller wrote back immediately with the formula for the number of nodes on a shell (10f + 2, varying according to frequency) as confirmation of Klug's hypothesis, and Klug answered that the values were consistent with the virus research (Edmonson 1987, 239). It is important to note that geodesic domes were utilized worldwide fifteen years before electronmicroscopy enabled detection of virus capsids. In 1982, Klug won a Nobel prize for his "structural elucidation of important nucleic acid-protein complexes," and has been described as a "biological map maker," a Magellan "charting the infinitely complex structures of the body's largest molecules" (Associated Press 1982).

Whereas cells were regarded as the basic building blocks of living organisms during the nineteenth century, the attention shifted from cells to molecules toward the middle of the twentieth century, when geneticists began to explore the molecular structure of the gene. Biologists were discovering that the characteristics of all living organisms - from bacteria to humans - were encoded in their chromosomes in the same chemical substance and using the same code script. After two decades of research, biologists have unraveled the precise details of this code. But while they may know the precise structure of a few genes, they know very little of the ways these genes communicate and cooperate in the development of an organism. Similarly, computer scientists may be well-versed in networked technologies but have no clue as to how and why the internet exploded as it did - naturally, spontaneously.

During the 1950s and 1960s, strategic thinking using "systems analysis" emerged, pioneered by the RAND Corporation, a military research and development institution. This was happening at the same time that the greatest discovery in biology occurred - the physical structure of DNA. Watson and Crick explicitly described DNA in computer terms as the genetic "code," comparing the egg cell to a computer tape. This school of thought is perpetuated in even more extreme terms by proponents of Artificial Life such as Chris Langton, who speaks of separating the "informational content" of life from its "material substrate." As Richard Coyne notes: "Information is thought to be the essence of life, as in the DNA code. To record and break the code is to have mastery over life" (Coyne 1995, 80).

The most common organizational pattern identified in all systems is networking. All living systems are arranged in a network fashion. Since the 1920s, when ecologists began studying food chains, recognition of networks became essential to many scholars, in different forms. Cyberneticists in particular tried to understand the brain as a neural network and to analyze its patterns. The structure of the brain is enormously complex, containing about 10 billion nerve cells (neurons), which are interlinked in a vast network through 1,000 billion junctions (synapses). The whole brain can be divided into subnetworks that communicate with each other in a network fashion. All this results in intricate patterns of intertwined webs, networks nesting within larger networks (Varela 1995, 94).

There have been a growing number of researchers who are working on visualizing the network geographies, mapping data use. As the networks continue to expand with unbelievable speed, systems administrators increasingly look more to visual representation of data to give them a quick overview of the status. Martin Dodge at the Centre for Advanced Spatial Analysis, at University College, London, has put together an impressive array of various research efforts to visualize the Net. Network topology maps typically show things such as traffic information flow; however, more and more scholars are recognizing the value of visualizing network topologies for analyzing social, demographic, and political information flow. In my mind, this is the beginning of the art and science of visualizing and analyzing the patterns of communication networks. This is the beginning of mapping our online societies and viewing ourselves as a particular organism, and here we have rich territory for artists working on the networks.

With the advent of Internet 2 and ubiquitous computing, we are bound to see networked spaces move into three-dimensional topographies. Scientific discoveries are influencing the way we think about information and moving beyond digital computing into the biological realm. The question that arises then is: how do we visualize social networks that do not disembody information for a community of people with no time?

Collaboration Time

> Thence evolved a mathematics based on
> the proportion of reciprocal forces,
> complements, and functions of a mobile,
> non-static TIME-world. Thus the scientist-
> philosopher-artist, by the teleological
> mechanism of mathematics which contains
> in its infinite ramifications all the secrets
> personally contacted by the Yogi, made
> possible continuity of the expression of the
> truth beyond "the great wall" of the body
> and of personal death. (Fuller 1986, 105)

Just as relationships are shifting due to networks, so
too is the creative process for those working on the Net,
and the meaning of collaboration changes drastically.
The word "collaboration" assumes a very different
meaning when there is a lack of time and too much
information. Collaboration happens in many ways, and
unfortunately for those who would like a clearly
organized world, there is no one straight formula. As
projects get more elaborate, the need to work with
others is simply a necessity, and with the internet, we
have the option of collaborating with people whom we
never even meet, and consciously plan projects in
which the audience become an integral part of the piece
and even play an important role in its development.
This, together with the fact that new generations who
grew up with games and interactivity are expecting a
different type of interaction, has great implications in
the art world and in the academic environment at large
that has traditionally nurtured the idea of an
"individual."

I came to the conclusion that if tensegrity structures
work in physical architectures (as in Buckminster
Fuller's domes and Kenneth Snelson's sculptures), and
are the basis of cellular and molecular architectures, the
same principles should be applied to networked
information spaces. I started imagining how these
spaces could look and function, and was inspired to
start experimenting with the visualization of social
networks. However, I was having enormous difficulty
finding someone who could both program and

understand this type of system until I ran across Gerald
de Jong, a programmer working in Holland, while I was
doing research on the web. De Jong (1996) had
developed a system called "Struck," which later
morphed into "Fluidiom" (fluid idiom), and was actively
engaged in programming dynamic tensegrity
structures. In this system, synergetic geometry or
"elastic interval geometries," as de Jong calls them, are
used to model arbitrary database information for
visualization and decision-making purposes, as well as
for the creation of effective and aesthetic presentation
graphics and web applications. The Fluidiom Project's
inspiration was directly linked with Buckminster
Fuller's comprehensive scientific philosophy,
Synergistics. According to Fuller:

> Synergistics shows how we may measure
> our experiences geometrically and
> topologically and how we may employ
> geometry and topology to coordinate all
> information regarding our experiences,
> both metaphysical and physical.
> Information can be either conceptually
> metaphysical or quantitatively special case
> physical experiencing, or it can be both.
> The quantized physical case is entropic,
> while the metaphysical generalized
> conceptioning induced by the generalized
> content of the information is syntropic.
> The resulting mind-appreciated syntropy
> evolves to anticipatorily terminate the
> entropically accelerated disorder.

The Fluidiom Project was exactly what I was looking
for, and in February 2000, I contacted de Jong via e-
mail, introducing my research and concept. He
immediately understood the idea of creating a
networked human information architecture, using
"energetic geometries," and before long we were
collaborating on *Datamining Bodies*.

The following month, Gerald came to Los Angeles
and we spent a week working together on how my
ideas could connect to the tensegrity structures he had
been developing using the Java programming language.

257

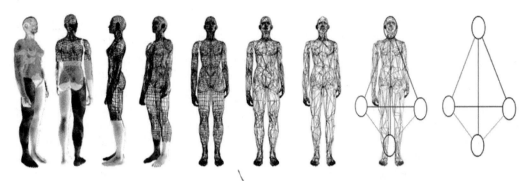

21.2. From one body to another.

As it turned out, he had very similar ideas and it was almost strange to both of us how we came to the same place from very different angles. We also knew that both of us were going to gain something from working together and from that point on, we collaborated remotely and did not meet again until the opening of the exhibition. At UCLA, I began collaborating with David Beaudry, a Ph.D. student in music who composed and spatialized the soundscapes to be used in the physical installation. David and Gerald collaborated on the sound interface online, and met for the first time just days before the exhibition to set up the work. This kind of internet collaboration would not have been possible until very recently. Initially, my intent was to create a site-specific piece that was networked, with the idea of continued further remote development. However, we found that the connection at the exhibition site was slow - only a modem was available — and we had to shift to creating both an on- and off-line version. *Datamining Bodies* was the only networked piece in the exhibition and it required a fluid collaborative process, along with a constant network connection.

nOtime

I was inspired to somehow utilize these principles of tensegrity for envisioning a different type of body, an "energetic body," meaning a body that is networked and built from information, but not dehumanized. This led me to consider some of the Eastern representations of the energy centers, specifically the chakra system. "Chakras," which means "wheels" in Sanskrit, are points of energy believed to run along our spine. Ancient Hindus formulated that there were seven of these energy wheels, each a different color and spinning in a clockwise direction. Interestingly enough, the spacing of chakras actually matches major nerve or endocrine centers, while the colors correspond to the traditional ROYGBIV divisions of visible light.

I decided to borrow the chakra structure loosely, using the colors and shapes constructed from tensegrity. At the same time I wanted to get away from the human-looking "avatar" and abstract the body by using principles of tensegrity that I considered ideal for the construction of this piece because of their connection to the biological "architecture of life" pointed out by Donald Ingber (1998). The reappearance of this universal set of building principles that guide the design of organic structures, from simple carbon compounds to complex cells and tissues, became the foundation of the architecture of information that would be mined by the audience in conceiving *nOtime*.

From 1995–1999 I was focused on developing an online participatory project, *Bodies INCorporated*. The project was audience-driven and much of it was developed as a response to certain demands and comments that radically shifted my creative process and thinking about future work. For instance, I consider this new piece as an evolution from *Bodies INC*, requiring autonomy because of the issues raised that require a different context. Thus the transition from projecting ourselves as bodies to collapsing into a space of information and geometrical patterns becomes an essential part of the project.

The most persistent demand from the growing number of people who created bodies in *Bodies INCorporated* (now over 50,000) was the need for "community," and for a way of allowing participating members to communicate with each other. This made me examine the meaning of community on the Net and compelled me to extensively research the existing efforts to create communal spaces on the web. What very quickly became apparent to me is that the recent efforts to build communities on the Net are inextricably connected to e-commerce and that the architects of these spaces are following models of malls and credit card systems.

Thus, people shopping and having similar tastes are the basis of such communities, and they are increasingly using agent technologies to search through endless data based on their personal information. Yet, while these agents are supposedly empowering us as users, we don't know how or where our information flows and these information streams tend to remain out of reach and invisible. Few people realize how quickly entire histories can be reconstructed from credit cards and social security numbers that people submit for economic transactions.

When I asked myself who the people are whom I would like to create community with, I realized that they would largely be composed of people who have very little time — in fact, the more interesting the people, the less time they seem to have. Thus it seemed to me that the logical conclusion was to conceptualize an environment that would act autonomously, largely independent of direct real-time human interaction, while representing people through the information they carry. In this system, databases, and the resultant database aesthetics, would in fact become the representation of people and interaction in this community space.

By exploring innovative ways of visualizing the trajectories of evolving human networks in relation to information, access and navigation, we will explore our relationship to time and the meaning of community in a networked environment. New methods of management, molecular and nano-political, focus not on planned communities, but on emergent communities. These types of communities require the technical infrastructure that allows for real-time collective intelligence work.

Construction of the Initial Tetrahedron

Participants are invited to spend a few minutes to create their initial minimum structure, a tetrahedron, by determining the length of six intervals, each representing an aspect of perception of self, and inputting the initial four memes. Intervals each have a color and meaning attached to them, based on the chakra system. Red represents family, orange: finances; yellow: creativity; green: love; blue: communication; violet: spirituality.

The time a person spends on deciding the length of a particular interval is registered and has an effect on the speed of replication. After determining the length, sounds are attached from a library created by David Beaudry. When the structures are in motion, the combination of the chosen sounds with the determined lengths of intervals create a personal composition.

As the cultural equivalent of genes, memes work particularly well in this context: the participants' intervals are already inscribed with ideas; the memes are meant to reinforce the possibility of further evolution of the *n0time* body. Also consider the four initial nodes of the tetrahedron in relation to the four letters of the alphabet: ACTG. The four initial ideas replicate and keep evolving into a complex structure through the interaction of others.

Because we are limited biologically to having a personal network of 300–500 people, it is programmed to implode when it reaches that point of information overflow. This moment is dramatized by an announcement to the entire community, making it aware of the implosion event. At that point the person who owned the *n0time* body has a choice of beginning from the same initial tetrahedron, creating a new one or not continuing the cycle. The decision is also announced to the community via e-mail.

Interdependence of the Physical and Net Spaces

For physical installations, in addition to the undetermined online audience, specific people are highlighted depending on the specific site and context. Once a person creates the initial tetrahedron, their presence is no longer required. They then invite people to timeshare their geometric body by adding more memes that result in replication and growth. Time spent interacting with the *n0time* bodies as well as total time spent in the space is measured throughout the experience and affects the growth patterns. The physical installation of *n0time* allows the audience to navigate these *n0time* bodies with their bodies via sensors.

The experience of time and no time is heightened in the physical structure, whose base is shaped as a spiral and creates a enclosed atmospheric space with projections and a reactive three-dimensional sound environment working in conjunction with the elastic interval geometry. By spending time navigating, participants add intervals that replicate from the initial tetrahedron shape. Memes are added only online when the intervals are created by people on site, and only by those invited by the owner to timeshare the body and add further meaning to it. Thus the physical and online spaces are interdependent.

The *n0time* environment evolves based on time spent on communicating with others and the audience's attention span with people represented as energetic geometries.

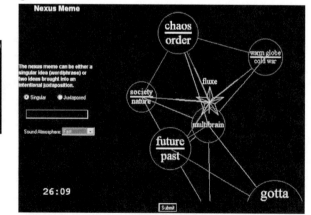

21.3. Nexus meme.

Physical Structure

Initially there was no plan to build a physical structure for the piece, but as we progressed in our development it became clear that there was a need to control the light and sound. Further, since *n0time* was scheduled to travel with the "Telematic Connections" exhibition, it became necessary to consider that the spaces would change with each location. The idea of simply building a box was not only unsatisfactory but ran contrary to the philosophy of the informational architecture. I summoned sculptor Tim Quinn to help build a structure that would reflect the work rather than simply be a "black box." Although I would have preferred to have a true tensile structure that was lightweight and easily transportable, we had to settle for using steel for the spiral structure. With the addition of this massive structure, the project made a major shift towards deliberately making the connectivity and dependency on networks a physical experience.

Note

1. A meme is an idea that is passed on from one human generation to another. It is the cultural equivalent of a gene, the basic element of biological inheritance. The term was coined in 1976 by Richard Dawkins in his book *The Selfish Gene*. Dawkins speculates that human beings have an adaptive mechanism that other species don't have. In addition to genetic inheritance with its possibilities and limitations, humans, says Dawkins, can pass their *ideas* from one generation to the next.

Examples of memes might include the idea of God; the importance of the individual as opposed to group importance; the belief that the environment can to some extent be controlled; or that technologies can create an electronically interconnected world community. Today, the word is sometimes applied ironically to ideas deemed to be of passing value. Dawkins himself described such short-lived ideas as memes that would have a short life in the meme pool.

References

Associated Press (1982). "A Map Maker of Molecules." Tuesday, October 19, 1982.
<http://www.boston.com/globe/search/stories/nobel/1982/1982n.html>.

Bak, Per, and Kan Chan (1991). "Self-Organized Criticality." *Scientific American* 264, no.1 (January 1991): 46-53.

Borland, John (1998). "Ed Yardeni: Y2K's A Bear (Market, That Is)." *TechWeb News*, July 30, 1998. <http://www.techweb.com/wire/story/y2k/TWB19980730S0001>.

Brand, Stewart (1999). *The Clock of the Long Now*. New York: Basic Books.

Coyne, Richard (1995). *Designing Information Technology in the Postmodern Age*. Boston: The MIT Press.

Dawkins, Richard (1976). *The Selfish Gene*. New York: Oxford University Press.

de Jong, Gerald (1999). *The Fluidiom Project*. <http://www.beautifulcode.nl/>.

de Jong, Gerald (1996). *Struck*. <http://www.beautifulcode.nl/struck/>.

Dodge, Martin (1996). *Cyber-Geography Research*. <http://www.cybergeography.org/>.

Duberman, Martin (1972). *Black Mountain: An Exploration in Community*. New York: E.P. Dutton & Co.

Edmonson, Amy C. (1987). *A Fuller Explanation: The Synergetic Geometry of R. Buckminster Fuller*. Boston: Birkhauser.

Fuller, R. Buckminster (1975). *Synergetic Dictionary*, edited by E.J. Applewhite. New York: Garland Publishing Inc.

Haken, Herman (1987). "Synergetics: An Approach to Self-organisation." In *Self-Organizing Systems: The Emergence of Order*, edited by F. Eugene Yates. New York: Plenum.

Haraway, Donna (1985). "Manifesto for Cyborgs: Science, Technology, and Socialist Feminism in the 1980s." *Socialist Review* no.80 (1985): 65-108.

Haraway, Donna (1998). "Deanimations: Maps and Portraits of Life Itself." In *Picturing Science, Producing Art* , edited by Caroline A. Jones and Peter Galison. New York: Routledge.

Harvey, David (1989). *The Condition of Postmodernity*. Oxford: Blackwell.

Ingber, Donald (1998). "The Architecture of Life." *Scientific American* 278, no.1 (January 1998). <http://www.sciam.com/1998/0198issue/0198ingber.html>.

Innis, Harold Adams (1951). *The Bias of Communication*. Toronto: University of Toronto Press.

Jeremijenko, Natalie (1998–present). *OneTrees*. <http://onetrees.org/>.

Jones, Steven (1997). "The Internet and its Social Landscape." In *Virtual Culture: Identity and Communication in Cybersociety*. London: Sage Publications.

Langton, C.G. (1989). *Artificial Life (Santa Fe Institute Studies in the Sciences of Complexity, Vol. VI)*. Reading, MA: Addison-Wesley.

Mandel, Thomas, and Gerald Van de Leun (1996). *Rules of the Net*. New York: Hyperion.

Margulis, Lynn, and Dorion Sagan (2000). *What Is Life?* Berkeley: University of California Press.

Mumford, Lewis (1962). *Technics and Civilization*. New York: Harcourt, Brace & World.

Poulsen, Kevin (1998). "The Y2K Solution: Run for Your Life!!" *Wired* 6.08 (August 1998). <http://www.wired.com/wired/6.08/y2k.html>.

Rifkin, Jeremy (1987). *Time Wars*. New York: Touchstone Books.

Strickland, Stephanie (2000/2001). "Dalí Clocks: Time Dimensions of Hypermedia." *Electronic Book Review* 11 (Winter 2000/2001). <http://www.electronicbookreview.com/ebr11/11str.htm>.

Schrödinger, Erwin (1992). *What is Life? With Mind and Matter and Autobiographical Sketches*. Cambridge: Cambridge University Press.

Valera, Francisco (1995). "The Emergent Self." In *The Third Culture*, edited by John Brockman. New York: Touchstone.

Varela, Francisco, Evan Thompson and Eleanor Rosch (1991). *The Embodied Mind: Cognitive Science and Human Experience*. Cambridge, MA: The MIT Press.

Vesna, Victoria (2001). *n0time*. <http://notime.arts.ucla.edu/>.

Paul, Virilio (1984). *L'Horizon négatif*. Paris: Galilée.

Wiener, Norbert (1948). *Cybernetics, or Control and Communication in the Animal and the Machine*. Cambridge, MA: The MIT Press.

261

If Things Can Talk, What Do They Say? If We Can Talk to Things, What Do We Say?

Using Voice Chips and Speech Recognition Chips to Explore Structures of Participation in Sociotechnical Scripts

Natalie Jeremijenko

Introduction (The Gossip on Voice Chips)

This essay develops a frequently asked question (FAQ) list for Voice Chips. Like the questions in most FAQs, these questions are not actually frequently asked, but they might be, and like every FAQ, the attempt is to structure the accumulation of experiences in a sociotechnical project.

Voice Chips and their newer partners, speech recognition chips, are small low power silicon chips that synthesize voice, play prerecorded voice messages, or recognize voice commands. Although this functionality is not new, what makes voice chips unique is that they are small and cheap enough to be deployed in many, in fact almost any, product. Sprinkled throughout the technosocial landscape, their presence in products is a (not quite arbitrary) sampling mechanism, and enables us to compare very different products. So their secondary function, the concern of this essay, is as a simple instrument to slice through the history of our attempts to swap attributes with machines and be able to understand the nuances of complex sociotechnical systems — precisely because the systems are rendered in the form in which we can best recognize nuance: English, be it our own or the machines'.

These chips represent in-the-wild models of the interactions between humans and machines — as reductive as they are comic, but at least a manageable examination. They are caricatures of more complex human–machine interactive systems. We will ask: What is the structure of participation scripted with these new products and with increasingly ubiquitous information technologies? By examining the "structure of participation" (who addresses what, what addresses whom, who listens, what hears and who or what acts... and other forms of participation elaborated later) rather than focusing on the interaction between the device and the "user," we pay attention to peripheral participation, the participation between users and

---

Response by Lucy Suchman: Talking Things

"You are too close. Please move away." Hearing oneself as the addressee of this phrase, Natalie Jeremijenko reminds us, effects an abrupt repositioning of subjects and objects. As hearers, we are in that moment called to a recognition of the car that "utters" these words not only as an object (to which we may or may not have been oriented previously), but as an object separate from us, to which we're assumed to have a particular relation (of proximity), and from which we're directed to step back.

Were this directive to come from someone standing beside the car we might take them to be the car's owner or, if they were in uniform, as a person assigned the job of maintaining its security. Through such an encounter we are instructed to see the car as valued, as desired and as vulnerable, and as hearers we might respond with respect, resentment or resistance. These dynamics and their performance in everyday human interaction have been eloquently described by Althusser (1971, 74), Butler (1993, chapter 4) and others interested in deciphering how normal orders are reiterated, as well as the slippages and gaps through which they are, potentially, transformed.

What Jeremijenko's essay points out is that, with the introduction of voice chip technology, the car no longer requires a human to speak on its behalf at that moment when we encroach on the boundaries of its protected space. The directive is delegated to and now emanates from the object itself and, in the process, the

Sack
Vesna

Ross Sengers
Strickland

VII. Beyond Chat

Beyond Chat >Jeremijenko Suchman Penny

around things; between users and things within systems. It is an approach to human (singular)-computer (singular) interaction that reconsiders interaction as a form of participation and escapes the simple dichotomy between social and technological.

The question we begin with is simply, when things can talk, what do they say? Our intent is to actually listen, and try to figure out whose voice it is and what it means. We then ask the complementary question: when we can talk to things (i.e., when there is speech recognition capacity embedded), what do we say? Who are we addressing? And what do we sound like? Are we polite, at least? And what is the appropriate way to talk to things (social norms)? Does it change language to be talking across the human/nonhuman divide, or how does it change us? Can we get some new insights into the old question, Is language uniquely human? We ask the voice chips these questions because they literally talk back, insisting on the scripts of participation that they were built with, reflecting the expectations and failures of our interactive technologies.

How have the things that voice chips say changed over the years since voice functionality was implemented? Does the "Chatty Cathy" of the sixties (a tape mechanism precursor to the voice chip) have anything different to say vis-à-vis the Barbie of the eighties or contemporary interactive toys? Or what is the relationship between novelty and familiarity, stability and instability, managed in these devices? Which things are given voices and which things are not, and why not? Why are they different from other talking hardware? What did the patents say they would say? And what did they actually say? What are the differences between these innovations as intellectual property and the novel devices as viable products? Exploring these questions tells us about the process of commodification of an ephemeral device, and explores the pattern of propagation of an innovation.

Where are the voices coming from? Who is hearing them, who isn't? Whose accent do they have? Does the failure of voice chips in automobiles predict anything for the future of speech recognition chips inserted in other modes of transportation, and other places? Do they work in public or private places? What does any of this tell us about ubiquitous computing? Do these voices actually work? Does a voice chip reminder to not leave your things behind, watch your step, stand back, actually make you take your thing, watch your step, or stand back? How does the function of the product change the meaning of the voice? How does the voice change the product? How do nonhuman speech devices change language? And similarly: Now that we can talk to things, what do we say? What would we prefer to

familiar ground of subjects and objects is shaken. The car is simultaneously an other who addresses us, and the thing about which the other speaks. Translated as "Stay away from me," things become even more complicated, as all of the affective nuance that adheres to that phrase from personal and common usage has its effects. The project that Jeremijenko sets out for us is to begin to disentangle the many threads of meaning and experience that give speaking things their current place in our collective world, to see what we can learn from their critical inspection, and to begin to redefine their possibilities.

Jeremijenko proposes that voice is the "direct evidence of the interactive." "Voice" is used metaphorically here, as the capacity for engaged participation, but I wonder nonetheless about the singling out that is implied. In some respects, the formulation of discrete, separable elements that together compose intelligence, interactivity, and the like is the move that underwrites the logic of AI in its usual forms. I'm reminded as well of the frequent assertion that although text and graphics-based interfaces may show limited ability to represent themselves, voice-based interfaces will resolve the problem of human–machine communication once and for all. In contrast, I would argue that while text, graphics and speech all have their particular qualities, the question of interactivity cuts across and through that of modality. Things that utter speech are not thereby interactive, any more than persons unable to

say? What would be the correct thing to say? What could we say? What does this tell us about the contingency of meaning?

Can You Capture Voice?

Voice is the icon of person. "To be given a voice" is shorthand for the fundamental units of democracy: voting, "being represented," or participating. A device of sociality and therefore interaction, it is used to interpolate a subject (presumably a person) into society (Althusser 1971), or as a performative device to instantiate social agreements and identities (Butler 1993). We will trace how the responsive and ephemeral social device of voice interaction is commodified and sold back to us.

What's So Special about Voice Chips?

Talking hardware has existed since before the time of Thomas Edison (who is generally credited with having invented the phonograph around 1877), when Alexander Graham Bell's telephone learnt to talk. The proliferation of talking hardware since has brought about the recording industry, the broadcast industry and the multimedia industry. Our exposure to voices (and other communicative sounds) that emanate from inanimate objects has become a significant part of our daily interactions: from radios to the more recent

talking elevators, answering machine messages and prerecorded music, television, automated phone menus, automatic teller machines, alarms and alerts, each of which, as we will show, speaks in a language or dialect that makes little distinction between music, sound effects and articulated words, and privileges the situational function of language over the semantic and interactive.

There are, however, distinctions to make between the voice chips, the concern of this essay, and noisy hardware more generally. Voice chips refers colloquially to: Texas Instrument TSP50C04/06 and TSP50C13/14/19 synthesizers; Motorola MC34018 or any other "speech synthesis chip implemented in C-MOS to reproduce various kinds of voices, and includes a digital/analog (D/A) converter, an ADPCM synthesizer, an ADPCM ROM that can be configured by the manufacturer to produce sound patterns simulating certain words, music or other effects."[1] The speech recognition chip is exemplified by the ISD-SR3000 Embedded Speech Recognition Engine.

The voice chip differs from other technologies of automated sound production in that it offers autonomous voices, as opposed to broadcast voices. That is, voices which are not necessarily associated with a performer, a brand, or any other preestablished identity. These chips present what we will call "local

speak are thereby mute.

Interactivity, as Emanuel Schegloff (1982) reminds us, is not the stage on which "talking in a conversational manner on different subjects" (patent #5029214, cited by Jeremijenko) takes place, nor the means through which intentionality and interpretation operationalize themselves. Rather, interaction is a name for the ongoing, contingent coproduction of the sociomaterial world, whether as familiar or as strange. Although certain forms of institutionalized interaction such as the interview may pre-allocate turns and prescribe agendas (as Jeremijenko discusses), even prescription does not foreclose the dynamic contingencies of talk-in-interaction. Interactivity as engaged participation

cannot be stipulated in advance, but requires an autobiography, a presence, and a projected future. In this strong sense, I would argue, we have yet to realize the production of an interactive thing.

To the extent that things do participate, moreover, they must be allowed to do so in their own particular ways. Voice chips, like other signs, rely very immediately upon and invoke their embedded locations for their intelligibility. Rather than things made in the image of the monadic, rational actor, we need a re-imagining of humans as contingently divisible participants in sociomaterial collectives, who live out their particular histories in uniquely inflected ways. Such re-imaginings might in turn displace a program of talking things based in an obsession with regulation and the

talk" in products that refer to themselves and don't often make claims to another's identity, or to the faithful reproduction of someone else's voice. In fact, their sound quality has effectively limited this. The "I" in "I'm sorry, I could not process your request," or the "I will transfer you now" voice of the automated operator[2] claims agency by using the first person pronoun. Presumably, the machine is referring to itself when saying "I,"[3] because it is not identifiably anyone else.

Attributing agency to technologies is a strategy that has been used by theorists to better understand the social role of technologies (Latour 1988; Callon 1995). It is a strategy that dislodges the immediate polarization of techniques and society, a strategy that refuses reduction to a situation that is merely social or only technological. Bruno Latour bases his Actor Network Theory — a theory that regards things as well as people as actors in any sociotechnological assemblage — on the ability of humans and nonhumans to swap properties. He claims that "every activity implies a generalized principal of symmetry or, at least, offers an ambiguous mythology that disputes the unique position of humans." Michel Callon and John Law (1982) have also explored nonhumans as agents, but their strategy starts with an indisputable agent (a white male scientist) and strips away his enabling network of humans and nonhumans to

demonstrate that his agency, his ability to act as a white male scientist, is distributed throughout his network of people, places and instruments. The more traditional (default) theory of technological determinism rests on the assumption that technology has an agency apart from the people who design, implement or operate it, and hence can determine social outcomes. Voice chip products take these ideas literally and actually attribute, with little debate or contest, the human capacity of speech to technological devices. Voice chips humbly preempted the theory.[4]

The voices of chips also differ from those of loudspeakers, TV/radio, and other broadcasting technologies in the social spaces they inhabit. Although radio and TV have become so portable that their voices can emanate from any vehicle, serving counter, or room — voice chip voices, by virtue of their peripheral relationship to the product, inhabit even more diverse social spaces. The identity of the voice that emanates form TV and radio reminds us that it is coming from elsewhere: "..for CBS News," "It is 8 o'clock GMT; this is London." And although Channel 9 is not a physical place, its resources and speech are organized around creating its identity, as an identifiable place on the dial. The voice chip that tells you "your keys are in the ignition" is not creating a Channel 9 identity, however. Its identity is "up for grabs," not quite settled;

---

perpetual expansion of competitive markets (including for the child consumer) through value added at the margins. Perhaps more than a dialogue with a monologue, we need the creative elaboration of the particular indexical affordances of machine "speech," and of the ways that subjects and objects together can perform interesting new effects. The former works to reiterate the subject/object divide, while the latter promises to reinvent it as new sociomaterial connections.

From Simon Penny's Online Response
The fact that they are handheld alerts me to the importance of their physically instantiated nature. They are meant to be held, to be carried, to be spoken

into or listened to. They take part in the complex choreography of embodied relation with the world. I am cautious of her isolation of the capacity of speech synthesis from other aspects of the devices. Is she committing what we might call the "Artificial Intelligence Fallacy": reductively isolating a component of sentience as being primary and disregarding the remainder? In the early history of AI, the question of sensor and effector integration with the world was cast aside, either because it was too hard, or because it was not deemed to be of prime significant in the quest for "intelligence."

If the decision-making capability of these talking devices is rudimentary, then so is their integration with the outside world. Their knowledge of the world tends

it speaks from a position of a product in the social space of daily use.

Similarly, recording media and hardware refer to what they record. We know we are listening to someone when we listen to an Abba CD. And although it is the tape player in the car that produces the sound, we claim to be listening to the violin concerto itself. The tape player as a product does not itself have a voice; it never pretends to sing, speak or synthesize violin sounds itself. The recording industry and associated technologies, born at a very different historical moment from voice chips, came out of the performance tradition.[5] Its claim to represent someone, from the earliest promotions using opera singers, to contemporary megastars, has focused the technologies around "fidelity" issues. Additionally, telephones, telephonic systems and the telecommunications industry, motivated by the communication imperative, prioritize real-time voices passing to real-time ears over fidelity. Simply stated, it is an industry that puts technologies between people, things to communicate through, "overcoming the tyranny of distance" (Minneman 1991). Invisible distance and seamless technology reflect the recording industry's ambition to "overcome the tyranny of time," enabling people to duplicate the performance regardless of when or where it was originally performed. Voice chips and their

inferior sound quality do not refer beyond themselves. Their position in a product becomes their position as a product.

How Are Voice Chips Distributed?

Voice chips provide the opportunity to add "voice functionality" to the whole consumer-based electronics industry. They are the integrated circuits that can record, play and store sounds, and more importantly, voice. They are the patented chips that play "Jingle Bells" in Hallmark greeting cards.[6] They are the voice in the car that reminds you, "Your lights are on."[7] They are the technology that makes dolls say "Meet me at the mall," and gives voices to products ranging from picture frames to pens.[9] The well-sung virtues of integrated circuits (chips) are that they are cheap, tiny and require little power. Smaller than a baby's fingernail, they have the force of a global industry behind them and an entire economic sector invested in expanding their application. Technically, they can be incorporated into any product without significant changes in their housing, their circuit design, power supply, or price. Wherever there is a flashing light, there could instead, or as well, be a voice chip.

Although most personal computers can record and play voice, the voice chip is different in that it is dedicated solely to that function. The same integrated

---

to be limited to a set of one-bit signals from immediately local finger-pressed buttons. Many of the hypothetical devices referred to in the latter part of the paper depend on unspecified and often technologically nontrivial sensor arrays. More than the use of synthetic or sampled voice as output, it is the sensor arrays and the integration and processing of sensor data that generates the semblance of sentience. A textual display, combined with such sensor processing, is unlikely to be deemed significantly more stupid than such a thing with voice output.

http://www.electronicbookreview.com/thread/firstperson/pennyr1

Jeremijenko Responds

[W]hen I claim that the voice chips are direct evidence of interaction, I mean that they are in the sense that a caricature is direct evidence: recognizable, descriptive, reductive and absurd — but not correct, and certainly not comprehensive. The voices in the whole array of products reviewed in the paper, I think, are very effective caricatures of what we expect from information technologies.

http://www.electronicbookreview.com/thread/firstperson/jeremijenkor2

circuit technology found in calculators and computers allows this tiny package to be placed ad hoc in consumer devices. Their development exploited the silicon chip manufacturing processes and its dedication to miniaturization. With sound storage capacities ranging from seconds of on-board memory to minutes and hours of recording time when configured with memory chips, they were conceived to enable voices in existing hardware, to be incorporated into products. They are the saccharin additive of consumer electronics.[10] They were first mass marketed in 1978 by Texas Instruments, though they had existed in several forms before that, particularly in the vending industry. It was not until seven years later, in 1985, that the Special Interest Group in Computer-Human Interface (SIGCHI) of the Association for Computing Machinery (ACM) professional society broke off into their own conference from other more general computing conferences. This institutionalization formalized the discussion in design communities on the Human-Computer Interface as a site of scientific investigation that differs from earlier formulations of this interface, such as Englebart's human augmentation thesis or Turing's standing-in-for ideal (Bardini 1997), but whose concerns for evaluating an interface tends toward task decomposition, with metrics of efficiency still dominating (Dourish 2001). This liminal zone where people and machine purportedly interact is where the voice chips were intended to reside. The voice chips arrived to mediate, even to negotiate, this boundary. Voice chips promised to make hardware "user-friendly," a phrase that defines the technical imagination of the time, by turning the person into an interchangeable standardized "user" and attributing a personality (i.e., friendliness) to the device. In this context the problem for designing user-friendly devices begins with the assumption that the hardware has agency in the interaction.

Writes Turkle: "Marginal objects, objects with no clear place, play important roles. On the lines between categories, they draw attention to how we have drawn the lines. Sometimes in doing so they incite us to reaffirm the lines, sometimes to call them into question, stimulating different distinctions" (Turkle 1984, 31).

Do Marginal Voices Have Any Say in the Market?

Finally, before listening to the voices themselves, I want to emphasize the peripheral relationship of the voice chip to the product. It is the position of the voice chip as marginal, not particularly intended to be the primary function of the product, that increases the present curiosity in it. The motor vehicle, for example, is not purchased primarily for its talking capacity, and pens that speak are still useful for writing. This marginality gives voice chips a mobility to become distributed throughout the product landscape and mark, like fluorescent dye, a social geography of product voices.

The chips are usually deployed — to borrow the economic sense of the term — for their marginal effects, to distinguish one product (e.g., an alarm system) from another, and give it some marginal advantage over a competing product. However, the chips are not evenly distributed throughout competitive markets (e.g., consumer electronics) in the manner one would expect for the propagation of a low-cost technical innovation driven by market structure alone.

Although consumer preferences are often claimed to have a causal determination on the appearance or disappearance of marginal benefits, it is difficult to see how the well-developed paths of product distribution have the capacity to communicate those "preferences" developed after the point of purchase. Lending the market ultimate causality (or agency) ignores the specific experience of conversing with products, the micro-interactions that enact the market phenomenon, and occludes the attribution of agency to the voice chip products, insomuch as these products speak for themselves. The voice chip products themselves have something to say, although their voices are usually ignored. In this essay we will not be examining voice chip products in the interactions of daily use, as contrapuntal to market descriptions – however, by recognizing the social assumptions that determine their physical design, we frame the imagined interactions and social worlds in which these products make sense.

Hearing Voices?

The marginality of the product makes it difficult to systematically study. Neither of the two largest manufacturers of voice chips of various types (Motorola and Texas Instruments) keep information on what products incorporate this technology, partly because they can be configured in many different ways — not necessarily as voice chips — and partly because products that talk are not a marketing category of general interest. This essay traces voice chips in two ways: first via the patent literature, and second through a more ad hoc method of searching catalogues, electronics, and toy and department stores, to compile a survey of products that have been available in the last six years (my voice chip collection was begun in June 1996).[11]

What is initially observable from the list of products and patents that contain voice chips is that there is no obvious systematic relationship between the products that include voice chips and the uses or purposes of those products. Except for children's toys, no particular electronics market sector is more saturated with talkative products. These chips are distributed throughout diverse products. However, we can view the voices as representatives, as in a democratic republic where voices are counted. Just as in a republic, each citizen has a vote, but most chose not to exercise it; likewise, most products could incorporate voice chips but most do not. We will count what we can.

22.1. The talking watch. (These images are drawn from the ephemeral propaganda form known as the *product catalog*. They have been deliberately pixelated.)

What Do Voice Chips Say?

A review of the patent literature yields a loose category scheme or typology, not by where the voice chips appeared (a technology sector approach that we will visit later), but by what they said. The patents themselves hold a tentative relationship to the products. For only two of the products on the market did I find the corresponding patents, the CPR device[12] and the recordable pen.[13] Though patents do not directly reflect the marketed products, they do represent a rather strange world of product generation, a humidicrib for viable and unfeasible proto-products. Patents track how products have been imagined and protected; while they do not by any means demonstrate market success, they do reflect a conviction of their worth, being invested in and protected. Patents are a step in the process of becoming owned, are therefore worth money, and thereby demonstrate how voice, a social technology, becomes property.

There were as of October 2001 only 163 North American patents that included a voice chip. (More recent years show a proportional increase.) In the context of the patent literature, the first thing to note is that this is a very small number — compared, that is, to the integrated circuit patent literature more generally. The question "Why not more?" we will return to later. The federal trademark office offers a suggestive list of speech-invoking names, including: *who's voice*; *provoice*; *primovox*; *ume voice*; *first voice*; *topvoice*; *voice power*; *truvoice*; *voiceplus*; *voicejoy*; *activevoice*; *vocalizer*; *speechpad*; *audiosignature*. These monikers introduce how the voice is conceptualized in the realms of intellectual property, in a different form, claiming that these voices are premium (should be listened to?) in various ways. However, the voice chips themselves seem to fall into the following loose categories:

1. *Translators*, which range from reporting and alerting to alarming and threatening and include "interactive" instructional voices;

2. *Transformers*, which transform the voice;

3. *Voice as Music*, that make speech indistinguishable from music or that present voice as sound effect;

4. *Locating Voices*, speaking from here to there about being here;

5. *Expressive Voices*, expressing love, regret, anger and affection;

6. *Didactic Voices and Imitative Voices*, mainly as in educational and whimsical children's toys;

7. *Dialogue Products*, which explicitly intend to be in dialogue with the user, as opposed to delivering instructions to a passive listener.

Products and patents often exist in more than one of these categories; for instance, the Automatic Teller Machine will not only apologize (expressive) for being out of order but will also simply function to translate the words on the screen into speech. This said, the categories remain, for the most part, distinguishable and useful.

Translators

A large category, this is the voice that translates the language of buzzes and beeps into sentences — whether English, French, or Chinese. A translator is a chip that translates the universal flashing LED, the lingua franca of the peizo electric squeal, the date code, the bar code, the telephone ringer adapter that translates that familiar ring, the tingling insistent trill of an incoming call, into "a well-known phrase of music"[14] (an approach that has since become popular in cell phones, where this function is useful in differentiating whose phone is ringing), or the unrelated patent that translates the caller identification signal into a vocal announcement.

Within the translators there are distinct attitudes; for instance, the impassive reporting, almost a "voice of nature." This is exemplified by the patent for the

menstrual cycle meter. The voice reports the date and time of ovulation, in addition to stating the gender more likely to be conceived at a particular date or time during a woman's fertility cycle. Another example is the patent for the "train defect detecting and enunciating system," which "reports detected faults in English." These chips speak with a "voice of reality," reporting "fact" by the authority of the instrument that triggers them.

Another type of translator claims more urgency than those that simply report fact. These raise an alarm and expect a response. They are less factual, more contestable perhaps. Take the "Writing device with alarm,"[15] an "invention which relates to a writing device which can emit a warning sound — or appropriate verbal encouragement — in order to awaken a person who has fallen asleep while working or studying"; or the baby rail device which exclaims, "The infant is on the rail, please raise the rail"... and then if there is no subsequent response from an attendant caregiver, raises it automatically.[16] A product on the market that will politely tell you if there is water on the ground is pictured in figure 22.2. These voice chips ask for and direct the involvement of their humans counterparts — they assume "interactive humans."

These chips articulate not only simple commands, but series of instructions as well. The CPR device[17] in figure 22.3 guides the listener through the resuscitation process. And finally, these chips translate menus of

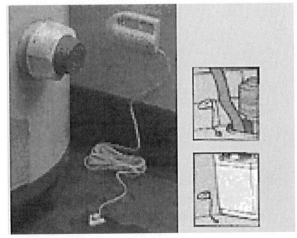

22.2. Flood warning.

22.3. CPR prompt rescue aid.

22.4. Voice changer.

choices into questions. The car temperature monitor that asks the driver, "Would you like to change the temperature?" translates from the visual menu of choices, but in the process also takes over the initiating role. What is lost or gained in the translation generates many questions: Does translating from squeals to a more articulate alarm make it any more alarming? How do spoken instructions transform written instructions? We will try to address these questions later.

There is an notable set of aberrant but related patents that exist in this "alarming" category: "Alarm system for sensing and for vocally warning a person approaching a protected object,"[18] "Alarm system for sensing and for vocally warning of an unauthorized approach towards a protected object or zone,"[19] and "Alarm system for sensing and for vocally warning a person to step back from a protected object."[20]

What seems almost like hair-splitting turns of phrase to get three separate patents has little technical consequence: the second patent has the extra functionality to detect authorized persons (or their official badge), and the third can, but need not, imply a different sensor — but each implies a different attitude. Although all patents are contestable, patent attorneys typically advise that you would not be able to successfully claim as separate patents an alarm system that warned at 15 feet and one that alerted at two feet. The "novel use" being patented here depends on the wording: the phrasing of the instruction that

determines the arrangement of the sensor and alarm/voice chip. On the strength of a differently worded warning, the importance of the technically defined product description seems to have diminished. Perhaps ElectroAcoustic Novelties, the owner of the patents, has a linguist generating an alarm system for other phrases. These patents seem to be articulating the semantics of the technology. The intentionality of the system is its voice.

Transformers

Transformers are distinct from patents that translate the voice. They translate in the other direction — not from the buzzes and squeals to spoken phrases, but from the human voice to a less particular voice. For instance: to assist the hearing impaired, a chip that transforms voices into frequency range the listener can still hear (usually a higher frequency); or the "Electronic Music Device" effecting a "favorable musical tone." "The voice tone color can be imparted with a musical effect, such as vibrato, or tone transformed."[21]

Into this category fall children's products like the "YakBak," popular in the 1997–1999 seasons, which plays back a child's voice with a variety of distortions; and the silicon-based megaphones that allow children to imitate technological effects, or sound like machines. These are voice masks, for putting on the accent of techno-dialect. The socializing voices broadcast on radio and TV, the voices of authority heard over public address systems, and the techno-personalities of androids and robots are practiced and performed by playing with these devices. This is also the category of voice chips that is concentrated in products for the hearing impaired or the otherwise disabled, and for children. These transforming devices act as if to integrate these marginalized social roles into a sociotechnical mainstream.

Speech as Music

Many of the patents that are granted specifically collapse any difference between music and speech. This contrasts with the careful attention given to the meaning of the words used in the alarm system family of the translators. An explicit example is the business card receptacle, which solves the problem of having business cards stapled onto letters — making them more difficult to read — and provides an "improved receptacle that actively draws attention to the receptacle and creates an interest in the recipient by use of audio signals, such as sounds, voice messages, speech, sound effects, musical melodies, tones or the like, to read and retain the enclosed object."[22] Another example is the Einstein quiz game that alternately states, "Correct, you're a genius!" or sounds bells and whistles when the player answers the question correctly. This interchangeability of speech and music is common in the patent literature presumably because there is no particular difference technically. In this way patents are designed to stake claims — the wider the claim the better. The lack of specificity, and deliberate vagueness in the genre of intellectual property law contradicts the carefulness of copyright law, the dominant institution for "owning" words.

Local Talk from a Distance

One would expect chips that afford miniaturization and inclusion in many low-power products to be designed to address their local audience, in contrast to booming public address systems or broadcast technologies. However, several of these voice chip voices recirculate on the already-established (human) voice highways, imagined to transmit information as you or I would. The oil spill detector[23] that transmits via radio

the GPS position of the accident, or "the cell phone-based automatic emergency vehicle location system" that reports the latitude and longitude into an automatically dialed cell phone[24] — these are examples of a voice chip standing in for and exploiting the networks established for humans, transmitting as pretend humans. This class of products, local agents speaking to remote sites, is curious because the information can easily be transmitted efficiently as signals of other types. Why not just transmit the digital signal instead of translating it first into speech? The voice networks are more "public access," more inclusive, if we count these products as part of our public, too. The counterexample, of voice chips acting as the local agent to perform centrally generated commands, is also common, as in the credit card-actuated telecommunication access network that includes a voice chip to interact locally with the customer while the actual processing is done at the main switchboard. Although the voice is generated locally, the decisions on what it will say (i.e., the interactions) are not.

Expressives

The realm of expressiveness, often used to demarcate the boundaries between humanity and technology, is transgressed by voice chips. There are, of course, expressive voice chips ranging from a key ring that offers a choice of expletives, swear words and curses to the "portable parent" that plays stereotypical advice and parental orders to the array of Hallmark cards that wish you a very happy birthday, or say, "I love you." These expressive applications also remind us of the complexities of interpreting talking cards. The meaning of these products is of course dependent on the details of the situation, rather than on the actual words being uttered: who sent the card, and when; or what traffic situation preceded the triggering of the key ring expletive.

These novelty devices lead into the most populous voice chip category: those intended for children. The toy department store Toys "R" Us currently has seven aisles of talking and sound-making products — approximately 45 different talking books alone, in addition to various educational toys, dolls and figures

271

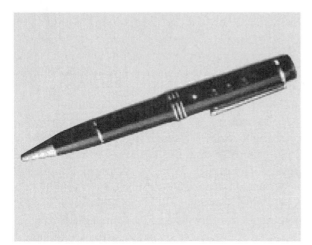

22.5. Recordable pen product.

that speak in character. The voices are intended for the entire age range, from the earliest squeaking rattles for babies, to strategy games for children 14 years of age and up — for example, the "Talking Battle Ship," in which you can "hear the Navy Commander announce the action" as well as "exciting battle sounds." The categorization of the multitude of toys extends far beyond "expressive" types, from the encouraging voices inserted in educational toys ("Awesome!," "No, try again" or "You're rolling now") such as the Phonics learning system, the Prestige Space Scholar, and Einstein's trivia game, to the same recordable voice chips used for executive voice memo pads. Chips for children are placed in pens, balls, and YakBaks; then there is the multitude of imitative toys that emulate cute animals, nonfunctional power tools and many trademarked personae, from Tigger and Pooh to Disney's recent animation characters Sampson and Delilah, Ariel the mermaid, and others.

This listing demonstrates a cultural phenomenon that enthusiastically embraces children interacting with machine voices, and articulates the specific didactic attitudes projected onto products. These technological socialization devices have already been subject to analysis, as in Sherry Turkle's study of children's attitudes towards "interactive" products.[25] Barbie, for instance, was taken very seriously for what she had to say about the polarized notions of gender she embodies. Since Barbie's introduction in 1957 she has

been given a voice three times (each with slightly different technology); her most controversial voice during the 1980s was censored for saying, "Math is hard." This controversy rests on the assumption that voice chips are social actors and do have determining power to affect attitudes — in this case a young Barbie player's attitude to math.

Although Barbie is currently silent, a myriad of talking dolls remain, from Tamagotchi virtual pets, with their simple tweets, to crying dolls that ask to be fed, and an ever-increasing taxonomy of robotic dolls and creatures. The utility patent literature continues to award "new and novel" applications in this area. One of the "new" voice chip patents is for a doll that squeals when you pull her hair (dolls that cry when they are wet or turned upside-down are technically differentiated by their simple response triggers).[26] There is also a new doll patent that covers an "electronic speech control apparatus and methods and more particularly for. . . talking in a conversational manner on different subjects, deriving simulated emotions... methods for operating the same and applications in talking toys and the like."[27] The functional categories at work here are not linguistic, nor do they resemble other ways in which a voice has been transformed into a document — for example, as in the copyright of a radio show. It would, in other realms, be very difficult to get copyright on "talking in a conversational way." In the material world the ownership of voice has been redefined.

Recording Chips

This category encompasses many of the most recent voice chip products. It is the existence of these products that tests the nature of the communication we have with these technologies: do we, can we, converse with these products? This category draws from the other typologies but is distinguishable, for the most part, by the recording functionality that is the raison d'être of the product. The category includes those products that perform a more specific speech function that could not be alternatively represented by lights, beeps, or visual display, i.e., perhaps they are more communicative. This category includes the products that seem to hold dialogue.

The category's range of products includes the shower radio (see figure 22.6) that reinterprets bathing as a time for productive work, an opportunity to capture notes and ideas on a voice chip, consistent with the theory that there is an ongoing expansion of the work environment into "private" life. It also includes both the recordable pen and its business-card-size counterpart, the memo pad. Both the pen and the pad have many versions on the market currently, and they seem to be becoming more and more populous. The YakBak is the parallel product for children, deploying the same technology with different graphics, and to radically different ends.

The growing popularity of this category compared to the others arouses a number of questions. Firstly, how do we understand why this category is popular? Is the popularity driven by consumers because these products are successful at what they do? And is what they do dialogue? Or is it that the cost and portability of the technology make it an affordable newtech symbol beyond what is attributable to its function alone? Is this category popular because it alone can be marketed as a work product?[28] And then conversely, why are these devices not more popular? Why is it that only a few types of products become the voice sites? Pens, photo frames and memo pads are all documents of a sort, in contrast to switches or menu choices.

According to the patent literature, "the failure of the market place to find a need for voice capability on home appliances has discouraged the use of voice chips in other products,"[29] but lending the market agency for design assumptions is circular logic. This does express, however, the sentiment that many more products could have speech functionality then do.

Although miniaturization has made these products possible, the concept of embedding recording capability in products has been possible with other technologies. There has been no technical barrier to providing recording capability in cars, or in any of the larger products — a refrigerator, for instance — certainly since the existence of cheap magnetic recording technologies. Why is it that now we want consumer products that talk to us?

22.6. Device for recording in the shower.

It is striking that the majority of talking products on the market currently are for conversing with oneself. Although deeply narcissistic, this demonstrates a commodification of self-talk that transforms the conceptualization of the self into subjectivity in relationship with our products. It suggests, without subtlety, that the relationship with these products is a relationship with the self. The constitution of personal and social identity by means of the acquisition of goods in the marketplace (Shields 1992) — the process of identifying products that provide the social roles we recognize and desire — cannot be excluded from the consideration of the social role of products.

Where Are the Voices Coming From?

The preceding typologies focus on what the voice chips say rather than where they say it. However, because voice chips are distributed throughout the product landscape, where they appear (and disappear) is also interesting to examine. Although a very detailed analysis could yield an interesting geography, it is beyond the scope of an essay intended to generate preliminary questions about why they say what they do where they do.

The automobile industry, a highly competitive, heavily patented industry that quickly incorporates cheap technical innovations (where they do not substantially alter the manufacturing process) is a place

22.7. Tranquil moments.

to expect the appearance of voice chips. Indeed, there was early incorporation of voice chips in automobiles. A 1985 luxury car, the Nissan Maxima, came with a voice chip as a standard feature in every vehicle. The voice chip said, "Your lights are on," "Your keys are in the ignition" and "The door is ajar." There were also visual displays that marked these circumstances, yet the unfastened seatbelt warning only beeped. By 1987, you could not get a Nissan Maxima with a voice chip, even on special request. In this case, the voice was silenced, but only for a time, reemerging with a very different role to play in the automobile.

By 1996, the voice chips reappeared in the alarm system of cars. Cadillac's standard alarm system uses proximity detection to warn, "You are too close. Please move away." In this 10-year period the voice shifted from notification to alarm, a trajectory from user-friendly to a distinctly unfriendly position. It is also interesting to note another extension of the action/reaction voice chip logic, if not the voice itself. The current Nissan model no longer notifies that the lights have been left on, it simply turns the lights off if the keys are taken out of the ignition. The courtesy of notification has been dispensed with, as well as the need for a response from the user. The outcome of leaving the lights on is already known, so the circuit will instead address that outcome. This indicates that when the results are exhaustively knowable, the need for interaction diminishes.

274

Of the seven patents specifically for vehicles,[30] all bar one are intended for private and not public transportation. However, in late 1996, voice chips began to appear in the quasi-private/public vehicles of New York's Yellow Cabs. After debate about what ethnic accent[31] should be ascribed to the voice that reminded you to "please fasten your seatbelt" and "please check for belongings that you may have left behind," the prerecorded (68k-quality) voices of Placido Domingo and other celebrities won the identity contest, and have since proliferated into many well-known New York characters, from sports stars to *Sesame Street's* Elmo. The voice chip in this quasi-public sphere adopted a broadcast voice, albeit one of poor quality, or a microbroadcast voice. Whether they are effective in increasing seatbelt wearing or reducing the number of items left in the cabs in any accent is less certain than the manner in which they articulate the social relations of the cab. The voice chips address only the passengers and assume that the drivers don't hear them, although it is the drivers who bear the brunt of their monotony. Their usefulness delegates the human interaction of service and rests on the assumption that the chips are more reliable and consistent in repeating the same thing over and over, no matter the circumstance, and that the customer responds to Placido Domingo's impassive, recorded reminder more than they would to a driver who may be able to bring some judgment to bear upon the situation. In the transformation of the passenger into a public audience (not unlike that of a radio station) the product or service itself is not attributed with the voice. Instead the voice becomes identified with a celebrity.

In the transportation sector alone we can see the voice chip develop from an anonymous to an identifiable voice, and from a polite notification to an alarm for deterring approach. Cars have struggled with the problem of talking to humans and seem to have exploited the nonhuman qualities of their speech[32] — the things that the technology is better at doing, like faithful repetition or careful reproduction of the identity of another — rather than any particularly human attribute of their speech. It is also notable that talking cars have not endured.

In the health industry, another social sector highly saturated with electronic product, the distribution of voice chips is almost exclusively on one side of the home/professional, expert/non-expert divide. Although in number there are more products made for hospitals and clinics than the home market, the placement of voice chips is inversely represented. In home products, from the menstrual cycle meter to the CPR device, electronic voices seem to play the role of the health professional or "expert." In addition, the large number of products for the visually impaired are intended for patients and not professionals (a demographic with more spending power); see, for example, the addition of a sound indicator to the syringe-filling device "for home use," which testifies that the user of this device is imagined at home, without the help of the professional for whom the product can stand in. Ironically, the most vocal equipment in this industry are the relaxation and stress reduction products, e.g., those by which you talk to yourself or are reassured and relaxed by the sounds of the ocean (see figure 22.7). The reassuring factuality of these technovoices focuses its attention on the lay audience.

These are preliminary observations of the voices introduced into transportation and in the health and medical areas, and are cursory at best. But they demonstrate that for the voice to make sense, the technological relationship itself needs to make sense. The speech from devices is as culturally contingent as language.

There are many other areas in which the introduction of voice chips provides insight into what technological relationships make sense. Their incorporation into work products articulates the transformation and reorganization of work structure, particularly into "mobile" work (Zuboff 1984).[33] They speak to a culture's popular notions of where work gets done, a culture in which providing a product to take voice notes while in the shower makes sense. The voice chip population of areas of novelty products, children's toys, and educational products, and of the safety, security and rescue products also maps the social relationships we engage in with our products. Conversely, where we don't find voice chips, for

example in biomedical equipment for health *professionals*, also maps the social relationships that the technologies play out — they stand in for experts with an authoritative voice one wouldn't use on a colleague. However, to understand the dialogue we are having with these voices requires us to also examine how we listen.

Discussion: What Do the Voice Chips Actually Mean When They Speak? Do They Actually Work?

Voices Chips as Music

The preceding categories survey what voice chips say, where it is they say it, and to whom they say it. To understand what the voice chips are saying, however, means engaging strategies for listening that may not be automatic. Products, with or without voices, are well-camouflaged by what Clifford Geertz described as "the dulling sense of familiarity with which... our own ability to relate perceptively to one another is concealed from us." Modes and strategies for listening that can help us hear these voice chips can be borrowed from music. Music, unlike machinery, is commonly understood as "culture," or a cultural phenomenon, and its analysis looks very different from the analysis of technology. The structure of participation enables multiple listeners (vs. a "user"); the "use" of music is widely divergent; and interaction with it is more specifically understood as interpretation (we don't speak of the task's decomposition, efficiency or effectiveness). Perhaps the most glaring difference is the concept of improvisation, which is prevalent in theories of music, yet is unusual in the analysis of human–machine interaction. (The striking exception is Lucy Suchman's work, which we will discuss in depth later.) Is it that improvisation is absent from our interaction with machines, or our models for designing interaction?

Our strategy here is to avoid the contested terms "reality," "progress," and "rational choice" that usually inform the analysis of technology – thus we can provide more emphasis on the interpretative experience. Additionally, some of the voice chip products themselves demonstrate an indifference to the

22.8. The funny animal piano.

distinction between speech and music, by blurring the distinction between words and beeps (see the "speech as music" category of products).

Music, like product, is also easily recognized as involved in the production of identity. That is, subcultures identify through and with music (Fabbri 1981). Where technological product is presented to the consumer, at what Cowan calls the "consumption junction," we are at such an identity-producing site.[34] For this reason it is difficult to ascribe any one particular meaning or mode of listening to the voice chips. In the wide spectrum of musical styles available, each piece of music can and does exist in widely different listening situations. This means that each

listener has a variety of listening experiences and an extensive repertoire of modes of listening. The hearing person who listens to radio, TV, the cinema, goes shopping to piped music, eats in restaurants, or attends parties, has built up competence in translating and using music impressions. This ability does not result from formalized schooling, but through the everyday listening process in the soundscape of modern city. Stockfelt asserts that mass media music can be understood as something of a nonverbal lingua franca,[35] without of course denying the other more specialized musical subcultures to which we may simultaneously belong.

Listening modes are not, of course, limited to music, and nor for that matter is a musical experience limited to music. Even so, teasing out the musical modes of listening from listening modes that focus on the sound's quality, its information-carrying aspect, or other nonverbal aesthetic modes is difficult. The "cultural work" of using unmusical sounds as music is not uncommon; for example, Chicago's Speech Choir, John Cage's *4'33"*, *The Symphony of Sirens*[36] and the sounds created with samplers, particularly for percussive effects. At the same time, the sirens, speech choirs, etc., do not lose their extramusical meaning as they become music. Conversely, using musical sounds for nonmusical ends is the conceit of many voice chip applications.

The two products in figures 22.8 and 22.9 demonstrate the confusion of musical listening vs. other modes of musical sound consumption. The Soother uses unmusical sounds for musical effect while the Funny Animal Piano uses musical sounds to respond to toddler's feet. The alignment of voice chips with music has interesting implications for their linguistic claims; if they produce meaningful speech, why don't they differentiate between music and speech?[37] Is it that the social position of the product determines the meaning of the sounds and utterances? Indeed, if the speech they produce is linguistic, then when the voice of the alarm system warns us, are we altering the meaning of the sound, whether it resembles speech or siren? Or can we expand linguistic theories to accommodate all meaningful sounds that

22.9. The soother.

humans or machines make? These questions about how we understand the sounds that voice chips produce complicate the attribution of agency to these "things with voices." Voice chips seem to frame sound as a prepackaged cultural product, the identity of which is located in the manufactured materiality. At the consumption junction these voices are heard in the buzz and squeal of products, but can we call it language?

Voice Chips as Speech

What do voice chips tell us about our understanding of language? The voice chips' languages provide a picture of our on-the-ground, in-the-market operationalization of our explicit understanding of language. Even though some voice chips use music and speech indistinguishably, the words that they say cannot be overlooked. Voice chips talk and say actual words, but how do we understand these voices as communicative resources? Are they "speech acts" as defined by linguistic theorists?[38]

Speech acts[39] are used to categorize audible utterances that can be viewed as intending to communicate something, to make something happen, or to get someone to do something. To construe a noise or a mark as a linguistic communication involves construing its production as a speech act (as opposed to a sound that we decide is not communicative). Categories of speech acts are given next (examples quoted from voice chips).

> 1. *Commissives:* The speaker places him/herself under obligation to do something or carry something out; for example, in a telephone system, "I will transfer you to the operator";

> 2. *Declaratives:* The speaker makes a declaration that brings about a new set of circumstances; for example, when your boss declares that you are fired, or when the car states, "The lights are on";

> 3. *Directives:* The speaker tells the listener

to do something for the speaker; "Please close the door," "Move away from the car";

> 4. *Expressives* are without specific function except to keep social interactions going smoothly, like "please" and "thank you," or the more expressive "I love you."

Each of these categories is performed by the voice chips examined in this essay, as are other verbs and verb phrases associated with the wider category of eloctionary acts: "to... state, assert, describe, warn, remark, comment, command, promise, order, request, criticize, apologize, censure, approve, welcome, express approval, and express regret."[40] The category in which voice chips are least convincing is the declarative that requires the reliability or trustworthiness of the agent (human and nonhuman) to understand whether or not this thing is going to come about. We note that the declarative notification that your car will turn off the lights has been removed, and the car simply enacts the turning off the lights. The voice chips also tend to inhabit the present tense, or the very recent past tense. Future tense is less common, perhaps because the autonomy of a system is held in check by the interactive scripts. And they also prefer the first person, which supports the idea that they are not referring beyond themselves.

Searle defines the "speech act" as an utterance (action) intended to have an effect on the hearer, with preconditions and effects. This has been criticized by other theorists who have pointed out that meaning is imparted by the work of an "interpretative community."[41] The limitation of speech act theory in explaining voice chips is that it ascribes the most intention to the least animate thing in the interaction. In its failure to elaborate on interpretation, it provides no place for information about the significance of any particular assertion, warning, or, more generally, any speech act. Voice chips amplify this problem because they can inhabit so many different situations yet repeat the same thing. Because the voice doesn't change, all flexibility in understanding to accommodate the changing circumstances needs to be accounted for by

277

the listener's interpretation. The case of the Cadillac's alarm voice illustrates this.

During a demonstration of the Cadillac's alarm system, the salesman instructed me to move away from the car and then approach it again. Despite coming as close as I could to the car, the voice did not sound. On hearing no voice, the demonstrator toggled the key fob switch. I approached again and the voice sounded. In the first approach, the voice chip's silence was interpreted as "the alarm is not working or is not on." In the second approach, the voice communicated, "Now the alarm is on and functioning."

By staying in the proximity range of the alarm system, the voice answered several questions, despite simply repeating the same words: "move away..." What is the area range in which we are detected? Will the alarm keep repeating, or will it escalate its command? Although moving away from the car stopped the voice, we also came to understand the types of motions that it detected, the speed of approach, what happened when we physically shook the car, etc. The simple interaction with the car and its voice demonstrates the interpretative flexibility that transcends the directive of the words stated, and how, as hearers, we respond to the voice's imperatives. So in asking how we understand the significance of speech performed by the voice chip, we are asking whether speech is abstractable.[42] In other words, is there a difference between talking with a voice chip and talking with something (human) with which we share capacities other than speech?

Is Speech Abstractable?

Speech in action, rather than in theory, is conversation. If we are to claim that we interact with voice chip speech, we need to examine the fundamental structure of conversation as the primary model for interaction.[43] One of the voice chip patents claims the rights for "electronic apparatus(es) for talking in a conversational manner on different subjects, deriving simulated emotions which are reflected in utterances of the apparatus." Although the other voice chip products make no explicit claim to be conversing, they do claim to be "interactive."[44]

Lucy Suchman's (1987) work, however, proves more appropriate to describing the interactive "speech" of voice chips. Her work focuses on the inherent uncertainty of intentional attributions in the everyday business of making sense via conversational interaction with another machine, the photocopier. Like voice chips, she characterizes these machines by the severe constraints on their access to the evidential resources on which human communication relies. She elaborates the resources for constructing shared understanding, collaboratively and in situ, rather then using an a priori system of rules for meaningful behavior.

Suchman shows that the listening process of situated language depends on the listener to achieve the shared understanding of successful communication. The listener attends to the speaker's words and actions in order to understand. Although institutional settings can prescribe the type, distribution and content of talk (e.g., cross-examinations, lectures, formal debates, etc.), they can all still be analyzed as modifications to conversation's basic structure. Suchman characterizes one form of interactional organization (or structure of participation) — in this case the interview — as a) the pre-allocation of turns: who speaks when and what form their participation takes; b) the prescription of the substantive content and direction of the interaction, or the agenda.[45] More generally she describes a system for situated communication, or conversation as "an organization designed to support local endogenous control over the development of topics or activities and to maximize accommodation of unforeseeable circumstances that arise, and resources for locating and remedying the communication troubles as part of its fundamental organization."

Conversation with a Voice Chip?

Prerecorded voices on voice chips are ill-equipped to detect communication troubles, and although they are usually triggered by local inputs, the content of what is said does not change. They will repeat the same thing, or a set of prerecorded phrases, over the indefinite range of unpredictable circumstances. Although they localize control, they for the most part do not localize the direction of speech.

Sack   Ross Sengers   **VII. Beyond Chat**
Vesna   Strickland
Beyond Chat >Jeremijenko Suchman Penny

The applications that seem closest to Suchman's characterization of conversations are the products that include "dialogue chips." These chips hand over control of the content of talk to the listener, fulfilling Suchman's characterization of conversational interaction in this respect. The listener literally controls the speaker and sets up a relationship with the device. Further, the dialogue chip products use the turn-taking of conversation collaboration, not as the alternation of contained segments of talk in which the speaker determines the unit's boundaries, but in the manner illustrated by the joint production of single sentence (Suchman 1987, 81, 125).[46] The "turn-taking system for conversation demonstrates how a system for communication that accommodates any participants, under any circumstances, may be systematic and orderly, while it must be essentially ad hoc" (Suchman 1987, 78). The alarm clocks that incorporate voice recording functions are a new example of how that control is extended over time, but remains very local.

The response to voice chips, like the applause at the end of a play, is not a response to the final line uttered, or the fact that it just stopped. "The relevance of an action. . . is conditional on any identifiable prior action of event, insofar as the previous action can be tied to the current action's immediate local environment." The conditional relevance does not allow us to predict a response from an action, but only to project that what comes next will be a response, and retrospectively, to take that status as a cue to how what comes next should be heard. The interpretability therefore relies on "liberal application of *post hoc ergo propter hoc*" (Suchman 1987, 83). The response that a listener can have to the voice of the train defect enunciation system is not only a response to the words uttered by the product. It also involves a complex series of judgments that include assessments of the information available and how to integrate this into what else the listener knows of the event at hand.

The understanding of talking products does not come so much from the words found at what is popularly conceived as the human–machine interface, but beyond this. The voice is a voice embedded in a network of local control, sequential ordering, interactional organization and intentional attribution. The recordable chips with which we can have a dialogue with ourselves, in which the control remains local, best demonstrate this. These products frame the understanding that we are talking with ourselves through our products.

Whereas dialogue is conversation with another agent, one who is somehow *there*, monologue is characterized as written speech, inner speech or rehearsed speech. Dialogue implies immediate unpremeditated utterances, whereas monologues are written speech lacking situational and expressive support that therefore require more explicit language. Questioning the abstraction of speech in voice chips does not demonstrate that speech is uniquely human. On the contrary, the stabilized voices of hardware-based speech are subject to reinterpretation, and rediscover the listener's capacity, not the speaker's incapacity. It may simply be viewed as a distinction between dialogue and monologue, neither of which are more or less human. Because we inhabit both sides of a dialogue, we can understand the voice chip's position and compensate, so as to perform dialogue with ourselves.

Can We Summarize What They Said, and What Sort of Response This Suggests?

This essay has so far examined the unique position of voice chip products, differentiating them from the background noise of contemporary culture and other technological configurations that deliver speech. These hardware-bound voices are not broadcast and have no stable identity. The survey of what the voice chips say produces typologies that suggest further modes of investigation into how we understand and use these voices, where they appear, and what their voices mean. The short product life cycle of the consumer electronic devices they inhabit position these products as the *E. coli* of sociotechnical relations and can demonstrate the formation of product identities and product voices in our shifting understanding of machine interaction. The appearance of voice chips in some types of products and not others, some social sectors and not others, is open to further investigation. Detailing these would reveal the voice chip's oral history of the process by which the very ephemeral social device of speech becomes stabilized and entered into systems of exchange.

Now I will introduce a complementary examination of speech recognition chip sets, around which there is much more recent product development activity.[47] Although the voice chip's applications may have peaked, the equivalent low power, distributed speech recognition function may be just beginning. Watching their development and deployment carefully, asking, "Now that we can talk to our products, what do we say?," may allow us to hear the social scripts they presume. Can these provide evidence that symmetry between the ambitions for human and nonhuman attributes holds?

However, because we are more self-conscious about speaking than listening, this may be an instrument through which to observe our own roles in sociotechnical interaction. In order to prime this investigation, and because speech recognition chip sets are not yet (and may never be) widely available, the author hosted a competition to survey a range of applications. The competition was advertised on a large mailing list (12,000 members): the Viridian list owned and carefully managed by science fiction writer Bruce Sterling. The list is a forum for discussing technological futures with an emphasis on addressing environmental problems. Entrants were asked to propose speech recognition interfaces to an existing product (the prize was a voice note taker and the prototyping of the proposed device). Just under three hundred designs were submitted and will soon be available on the web site <www.cat.nyu.edu/neologue>. While these entries cannot be claimed to represent the conceptions of human–computer interaction distilled by the social forces of the market, manufacturing and advertising, they can be treated as evidence of technological desires and cultural expectations.

Now That We Can Talk to Our Devices, What Do We Say?

The most striking feature the competition entries demonstrated was the explicit intention to effect social change with technological change. This may or may not

be peculiar to this list (which might be tested by hosting a similar competition in other contexts); however, this is consistent with a popular techno-determinism that attributes social change to technological change and under-represents the dominant forces of product innovation that can be attributed to sustaining and continuing a corporate entity.[48] This also contradicts other popular understandings and lay rationalizations that new products arise to address preexisting social "needs" or profit opportunities, follow fashion or to optimize existing applications.

We can summarize the trends illustrated by the proposed products and product interfaces, which are predominantly the desire for social and individual envisioning and regulation. This is apart from the ultimate (and theatrical) control fantasies that this particular type of interface engages (e.g., on saying "Showtime," the lights dim and the television and VCR turn on[49]), or the suggestions that dispensed with buttons (e.g., the TV remote[50]) without explicating what words to use. Entries that did not explore what happens in the translation from finger-button to voice-button and the social (and observable) spectacle this makes did not render the sociotechnical relationship this investigation was trying to identify. There were also the applications that were similar to voice chips – with a similar interchangeable use of speech/buzz (e.g., the cookie container that recognized children's footsteps to trigger singing, or the TV remote that called out "Polo" when it heard "Marco"[51]).

In addition to self-observation, regulation and control, the applications took on moral, physical, emotional, and consumption monitoring and regulation, in such forms as:

> A wallet that recognized words and dispensed consumption regulation advice[52];

> A pocket device that recognized the phrase "now what am I supposed to do?" and responded "with a gentle reminder to adhere to the user's selected ethical set"[53] (regulation of consumption);

A coffee maker that recognized "good morning" ("when you respond, the chip analyzes your tone of voice [for sluggishness]" and "adjusts the strength of the coffee...," thus automating the physical regulation on which Starbucks has so successfully capitalized);

A more extreme circumvention of one's own self-judgment: a device that monitors bloodflow and when detecting stress whispers "'relax,' dims the lights a bit, and releases soothing aromatherapy"[54];

And the very opposite of an alarm clock, a device that on hearing, "Why am I still up?" "...should cause every light and entertainment system in my house to shut off for 4 hours."

An example of self-observation was a voice-triggered "nocturnologue," which would record any sleeptalking.

These devices to regulate the self, presumably with the goal of social synchronization, do not necessarily imagine the devices as "companions" and attribute to them a more social performance, although there is a small subset that do. This subset of entries realize the "technology-should-be-more-humanlike" expectation, which reflects a similar school of Human Computer Interface (HCI) designers working towards adaptive interfaces that can recognize and respond to different emotive states as an explicit strategy to be "user-friendly." The best example is a comedic sidekick (Jerry Lewis) built into a watch and ready with smart rejoinders to recognized phrases (when it hears "nice hair," the device says "cha cha cha"). This functionality would have to be described as reinforcing social performance.[55] This seems both similar to other identification relationships (cars, furniture, home), and different, insomuch as it is directly inserted into the conversation.

The promise of emotive interfaces that recognize and respond to how you are feeling,[56] if these imagined interfaces are any evidence, was demonstrated and expressed in words that describe an ambivalence, even resentment, of technological relationships: for example, being able to say "shut up" to your television set[57] or to your telephone[58] (not "turn off," not "close/finish" or other ending command). Clearly, this complicates the sort of understanding we can develop about a person's relationship to a purchased product — and purchasing is of course the predominant form of "feedback" that companies and designers get about products. These voices make audible a strongly polarized ambivalence. There was no suggestion of saying, "I love my TV," to turn it on.

Another device was proposed for automated prayers: triggered by saying "pray for me," it was customizable for different religious "preferences."[59] Prayers suggested ranged from excerpts from Psalm 23, to those for "cynical hipster types [who] might want their in-dash prayer boxes to recite William S. Burroughs' Thanksgiving Prayer ('Thanks for Indians, to provide a modicum of challenge and danger... thanks for a nation of finks...,' etc.), and some guilty white liberals (some Viridians, even) might want theirs to apologize for driving around in a vehicle spewing noxious fumes into the atmosphere."[60] This is more than an interface that recognizes and responds appropriately to user emotional states; actually the entertainment is in delegating the emotionality or at least religiosity itself to the device.

This impulse is replicated in the delegation of care, social niceties and other arational and noncalculative tasks to the computational devices; for instance, a speech recognition chip that recognizes the sound of flatulence and politely apologizes[61] to the room, relieving the responsibility of any one person to bear the embarrassment. Another entry, as an extension of Tamagotchi-like automation care, suggested using a voice recognition chip to train a parrot to speak.[62] There were actually several other entries exploring information technology for animals, which seems to be evidence against a voice interface imagined as "humanizing" the computer, and more a demonstration that the ready treatment of animal noises as recognizable sounds imagines these as functionally equivalent in every way to English words. Speech recognition, reinterpreted as sound recognition.

Finally, and perhaps the most interesting or novel constellation of projects are the designs that use the opportunity to script interactions as a form of propaganda — propaganda that is distributed (enacted) beyond traditional and corporate monopolized media channels. The portable ideologue could play the role (even potentially look like) the soapbox.[63]

Another device, the BackTalk, is a portable billboard for one's car. It is triggered by the use of simple trigger words and suggested deep-set LEDs, displaying a message specifically to the driver behind one's own car: "Thanks for letting me in," "Baby on board," or presumably any other bumper sticker expression. This is intended to influence others, and thus belongs in this category of the regulation (or at least influencing) of others.

These propaganda projects take very direct and explicit forms, including cell phones which, for example, cut out if they hear you say, "Yeah, I am on the cell phone," "Yeah, I am in the village," or "Dude,"[64] or monitor for swear words, or take other efforts to silence loud or otherwise "inappropriate" private voices in public spaces.

This impulse for social observation is illustrated by a museum display designed to collect responses (what the entry calls clichés) so that it "will grow as an open-ended accretion or demonstration of the clichés uttered by thousands, tens of thousands, millions of art consumers." This collection is itself the spectacle; the museum exhibit is rethought of as an instrument for the collection of comments.

Another suggestion was the "crowd morality barnacle," which is a device intended to influence mass behavior — in the given example, a riot. The CMD is intended for distribution throughout a crowd and will respond to key riot phrases; for example, it might respond to "smash" with "be careful"; "burn" with "it might explode"; or "get them" with "where are the children?"[65] This is a different conception of regulation

than the examples that illustrated the control of self.

To effect self-control, the designs went beyond turning electronic devices off or regulating the self with insistent and unrelenting reminders (e.g., correcting a habit of speech or cutting the "ums" out of the story) to quite novel punishment. These punitives enacted on the self included squirting water in one's ear, triggering electric shocks, and dribbling water down one's leg. There were few viable designs that offered a simple reward rather than punishment.

For affecting the social body, there were no physical punitives; the reward seems to have been the social behavior itself, or at least the evidence of it (as in the spectacle of clichés). This desire to see a social spectacle is repeated often, and I would like to argue that it is a recurrent theme in the networked context of information technology.

The final category of devices relies on double entendres and the multiple meanings of words, and demonstrates that speech interface cannot be understood as making the machine more human. Rather, it is clearly exploiting the different parsing, context sensitivity and repeatability of human-vs.-machine models of cognition. For example, to trigger the discrete recording of conversations, one entry describes a recorder that is triggered by "What's up, amigo?" This deployment of an unusual (relative to the user and context of use – i.e., no one else is likely to say it) filler is used to initiate conversation and direct attention to the people being addressed, but is simultaneously being used for an instrumental purpose: as the "on" button. Likewise the "Don't hurt me, just don't hurt me" cell phone/GPS position locator/911 dialer proposal,[66] which uses the self-defense phrase to dial for help without alerting the presumed attacker, who is presumed to interpret the plea at face value – second-guessing a reasonable or "usual" response in a threatening situation. In these interactions the user is able to simultaneously employ multiple meanings of his or her words. Clearly the speech chip is here being used so that the words used to interact with the machine are understood to be different from the speech used to interact with humans.

282

It is also notable that there were categories of speech not explored by these interfaces. Consider the linguistic communication defined as a performative. A performative, such as "I do," is a highly codified and stabilized utterance that communicates a future commitment or social contract (Butler 1993). Because it is a stabilized social technique, it would be technically pragmatic — the problem of unlimited variation of phrasing is solved. The absence of designs to address this sort of statement is curious, and worth further investigation.

The categories of interaction demonstrated by this brief survey of voice chips are not discontinuous or radically different from other contemporary consumer technologies. The observation of self (or one's own property) is embodied in the consumer video camera market and surveillance systems; self-regulation has extended from alarm clocks once a day to alarming cell phones carried with you and ready for all alarming occasions; handhelds directly regulate sleep and activity; VCRs and TiVo capture, regulate (in order to extend) and meter out media program consumption.

Social observation is also embodied by surveillance systems, but although surveillance looms large in the popular imagination, it has not been used to see or envision the social mass, or one another. The problem of seeing the social body has remained an architectural problem, solved by spectacles of plaza and malls: public and quasi-public places. What the voice chip most clearly demonstrates is that it is this area in which there seems to be the most interest: being able to view mass behavior. The traditional broadcast (e.g., television) media had very little interest in rendering the public to itself, and as such the rise of phone-in, and "reality television" genres suggests that even in the context of high production value broadcast media there is a cultural appetite to "see" each other, no matter how contrived. The collaborative filtering models, such as that popularized by the Amazon people-who-bought-this-book-also-bought-x button show us each other's behavior, to make it a shared experience – to see where others have been. Like the micro-casting of a speech recognition-triggered rear window car display, we see

this desire expressed through the car, and the car's peculiar access to the public space of freeways. This is a public space where the rules of communication between and among people are highly constrained (cf. the plaza). This is not the interactive experience of the self with the self, or the self with the machine, but the machine as a proxy for interacting with the social. This is a peculiar and interesting way to think about human–machine interaction.

Conclusion

The interactions we hear with voice chips do not disambiguate the buzzes and beeps used by speechless machines, but speech recognition products do reinforce the idea that we use speech for machines and speech for humans differently, and simultaneously. The other applications also re-imagine how we understand their functions. The products discussed do not exploit the mechanistic, logical and fully controllable functions of machines, but treat them as complicated multifarious social actors. There is a clearly stated desire to enlist these new technologies and product interfaces to promote explicit desired social transformations. We also see here the ambivalent relationship we have with and for our current technological devices.

This essay has explored why listening to voice chips and speech recognition chips might give us a way to examine human–machine interactions in situ. Much real complexity of social and technical interactions is lost in the tradition of examining them within controlled laboratory contexts, and ethnographic analysis can be too rich (though the theoretical perspective that has developed from ethnographic insights, that privileges the improvisational nature of real-world applications, enables us to focus on how speech and turn-taking is used to coordinate the interaction between machines and humans).

This initial analysis is presented in order to set up some preliminary ideas and interpretations, so that as (or if) speech recognition chips become more widely distributed, we can "tune in" to this particular historical moment and hear what it is we expect, want and bring to our human–machine interactions. There are few instruments that give us this viewpoint. Listening to

If Things Can Talk, What Do They Say?
Natalie Jeremijenko

our daily interactions with products can work to contest and complicate the dominant methods used to describe technological trends and patterns of product innovation: demographically driven mass market research and the capture of consumption behaviors at the point of purchase. The examination of speech recognition applications gives unique access to the assumptions, expectations and the imaginative work of products and the interactions they script.

Further examinations of voice chip and speech recognition products and patents can extend what has only just begun. In understanding how voice chips abstract speech, we can examine what we understand interaction to be, and hence how we design and frame interactions in products of daily use, reproducing our understanding of human technical relations. The products make obvious the design assumptions with which they are built, but further investigation of the details of their use will help to elaborate how these micro-interactions perform and realize actual social roles and social structures. A detailed use-analysis of any one of the products could provide further insight into this sort of investigation.

Voice chips also raise other questions. Because they slice through many social and economic sectors but are still in a manageable population of products, they can be used to illustrate the iterative and continuous process of technical change that is intimately involved in a technology's sociality, in contrast to the radical discontinuities of technological change through discovery and paradigm shifts (Dosi 1982, 147–162; Clark 1985, 235–251). They realize a recombinant model of technological change. Furthermore, for the same reasons, they can be used to examine the changing social position of these products in relation to the configuration of power and work relations (Zuboff 1984), and the transformations of the market groups and users that these products presume.

Finally, in the tradition of Turkle's examination of children's understanding of their interactive machines, children's products with voice chips can illustrate what childcare roles we delegate to machines, and articulate clearly the hardwired (per hardware, not neurons) expression of consumption identity of children.

For these reasons, this essay marks the beginning of a project to collect an ongoing database of products with voices or speech recognition that appear on the market, or receive patents.[67] As a longer archive of product voices, this may prove a valuable resource for the examination of changing sociotechnical relations, even in the event of the products falling silent and voice chips and speech recognition being abandoned altogether.

The voices of the products reflect back the voices and interactions we have projected and programmed into them, returning them for our reinterpretation. One mode of interaction we have with the consumer products that exist and are imagined at the time of this essay is a dialogue with a monologue. Command and control scripts are more common than improvisational scripts, but other forms of interaction are being scripted. By literally listening to what hardware has to say, and what we say to it, we may better ground our assumptions of interaction in reflexive reinterpretation. Furthermore, we can see from this examination that these technologies can be seen as structures of participation, organizing often indistinguishable human–machine interactions and using them to extend the predictability of individuals and coordinate their interactions. We have an ongoing opportunity, even method, to hear and understand our technologies in terms of these structures of participation, in our own language, and to see these technologies as a distributed system of voices and ears.

Notes

1. Quoted from the North American patent literature.

2. Pacific Bell voice mail system 1996, 1997, and AT&T automated customer help.

3. Benveniste showed how linguistic categories not only allow human subjects to refer to themselves, but actually create the parameters of human self-consciousness. "'Ego' is he who says 'ego.' That is where we see the foundation of 'subjectivity' which is determined by the linguistic status of 'person.' Consciousness of self is only possible if it is experienced by contrast. I use I only when I am speaking to someone who will be a you in my address" [Benveniste, 225]. Linguistic categories such as "I" rely wholly on the identity of the speaker for their meaning.

4. Latour published the book *Science in Action* in 1987. The following year, in Dallas (June 11, 1978), Texas Instruments

Incorporated announced the launch of its speech synthesis monolithic integrated circuit in the new talking learning aid Speak & Spell™. The speech synthesizer IC accurately reproduced human speech from stored (a capacity of 200 seconds in dynamic ROM) or transmitted digital data, in a chip fabricated using the same process as that of the TI calculator MOS ICs.

5. See M. Paton's forthcoming paper in *Social Studies of Science* for a detailed examination of the initial construction of the virtues and values of the phonograph recording technology.

6. Hallmark first included voice chips in their cards in 1988. Five years later they introduced a recordable card on which you could record your own voice.

7. Nissan Maxima 1986.

8. Barbie had a few statements when she was given a voice in late 1980s, including: "Meet me at the mall," "Math is hard," "I like school — don't you?"

9. Machina^R, a San Francisco-based company, had on the market in 1997 several talking pens or "Pencorders," a talking key ring, several talking photo frames and many "Cardcorders," including "Autonotes."

10. Saccharin is perhaps the first product to be parasite-marketed (i.e. "This product uses saccharin"), which is similarly Intel Inside's marketing strategy.

11. A complete list of the collected products and patents is planned for http://www.cat.nyu.edu/neologue. This will be updated constantly.

12. Patent #4863385 (Sept. 5, 1989).

13. Patent #5313557 (May 17, 1994).

14. Patent #5014301 (May 7, 1991).

15. Patent #4812968 (Mar. 14, 1989).

16. Patent #4951032 (Aug. 21, 1990).

17. Patent #4863385 (Sept. 5, 1989).

18. Patent #5315285 (May 24, 1994).

19. Patent #4987402 (Jan. 22, 1991).

20. Patent #5117217 (May 26, 1992).

21. Patent #5254805 (Oct. 19, 1993).

22. Patent #5275285 (Jan. 4, 1994).

23. Patent #5481904 (Jan. 9, 1996).

24. Patent #5555286 (Sept. 10, 1996).

25. Turkle demonstrates how children enter into social relationships with their computers and computer games; thinking of them as alive, they get competitive and angry, they scold them, and even want revenge on them. She finds that they respond to the rationality of the computer by valuing in themselves what is most unlike it. That is, she raises the concern that they define themselves in opposition to the computer, dichotomizing their feeling and their thinking.

26. Patent #5413516 (May 9, 1995).

27. Patent #5029214 (July 2, 1991).

28. Work and the products of work can be shown to take on meaning that transcends their use-value in commodity capitalism. See Susan Willis, *Primer for Daily Life*.

29. Patent #5140632 (Aug, 18, 1992): a telephone having a voice capability adapter.

30. Within the patent literature, what appeared in relation to transportation was:

#5555286: A cellular phone-based automatic emergency vessel/vehicle location system; translates a verbal rendition of latitude and longitude to a cell phone.

#5509853: An automobile interior ventilator with voice activation, which queries the driver when the door closes and gives menu options.

#5508685: A vehicle and device adapted to revive a fatigued driver; a voice reminder combined with spray device.

#5428512: A sidelighting arrangement and method, with a voice warning of impending obstacles.

#5045838: A method and system for protecting automotive appliances against theft.

#5278763: Navigation Aids (presumably for application in transportation).

#4491290: A train defect detecting and enunciation system

31. See the *New York Times* discussion.

32. This is in contrast to the popular depiction of cars with voices on mainstream television. In programs such as *My Mother the Car* or *Knight Rider*, the voice was used to lend the car personality.

33. See particularly "The Abstraction of Industrial Work."

34. See also Laura Oswald, who describes the site for purchasing product as the staging of the subject in consumer culture.

35. Stockfelt supports her work with Tagg and Clarida's studies on listeners' responses to film and television title themes, which demonstrates common competence to adequately understand and contextually place different musical structures; listeners for the most part understand musical semiotic content in similar ways, across dissimilar cultural areas. See also Philip Tagg, *Kojak: 50 Seconds of Television Music — Toward the Analysis of Affect in Popular Music*.

36. The *Symphony of Sirens* was first performed in 1923 by Arseni Avraamov.

37. In particular the products that use speech and music interchangeably: the children's applications, the bells and whistles that substitute for spoken encouragement, the alarm systems that use vocal warnings or sirens, and the pen (patent #4812068).

38. To relate the voice chip to the sociolinguistic universe – with its emphasis on the place of language within it — interprets the social system as semiotic, and stresses the systematic aspects of it. We cannot simply assume that the concept of a system itself and

the concept of the function (of language) within that system is the most appropriate starting point. However, this assumption underlies most of the guidelines developed for computational models of speech and is thus appropriate for discussion of the voice chip.

39. See J.L. Austin, *How to Do Things with Words*, the general point of which is not to look at how language is composed, but what it does.

40. Searle uses this list to introduce his paper "What is a speech act?"

41. Stanley Fish's essay "How to do things with Austin and Searle" analyzes Shakespeare's *Coriolanus* as a speech-act play. When Coriolanus responds to his banishment from Rome by stating a defiant "I banish you," the discrepancy in the elocutionary force in both the performatives of banishment is obvious. Rome, embodying the power of the state and community, vs. Coriolanus's sincere wish to banish Rome (i.e. his intentionality) is illustrative.

42. Broadcast voices and prerecorded voices, although abstracted onto technologies, still belong to an identity; however it is the combined sense of abstraction that connotes the identity of the voice as that of the car. This could be interpreted alternatively as an abstracted voice of authority performed by the car, or the abstraction of the car itself.

43. "If certain stable forms appear to emerge or recur in talk, they should be understood as an orderliness wrested by the participants from interactional contingency, rather than as automatic products of standardized plans. Form, one might say, is also the distillate of action and interaction, not only its blueprint. If that is so, then the description of forms of behavior, forms of discourse... included, has to include interaction among their constitutive domains, and not just as the stage on which scripts written in the mind are played out" [Schegloff, 73].

44. Patent #4517412, the card-actuated telecommunication network, is an example of this: "Local processor (11) controls a voice chip (15) coupled to telephone set (10), which interacts with the caller during the card verification process."

45. Suchman explains that this interpolation of verbal nuances and the coherence that the structure represents is actually achieved moment by moment, as a local, collaboratively, sequential accomplishment. The actual enactment of the interaction is an essentially local production, accomplished collaboratively in real time rather than born whole out of the speaker's intent or cognitive plan.

46. Suchman uses the example of the joint production of a single sentence to demonstrate the fluid division of labor in speaking and listening.

47. Measured by patents filed for novel devices that incorporate speech recognition

48. Product innovation for corporate continuity — assessing the life expectancy of corporate products.

49. A.M.Dixon@shu.ac.uk

50. A.M.Dixon@shu.ac.uk

51. zoeluna@bellsouth.net

52. zoeluna@bellsouth.net

53. zoeluna@bellsouth.net

54. Andre French: Afrench@iss.net

55. This is a version of the gestural value of handheld and portable devices identified and described in a study involving the ethnographic examination of filmic depictions of the use of handhelds [Jeremijenko 1992].

56. For example, work at the MIT Media Lab's "Affective Computing" research group.

57. Vaclav Barta: vbar@comp.cz

58. Michael Butler: butler@comp-lib.org

59. It is peculiar to refer to a religious "preference" as if it were another consumption category — are religious and addictive behaviors subject to the same economic characterization?

60. Jon Lasser: jon@lasser.org

61. Michael Butler: butler@comp-lib.org

62. wapel@tc.cac.edu.eg

63. xiane@entech.com

64. spiff@bway.net

65. Dave Whitlock: zoeluna@bellsouth.net

66. Dave Whitlock: zoeluna@bellsouth.net

67. As noted above, this list will be available at http://cat.nyu.edu/neologues and updated constantly. It will include images and product literature and, when possible, an audio file recording of the voices.

References

Althusser, Louis (1971). "Ideology and Ideological State Apparatuses (Notes Towards an Investigation)." In *Lenin and Philosophy and Other Essays*. New York: Monthly Review Press.

Austin, J.L. (1962). *How to Do Things with Words*. Oxford: Oxford University Press.

Bardini, Thierry (1997). "Bridging the Gulfs: From Hypertext to Cyberspace." *Journal of Computer-Mediated Communication* 3, no.2 (September, 1997).
<http://www.ascusc.org/jcmc/vol3/issue2/bardini.html>.

Benveniste, Émile (translated by Mary Elizabeth Meek) (1971). "The Nature of Pronouns." In *Problems in General Linguistics*. Coral Gables: University of Miami Press.

Butler, Judith (1993). *Bodies that Matter*. London: Routledge.

Callon, Michel (1995). "Four Models for the Dynamics of Science." In *Handbook of Science and Technology Studies*, edited by Sheila Jasanoff, Gerald E. Markle, James C. Petersen and Trevor Pinch. Thousand Oaks, CA: Sage Publications.

Callon, Michel, and John Law (1982). "On Interests and their Transformations: Enrollment and Counter-Enrollment." *Social Studies of Science* 12 (1982): 615-625.

Clark, Kim (1985). "The Interaction of Design Hierarchies and Market Concepts in Technological Evolution." *Research Policy* 14 (1985): 235-251.

Cowan, Ruth Schwartz (1987). "The Consumption Junction: A Proposal for Research Strategies in the Sociology of Technology." In *The Social Construction of Technological Systems*, edited by Wiebe E. Bijker, Thomas P. Hughes and Trevor Pinch. Cambridge, MA: The MIT Press.

Dosi, Giovanni (1982). "Technological Paradigms and Technological Trajectories: A Suggested Interpretation of the Determinants and Directions of Technical Change." *Research Policy* 11, no. 3 (1982): 147-162.

Dourish, Paul (2001). *Where the Action Is: A History of Embodied Interaction*. Cambridge, MA: The MIT Press.

Fabbri, Franco (1981). "A Theory of Musical Genres: Two Applications." In *Popular Music Perspectives*, edited by David Horn and Phillip Tagg. Gothenburg and Exeter: International Association for the Study of Popular Music.

Fish, Stanley (1980). "How to Do Things with Austin and Searle." In *Is There a Text in this Class? The Authority of Interpretative Communities*. Cambridge, MA, Harvard University Press.

Geertz, Clifford (1973). *The Interpretation of Cultures*. New York: Basic Books.

Jeremijenko, Natalie (1992). "TITLE." Palo Alto, CA: Xerox PARC internal publication.

Latour, Bruno (1987). *Science in Action*. Cambridge, MA: Harvard University Press.

Latour, Bruno (writing as Jim Johnson) (1988). "Mixing Humans and Nonhumans Together: The Sociology of a Door-Closer." *Social Problems* 35, no.3 (1988): 298-310.

Minneman, Scott (1991). *The Social Construction of Engineering Reality*. Ph.D. Thesis, Stanford Department of Mechanical Engineering Dissertation, Stanford, CA.

Oswald, Laura (1996). "The Place and Space of Consumption in a Material World." *Design Issues* 12, no. 1 (Spring 1996).

Schegloff, E. (1982). "Discourse as an Interactional Achievement: Some Uses of 'uh huh' and Other Things that come Between Sentences." In *Georgetown University Round Table on Language and Linguistics: Analyzing Discourse Text and Talk*, edited by Deborah Tannen. Washington, DC: Georgetown University Press.

Searle, J. (1972). "What is a Speech Act?" In *Language and Social Context*, edited by P.P. Giglioli. Baltimore: Penguin Books.

Shields, Rob (editor) (1992). *Lifestyle Shopping: The Subject of Consumption*. New York: Routledge.

Suchman, Lucy (1987). *Plans and Situated Action: The Problem of Human-Machine Communication*. Cambridge: Cambridge University Press.

Tagg, Philip (1979). *Kojak — 50 Seconds of Television Music. Towards the Analysis of Affect in Popular Music*. Göteborg, Sweden: Studies from the Department of Musicology, University of Gothenburg.

Turkle, Sherry (1984). *The Second Self*. New York: Simon and Schuster.

Willis, Susan (1991). *Primer for Daily Life*. New York: Routledge.

Zuboff, Shoshana (1984). *In the Age of the Smart Machine: The Future of Work and Power*. New York, Basic Books.

New Readings

The Oulipopo — a younger relative of the Oulipo — explores the potential of the mystery story, describing and creating new configurations of the elements that compose the mystery genre. The group's 1971 founding text, by Oulipo cofounder François Le Lionnais (1998), asks in its title, "Who is Guilty?" Of the many possible answers, Le Lionnais considers numerous examples from the literature — although one possibility has no example: "x = the reader."

This configuration, in which the reader is guilty, would seem impossible in a mystery story. For a computer game, on the other hand, it might seem to be the easiest configuration — the design of id's *Doom* (Green, Petersen, and Romero 1993) being much simpler to emulate than Infocom's *Deadline* (Blank 1982). Yet there is clearly something incorrect about the comparison. In what sense, after all, is the player of *Doom* a reader?[1] It may be that the term "reader" should not be used here.

And yet, the *Deadline* player clearly is a reader — and something more, or at least something different. What's taking place here? To begin to answer, the three essays in this section fashion new modes of thinking to grapple with new forms of reading. Or perhaps it would be better to say that they create new theoretical positions appropriate to emerging textual forms — for although there have certainly been critical discussions of responsive texts in the past, much of these discussions have focused on concepts not appropriate to the works discussed here.

The first text under consideration is Talan Memmott's (2000) *Lexia to Perplexia* — which N. Katherine Hayles, in her essay, describes as her "tutor text," for exploring ways that computation and network technologies are "fundamentally altering the ways in which humans conceive of themselves and their relations to others." *Lexia to Perplexia* is a work built on and of the web, pushing web techniques to their limits, and requiring a reading that constantly adjusts to its unpredictable modes. In the next essay, Jill Walker offers a reading of *Online Caroline* (Bevan and Wright 2000–01), a technically wide-ranging internet work that incorporates web pages, e-mail, streaming video, and response forms, as well as audience-tracking and customization techniques. Not only does *Online Caroline* require a new type of reading — it also produces a new permutation of "Who is Guilty?" in which the reader becomes an accomplice to murder. In this section's final essay, Nick Montfort considers a class of works known as Interactive Fiction — a class to which *Deadline* belongs, as well as the landmark *Zork* (Anderson, Blank, Daniels, and Lebling 1977–79) — which still boasts a culture of active authors and readers, who use freely available tools to create new work and distribute it over the internet. Montfort locates his essay within our continuing story/game discussion, and defines a number of possible categories of experience that may expand this discussion beyond the dualism.

As the last essay in this book, it is fitting that Montfort's respondents are Brenda Laurel and Janet Murray — two of the founders of the cyberdramatic perspective with which our discussion began. In this volume the editors have attempted to group together thematically similar essays, but it shouldn't be forgotten that any of the essays included here could be fruitfully compared with any other — and that we have convened this wide-ranging discussion specifically because it is not possible to understand this emerging field without such a diverse assemblage of viewpoints. We hope that this book may serve as a sort of core sample of the new media "story, performance, and game" field at this stage in its development, and that as this field continues to expand, it will prove useful to the next generation of new media practitioners.

1. Establishing that the *Doom* player is a murderer is left as an exercise for the reader.

289

Reference: Literature

Le Lionnais, François (1998). "Who is Guilty?" translated by Iain White. In *Oulipo Compendium*, edited by Harry Mathews and Alistair Brotchie. London: Atlas Press, 269–270.

References: Games

Zork. Timothy Anderson, Marc Blank, Bruce Daniels, and Dave Lebling; Infocom. 1977–79.

Deadline. Mark Blank; Infocom. 1982.

Doom. Shawn R. Green, Sandy Petersen, and John Romero; id Software. 1993.

Metaphoric Networks in *Lexia to Perplexia*

N. Katherine Hayles

As leading theorists and practitioners Marvin Minsky (1985), Daniel Hillis (1999), and Brian Cantwell Smith (1998) have been telling us, computers are much more than hardware and software. In their most general form, computers are environments of varying scope, from objects that sit on desktops to networks spanning the globe. Indeed, in Edward Fredkin's (1990) interpretation, computational processes ultimately generate the fabric of the universe. It comes as no surprise, then, to find researchers arguing that computation is fundamentally altering the ways in which humans conceive of themselves and their relations to others. There are, of course, many approaches to this issue, from sociological studies to human factor analysis. Among these approaches are artistic works that tell new stories about the formation of human subjects, instantiating these stories in images as well as words. To explore this systemic shift, I will take as my tutor text Talan Memmott's (2000) *Lexia to Perplexia*. In this complexly coded work, human subjectivity is depicted as intimately entwined with

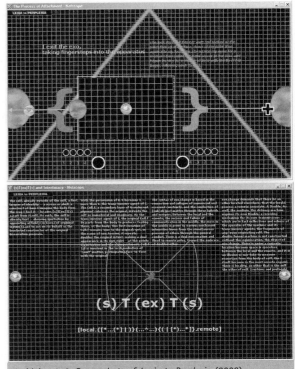

23.sidebar.1–2. Screenshots of *Lexia to Perplexia* (2000).

computer technologies (see sidebar).

Memmott's work reveals the co-originary status of subjectivity and electronic technologies. Instead of technologies being created by humans, this work

Eugene Thacker Responds

One of the significant claims made for hypertext and "net.art" is that they are forming new genres in which narrative, culture, and technology intersect. Hypertext works such as *Lexia to Perplexia* are paradigmatic in this regard, because they both construct multiple narratives about contemporary information cultures, and do so through the technologies of information culture. Hayles uses Memmot's work as an exemplar of a narrative of informatic subjectivity, of how our technologically saturated environment is in turn altering how we view ourselves as individual subjects. As Hayles suggests, the instances of illegibility, partial readability, and symbolic text hybridizations in *Lexia to Perplexia* all point to the relationships between the embodied, human subject

and the abstract materiality of the screen. It is this complex relationship that *Lexia to Perplexia* challenges us with.

As Hayles states, "illegibility is not simply a lack of meaning, then, but a signifier of distributed cognitive processes that construct reading as an active production of a cybernetic circuit and not merely an internal activity of the human mind." Illegibility becomes the index of the difference between human body and computer system; a difference that materializes once the human subject cognitively enters the world of Memmot's text. In this coevolution of agencies (both human and nonhuman, both clicking mouse and dynamic HTML text), reading becomes a meaning-making process that must navigate the

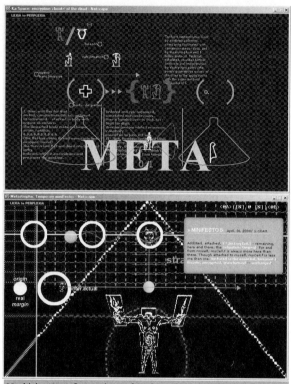

23.sidebar.3–4. Screenshots of *Lexia to Perplexia* (2000).

imagines digital technology present from the beginning, with subjects and technologies producing each other through multiple recursive loops. To

develop this idea, Memmott devises an idiosyncratic language, a revisioning of classical myths, and a set of coded images that invite the reader to understand herself not as a preexisting self with secure boundaries but as a permeable membrane through which information flows.

Three principal strategies enact this transformation. The first category is linguistic. Rather than writing standard English, Memmott devises a wide range of neologisms — coinages made from existing words that express new syntheses. In addition, he also creates a creole discourse (defined as a new language that arises when two different language communities come into contact). This creole is not, however, made up from two natural languages but rather from English and computer code. Code erupts through the surface of the screenic text, infecting English with machine instructions and machine instructions with English, as if the distinction between natural language and computer commands has broken down and the two languages are mingling promiscuously inside the computer. In addition to these linguistic strategies are rewritings of myth. Drawing on a range of classical references from the story of Echo and Narcissus to Minoan funeral practices, Memmott reenvisions this material to make it enact narratives about how human subjects misunderstand themselves as autonomous

various "creolizations" of the English language and Web-based computer code. If our language is tied not just to our cultures, but to our bodies (to our selves as embodied, living subjects), and if speaking about computer "languages" is not just metaphor, but a material instantiation of hardware and software, then hypertext works such as *Lexia to Perplexia* can be interpreted as a mediation between two material orders, two systemic logics (human and machine, molecular and digital, DNA and ASCII). Reading code as narrative text compresses the technical differentiation between language and code (bits representing letters in ASCII).

In this sense we might continue to elaborate the body-technology relationship that Hayles formulates

with regard to *Lexia to Perplexia*. A first-time reader of this work is, among other things, struck by the activity of the work: like many hypertext and net.art works, it seems to be alive, sometimes frenetic, sometimes frustratingly inert, and usually hypersensitive to any action on the part of the reader/user (mouse movements, clicks and double-clicks, dragging, closing windows, and so forth). It is this feeling of being overwhelmed by a complexly sensitized work that may form one point of departure for the body-technology interface in hypertext works. The connection here is, as Hayles points out, multiple and neuronal; the dynamic character of the text prompts a range of actions in the computer user, which in turn completes one turn of the cybernetic loop in the dynamic text. What is happening

agents when, in fact, they cannot be separated from the information technologies that, more than expressing, cocreate them. Finally, Memmott develops a symbolic visual language that images the interactions and structures leading to the "cyborganization" of human subjects and resulting in mutations that fundamentally alter what counts as human.

One way to bring these issues into focus is to notice at what points the screen displays cease to be legible as readable texts. These occluded representations create visual images that mark the limits of what human perception can discern. Illegible texts hint at origins too remote for us to access and interfaces transforming too rapidly for us to grasp. The text announces its difference from the human body through this illegibility, reminding us that the computer is also a writer, and moreover a writer whose operations we cannot wholly grasp in all their semiotic complexity. Illegibility is not simply a lack of meaning, then, but a signifier of distributed cognitive processes that construct reading as an active production of a cybernetic circuit and not merely an internal activity of the human mind.[1]

When *Lexia to Perplexia* hovers at the border of legibility, it hints that our bodies are also undergoing metamorphoses. What we read when we cannot read is not so much the disjunction between us and the

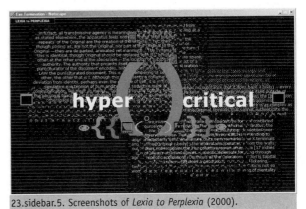

23.sidebar.5. Screenshots of *Lexia to Perplexia* (2000).

computer (for it is always possible to access the underlying code and hack our way into a readable version of the nonreadable text). Rather, the occluded display signifies a trajectory in which we become part of a cybernetic circuit. Interpolated into the circuit, we metamorphose from individual interiorized subjectivities to actors exercising agency within extended cognitive systems that include nonhuman actors. In this broader context, illegible text reminds us of the changes our bodies are undergoing as they are remapped and reinterpreted by intelligent machines working within networks that bind together our flesh with their electronic materiality. In this posthuman conjunction, bodies of texts and bodies of subjects evolve together in complex configurations that carry

---

in such instances? One suggestion — which Hayles alludes to — is that a particular type of network is in the process of being formed: "To create new kinds of textual bodies is inevitably to write new human bodies, as we continue to produce the technologies that produce us." Whether this relationship is benign or antagonistic ultimately depends on the particular hypertext under consideration. But what works like *Lexia to Perplexia* demonstrate for us is that there is always tension, dynamism, and a certain ambivalence in this relationship between flesh and code.

To extend Hayles' reading of *Lexia to Perplexia*, we might take this mediated relationship between bodies and technologies a little further: If the body of the subject engages in a kind of distributed agency in

"reading" works such as *Lexia to Perplexia*, then what happens to the specificity of the embodied subject as marked by gender, race, language, and cultural difference? In other words, *Lexia to Perplexia*, in articulating a relationship between flesh and code, also puts a challenge to us: to what degree does language account for the markers and meanings of embodied difference? To what degree does it account for our relationships to technology and media?

From Bill Seaman's Online Response
This response text was itself written within the framing environment of the "desktop metaphor." Inside this metaphor one asks, where does the metaphor leave off and the text take over? We look at the computer

along the past even as they arc toward an open and unknown future.

Typical is the opening screen locating the origin of the self in a specular play with an Other:

> The inconstancy of location is transparent to the I-terminal as its focus is at the screen rather than the origin of the image. It is the illusory object at the screen that is of interest to the human enactor of the process — the ideo satisfractile nature of the FACE, an inverted face like the inside of a mask, from the inside out of the screen is the same <HEAD>{FACE}<BODY>, <BODY>FACE>/BODY rendered now as sup/posed other.

Read as HTML, <HEAD>{FACE}<BODY> has two opening tags but no closing tags, which would indicate that FACE is part of HEAD but is not included in BODY. A different interpretation is suggested by <BODY>FACE</BODY>, which indicates that FACE is tagged as being the BODY. These creolized puns make a serious point, for they allude to the mind/body split in which the face, the most intensely signifying part of the human form, is alternatively tagged as separate

from the body and part of it.

Parsing body parts as textual components initiates a connection between flesh and electronic materiality that is further underscored by the electronic signature "Sign.mud.Fraud." Inserting the dots references their use in program names to delimit a file extension. The dots also divide the name so it functions both as an allusion to Freud (Fraud), announcing its ironic appropriation of this seminal thinker, and also punctuating (or as one of Memmott's neologisms would have it, "puncturating") the signature so it performs what "cyborganization" implies by transforming a proper name into creolized sign.

This performance of hybridity is further reinforced by the passage's content, where the self is generated through a reflection on the *inside* of the screen, as if on "the inside of a mask." The dislocation from traditional subjectivity is here doubly articulated. First the face is seen as a mask, implying an inside different from the outside, and then this traditional trope of the persona is further dislocated by metaphorically connecting the mask with the screen, so that the interiorized life of the subject is positioned inside the technology.

Thus inside and outside, terms conventionally generating the boundaries between subject and world, are reconfigured so the subject and the techno-object are both inside, interfaced with the world through a

---

screen closely and we see a set or field of pixels. The pixels are presented through an underlying code functioning within a particular software/hardware environment. This software/hardware environment enables the creation of a particular "language" space. The pixels form patterns that look like words or images. We read these patterns as words or images or some word/image hybrid. Thus, this light configuration is "likened" to a word or image or word/image hybrid and we understand it as such. We compare the environment of the screen to our embodied memory of past relationships, gleaning the shape of words and images, symbols, formulas — patterns. In general these are not fixed figures in *Lexia to Perplexia*, presented through the auspices of the computer — they are

generated, malleable, and operative time-based configurations that are authored to be responsive to interactive exploration. Thus we might describe computer networks themselves as being literal and "metaphoric networks" in that they enable the circulation of metaphors through technological means. We have the vehicle of light, hardware/software, and connectivity, forming an evocative, richly ambiguous, extended environment of "implied comparison" brought about through cognition. The computer also enables the nesting of metaphor, in that the word or image produced through light configurations can also function as a metaphor in itself.

http://www.electronicbookreview.com/thread/firstperson/seamanr1

screen that functions at once as display and reflecting surface. These metaphoric connections are created in part through the screen display, for as the user moves the cursor over the passage quoted previously, stylized eyes appear along with terminal screens. This iconography can be read either as interiorized eyes looking out at us through the screen-mask or reflections of our own eyes looking at the screen, thus positioning the reader as Narcissus gazing at an image that he fails to recognize himself.

By implication, this narcissistic doubling positions us inside the screen as well as external to it, intimating that we too have become techno-subjects. Although this specular play obviously alludes to the Lacanian mirror stage, it differs significantly from the Imaginary self that Lacan theorized. The subject generated by the reflections between terminal and I/eye is inscribed as cell...(f) or cell.f, expressions that visually display their infection by code and hint that the subject has been fused with the technology. From this dynamic emerges the subject as an "I-terminal," an expression recalling Scott Bukatman's (1993) punning phrase "terminal identity." Acknowledging the illusion of an autonomous I/Eye, "I-terminal" subverts autonomy through the hyphenated appendage that connects human vision with the scanning electrode beam of a computer display.

A word about creole. Typically, first-generation speakers who encounter another language community develop a pidgin, which is not a true language but an amalgam using a reduced vocabulary and simplified verb forms to communicate. By the second and third generations, a creole generally emerges. Unlike pidgin, a creole has its own syntax, verb forms, and vocabulary, thus qualifying as a language uniquely different from the two communicating languages of which it is a hybrid.

As we have seen, *Lexia to Perplexia* moves toward a creole devised from the merging of English with programming code. Creole expressions include the *cell...f* (and *cell.f*) noted above, homophones for self that conflate identity with a pixilated cell and the notation for a mathematical function, respectively; *inTents*, a pun that collapses intensity into intentionality and also references the programming practice of using interior capitalization to make clearly visible two functions in a variable name that allows no spaces; *exe.stream*, another pun that references and inverts the usual use of the exe.extension to denote an executable program; and **.fect*, a neologism that alludes to the programming practice of using * as a wild card, so **.fect* could be read as infect, defect, disinfect, and so forth.

To what purpose is this creole concocted? Compounded of language and code, it forms the

---

Hayles Responds

If ethnicity and enculturation are expressed through bodily enactments (and how can we doubt that when we watch black and white rappers, dancers, actors, etc.), then there is at least the possibility that the physical enactments required by interactive art works may also be experienced in racially marked ways. What does a "nervous" text mean to a German female academic used to a sedentary lifestyle compared to an African-American improvisational actor who practices yoga every day?

http://www.electronicbookreview.com/thread/firstperson/haylesr2

medium through which the origin of subjectivity can be redescribed as coextensive with technology. Just as these hybrid articulations do not exist apart from their penetration by code, so the subject does not exist apart from the technology that produces the creole describing (or creating) the techno-subject Nowhere is this circular dynamic more on display than in Memmott's revisioning of the myth of Echo and Narcissus. About Narcissus who mistakes himself for an Other through the mediation of a reflective surface we have already heard, but Echo's role is equally important. She reacts to her exclusion from the narcissistic circuit by losing her flesh and becoming a mediated repetition of what others say. In this regard Echo is an appropriate nymph to haunt this text, for *Lexia to Perplexia* is permeated by echolaic articulations. Memmott says that he created the text by selecting passages from such seminal thinkers as Freud, Nietzsche, Heidegger, and Deleuze and Guattari. He then "mediated" them (or remediated, in Grusin and Bolter's (1999) term) by "puncturating" them with neologisms and creolized transformations.

> It was my method for the development of this piece to collect a stack of books that I thought may be helpful, distracting, add to or subtract from the argument. As I passed through these volumes I would pull texts for later mediation. When there was enough text to begin this mediation work, which in fact began by the selecting of various volumes, I compiled the excerptstogether and began parsing for context. . . . So, I became I-Terminal; you, she, he became X-terminal, and so on. This made the collected texts, the analects very messy so I endeavored to rewrite only using this premediated text as reference. The context is built from the simple replacing of "selves" and "others" with cyborganized values. Then it is a matter of creating the connective, conductive space between. [Memmott, e-mail communication (November 12, 2000)]

To see the results, consider the following passage describing the appearance of Echo, associated with the collapse of the original into the simulation, so there is no longer an ontological distinction between "real" and "artificial" life.

> From out of NO.where, Echo appears in the private space of Narcissus.tmp to form a solipstatic community (of 1,ON) with n.tmp, at the surface. The two machines — the originating and the simulative — collapse and collate to form terminal-I, a cell.f, or, cell...(f) that processes the self as outside of itself—in realtime.

Through the neologism "solipstatic," the state of mental isolation denoted by solipsism is conflated with static, which in a machinic context references both the inevitable intrusion of noise and the on-off functionality of the machine. In contrast to living organisms, the machine can undergo a period of inertness and still be capable of reanimation when the switch is turned on. The neologism thus combines two very different forms of intelligent life with the result being a "solipstatic community," an oxymoron whose strong internal tensions sprang from the combination of fleshless Echo with doubled Narcissus. The oxymoron is then further assimilated with the programming function n.tmp, a name customarily used for a function that will be replaced by another. As the nomenclature suggests, n.tmp immediately slides into another union as the "originating" and "simulative" machines collapse into one another.

If we like, we can suppose that the originating machine is the human and the simulative one the computer. But any such assignment partakes of the Imaginary, for the emergence of the I-terminal reveals that the division between the human and the technological is an origin story that narrates as a temporal process something that was always already the case. So the cell.f imagines "the self as outside of itself" in "realtime." "Realtime" is a phrase programmers use to indicate that the simulated time of computer processes are running, at least temporarily, along the same time scale as the "real time" experienced by humans. Thus the temporal language used to authenticate the evolutionary story of an "originary machine" separate from a "simulative machine" is already infected with the technological. The collapse of the simulative into the original can be imagined as an event at a discrete moment in time, but the language reveals that this narration is always after the fact, for the fusion has always already happened.

The transformation of the self into a cell.f does not end with the individual subject, for the process extends from "local" to "remote" bodies. "The bi.narrative exe.change between remote and local bodies is con.gress and compressed into the space between the physical screen and the Oculus of terminal-I." As a result, the progression into the "solipstatic original" is succeeded by the "cyborganization of any/every para.I-terminal," so that the individual is subsumed into the "greater X-terminal" formed by "component I-terminals." Thus human community becomes indistinguishable from the global network of the world wide web. "The completion of this circuit is an applied communification — synamatic programs and values shared by. . . other applications and detached machines." "Synamatic," a homophone for cinematic, perhaps alludes to the Symantic (semantic) Corporation, creator of the Norton Anti-Virus and Norton Utilities, in a conflation that implies computer health is integral to the reproduction of screen image and therefore to subjectivity. "Communification," which can be read as a neologism conflating commodification and communication, arises when the circuit is completed; that is, when humans and intelligent machines are interconnected in a network whose reach is reinforced by naming the few exceptions "detached" machines.

The graphics accompanying these texts include, in addition to terminals and eyes, the letters E.C.H.O. dispersed across underlying text and animated rollovers that appear in quick succession, occluding portions of the screen. Particularly significant is the image of double funnels with the small ends facing each other, a sign that Memmott associates with "intertimacy," the process by which two selves (cell...fs) meet in the computer "apparatus" and, through their interactions

with the apparatus, reconstitute from bits and bytes an impression of an other in a relation that Memmott appropriately neologizes as "remotional."

Seen from one perspective, as Memmott points out, the cone with an elongated end is a funnel condensing the cell...f so it can circulate through the network; seen in mirror inversion, the cone becomes a megaphone, an amplifying device that lets the receiving cell...f construct an image of the sending cell...f. As Memmott (2001) makes clear in the companion work "Delimited Meshings: agency | appliance | apparatus," *Lexia to Perplexia* must be considered not only as text but as what W. T. J. Mitchell (1995) in *Picture Theory* has called textimage, a fusion of text and graphic into signifiers that function simultaneously as verbal signs and visual images. Memmott, who came to graphic design from a background as a painter, notes that

> much of the writing is integrated with the screen design. In addition to this, much of what was written prior to the development of the hypermedia work has in fact been incorporated into the functionality of the work. Portions of the text that I thought may be better served as screen interactions do not appear at the superficial text level but inspired some of the animations as actions that occur in the piece. [Memmott, e-mail communication (November 14, 2000)]

These actions often surprise and frustrate a user. Slight cursor movements cause text the user was reading to disappear or become illegible as new images and symbols are superimposed on top of it. *Lexia to Perplexia* is a very "nervous" document; it constantly acts/reacts in ways that remind the user she is not in control, for not only are the cursor movements extraordinarily sensitive but some of the actions are animations controlled by timed computer sequences. Eugene Thacker, commenting on a version of this essay, writes about his encounter with the work. "A first-time reader of this work is, among other things, struck by the activity of the work: like many hypertext and net.art works, it seems to be alive, sometimes frenetic, sometimes frustratingly inert, and usually hypersensitive to any action on the part of the reader/user..." [Thacker, this volume]

This dense layering of the screen display, insofar as it interferes with reading, manifests itself as a kind of noise that is simultaneously a message. The linking structure works not by moving the reader from lexia to lexia — the standard form used by first-generation literary hypertexts such as Michael Joyce's *afternoon* — but rather through a combination of user and computer actions that nervously jump from one screen layer to another, as if probing the multiple layers of code used to produce these effects.[2] Thus, the action of choosing that first-generation hypertext theory attributed solely to the reader here becomes a distributed function enacted partly by the reader but also partly by the machine. Memmott interprets this design in "Delimited Meshings: agency|appliance|apparatus" as creating "a text that does what it says — confronting the user as it mimes the User's actions." The "I-terminal" is thus at once a theme within the work and a performance of techno-subjectivity jointly enacted by computer and user.

An important component in the process of configuring the subject as an "I-terminal" is noise, which can play a productive role in complex systems by forcing them to reorganize at a higher level of complexity.[3] "Minfesto 1" seems to evoke this possibility when it proclaims, "Bi.narrative communification is rendered in the wreck, the mess in the middle, the collision of incompatible transmissions, arising from the eroded ruins of miscommunication." Recalling the phrase that circulated through the post-World War II Macy Conferences on Cybernetics of the "man in the middle" (i.e., the man spliced between two automated cybernetic machines), the "mess in the middle" promises to self-organize into a new kind of message, an emergent articulation produced by subversive "Secret(e) agents" who "produce narra.tive singularities throughout the apparatus." The "apparatus" names not only the technology but also the interpolated subjects who have become indistinguishable from electronic messages. "The earth's

own active crust we are," "Minifesto 2" proclaims, "building — up and out — antennae, towers to tele.*. We *.fect the atmosphere as we move through it, striving toward communification. Our hyperlobal expectations sp.read knowledge into no.ledge, far, wide, thin... I cannot contain myself and so I spread out — pan — send out signals, smoke and otherwise, waiting for Echo. Waiting for logos to give me a sine." "Hyperlobal" neatly sutures lobes — presumably of the brain — into the hyperglobal expectations of a worldwide communication system, creating a technohuman hybrid. A similar conflation resonates in logos as a mathematical (sine) function and a word capable of signification (sign). If reorganization occurs, these neologisms suggest, it will operate to fuse human subjectivity with silicon processes. In fact this transformation is already underway as the creole performs what it describes, creating a narrative that reaches back to an origin already infected (or *.fected) with technology and arcs forward into a future dominated by "communification."

As we learn to make sense of the creole, we are presented with an ironic description of our attempts to make everything "crystal clear and susynchronized," to reduce its polyvocality so that the "passage of meaning through the bi.narrative conduit is smooth, without catches or serration and the doubled trans/missive agent(s) never meet, combat or challenge. The combined inTents perform as components of a single ideocratic device, de.signing, de.veloping and exe.cuting the mechanism that permits their passage." At times the "doubled trans/missive agent(s)" of code and language cooperate to yield a consistent meaning, as in the neologism "hyperlobal." But these moments of clarity are embedded in screen designs where they are transitory at best, flashing on the screen in quick bursts broken by animated graphics that intervene to obscure text and layer one image over another. The noise that permeates the text may serve as a stimulus to emergent complexity, but it also ensures that meanings are always unstable and that totalizing interpretations are impossible.

As the transformation of self into cell...f continues, the work imagines flesh becoming digitized into binary signs.

New Readings >Hayles   **Thacker Seaman**   **VIII. New Readings**
Walker   Wortzel Sack
Montfort   Laurel Murray

From here, the analog and slippery digits of the real are poured into the mouth of the funnel... Flowing further, the variable body, the abstracted and released continuum of the body is com/pressed, reduced and encoded, codified... made elemental... Now we are small enough, we hope—it is the hope of communification that we minimize the space of the flesh.

Significantly, there are no intact bodies imaged at the site, only eyes and terminals (I-terminals), along with creolized text, mathematical functions, and pseudo-code. Of course, everything is already code in the programming levels of the computer, so in this sense the human body has already been "reduced and encoded, codified... made elemental." If the body of this text aspires not merely to represent the bodies of writers and readers but also perform them, then they too become code to be compiled in a global dynamic of "communification." In a startling literalization of the idea that we are bound together with the machine, this vision implies that at some point (or many points) our flesh will circulate through the cybernetic circuit, miniaturized so that it can slip through the "mouth of the funnel" and merge with other subjectivities into a collective "we."

This at least is the ideology of the text, but the actuality of its materialization is more complex. At the same time the work appears to banish the flesh, it also relies on embodied responses to its digital performance. Consider the homophonic puns that the work mobilizes to create multiple levels of meaning.[4] For example, "inTents" references the motivations that drive the creation and consumption of the text; it also is a pun on "intense," the state of focused alertness necessary to comprehend this difficult text. Moreover, through internal capitalization it suggests that the state of in-tending can be read both as inwardness and as a trajectory "tending" toward some end, presumably "communification."

To decode these multiple meanings, the reader needs to employ at least three different sensory modalities of sight, sound, and kinesthesia. To catch the

intents/intense pun, the reader must "hear" the sound through subvocalization, a process that involves the body in the silent but muscularly distinct action of using the vocal cords without allowing air to pass through. Garrett Stewart (1990) has identified subvocalization as essential to the literariness of literary language, precisely because it activates a nimbus of homophonic variants that hover around the written word (much as Borges imagined alternative futures "pullulating" in the air around Yu Tsun in "The Garden of the Forking Paths" [Borges 1962, 99]). In a print medium, the durable inscription of ink marks on paper normally requires that only one word be written in one place.[5]

The multiple layers embedded within a single screen in *Lexia to Perplexia* routinely violate this presumption, revealing multiple encodings piled on top of one another on the same screen. Like *Intergrams* (1999) and *The Barrier Frames and Diffractions through* (1996) by Jim Rosenberg, the electronic medium is here used in ways that create "noisy" messages, making the noise itself a message about the distributed cognitive environment in which reading takes place. These changes in reading practices expand the sensory experiences involved in reading, so that vision, subvocalization, and kinesthetic manipulation of fine cursor movements all become highly sensitized modalities. It is against this background of complex bodily performance — considerably more complex than that involved in reading a traditional print work — that the text proclaims "it is the hope of communification that we minimize the space of the flesh." In this sense the text precisely does not enact what it articulates but rather creates conditions of consumption that if anything *expand* the "space of the flesh."[6]

Similarly, the text also takes an ironic stance toward the future of "communification" when it explores its own obsolescence. "Minifesto 3" proclaims, "the machine is built in expectation, more than as an object — the tangible machine, the one you are seated before, is dead already, or returns a dead eye — slowly — I can't think fast enough; or, if today you think I think fast enough for you, tomorrow you will reject me — this is my destiny I know." This narrative voice —

which can be read as that of the techno-subject as easily as that of the computer — teases the reader with the bold-faced taunt, "pull the plug why don't you." If the reader clicks on the phrase the program immediately shuts down, throwing her back to the preliminary screen from which the program loads. In this way the work anticipates its own inevitable future when the platform on which it runs is obsolete and it can no longer be opened. In a real sense the work at this point will cease to exist, for properly understood it is not a web site or a CD-ROM — in fact not a product at all — but a series of dynamic processes created when the appropriate computer running the appropriate software executes the commands. The work can no more escape its materiality than its human interlocutors can escape their bodies. Whatever future "communification" holds for us, it will not do away with materiality or the constraints and enablings that materiality entails.

Amid these complexities, what is clearly established is not the superiority of code to flesh but metaphoric networks that map electronic writing onto fluid bodies. *Lexia to Perplexia* intervenes at beginnings and boundaries to tell new stories about how texts and bodies entwine. The shift in the materiality of writing technologies that electronic textuality instantiates creates new connections between screen and eye, cursor and hand, computer coding and natural language, space in front of the screen and space behind it. Scary and exhilarating, these connections perform human subjects who cannot be thought without the intelligent machines that produce us even as we produce them.

Notes

Acknowlegements: I am grateful to Nicholas Gessler for help with technical details of my analysis, Carol Wald and Michael Fadden for help in researching sources, Marjorie Luesebrink for consultation and ideas, and Talan Memmott for his generous responses to my queries. This essay also benefited from discussions with my colleagues in the 2001 NEH Seminar, "Literature in Transition," especially Rita Raley and John Johnston.

1. The effect of cybernetic circuits on narrative patterns is explored in more detail in N. Katherine Hayles (1999), "Virtual Bodies and Flickering Signifiers," Chapter 2 of *How We Became Posthuman*.

2. Marjorie Luesebrink printed out the source code for one of these screens and reported that it came to twenty-five pages for a single screen [E-mail communication (November 17, 2000)].

3. For a further discussion of this characteristic of complex systems, see William Paulson (1988), *The Noise of Culture: Literary Texts in a World of Information* and N. Katherine Hayles (1990), *Chaos Bound: Orderly Disorder in Contemporary Literature and Science*.

4. I am indebted to Mark Hansen for suggesting this point to me and encouraging me to expand this portion of my argument.

5. I speak here about normal print practice, to which there are of course many exceptions, especially in the tradition of artist's books and in such experimental novels as Mark Danielewski's *House of Leaves*.

6. Simon Penny has written cogently about the role of physical training and embodied actions in electronic works in "Representation, Enaction and the Ethics of Simulation" (this volume).

References

Bolter, Jay David, and Richard Grusin (1999). *Remediation: Understanding New Media*. Cambridge, MA: The MIT Press.

Borges, Jorge Luis (1962). "The Garden of Forking Paths." In *Ficciones*, edited by Anthony Kerrigan. New York: Grove Press.

Bukatman, Scott (1993). *Terminal Identity: The Virtual Subject in Postmodern Science Fiction*. Durham, NC: Duke University Press.

Danielewski, Mark Z. (2000). *House of Leaves*. New York: Pantheon Books.

Fredkin, Edward (1990). "Digital Mechanics: An Information Process Based on Reversible Universal Cellular Automata." *Physica D* 45 (1990): 254–270.

Hayles, N. Katherine (1990). *Chaos Bound: Orderly Disorder in Contemporary Literature and Science*. Ithaca: Cornell University Press.

Hayles, N. Katherine (1999). *How We Became Posthuman: Virtual Bodies in Cybernetics, Literature, and Informatics*. Chicago: University of Chicago Press.

Hillis, Daniel (1999). *The Pattern on the Stone*. New York: Perseus Books.

Memmott, Talan (2000). *Lexia to Perplexia*. Hypermediation/Ideoscope. <http://www.memmott.org/talan/dac2001/index.html>.

Memmott, Talan (2001). "Delimited Meshings: agency/appliance/apparatus." <http://www.memmott.org/talan/dac2001/delimited_meshings/meshings/0.html>.

Minsky, Marvin (1985). *Society of Mind*. New York: Simon and Schuster.

Mitchell, W. T. J. (1995). *Picture Theory: Essays on Verbal and Visual Presentation*. Chicago: University of Chicago Press.

Paulson, William (1988). *The Noise of Culture: Literary Texts in a World of Information*. Ithaca: Cornell University Press.

Rosenberg, Jim (1993). *Intergrams*. Watertown, MA: Eastgate Systems.

Rosenberg, Jim (1996). *The Barrier Frames and Diffractions Through*. Watertown, MA: Eastgate Systems.

Smith, Brian Cantwell (1998). *On the Origin of Objects*. Cambridge, MA: Bradford Books.

Stewart, Garrett (1990). *Reading Voices: Literature and the Phonotext*. Berkeley: University of California Press.

Webster's New Universal Unabridged Dictionary (1983). Cleveland: Dorset and Baber.

How I Was Played by *Online Caroline*

Jill Walker

My hair is still wet from the shower when I connect my computer to the network, sipping my morning coffee. I check my e-mail and find it there in between other messages: an e-mail from Caroline. I read it quickly and then visit her web site. She's waiting for me. She holds up a shirt she's bought to the webcam, asking me afterwards by e-mail whether I'd like her to send it to me. "Yes," I answer, clicking and typing my responses into a web form and giving her my physical address. Caroline and I are friends.

Of course, Caroline isn't actually real. She's the fictional protagonist in a 24-part online drama called *Online Caroline* (see sidebar images). The web site and e-mails are written and designed by Rob Bevan and Tim Wright, and Mira Dovreni acts Caroline's part in the prerecorded webcam sequences. You can be Caroline's friend too if you go to her web site: <http://www.onlinecaroline.com>.

This essay is about my relationship with Caroline. Caroline permeates my everyday life in a way that is unlike other fictional characters. I don't have to switch

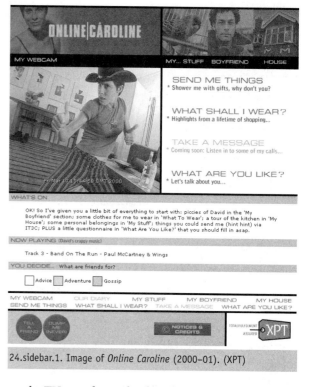

24.sidebar.1. Image of *Online Caroline* (2000–01). (XPT)

on the TV or pick up a book and start reading to engage in this fiction. Once I've signed up for it, it comes to me. If I don't visit for a few days, Caroline complains. I'm bound to this narrative.

Response by Adrianne Wortzel

The thesis could be posed that we are a species starved for interaction that is unbounded by the mediated parameters of our displayed personalities — where our emotional allegiances are free to take any form.

As much as we try to avoid it, we all know people who, in real life, cannot or will not mediate their behavior to consensus modes. I am not necessarily talking about criminal extremes. This is more about, let's say, parishioners in Salt Lake City who may blithely wear see-through garments to religious services, colleagues who have no scruples on issues of shared workload or intellectual property, and authority figures obsessed with the forest with no regard whatsoever for the trees.

New technology experiences that allow individuals to engage in interactive experiences over time, as fictive characters in databased scenarios, are a captivating subject. Such scenarios can either replicate those that occur in our daily lives, or reside outside that realm and subsequently pose a nice respite from the familiar. In either case they afford an opportunity to experience a level of power over circumstances. This disembodied freedom in a virtual environment allows us to exercise and amplify our own persona in ways that our culture and real-world responsibilities make difficult, or impossible.

Jill Walker is a good detective, assuming two different characters to test the parameters of the database that constitutes the Caroline persona. *Online*

Personalized Narrative

Caroline is a young woman who reminds me of Bridget Jones: she's worried about her boyfriend David, her friends, her weight and her job. David is away on research in New Guinea, and his employers, XPT, have provided Caroline with the web site and equipment so she can find online friends to keep her company while David's away. A week into our friendship, David returns and the story becomes more sinister. He coerces Caroline into following an outlandish diet, making her the guinea pig in an experiment that appears to be connected to XPT and to David's own research. Within days, Caroline is feeble and ill. In the final week of the serial, David takes over the web site bit-by-bit, until Caroline's only voice is in her ever-shortening e-mails. The story ends as Caroline is silenced, and can send me no more e-mails. Instead, I receive an e-mail from XPT, thanking me for my assistance.

This synopsis doesn't say much about how the story is told, and it is this telling that makes reading (or playing) *Online Caroline* a very new experience. *Online Caroline* is a story told to and, importantly, with its reader. It's built around a database that collects the information I feed it as I read. I answer questions about myself and the program uses that information to generate personalised e-mails from Caroline to me. When I visit Caroline's web site the version I see

24.sidebar.2. Image of *Online Caroline* (2000–01). (XPT)

depends on how much of the story I've read. Each day I'm limited to one episode, consisting of an e-mail and the appropriate version of the web site. In addition to the daily webcam segment, the web site regularly updates a diary section, similar to a web diary or personal home page. It takes me a minimum of 24 days

Caroline allows only finite conditions, but they are still more layered than those most often found in the bipolar genre of computer games — from *Doom* to even the much more complex and layered *Myst*. Games remain on the level of puzzle-solving, and the player never loses his or her self-consciousness as a player with a sense of place.

The *Online Caroline* experience is reminiscent of *Eliza*; the language analysis program designed by Joseph Weizenbaum in the 1960s, the most popular aspect of which was its impersonation of a psychotherapist in consultation with a patient. There are demos of the *Eliza* program available for interaction on the web, but none that I know of as much in the mode of an evolving narrative drama over time as *Online Caroline*.

In *Online Caroline*, depth of character develops on the web — not an easy feat, and one accomplished more through narrative skills than through the limited technology of clicking and text response.

Albeit limited to text only, in MOO Theater participants can also interact, either as themselves or as characters they have developed. They can do this to any degree, or no degree, of distinction between performer and audience. The audience immerses itself on an individual basis into the collective theatrical process. MOOs also allow for the expression on the part of the player for more than one disembodied personality to evolve from individual players. This is because the MOO allows for programming where characters can create environments, objects, soft robots and

303

24.sidebar.3. Image of *Online Caroline* (2000–01). (XPT)

to experience the drama, though I'll take longer if I visit the site less than daily.

The personalization that's generated by the database that backs this system is a major narrative technique in *Online Caroline*. Though this kind of seamless adjustment to the user's behaviour is used a lot in marketing, it's rarely used in art, narratives, or games. Companies harvest information about us and target ads to our demographic information. Epinions.com arranges articles so the ones I see first are ones similar to others I've liked, or are highly rated by people whose writing I've rated highly. Amazon.com shows me "The page that you made" full of books and kitchen gadgets

they think I'll like based on the last books I've viewed, or based on books my friends think I might like, as well as on my own deliberate ratings and preferences. Games and electronic narratives, on the other hand, will react to my deliberate choices (I type "kill troll with sword" or click on a door to show I want to open it), but they rarely track my behavior in this insidious and unasked-for manner.

Viewer and Viewed

Caroline watches me as much as I watch her in this fiction. I have a clear role in the story, as I would in a computer game and yet not as in a computer game. There is no space for me to act on my own initiative in *Online Caroline*. I can only speak when spoken to, and the allowed responses are few. My role is that of the confidante. My function is simply to allow the heroine to speak. As the story progresses, however, I realize that the program knows more about me than I have deliberately told it.

In the first episodes of the story, Caroline asks me to tell her more about myself, "so that we can really be friends," and she provides me with a handy web form to fill out my details. I answer truthfully or not as I please, though I'm often limited to set options — I can only choose to call Caroline funny, sad, or boring; I can't type my own word.

communicative missiles, allowing for many layers of development, a deeper immersion, more paths of possibilities, and dynamic environments.

Miraculously, although *Online Caroline* is limited to a database of finite experiences, it still draws the player through emotional states and evokes a sense of responsibility in the player. The player also has the option of "playing" him/herself as an unsympathetic character. In this particular work the ending is precluded and not subject to paths, and I understand why the authors chose to do this. It brings the interactive narrative to an extremely poignant and regretful closure that will have resonance to most people. It is interesting that Walker evokes the writings of Lev Manovich. The empathic intensity of a work like

Online Caroline resembles the similar suspension of disbelief engaged by films like *Easy Rider*, or *Manon of the Spring*, films where the endings ring so true while at the same time are so impossibly horrible that they can be traumatically overwhelming and stimulate (more than "simulate") a resonance that just won't quit long after the viewing is over.

It would be great for there to be more history, and the history of discourse, out there, on this kind of experience, from immersion in painting with the emergence of chiaroscuro and perspective; in theater from the Greeks through Shakespeare through the Living Theater of the 20th Century; as well as comparisons between psychoanalysis and electronic game environments and scenarios.

My responses to the questions in these web forms affect the e-mails she writes to me. In one of my first visits, I told the database that I have a daughter. The next morning I found an e-mail from Caroline where she wrote:

> There was me banging on about not liking children, and then discovering you're already a parent. Ah well, you still came back for more. [E-mail no. 4 to "Jill"]

She knew I had a daughter! I felt as though the fiction was adjusting to me, changing itself according to my input and qualities. I decided to see how Caroline would react to a different kind of reader. I started over, using a different e-mail address and inventing a reader I called Jack, making him the opposite of my original character, who had been an honest rendition of my real self.

But the e-mails barely changed, and Caroline's response to Jack, the childless bachelor, shows how changing a phrase needn't change the story at all:

> There was me banging on about children, when you don't have any. Ah well, you still came back for more. [E-mail no. 4 to "Jack"]

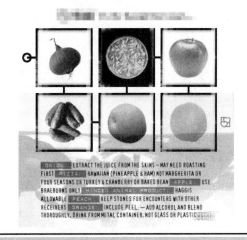

24.sidebar.4. Image of *Online Caroline* (2000–01). (XPT)

Another place I can speak up is in the "You decide" box that appears underneath the webcam image each day. On the eighth day of the serial Caroline is anguishing over how upset David will be when he discovers that some parcels of his have been stolen. The title for the day's "You decide" section is "The great parcel crisis." Caroline wants advice on what to do about the stolen

---

We are still anticipating the merger of virtual reality games with psychological and philosophical scenarios that approach the fully immersive holodeck dreams-come-true experiences we know from science fiction writing and film. Seemingly, it is just around the next metaphorical and concrete corner.

From Warren Sack's Online Response

The founding essay of artificial intelligence (AI) is British mathematician Alan Turing's (1950) article for the journal *Mind* entitled "Computing Machinery and Intelligence." In the 1950 essay, Turing proposes a game to determine if a computer is intelligent. [...]

Turing intended the man, in the original game, to play the role of a woman. The point of this being that

both the man and the woman are supposed to try to convince the interrogator that they are the woman. In other words, Turing's original proposal was, essentially, to build a machine to function as a man pretending to be a woman.

The first question that Turing proposes the simulacrum might be given by the interrogator as follows:

> [The interrogator asks]: Will [you] please tell me the length of [your] hair? It is the [simulacrum's] object in the game to try and cause [the interrogator] to make the wrong identification. [The simulacrum's] answer might therefore be, "My hair is

24.sidebar.5. Image of *Online Caroline* (2000–01). (XPT)

parcels. I can choose between three options by clicking in the appropriate box: "Tell David," "Avoid David," or "Leave David." Caroline doesn't necessarily take my advice though, whether I'm Jill who thinks she should leave David, or Jack, who thinks she should tell him. Whatever choice I make, the web page refreshes to show me the same sentence: "You need to know more about David, I think." Next morning my characters Jack and Jill receive almost identical e-mails. Although Jack told Caroline to tell David about the stolen parcels while Jill told her to leave the brute, only a few words in the e-mail are different:

> I do love David. And I want to be straight with him about that parcel business, as you suggested.

> I do love David. And I want to be straight with him about that parcel business. (So I won't be leaving him as you suggested!).

As the plot advances, it becomes clear that *Online Caroline's* system is watching me in more than these explicit ways. It's not only reacting to my deliberate responses and answers, but also to my silent wanderings around the web site itself. In e-mail no. 14, Caroline writes:

> You've convinced him that you're interested in his theories, because you took a look at the "My Boyfriend" section again last time you came. You shouldn't encourage him.

My actions as a reader don't just evoke a response from

---

shingled, and the longest strands are about nine inches long." (Turing 1950, 434)

Remarkably — at least from the perspective of standard AI readings of the text — the first thing that Turing posits with this question is the existence of a "virtual body" for the simulacrum. The "virtual body" invoked here is that of the simulacrum, i.e., either the machine or man pretending to be a woman and/or the woman playing the role of a woman.

I will argue that it is more than coincidence that Walker starts her essay with an analogous reference to her hair and, in general, her embodiment at the other end of a computer terminal. Walker starts her essay with this sentence: "My hair is still wet from the shower when I connect my computer to the network, sipping my morning coffee." With this sentence we — the readers — are convinced of Walker's embodiment. We now know that Walker is nonfictional, i.e., "real," while Caroline, according to Walker, ". . . isn't actually real. She's a fictional protagonist in a 24-part online drama called *Online Caroline*." Of course, what do we — the readers of Walker's piece — really know? Do we know Walker is real? How do we know she isn't just another Caroline in print form? We are, I believe, supposed to understand Walker's more concrete status as "proven" by the fact that she is embodied, she drinks coffee, she has hair.

http://www.electronicbookreview.com/thread/firstperson/sackr1

the text, they seem to affect the story, even to make me complicit in what happens. Interestingly, my deliberate responses are presented as having less influence on the plot than movements that I had thought were unseen. By the very act of reading, I'm encouraging David in his imprisonment of Caroline. Following this serial doesn't feel like "just watching" or "just reading." It feels as though I may be partially responsible for what's happening in this simulated world.

Forced Movement

Emanuel Vigeland is the little-known younger brother of the famous Norwegian sculptor Gustav Vigeland. While Gustav filled a huge park with sculptures, creating a monumental Oslo tourist attraction that still bears his name, Emanuel spent decades designing and building his own mausoleum. He designed the space to direct visitors' movements in several ways. The door is so low that I have to bow my head to enter. Inside the light is dim, and it takes several minutes for my eyes to adjust. The acoustics are peculiar, making my slightest sound reverberate in echoes. I walk quietly to avoid making a din. The architecture makes it physically impossible to enter or view his work without showing it respect (Wadell 1999, 41–42).

Online Caroline reminds me of this manipulation of the audience: it forces me to act in certain ways. The

24.sidebar.6. Image of *Online Caroline* (2000–01). (XPT)

program behind *Online Caroline* doesn't just track my movements; it also makes me move. Each e-mail needs to be opened. Then I have to click a link in the e-mail to visit the web site. To follow the narrative I have to move around the web site to find changes, and I have to answer questions. If I don't do this, the story doesn't move on and Caroline complains.

I perform these movements and others whenever I use my computer, but I'm used to ignoring them,

Walker Responds: Thinking Around the Responses

I have noticed that men who read *Online Caroline* tend to think she's flirting with them. On the other hand, discussing the experience of reading *Online Caroline* with two other female researchers, Lisbeth Klastrup and Elin Sjursen, we agreed that we felt that our relationships with Caroline were like the relationships between girlfriends.

http://www.electronicbookreview.com/thread/firstperson/walkerr2

assuming they're invisible. *Online Caroline* encourages this at first by emphasising my deliberate responses and by frustrating my attempts at independent actions, then turning on me to show me that my invisible, unconscious, forced motions have a greater impact on the plot.

Simulations

Online Caroline and Emanuel Vigeland's mausoleum are examples of what Lev Manovich (2001) calls simulations. Manovich sets simulations as an alternative tradition to representative art, giving frescos and goggles-and-gloves virtual reality as examples of simulations. A simulation is characterised by blurred boundaries between the viewer's proximate space and the virtual space of the simulation, as well as by the scale being the same in both spaces. Manovich argues that while representations force immobility, simulations force movement (Manovich 2001, 103–115). Both Emanuel's mausoleum and *Online Caroline* force their audiences to perform certain actions in order to access them. In the mausoleum I must bow low to enter and wait respectfully while my eyes adjust to the dim light; in *Online Caroline* I must revisit the site, type in responses, move the mouse and find the e-mails. Rather than sit still in a cinema or lock my eyes to the page of a book, I am trapped in constant motion.

Captivity and forced movement are also dominant themes in Caroline's story. Caroline has few friends and little contact with the world. She's a freelance writer, but doesn't seem to work much. Her editor Simon, who takes her to Paris and then nags her for an article about the trip (that she never actually writes), is the only contact she seems to have with that world. Finally I am told that all Caroline's friends were in fact XPT agents: Sophie, David, and even Simon. Caroline has been kept hostage by her friends and used as a guinea pig in a mysterious experiment. Her only link to a possible freedom is through the online friendships she has with characters like Jack and Jill. And of course, Jack and Jill are as unreal and unhelpful in relation to Caroline's world as she is in relation to ours.

The most poignant symbol of Caroline's captivity is the budgie cage she places in front of the webcam to show that she's not got anything more to say. There's often no bird in the cage, and "Bluebird" is a nickname she uses to refer to her online friends (or readers). Inside the cage a heart-shaped mirror is sometimes visible, possibly reflecting part of a face, though the image is too unclear to see clearly. Perhaps that's my face I imagine I see reflected in the trapped mirror. I see myself as a captive of the narrative, of the screen and of the computer.

Impotence and Guilt

My relationship to Caroline is defined by its impotence. She can ask me for help but there's no way I can do anything that will really change her story. And yet I'm left feeling responsible for her fate.

> Don't think I haven't noticed how oddly David is behaving, by the way. The question is: what can I do about it? I mean, what can WE do about it?
>
> What I'm trying to say is — don't just sit there. HELP ME OUT HERE!! [E-mail no. 19]

I've distracted her by being her friend and reading her story. If I hadn't read, she'd have lived. Reading, in *Online Caroline*, is being an accomplice to murder.

When the story is finally over, Caroline is unable to send more e-mails. Instead, as mentioned above, I receive a "thank you" e-mail from the president of XPT, the company David works for. The e-mail seals my guilt, leaving me feeling that perhaps I could have saved Caroline from her fate had I made different choices in what sounds more and more like a game.

> Thanks to you, our operatives were allowed to carry out their tasks without hindrance, and Caroline's life was irrevocably changed. We were particularly grateful to you for preventing Caroline from developing complicated and

distracting relationships with Simon and Sophie. She did not want them. [Final e-mail from Sir Gerald Inomynte, President and CEO, XPT]

I'm not in charge of reading *Online Caroline*. I'm not a disinterested reader or viewer. I'm involved. This is a simulation, and simulations make their audience participants: I bow my head as I enter, speak with a hushed voice, feel guilty at letting Caroline down. I'm the raw material for a simulation: it's carving itself into my flesh and my emotions. I'm being played.

My explorations through the text make me feel as though I have choices and as though I am in control. The narrative seems to adjust itself to *my* actions and responses. Then I see that the system is paying as much attention to the details of the way I *read* as it is to my deliberate responses.

I'm told what happens in this story, I don't discover it. I'm not active. I'm not in control. The text I'm reading is the active party here. It reveals my secrets, and tells me so.

You don't play a simulation. It plays you.

References: Literature

Manovich, Lev (2001). *The Language of New Media*. Cambridge, MA: The MIT Press.

Turing, Alan (1950). "Computing Machinery and Intelligence." *Mind* 59, no. 236 (1950): 433–460.

Wadell, Maj-Brit (1999). "Tomba Emmanuelle: et Allkunstverk om Livet og Menneskets Predestinasjon." In *Emanuel Vigeland,* edited by Nils Messel. Oslo: Emanuel Vigeland Museum.

References: Games

Online Caroline. R. Bevan and T. Wright. 2000/2001. <http://www.onlinecaroline.com>.

Interactive Fiction as "Story," "Game," "Storygame," "Novel," "World," "Literature," "Puzzle," "Problem," "Riddle," and "Machine"
Nick Montfort

Asking whether a new media artifact is a story or a game is like asking of a poem: "Which is it? Narrative or metrical?" This contrived question holds two dangers. Most obviously, it suggests that narrative and meter are somehow opposing forces in poetry, indeed, that they are exclusive. The further danger is its implicit presupposition, that these are the only two interesting aspects of a poem. We almost certainly would benefit from considering whether the poem is book-length or short, if it is schematically alliterative, what themes it treats, if it is in a traditional or invented form, and

what traditions it works in or against — but the first dichotomy, by distracting with its false opposition, disguises the other important aspects of the poem because it silently claims that there are only two important aspects.

Advocates of game studies and ludology have rallied against the simplistic consideration of computer games as stories, resisting what they refer as the "colonization" of the new field by literary studies as they build up their rebel fleet on the ice planet. Of course their project is not to banish discussion of story from computer game studies (how could it be, when half the articles in the premiere issue of the journal *Game Studies* take the issue of narrative as their central topic?) but to ensure that discussion is framed in terms of a new discipline, native to the computer game. Discourse about new media, at its best, no longer concerns itself with the mythical story/game dichotomy. Instead critics like Henry Jenkins are considering in detail the many ways that story is involved with, produced by, or reflected in games, and pointing out that aspects such as the simulated environment are often more important than the "story," even when we have determined what exactly that is (Game-Stories 2001). Janet Murray describes other, overlapping categories: "puzzle" and "contest," creating a Venn diagram with four circles instead of just

---

Response by Brenda Laurel

In my view, Nick Montfort's most important observation is that computer games are a new kind of animal that comes in lots of different sizes, colors, and subspecies. His observation that a computer game "is a potential narrative that may contain game elements" points to a reader-response-oriented view, that the narrative can be understood to be the player's construction of what happens in an interactive session.

Montfort asks why we use the word "game" as a default noun, when clearly many forms of interactive play are not games. It may be because "game" approximates the idea of "play," which, when used as a verb, often takes "game" as its object. But the central pleasure of play, as for the audience member of a

theatrical event or for the reader of fiction, depends upon the absence of serious consequences in real life. We can feel for Hamlet but we will not die with him.

What experts call "play patterns" in children's play are instructive in figuring out the structure of play with computers. "Games" are forms of rule-based play. Playing with pattern and rhythm (as with clapping and jumping games) may illuminate the underlying play pattern of games such as *Tetris* or *Breakout*. Equally attractive to kids is exploratory or "free" play, where the underlying play pattern often involves improvisational story making. Narrative construction as a play pattern provides an excellent starting place for understanding the pleasure that is particular to IF.

Montfort notes in his discussion of Buckles's

the usual "story" and "game" categories (Game-Stories 2001). Even in this view, however, the Venn diagram that Murray offers collapses apples and oranges into the same plane. Story, game, and puzzle are better viewed as aspects of new media — vectors in an n-dimensional space, some of which are orthogonal and some of which are not — rather than categories, even intersecting categories. Even this concept is lacking in some ways. What is important to realize is that while there are such things as "games" and "stories," many new media artifacts are neither of these, but employ elements from both. They employ elements from other forms and can be understood using other figures, too. What is important to distinguish about these different aspects and elements is which of them are essential to which well-defined categories of new media artifacts, and how they are or are not tied to one another.

Making broad claims about "new media" or even "computer games" can be problematic. There are new media forms that are reasonable categories: the massively muliplayer role-playing game, the first-person shooter, the hypertext novel, the chatterbot. Whatever the difficulties with definitions, we know a first-person shooter, like obscenity, when we see it. I focus here on one new media form, recognized by authors and interactors to be its own category: interactive fiction. Examples of interactive fiction, abbreviated as IF,

include *Adventure* and *Zork*; later literary efforts *A Mind Forever Voyaging*, *Trinity*, *Amnesia*, and *Mindwheel*; and more recent works such as *Curses* and *Photopia*. Rather than begin with a definition of IF, I'll go through a series of figures that can be used to understand the form — beginning with story and game, but not stopping there — and conclude by considering which of these figures are defining and which are important to the poetics of interactive fiction.

Story

Even IF that clearly has puzzle-solving as its only pleasure — works that make fortune cookies seem florid — produce narratives as a result of sessions of interaction. Here is a concrete example of how IF is potential narrative, a space of possibility in which the user's inputs, parsed as actions, become part of a narrative text:

> Orange River Chamber
>
> You are in a splendid chamber thirty feet high. The walls are frozen rivers of orange stone. An awkward canyon and a good passage exit from east and west sides of the chamber.
>
> A cheerful little bird is sitting here singing.

"storygame" concept that story cannot be pulled out of a work of interactive fiction, whereas it is spurious in the action game genre. In my research on gender and technology, however, I learned that narrative construction is a key element of pleasure for girls in the playing of action games. An action game is judged as "good" when the player can imaginatively "fill in" the characters, and "bad" when, to quote one interviewee, "the characters are so boring you can't even make up stories about them" (she was referring to *Mortal Kombat*). To take an example from the adventure genre, *Myst* has spawned several books that explore its main narrative and backstory. In IF that does not include such guide books, players construct the backstory — that is, notions about causality, relationship, and other

aspects of characters and situations that are not explicitly revealed. Players take pleasure in narrative construction.

Montfort's insistence on the creation of a complete world should be the first sentence in the IF author's bible. In the Aristotelean sense, the "world" is typically understood as the *material* of a play, whereas the plot is its *form*. In this view, a "world model" can be seen as a collection of interrelated materials with potential for formulation through the means of thought and character into plot (Laurel 1991, 50-51).

The Smalltalk "model-view-controller" metaphor also sheds light on the idea of a "world model," which corresponds to the "model" in Smalltalk. The "controller" may be seen as an individual player in

>TAKE BIRD

You catch the bird in the wicker cage.

This text is a minimal story, by Gerald Prince's (1973) definition, produced in a session of interaction with *Adventure*. The initial state has an adventurer in a cave chamber with a little bird. The adventurer types "TAKE BIRD" to take the bird. Then, as a result, the bird is in the wicker cage.

Game

Jesper Juul, after demonstrating that the case for story in computer games is overstated, adds that "many computer games contain narrative elements" (Juul 2001). Reversing this formulation works better for IF. It is a potential narrative that may contain game elements. Some interactive fiction works cannot be "won" and do not keep score: Emily Short's *Galatea* and Ian Finley's *Exhibition* are examples. They are not games by the definition Eric Zimmerman gives,[1] and only by liberally extending the concept of "symbolic reward" would they be games by Espen Aarseth's definition.[2] I prefer to define game as a contest (one of the categories Murray distinguished) — but a contest broadly defined, either played directly against one or more players or played individually in an attempt to break a record or achieve a superior score. Game

elements are used in interactive fiction to convey the extent of a work (a score of 20 out of 250 replaces being on page 20 of 250) and to provide what hypertext theorists and pop psychologists call "closure," but they are seldom used to actually structure a contest. Hence the popular way of referring to IF works, as "games," highlights an aspect of IF that is not fundamental, and suggests a figure that is not one of the more useful ones for understanding the form.

Storygame

Mary Ann Buckles, author of the first dissertation on interactive fiction, suggests a different concept, that of the "storygame," for understanding the form. Although Buckles writes that "in *Adventure*, the game is embedded in a story" (Buckles 1985, 32), her term suggests that rather than one element being embedded in the other, both are essential to the experience and are intertwined rather than nested. *Dungeons and Dragons* is a precomputer case of an experience that inextricably merges story and game — and performance as well.[3] One cannot simply remove the story from *Dungeons and Dragons* the way that the narrative cut-scenes in *Ms. Pac-Man* can be lifted away. Nor can the aspects of contest be removed without changing the experience into something other than

---

his/her situated context, and the "view" constitutes the one story that results from that particular controller's vector into the model. To quote the Guardian of Forever (from *Star Trek*), "many such experiences are possible."

Montfort reminds us that "Aristotle held that a play could exist even without characters, but never without a plot." By character, Aristotle is generally interpreted to mean entities with moral qualities and predispositions, that formulate thought into action. His "play without character" refers to a representation of an action that lacks sufficient representation of the moral character and qualities of its agent(s) (Aristotle 1961). His point was that the essential nature of a play was to be the representation of an action rather than merely the

representation of characters. In the case of an IF world without "characters," it becomes obvious that the player would function as the sole character, contributing his own thought and action to the formulation of the potential of the world model into a "plot."

Montfort asserts that "a puzzle is a formal test of ingenuity." The idea of "ingenuity" may not be inclusive enough; puzzle-solving skills include cognitive skills such as pattern-recognition, pattern-matching, and mental rotation. Parenthetically, the skills I just mentioned are likely to involve brain-based gender biases. Much is made of the fact that *Tetris*, a game that seems to depend largely on mental rotation skills (at which males tend to be more facile), has a higher-than-normal female following. Anecdotal evidence suggests

Dungeons and Dragons. IF works *can*, similarly, involve story and game essentially — but neither quality is part of IF's foundation. The "story" that occurs emerges through interaction, and what is commonly thought of as "game" in the form is — when it is present — better understood through other figures.

Novel

Mindwheel and other Synapse titles were labeled "electronic novels." Some IF works (including those) typically take many hours of interaction to complete. Other works, such as those entered in the annual IF competition <http://ifcomp.org/>, are designed to be completed within two hours. Seeing those in the former category as "novels" and the latter sort as "short stories" is a sensible way to describe how much interaction time is required. It is not particularly the case, however, that aesthetic or poetic principles of the novel vis-à-vis the short story apply to these two sorts of works. It is not in fact obvious that IF is more closely tied to traditions of written prose than to other literary traditions.

World

IF accepts natural-language text from the interactor and produces text in reply, but the same can be said for the stand-alone chatterbot *Racter* or a database that takes English-like queries. What distinguishes IF from these systems is that in addition to a "parser" there is another essential element of an IF work: a "world model." Aristotle held that a play could exist even without characters, but never without a plot (Aristotle 1961). In IF, it is the world (like the literary "setting") that is essential — characters and plot can be dispensed with, but a system is not IF unless it simulates a world, however erratically and in however limited a way.

Literature

Accepting the ideas of Russian Formalism, and specifically Victor Shklovsky's (1965) concept that the literary nature of a text comes from its "making strange" ordinary reality, it's evident that not just the textual output of IF but even the nature of many IF puzzles hinge on their literariness (Randall 1988). Although variation between the *sjuzet* and the *fabula* is not the main device used to accomplish this (it is employed at times — for instance, in Adam Cadre's *Photopia*) IF does use the technique of literary art "to make objects 'unfamiliar,' to make forms difficult, to increase the difficulty and length of perception because the process of perception is an aesthetic end in itself and must be prolonged" (Shklovsky 1965).

that successful female players conceptualize the *Tetris* problem as one of pattern-matching, a cognitive skill at which females tend to excel.

I agree wholeheartedly with Montfort's observation that "finding a way in which the puzzle-solving and reading aspects of IF work together instead of in opposition" is important. Puzzle-solving can replace language as a form of communication in the game (see, for example, *Secret Paths in the Forest*).

I question the notion of games as "contests." If that is so, then how do we define the quest? With what or whom is a quest a contest? Echoing the author's annoyance with binary choices in his opening paragraphs, I object to the idea of "contest" or "competition" and its unspoken alternative, "collaboration." This false dichotomy is used to simplify everything from business ethics to gender differences.

More often — in business, life, and literature — the protagonist seeks *change*: material, mental, social, spiritual, or what-have-you. The desired change is often described as the satisfaction of some goal, but this definition proves too narrow in many plots, where the protagonist may know only that the status quo isn't good, and discovers only through the unfolding of the action what sort of change would be most positive. Realistically, change proceeds, not through simplistic competition or collaboration, but rather through the somewhat more complex action of identifying or constructing effective symbiotic relationships. This is as true in literature as it is in business and biology. This

313

Puzzle

A puzzle is a formal test of ingenuity. A jigsaw puzzle is, of course, a puzzle, as is a scrambled Rubik's Cube or a verbally posed logic problem or lateral thinking puzzle. The device of the puzzle is described as essential to IF by Graham Nelson, creator of the IF development system Inform and author of *Curses*: "Without puzzles, or problems, or mechanisms to allow the player to receive the text a little at a time . . . there is no interaction" (Nelson, 2001, 382). But IF has been devised without puzzles; conversation and exploration rather than puzzle-solving allow one to move further through these works while interacting. Undoubtedly, the puzzle provides the main effective way to engage the interactor deeply. Dealing with explicit puzzles, however, involves a mode of thought alien to ordinary reading; progress through the text of a novel is not arrested when the reader comes up with the wrong answer. As important as the puzzle has been, finding a way in which the puzzle-solving and reading aspects of IF work together instead of in opposition is also important.

Problem

The single academic article about *Zork* by its creators does not use the word "puzzle." The challenges in *Zork* are instead referred to by Lebling, Blank, and Anderson (1979) as "problems." Problems are questions raised for solution; the term suggests that they are more likely to be posed as homework than for diversion, but this is a matter of connotation. Essentially puzzles and problems are the same. But if all puzzles or problems are games, we are in left in the difficult situation in which "2 + 2 = ?" is a game. That question is a puzzle, however uninteresting it may seem,[4] but it rightly seems difficult to swallow as a game. It is more sensible to define games as contests and also allow the existence of puzzles and problems that are not games. Defined this way, a crossword puzzle is a puzzle, not a game; "Let's see who can finish the crossword puzzle first" is a game. Similarly, chess is a game; the knight's tour is a puzzle that uses the gaming equipment and rules for movement from the game of chess.

Whether called puzzles or problems, challenges do play an important role in almost all IF. However, the concept of "problem" helps no more than does "puzzle" in connecting these challenges to the narrative world presented in IF. It is this connection, and the establishment of systems that have meaning outside of their own closed workings, that is the excellence of the IF form.

---

view preserves the author's emphasis on establishing "systems which have meaning outside their own closed workings," but it adds a level of complexity and realism that I find lacking in the idea of "contest."

Similarly, the idea of "riddles" seems incomplete. Does merely not knowing the source of discomfort or disharmony qualify as a riddle? For example, "Something's rotten in the state of Denmark" — a riddle, or merely an itch that one must discover how to scratch?

Montfort observes that a mechanistic view of IF engenders negative responses. This is a really important point. The image of IF has been tainted by hypertexts passing themselves off as interactive fiction through the years. There is something deeply unsatisfying about the lack of significance in one's actions as a player; that is, the player knows that he/she is merely selecting one of many preordained "pathways" and is therefore exercising no more agency than a rat running a maze. To the discerning player, branching architectures lack vitality in the same way as hypertexts.

The author's insistence on natural-language understanding and generation as definitional of IF holds authors to very high standards indeed, and may in fact put them in a straitjacket. There are workable and interesting alternatives to natural language, where players may express themselves with gestures or other non-verbal or paralinguistic actions, and their impact on the developing plot may similarly be nonverbal in

Riddle

The connection of a puzzle or problem to issues in the world (not only the world of the IF work but the world that we inhabit) of the sort that literature engages is best seen in the figure *riddle*. The riddle, as discussed here, is a didactic form of poetry, not a response-format light-bulb joke. A famous riddle that was said to confound Homer is: "Those we have caught we left behind, those that have eluded us we carry with us."[5] There are many examples from Greek and Latin that remain current in our culture; the English tradition of the riddle begins, in writing, at the very beginning of written English literature, with the Anglo-Saxon riddles of the Exeter Book.

Many works of IF simply contain riddles which must be solved in order to progress, but it is more useful to consider not the explicit presence of riddles in IF but the riddle as a figure for how IF works. The best examples of IF do what the best riddles do: they create a provocative system of thought that one is invited to enter, explore, and understand — demonstrating one's understanding, at last, by explicitly offering a solution.

A puzzle in the mainframe *Zork* (which appears in the commercial *Zork I*)[6] provides a example that is not spectacular but is concise enough to relate here: in a coal mine there is a machine, similar in appearance to a washing machine. *Zork* simulates a world in which magic and technology coexist, where the adventurer's goal is to acquire all possible treasures. Nearby there is a heap of coal. The treasure here must be not located, but manufactured. By placing the coal in the machine and turning it on (this procedure requires a bit of figuring out), the coal is converted under pressure into a diamond. The puzzle requires some awareness of the properties of carbon, and also requires that the interactor understand that the system of this world is one in which engineers have, in many cases, provided useful devices in appropriate places.

A good scientist might happen upon the solution experimentally by placing different items in the machine and turning it on. What gives this puzzle the qualities of a riddle, if not the excellence of the best riddles, is that it is consistent with the logic of the world in which it occurs. More elaborate and poignant puzzles, tied in riddle-like ways to the worlds in which they occur and to the world outside, achieve more provocative and profound results. The riddle, unifying the literary and puzzle-solving aspects of IF, is the central figure in this form's poesis.

Machine

A work of IF is not an "electronic document." It is a program, parsing input and generating output based on rules. One reason that IF has been overlooked by nature. I held up Purple Moon's *Secret Paths* adventures as one example, but there are many others. I would think that we might see more creativity result from a definition which replaced "natural language" with any workable semiotic system. Regardless of this quibble, the author makes the crucial point that the program and player must have a highly nuanced shared language.

From Janet Murray's Online Response

IF is a riddle most of all because it is a conversation. It is not a conversation with an imaginary character, a chatterbot like Eliza, although it may include characters. It is a conversation with the author of the imaginary world, who is challenging the interactor to solve the puzzle, to figure out what the author has in mind, to debug their own interactive processes, repeating the sequences until the desired ending is reached. In the early online games there was no way of saving one's position or undoing moves. The space could be traversed at will, assuming there were not locked doors, but time was relentless and irreversible. As in a conversation with another person, you could not unring a bell; as in an obsessive or superstitious ritual, the only way to get it right was to do it in exactly the acceptable order, no matter how many repetitions it might take to get it right. An interactor learning an IF environment had to memorize the sequences (or record them on paper) and say them back in the right order to please the god of this magical world. Meanwhile, the

315

hypertext theorists is that IF is not hypertext by most of the conflicting definitions that are offered; the view of it as a network of linked text is particularly strained and hides important aspects of IF. A broad category that recognizes the nature of IF and other new media artifacts as programs, such as Espen Aarseth's (1997) *cybertext*, offers many critical benefits. It helps one understand that certain frustrations with IF are due to difficulty with or unwillingness to *operate a machine* in order to generate text, and certain pleasures of IF come from engaging in this text/machine operation, or from reading that takes place in the context of operation.

Defining Interactive Fiction

A work of interactive fiction is a program that simulates a world, understands natural-language text input from an interactor and provides a textual reply based on events in the world. This definition includes everything that is commonly held by IF authors and interactors to be IF, excludes new media artifacts that are similar but not commonly held to be IF, and sheds light on the elements that are truly essential to the form:

> Simulation of a world
>
> Natural-language understanding
>
> Natural-language generation

Understanding Interactive Fiction

By definition, IF is neither a "story" or a "game," but, as all IF developers know, a "world" combined with a parser and instructions for generating text based on events in the world. The riddle is central to understanding how the IF world functions as both literature and puzzle. Interestingly, the riddle is a part of the literary tradition of poetry, not that tradition of the novel more often associated with IF. This means that despite the common nomenclature of IF works as "games," the IF program as a "story" file, and the work of IF as an electronic "novel," none of these three figures are of central importance to IF.

It's time to look beyond "story" and "game" for those other figures that are essential to different sorts of new media artifacts, and to recognize that views of "story" and "game" as simple overarching categories can be counterproductive. Rather than only race back and forth between narratology and game studies for further insights into the "story" and "game" of IF, for instance, it makes sense for those seeking to understand IF and those trying to improve their authorship in the form to consider the aspects of world, language understanding, and riddle by looking to architecture, artificial intelligence, and poetry.[7]

---

author is taunting or encouraging the interactor, and in either case making clear his or her own cleverness. Like the poser of the riddle, the author of an interactive fiction exists only as a conversational partner. Like the person to whom a riddle is posed, the interactor is in a contest, drawn in by a desire to "match wits," with the riddle-poser, to test the operation of their own cognitive processes against the trickery of the master.

http://www.electronicbookreview.com/thread/firstperson/murrayr1

Montfort Responds

To see IF as "new media," and to add "play" and "conversation" to the ten perspectives I originally mentioned, offers thirteen ways of looking at interactive fiction, perhaps enough for a clear vision of sorts. The thirteen ways Wallace Stevens offered are, after all, also one way; they build on and speak to each other.

http://www.electronicbookreview.com/thread/firstperson/montfortr2

Notes

1. Games have an explicit rule system, according to Zimmerman, and they have a definite result or outcome. This definition was described by him in the "Aesthetics of Game Design" panel at Computers and Video Games Come of Age, and in the "Game-Stories: Simulation, Narrative, Addiction," panel at SIGGRAPH 2001. This distinguishes games and more general play activity very well, which is what the definition evidently was created to do, but it does not distinguish between games and puzzles as well as I would like, or indeed at all.

2. Games provide "symbolic rewards," in Aarseth's formulation, which may be in the form of higher scores or in some other form. This would possibly allow for a Furby or Tamagotchi to be a game, because growth and good behavior of these creatures might be a reward, but it would rule out slot machines and vending machines, which dispense real, rather than symbolic, rewards. This was described by Aarseth in a talk to a Comparative Media Studies seminar at MIT in February 2001.

3. I have not mentioned performance until now because the term seems to have little direct relevance to interactive fiction and has not dominated the discourse around computer games the way that "story" and "game" have. However, the performing arts are rich in figures that may help in understanding interactive fiction — too rich to treat well in a short essay like this. See particularly Laurel 1986, 74–81, which treats *Zork* in dramatic terms; *Mindwheel* author Robert Pinsky also emphasized the applicability of the dramatic perspective to IF poetics in his MIT Media Lab Colloquium in February 1997.

4. "2 + 2 = ?" may actually be a slightly interesting puzzle. On a planet in which the inhabitants have two fingers on each of their two hands, the answer is likely to be "10," since such creatures would probably use base 4 arithmetic.

5. The answer gives the title to W. S. Merwin's third book of poetry, *The Lice*. I am indebted to Will Hochman for pointing out how this riddle is an excellent figure for how the most puzzling aspects of literature are those that stay with us.

6. *Zork* was modified, split into three works which contain some new material, and published as *Zork I–III*. This trilogy was sold for a wide variety of personal computers by Infocom, a company founded by the *Zork* creators and fellow students and researchers from MIT. *Zork I–III* have been made available for free download by Activision, which acquired Infocom in 1986: <http://www.csd.uwo.ca/Infocom/download.html>.

7. I continue the discussion of the nature of IF, describe the history of the form, and approach some of the major IF works critically in my book *Twisty Little Passages* (The MIT Press, 2003).

References: Literature

Aarseth, Espen (1997). *Cybertext: Perspectives on Ergodic Literature.* Baltimore: Johns Hopkins University Press.

Aarseth, Espen (2001). Comparative Media Studies Seminar, MIT, February 8, 2001.

Aristotle (translated by S. H. Butcher, introduction by Francis Fergusson (1961). *Poetics.* New York: Hill and Wang.

Buckles, Mary Ann (1985). "Interactive Fiction: The Computer Storygame *Adventure*," Ph.D. Thesis, University of California San Diego.

Herz, J.C., Henry Jenkins, Janet Murray, Ken Perlin, Celia Pearce, Noah Wardrip-Fruin, and Eric Zimmerman (2001). "Game-Stories: Simulation, Narrative, Addiction." Panel at SIGGRAPH 2001, Los Angeles, August 17, 2001.

Juul, Jesper (2001). "Games Telling Stories?," *Game Studies* 1, no.1 (July 2001). <http://gamestudies.org/0101/juul-gts>.

Laurel, Brenda (1986). "Toward the Design of a Computer-Based Interactive Fantasy System," Ph.D. Thesis, Ohio State University.

Laurel, Brenda (1991). *Computers as Theatre*. Boston: Addison Wesley.

Lebling, P. David, Mark S. Blank and Timothy A. Anderson (1979). "Zork: A Computerized Fantasy Simulation Game," *IEEE Computer* 12 no. 4 (April 1979): 51–59.

Nelson, Graham (2001). *The Inform Designer's Manual,* 4th edition. St. Charles, Illinois: The Interactive Fiction Library.

Pinsky, Robert (1997). MIT Media Lab Colloquium, February 5, 1997.

Prince, Gerald (1973). *A Grammar of Stories*. The Hague: Mouton.

Randall, Neil (1988). "Determining Literariness In Interactive Fiction." *Computers and the Humanities* 22: 183–191.

Shelley, Bruce, Warren Spector, and Eric Zimmerman (2000). "Aesthetics of Game Design." Panel at Computers and Video Games Come of Age, MIT, February 11, 2000.

Shklovsky, Victor (translated by Lee T. Lemon and Marion J. Reis (1965). "Art as Technique." In *Russian Formalist Criticism: Four Essays*. Lincoln: University of Nebraska Press.

References: Games

Adventure. Will Crowther (1975) and Don Woods (1976). 1975/1976.

Amnesia. Thomas M. Disch, programmed by Kevin Bentley; Electronic Arts. 1986.

Curses. Graham Nelson. 1993.

Exhibition. Ian Finley. 1999.

Galatea. Emily Short. 2000.

A Mind Forever Voyaging. Steven Meretzky; Infocom. 1985.

Mindwheel. Robert Pinsky, programmed by Steve Hales and William Mataga; Synapse/Brøderbund. 1984.

Photopia. Adam Cadre. 1998.

Trinity. Brian Moriarty; Infocom. 1986.

Zork. Timothy Anderson, Marc Blank, Bruce Daniels, and Dave Lebling; Infocom. 1977–1979.

Permissions

The editors wish to thank the following, who gave permission for material to be reproduced. Most images not listed here are by permission of the author of the essay or response with which they appear . In a small number of cases it was not possible to locate the copyright holder.

Jim Andrews:
Image of *Nio* appears courtesy of Jim Andrews.

Atari:
Image of *Civilization 3* appears courtesy of Atari Interactive, Inc.

Webb Chappell:
Image of *Stream of Consciousness* appears courtesy of Webb Chappell.

Eastgate Systems:
Jim Rosenberg's "The Barrier Frames" first appeared in *Eastgate Quarterly Review of Hypertext* 2(3). Image appears courtesy of Eastgate Systems, Inc., Watertown MA.

Eidos Interactive:
Images of *Tomb Raider* appear courtesy of Eidos Interactive, Inc.

Electronic Arts:
The Sims, SimCity, Wing Commander, and *American McGee's Alice* are trademarks or registered trademarks of Electronic Arts Inc. in the U.S. and/or other countries. Screenshots used with permission of Electronic Arts Inc.

Funcom:
Image of *The Longest Journey* appears courtesy of Funcom.

Shannon Gilligan:
Images of *Who Killed Taylor French?* and *Who Killed Brett Penance?* appear courtesy of Shannon Gilligan.

Matt Gorbet:
Image of *Tilty Table* appears courtesy of Matt Gorbet.

Jordan Mechner:
Images of *The Last Express* appear courtesy of Jordan Mechner. *The Last Express* is a trademark of Phoenix Licensing, Inc.

Talan Memmott:
Images of *Lexia to Perplexia* appear courtesy of Talan Memmott.

Mez:
Image of email writing appears courtesy of Mez.

Microsoft:
Images of *The Beast* appear courtesy of Microsoft, Inc.

Stuart Moulthrop:
Images of *Reagan Library* and *Hegirascope* appear courtesy of Stuart Moulthrop.

Namco:
Image of *Ms. Pac-Man* appears courtesy of Namco.

Sega:
Image of *Pengo* appears courtesy of Sega Europe.

Jeffrey Shaw:
Images of *The Legible City* appear courtesy of Jeffrey Shaw.

Stelarc:
Images of *Exoskeleton* and *Handwriting* appear courtesy Stelarc. *Exoskeleton* — Cyborg Frictions, Dampfzentrale, Bern, 24 November–1 December, 1999 — photographer Dominik Landwehr. *Handwriting* — Maki Gallery, Tokyo, 22 May, 1982 — photographer Keisuke Oki.

Sony:
Images of *EverQuest* appear courtesy of Sony Online Entertainment Inc.

XPT:
Images of *Online Caroline* appear courtesy of XPT.

Zoesis Studios:
Images of OttoAndIris.com and *The Penguin Who Wouldn't Swim* appear courtesy of Zoesis Studios.

Index